D1461898

The Daily Telegraph
Chronicle of Horse Racing

Compiled & edited by
Norman Barrett

GUINNESS PUBLISHING

First published 1995
Reprint 10 9 8 7 6 5 4 3 2 1

Copyright © 1995 The Telegraph plc

The right of Norman Barrett to be identified as the Author
of this Work has been asserted in accordance with the
Copyright, Designs and Patents Act 1988.

Published in Great Britain by Guinness Publishing Limited,
33 London Road, Enfield, Middlesex

Front cover illustrations: Desert Orchid *(Allsport/Dan Smith)*
and Sir Gordon Richards *(Hulton Deutsch)*

Design and layout by John Mitchell

Printed and bound in Great Britain by The Bath Press,
Bath, Avon

A catalogue record for this book is available from
the British Library

ISBN 0-85112-649-9

Contents

Foreword

By Lord Oaksey

O ld Men Forget, Duff Cooper wrote – and this book can, among many other things, be a reminder of just how much you have forgotten. Don't be insulted; you may not be old or forgetful enough to need reminding. But even then, I believe you will find on these pages some powerful mental pick-me-ups.

Suddenly a fact or opinion or scene or sight or race or name of a jockey, trainer or horse will leap out and jog your memory. How closely does Hotspur's description fit the picture which lingers in your mind's eye? How much does he (or she or whichever Telegraph scribe you happen to be reading) add to your knowledge – or what you thought was knowledge?

How much *can* you remember – and was that *really* how you heard the story first? Best of all, thanks to the Chronicle's year-by-year format, how does that performance or record compare with those of other seasons?

In my admittedly prejudiced view, there is scarcely a page of this book – not even those I contributed to – on which one or more of those questions does not ask itself. I hope and believe that you may find trying to answer them as much fun as I did.

If, of course, you are lucky enough to be too young even to have heard of some of the events recorded here – well, there has to be a first time. There is an awful lot of racing history between these covers and the Chronicle has already settled three heated arguments in my house! I was only right in one of them but that's what I mean about forgetting . . .

Of course it can be infuriating too – when the story goes on too long, or not long enough or something you need is left out altogether. But if all those complaints were going to be avoided this would be an even bulkier volume.

It begins in the days when "Racing Correspondents" were widely regarded as "touts" and, if they had any sense, kept their heads down. Did someone really use the *nom de plume* "Roughscratcher" in 1855? I never knew that "Betting Offices" were closed by law in 1853 – just possibly a law which should never have been repealed . . .

Lucky old Hotspur saw Kincsem win the Goodwood Cup in 1878 – although, by the sound of it, the great Hungarian mare, unbeaten heroine of 54 races, was grossly maltreated by her jockey that day – "spurred up to her shoulders" if you please . . .

The fight against cruelty in all its forms – from unfairly difficult fences to excessive use of the whip – has, I'm glad to say, been regularly covered in the Telegraph. The Jockey Club's courageous attempts to control the whip have been at least partly successful while modifications to deceptive obstacles like Becher's Brook and the water jump have made them a fairer test with horses able at least to *see* what they are jumping.

But what days those were in the last quarter of the 19th century. Fred Archer majestic and invincible on Ormonde and then, only five months later, shooting himself in a fit of depression aggravated by typhoid and his constant battle with the scales.

Weight was equally vital in a different but equally deadly way at the turn of the century – arguably the golden age of the Grand National. After Cloister, twice second, defied 12st 7lbs to win in '93, the immortal Manifesto began a sequence of eight National heroics in 1895. One fourth, a fall, two wins, and three thirds, one of them beaten only three lengths under 12st 13lbs. They would be calling out the RSPCA nowadays – but Manifesto's cumulative achievements have never been surpassed.

Or have they? The beauty of this book is that you can quickly form your own opinion. Turn to Golden Miller's record time in 1934 – and, much more relevantly, to the five-year reign of Red Rum from 1973-77.

Comparisons may be odious but they are also fun – and the Chronicle gives endless opportunities. You can compare Arkle with Golden Miller, Petite Etoile with Pretty Polly, Tod Sloan with Steve Cauthen, Lester Piggott with Gordon Richards, Fred Winter with John Francome, Persian War with Sir Ken and Vincent O'Brien with Noel Murless. They and their greatest triumphs are all here.

Another source of fascination, for me, has been to be reminded how often great events coincided or closely succeeded one another. I had, for instance, forgotten that Sceptre was only two years older than Pretty Polly – just as Nijinsky was born only a year before Brigadier Gerard and Mill Reef. The sad, commercial custom of premature retirement to stud has robbed us of what could have been some mighty confrontations.

But there's no harm in dreaming and for anyone who, whatever their age, cares about racing and riding or horses and jockeys, this book will surely provide the stuff that dreams – or memories – are made of . . .

Introduction

Irst published in June 1855, The Daily Telegraph has from the very first provided a comprehensive coverage of the 'Sport of Kings'. All of the reports in this Chronicle since that date have been taken from the newspaper, mostly in the form of extracts. This is unavoidable in view of the wordage devoted to racing, especially to the big events, such as the Derbys and Grand Nationals.

Before the advent of broadcasting, when the printed word was the only medium of communication, every facet of the race was dissected in the minutest detail. First there would be a discursive piece by a "Special Correspondent", musing on Derbys, say, in general before describing the scene, with the arrival of the crowds by their various means of transport, their behaviour, the organisation, the appearance of the racecourse and, of course, the weather. He might then focus on the race, describing the highlights and the crowd's reactions, before summarising the event, criticising and praising as appropriate. All this would cover two or three columns of small, closely spaced type and amount to three or four thousand words. Likewise, "Our Own Correspondent", describing the race – the betting, the appearance of the horses in the paddock and on the way down to the post, the start, the running and the finish – would enjoy the luxury of another thousand or two words. The card and the betting would then be followed by a race-reader's report of perhaps five hundred words and a piece of similar length detailing the winner's pedigree, past performances and future engagements. That's a total of nine or ten thousand words.

In this book, with an average of a thousand words per page to cover three or four events, it has not been possible to do those early reports justice, but every effort has been made to convey the enthusiasm and descriptive skills of those first correspondents, all of whom practised their art under anonymous banners.

It was not until the 1960s that the by-lines were identified in the Telegraph racing pages, and one could put a name to the ubiquitous "Hotspur" – and the blame, too, when his selections failed to come up. Among the Hotspurs to acknowledge for their contributions to this Chronicle have been B.W.R.Curling, Peter Scott and the present incumbent J.A.McGrath, while Lord Oaksey (formerly John Lawrence) has been setting new standards in racing journalism as Marlborough for more than thirty years, and Tony Stafford's perceptive analysis of horses and races is second to none.

Thanks are also due to Robert Carter of the International Racing Bureau for supplying some of the elusive overseas statistics used in the tables. Although it has not been possible to reproduce the full race results with the reports, starting prices have been inserted where relevant. The date included in the strap line above each report is the date of the race or event, unless otherwise indicated.

Final thanks are owed to Simon Barrett and Isabel Boothby for diligent cuttings research and Charles Richards of Guinness for his help and encouragement.

Norman Barrett
June 1995

Picture acknowledgements

Allsport UK Ltd 110-1, 132-3, 178-9, 194, 196, 198, 201, 204, 205, 232, 243 (bottom), 244
Shaun Botterill 234
Howard Boylan 226
Simon Bruty 167, 228
David Cannon 211, 219
Phil Cole 166 (both), 248, 249
Chris Cole 200, 202, 230, 231, 233, 238
Anton Want 247
Dan Smith 220, 242
Phil Smith 214

Allsport Historical Collection 68, 69 (bottom), 83, 85, 93 (top), 98-9, 100, 103, 104, 107, 108 (right), 112, 117, 118, 121, 127, 142, 158, 161, 168, 171, 177, 181, 186

Hulton-Deutsch Collection 56, 58, 71, 76-7, 91, 96, 108 (left), 131, 136, 141, 145, 147, 149, 152, 154-5, 164

Illustrated London News 42, 45

Popperfoto 113, 115, 123, 126, 129, 137, 138, 144, 150, 154 (inset), 157, 162, 165, 172, 183, 185, 188, 193 (both), 203, 206, 208, 209, 212, 215, 217, 218, 222-3, 224, 241, 243 (top)

Syndication International 59, 119, 124, 148, 156

Telegraph Newspapers 240

Other photographs from the Norman Barrett Collection

Early Days

Racing owes it early development to the participation and patronage of royalty. It has always been the "Sport of Kings", enjoyed as much by politicians and princes as by the ordinary country-folk and townspeople.

Among those whose influence on racing was crucial were the 12th Earl of Derby and Sir Charles Bunbury, the prime movers in the establishment of the Derby and Oaks in the late 18th century. They had been impressed by the success of the St Leger in the north, and the popularity of races for younger horses, run all out over shorter distances. Before these "Classics" for three-year-olds came along, most races were for mature horses over longer distances, often run in best-of-three heats or as matches between individuals.

Bunbury was particularly active within the Jockey Club, which grew from a loose association of gentlemen in the mid-18th century into the regulating body for the sport, publishing, under the aegis of James Weatherby, the first racing calendar and first stud book.

Another great innovator and reformer of the Turf was Lord George Bentinck, a self-appointed vigilante who, in the first half of the 19th century, waged his own private war on the scoundrels whose dishonesty threatened to destroy the sport. While the Jockey Club dithered, he acted, and his success in exposing the skulduggery behind the "Running Rein" affair of 1844, in which, probably not for the first time, a four-year-old "won" the Derby, was a landmark in the fight against corruption.

Steeplechasing first became organised by Tom Colman at St Albans in the early 1830s, and by the end of that decade William Lynn had established the tradition of the Grand National at Aintree.

The import of Arab stallions in the late 17th and early 18th centuries led to the development of the Thoroughbred, and their blood survives, through the great sire lines of Eclipse, Herod and Matchem, to the present day.

Jockeys began to be stars of the Turf in the late 1700s, and outstanding among the early "Knights of the Pigskin" were Sam Chifney Sr, Frank Buckle and Jem Robinson.

August 24.1684.
The last Horse Race
Run before
CHARLES the. Second of
Blessed Memory
By Dorsett Ferry
near
Windsor Castle.

680 BC – AD 1849

680 BC Chariot racing, popular for centuries, is introduced into the ancient Olympic Games.

648 BC Racing on horseback is introduced at the 33rd Olympics. Horses are ridden without saddles or stirrups. The horses are lighter than those used in chariot racing, probably of Arab origin, introduced into Greece between 2000 and 1500 BC.

68 BC Soon after the transfer of the Olympic Games to Rome **(80 BC)** horseracing is dropped from the programme.

AD 210 Horses at the Roman encampment at Wetherby, in Yorkshire, are matched against Arabian horses brought to England by Roman emperor Severus Septimus.

A Roman horserace: at the start.

1540 Racing takes place at The Roodee, Chester, the oldest surviving course in England.

1580s Queen Elizabeth I attends races on Salisbury Plain.

1591 Earliest reference to racing in Scotland, at Leith, in the memoirs of the Earl of Huntley.

1595 A map of Doncaster shows a racecourse at Town Moor.

1619 The earliest known rules of racing are drawn up, at Kiplingcotes, Yorks.

1622 The first recorded race at Newmarket is a match for £100 between horses of Lord Salisbury and the Marquess of Buckingham.

1636 Newmarket racecourse is founded.

1640s Racing takes place at Epsom.

1660s Thanks to the patronage of King Charles II, Newmarket becomes the centre of racing in England.

1671 Charles II becomes the first (and only) reigning monarch to ride a winner, in Newmarket's Town Plate, a race he founded about six years earlier.

c.1689 William III founds the Royal Stud at Hampton Court.

The Byerley Turk, brought to England in 1689, was foaled in the late 1670s. Captain Byerley is said to have ridden him in the Battle of the Boyne before the stallion became the sire of Jigg and, through him, the great-great-grandsire of Herod, the greatest stallion in the latter 1800s.

The Darley Arabian was foaled in 1700, and, like the "Turk", never raced. From the age of four until he died at 30 he was a prolific stallion at Aldby Park, although he stood barely 15 hands. He sired Flying Childers, arguably the first great racehorse, and he was the great-great-grandsire of the incomparable Eclipse.

£50 Plate Epsom: 3 May 1769

'Eclipse first, the rest nowhere'

A bizarre bet was struck at Epsom after Mr William Wildman's Eclipse, making his first appearance on a racecourse but starting at 4-1 on, had easily won the first heat of the £50 Plate for horses who have never won. The self-styled "Captain" Dennis O'Kelly bet that he would correctly forecast the result of the second heat, placing all five runners. His bet was: "Eclipse first, the rest nowhere" – in other words, he wagered that Eclipse would win the four-mile heat by a distance (240 yards).

The frisky five-year-old, who manifestly loves racing, almost pulled jockey Jack Oakley's arms from their sockets, and there was never any danger that O'Kelly would lose his bet. The second horse, Gower, was almost out of sight when Eclipse crossed the finishing line.

Eclipse was bred by the Duke of Cumberland, second son of King George II, and is by Marske out of Spilletta. He was foaled in 1764 during an eclipse of the sun.

On the death of his owner a year later, he was put up for auction and bought by Wildman for 75gns. Such was Eclipse's disposition that it was thought at one time that he might be gelded. But Wildman refused to curb the colt's fiery spirit in this way and put him in the hands of a notorious rough-rider, who worked him day and night and finally tamed him.

A few days ago, it is understood, Eclipse was turned out for a trial over the gallops at Mickleham, too early for the touts to catch sight of him. But, as luck would have it, they met an old woman collecting faggots, and asked whether she had seen the horses. "Oh yes," she replied, "there were two of them. The one racing behind would never have caught the one with the white leg if they had run to the world's end."

The secret was out. The white-legged horse, standing 15 hands 2 inches, was Eclipse, and that is why he started at such short odds in his first race.

1689 The Byerley Turk, thought to be an Arabian and obtained by Captain Robert Byerley when fighting against the Turks in Hungary in 1687, is imported into England, and is to become the first of the three male-line ancestors of the Thoroughbred.

1704 The Darley Arabian is bought for Mr James Darley by his son, a merchant in Aleppo, and is the second of the male-line ancestors of the Thoroughbred, the paternal great-great-grandsire of Eclipse.

1711 First meeting held at Ascot.

1713 First use of the term "thro-bred" to describe horses.

1721 Flying Childers, the fastest horse of his day and the first to catch the public imagination, beats Speedwell over 4 miles in a match at Newmarket.

1727 The first account of all "horse matches run", the model for the world's racing annuals, is produced by John Cheny.

1729 The Godolphin Arabian, believed to have been a present from the Sultan of Morocco to King Louis XV of France, is purchased in Paris by Edward Coke of Derbyshire, subsequently coming into the possession of Lord Godolphin and becoming the third of the founding fathers, the paternal grandsire of Matchem.

1730 Bulle Rocke, a son of the Darley Arabian, leaves for Virginia, the first export of a Thoroughbred to America, where racing is becoming increasingly popular.

1731 Three-year-old races are introduced in England, at Bedale, Yorks.

c.1750 The Jockey Club is founded in London, at the Star and Garter, Pall Mall, originally as an association of gentlemen with the common interests of racing at heart.

1752 The first recorded steeplechase is held over 4 1/2 miles of hunting country at Cork, in Ireland, the name deriving from the fact that it takes place between Buttevant Church and St Leger Church.

1758 The Jockey Club, with jurisdiction over Newmarket, passes its first resolution, that all riders must weigh in after a race.

1762 Racing colours are registered at Newmarket.

1766 Tattersalls is founded, as Richard Tattersall organises bloodstock sales at Hyde Park Corner.

1769 A 2-year-old raced for the first time and won at Newmarket.

1773 James Weatherby, secretary of the Jockey Club and keeper of the Match Book at Newmarket, publishes the first Racing Calendar.

1776 The first running of the St Leger (not so-called until 1778), at Doncaster, is won by Allabaculia (1-2f). There are 5 runners, and the distance is 2 miles (until 1812).

1779 First Oaks.

1780 First Derby.

1784 The Derby is run over a mile and a half for the first time.

1786 Newmarket sees the first running of the July Stakes, now the oldest 2-y-o race in the world.

Newmarket: 4 October 1770

Farewell to a champion

A huge crowd turned up at Newmarket to see the last appearance on a racecourse of the mighty Eclipse *(pictured above)*, even though, as he has done seven times before in his 18-race career, he walked over.

In his two active seasons, there has not been a horse in the country to extend him. With seven of his races run in heats of as much as 4 miles, he has raced 17 times, often with the burden of 12 stone on his shoulders, and usually winning by at least 200 yards. In all, only 20 different horses have had the temerity to challenge him, and he has always started at odds on.

Only the gallant Bucephalus, in the match at Newmarket in April, has got anywhere near Eclipse, and he has now had to be taken out of training, such was the effort. Eclipse has won 11 valuable King's Plates, two of them at Newmarket. In August, in the Great Subscription at York, he trounced two first-class horses, Tortoise and Bellario. Starting at 20-1 on, he was over a furlong in front after two miles and went on relentlessly to win in a canter by a distance.

Soon after his famous bet last year on Eclipse's début, Mr Dennis O'Kelly purchased a half-share in Eclipse for 650gns, and later gave 1,150gns for the other half. With nothing more to prove on the racecourse, Mr O'Kelly has decided to send his brilliant stallion to stud.

[Eclipse died in 1789, at the age of 25, a year after Mr O'Kelly. His fame as a racehorse has been exceeded only by his fame as a sire. Surprisingly, he headed the list of leading sires only once, in 1786, in his own time, coming second nine times, either to Herod or Herod's son Highflyer. But he founded several undying male lines, and some 90 percent of modern Thoroughbreds descend from him.]

The Oaks Stakes Epsom: 14 May 1779

Lord Derby wins race for 3-year-old fillies

Lord Derby's Bridget appropriately won the first running of The Oaks Stakes, a race for three-year-old fillies over the last one and a half miles of the Epsom course. The race was named as a compliment to the 12th Earl of Derby, who was largely instrumental in organising the contest, and whose house is called The Oaks.

Lord Derby's house is leased to him by his uncle and great friend, General Burgoyne, who advises him on his bloodstock interests. The general had been impressed with the success of his military acquaintance Anthony St Leger, who inaugurated a race for three-year-olds at Doncaster three years ago.

Bridget, who started as 5-2 favourite, was ridden by Dick Goodison. She is a bay filly by Herod.

1788 Sir Thomas (5-6f), ridden by 54-year-old William South and owned by the Prince of Wales, is the first Royal Derby winner.

1788 Trainer and jockey John Mangle rides his 3rd consecutive St Leger winner for Lord Hamilton (almost making it four next year but is disqualified from 1st place for jostling).

1789 Sam Chifney is the first jockey to land the Epsom Classic double, winning the Derby on Skyscraper (4-7f) and Oaks on Tag (5-2jf).

1791 The first handicap, the Oatlands Handicap, is held at Ascot.

1791 The first volume of the General Stud Book appears.

1791 St Leger winner Young Traveller (3-1) wins the Doncaster Gold Cup at the same meeting, beating three other St Leger winners, Spadille (1787), Pewett (1789) and Ambidexter (1790).

1791 Cash, receiving 3st, is the first yearling to race in public, beating a 3-year-old in a match at Newmarket.

1792 The first recorded steeplechase in England takes place in Leicestershire, 3 runners racing from Barkby Holt to Billesdon Coplow and back, a total distance of 8 miles.

1794 Only 4 horses take part in the Derby won by Frank Buckle on Daedalus (6-1), a record low still standing today.

1794 Beningbrough wins the St Leger and Doncaster Gold Cup on consecutive days.

1795 The first bookmaker, Ogden, sets up at Newmarket.

1795 Hambletonian (4-6f) wins the St Leger for Sir Charles Turner, who wins 6 of the 7 races at the 3-day Doncaster meeting.

1798 Sir Harry is the first Derby winner to be sired by a previous winner, Sir Peter Teazle (1787).

1799 Frank Buckle rides northern champion Hambletonian to a half-neck victory in a match with Diamond at Newmarket, some £250,000 being wagered on the race.

1807 First running of the Ascot Gold Cup.

1809 Wizard (4-5f), ridden by Bill Clift, wins the first running of the 2,000 Guineas, at Newmarket, from 7 other runners.

1810 The first race meeting in Australia takes place at Hyde Park, Sydney, on a prepared racecourse, starting on Monday, 15 October, and continuing on the Wednesday and Friday.

1811 The first race over manufactured fences is held at Bedford, with more than 40,000 spectators, Fugitive beating Cecilia over a 3-mile course in which 4 fences (4ft 6in high) are each jumped twice.

1812 The Goodwood Cup is run for the first time, 10 years after the racecourse was opened.

1814 There are only 5 runners in the first 1,000 Guineas, at Newmarket, won by Charlotte (11-5f), ridden by Bill Clift, who won the first 2,000 5 years earlier.

The Derby Stakes Epsom: 4 May 1780

Sir Charles Bunbury's colt successful at Epsom

Lord Derby

Sir Charles Bunbury's Diomed won the new race over a straight mile at Epsom from nine other three-year-olds. Diomed, who started as 6-4 favourite, was ridden by Sam Arnull. He is a strongly built chestnut by Florizel, and was bred by Mr Richard Vernon at Newmarket.

The race, which was worth £1,065 to the winner, started in the Parish of Banstead (about half a mile east of Tattenham Corner). It was the first event on the programme.

Last year, on the night of Lord Derby's success with Bridget in the fillies' race, The Oaks, guests at Lord Derby's home resolved to establish a race for three-year-old colts. Sir Charles, the Senior Steward of the Jockey Club, was particularly anxious to discourage the customary four-mile or over races, and was, with Lord Derby, a prime mover in the inauguration of this new race. What to call it was resolved, it is understood, by the toss of a coin, and Derby's name was given to the race.

[Dennis O'Kelly, owner of Eclipse, won the second running of the Derby

with Young Eclipse, and also the first to be run over 1 1/2 miles, its present distance, with Serjeant in 1784. Diomed continued racing successfully until he broke down as a 6-year-old. Initially, he had little success as a sire, and his stud fee had diminished to 2gns by the time he was sold to America in 1798 for 50gns. Extraordinarily, in Virginia he founded a dynasty that includes some of the greatest horses in American racing history, and his death at 31 was greeted as a national catastrophe.]

Diomed: winner of the first Derby

Jockey Club Enquiry Newmarket: October 1791

Royal jockey accused of pulling Escape

Sam Chifney, jockey to the Prince of Wales, was hauled before the Jockey Club to explain the discrepancy in the running of the Prince's horse Escape on consecutive days at Newmarket. The Enquiry, conducted by Sir Charles Bunbury, did not accept the jockey's explanation, and the Prince is understood to have been informed that no members of the Jockey Club will henceforth make matches or run horses in any stake where Chifney rode.

In Chifney's defence it must be said that Escape has proved an erratic runner. Only last June, Chifney chose to ride him in the valuable Oatlands Stakes at Ascot, backed him heavily, and then on the day did not like the look of him, so, with the Prince's permission, switched to another Royal horse, Baronet, and won high praise for bringing him home by half a length, with Escape well down the field. Both jockey and owner had backed Baronet heavily at 20-1. Escape won two matches at Newmarket in early October, but on Thursday the 20th – in the race in question – he started at 2-1 on and finished last of four over two miles. In front of him was Skylark, a horse he had beaten in the spring. Now, the very next day, again at Newmarket, Escape turned the tables on Skylark and won easily from a field of six at odds of 5-1.

Chifney admitted to the enquiry that he had backed Escape on the Friday for 20gns, but not on Thursday. He explained that the horse had needed the run, and, more importantly, preferred the four miles over which the second

race was run. Convincing as these arguments sound, it appears that Chifney's reputation has perhaps counted against him in this instance.

[The Prince stood by his jockey, and sold all his horses, deserting the Turf for five seasons. He continued to pay Chifney his annual retainer of 200gns, an extremely generous amount in those days. Chifney, however, sold the annuity for 1,200gns, moved to London and eventually died in a debtors' prison in 1807, aged 53.]

Doncaster: 25 September 1793

Remarkable resilience of the Thoroughbred

The meeting at Doncaster has demonstrated the remarkable resilience of the Thoroughbred horse. Yesterday, Bill Peirse brought home Mr J.Clifton's most aptly named Ninety-three (15-1) in the St Leger Stakes. Then to-day, the bay colt by Florizel ran again in the Gold Cup over four miles and finished a gallant third.

Yet yesterday's exertions cannot be put forward as an excuse for to-day's defeat, because the winner of the Gold Cup, Mr John Hutchinson's Oberon (2-1), had only one hour earlier run in the four-mile Doncaster Stakes, and won at 4-1. Rarely, if ever, can there have been such a fine performance in races of such importance.

THE DERBY

Year	Horse	Jockey	Odds
1780	Diomed	S Arnull	6-4f
1781	Young Eclipse	C Hindley	10-1
1782	Assassin	S Arnull	5-1
1783	Saltram	C Hindley	5-2jf
1784	Serjeant	J Arnull	3-1f
1785	Aimwell	C Hindley	7-1
1786	Noble	J White	30-1
1787	Sir Peter Teazle	S Arnull	2-1
1788	Sir Thomas	W South	5-6f
1789	Skyscraper	S Chifney Sr	4-7f
1790	Rhadamanthus	J Arnull	5-4f
1791	Eager	M Stephenson	5-2
1792	John Bull	F Buckle	4-6f
1793	Waxy	W Clift	12-1
1794	Daedalus	F Buckle	6-1
1795	Spread Eagle	A Wheatley	3-1
1796	Didelot	J Arnull	–
1797	unnamed colt	J Singleton Jr	10-1
1798	Sir Harry	S Arnull	7-4f
1799	Archduke	J Arnull	12-1
1800	Champion	W Clift	7-4f
1801	Eleanor	J Saunders	5-4f
1802	Tyrant	F Buckle	7-1
1803	Ditto	W Clift	7-2
1804	Hannibal	W Arnull	3-1
1805	Cardinal Beaufort	D Fitzpatrick	20-1
1806	Paris	J Shepherd	5-1
1807	Election	J Arnull	3-1f
1808	Pan	F Collinson	25-1
1809	Pope	T Goodison	20-1
1810	Whalebone	W Clift	2-1f
1811	Phantom	F Buckle	5-1
1812	Octavius	W Arnull	7-1
1813	Smolensko	T Goodison	1-1f
1814	Blücher	W Arnull	5-2f
1815	Whisker	T Goodison	8-1
1816	Prince Leopold	W Wheatley	20-1
1817	Azor	J Robinson	50-1
1818	Sam	S Chifney Jr	7-2
1819	Tiresias	W Clift	5-2f
1820	Sailor	S Chifney Jr	4-1
1821	Gustavus	S Day	2-1f
1822	Moses	T Goodison	6-1
1823	Emilius	F Buckle	11-8f
1824	Cedric	J Robinson	9-2
1825	Middleton	J Robinson	7-4f
1826	Lap-dog	G Dockeray	50-1
1827	Mameluke	J Robinson	9-1
1828	Cadland	J Robinson	4-1
1829	Frederick	J Forth	40-1
1830	Priam	S Day	4-1f
1831	Spaniel	W Wheatley	50-1
1832	St Giles	W Scott	3-1f
1833	Dangerous	J Chapple	30-1
1834	Plenipotentiary	P Conolly	9-4f
1835	Mündig	W Scott	6-1
1836	Bay Middleton	J Robinson	7-4f
1837	Phosphorus	G Edwards	40-1
1838	Amato	J Chapple	30-1
1839	Bloomsbury	S Templeman	25-1
1840	Little Wonder	W Macdonald	50-1
1841	Coronation	P Conolly	5-2f
1842	Attila	W Scott	5-1
1843	Cotherstone	W Scott	13-8f
1844	Orlando	E Flatman	20-1
1845	The Merry Monarch	F Bell	15-1
1846	Pyrrhus the First	S Day	8-1
1847	Cossack	S Templeman	5-1
1848	Surplice	S Templeman	1-1f
1849	The Flying Dutchman	C Marlow	2-1jf

The Derby Epsom: 21 May 1801

Bunbury's filly Eleanor wins the Derby: 'A hell of a mare'

For the first time, in its 22nd running, the Derby has been won by a filly. Sir Charles Bunbury's Eleanor *(pictured above)*, a bay filly by Whiskey, started the 5-4 favourite in a field of eleven, and there was not a colt who could catch her.

Eleanor was ridden by J.Saunders, and is the second success for Sir Charles, who won the first Derby with Diomed in 1780. The celebrations were muted, however, by the tragic death of the filly's trainer Cox, who was taken ill just hours before the race. With his very last breath, the poor man gasped to the parson by his side: "Depend upon it, Eleanor is a hell of a mare."

[Eleanor underlined her special place in racing history the next day by winning the Oaks, starting as 7-4 on favourite and ridden by the same jockey. She continued racing, but ended her career contesting unimportant events at minor meetings before she was retired to stud at the age of 7.]

The St Leger Doncaster: 16 September 1822

Outsider wins St Leger: '£1,000 to a walking stick' laid

James Croft achieved perhaps the most remarkable training feat in the history of racing at Doncaster when he saddled the first four to finish in the St Leger out of a field of 23. But even he made no secret of the fact that he fancied the winner, Theodore, least of all. Mr E.Petre's bay colt by Woful was returned at 200-1, the longest odds for any winner of an important race. He was reckoned to have so little chance of success that one bookmaker laid an optimistic punter £1,000 to a walking stick.

Croft, who trains at Middleham, in Yorkshire, must have been astonished to see Theodore lead Violet, Professor and Corinthian home. Apart from anything else, Theodore was suffering badly from corns. It is reported that his jockey, John Jackson, was so put out at having to ride a lame horse that he was in tears just before the start, complaining bitterly about riding "such a cripple as that". That "cripple" came home by four lengths to give Jackson his eighth success in the race.

The St Leger Doncaster: 18 September 1827

Majestic ride by Robinson in Leger: Filly beats Derby winner

The Hon.E.Petre's filly Matilda won a thrilling race for the St Leger at Doncaster, beating the Derby victor Mameluke by half a length after a long battle in the straight. The winner's jockey, Jem Robinson, deserves the utmost praise for riding a masterly race.

There were seven false starts before the field of 26 finally got away, and Robinson sprang the little bay filly into the lead almost immediately. Because of Matilda's disposition, he rode her without spurs, and did remarkably well as the huge colt Mameluke chased her up the straight, almost getting his nose in front, before Robinson managed to get clear again with a final effort.

Matilda *(pictured right)*, who started at 10-1, is by Comus and was trained by John Scott.

[This was the first leg of a St Leger treble for owner and trainer, who followed up with The Colonel (3-1f) and Rowton (7-2f), although both of these were ridden by the trainer's younger brother Bill Scott.]

1819 Antonio (100-3) is a third successive St Leger winner for trainer J.Lonsdale, but he has to wait more then a fortnight for confirmation, as 5 runners missed the start, causing the stewards to order a re-run in which Antonio does not take part. But the Jockey Club later overrules this decision.

1821 The first recorded hurdle race takes place at Durdham Down, near Bristol, with 5 hurdles on the mile-long course, and is run in 3 heats.

1821 The 10-y-o Doctor Syntax wins the Preston Gold Cup for the 7th consecutive time (a record that has never been equalled in any race). He has never had more than 3 runners to beat, but numbered 3 St Leger winners among the vanquished, over distances ranging from 3 to 4 miles.

1822 The Duke of Grafton's Pastille, a bay filly by Rubens, wins the 2,000 Guineas (4-6f) and the Oaks (7-2), the only time this particular combination of Classics has been achieved. [She was ridden in the 2,000 by Frank Buckle, who was completing a hat-trick in the race.]

1824 Jockey Jem Robinson gets married to complete an unusual 100-1 treble, having bet that he would win the Derby and Oaks and get married within a week. Cedric (9-2) is the first of 4 Derby winners for Robinson in 5 years, Cobweb (8-11f) obliges in the Oaks, and when a certain Miss Powell says "Yes" the following day, he collects £1,000.

1825 The Duke of Grafton's Tontine walks over in the 1,000 Guineas, the only such instance in an English Classic. No jockey is recorded, but as the filly was trained by Robert Robson, it is likely that Frank Buckle was up.

1825 The St Leger, reaching a peak of popularity with 30 runners, is won by Bill Scott on Memnon (3-1f), and the news is carried to Manchester by a team of dogs and to London by carrier pigeon.

1826 The St Leger, won by Tarrare (20-1), is run for the first time over its present distance of 1mi 6f 132yd.

1827 Frank Buckle, an honest jockey in an age when this was the exception, rides his last Classic winners, Turcoman (5-1) in the 2,000 and Arab (8-1) in the 1,000, for a total of 27, more than twice as many as any of his contemporaries and a record that is to last for more than 150 years. It is thought that he might well have ridden two more, both in the 1,000, but the riders were not credited.

1828 In a rerun after the first dead-heat in Derby history, Jem Robinson cleverly gets Cadland (4-1) home by a neck from The Colonel, partnered by Bill Scott.

An appreciative crowd looks on as Squire Osbaldeston performs his amazing and unprecedented feat at Newmarket.

Newmarket: 5 November 1831

Squire Osbaldeston's ride

That great sporting gentleman Squire Osbaldeston has brought off a most unusual bet at Newmarket despite the most trying conditions of the weather.

The Squire, who is as well known for his fast underarm bowling on the cricket field, as a Master of Hounds and as an expert shot as he is for his exploits on the Turf, has won a wager of 1,000 guineas that he would ride 200 miles in under 10 hours.

Using 29 horses and riding round the Newmarket course, he completed the ride in the remarkable time of 8 hours 42 minutes despite the fact that for the first three hours it rained heavily without stop.

The Derby Epsom: 1834

'Plenipo' victory a blow for the Chifneys: Shillelagh beaten

The Chifney brothers, Will the trainer and Sam Jr the jockey, had a long, sad walk back to Newmarket after Shillelagh, the horse they thought could not lose, was beaten by the massive Plenipotentiary *(pictured right)* at Epsom in the Derby. For once, their judgement was at fault, and Mr S.Batson's chestnut colt justified his favouritism, coming home in a canter at 9-4. Glencoe, the Two Thousand Guineas winner, was third. It is no secret that the Chifneys, who have had their share of success at Epsom, backed Shillelagh heavily.

Plenipotentiary, who is by the 1823 Derby winner Emilius, was ridden by P.Connolly. He did not race as a two-year-old. He won a small race at Newmarket's Craven meeting, and then two days later registered an impressive win over Glencoe in the Craven Stakes.

[The Chifneys gambled heavily on Shillelagh again in the following year's Ascot Gold Cup, in which he was well beaten by Glencoe. The

disillusioned Will sold up and left Newmarket, while Sam Jr soldiered on for several years and won his 9th and last Classic, the 1,000 Guineas on Extempore, in 1843 – 36 years after his first. It could have been so many more for this talented son of Sam Sr had he not been so lazy and, as was widely believed, pulled a few potential winners.]

The St Leger Doncaster: 16 September 1834

Outsider wins St Leger: Mystery failure of favourite

Derby winner Plenipotentiary did not look in the peak of fitness during the parade for the St Leger, but one comment heard that he was carrying "enough blubber to sink a South Sea whaler" was a cruel exaggeration, and he went off a 12-10 on favourite. His running, however, was difficult to explain and he finished tenth of the eleven runners.

The race was won by Lord Westminster's 40-1 outsider Touchstone *(pictured, above right).* A brown colt by Camel, he was ridden by G.Calloway and trained by John Scott.

[Plenipotentiary, it was discovered, was

almost certainly poisoned, which accounted for his poor showing, but he was a failure at stud. Touchstone, on the other hand, went from strength to strength, winning the Ascot Gold Cup twice and becoming the most influential sire of the mid-19th century with a then record 12 Classic winners, including 3 Derbys.]

The St Leger Doncaster: 15 September 1835

Queen of Trumps makes history

Queen of Trumps: unique double

In front of the Duchess of Kent and her daughter, Princess Victoria, the Hon. Edward Mostyn's filly Queen of Trumps won the St Leger at Doncaster to become the first winner of the Oaks to complete this classic double. A brown filly by Velocipede, Queen of Trumps started as 11-8 on favourite and was ridden by Tommy Lye.

There were only 11 runners again for this important race for the cream of this season's three-year-olds, largely because the hard ground experienced all summer has been responsible for crippling so many of the 67 horses originally entered. In addition, only two of the 19 entered by John Scott's Malton stables started.

Behind Queen of Trumps were two other classic winners, the Derby winner Mündig and Preserve, winner of the Thousand Guineas and beaten favourite by Queen of Trumps in the Oaks. The rivalry between these two top fillies has intrigued followers of racing all season. Preserve, owned by Charles Greville, unofficially in partnership with his younger cousin Lord George Bentinck, was unarguably the best two-year-old last season, and was an impressive three-lengths winner of the Thousand Guineas, ridden by Nat Flatman. She was regarded as a certainty for the Oaks and, despite the intricate machinations of Bentinck to extend her starting price by giving the impression she was suffering from influenza, she went off at 7-4 on. But Queen of Trumps beat her easily into second place.

Bentinck, who fell out with his cousin over the running of Preserve in the Oaks, nevertheless was satisfied that Queen of Trumps had won entirely on merit and set about recouping his losses, first by backing her for the St Leger and then by making sure she came to no harm. He did this by persuading her owner to transfer her final training to Hednesford, where the softer downs would be kinder on her legs than the sandy soil of Holywell. Whether or not this was necessary, Queen of Trumps was certainly in the peak of fitness at Doncaster, and a convincing winner.

[As an epilogue to this story, three days later Queen of Trumps came out again at Doncaster, where she was made 10-1 on favourite to beat a couple of moderate opponents in the Scarborough Stakes. But just as she was making her challenge with 100 yards to go, a bulldog ran on to the course and brought her to her knees, leaving Ainderby to win the race and a substantial bet for her owner Capt. Frank Taylor. Such strokes of fate even Lord Bentinck could not legislate against.]

The Derby Epsom: 1836

Jem Robinson tames Bay Middleton to win 6th Derby

Leading in Bay Middleton after the 1836 Derby

The great jockey Jem Robinson won his sixth Derby, to make his own the record he shared with Bill Clift and Frank Buckle. To do so he not only held off the other 20 runners but he had to tame the fearsome temper of his mount, Lord Jersey's Bay Middleton.

A Bay colt by Sultan, Bay Middleton did not run as a two-year-old, as was his owner's policy. Despite his fractious temperament and a doubtful leg, he won the Riddlesworth Stakes at Newmarket's Craven meeting and then the Two Thousand Guineas, with odds of 6-4 laid on him, although he beat the useful Elis by only a neck. With the imperturbable Robinson up and Elis not running, Bay Middleton started as 7-4 favourite for the Derby and won the race impressively.

[A tragic footnote to the result of the Derby was the suicide that evening of the Hon. Berkeley Craven, whose unsuccessful wagering on the race had turned a serious position with his creditors into an impossible one. Bay Middleton continued in winning vein and was bought by Lord Bentinck for the then huge sum of £4,000, but his leg gave way and he was retired unbeaten in his 7 races. Unsuccessful at stud at first, he became champion sire twice in the 1840s.]

1828 Leading trainer Robert Robson retires with a record 34 Classics to his credit, including 12 Oaks and 9 Thousand Guineas (both still records), 7 Derbys (since equalled), but no St Legers.

1829 The first meeting at Aintree, the new course at Liverpool, is held.

1830 Tom Coleman (known later as the "Father of Steeplechasing") institutes the St Albans races, a series of steeplechases that puts this branch of the sport on the map. Before now, almost all the races had been matches between gentlemen.

1833 The first meeting takes place at Randwick racecourse, Sydney.

1834 Horses based at Newmarket from now on have their official birthday on 1 Jan, a convention adopted universally 24 years later.

1836 The Duke wins the first steeplechase held at Liverpool (Aintree), ridden by a certain Captain Becher.

1836 The first Prix du Jockey Club (French Derby) is run, at Chantilly, 2 years after the opening of the course.

1837 Riding Mango (13-2), Sam Day Jr, son of leading trainer-jockey J.B.Day, is the youngest ever winner of the St Leger. [He dies at 19, the next year, after a fall when hunting.]

1837 The Hampton Court Stud is put up for auction after King William IV's death, despite fulminating MPs and a Jockey Club petition, and the cream of the country's bloodstock departs overseas.

1838 In Australia, the first meeting at Melbourne takes place on 6 March.

1838 The Epsom-trained Amato (30-1), making his first and only acquaintance with a racecourse, wins the Derby. [His bones are buried in the plantation between The Durdans and the Epsom paddock.]

1838 Bill Scott rides his 5th St Leger winner (of a record 9, and the 1st of 4 on the run), guiding Don John (13-8f) to a 12-length victory in record time.

1839 The first Grand National, called initially the Grand Liverpool Steeplechase, takes place at Aintree.

1840 Flemington, Melbourne, is first used as a racecourse.

1840 Last year's National winner Lottery carries 13st-3 to victory in the 4-mile Cheltenham Cup Chase, a win that earns him an 18lb penalty in the next two Nationals!

1840 The young Queen Victoria visits Epsom for her first and only Derby, and sees it won by 50-1 shot Little Wonder, sent down from Berwick-on-Tweed. The unscrupulous Bill Scott, having backed his mount Launcelot to win a fortune and finding himself being overtaken by Little Wonder close to home, loudly offers the winner's jockey £1,000 to stop him – to no avail. At 14 hands 3 1/2 inches, Little Wonder is the smallest horse to win a Derby, despite, as is later discovered, almost certainly being a 4-year-old!

The 1836 St Leger winner Elis, with, on the left, his unconventional transport – the first horse-box

The St Leger Doncaster: 20 September 1836

Elis reaches Doncaster in record time to carry off Lord George's coup

When Lord George Bentinck's chestnut colt Elis won the St Leger, he brought off an audacious betting coup for his owner. Bentinck's penchant for honesty, as a zealous reformer of the Turf, is legendary, but it stops short of fairness to bookmakers.

Bentinck felt sure Elis was the second-best three-year-old in the country. Only Derby winner Bay Middleton, who beat him in the Guineas, was superior, and he was not running in the St Leger. Bentinck took advantage of the fact that the odds are against southern-trained horses attempting to win important races in the north, because of the travel by foot and the change of stables and feed. With Elis in Goodwood a few days before the St Leger, he was given little consideration by the bookies, so Bentinck had his commission agents working overtime getting his money on.

What the unsuspecting layers did not know was that Bentinck had arranged to have a special van constructed, padded inside and with a hard mattress to cushion the horse's knees if it fell. This cumbersome vehicle required six post horses to pull it, but, using relays of teams, Bentinck's trainer got Elis the 250 miles from Goodwood to Doncaster in just three days.

Elis started at 7-2, the bookies' losses being somewhat assuaged by a huge gamble made by the Scotts of Malton, who thought their horse Scroggins was unbeatable. But Bentinck's judgement was the equal of his cunning, and Elis duly came home two lengths ahead of the Malton colt.

The Grand Liverpool Steeplechase Aintree: 26 February 1839

New 'chase an outstanding success: Favourite Lottery wins

They came from far and wide, thousands of visitors pouring into Liverpool by road, rail and canal, in stately carriages, the new steam trains and paddle-boats, on horseback and on foot. Hotels for miles around were crammed to bursting point. The attraction was the great steeplechase at Aintree, and the talk for days had been about nothing else.

On the day, the crowd grew impatient at the delay caused by the weighing out and several false starts. Due to start at one o'clock, the race did not get off until three. But it did not disappoint. There were seventeen runners, all carrying 12 stone, tackling a cross-country course of more than four miles over open farmland, the severest obstacles being a high brick wall and, to be jumped twice, two difficult fences with brooks.

Conrad, ridden by the redoubtable Capt.Martin Becher, led over the first fence, a high obstacle of gorse and hawthorn. The Irish horse Daxon took the lead, with Conrad close up. But after racing across heavy plough to the first brook both hit the rails. Daxon somehow managed to negotiate the obstacle, but Conrad tipped Capt.Becher into the brook. After allowing several horses to jump clear, the gallant captain caught and remounted Conrad, but came to grief in the next brook.

Meanwhile, other runners were falling, Daxon twice before he went out, and the favourite Lottery began to look good, jumping beautifully as the field went into the country for the second time. Ridden by Jem Mason, Lottery was in command as they finally entered the straight, and a prodigious leap at the last fence left him well clear. He won by three lengths and the same from Seventy Four and Paulina. Seven horses finished, including one who was remounted, and one horse, Dictator, burst a blood vessel and died taking the second brook on the final circuit.

The race was a triumph for Mr William Lynn, proprietor of the Waterloo Hotel, who in 1836 began organising steeplechases at Aintree and then nearby Mughall, on the lines of the Great St Albans Steeplechase. With Mr Lynn's failing health, the organisation of this year's grand event was undertaken by a syndicate of some of the most prominent men of the Turf, including the Earls of Derby and Sefton and Lord Bentinck. The sport of steeplechasing, which, it must be remembered, had its origins across the Irish Sea, has taken a great leap forward with this successful venture at Aintree.

Captain Becher (left) struggles out of the brook that took his name after Conrad had spilled him in what was the first Grand National

Mr Powell on Railroad leads Jem Mason on Lottery over the formidable-looking stone wall

Mr John Elmore's 9-year-old gelding Lottery, the first winner of the Grand National. Lottery, out of Lottery, reputedly descended from the great Eclipse, was named Chance before Mr Elmore bought him for £120 and renamed him after his sire. Before the National, he had made a good impression when winning the Cheltenham Steeplechase, and started 5-1 favourite. For some reason, he hated Mason, and the leading jump jockey had to wear a coat over his colours every time he mounted him.

1841 The 11-y-o mare Catherina, the most prolific winner in the history of British racing, is retired after winning 79 races (48 2nds and 17 3rds) out of 176 starts. A daughter of the 1815 Derby winner Whisker, she ran only once in high-class competition, when unplaced in the 1833 Oaks. She picked up just over £5,000 in prize money, chiefly on Northern, Midlands and Welsh racecourses, and, including all the heats, she faced the starter nearly 300 times.

1842 Australian Jockey Club founded. First recorded meeting takes place in New Zealand, on the Epsom racecourse.

1843 The Grand Liverpool Steeplechase (later the Grand National) is made a handicap for the first time and renamed the Liverpool and National Steeplechase. Edward William Topham frames a handicap ranging from 11st to 12st-8, although, with a 5lb penalty, the in-form Peter Simple (3-1f), 3rd in the last two years, carries 13st-1 and can finish only 8th in the race won by Vanguard (12-1).

1843 Knight of the Whistle (5-1), ridden by Nat Flatman, wins the first running of the Royal Hunt Cup, at Ascot, in front of three horses dead-heating in 2nd place.

1844 The Ascot Gold Cup is won by a chestnut colt by Defence, owned by Lord Albermarle, who immediately names him The Emperor, in honour of the visiting Nicholas I, Tsar of All the Russias. The Tsar is so delighted that he asks to be allowed to present an annual prize, a piece of plate worth £500, to be called the Emperor's Plate. It is so known until 1853, after which, with England plunged into war with Russia, it reverts to being the Ascot Gold Cup.

1846 Bill Scott, coming to the start drunk on his own horse, Sir Tatton Sykes, 2,000 Guineas winner and now Derby favourite, loses 60 yards at the break yet goes down by only a neck to Pyrrhus the First, in the first officially timed (2min 55sec) Derby. (As Sir Tatton Sykes goes on to give Scott his 9th St Leger and his 19th and last Classic, it is fair to say that he would have achieved the first Triple Crown success had he not hit the brandy.)

1847 The Grand National, so named officially for the first time, is won by 9-y-o gelding Matthew (10-1jf) by a length from St Leger (15-1). The first Irish horse to win the race, Matthew, making his first appearance with only 10st-6 to carry, had been a 4-1 favourite until just before the start, when his odds inexplicably drifted out to the generous starting price.

1849 A triple dead-heat is recorded at Goodwood on 3 Aug in the March Stakes between Besborough, Sagacity and Nautch Girl.

The Oaks Epsom: 5 June 1840

Crucifix wins historic Oaks despite poor start

Lord Bentinck's remarkable filly Crucifix made racing history at Epsom when she won the Oaks to complete a unique treble, having already won both Guineas at Newmarket. This was her hardest race, for there were 16 false starts before the field got off an hour late, and Crucifix was badly away. But her jockey, John Day, who also trains her, got her up to win by half a length.

This ungainly bay filly by the 1830 Derby winner Priam started at 3-1 on. Because of her palpable superiority to fillies and colts alike from the very start, Bentinck has not been able to work any betting coups. But such has been his confidence in her, he doubled up several of her two-year-old races with the Oaks, so must have profited considerably from this latest triumph.

Bentinck bought the twenty-year-old mare Octaviana for £60 in 1837, when she was in foal to Crucifix. The young filly's first trial gallops at Danebury astounded the Day family, but news of this "world-beater" leaked out before her first planned race as a two-year-old, the July Stakes at Newmarket.

Furious at having had his "market" stolen, Bentinck almost withdrew her, but in the event she did run, and won hard held by two lengths at 6-5 on. Her only "defeat" came in her next race, the Chesterfield Stakes, for which she carried a 9lb penalty. Most of the runners covered the length of the course, Crucifix finishing second to Iris, before being recalled because of a false start – she won the re-run comprehensively. Then came two

Crucifix wins the Oaks, hard pressed for the only time, but in extenuating circumstances.

victories at Goodwood, followed by a rest and another five successes at Newmarket (including a walk-over and a dead-heat), all of these at odds on.

For such a magnificent racer, Crucifix is a strange filly to behold, standing nearly sixteen hands, with a long, light neck, thin shoulders, narrow chest, drooping quarters and small legs. In addition, she has a shambling gait and a tendency to cross her legs!

As a three-year old, Crucifix came out to win the Two Thousand at 11-8 on and the Thousand at 10-1 on, with only three opponents taking her on. Now the Oaks makes it twelve races unbeaten, and she is already a strong favourite for the St Leger.

[As Bentinck already knew, the Oaks was Crucifix's last race, as she had jarred her legs on the hard ground at the Guineas meeting. So she was retired and later, mated with Touchstone, she produced the 1848 Derby and St Leger winner Surplice.]

The Grand National Aintree: 5 March 1845

Unquoted Cure-all wins National after walking from Grimsby

The 1845 Liverpool and National Steeplechase has been a benefit indeed for the bookmakers. The original favourite was pulled out at the last moment, and the winner was virtually ignored in the betting. Indeed, Cure-all had been walked from Grimsby for the race, and it was only because of a withdrawal that he ran at all.

Cure-all ran in the name of Mr W.Sterling Crawford, a condition of the transfer of the nomination of his own horse, who had met with an accident in training. But he was ridden by his true owner, Mr William Loft. And had the latter had his way, the race would not have been run at all, for such were the icy conditions (the Leeds and Liverpool Canal was frozen over) that he and another owner protested to the stewards. However, a vote was taken and the race eventually got off late, at nearly five o'clock.

The 5-1 ante-post favourite The Knight Templar was said to have met with an accident

Aintree is packed for the 1845 Liverpool and National Steeplechase.

and withdrawn just before the start, and Vanguard was made the new 4-1 favourite. Cure-all was done at 15-1, but only for a very small amount, not enough for an official price.

Vanguard led from the start, but could not handle the ground and had to be pulled up. Loft found a strip of stubble to race on, rather than the testing plough, and this might have been the vital factor. As The Exquisite suddenly ran out of steam, Cure-all drew level with Peter Simple (9-1) at the last fence and won by two lengths, with The Exquisite third, another two lengths back. Only Tom Tug of the other 12 starters finished. It was the gallant Peter Simple's fifth unsuccessful attempt to win the race.

A great deal of credit is due to the winner's groom, Kitty Crisp, who patiently nursed him back to fitness after he was lamed in a heavy fall – and walked him to Liverpool and back to Grimsby again.

THE GRAND NATIONAL		
1839 Lottery	Jem Mason	5-1f
1840 Jerry	Mr Brethertom	12-1
1841 Charity	Mr HN Powell	14-1
1842 Gaylad	T Olliver	7-1
1843 Vanguard	T Olliver	12-1
1844 Discount	Mr H Crickmere	5-1jf
1845 Cure-all	Mr W Loft	*unqtd*
1846 Pioneer	W Taylor	*unqtd*
1847 Matthew	D Wynne	10-1jf
1848 Chandler	Mr J Little	12-1
1849 Peter Simple	T Cunningham	20-1

The Derby Epsom: 22 May 1844

Sordid events of the Derby

Stakes held pending inquiry: Winner Running Rein alleged to be 4-year-old

The running of the 1844 Derby has opened up a nasty can of worms, but the stewards cannot say that they were not warned. That denizen of the Turf Lord George Bentinck has been labouring long and hard to uncover the scandal of the horse running under the name of "Running Rein", and did indeed present a petition to the Epsom stewards five days ago to have the colt's mouth examined. But they ignored the warning, and allowed him to run with the proviso that the stakes would be withheld pending an inquiry if he won.

Well, he has won, and now complete chaos reigns. Colonel Peel, owner of the second and third horses, Orlando and Ionian, respectively, lodged an immediate objection on the grounds that the winner was in fact the four-year-old Maccabeus. The owner of the winner, Mr Alexander Wood, an honourable and respected Epsom corn merchant, replied straight away by bringing an action against Colonel Peel.

Nor is the cloud over Running Rein the only sordid circumstance of this sorry affair. Mr William Crockford's Ratan, the ante-post favourite, was undoubtedly nobbled in his box overnight despite the strictest precautions, and

another horse, Leander, was suspected of being a four-year-old,

When the 29 starters went to the post, the Two Thousand Guineas winner The Ugly Buck had been made favourite at 5-2, with the obviously distressed Ratan having gone out to 3-1, then came Running Rein, who had been backed down from 20-1 to 10-1, Leander at 14-1, Ionian 15-1, with Orlando among those on 20-1. The race was the first on the card and, after two false starts, was off at three o'clock.

Leander set a furious pace and was joined by Running Rein after half a mile. An extraordinary incident then occurred, at the top of the hill, which might have got the stewards off the hook, as Running Rein struck into the off hind leg of Leander. The latter, with his leg smashed, fell to the ground and had to be destroyed, but Running Rein was apparently not affected and stormed on. He led by several lengths as he reached the straight and, although this was considerably cut back, he could not be caught.

Col. Jonathan Peel, brother of the Prime Minister and a man of acknowledged integrity, has lodged his objection, and the world awaits the outcome.

CHAMPION JOCKEYS	
1846 E Flatman	81
1847 E Flatman	89
1848 E Flatman	104
1849 E Flatman	94

Wood v Peel Court of Exchequer, Westminster: 1 July 1844

"Running Rein" established as the 4-year-old Maccabeus: Orlando is the Derby winner

The case of Running Rein and the Derby is over, although much of the mystery remains. On the second day of Wood v Peel, the plaintiff, Mr Wood, has withdrawn, admitting there was a fraud concerning the horse, although asserting he had no part in this fraud himself and was indeed just as much a victim of it.

Mr Wood, much to his embarrassment, could not produce the horse in question, who had vanished from his trainer's stables at Epsom. Nor could he be found at the stables of former owner, and perceived villain of the piece, Levi Goodman, at Sutton.

The judge, Baron Alderson, in his summing up, expressed his regret and disgust at "noblemen and gentlemen of rank associating and betting with men of low rank and infinitely below them in society". He added: "In doing so, they have found themselves cheated and made the dupes of the grossest frauds."

[Running Rein and Maccabeus – both bays, with four black legs and a small white star on the forehead – were originally owned by Goodman, who switched them when Running Rein was a 2-yr-old. The new "Running

Running Rein: a "ringer", disqualified after the Derby

Rein" was heavily backed by those in the know when he won a 2-y-o race, and in a subsequent inquiry Goodman produced a key witness to identify the horse as the true Running Rein. He then contrived to give the colt to the honourable Wood as payment for a spurious debt, but kept control of his racing arrangements. Goodman was able to snap up early odds of 33-1 about the horse and would have made a fortune had his subterfuge come off. Thanks largely to Bentinck it didn't, and the Jockey Club conveyed their thanks to the latter for "the energy, perseverance and skill he has displayed in detecting, exposing and defeating the atrocious frauds" and presented him with a valuable piece of plate subscribed to by the higher echelons of the racing fraternity in their gratitude.]

The Derby Epsom: 25 May 1848

The "Blue Riband of the Turf"

It must indeed have been a bitter-sweet day for Lord George Bentinck as he watched Surplice win the Derby. The colt, son of his beloved triple Classic winner Crucifix, was sold to Lord Clifden two years ago when Lord Bentinck disposed of his entire racing interests, which were becoming a burden both financially and on his time.

So he has not fulfilled what had been his burning ambition, to win the Derby, although he had backed the

even money favourite at long odds before Christmas. And he was largely instrumental in getting Surplice to the post, as, after a trial at Goodwood two weeks ago in which Surplice established himself as a virtual certainty for the Derby, there was every incentive for certain shady characters to prevent him starting.

In the event, Surplice's biggest danger was his tendency to run lazily when in the lead, but he hung on to fend off a

late challenge from Springy Jack and win by a neck.

Epilogue: Two days before the Derby, Bentinck had lost a long and hard-fought campaign in the House of Commons. On the day after the Derby, as he was standing dejectedly in the Commons library, his friend and colleague Benjamin Disraeli, approached him to offer consolation. Bentinck asserted that Disraeli did not appreciate the importance of the Derby. Disraeli, who was

very proud of the blue Garter sash he had recently been accorded, made his famous reply: "Indeed I do, it is the blue riband of the Turf."

[Surplice, starting at 9-4 because of two listless displays at Goodwood, became the first Derby winner to win the St Leger since 1800. It was the last Classic Lord George ever saw, as six days after the Derby meeting he died of a heart attack aged 46. Disraeli, two years his junior, became Prime Minister in 1868.]

The Latter 1800s

T he development of the railways in the mid-1800s made racecourses more accessible to the general public – Ascot, Epsom, Goodwood and Newmarket in the south, Chester, Doncaster and York in the north, all flourished. The active interest taken by the Prince of Wales in the Turf was a great boost for the sport. He became a member of the Jockey Club in 1864, and two years later a patron of leading trainer John Porter. Racing had indeed become a respectable pastime, along with the betting that went with it – although betting offices were closed down in 1853.

Racing began to flourish abroad, too. In France, Longchamp was opened in 1857, and the pari-mutuel system for betting was devised in 1865, the year that the French colt Gladiateur came over to win the English Triple Crown – to the horror of the patriotic British racegoers. The first Melbourne Cup was held in 1861, the first Irish Derby in 1866, and in the United States the three races that make up their Triple Crown were inaugurated from 1867 to 1875.

Racecourse innovations included the banning of yearling races in 1859 and the introduction of the draw for starting positions in 1877. Among the great thoroughbreds to grace the scene in this period were West Australian, the first Triple Crown winner (1853), the fillies Blink Bonny (1857) and Formosa (1868), and those two outstanding, unbeaten colts of the 1880s, St Simon and Ormonde.

The Grand National Steeplechase Committee was founded in 1866, becoming the National Hunt Committee in 1889, and steeplechasing's equine heroes included The Lamb and The Colonel, who shared the four Nationals between 1868 and 1871.

The jockeys' championship was dominated for a decade and a half by George Fordham, who won 13 of the 15 titles from 1855. Fred Archer reigned supreme from the mid-1870s, and became one of the most loved and respected personalities in the country – so much so that his suicide in 1886 overshadowed everything else that happened on the Turf in the latter part of the century.

Fred Archer (inset) drives Bend Or to victory (main picture) in the 1880 Derby

1850s

1850 Derby winner Voltigeur starts as 13-8 on favourite for the St Leger, but needs a run-off to beat Russborough after a dead-heat.

1851 The first recorded quadruple dead-heat takes place, on 26 April at The Hoo, where Defaulter, Squire of Malton, Reindeer, and Pulcherrima finish in line in the Omnibus Stakes.

1851 A meeting on 16 December heralds the start of racing at Canterbury, in New Zealand.

1853 The Betting Houses Act becomes law in England, resulting in the closing down of betting offices.

1854 Hot Grand National favourite Miss Mowbray, winner in 1852 and runner-up in 1853, is "got at" and has to be withdrawn shortly before the race. Money

pours onto the new favourite, Bourton, who wins by 15 lengths at 4-1 in a field of 20. Unfortunately, there is no ruling body to investigate the scandal. The next year, Miss Mowbray (4-1 second favourite) has to be destroyed after breaking her neck and back.

1854 The Great State Post Stake, run in 4-mile heats, takes place at Metairie, New Orleans, on 1 April, with four runners. Four states muster a starter at $5,000 each, making it the richest race yet, and it is won in straight heats by Lexington, the representative of Kentucky.

1854 The filly Virago, raced only once as a 2-year-old, begins her 3-year-old career at Epsom with two races – and two wins – on the same afternoon, remarkably following victory in the 1 mile 2 furlong City and Suburban Handicap with another in the 2 mile 2 furlong Great Metropolitan. Trained by John Barham Day, who bought her as a yearling for £300, she goes on to win 10 of her 11 races, including the 1,000 Guineas.

1855 Thirsk stages its first race meeting, on 15 March.

1855 Lord of the Isles beats St Hubert by a neck at Newmarket in the 2,000 Guineas, the two colts being trained by son and father, William and John Barham Day, respectively. The owners, on hearing that this was an arrangement, to be reversed for the Derby, make other training arrangements for Epsom.

1857 Emperor Napoleon III opens Longchamp racecourse on 27 April.

1857 The 34-horse Cesarewitch on 13 October finishes in a triple dead-heat between Prioress (100-1), El Hakim (8-1), and Queen Bess (30-1). A re-run takes place at the end of the programme over another 2 miles 2 furlongs, but not before shrewd bookmaker George Hodgman persuades American owner Richard Ten Broeck to drop Prioress's jockey, who, he considered, had not given her the best of rides. Backed heavily by Hodgman, Prioress, under ace jockey George Fordham, wins the decider at 2-1, beating El Hakim (5-4f) by 1½ lengths.

1858 From this year, horses celebrate their official birthday on 1 January.

1858 Little Charley (100-6) wins the Grand National at his 4th attempt, ridden by former jockey and stud manager for the Emperor of Russia, William Archer, whose 14-month-old youngest son Frederick James will go on to win undying fame on the flat.

1858 The Craven Plate at Salisbury on 29 April finishes in a triple dead-heat between Pinsticker, Polly Johnstone, and Bar One, the first two mentioned dead-heating again in the run-off before Pinsticker finally won a second run-off.

1858 Vatican walks over after twice dead-heating with Lustre in the Revival Stakes at Chesterfield on 28 September.

1859 Yearling races are banned in Britain.

1859 Mayonaise (9-2), George Fordham up, wins the 1,000 Guineas (4 runners) by 20 lengths, a record for any Classic.

1859 Fisherman ended his career with nearly 70 wins, including a record 23 as a 3-year-old in 1856, 22 in 1857, and 21 in 1858 – over distances from 4 furlongs to 3 miles.

Grand National Aintree: 1850

No betting on little winner Abd-el-Kader

Of the record 32 starters for the Grand National, tiny Abd-el-Kader was ignored in the betting, and when the 8-year-old bay came home a length clear of the field, the bookmakers rejoiced. Home-bred in Ireland by Henry Osborne of County Meath, the winner was foaled by a mare "plucked" for 40 guineas by the owner in 1827 from a coach he was travelling in.

Last year's winner, Peter Simple, the 5-1 favourite, and The Knight of Gwynne led the field after the first circuit. But Chris Green jumped "Little Ab" into the lead at Bechers

second time around, and the little horse put on a dazzling display of jumping before holding off the challenge of The Knight of Gwynne at the line. Peter Simple, who with 12 st 2 lb was giving 32 lb to the winner, failed to finish. The winner's time, 9 min 57 1/2 sec, was a new course record.

[Abd-el-Kader, carrying only 6 lb more the following year, became the first horse to win the National twice, this time at 7-1 and by only half a neck. He ran thrice more, pulling up in 1852, finishing 5th in 1853, and falling in 1858.]

CHAMPIONS

1850	E Flatman	88	
1851	E Flatman	78	
1852	E Flatman	92	
1853	J Wells	86	
1854	J Wells	82	
1855	G Fordham	70	
1856	G Fordham	108	
1857	G Fordham	84	
1858	G Fordham	91	
1859	G Fordham	118	

Match York: 13 May 1851

'Dutchman' wins re-match

The long-awaited re-match between Lord Eglinton's The Flying Dutchman and Lord Zetland's Voltigeur took place at York this afternoon over 2 miles and for a stake of 1,000 guineas. When they last met, both unbeaten, in last year's Doncaster Cup, Derby and St Leger winner Voltigeur, carrying 7 stone, won by a neck from the 1849 Derby and St Leger winner, who started 4-1 on favourite but was conceding 26 pounds. They were the only runners, and it is said that the "Dutchman's" jockey Charles Marlow was

"tight as a tick", a handicap he could ill afford against a match rider of Nat Flatman's renown.

This time, however, with the betting even and Flatman making the pace, the Dutchman emerged victorious by a short length in 3 min 55 sec, conceding 8 1/2 pounds to the younger horse. It was a desperate struggle, and at the finish supporters of the Dutchman, said to have wandered about "pale and silent as marble statues" after the defeat at Doncaster, greeted their hero with tumultuous cheering.

GRAND NATIONAL

1850	Abd-el-Kader	Mr C Green	unqtd
1851	Abd-el-Kader	T Abbott	7-1
1852	Miss Mowbray	Mr A Goodman	unqtd
1853	Peter Simple	T Oliver	9-1
1854	Bourton	Tasker	4-1f
1855	Wanderer	J Hanlon	25-1
1856	Freetrader	G Stevens	25-1
1857	Emigrant	C Boyce	10-1
1858	Little Charley	W Archer	100-6
1859	Half Caste	C Green	7-1

Grand National Aintree: 1853

Old stager Peter Simple wins National again

That grand old steeplechaser Peter Simple, now 15 and tackling his fifth national, won it for the second time, beating last year's winner Miss Mowbray by 3 lengths, with Abd-el-Kader, winner the previous two years, in fifth place. It was a popular victory, for the price of 9-1 about a horse that had failed to finish in his last three attempts could only have been that short because of public sentiment.

Mr T.F.Mason's two entries, Miss Mowbray and Oscar, led the betting, and despite the owner's declared preference for the latter, it was the mare who started favourite at 5-1. Approaching Bechers in the lead, Peter Simple was buffeted by a loose horse but bounced back on course by top weight Sir Peter Laurie, coming up on his inside. He regained the lead, but

suddenly Abd-el-Kader made a characteristic surge to the front and opened up an enormous gap, clearing the Water 100 yards ahead of the field. Coming out of the country, however, "Little Ab" began to lose momentum, and by the time they reached the last it was a three-horse race, with the powerful Tom Oliver easily holding off challenges from Miss Mowbray and Oscar to record his third success in the race and bring home the oldest winner to date.

Peter Simple was carrying 10 st 10 lb, 4 lb less than when he won in 1849 and considerably less than the burdens he had to shoulder in the intervening years.

[Peter Simple ran once more in the National, understandably failing to finish the following year having been unreasonably asked to carry an additional 32 lb.]

West Australian and Sittingbourne, by H Hall, Newmarket

St Leger Doncaster: 15 September 1853

'The West' is first Triple Crown winner

Mr John Bowes' West Australian cantered in at Doncaster to win the last Classic of the season and become the first horse to complete the coveted Triple Crown – 2,000 Guineas, Derby and St Leger. Starting as 6-4 favourite, "The West", as he is now affectionately known, gave Frank Butler an easy ride and the partisan Yorkshire crowd a day to remember. For trainer John Scott, the "Wizard of the North", it was a 12th St Leger win in 27 years.

After the Derby, in which The West had started at 6-4 on and only just got up to beat Sittingbourne and Cineas by a neck and a head, backers were able to get odds about him. But he has obviously reached his peak, and after cruising in by 3 lengths, jockey Butler said: "I only touched him with the whip once and was glad to get him stopped." So Butler, nephew of the great Sam Chifney, has achieved something his uncle never managed – the Triple Crown.

[West Australian won all three of his races as a 4-year-old, including the Ascot Gold Cup in record time, before being retired to stud.]

Derby Epsom: 27 May 1857

Filly triumphs in close Derby finish

Winter favourite Blink Bonny, starting at 20-1 after her dismal odds-on defeat in the 1,000 Guineas at Newmarket, made a dramatic return to form at Epsom to win the Derby. Six horses were involved in the finish, but none of the colts could catch the flying filly once she got her head in front. The only other filly to have won the Derby was Eleanor in 1801.

When the horses had taken their preliminary canters, the police, with admirable discipline and tact, marched shoulder to shoulder up the course, driving all loiterers before them, and leaving the running ground stretched out between the serried ranks of people like a long green belt, and as smooth and as clear as a billiard table. In the meantime, the din of tongues in the ring had swelled into a deafening noise. Book-makers were dodging in and out the crowd, and layers and backers generally seemed to be indulging in a complicated game of hide and seek. Amidst the noise and the excitement, the pushing and driving, it was somewhat difficult to ascertain the real tone of the market. It was evident, however, that Tournament held his position firmly, while Skirmisher, who had been slightly depressed, was again in high favour. The advance of M.D. to 7-1, and the desire evinced to back Blink Bonny by those persons who wished to "get out", and by others who remembered her two-year-old running, and were, despite her very wretched exhibition at Newmarket, determined to get on, were the principle incidents which marked the end of speculation.

As the horses emerged from the paddock on to the course, the shouting and bawling in the ring suddenly ceased, and a prolonged confused roar of curiosity and excitement broke out from the multitude as they approached the starting-post. No sooner had the starter taken command of them than the ranks were scattered by the breaking away of certain horses. A long series of failures followed, before the horses could be got off, and as one false alarm after another was raised, the impatience and excitement of the spectators were displayed with an intensity which was striking and impressive. At length a simultaneous shout of "They are off!" was sent up for the last time, and this shout subsided into a kind of murmur as the horses streamed up the hill, and again swelled into a roar as they turned round Tattenham Corner.

When they had fairly landed in the straight, Lamborne and Anton were in the lead, with Black Tommy, Adamas, Arsenal, M.D., Wardermarske, Blink Bonny, and Strathnaver showing nearly in a line behind. On nearing the stand, Strathnaver headed Anton, with Blink Bonny waiting upon them, Adamas, Arsenal, and Black Tommy going on in close attendance. In a few strides further a most exciting set-to ensued, and Charlton "let out" Blink Bonny, who immediately rushed to the front. She stayed there to the line, a neck in front of the 200-1 shot Black Tommy, with Adamas and Strathnaver a further head and neck in third and fourth, just ahead of Anton and Arsenal.

The result in some ways was scarcely unexpected, for the winner had throughout the winter been the leading favourite, and had only lost her position in the betting by her defeat at Newmarket for the 1,000 Guineas, a defeat which is now inexplicable, and which perhaps can only be attributed to the glorious uncertainty of the turf.

Newmarket: 22 October 1855

Quadruple dead-heat

By Roughscratcher

The first day of the Newmarket Houghton meeting, the last of the season, produced a rare occurrence in racing, a quadruple dead-heat, the only other recorded instance of which took place four years ago at The Hoo.

In the fifth race, a Sweep- stakes of 10 Sovereigns for 2-year-olds, four of the five runners – Gamester, Lady-go-Lightly, Unexpected, and Overreach – could not be separated at the finish. Overreach won the deciding heat, with Unexpected placed second.

Oaks Epsom: 29 May 1857

Derby heroine Blink Bonny captures Oaks

[From our own correspondent]

The certainty of Blink Bonny's success diminished the attraction of Oaks day. In the Ring, an enquiry was made now and then about another filly, but all who had the money to spend laid it out on Blink Bonny, and her party never feared the field for an instant. The race itself, in which the 5-4 on favourite was seen coming in by herself, 8 lengths ahead of Sneeze in second, scarcely stirred the spectators to activity. It will long be remembered, however, for not since the year 1801 have the Oaks and Derby been carried off by the same animal.

[Blink Bonny was "pulled" by jockey John Charlton in the St Leger.]

DERBY			
1850	Voltigeur	J Marson	16-1
1851	Teddington	J Marson	3-1f
1852	Daniel O'Rourke	F Butler	25-1
1853	West Australian	F Butler	6-4f
1854	Andover	A Day	7-2
1855	Wild Dayrell	Robt Sherwood	1-1f
1856	Ellington	T Aldcroft	20-1
1857	Blink Bonny	J Charlton	20-1
1858	Beadsman	J Wells	10-1
1859	Musjid	J Wells	9-4f

1860s

1860 Yearlings are no longer allowed to race in Britain

1861 The first Melbourne Cup takes place, on 7 Nov. An all-age handicap over 2 miles, run at Flemington, the inaugural race is won by a 5-y-o called Archer (6-1), carrying 9st 7lb. Starting out nearly a month earlier, the winner had been walked some 550 miles from the stables of his trainer Etienne de Mestre, in New South Wales. [Archer became a popular hero, winning again in 1862 under 10st 2lb, and the race became the biggest event on the Australian sporting calendar.]

1863 The Grand Prix de Paris is first run, at Longchamp. At the instigation of Emperor Napoleon III, it is, unlike the French Classics which are closed to foreign opposition, open to all. It is won by the English horse The Ranger.

1864 Lord Coventry is unable to run last year's Grand National winner, the 8-y-o Emblem, but he wins it just the same, with her 6-y-o full sister, Emblematic – their sire was the 1851 Derby winner, Teddington.

1864 Fille de l'Air (6-4f) wins the Oaks to become the first French-trained winner of an English Classic.

1865 The first pari-mutuel betting system is devised, by Parisian Pierre Oller.

1865 The French colt Gladiateur becomes only the second horse to win the Triple Crown – 2,000 Guineas (7-1), Derby (5-2f) and St Leger (8-1f).

1866 The Grand National Hunt Steeple Chase Committee is founded [name changed to the National Hunt Committee in 1889].

1866 The first Irish Derby takes place, at the Curragh over an extended 1 3/4 miles [it came down to its present 1 1/2 miles in 1872] and is won by Selim (5-4) in a field of 3.

1866 Triple Crown winner Lord Lyon is returned the odds-on favourite for all 3 Classics – 4-7, 5-6 and 4-7.

1866 Jockey Harry Grimshaw, 25, who won the Triple Crown on Gladiateur last year, is killed on 4 Oct when his trap overturns on his way home to Newmarket.

1866 Stockwell, 2,000 Guineas and St Leger winner in 1852, is champion sire for the 6th time with £69,391 [a total unsurpassed until Blandford in 1934].

1867 John Day Jr trains 146 winners in the Flat season [a record that stood for 120 years, until beaten by Henry Cecil].

1867 The first Belmont Stakes, run over 1mi 5f at Belmont Park, is won by the filly Ruthless in a field of 4.

1868 The filly Formosa (100-30jf) wins the St Leger to complete a remarkable 4-timer in this year's Classics, having won the 1,000 Guineas (10-11f) and the Oaks (8-11f) and dead-heated for the 2,000 Guineas (5-2f).

1869 Last year's Derby winner Blue Gown beats Formosa, the winner of the other 4 Classics (one jointly), in the Trial Stakes, an optional selling race worth the grand sum of £135 to the winner!

Gladiateur: successful French raider

The St Leger Doncaster: 16 September 1863

The great St Leger day

The excitement, which has been growing and growing, culminated on the Doncaster Town Moor this day, as the steeds were mounted and saddled. The race for the Derby, as usual, left certain questions undecided. Lord Clifden, it will be remembered, was second by only a head to Maccaroni, who was not amongst the St Leger nominations, and when he stretched himself down for his canter the magnificence of his stride once more revived the recollection of the splendid form he exhibited that day.

But directly the flag fell, Lord Clifden was over one hundred yards behind everything, and a derisive roar broke from the members of the ring as they saw the horse, for another mile, last of all. At this moment any price could have been obtained about him, £100 to a shilling having been absolutely laid.

As they approached the Red House turn, Lord Clifden (100-30f), striding on, bore down upon his horses, and passing them one by one, drew up alongside of Queen Bertha, Borealis, Golden Fledge. and The Ranger. At the distance The Ranger retired, and the spectators were fairly electrified to find Lord Clifden with the race in hand. Johnny Osborne sat quite still until within a few strides of the chair, where he just roused his horse, who came away, and he won in the most gallant style by half a length from Queen Bertha (7-1).

The Derby Epsom: 31 May 1865

Blue Riband crosses the Channel: Gladiateur pride of France

The deed is done! Count de Lagrange has carried away from perfidious Albion the blue riband which she never expected to see depart from the shores. The news has flown already by the wings of electricity over all England, that "the Frenchman" yesterday defeated our native-born cracks, and that, too, in a style so splendid that admiration must mingle with patriotic regret. The eighty-sixth Derby will henceforth be remembered as "Gladiateur's year", and Gladiateur – alas for the pride of the land that taught France what horse-racing meant! – is a French-bred horse.

Never mind if he be proved one of the best animals that was ever foaled, the good old school can never be consoled for such a reverse. There is some comfort, perhaps, in the fact that an English jockey rode him; and in his pedigree, which brings him back to us, through Irish blood; but that is merely to be reminded that, like the eagle, we are wounded by an arrow feathered from our own wing.

By and by the boards go up, and the bell rings to clear the course for the Derby of 1865 – here, at last, is the "horse of vengeance" – this is Breadalbane, and "eleven thousand pounds" isn't the only recommendation of that brilliant son of Blink Bonny, pure warm chesnut, who takes every eye away. The hand upon his snaffle is loosed – and "There is the winner!" people cry, as Aldcroft bends over his beautiful and proudly carried head, and humours him with a great stride or two.

Here, too, at last are the "Gauls" – Gladiateur and Le Mandarin. We look for a fault in the foreigner, and can't see one, and the traitor Grimshaw sits him like a statue – coloured after Gibson. Then they all come back together, and Breadalbane is vociferously backed at 5-4 for a place – though the terrible Frenchman, that won the Two Thousand, always keeps his insulting place at the head of the odds, at 5-2.

As to the false starts, twelve times the pencil marked miscarriages of this sort. But the flag falls at last, and soon, as the faces turn and the riders pass, the agony of the year is at its height abreast of you, and a brown horse with a white and black jockey wins, with another in white, black, and gold belt, madly whipped, at his saddle-flaps. Not so! – by Neptune, God of horses, and all the Centaurs! – Gladiateur has been closing like Fate upon them from the Corner! The "whites and blacks" spur and lash, and roll in their saddles – vainly! - for the French horse, with Grimshaw cool and conquering, "draws out like a telescope", reaches, collars, passes Christmas Carol (100-7) and Eltham (1,000-8), and, with the finest specimen of a winning stride that can be imagined, carries the fatal red cap past the judge's chair, two lengths and more in advance of all. Breadalbane (7-2) – done with, defeated, disgraced – *[contd]*

[contd] was it the taint of his foster-mother, the cart-mare's milk? – pants past us eleventh or twelfth in the race, to win which his owner risked so much.

The cheers of his backers greet Gladiateur. We are beaten by the Frenchman and we are staunchly determined to sustain our defeat valiantly. Grimshaw, escorted by mounted police to the scales, gets a round of applause for his magnificent riding, and Gladiateur is pronounced to be a horse worthy to carry the great English prize – in hard cash nearly £7,000 – to France. Thus the blue riband must cross the Channel.

CHAMPIONS

1860	George Fordham	146	1865	George Fordham	142
1861	George Fordham	106	1866	S Kenyon	123
1862	George Fordham	166	1867	George Fordham	143
1863	George Fordham	103	1868	George Fordham	110
1864	J Grimshaw	164	1869	George Fordham	95

Stockbridge: 18 June 1867

Six winners for Fordham

From HOTSPUR

Magnificent weather inaugurated the meeting in the beautiful Hampshire valley. The towns in the Stockbridge districts, even as far down "the line" as Southampton, are filled with racing visitors, and the quaint and interesting old city of Winchester wore a most animated appearance this morning, as four-in-hands, wagonettes, and flys rattled up the narrow streets in the direction of the Stockbridge-road.

My remark yesterday, that it would be a "Fordham and John Day week", and the suggestion that all who wished to get rich should follow the Danebury trainer and jockey, was wonderfully confirmed the first day. Fordham quite surpassed himself. There were eight races on the card, and in seven of these the great jockey rode six winners and a dead heat.

The meeting of the crack two-yr-old fillies, Leonie and Athena, created great interest and excitement. Odds of 5 to 2 were laid on Fordham's mount Athena, and a distance from home Leonie seemed beaten; but she went on, and, sticking to the Marquis's filly, made a dead heat. In the "decider", Leonie cut down her antagonist, now 11-8 on, with great ease at the finish, and won by a length and a half to spoil Fordham's perfect day.

The 2,000 Guineas Epsom: 28 April 1868

A dead heat in the Guineas

An enormous attendance, which could only be compared to the mobs which assembled in Gladiateur's year, witnessed the first dead heat for the Two Thousand on record, between Moslem (14-1) – an animal who only a few weeks ago was unheard of – and Mr Graham's mare Formosa, the 5-2 favourite.

Moslem retained a slight advantage of Formosa, and it was apparent at the dip that the race was a match between the pair, who were three lengths clear of the field. Fordham rode the mare in the most artistic manner, closing on Moslem inch by inch. Formosa got on even terms with him a few strides from the chair, a splendid struggle resulting in a dead heat between the pair.

Much disappointment was manifested that the dead heat was not run off, but the owners agreed to divide the stakes, which was, perhaps, sound policy on both sides, as Formosa has the One Thousand staring at her in the face – a race she might, by a second "bucketing", have placed in jeopardy.

Grand National Aintree: 4 March 1868

National favourite shot: The Lamb wins

By HOTSPUR

On Tuesday night, on the eve of the Grand National, speculators interested in wagering used to block up the dingy avenues of a little "public" in Liverpool; but the venue of betting is now changed to the "Washington Hotel". Standing upon the stately stairs at midnight was a crowd of conspicuous sportsmen, including the Duke of Hamilton and Lord Westmorland and several "amateurs". Towards midnight real business was transacted, and Chimney Sweep was backed in hundreds at 7-1. At the break-up, the sooty gentleman had decidedly the honour of enjoying the rank of firm favourite.

The morning opened dull and mistily, but it became more agreeable towards noon. They had scarcely settled in their places and had only, in fact, reached the lane, when Chimney Sweep trod on a large stone that lay in the course, and in consequence fell and broke his leg. The accident caused immense excitement and consternation to prevail in the stand, from which point Adams, the jockey, was seen first to vault out of the saddle, and next to return to the enclosure on foot. So serious was the injury sustained by Chimney Sweep, that Lord Coventry, to put an end to the horse's sufferings, ordered him to be shot, and this was immediately done.

In the last mile, the issue was entirely between The Lamb (9-1) and Pearl Diver (10-1), and both were so completely exhausted that they knocked down the last hurdles. The Lamb, the "little iron-grey pony", finished the strongest, and having the Diver fairly settled at the distance, Mr Edwards went on and won amidst uproarious cheering by a couple of lengths, with Alcibiade (16-1), the winner of 1866, third. Tremendous was the enthusiasm of the Irish sportsmen at the victory of the little representative of the Emerald Island.

GRAND NATIONAL

1860	Anatis	Mr Thomas	7-2f
1861	Jealousy	J Kendall	5-1
1862	Huntsman	H Lamplugh	3-1f
1863	Emblem	G Stevens	4-1
1864	Emblematic	G Stevens	10-1
1865	Alcibiade	Capt Coventry	100-7
1866	Salamander	Mr A Goodman	40-1
1867	Cortolvin	J Page	16-1
1868	The Lamb	Mr Edwards	9-1
1869	The Colonel	G Stevens	100-7

DERBY

1860	Thormanby	H Custance	4-1
1861	Kettledrum	R Bullock	16-1
1862	Caractacus	J Parsons	40-1
1863	Macaroni	T Chaloner	10-1
1864	Blair Athol	J Snowden	14-1
1865	Gladiateur	H Grimshaw	5-2f
1866	Lord Lyon	H Custance	5-6f
1867	Hermit	J Daley	1000-15
1868	Blue Gown	J Wells	7-2
1869	Pretender	J Osborne	11-8f

1870s

1870 The Jockey Club restricts the length of the Flat season.

1870 Amateur jockey George Ede, who rode as "Mr Edwards" and who partnered The Lamb to victory in the 1868 Grand National, is about to go home after an unsuccessful National when a trainer begs him to ride Chippenham in the Sefton 'Chase over a single circuit of the course the next day. His friend, Arthur Yates, implores him: "Don't ride the brute, George, he'll kill you." But Ede, soon to retire from competitive racing to marry, does ride him, and is killed in a terrible fall.

1871 Leading jump jockey George Stevens, winner of a record 5 Nationals, is killed while out riding his hack. The horse, startled in a high wind, whips round and unseats Stevens, who hits his head on a boulder.

1871 In the absence of "Mr Edwards", Lord Poulett asks Tommy Pickernell to ride The Lamb in the National, for the sole reason that he dreamt "Mr Thomas" rode him to victory. Tommy obliges and brings the little horse home in record time, the 4th dual winner of the race.

1871 Malton trainer John Scott, 77, dies. He saddled a monumental 40 Classic winners (1827-63), including 5 Derbys and a record 16 St Legers, his most famous horse being West Australian, the first Triple Crown winner (1853).

1872 The Derby is run over its present course for the first time.

1873 The Preakness Stakes, the 2nd and shortest of the US 3-y-o classics, is run for the first time, on 23 May at Pimlico, Maryland, and won by Survivor by 10 lengths. The race was named after the double-winner at the inaugural Pimlico meeting in 1870.

1875 Sandown Park, the first enclosed course in Britain, is opened on 22 April.

1875 The first Kentucky Derby is run on 17 May at Louisville over 1 1/2 miles, and is won by Aristides, "The Little Red Horse". It was founded by Col M.W.Clark, who had studied the racing business in Europe for two years and who named it after the famous Epsom race.

1876 Regal gives owner Capt James Machell his 3rd Grand National winner in 4 years. Machell, who resigned his commission in 1863 after being refused leave to attend the Doncaster races, sent out the 1st, 4th and 6th in the 1874 National.

1877 Jockey Club rules provide for a draw for starting positions.

1877 Amateur rider Fred Hobson, whose curious habit of clutching the saddle at every fence caused consternation among the purists, ignores strong advice and partners his own horse Austerlitz in the Grand National – and wins it in his only National ride.

1877 Fred Archer wins on all 6 of his mounts in the 7-race card at Newmarket on 19 April, only two of which are favourites, for a 504-1 accumulator. He won the first race, a stakes for 4-yr-olds over 2mi 105yd, in a canter by 6 lengths on Skylark (6-4) in a field of 3, and the last, a similar race over the same distance, by 4 lengths on the same horse, this time at 6-5 on, against one other runner.

1878 Fred Archer wins the St Leger on Oaks winner Jannette (5-2f), having won last year on Silvio (65-40f), both for Lord Falmouth, who also owned the runner-up in each year.

1878 The French pari-mutuel system is operated for the first time at the Kentucky Derby.

1879 Jockeys in Britain must be licensed.

1879 Sir Bevys wins the 100th running of the Derby.

Grand National Aintree: 9 March 1870

Second National for The Colonel, fifth for George Stevens

By HOTSPUR

People who declare that the public are losing their regard for the national pastimes should have been present at Aintree. Never had so many thousands of spectators been congregated on the course. Every elevated spot or position from which a view of the struggle could be obtained was secured. Sportsmen whose experience went back many years, and to the palmy days of steeplechasing, declared that they had never witnessed such a spectacle at Liverpool.

It would be impossible here to do justice to the brilliant race, which ended in The Colonel's emulating the achievement of Abd-el-Kader, and winning for a couple of years in succession, while George Stevens became the first horseman to ride five Grand National Steeplechase winners, and two consecutively. The departure of the train containing my despatch compels me to be brief in my notes, further criticism being reserved until Monday.

Mr Topham had wisely modified some of the most dangerous jumps, and the result was a race of deep interest, and unattended with any mishap – Fan and Traveller being the only two refusers.

Intense excitement was aroused when The Doctor appeared so formidable a quarter of a mile from home, and when the last struggle took place between the Soldier and the Surgeon the furore was wonderful. The Colonel, outlasting The Doctor, and disputing every inch to the winning post, won by a neck only. Primrose, third by three lengths, ran a splendid race, and after the first two hundred yards she was either first or second until passed by The Colonel and The Doctor when nearly home.

Just below the distance, The Doctor had appeared to have so much the best of it that shouts of a deafening nature proclaimed his anticipated victory. The Colonel, however, ran with surprising gameness, and George Stevens, by his magnificent riding, landed him the winner amidst a scene of extraordinary enthusiasm.

CHAMPIONS

1870	W Gray	C Maidment	76	1875	F Archer	172
1871	G Fordham	C Maidment	86	1876	F Archer	207
1872	T Cannon		87	1877	F Archer	218
1873	H Constable		110	1878	F Archer	229
1874	F Archer		147	1879	F Archer	197

GRAND NATIONAL

1870	The Colonel	G Stevens	7-2f
1871	The Lamb	Mr Thomas	11-2
1872	Casse Tete	J Page	20-1
1873	Disturbance	Mr J Richardson	20-1
1874	Reugny	Mr J Richardson	5-1f
1875	Pathfinder	Mr Thomas	100-6
1876	Regal	J Cannon	25-1
1877	Austerlitz	Mr F Hobson	15-1
1878	Shifnal	J Jones	7-1
1879	The Liberator	Mr G Moore	5-1

The St Leger Doncaster: 13 September 1871

Third Classic for Hannah

From HOTSPUR

The result of the St Leger was altogether in accordance with the sympathies of the vast concourse that assembled to witness the last of the great three-year-old contests on the Doncaster Town Moor. Yorkshire itself was compelled to discard "home influences" for the nonce, and to join in the congratulatory roar that proclaimed Baron Rothschild's Hannah – the victress of the One Thousand Guineas and of the Oaks – the successful combatant for the much-coveted Northern prize.

After years of patient perseverance, during which he has experienced many sore disappointments, Baron Rothschild has reached the very pinnacle of racing prosperity, having in one short season succeeded in carrying off four such glorious prizes as the One Thousand Guineas and the Oaks with Hannah, the Derby with Favonius, and now the St Leger with the beautiful daughter of King Tom. Such a run of good fortune has never been equalled by any one owner of horses in the same season.

Orator made the pace a hot one from the outset for his stable companions Ringwood and Bothwell, until his mission was accomplished, and then, after Digby Grand, Rose of Athol, and Général had each for a brief moment raised the hopes of their backers by showing formidably, an exciting finish was left to Hannah (2-1), Albert Victor (3-1), and Ringwood (10-1), the Baron's filly winning very cleverly by a length.

The ovation that greeted the mare and her rider, Charlie Maidment, who was also on her in the 1,000 Guineas and Oaks, on their return to weigh in was exceeded only by a whirlwind of cheering that burst out when Baron Rothschild was recognised. Such a scene of genuine and spontaneous enthusiasm has indeed been rarely witnessed on a racecourse.

Grand National Aintree: 18 March 1875

Third National for Mr Thomas

FROM OUR SPECIAL CORRESPONDENT

Mr Thomas rode his third Grand National winner this afternoon, and although he fancied his Liverpool chances very greatly, and the party backed him, Pathfinder was not a public horse, and consequently started at 1000 to 60. Mr Thomas [Tommy Pickernell] has been accurately styled one of the first gentlemen jockeys of the Turf, and it may be doubted whether any professional surpasses him either in horsemanship or in good fortune.

The start was a good one, and the first round of the course was accomplished at a very quick speed, with but few casualties. The second round commenced, and again the phalanx was a close one, and the field but slightly diminished. Two colours began to show themselves prominently – green the one, chocolate the other. For a time it appeared as though the Grand National would really go to the favourite La Veine (6-1). Close pressing the French mare, and passing her, came Dainty (25-1), her jockey conspicuous in bright green.

The horses were nearing home when a new colour rushed to the front – one that had been all but unnoticed during the race – violet and white hoops. This horse was Pathfinder, and the race now, in fact, lay between two outsiders, La Veine lying third. The last jump was cleared, and Mr Bird's Pathfinder was declared the winner of the 1875 Grand National, to the surprise of all and the intense disgust of not a few.

An objection on the ground of insufficient description fell to the ground, being frivolous, and the Stewards ordered the £5 to be forfeited.

The Oaks Epsom: 2 June 1876

French fillies dead-heat in Oaks

BY OUR SPECIAL CORRESPONDENT

English owners are having decidedly the worst of it just now, for whilst a Hungarian-bred colt has run away with the Derby, a couple of French fillies have passed the post locked together a long way in front of the rest of a very "ragged" field for the Oaks.

Since her victory in the One Thousand, Camelia has been greatly fancied, and from 3 to 1 has found partisans bold enough to back her down to 5 to 4, at which rate of odds she started. Enguerrande (4-1), who caught her in the last few strides, has, after being a moderate two-yr-old, improved greatly, and done extremely well this season in France, her second to Kilt in the Chantilly Derby last Sunday stamping her amongst the best.

After entering the straight the favourite took up the running, attended by Merry Duchess, with Enguerrande drawing closer on the outside. At the Bell it looked any odds on Count de Lagrange's mare, but Glover began to ride her directly after, and Hudson, setting to very resolutely on M Lupin's filly, got up on the post, and made a dead heat of it. Merry Duchess (33-1) finished third four lengths off.

In the absence of M Lupin the party were in a difficulty whether to run the race off or not, but this was eventually surmounted, and an official announcement was made that stakes would be divided, as also, of course, are the bets.

Kincsem: extraordinary record

Goodwood Cup 1 August 1878

Unvanquished Hungarian mare wins at Goodwood

From HOTSPUR

A tamer Goodwood Cup has never been known, as of the nine coloured on the card only three went to the post. Betting at the outset had been 7 to 4 against Pageant and 3 to 1 each against Kincsem and Lady Golightly; but when the fact became known that they alone would form the field, layers reduced the prices to 5 to 4 against Pageant and 2 to 1 against Lady Golightly, the Hungarian mare being the worst favourite at 3 to 1 (offered freely). She was not liked when stripped, good judges pronouncing her too lengthy, but she looked very hard and well.

Pageant settled down with the lead a couple of lengths in advance of Lord Falmouth's mare, the foreigner lying off. In this way they ran round the loop, but about six furlongs from home Kincsem began to close up, and as Archer was hard at work on Lady Golightly before entering the straight, the contest became reduced to a match.

Half-way down the hill 10 to 1 was freely offered on Pageant, on whom Cannon was sitting still, whilst Madden was flogging Kincsem, and the Kingsclere horse appeared to be having it all his own way. The mare, however, stuck to her work, and as when finally called upon Pageant proved unequal to the effort of drawing away, Kincsem, amidst the cheering of the fielders, won in a canter by two lengths after having been spurred up to the shoulders. She is obviously a rare animal, and little need be said to recommend her further than that she has now won 37 consecutive races.

Mr E.Blascovitz purchased her at the break-up of Prince Esterhazy's stud, and has been amply repaid by her unprecedented successes. Her stamina is undoubtedly her strong point, and in a fast-run race she would have won by a hundred yards. She was, however, very severely punished with both whip and spur, and will remember her Goodwood Cup race for a long time to come.

[This was Kincsem's only race in England, but she travelled all over Europe and retired undefeated in 1879, with a record 54 wins to her credit. The name is Hungarian for "My treasure".]

1880s

1880 Three Beasley brothers, all amateur jockeys, spearhead a raid on the Grand National from across the Irish Sea, and the eldest, Tommy, who was 2nd and 3rd the previous two years on Martha, wins it this time on Empress (8-1), trained by Henry Linde, while Harry finishes 5th on Woodbrook [who wins it next year with Tommy up] and John 8th on Victoria, 10 of the 14 starters completing the course.

1882 Tommy Beasley is deprived of a National hat-trick by an extraordinary ride in a blizzard by the inexperienced Lord John Manners on his own horse Seaman, a horse whose previous trainer Henry Linde and current trainer James Machell both felt was not robust enough for such a race. Coming over the last, Seaman (10-1) is just behind Beasley's mount Cyrus (9-2), with the only other of the 12 starters still standing, Zoedone, well beaten. Seaman has obviously broken

down, though, yet despite running virtually on three legs, he gets up to beat Cyrus by a head.

1882 Fred Archer rides 6 winners in 6 mounts at Lewes on 5 Aug, the 2nd time he has accomplished this feat.

1882 For the first [and only] time, all 5 Classics are won by fillies, Shotover the 2,000 (10-1) and Derby (11-2), St Marguerite the 1,000 (10-1), Geheimniss (4-6f) the Oaks and Dutch Oven (40-1) the Leger.

1883 In the smallest ever field for the Grand National – 10 – Zoedone (100-7) wins from 6 other finishers, ridden by the first foreigner to win, Austrian diplomat Count Charles Kinsky, at his first attempt.

1884 The 6-y-o Voluptuary - bred by Queen Victoria, 6th in the 1881 Derby and whose only public jumping experience was a couple of minor hurdle races – wins the Grand National.

1884 Buchanan (3-1) wins the Kentucky Derby on his first public outing.

1884 The Derby is shared for the first time, between dead-heaters Harvester and St Gatien, the only other instance of a dead-heat having been in 1828, when there was a run-off.

1885 Zoedone, 5-1 2nd favourite to repeat her 1883 National triumph, is "got at" shortly before leaving the paddock, injected with a poison. Although she falls on attempting the preliminary hurdle, Count Kinsky decides to give the public a run for their money (she has been coupled in doubles with the Lincoln winner), but she finally falls on the second circuit when well behind. [This was Zoedone's last race and the Count's last appearance in the National; he is later made an honorary member of the Jockey Club and elected to the National Hunt Committee.]

1885 The Bard sets a record number of wins for a British 2-y-o – 16 (including one walk-over).

1886 The first £10,000 race in England, the Eclipse Stakes, takes place on 23 July at Sandown Park and is won by Bendigo.

1886 The great Ormonde wins the St Leger, the shortest priced favourite to date (1-7) and Fred Archer's 6th success in 10 years. He is the fourth horse to complete the Triple Crown, the first for 20 years, having won the 2,000 Guineas (7-2) and Derby (4-9f).

1886 Newmarket closes 12 Nov for the funeral of jockey Fred Archer.

1887 Bendigo wins the inaugural Jubilee Handicap, at Kempton Park.

1877 Merry Hampton wins the Derby on his first appearance in public.

1887 The Duke of Westminster's 4-yr-old Ormonde (3-100f) wins the Imperial Gold Cup at Newmarket's July meeting and retires undefeated after 16 wins.

1888 Jim McLaughlin rides his 6th Belmont Stakes winner in 7 years.

1888 First meeting at Leopardstown, in Ireland.

1889 Racing colours, or silks, become compulsory.

The Derby Epsom: 1 June 1881

Archer steers American-bred colt to Derby victory

[FROM OUR OWN CORRESPONDENT]

The most remarkable feature of yesterday's Derby was Archer's reception immediately after his victory on Iroquois, the first American-bred colt to win England's "Blue Riband". People literally threw their caps in the air and waved their handkerchiefs as the successful jockey passed through the elbowing crowd to weigh in. When he won race after race on Tuesday and Wednesday, the crowd seemed to ascribe something super-human to the great man.

The 2,000 Guineas winner Peregrine started 6-5 favourite, with Iroquois, second in the Guineas, 11-2 second favourite. As the field came into the straight, Voluptuary took up the running, with Peregrine and Iroquois in a group of six close up.

Webb, who had gone a little wide at the turn, got splendidly placed in the line for home, and terrific shouts of "The favourite wins!" were hardly raised when Archer was seen in pursuit. To head and shake off Peregrine was the work of a few strides only, and the stars and stripes had won the day.

The Derby Epsom: 26 May 1886

Ormonde wins the Derby

From HOTSPUR

It is "Ormonde's year" and no mistake. If anything could add popularity to the triumph of the favourite (4-9) and 2,000 Guineas winner *(pictured)*, it is the fact that he had to put in some good work before he could shake off his sturdy little opponent, The Bard (7-2), who, on his 17th appearance before the public and his first this year, sustained his first defeat.

When Ormonde and The Bard came out nearly half a mile from home, we saw a triumphant vindication of public form, as from that point the remainder had really no share in the race. The crucial test did not come until 200 yards from home.

Then it was that the superiority of Ormonde manifested itself in a striking degree, as, although The Bard had drawn a neck in front, Archer no sooner sat down in earnest than the "boy in yellow" drew out and secured the verdict easily by a length and a half. The farther he had gone, the farther would he have won.

The Duke of Westminster can now boast of his third Derby in the short space of seven years, and the success of Ormonde is rendered the more complete seeing that he belongs to the first of the Bend Or crop. John Porter can now claim to have trained four Derby winners, while Archer has ridden one more.

Ascot Gold Cup: 12 June 1884

St Simon wins Gold Cup in a canter

[FROM OUR SPECIAL CORRESPONDENT]

The struggle for the Gold Cup showed in his finest form a horse that is beyond all question the grandest three-year-old in Europe. The bookmakers actually took 75-40 that St Simon would not win. Yet this really looked a foregone conclusion, as he had simply made a hack of the six-year-old Tristan in their trial match at Newmarket, while Faugh-a-Ballagh, who would have been more at home in the Alexandra Plate, belonged to an entirely different class.

How St Simon's performance was watched by thousands from all points commanding a view of the course, from the start to the finish; how every eye was strained to mark for a time C.Wood's confident tactics in lying off from the field, while Friday, attended by Iambic, took the lead, the latter being counted on to make the running; how the favourite still kept back, cautiously lessening his distance, till the time came for the rush; how, within a quarter of a mile from home, St Simon flew past Tristan (100-30), then the leading horse; and how, from that moment, the favourite cast off his pursuers in a scattered group, winning by a score of lengths, will be told in the chronicles of Ascot and in the history of a horse who now confirmed his reputation.

[St Simon, who had not been entered for the Classics, retired unbeaten at the end of the season and became the greatest sire of the 19th century.]

Report: Tuesday, 9 November 1886

Suicide of Fred Archer

When this startling announcement was displayed in Fleet-street yesterday afternoon it was at first received with incredulity, although it was known that the famous jockey was suffering from severe cold at his home at Newmarket and his health was in a weak state from wasting. The information was soon verified, and when the details of his untimely decease by his own hand became known the shock was of an even more startling character.

The name of Fred Archer was so well known all over the world that his sudden demise was looked upon as a great calamity, and was the chief topic of conversation among all classes during the evening.

On Thursday Archer was in the saddle at Lewes, where he caught a cold. On Sunday it was found he was suffering from an attack of typhoid fever. Early yesterday morning a bulletin announced his condition as much more favourable. About one o'clock Archer was attended by his sister, Mrs Coleman, and the nurse, when he desired the latter to retire. A short time later, Mrs Coleman, who was at the window, hearing a movement, turned, and was horrified to see Archer staggering across the room with a revolver in his hand. She at once attempted to disarm him, but before she could do anything, Archer, while holding her tightly with one hand, deliberately placed the muzzle of the pistol in his mouth, fired and fell, bleeding and dying, in his sister's arms.

Frederick Archer was the son of William Archer, a steeplechase rider, living at Cheltenham, and was born at

Fred Archer's grave

Prestbury, near that town, on Jan 11, 1857. So well did he figure in the saddle that when only eleven he was apprenticed to Mr Matthew Dawson, of Newmarket, and at that time he scaled only 4st 11lb. After going through the usual routine of a jockey's apprenticeship, he appeared in the saddle at Chesterfield races in 1870, where he began his brilliant record by steering Athol Daisy to victory in a nursery handicap.

In 1873, he rode 107 winners, only three behind the champion jockey, H.Constable, and the following year, at 17, won the title for the first time. He never lost it. In 1875, he had 172 winning mounts, a new record, and eight times exceeded 200 winners in a season, last year's total of 246 setting a new record. In all, he rode 2,748 winners from 8,084 mounts. He rode 21 Classic winners – six St Legers, five Derbys, four Oaks, four 2,000 Guineas and two 1,000 Guineas – and would surely have gone on to beat Frank

Buckle's record of 27.

It is needless to say that the tragic end of a man so greatly beloved and so universally admired in the sporting world has elicited the deepest emotions of surprise and sorrow. In Newmarket every person is talking of his kindness of heart, and his incomparable achievements.

Archer was a widower, his wife having died in childbirth two years ago, her loss being keenly felt by her husband. He leaves the one child, a little girl.

He returned from a successful trip to Ireland last month in order to ride St Mirin for the Cambridgeshire, the only big race he had never won. In order to get down to the handicapped weight, Archer underwent great privation, and for three consecutive days went without food, whilst on the other hand he dosed himself with trying medicine, and spent the best part of his time in the Turkish bath attached to his private residence at Falmouth House. By these means he was able to ride St Mirin at 8st 7lb, one pound overweight, and was bitterly disappointed to lose by a head. The effort probably cost him his life.

DERBY

1880	Bend Or	F Archer	2-1f
1881	Iroquois	F Archer	11-2
1882	Shotover	T Cannon	11-2
1883	St Blaise	C Wood	5-1
1884	St Gatien*	C Wood	100-8
	Harvester*	S Loates	100-7
1885	Melton	F Archer	75-40f
1886	Ormonde	F Archer	4-9f
1887	Merry Hampton	J Watts	100-9
1888	Ayrshire	F Barrett	5-6f
1889	Donovan	T Loates	8-11f4

Dead-heated.

The St Leger Doncaster: 14 September 1887

Left at start, Kilwarlin wins St Leger
By HOTSPUR

Kilwarlin, the winner of the St Leger, may be said to have won under serious disadvantages, as, at the fall of the flag, he stopped behind until all the others had travelled quite 150 yards. In a strongly run race, this must have been fatal to the chance of the 4-1 favourite.

It was fortunate for all those with an interest in Kilwarlin that the pace was for more than half the

journey no better than an ordinary canter, and the upshot was that Kilwarlin passed Eiridispord (85-20) and Timothy (100-8) before climbing the hill. Kilwarlin drew ahead a distance and a half from home and retained his advantage to the end, winning by half a length from Timothy, a head separating second and third, Derby winner Merry Hampton (6-1).

CHAMPIONS

1880 Fred Archer................................120	1885 Fred Archer................................246
1881 Fred Archer................................220	1886 Fred Archer................................170
1882 Fred Archer................................210	1887 C Wood 151
1883 Fred Archer................................232	1888 F Barrett....................................108
1884 Fred Archer................................241	1889 T Loates....................................167

GRAND NATIONAL

1880	Empress	Mr T Beasley	8-1
1881	Woodbrook	Mr T Beasley	11-2jf
1882	Seaman	Lord Manners	10-1
1883	Zoedone	Count C Kinsky	100-7
1884	Voluptuary	Mr E Wilson	10-1
1885	Roquefort	Mr E Wilson	100-30f
1886	Old Joe	T Skelton	25-1
1887	Gamecock	W Daniels	20-1
1888	Playfair	G Mawson	40-1
1889	Frigate	Mr T Beasley	8-1

The 1890s

The glamour of racing received further fillips in the 1890s when the prime minister, the Earl of Rosebery, won the 2,000 Guineas and Derby in 1894 with Ladas, and the Prince of Wales the Derby and St Leger in 1896 with Persimmon. The latter was the son of St Simon, who was champion sire for the first seven years of the decade and by 1900 had sired 17 Classic winners to equal the record of Stockwell some thirty years earlier.

There were an extraordinary number of Triple Crown winners in the decade – Common (1891), Isinglass (1893), Galtee More (1897) and Flying Fox (1899), as well as La Flèche, who won the fillies' equivalent in 1892. Two legendary names from steeplechasing also graced the nineties. Cloister, after twice finishing second, finally won the Grand National in 1893, the first horse successfully to carry 12st-7, and in a record time that stood for forty years. Who knows what he might have accomplished had he not been almost certainly nobbled in both succeeding Nationals when hot ante-post favourite? But Manifesto restored the damaged image of the sport with hugely popular victories in 1897 and 1899, elevating the prestige of the National to new heights.

Morny Cannon was six times champion jockey in the nineties, but the arrival in 1897 of the American jockey Tod Sloan had an immense impact on the English scene. His "monkey-on-a-stick" seat, his streamlined crouch over the horse's neck, and above all his tactics of racing the whole distance, revolutionised English jockeyship.

Starting tapes were used for the first time in Britain at Newmarket in 1897, and new racecourses included Lingfield (1890) and Haydock Park (1899).

Main picture: The Prince of Wales leads Persimmon in after his 1896 Derby victory and, as The Daily Telegraph put it, "... in superabundant gratification at this right royal triumph all conventionality was thrown to the winds. Hats rose in the air, and the crowd delivered such volleys of cheers as have never before been heard."

Inset: Persimmon's sire, St Simon, whose progeny enjoyed prolific success in the Classics of the 1890s.

ST. SIMON

1890

28 Aug In a race set up against the clock, the 4-y-o Salvator records 1min 35 1/2sec to break the world mile record by 3 3/4sec on Monmouth Park's straight course in the USA.

10 Sep Memoir provides a second St Leger in succession for the Duke of Portland and trainer George Dawson, and the 3rd Leger win for jockey

Jack Watts, his 4th Classic this season.

4 Nov Carrying a massive 10st 5lb, the former New Zealand 2-y-o champion Carbine, now 5 and a great public hero in Australia, has to be pushed and dragged to the start for the Melbourne Cup, but proceeds to win the race in record time, 3min 28 1/4sec for the 2-mile handicap.

Grand National Aintree: 28 March

National won by hot favourite

From HOTSPUR

The fences of the Grand National were reckoned smaller than in previous years, and yet the majority of the combatants failed to complete the long journey.

The question of supremacy in the betting was decided in the most distinct manner, as the confidence of all connected with Ilex continued to the eleventh hour, and he closed at 4 to 1. Without being overdone in condition, Mr Masterman's horse was fit to run for his life. Curiously enough, the first three of last year, Frigate, Why Not and M.P., were all easy at the finish.

The pace was far from fast at the commencement, and the chase progressed as smoothly as possible to the fence before Becher, when Why Not fell, and although Mr Cunningham soon remounted, he never went smoothly afterwards. Other casualties were in store,

and when the racecourse was reached the first time the backers of Frigate, Gamecock, Bellona and Hettie searched for them in vain.

Jumping boldly and safely, Ilex cleared the stand in front of M.P., and when Voluptuary fell and broke Skelton's collarbone at Valentine's the second time round the issue was reduced to Ilex, M.P. and Pan.

With a mile to go, M.P. was well beaten and the race resolved itself into a match between Ilex and Pan. Ilex soon got the upper hand and he won easily by 12 lengths.

The belief that weight would tell in his favour has been strongly urged in these columns from the outset, and his owner deserves credit for having expressed his confidence in the most open manner.

The Derby Epsom: 4 June

Sainfoin wins in the rain

By HOTSPUR

Sainfoin's Derby will go down to posterity as the most soaking and incessantly wet holiday that the oldest London inhabitant can recall for nearly forty years. It was surprising to find so much enthusiasm evoked by the result of the big race. The thousands who occupied the Downs without being able to obtain the least respite stood their ground resolutely until Sainfoin had been proclaimed the hero of the hour.

The field of eight, falling one short of the totals when Ormonde and Ayrshire were the winners, was the smallest on record for close upon a century. The critics who assembled at the paddock and trudged through the wet grass in search of Sainfoin fell in love with him at first sight as, if not framed on a big scale, he is full of quality and has been trained to the hour. Le Nord seemed none the worse for his trip to Chantilly and back, and Rathbeal, who was a tremendous eleventh-hour tip, has grown into a charming colt.

For the first three-quarters of a mile the pace was wretchedly slow, and whereas in the Two Thousand Liddiard could hardly hold Surefoot to the Bushes, he now managed to place him at the heels of Kirkham, who followed Orwell, Golden Gate, and Sainfoin to the top of the hill. This sort of work did not suit Surefoot and, besides attempting to savage Sainfoin and Rathbeal, he nearly laid hold of the latter's jockey.

The despised Orwell was a thorn in the side of his stable companion, Sainfoin, until passing the distance, when Le Nord challenged boldy on the upper ground and Surefoot made a final effort.

For a few strides Sainfoin (100-15) looked like winning easily, but Le Nord (100-7) came with a rare rattle, and, creeping up at every stride, only succumbed by three-parts of a length; Orwell (100-1) lost second place by a neck and finished a head in front of Surefoot (40-95f), who was placed fourth.

The St Leger Doncaster: 10 September

Memoir has smooth win in rough St Leger

From HOTSPUR

The overnight calculation of sixteen runners for the St Leger was spoilt by the absence of Hebrides, which left the Manton stable without a representative. Just one-third of the number came from Kingsclere, and full as John Porter's hands may have been, all his charges stripped in the bloom of health and conditions.

Blue Green came back to tens as, though like Memoir (also 10-1) he wore blinkers,

his behaviour in the preliminaries was all that could be desired. Both Heaume (5-2f) and Sainfoin (4-1) left off in strong demand.

The pacemaker from Hampshire, Orwell, found a travelling companion in Odd Fellow, and to such a merry tune did they gallop that the field soon opened out. As they approached the bend Surefoot was dying away, and with St Serf then striking into his heels, Loates had a very

narrow escape of a spill. He only saved himself through being held up by Alloway. The chances of the pair were completely destroyed, and a second scrimmage occurred at the bend, where Heaume was badly cut into and Blue Green was forced against the rails.

Memoir had the good fortune to avoid even the slightest interference, and, to the surprise of those who expected to see her signally

fail to stay the course through want of condition, she passed Sainfoin and Heaume full of running below the distance. In the meanwhile Blue Green had extricated himself from trouble, and, with the blinked pair first and second, the verdict, to which Memoir could perhaps have made no addition, was a couple of lengths. So stoutly did the despised Gonsalvo (200-1) finish that he beat Sainfoin for third place.

1891

19 Apr On his first racecourse appearance, Common, trained by John Porter at Kingsclere, wins the 2,000 Guineas at Newmarket by 3 lengths from Orvieto, to clinch the first leg of the Triple Crown.

The Derby Epsom: 27 May

A dismal Derby

From HOTSPUR

Few of the members of the House of Commons who voted against the adjournment for Derby Day assisted, it may be presumed, at the great summer carnival. By staying away they acted with discretion, as, instead of the "sink of iniquity", we had some experience of "the Slough of Despond". The sunshine of the early morning was a snare and a delusion, and old stagers travelled back in memory to Daniel O'Rourke's year for a scene of similar wretchedness.

The heavy rain, which ceased soon after the Town Plate, was little more than a preliminary, and the jockeys engaged in the Derby were kept prisoners in the weighing-room by a storm of hail that for a few minutes covered the course with a white carpet. This had scarely passed before black clouds rolled up from the south-west and discharged themselves in volumes as the great event of the day was in progress.

Fractional odds were at the last moment entrusted to Common. Gouverneur (100-9) carried his colours well to the fore at the mile post, and, sailing along at a fair pace considering the state of the ground, was not caught until a quarter of a mile from home. Then Common, who had parted from Dorcas and Martenhurst in rounding Tattenham Corner, collared him without a perceptible effort, and gave George Barrett the great satisfaction of knowing that he was on the back of his first Derby winner. So decisive was the result that Common won by a couple of lengths under half-steam only.

As in 1882 and 1883, John Porter can boast of having trained the winner in successive years, and with Bend Or and Ormonde to remember in the bargain, he has an Epsom record of which he may well be proud.

Grand National Aintree: 20 March

Come Away survives objection to win National

From HOTSPUR

Most admired perhaps of the twenty-one competitors was last year's winner, Ilex. Still, the favouritism which he resigned to Come Away he never recovered, and in spite of the frequent hints to the detriment of the latter, the money told a tale of unimpaired confidence in the newcomer, which he justified at the winning post.

A mile from home Come Away assumed the command, and entered the inner circle of the racecourse slightly in advance of Cloister, Ilex and Why Not. All four were being ridden hard at this point, and when Why Not came to sad grief two fences from home it is more than probable that Mr Cunningham missed the

great object of his ambition, namely, to steer the winner of the Blue Riband of the chase.

Between the last two fences Ilex was completely spun out. Cloister struggled with such stoutness that he reduced the verdict of Come Away to half a length. Captain E.R.Owen lodged an objection on the grounds of a jostle when approaching the bend at the distance. Without saying that this was frivolous, I did not see sufficient grounds for a reversal of the verdict and when the stewards confirmed the judge's decision, they took a popular view.

Come Away pulled up very lame and his days of hard work are, perhaps, numbered.

CHAMPIONS

Jockey	Morny Cannon	137
Leading Owner	Mr N Fenwick	
Horse	Common (3)	

BIG RACE RESULTS

2,000 Guineas	Common	G Barrett	9-1
1,000 Guineas	Mimi	F Rickaby	7-1
Derby	Common	G Barrett	10-11f
Oaks	Mimi	F Rickaby	4-7f
St Leger	Common	G Barrett	4-5f
Grand National	Come Away	Mr H Beasley	4-1f

The St Leger Doncaster: 9 September

Common has to work for Triple Crown

From HOTSPUR

In the dull days of Winter, when the racing season, which is fast speeding onward, becomes subject of retrospective writing, it will be impossible to revert to the feast of St Leger otherwise than in most pleasant words. What with the magnificent weather of the purest Autumn type, a company that has seldom been equalled in point of size, and the triumph of a long-reigning and popular favourite, there was not a single flaw.

Common, who after his Derby triumph sustained his first defeat, finishing third to Surefoot and Gouverneur in the Eclipse Stakes at Sandown Park, stripped as hard as nails in the parade and 5 to 4 was freely laid on him. Matthew Dawson reckoned that Mimi had quite come back to her Spring and Summer form, when she won the 1,000 Guineas and Oaks, and she

Triple Crown winner Common

started second favourite of the nine runners at 5-1.

It was no easy race, and Common, only the 5th colt to win the Triple Crown, had a long struggle to gain the verdict by a length from Révérend (11-2) with St Simon of the Rock (50-1) losing second place by a neck. A neck behind the latter came Bosphorus (33-1), with Mimi fifth. This was one of the gamest St Leger performances within my recollection, and the Yorkshire roar that awaited Common on the return to scale was richly deserved.

The Oaks Epsom: 29 May

Mimi wins Oaks in a canter

From HOTSPUR

Has the glory of Epsom departed, or is the capricious state of the weather or the presence of influenza to be held responsible for the poor assemblage which gathered together to witness the race for the Oaks Stakes? Whatever be the reason, there can be no doubt but that the "Ladies' Day" was shorn of most of its traditional splendour and gaiety. Champagne itself could not arouse the general listlessness, for the ladies had no new dresses and hats to criticise and if necessary (metaphorically) tear to pieces.

No excitement was possible over a race which, bar accidents, was a foregone conclusion for the 1,000 Guineas winner, Mimi. With

exquisite feminine reasoning, one damsel inquired anxiously of another, "Why doesn't Common run in the Oaks?" On it being pointed out that the contest was for ladies only, she immediately retorted with a shrug of her shoulders, "Dear me, how stupid the fillies must find it!"

The history of the race is brief. After St Kilda and Sabra had played conspicuous parts for three-quarters of the course, Mr Fenwick's beautiful mare cantered away from the other competitors and passed the winning-post at a hand gallop, four lengths ahead of her rivals, with Rickaby turning round in his saddle, possibly to see who would be second and third.

1892

25 Mar Cloister (11-2f) is 2nd again in the National, but his jockey of last year, Capt Roddy Owen, is this time on the 20-lengths winner, Father O'Flynn.

3 Jun Two days after just failing to land the Derby, the Porter-trained La Flèche (8-11f) pips Smew (100-6) in the Oaks by a short head.

31 Oct The great Ormonde, 1886 Triple Crown winner and sire of Orme, at stud

overseas, is bought by Mr M'Donough of San Francisco from Don Juan Bocau of Buenos Aires for $15,000 (£30,000).

17 Dec Covert Side, the 20-1 outsider of 3 in the 3-mile Ovingdean Steeplechase at Plumpton, declines to go farther than half-way and his rider takes him back to the paddock, but with the other 2 also persistently refusing, he returns to the course to win.

The Derby Epsom: 1 June

A delightful Derby

From HOTSPUR

Not for very many years have so many ladies graced the Derby scene with their presence. It looked as though the Oaks, and not the contest usually devoted to the sterner sex, were going to be decided. Was their attendance due to the fact that a filly was the favourite for the competition; was it because of the increased animation in the interests of woman's rights; or was it by reason of the delicious atmosphere tempting every owner of a pretty frock or tasteful bonnet to come and be seen and admired on the Hill, by the rails, or in the boxes of the Grand Stand?

What a weary time is taken up by the start, chiefly owing to the bad behaviour of Thessalian and Galeopsis! It is half-an-hour after time when the flag falls and the bell rings. Up to the mile post Persistive, St Damien and Thessalian are going ahead, then, when the corner is turned, and the shout of "Hats off" has gone up, Bucentaure appears to have the best of it and "the Frenchman wins!" is heard on every side. "The favourite! The favourite! La Flèche! La Flèche!", is the next shout, but Allsopp on Sir Hugo (40-1) staves off the mare's gallant challenge and Lord Bradford's white, scarlet sleeves and cap, catch the judge's eye three-quarters of a length before the citron and turquoise of Baron Hirsch.

There is not much cheering at the result, for the public in general has been hard hit by the defeat of the 11-10 favourite.

The St Leger Epsom: 7 September

Fillies' Triple Crown for La Flèche: Orme fails to stay

From HOTSPUR

There was no outward sign in the paddock for the marked hostility to the Derby winner; the nearer the end, however, the worse he travelled in the market, and as the numbers went up Sir Hugo was out to 10-1, while of the Kingsclere trio Orme was firmly set at 6 to 5 on, with 9 to 2 procurable about La Flèche.

When the field came round the bend, May Duke joined Orme, and the pair were closely attended by La Flèche, Watercress and Sir Hugo. The first beaten was Orme, and with May Duke in trouble almost simultaneously, La Flèche took up the running followed by Watercress and Sir Hugo. Of these Watercress was done at the distance, and Sir Hugo could never get on terms with La Flèche, who turned the tables on the Derby winner and won rather easily by two lengths for a third Classic triumph.

Chester: 2 May

The "nobbling" of Orme

FROM OUR SPECIAL CORRESPONDENT

The Duke of Westminster had declared that Orme was "foully poisoned on Thursday week". On Saturday I had occasion to run down to Chester upon another mission, and finding myself, on a beautiful afternoon, within four miles of the Duke's magnificent country seat at Eaton Hall, I gladly seized the opportunity of obtaining such information upon the all-absorbing topic of the day as the Duke might think proper to impart to me.

Quiet, calm, and undemonstrative about passing events which to most men would seem catastrophes of the deepest dye, the Duke has (to use the language best filled to the occasion) never "turned a hair" since the first disastrous tidings about Orme reached him. Doubtless his first impulse, had health permitted, would have been to repair instantly to Kingsclere to inspect the interesting patient, whom every racing man of common sense has long regarded as the winner of the Two Thousand, the Derby and the St Leger in 1892.

Accordingly, he sent his nephew, Captain Arthur Lawley, to see John Porter, the able and upright head of the Kingsclere establishment for some thirty years. Of an easy-going, unsuspicious nature, and believing in optimistic fashion that poisonings of favourites, tappings of shins or of hocks – in short, "nobblings" – of racehorses in training are "such stuff as dreams are made of", John Porter was thunderstruck upon finding that the life of the most valuable horse in his stable was in danger, and that on Sunday, April 24, it was despaired of.

On Thursday, April 21, Orme was out, as usual, at exercise, and in the fast gallop which he took he appeared, as trainers say, "to tear up the ground". He returned to his stable, and at twelve (noon) Porter went into his box and examined him critically from stem to stern, and from head to heel. No horse could look fitter or seem in better health. He had cleaned out his manger to the last oat and there was nothing to indicate that anything was wrong.

At half past twelve his box was locked up; but when it was opened again for five o'clock stables the poor beast looked languid and uneasy, and slime was running from his nostrils. The first impression was that he had caught a slight chill, and on examination his throat was found to be very sore and much inflamed. Thus far no one dreamed of poison, and as the horse seemed to be better on the morning of Friday, April 22, he was sent out to gallop slowly for seven furlongs. On returning to his box Orme grew rapidly worse, and next day the horse dentist removed a tooth. For a brief space the poor horse seemed relieved; but graver symptoms soon supervened, and on Sunday, for two hours or more, it seemed as if every breath would be his last.

Antidotes suited for irritant poisons were plentifully administered, and by Monday morning their good effect, aided by the horse's naturally hardy constitution, became patent.

[Orme missed the first two Classics, then came back strongly at Sandown and Goodwood, but failed to stay in the Leger.]

BIG RACE RESULTS

2,000 Guineas	Bona Vista	WT Robinson	10-1
1,000 Guineas	La Flèche	G Barrett	1-2f
Derby	Sir Hugo	F Allsopp	40-1
Oaks	La Flèche	G Barrett	8-11f
St Leger	La Flèche	J Watts	7-2
Grand National	Father O'Flynn	Capt R Owen	20-1

CHAMPIONS

Jockey	Morny Cannon	182
Leading Owner	Baron De Hirsch	
Horse	La Flèche (3)	

1893

9 May The Chester course, under new management, is no longer free to the public, and a series of improvements and alterations are promised if the change is a success.

9 Nov Jockey R.Rowell meets his death riding in the Prix de Chasseurs, a selling hurdle, at Auteuil. His mount, Wisigoth, comes down at a hurdle, and with one of Rowell's feet trapped in the stirrup, drags him some 400 yards, while badly kicking him. When the horse is stopped and Rowell disengaged, it is found that he is dead, his neck broken and his body terribly mutilated.

10 Nov Captain James Machell, who saw three of his horses win the Grand National in the 1870s, is discovered outside the balcony of a fourth-floor hotel window Liverpool, crouching with his feet on the narrow ledge, his arm around the stone coping balustrade. He is eventually persuaded to come back, and is taken home to Newmarket by his valet. It is supposed that Captain Machell's mind is temporarily unhinged.

BIG RACE RESULTS

2,000 Guineas	Isinglass	T Loates	4-5f
1,000 Guineas	Siffleuse	T Loates	33-1
Derby	Isinglass	T Loates	4-9f
Oaks	Mrs Butterwick	J Watts	100-7
St Leger	Isinglass	T Loates	40-75f
Grand National	Cloister	W Dollery	9-2f

CHAMPIONS

Jockey	Tom Loates	222
Leading Owner	Mr H McCalmont	
Horse	Isinglass (3)	

Grand National Aintree 24 March

Cloister breaks National records

From HOTSPUR

Racecourse enthusiasm is, as a rule, very evanescent. There are times, however, when the excitement only subsides by slow degrees and this was most truly the case with Cloister's Grand National. For the remainder of the afternoon his brilliant work was the topic of continual conversation and congratulation, and in two ways he has cut the record. In the first place, his burden of 12st 7lb was by several pounds the highest ever carried to victory, and, in the second, he made the fastest time since the course was altered.

There were fifteen starters, ten below last year's total, but the loss in quantity did not extend to quality; and Cloister, the Midshipmite, Why Not, and Father O'Flynn were a representative sample of our best steeplechasers. One of the first to enter the paddock was Cloister, lighter in condition than when stripped in November for the Sefton Steeplechase, but full of muscle and very different in appearance to last year,

when he was runner-up for the second time in succession.

By the time they entered the country for the second time, only The Midshipmite, Why Not, Æsop, and Roman Oak were still in pursuit of Cloister, and it was soon clearly established that The Midshipmite and Roman Oak do not stay four miles and a half. After entering the inner circle of the course to terminate the journey, the placings of the leading trio were Cloister (9-2f), Why Not (5-1) and Æsop (100-12).

Of these Why Not, who had cut himself badly, laboured under difficulties for a long way, and between the two last fences he resigned to Æsop, leaving off a bad third; not that Cloister was even approached. With the clear lead taken after jumping the final fence, which he increased at every stride in the last three quarters of a mile, the verdict was forty lengths, and he passed the post to the accompaniment of terrific applause, which was again and again renewed.

Ormonde's arrival in England

Yesterday morning the Royal Mail steamer Clyde arrived off Southampton, having the famous stallion Ormonde on board. Between eight and nine o'clock, a party including Mr John Porter, Mr Somerville Tattersall (whose company have bought the former Triple Crown winner on behalf of an American breeder) and the Special Commissioner of the Sportsman, went out on the tender to meet the steamer, which was waiting outside the harbour for the tide. Dr Ross, who was in charge of the horse on his voyage from Buenos Ayres to England, was one of the first to be seen as the tender neared the liner, and his shout of "All right, not a scratch," was eminently satisfactory.

On boarding the Clyde the visitors had just a peep at Ormonde, the canvas from the fore part of the box being partially withdrawn. John Porter got on a truss of hay to see more fully into the box, and it was declared that the

horse recognised his old trainer; at any rate he took hay from his hand with considerable gusto.

When the Clyde got into dock, the box containing Ormonde was swung ashore by the hydraulic winch shortly before one o'clock. The front boards were taken down, the canvas was pulled up, and out walked the horse of the century on to his native soil. Few of the good people of Southampton knew what they were looking at as he passed in full view through the streets. Some guessed rightly, but before there was time for excitement or a crowd, Ormonde was safely under cover once more. The arrangements for Ormonde's future have not yet been definitely settled.

[Ormonde was not a success at stud in California, nor had he been in Argentina, but before he left England in the first place he sired Orme, who transmitted his influence to the modern thoroughbred by means of two powerful male lines in Orbe and Flying Fox.]

The St Leger Doncaster: 6 September

Isinglass again hero of the hour
From HOTSPUR

The first and most important half of the Doncaster week has been added to the past, and once again Isinglass reigns the hero of the hour in joining the five which had previously won the Two Thousand, Derby, and St Leger, namely, West Australian, Gladiateur, Lord Lyon, Ormonde, and Common. He is not the least illustrious member of the band. Like Ormonde, he came North with an unbeaten certificate, and put in such fine work that a reputation already high has been further increased. No race of his career has, perhaps, been carried off so easily, and the enthusiasm which greeted him was a welcome break in a singularly tame and quiet afternoon.

In the early stages of the race, Ravensbury and Isinglass had settled down with

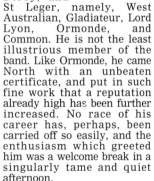

Triple Crown winner Isinglass

the rearmost berths, and as long as Khartoum and Glengall could keep going there was no necessity to hurry. Still, they swept up to Self-Sacrifice without an effort below the bend, and it was quite a new thing on the part of Isinglass (40-95) when he came round the bend in slight command, pulling double. There was, in fact, so much to spare that Loates stopped him from the distance, and the verdict of half a length from Ravensbury (11-2) by no means represents the full measure of the easiest victory that Isinglass has scored in an unchequered career.

1894

14 Mar A large sale takes place at Badminton, the Duke of Beaufort having decided to dispose of most of his horses. The total sum realised is 15,849gns, the highest price being obtained for the 4-y-o Son of a Gun, knocked down to John Porter for 2,800gns. The brood mare Rêve d'Or, with a filly foal by Petronel, goes for 2,700gns.

6 Jun, Lord Rosebery becomes the first Prime Minister of the UK to own a Derby winner, as Ladas (2-9) beats Lord Alington's Matchbox (9-1) in a field of 7.

27 Sep Barely 700 people turn up for the opening of the original Aqueduct track at Queen's, New York.

The Grand National Aintree: 30 March

Why Not wins National: Cloister mystery

From HOTSPUR

If it were necessary to summarise the Blue Riband of the Chase in a few lines I should say that the field was weak in quality, and that the result of a punishing race in favour of Why Not was entirely due to the jockeyship of Arthur Nightingall.

How Captain Fenwick's veteran would have fared had Cloister been delivered at the post fit and well admits of no kind of doubt. This was not to be, however, and the most popular chaser of the last four or five years went to the wall, after being peppered in the market to a considerable tune.

Let me hasten to add that I have no desire to discuss the Cloister case in this column, but all sensible men will desire to see a correspondence closed which can serve no good. We have now been told that never was any sound justification for the taking of 7 to 4 about the hero of last year, and that is all.

CLOISTER'S INJURIES: Professor Pritchard, the veterinary surgeon who examined Cloister last Monday, and whose opinion caused the horse's withdrawal from the Grand National – for which he had been one of the hottest favourites ever known – in an interview with a representative of the Sportsman last evening, maintained his opinion that Cloister's lameness was caused by injuries sustained in his long gallop on Saturday last. He does not think there could have been any serious injury before this. Referring to the trainer Mr Arthur Yates's letter which appeared in yesterday's Sportsman, Professor Pritchard entirely disagreed with Mr Yates in the idea that the present injury is the outcome of an old strain; while as regards the statement that the horse was lame after his gallop at Sandown Park about a fortnight ago, the Professor says that at the time he examined the horse no mention was made to him of any such lameness.

[A disconcerting aspect of the Cloister affair was that the bookmakers seemed to know in advance that there was something amiss with the horse.]

Jockey Club Stakes Newmarket: 27 September

Isinglass wins while Throstle bolts

From HOTSPUR

The presence of Throstle (100-12) at the post for the newly created Jockey Club Stakes was an added attraction, but the result was seriously disappointing, as instead of victory on the Town Moor curing the filly of the temper that she had so often betrayed before her St Leger, her second attempt to carry Morny Cannon out of the course proved successful, and she was galloping a circle round the exercise ground known as South-fields when Isinglass (2-5) added his third £10,000 to the account of Mr McCalmont.

Not since the days of Peter has a more ungovernable exhibition been witnessed in an important contest, and those who endeavoured to cover John Porter with ridicule after the St Leger can now see how easily a mistake could be made. The only wonder was that Throstle should take it into her head to secure the Doncaster spoils, and this sudden disposition to do the right thing must always be gall and wormwood to the backers of Ladas.

The St Leger Doncaster: 12 September

Throstle surprise
From HOTSPUR

The temperamental Throstle, shock St Leger winner

Never since a dozen years ago, to the dismay of a previously jubilant band, Dutch Oven swooped down upon Geheimniss and carried off the St Leger, has such a surprise been witnessed on the Town Moor as that which ended in the victory of Throstle.

After her smart performance in the Nassau Stakes at Goodwood, many arrived at the conclusion that she was a useful second string to the Kingsclere stable, and step by step Common's half-sister advanced to 100 to 6. Last week the market tactics were altered, and so badly had Throstle behaved herself in her gallops that any idea of success was abandoned. As far as could be judged of the pair in their clothes, Matchbox was capable of conceding her lumps of weight, and nobody may have been more surprised than Throstle's joint owners and her trainer, John Porter.

After the first hundred yards, Throstle had nothing to do with the pace-making, and Legal Tender did his level best until he resigned seven furlongs from home to Matchbox and None the Wiser. Here Ladas was very conspicuous in the rear. Although driven for a few strides below the bend, Ladas stood the pressure so well that he gave the leaders the go by as they approached the distance, and it then seemed the Two Thousand and Derby over again, Loates having taken a pull at Ladas, with his spring and summer rival, Matchbox, in turn taking care of Amiable

All of a sudden the situation was changed, and Throstle (50-1), who had been under hard pressure as far from home as the Rifle Butts, began to draw up hand over hand. The steersman of Ladas (10-11) was not slow to recognise the danger, but his efforts to get home proved of no avail, and he was beaten cleverly by three parts of a length

Matchbox (2-1) was two lengths further back, and Amiable (10-1), the One Thousand and Oaks winner, half a length away fourth. Such a staggering blow in a classic three-year-old race could not be recalled since the date already mentioned.

Time by Benson's chronograph: 3min 12 1/5sec, a new record.

BIG RACE RESULTS

2,000 Guineas	Ladas	J Watts	5-6f
1,000 Guineas	Amiable	W Bradford	100-8
Derby	Ladas	J Watts	2-9f
Oaks	Amiable	W Bradford	7-1
St Leger	Throstle	M Cannon	50-1
Grand National	Why Not	A Nightingall	5-1jf

CHAMPIONS

Jockey	Morny Cannon	167
Leading Owner	Mr H McCalmont	
Horse	Isinglass (4)	

1895

1 Jan The Duke of Portland, needing an outcross for his St Simon and Donovan mares, buys antipodean stallion Carbine for 13,000gns, and the great racing champion is given a wonderful send-off from Melbourne as he is shipped aboard the Orizata.

29 Mar In Cloister's controversial absence, Æsop becomes 5-1 favourite for the Grand National, but falls at the Canal Turn second time round, and the race is won by Wild Man from Borneo, ridden by Joe Widger and registered in the name of his brother John.

29 May The Derby is the first horserace to be recorded on film.

26 Jun Portmarnock (2-5) wins the Irish Derby by a record 12 lengths in a field of 6.

Carbine

CHAMPIONS

Jockey	Morny Cannon	184
Leading Owner	Mr L de Rothschild	
Horse	Sir Visto (3)	

Weatherbys: 25 March

Cloister and the Grand National
Remarkable coincidences

A great sensation was yesterday caused by the intelligence that Cloister, the favourite for the Grand National, had been scratched. The news was officially issued by Messrs Weatherby at 3.24 p.m.

It was at once remembered that very much the same thing had happened to the same horse, under the same ownership, when occupying the same position of favouritism, in the same race, and almost at the same hour on the same day last year – a series of most remarkable coincidences.

Many regrets were expressed that this great horse had not been allowed to retire after his grand victory in 1893. Mr C.G.Duff, his owner, is known to have backed the horse heavily on both occasions, and his disappointment must be the keenest.

Cloister was at exercise yesterday morning, and after seeming to go a little stiffly dropped as if shot, and lay with his tongue protruding. The lad riding him was pitched to the ground and when taken from under the horse was insensible. The trainer, Escott, hurried up to town to report to Mr Duff and soon the disastrous news was common property.

Prior to this the price against the favourite had lengthened, for whereas on Saturday and at the opening of the London market yesterday 5 to 1 was readily taken, 7 to 1 was as freely offered an hour or two later. Backers were tempted by the rate, and presently the market stiffened, only 6 to 1 being obtainable. Then came the announcement that Cloister had been scratched – an announcement that paralysed the betting. At the close of the day 600 to 100 was offered on the field.

It was ascertained at eleven o'clock last night that the eminent veterinary surgeon, Mr George Williams, had reported to Mr Duff that on examining Cloister he found the pulse all right and the temperature normal. The horse was lame in the near hind foot and very jaded. No sign of poisoning could be found. Dead tired and languid seemed to be all that was amiss with him.

[A further coincidence was that the bookmakers again appeared to have advanced knowledge of Cloister's "indisposition". The horse had made a full recovery since last year and, ridden by new trainer Harry Escott, had triumphed by 20 lengths in Aintree's Grand Sefton in November, encouraging his admirers to once again make him ante-post favourite.]

2,000 Guineas	Kirkonnel	J Watts	10-1
1,000 Guineas	Galeottia	FC Pratt	100-8
Derby	Sir Visto	S Loates	9-1
Oaks	La Sagesse	S Loates	5-1
St Leger	Sir Visto	S Loates	9-4f
Grand National	Wild Man from Borneo	Mr J Widger	10-1

The Derby Epsom: 29 May

Lord Rosebery's second victory
From HOTSPUR

The most "open" Derby within the memory of the present generation of racegoers has been lost and won, and Sir Visto is the hero of the same. It was quite in accordance with the topsy-turvy experiences of the Spring that the Blue Riband of the Turf should for the second successive year by secured by Lord Rosebery.

Although Sir Visto (9-1) could claim a certain degree of consistency, inasmuch as he ran third both for the Two Thousand Guineas and the Newmarket Stakes, he had succumbed to Kirkonnel and Laveno in the one and to The Owl and Solaro in the other. Upon all the four has he now turned the tables, and Kirkonnel (100-8) and Solaro (9-1) alone made a respectable fight. The only conclusion is that the three-year-olds taking part so far in the classic races are a moderate lot, and the best of them would have been unable to hold a candle last season to either Ladas or Matchbox.

Sir Visto came with a rattle in the last hundred yards, and, getting on terms with Curzon (33-1) half a dozen strides from home, he won by three-quarters of a length; half a length between second and third (Kirkonnel). The 5-1 joint favourites, Le Var and Raconteur, were sixth and seventh.

The St Leger Doncaster: 11 September

Victory of Sir Visto
From HOTSPUR

Sir Visto: punters' saviour in St Leger

All's well that ends well, and the popular victory of Sir Visto in the St Leger has carried many backers safely through a sea of trouble. In a double sense they had a narrow squeak, as, to begin with, there was the doubt in the morning as to Sir Visto seeing the post, which called to mind the sensational eleventh hour experiences of Apology's year; and, secondly, he had to be ridden home hard to win by three-quarters of a length.

Half a mile from home Match Maker took up the running, and was closely followed by Lord Chester and Butterfly, with Sir Visto well up on the outside. As they made for the bend Match Maker gave way, and Butterfly took up the running, followed by Sir Visto and Telescope, with Utica and Curzon next. A quarter of a mile from home Sir Visto (9-4f) took up the running, and Telescope (1000-35) took second place. Gamely as the latter struggled, he always had the worst of the fighting and suffered defeat by three-quarters of a length. The filly Butterfly (8-1) was a bad third.

1896

27 Mar Owner of the Grand National winner The Soarer, local businessman Mr William Hill-Walker has to ask a bystander which horse is his before the start, having only recently purchased the difficult 7-year-old gelding for 600gns from Mr David Campbell on the promise that Campbell would be allowed to ride him at Aintree.

9 Sep In the absence of St Frusquin, the St Leger is won for the first time by a Prince of Wales, Derby hero Persimmon carrying the Royal colours to a universally popular victory at Doncaster, where there is for once no trace of the old North-South jealousy. It is the 5th St Leger triumph for jockey Jack Watts.

The Grand National Aintree: 27 March

The Soarer's Grand National

From HOTSPUR

In the world of sport there are many who carry out the practice of praising the past at the expense of the present to an absurd degree. It cannot be gainsaid, however, that our steeplechase horses have sadly degenerated, and the Grand National field beaten a few hours ago by 40-1 outsider The Soarer was one of the weakest in quality that has ever contested the cross-country blue riband.

In the final workings of the market Rory O'More (7-1), Ardcarn (8-1), and Waterford (100-12) came well to the front, with best business in the second rank for Van de Berg and Biscuit. Of this quintet the last named alone finished in the first three, while only nine completed the journey.

Biscuit (25-1) and The Soarer, the first pair to come into the inner circle of the racecourse the second time, quickly changed places, and were followed over the next fence by Barcalwhey (1000-30) and Father O'Flynn (40-1).

From that point the last-named, with strong strides began to pick up rapidly the ground he had lost before leaving the canal side, and finished so full of running to justify the belief that had Mr Grenfell been able to get the last ounce out of him he would have repeated his victory of four years ago instead of succumbing by a length and a half. Beaten the same distance for second place, Biscuit just deprived Barcalwhey of a situation.

The Soarer, in the same stable as Why Not, had been sold to Mr W.H.Walker before he fell in the chase won by Westmeath at Hurst Park during the last week of February. He has shown himself one of the most uncertain performers in a season especially marked for inconsistency, and actually finished behind Bavarian and Ulysses at Lingfield in the middle of the winter. The favourites were too much routed for there to be .any display of enthusiasm.

The Oaks Epsom: 5 June

Outsider ruins double for the Prince

From HOTSPUR

An overwhelming majority of the visitors to Epsom on the fourth and concluding day were equally desirous and anxious to see the Prince of Wales win the Oaks, thereby completing a double event which has fallen to the lot of so few owners. They were, nevertheless, doomed to disappointment, and although Thaïs (13-8f) looked once to have the verdict in safe custody, she finished weak and was beaten easily at last by a comparative "outsider" in Canterbury Pilgrim (100-8), who was led back in silence.

After going half the journey, the Galop Filly (4-1) was showing the way, closely followed by Avilion, with Canterbury Pilgrim third, Thaïs fourth. As they came into the straight Avilion joined the Galop Filly, and directly afterwards headed her, with Thaïs taking third place in the centre, Canterbury Pilgrim being on the outside. A quarter of a mile from home Avilion was beaten, and then Thaïs took up the running. But at the distance Canterbury Pilgrim shot past and won easily by two lengths.

The Derby Epsom: 3 June

The Prince's Derby
A great race: Victory of Persimmon

Persimmon: popular royal Derby winner

The most popular Derby of modern times! No doubt whatever can be entertained of the fact, either by those who saw the sight on the Downs or those for whose benefit the great news was flashed to London, England and the world. The victory of the Prince of Wales was the one theme of talk and comment and congratulation wherever Englishmen collected together to discuss the events of a momentous day.

But if Persimmon's triumph made the pulse beat quicker fifty, a hundred, or a thousand miles from Epsom, how wonderful was the scene, how keen the excitement, how tremendous the roar of the delighted crowd who saw with their own eyes the final struggle, and heard with their own ears the welcome cry, "The Prince has won!" There has been nothing witnessed of the kind, probably, since the Derby commenced its brilliant career. For although another Prince has won besides the Prince of Wales, and other Prime Ministers, too, besides Lord Rosebery, we are growing to be more and more a democracy every year, and yesterday was a great people's holiday, in which a popular idol received his overwhelming meed of praise.

Persimmon and St Frusquin fighting out their rivalry inch by inch as they neared the winning post, the last seconds of a magnificent race, the final effort of the second favourite, the judge's verdict "by a neck", the Prince's success – all these accompanied throughout by the swelling thunder of applause which burst at last into a crash of reverberating yells – made up an ensemble of excitement and frenzy, the like of which has not been chronicled for many a day. It was something to have been a witness of at least once in a lifetime, a memory which will not easily fade away from those who saw the classic race of 1896.

A quarter of a mile from home Bay Ronald was beaten, whereupon St Frusquin drew out, with Persimmon in hot pursuit. From this point the issue was a match, and a desperately exciting battle ensued. St Frusquin (8-13) retained his advantage until opposite Tattersall's, when Persimmon (5-1) closed, and getting his head in front he always afterwards had a shade the best of it, and won, amidst a scene of indescribable excitement, by a neck; four lengths behind St Frusquin, Earwig (33-1) was third.

Persimmon, trained at Newmarket by R.Marsh, was bred by his owner, the Prince of Wales.

1897

4 Jun Limasol (100-8), on her first outing of the year, beats 5-2 on favourite Chélandry, winner of the 1,000 Guineas, by 3 lengths to win the Oaks.

13 Nov The first public test in Britain of the Carandini Starting Machine takes place at the Liverpool Autumn meeting in a 1 1/2-mile weight-for-age plate of that name. Worked with stout cords instead of webbing, it is regarded as "an improvement ... decidedly so on a rough day at Newmarket".

BIG RACE RESULTS

2,000 Guineas	Galtee More	C Wood	5-4f
1,000 Guineas	Chélandry	J Watts	9-4
Derby	Galtee More	C Wood	1-4f
Oaks	Limasol	W Bradford	100-8
St Leger	Galtee More	C Wood	1-10f
Grand National	Manifesto	T Kavanagh	6-1f

The St Leger Doncaster: 8 September

Galtee More wins: Joins select band
From HOTSPUR

To the select band of three-year-olds that have carried off in turn the Two Thousand, Derby, and St Leger, Galtee More is the latest addition. That the honours of the Town Moor would fall to the share of the Irish-bred son of Kendal seemed a very foregone conclusion, and thus there was an almost entire absence of excitement.

Everybody, in fact, anticipated a one-horse race or, in other words, that Galtee More (1-10) would come away by himself from the bend to pass the post pulling double. How different was the result? Of the five competitors, four were not divided by more than a length and, as the race was run, it would be absurd to say Galtee More ran in a style worthy of his Spring and Summer reputation.

On the other hand, extenuating circumstances can be advanced, and the pace proved so bad that the time was one-fifth of a second longer than the Rufford Abbey Handicap, decided over an extra quarter of a mile of ground. To pursue the time question a little further, the race was nineteen seconds slower than the record created by Throstle.

Entering the straight, St Cloud II (33-1) deprived Goletta (20-1) of the lead and was followed by Galtee More, but below the distance Galtee More took up the running, and at the same time Silver Fox (33-1)) began to draw up on the rails, with Chélandry on the outside. Inside the distance Chélandry (25-1) worked her way into second place, but she failed to reach Galtee More, who won by three-parts of a length; a neck separated the second and third, St Cloud II.

The Grand National Aintree 26 March

Manifesto's National: Easy win for Irish favourite
From HOTSPUR

The cross-country Blue Riband fully maintained its prestige, and today thousands of enthusiastic sportsmen assembled to participate in the stirring scene enacted on the historic Aintree track. The early promise of an enormous field was realised. The sensation created by the Wild Man from Borneo scare yesterday was partly evaporated this morning, and many who had backed the quondam favourite were to some extent reassured by the statements that the horse had done well at exercise, those who saw him reporting that he showed no signs whatever of his indisposition.

The executive were responsible for one public advantage, by supplying loin-cloths with the names of each horse worked in bold letters, rendering it unnecessary to inquire the names of the respective candidates. The innovation is one which might advantageously be followed at other meetings on big race days.

Manifesto was hard and full of muscle, and his owner at last made no secret of his confidence in the result of the contest. The Soarer has improved in appearance if anything. There was a tremendous amount of money for Manifesto, and the Irish division supported him with characteristic spirit.

It was a pretty sight when the competitors were despatched on their journey, but the phases of the race did not undergo many changes so far as the leaders were concerned, as Timon and Manifesto practically made all the running. Had it not been for a serious blunder he made two fences from home Timon would certainly have been in the first three.

At this point, however, it was evident that Manifesto had the issue in safe keeping, and he sailed home the easiest of winners. Cathal became second when Timon made his mistake, but he too came to grief at the last fence.

Manifesto (6-1f) then had matters all his own way and won by 20 lengths from Filbert (100-1), who, after a good race, beat Ford of Fyne (25-1) by a head.

CHAMPIONS

Jockey	Morny Cannon	145
Leading Trainer	R Marsh	£33,531
Leading Owner	Mr J Gubbins	£22,739
Horse	Galtee More (3)	

Manchester: 27 November

Remarkable success of "Tod" Sloan

In addition to the weather and the enormous fields, the close of the racing season of 1897 will be specially remembered by reason of the remarkable success attending the efforts of the American jockey "Tod" Sloan. Here was a stranger in a strange land – a young man whose acquaintance with England and the English climate extends to only six or seven weeks. Yet the winning average of Sloan is simply astonishing. The once ridiculed jockey scored no fewer than twenty successes out of fifty-eight mounts – more than one winning ride out of every three attempts.

The public, which has a keen eye for results, soon awoke to the fact that whatever theories might dictate Sloan's style of horsemanship he kept on winning races. On Saturday when "the curtain fell" – to quote the racing reporter – the American light-weight carried off four races out of five mounts; so, in spite of the weather, the Mancurians – horrible word! – thronged the open spaces in front of the paddock and gave the young man a gratifying send-off in recognition of his pluck and skill.

18 November

New racecourses

The necessary licence having been granted by the Jockey Club, the first meeting on the new Folkestone racecourse has been fixed for March 31, and will extend over the following day. The promoters are sanguine of success.

Certain influential members of the Jockey Club have just completed negotiations for acquiring a tract of land at Newbury, in Berkshire, with a view of constructing a racecourse, and establishing race meetings, to take the place of the Stockbridge meeting, which has so long been an important fixture in the racing world, but which is now to be discontinued.

The town of Newbury will obviously become an important racing centre, situated as it is in the immediate neighbourhood of many noted training grounds, and being only an hour's run from Paddington by express train.

1898

30 Mar John Gourley, who rode Manifesto in the 1896 National when he was knocked over, has his second ride in the famous chase, Drogheda, victor in the absence this year of the reigning champion.

30 Mar The inaugural meeting at Folkestone takes place, over jumps.

1 Aug The infamous "Trodmore Hunt" fraud is perpetrated, in which a spurious race-card is printed in the Sportsman, "results" are published next day, and some bets are paid out before the fraud is uncovered. (The culprits are never discovered.)

17 Aug The first Flat meeting takes place at Folkestone.

BIG RACE RESULTS

2,000 Guineas	Disraeli	S Loates	100-8
1,000 Guineas	Nun Nicer	S Loates	11-2jf
Derby	Jeddah	O Madden	100-1
Oaks	Airs and Graces	W Bradford	100-8
St Leger	Wildfowler	C Wood	10-1
Grand National	Drogheda	J Gourley	25-1

CHAMPIONS

Jockey	Otto Madden	161
Leading Trainer	R Marsh	£34,239
Leading Owner	Mr L de Rothschild	£30,267
Horse	Cyllene	

17 March

The Grand National favourite: Accident to Manifesto

Mr J.G.Bulteel, owner of Manifesto, writes to the Sportsman of today (Thursday) stating that the Grand National favourite met with an accident while at exercise at Weyhill on Tuesday. Mr E.Cooper Smith of Hollist, Midhurst, the veterinary surgeon who examined the horse yesterday morning, certifies that Manifesto is suffering from concussion of the cannon bone of the near foreleg. Mr Smith adds: "This may prevent his running in the Liverpool Grand National, but I have advised Mr Bulteel not to strike him out at present."

[Manifesto was struck out of the race, but any rumours that this was a repeat of the "Cloister affair" were scotched when it became known that a stable boy had negligently left the champion's door open and Manifesto, who had been recently sold to Mr Bulteel, went off to explore his new home and injured his fetlock when jumping a gate.]

13 May

Sale of Galtee More

In reference to the sale of Galtee More to the Russian Government, it is now stated that Mr Gubbins sold the colt with his engagements, and that if all goes well with him in the meantime the famous son of Kendal will run in the Ascot Cup next month in the name of the Grand Duke Dimitri, aide-de-camp of the Tsar. The purchase price was £21,000, not £25,000 as reported yesterday. The Sportsman of today announces, on the best authority, that Mr H.Bottomley yesterday refused an offer of £15,000 for the purchase of his horse Count Schomberg, without any contingency in respect to the big steeplechase at Auteuil on the 29th inst.

[Galtee More did not race again, but did well as a sire in both Russia and Germany, where he later moved.]

The Derby Epsom: 25 May

Victory of Jeddah: A "record" outsider
FROM OUR SPECIAL CORRESPONDENT

What lamentation and wailing was there last night over of the result of the greatest horse race in the world! Our old friend, "the glorious uncertainty of the Turf", after lying dormant for several years, came to the front yesterday – when unexpected, as usual – and won in a common canter, to the confounding of the wise and the envy of the avaricious. Reaching its apogee with the triumphs of a Prime Minister and a Prince, the Derby is now showing a disposition to fall into the hands of "small owners".

A little sighing may be excused on an afternoon when a "record" outsider has carried off the Blue Riband. Jeddah's win has never been paralleled. Eighty years ago Azor started at 50 to 1; Forth, the old trainer, a man over sixty years of age, rode Frederick (a 33 to 1 chance) when that colt won twelve years later; and the "dark"

Phosphorus scored in the year of Her Majesty's accession at 40 to 1. But a 100 to 1 winner beats the record. In recent years the nearest approach to such a coup was when Palm-bearer, at the same price as Jeddah, ran second to Sir Bevys, and Black Tommy, the runner-up to Blink Bonny in 1857, started at 200 to 1.

Both the first and the third places yesterday were filled by a pair so generally despised that in each instance the extreme odds of 100 to 1 could be obtained. That "glorious uncertainty" could not have received a greater illustration than Disraeli (2-1f), who had won the Two Thousand with scarcely an effort, dropped out of the race before it was half completed, In evidence that the pace was a good one, Calveley, who tried to make the running for Batt, failed to quite do so, and Elfin showed the way to the top of the hill, at which point Sam Loates picked up his whip to Disraeli. This was of

no avail, and either unable or unwilling, he dropped back stride by stride, until he was out of the race long before reaching Tattenham Corner.

In the meantime, Batt (10-1) and Wantage (33-1) had drawn well to the front, and crossed the road so far ahead of Heir Male, Pheon, and Archduke II, that both seemed quite safe, as far as place honours were concerned. The change that altered the complexion of the race took place a quarter of a mile from home, with Jeddah, who had been in the last four for a mile, drawing up in the centre, an example copied by Dieudonné (7-2) on the right, and Dunlop (100-1) in the track of the two leaders. This additional pressure caused Wantage to hang towards the rails, and with Dieudonné not sustaining the effort so long as his despised stable companion, Jeddah won by three-quarters of a length from Batt, and Dunlop just outlived Dieudonné and Wantage for the third money.

Although Jeddah, the property of Mr J.W.Larnach and trained by Mr R.Marsh, won the Craven Stakes, he could finish only fifth in both the Two Thousand Guineas and the Newmarket Stakes. Mr Larnach bought his dam Pilgrimage at the sale of the late Duchess of Montrose's stud for 190 guineas before she gave birth to Jeddah. In fact, the mare was not supposed to be in foal, and this explains the extraordinary nature of the bargain. Although faith in Jeddah had departed, it is evident now that the stable estimate of him before the Craven Stakes was soundly based, and Madden may congratulate himself that Mr Larnach decided to run. He was thereby enabled to ride his first Derby winner in a season which has so far seen him well established at the head of the list of successful jockeys, and this is the second time in three years that the training laurels have fallen to the share of Richard Marsh.

1899

10 Feb The inaugural jumping programme takes place at Haydock Park, postponed from last week.

2 Jun Mr Douglas Baird's Musa, a 20-1 chance, robs Lord Beresford of the Derby-Oaks double, beating his Sibola (4-7), winner of the 1,000

Guineas, by a head in the filly's Classic.

26 Dec Boxing Day sees the spawning of the eternal quiz question as a horse called Good Friday comes down in the Thorneycroft Steeplechase at Wolverhampton.

The Grand National Aintree: 24 March

A great performance: Manifesto's second National

From HOTSPUR

The magnificent victory of Manifesto adds considerable lustre to a contest which has been distinguished for equine performances such as The Lamb and The Colonel, and in later years Cloister. The event was not without its eleventh hour sensation, as the scratching of Drogheda at twenty minutes past one filled many with feelings of dismay, for last year's winner had the previous night left off virtually favourite for money.

Nothing created a better impression than Manifesto (5-1), and he finished up only a point behind Gentle Ida (4-1f). Backed by the unshaken confidence of those connected with him, Ambush II (100-12) had a large and gallant following, not merely because a loyal feeling prompted admirers of the Royal colours, but by the reason that he stripped a beautifully trained horse, and one who seems destined to grow into a

steeplechaser of the highest character. It was, however, setting a five-year-old an almost herculean task to beat such a field as went to the post today, though at some future time it would seem only a matter of ordinary luck for him to achieve a laudable ambition for the Prince of Wales.

The incidents of the struggle were exciting, though falls were not so frequent as usual. The leading parts were for most of the time played by lightly weighted candidates like Corner, Mum and Barsac. But in the last half-mile there was really nothing in it but Manifesto, who, with 12st 7lb, was carrying a stone more than any other. With the leading division running very wide approaching the last fence but one, he was able to take a nice place in the inside and win very easily by five lengths from Ford of Fyne (40-1), with Elliman (20-1) third.

The St Leger Doncaster: 6 September

Flying Fox wins the Triple Crown

From HOTSPUR

Loud, hearty, and genuine rang the cheers for the latest wearer of the "triple crown" as Flying Fox won the St Leger in the most hollow fashion, easing up, by three lengths from Caiman. The 7-2 on favourite got well away and, after lying forward the whole of the journey, came out below the bend and won in a common canter. Caiman (7-2) was a length in front of Scintillant (300-1) in the field of six.

So the Duke of Westminster's colt has added to his Newmarket, Epsom, and Sandown Park laurels in a style that should surely convince hostile critics of the mistakes they made in depreciating his three-year-old form. All distances come alike to him, and the frequently expressed belief in this column that he would pass through the season without the stain of defeat is in no danger of being upset.

Long before Flying Fox reached the goal, the Yorkshire "roar" began, and it increased in volume until the scene of enthusiasm almost "beggared description". It had been a matter of difficulty to get through the lane of people that surrounded him on his way to the paddock. But there was no moment of difficulty in any part of the race and Flying Fox pulled up as fresh as paint.

His superiority to all others of the same age, in both speed

Holocauste beaten

FROM OUR SPECIAL CORRESPONDENT

It is with the usual pleasure that we renew our acquaintance with Chantilly at this season. Trees and turf are at their most verdant, and a race meeting in the domain of the late Duc d'Aumale savours much of a gigantic picnic.

In the big event, the Prix du Jockey Club, or French Derby, as it is called, M de Brémond's Holocauste was far and away the favourite, and it was predicted with the utmost confidence in many quarters that the grey colt would not only emerge in easy triumph today, but would achieve further distinction in your Blue Ribbon of the Turf.

But cries of anguish rend the air as it becomes clear that Holocauste (2-5) is beaten, third by two lengths to

M Caillault's Perth (3-1). I had a good look at the beaten favourite just after the race, and he appeared as fresh as a new pin, with evidently any amount of running in him yet, and had not been called upon in time to get clear of the field.

What a bitter disappointment it has been for many besides his owners your readers can well imagine. But while there is life there is hope, and Holocauste may yet retrieve this defeat.

[Those last words prove painfully ironic as Holocauste, starting as 6-1 second favourite at Epsom, stumbles and falls after being headed by the favourite Flying Fox in the straight, and has to be destroyed after breaking a leg.]

BIG RACE RESULTS

2,000 Guineas	Flying Fox	M Cannon	5-6f
1,000 Guineas	Sibola	JT Sloan	13-8f
Derby	Flying Fox	M Cannon	2-5f
Oaks	Musa	O Madden	20-1
St Leger	Flying Fox	M Cannon	2-7f
Grand National	Manifesto	G Williamson	5-1

CHAMPIONS

Leading Trainer	J Porter	£56,546
Leading Owner	Duke of Westminster	£43,965
Horse	Flying Fox (3)	

Flying Fox on the way to the course in the Derby

and stamina, can hardly be estimated by pounds, and who shall say that the mantle of Ormonde has not fallen upon his grandson?

John Porter's first St Leger winner was Pero Gomez as far back as 1869, and in the interim came Ormonde, Common, La Flèche, and Throstle. Of these, Ormonde and Common stand on the platform to which Flying Fox has been raised as heroes of the three principal classic races, and this is a feat that no other trainer has accomplished. The share of Morny Cannon in this triumph was duly recognised, and few of his brother jockeys missed an opportunity of shaking him by the hand when the proclaiming of the welcome "All right" enabled him to leave the scale. It was a brilliant and popular victory, and that crowns the whole situation.

The Early 1900s

The first decade of the 20th century was marked by some extraordinary performances by fillies and by continued Royal success in the great races. Sceptre and Pretty Polly, foaled within two years of each other, are arguably the two greatest fillies ever to race in England. In 1902, Sceptre, a daughter of Persimmon, won every Classic except the Derby, in which, badly ridden, she finished fourth. Pretty Polly accomplished the fillies' Triple Crown in 1904 and would surely have won the other two Classics had she been entered. Of humble pedigree, she won 22 out of 24 races in a four-year career. Then, in 1908, Signorinetta achieved what her two great predecessors had not – she won the Derby, and at the odds of 100-1. Two days later she became the third (and last) filly to complete the Derby-Oaks Epsom double.

Yet even more popular were the victories won by "royal" horses. In 1900, the Prince of Wales's Ambush II became the first horse to carry royal colours to victory in the Grand National, and then Diamond Jubilee won the Triple Crown for the Prince, who was leading owner that year. But the climax was yet to come for the patriotic crowds, ever willing to acclaim a royal victory, when in 1909 Minoru gave Edward VII the distinction of becoming the first reigning monarch to lead in a Derby winner.

The American influence continued on the track, and in 1900 Lester Reiff was the first champion jockey from across the water. The next year, he rode the Derby winner, Volodyovski, and his brother John won on Orby in 1907, the first Irish victory in the race. Another US jockey, Danny Maher, won three Derbys in four years, including Rock Sand, Triple Crown winner in 1903.

However, in a decade with all these great horses, arguably the best two were Ard Patrick, Derby winner in Sceptre's year, and Bayardo, winner of the St Leger in 1909.

King Edward VII and trainer Richard Marsh lead Minoru in after their Derby triumph of 1909, and, as Hotspur of The Daily Telegraph put it: "It is no exaggeration to say that the excitement was even greater than when Persimmon and Diamond Jubilee respectively won the prize. For one thing, his Majesty had not then ascended the Throne, and that he should, as King of England, achieve the highest ambition of every sportsman marks a red-letter day in the annals of the Turf."

1900

9 Mar In the sale at Kingsclere of the late Duke of Westminster's horses, last year's Triple Crown winner Flying Fox goes to Frenchman M Edmond Blanc for 37,500gns, a British auction record for a horse in training until beaten by Vaguely Noble in 1967.

1 Jun John Porter saddles his 3rd Oaks winner when the Duke of Portland's La Roche (5-1) beats Merry Gal (100-7) easing up by 3 lengths, with Lady Schomberg (3-1jf) a bad 3rd.

12 Sep Diamond Jubilee wins the St Leger to clinch the Triple Crown for the Prince of Wales, who, with Ambush II winning the Grand National, pulls off a unique achievement in the annals of the Turf.

BIG RACE RESULTS

Race	Horse	Jockey	Odds
2,000 Guineas	Diamond Jubilee	H Jones	11-4
1,000 Guineas	Winifreda	S Loates	11-2
Derby	Diamond Jubilee	H Jones	6-4f
Oaks	La Roche	M Cannon	5-1
St Leger	Diamond Jubilee	H Jones	2-7f
Grand National	Ambush II	A Anthony	4-1

The Derby Epsom: 30 May

Victory of the Prince

From HOTSPUR

Royal favourite Diamond Jubilee wins the Derby

As long as memory sits upon her throne, the last Derby of the century will be held in vivid remembrance. The victory of Diamond Jubilee witnessed a renewal of the great scene when his brother Persimmon was proclaimed the hero of the hour three years ago, and a brighter page in Turf history has never been written.

The unanimity of opinion in the paddock that Diamond Jubilee must win the Derby quickly found reflection in the ring, and the next quarter of an hour saw him harden into a 6 to 4 chance.

Backers of Diamond Jubilee were surprised to see him nearer last than first in passing Sherwood's. This, however, was a matter of misfortune, and those who with one heart and voice were greeting Diamond Jubilee three minutes later as the winner little knew how narrow was his escape of being knocked down almost at the outset by Disguise II. Nor did the undesirable attentions of the American colt (ridden by Sloan) end there, as in

rounding Tattenham Corner he bumped Diamond Jubilee so hard that a collision took place with Chevening.

But Herbert Jones waited until Diamond Jubilee had settled down again, and then proceeded to overhaul Disguise II (3rd, 8-1) in a manner which speaks volumes for his coolness and nerve. And he resisted a late challenge from Simon Dale (100-6), to pass the post with his ears pricked, winning much more easily than the half-length verdict might suggest.

The cheering, which commenced in front of the stands, gradually spread the whole length of the course; flags that had already been used in connection with Mafeking Day were unfurled as if by magic; and when the Prince of Wales took up his position near the gate of the weighing-room enclosure to lead his champion in, the applause was deafening. It was a scene typical of England, and proof, if any were needed, of how deep are the roots which bind together loyalty and sport.

CHAMPIONS

Jockey	Lester Reiff	143
Leading Trainer	R Marsh	£43,321
Leading Owner	HRH Prince of Wales	£29,585
Horse	Diamond Jubilee (3)	£27,985

The Grand National Aintree: 30 March

Prince of Wales's victory: Enthusiastic reception

From HOTSPUR

That many familiar faces should be missing from the paddock in the hour that preceded the Grand National was only natural. The war has called for great sacrifices, and amongst those who eagerly accepted the call to arms are several of the best followers of 'chasing and hunting. None the less, the Grand National of 1900 will long be held in remembrance, and the reception accorded to Ambush II, when, after a long and exciting struggle, he placed the colours of the Prince of Wales in the van has only once been equalled on a racecourse. That occasion, it is almost superfluous to add, was the victory of Persimmon for the Derby.

Let it not be thought by this that the Grand National, in spite of the gallant effort of Manifesto, was one in which class shone forth prominently, and I shall always think that by keeping Drogheda in the stable Mr Bulteel missed the opportunity of carrying off the spoils for the second year in succession. Under the

circumstances, however, his retirement does not provoke the least regret, and rather am I rejoiced, in common with thousands and tens of thousands of good sportsmen, that the consummation of the Blue Riband of the Chase was so completely perfect.

The favourite Hidden Mystery (75-20) fell at the first fence in the second round when sailing along in the front rank and going great guns. When the racecourse had been reached, about five furlongs from home, the brunt of the battle was evidently between Ambush II (4-1) and Manifesto (6-1). Williamson had been compelled to raise his whip, and Manifesto, dwelling, as compared with Ambush II, over the final obstacle, the wearer of the Royal colours steadily drew away and established a decisive lead of four lengths. Manifesto (giving away 24lb) was completely pumped out inside the distance, and Barsac (25-1) came again to wear him down by a neck for second money.

6 December

American jockeys: Tod Sloan and his license

It having been reported to the Stewards of the Jockey Club that Sloan had accepted the offer of a large present from Mr F.Gardner in the event of Codoman winning the Cambridgeshire, and that he had betted on the race, they inquired into the case.

Mr Gardner, who was unaware of the regulations forbidding such presents, expressed his regret at having transgressed them, and the Stewards, fully accepting his explanation, fined him a nominal penalty of £25. They inflicted a similar fine on Mr C.A.Mills, who acted as commissioner to Mr Gardner, and finding both charges proved against Sloan, they informed him that he need not

apply for a license to ride.

[The charge resulted from a steward's overhearing Tod Sloan cursing the jockey that beat Codoman, the Irishman John Thompson. He had refused to be corrupted by Sloan's accomplices, who had fixed or nobbled all the other dangers. Sloan applied every year for 15 years for a renewal of his license to ride in Britain, but was always refused. The same inquiry investigated Sloan's compatriot Lester Reiff, but could find no foundation in rumours and suspicions that he had pulled certain horses. With 143 winners this year, he became the first American to win the jockeys' title, but he did not last another season.]

1901

17 Jul Thomas Lane, an English jockey who had settled in France, dies at 40 in Chantilly. He had wins in the French Derby and Oaks to his credit and established a peerless reputation in the Grand Prix de Paris, France's leading race, with 6 wins in 12 years, including 4 on the trot (1890-93).

1 Oct American Lester Reiff's riding of De Lacy at Manchester last Friday, when he is beaten a head by his brother John on Minnie Dee, after a series of suspicious defeats, proves the last straw for the Stewards of the Jockey Club, who withdraw the licence of the champion jockey and this year's Derby winner, and warn him off into the bargain.

14 Nov A man runs across the track at Northampton during the Compton Welter Handicap causing three horses to unseat their riders. Jockey Sam Loates is seriously hurt, breaking a thigh and a collar bone, while the man, a carpenter, receives fatal injuries.

The Grand National Aintree: 29 March

National run in snow despite protests

From HOTSPUR

When the time came for the numbers to be hoisted for the Grand National the course was covered with snow, and as it was still falling heavily the prospects of the race taking place seemed somewhat doubtful. Some of the owners and jockeys deeming it unsafe to race under such conditions, a protest was lodged with the Stewards, but, after inspecting the course, they decided that it would be perfectly safe.

The incidents of the chase were entirely hidden from view. About half the number were hors de combat in the first round. The first four to jump the water were Grudon, Covert Jack, Levanter, and Pawnbroker, of whom the last-named was "missing" when they quitted the country the second time. Along the canal-side Covert Hack, Levanter, and Drumcree in turn had a cut at Grudon, and the first-mentioned was going quite as well as the leader until entering the inner circle of the course. Here he lacked the speed of Grudon (9-1), who came into view behind the two last fences well in advance of Drumcree (10-1), Buffalo Bill (33-1), and Levanter (4-1f), and so the race ended, as, although Grudon was swinging his tail round in animated fashion, the others were too "baked" to get near him, and Arthur Nightingall added to his previous Grand National triumphs with four lengths to spare.

[The secret of Grudon's success was his owner-trainer Bernard Bletsoe's foresight in spreading a couple of pounds of butter into the horse's hooves to prevent snow building up there.]

BIG RACE RESULTS

2,000 Guineas	Handicapper	W Halsey	33-1
1,000 Guineas	Aïda	D Maher	13-8f
Derby	Volodyovski	L Reiff	5-2f
Oaks	Cap and Bells	M Henry	9-4f
St Leger	Doricles	K Cannon	40-1
Grand National	Grudon	A Nightingall	9-1

CHAMPIONS

Jockey	Otto Madden	130
Leading Trainer	J Huggins	£29,142
Leading Owner	Sir G Blundell Mapel	£21,370
Horse	Epsom Lad (4)	£18,242

The Derby Epsom: 5 June

Victory of the favourite
A record time for the Derby

From HOTSPUR

The hope that the first Derby under the machine would lead to no hitch of any kind was entertained in vain. From the commencement Orchid showed the greatest antipathy to facing the gate, and no sooner that Pratt forced him to line up than he jumped round the wrong way. This misbehaviour was again and again repeated until the infection spread to Lord Bobs, who used his heels so freely that those nearest him in the draw were not altogether happy.

When the twenty-five runners did get away, Olympian clapped on full sail to such an extent that it was not surprising that record time should be created. He was followed into the straight by Prince Charles II, Volodyovski and Revenue. When Volodyovski closed with Olympian on the inside, upwards of a quarter of a mile from home, they were out by themselves, and it was surprising to see Reiff thus early pick up his whip. In the end he resisted Morny Cannon's splendid late effort on the inside with William the Third (100-7) by three parts of a length, but it would surely have been more had Volodyovski (5-2f) kept "in his own water".

This was the first time that an American jockey had ridden the winner of the Derby. Reiff's compatriot Tod Sloan would have had the mount had he not been banned.

The Eclipse Stakes Sandown: 19 July

An exciting race

From HOTSPUR

Great indeed was the contrast between the conditions under which the Eclipse Stakes first took root fifteen years ago and the anniversary which forms the newest page of racing history. The success of the bold Bendigo was accomplished in a heavy rain storm, that of Epsom Lad beneath a burning sun, very provocative of various degrees of discomfort.

We should have seen a battle royal in the market between Diamond Jubilee and Epsom Lad. It was such common knowledge, however, that Epsom Lad had been almost constantly in the hands of the doctor that he declined rapidly until 7 to 1 was laid, and in the meanwhile Diamond Jubilee became a 6-4 on chance.

For some distance Diamond Jubilee did not seem inclined to take a firm hold of his bit, and more than half the journey had been completed before he drew into immediate attendance upon Epsom Lad. Both took a wide sweep round the bottom turn, the one in fault being Epsom Lad, and with Disguise II and Ian benefiting to the tune of two or three lengths a vigorous show of horsemanship on the part of Henry would in all probability have gained Disguise II the victory. As it was, he waited with Ian

Gomez holds on to his saddle to get home on Epsom Lad, the only gelding to win the Eclipse

until Epsom Lad had recovered himself, and from the entrance to the rails – where Gomez lost a pad, causing his saddle to slip back – the placed trio always had the best of Diamond Jubilee.

In the end Epsom Lad secured the verdict by a head from Ian (20-1), who in turn held a similar advantage over Disguise II (100-7), although the American was decidedly running the strongest of the three.

The closeness of the finish proved a redeeming feature in an Eclipse Stakes which could not compare to those won in successive years by Orme. The wonder to those who had grouped themselves near the unsaddling enclosure was that Argentinian jockey Pedro Gomez had preserved his balance, as the loss of the pad left him to finish bare-backed.

1902

21 Feb Bookmaker Victor Jackson is fined £20 at the London Police Courts for "inviting an infant to bet", said infant being Hastings Evelyn Beal, 19, of Balliol College, Oxford, one of 20 or 30 undergraduates who received circulars inviting them to open an account with Jackson and booklets outlining betting systems.

22 Feb The judge hands out heavy sentences in the Liverpool Bank Frauds case, in which a humble bank clerk, who began forging cheques to pay his gambling debts, got embroiled with shady characters of the bookmaking fraternity who blackmailed him into even greater excesses, to the tune of £160,000 defrauded from the bank.

21 Mar The 14-y-o dual Grand National winner Manifesto (100-6), carrying 12st 8lb and, in the disappointing absence of the favourite Ambush II, who split a pastern 10 days ago, conceding 35lb to the winner, is beaten 6 lengths into 3rd place by Shannon Lass (20-1) in a race that includes a 6-1 joint favourite called Drumree (knocked over) and a 10-1 chance called Drumcree (7th). *[The winning owner, bookie Ambrose Gorham, who had the 7-y-o mare trained at Telcombe, near Brighton, restored the village church with his winnings.]*

BIG RACE RESULTS

2,000 Guineas	Sceptre	H Randall	4-1jf
1,000 Guineas	Sceptre	H Randall	1-2f
Derby	Ard Patrick	JH Martin	100-14
Oaks	Sceptre	H Randall	5-2f
St Leger	Sceptre	FW Hardy	100-30f
Grand National	Shannon Lass	D Read	20-1

CHAMPIONS

Jockey	Willie Lane	170
Leading Trainer	RS Sievier	£23,686
Leading Owner	Mr RS Sievier	£23,686
Horse	Sceptre (3)	£23,195

Coronation Cup Epsom: 5 June

Lord Wolverton's success

From HOTSPUR

The Coronation Cup proved a powerful substitute for the Epsom Cup, and little wonder, therefore, that the company, which included the King and Prince Christian, was well maintained in size. The race is worthy of the great event it is intended to commemorate, seeing that a large sum had been added to a sweepstakes, which is very different to a subscription prize.

Much as we missed the opposition of some three-year-olds, the seniors formed a smart body, and Santoi (2-1f), Volodyovski (6-1), and Osboch (4-1) renewed their antagonism from the Jubilee Handicap at Kempton Park. On the strength of his failures in the City and Suburban and the Jubilee Handicap, it did not look unreasonable to partly despise Volodyovski. Lord Wolverton was very hopeful of Osboch, who, you will remember, was sixth in Volodyovski's Derby.

The pace was apparently very slow to commence with, and when they did get running in earnest Santoi never gave a flattering impression. When Osboch nicked in for the inside berth at Tattenham Corner, he was left to win quite comfortably from Volodyovski.

The St Leger Doncaster: 10 September

Sceptre's best on record

From HOTSPUR

The prediction often made that the victory of Sceptre in the St Leger would create a scene of great enthusiasm was fulfilled to the letter. Long before she reached the goal the cheers had commenced, and the depressing circumstances under which the battle was lost and won made no difference, few heroes or heroines of the St Leger having evoked greater applause. And whereas old stagers would point to Apology for a parallel, others would talk of Ormonde, Persimmon, and Diamond Jubilee.

The form of Sceptre in the "classics" had no exact counterpart, for although Formosa also secured the spoils of the One Thousand, the Oaks and the St Leger, she had to be content with only a half of the Two Thousand. The occasional failures of Sceptre have only served to accentuate the brilliancy of her triumphs.

Owing to the weather, the whole of the competitors were enveloped in waterproof sheets until the time arrived for saddling, and the inspection was less interesting than usual. The only approach to a crowd was in the extreme corner, which had been chosen for making the toilette of Sceptre, and whereas there were many with opinions formed beforehand who picked holes freely in her coat, others saw the filly through a different pair of spectacles. It was nothing against her that she should perspire freely, as this is characteristic of her blood. In the parade she carried herself quite easily.

As soon as the gates had been lowered in preparation for the start, Sceptre was again considerably on her toes. The efforts of

The Oaks Epsom: 6 June

Derby fourth Sceptre wins Oaks in a canter

From HOTSPUR

After a delay of nearly twenty-five minutes before the start, created partly by her own fractiousness, Sceptre (5-2f) made up for the disappointment of her fourth in the Derby on Wednesday by winning the Oaks in a canter by three lengths.

Many of Sceptre's backers may have quite prepared themselves for her defeat, and great must have been the relief, therefore, when the dual Guineas heroine threaded her way by degrees from the rear rank, and won with the same ease that had characterised the victory of Ard Patrick in the Derby.

In writing of the brilliant triumph of the Irish colt and his comparatively cool reception, I was inclined to wonder if things would have been different had Sceptre followed in the footsteps of Derby-Oaks winners Eleanor and Blink Bonny. The answer must now be given in the affirmative, as neither the rain nor an attendance apparently much below the average could check the display of public acclamation. The filly was the one that commanded the people's sympathies this week.

The great Sceptre, quadruple Classic winner

Ross-shire in the way of pacemaking were poor in the extreme, and passing the Rifle-butts he was tailed off. In this respect Caro proved a horse of another colour, and once out by himself a dozen lengths he was not caught by Rising Glass, Friar Tuck, and St Brendan until half a mile from home. At this stage, Sceptre, who was for a long time in the rear rank, became fourth. From the half-mile post the field fell all to pieces, and when they rounded the bend, the fatal spot to many St Leger favourites, Sceptre had joined Rising Glass, with Friar Tuck at their heels.

From this point, Sceptre (100-30f) shot out from Rising Glass (9-1) as if he were standing still. Any doubt that may have been left as to the issue vanished in the twinkling of an eye, and in the last quarter of a mile the St Leger could not have been won with greater ease. So much had Sceptre to spare that Hardy steered her with the greatest confidence, and the summing up of the situation is that, trained by an amateur and ridden by an apprentice only just emancipated from the allowance stage, she won with fully a stone in hand, the official verdict being three lengths.

1903

21 Jan Cloister, 19, one of the most brilliant steeplechasers of the last century, who won 18 of his 34 National Hunt races including the 1893 Grand National, is put down at Lower Forty Farm, Wembley.

17 Jul Three of the five runners in the Eclipse Stakes at Sandown line up with 7 Classic wins between them – the 5-4 favourite Rock Sand having won this season's 2,000 and Derby; the filly Sceptre (7-4), last season's Oaks, St Leger and both Guineas; and the colt Ard Patrick (5-1), who had beaten her in the Derby – and finish in reverse order of SP, Ard Patrick holding off Sceptre by a neck thanks to the fine jockeyship of Otto Madden, with Rock Sand trailing them by 3 lengths.

30 Sep Thanks to a dramatic campaign by the trainer the Hon George Lambton, the Jockey Club ban doping, adding the following to Rule 176: "If any person shall be proved to have administered for the purpose of affecting the speed of a horse drugs or stimulants internally by hypodermic or other methods, every person so offending shall be warned off Newmarket Heath and other places where these rules are enforced."

27 Oct The last two races at Newmarket throw up two of the greatest fillies in the history of the Turf, but each is opposed by only one runner, there to pick up 2nd money, as 4-y-o Sceptre (1-100) wins the 1mi 2f Limekiln Stakes and 2-y-o Pretty Polly (7-100) the 6f Criterion Stakes, by a "hollow" 8 lengths and an "easy" length and a half, respectively.

28 Oct Pretty Polly strolls to another 100-7 on victory at Newmarket, where earlier the 3-y-o filly Hackler's Pride (6-1) wins the Cambridgeshire to bring off a huge, but above-board, ante-post betting coup for trainer John Fallon and owner Capt Frank Forester that is said to have hit the bookies for upwards of £250,000.

Ard Patrick led in after his Eclipse triumph

British Dominion Plate Sandown: 27 June

Pretty Polly out by herself

From HOTSPUR

One event stood out alone on the second day of the Sandown Park meeting, which took place in an intense heat wave. It is needless to add that the British Dominion Plate claims the distinction, and the style in which Pretty Polly played the part of hare before the hounds may not be reproduced throughout the season.

Those who did not watch the actual start, and turned their heads down the course to find Pretty Polly "out by herself", jumped to the natural conclusion that she had poached a lot of start. This was not the case, and from the first furlong three or four were quite near enough to have fair chances. Then, however, in obedience to the vigorous tactics pursued by Trigg, she drew clean away, and having once led by a couple of hundred yards, the verdict was recorded by ten lengths after she had considerably slowed down.

It was the first time of Pretty Polly, a daughter of Gallinule and Admiration, wearing colours in public. She came from Newmarket with quite a smart reputation, but at 6-1 was only fourth in the betting. A big filly, a little inclined to coarseness, and far from ripe, she seemed nevertheless to possess the wings of the wind.

Grand National Aintree: 27 March

Visit of the King

From HOTSPUR

There was no novelty in the visit of the King to Liverpool in order to see the battle of the Grand National lost and won. Had the fates decreed that his Majesty's Ambush II should have rivalled the feats of Cloister and Manifesto by carrying home the top-weight, the reception when he scored three years ago would certainly have been exceeded. As it was, he retrieved himself grandly on the score of merit, and when he fell at the last fence the chance of his absolute triumph was far from exhausted. In fact, although I am unable to quite agree with the opinion of his jockey that he would have outstayed Drumcree on the flat, he was fighting bravely, and looked an even-money chance at the previous fence.

Ten of the competitors did not complete the first circuit of the course, and less than two lengths divided Ambush II, Drumcree, Detail, and Drumree little more than a quarter of a mile from home. On approaching the second fence from home Phillips took a "steadier" at Drumree, who shortly afterwards faltered without the slightest warning, and enabled Ambush II to jump first. Between the two last fences Drumcree (13-2f) and Detail (100-14) from my point of view were getting slightly the better of Ambush II (100-6), and were "in the air" at the last fence when he failed to rise and paid the penalty.

Detail was travelling the nearest way from the last fence, but Drumcree forged away again until the verdict was one of three lengths. The gallant 15-year-old Manifesto (25-1), carrying 12st 3lb, secured third money twenty lengths behind.

The St Leger Doncaster: 9 September

Rock Sand: An easy victory

From HOTSPUR

The extended interval allowed of plenty of time to inspect the St Leger candidates, and the prevailing opinion was that they were a common lot of horses, when judged from the highest standard of classic form, and the fact that Rock Sand (2-5f) stands out so immeasurably superior points to the conclusion that the three-year-olds are the most mediocre seen for several seasons.

The good fortune attending his owner Sir James Miller is such as falls to few men on the Turf, for at the very outset of his career he purchased Sainfoin, and won a lucky Derby with him immediately afterwards. Now he has bred a winner of the three classic races from the same horse after a lapse of thirteen years.

The story of the race is soon told, for after Persistence had made the pace under pressure for three-quarters of a mile he resigned the command to the favourite, who was never afterwards headed and won in a common canter by four lengths.

It was a meritorious performance on the part of the winner, and at the same time a triumph for his trainer, Blackwell, who has devoted the most careful attention to him throughout all his engagements. Maher, too, is to be congratulated upon the manner in which he has handled the colt, for it is a singular circumstance that on the only two occasions that he has been beaten the American jockey was not on his back.

BIG RACE RESULTS

2,000 Guineas	Rock Sand	JH Martin	6-4f
1,000 Guineas	Quintessence	H Randall	4-1
Derby	Rock Sand	D Maher	4-6f
Oaks	Our Lassie	M Cannon	6-1
St Leger	Rock Sand	D Maher	2-5f
Grand National	Drumcree	P Woodland	13-2f

CHAMPIONS

Jockey	Otto Madden	154
Leading Trainer	G Blackwell	£34,135
Leading Owner	Sir James Miller	£24,768
Horse	Rock Sand (3)	£18,425

1904

18 Jan In a hurdle race at Nice, Outlaw is killed in a fall and jockey Turner badly hurt, but it takes three hours to transport him to hospital. On arrival, the horses bolt with the ambulance, but fortunately not before the jockey has been removed.

29 Apr Pretty Polly (1-4) makes all the running and wins the 1,000 Guineas in a canter by 3 lengths from Leucadia (33-1),

beating Sceptre's record by 1/5sec with 1min 40sec.

1 Jun Mr George Thursby is the first amateur rider to be placed in the Derby when he guides John o'Gaunt (4-1) to 2nd money 3 lengths behind St Amant (5-1), who makes all the running, with 7-4f Gouvernant trailing in 7th of the 8 runners in a thunderstorm.

The St Leger Doncaster: 7 September

A record St Leger

From HOTSPUR

The triumph of Pretty Polly in the St Leger today was so thorough and complete, and her defeat of the Derby winner so absolutely emphatic, that the impression is now firmly established that she is possible the best filly of this or any other generation. It was not the

Pretty Polly: odds-on winner of three Classics without being extended

mere fact of her winning which confirms the theory, but the style in which she accomplished her victory, and it is a curious circumstance that throughout her brilliant career no animal has yet been discovered capable of adequately testing her superlative merit.

It is reasonable to assume that since the days of Ormonde no individual racehorse has created the interest or enjoyed the unique popularity of Pretty Polly. She was, as usual, fairly mobbed as she walked round the paddock at the heels of her faithful attendant, the cob, which is her constant travelling companion.

For a short distance Pretty Polly (2-5f) looked like setting the pace, but St Amant (4-1) quickly assumed the cutting-down tactics which were attended with such success in the Derby, and he held a clear lead of the filly until well in

the line for home, when Pretty Polly drew up to his quarters. The moment she did so, St Amant deliberately refused to struggle, and gradually dropped into the rear. As soon as he gave way the race was virtually over, for Pretty Polly drew out from Almscliff (100-6) and Henry the First (50-1), and won in the commonest of canters by three lengths.

It was a truly wonderful display on the part of Major Loder's filly, and seldom, if ever, has the St Leger been won in such a one-sided fashion. The time was the fastest on record, and when Pretty Polly returned to the unsaddling enclosure she had not turned a hair, and might, to all intents and purposes, have just completed an ordinary exercise gallop. It is now certain that had she been in the Two Thousand Guineas and Derby she would have added those events to her already remarkable record.

CHAMPIONS

Jockey	Otto Madden	161
Leading Trainer	PP Gilpin	£35,694
Leading Owner	Sir James Miller	£28,923
Horse	Rock Sand (4)	£19,719

The Grand National Aintree: 25 March

Moifaa's National

From HOTSPUR

Probably few noticed the ultimate winner of the Grand National, Moifaa, for there were so many to observe in the paddock that the great majority of the twenty-six runners were passed by without a thought. This remark does not apply to the veteran Manifesto, who the public have a positive affection for and who, though now sixteen years old, looked simply splendid.

Ambush II was brought into the unsaddling enclosure opposite the weighing-room door, where his Majesty came to see his final toilet adjusted. No one for a moment anticipated that the 1900 winner would come to grief at the very outset, but unfortunately he just touched the top of the third fence and rolled over.

Long before they jumped the water and passed the stand the first time the field had been greatly thinned. Moifaa was setting a wonderful pace, attended by Kirkland and The Gunner, while old Manifesto, if unable to keep up with the intense

pressure, was jumping with his accustomed brilliancy.

In the last mile of the journey there was nothing in it but the first three. As they came on the racecourse the name of The Gunner (25-1) was proclaimed as a likely winner, but Moifaa (25-1) had too much speed for him and Mr Spencer Gollan's horse, never making a mistake, practically won in a canter by eight lengths from Kirkland (100-7), who just deprived the Irish horse of second place. Manifesto (20-1), still burdened with over 12 stone, struggled on and completed the course, his performance being loudly cheered. The winner was not in the least distressed and, indeed, seemed capable of going round the course again.

[Before the National, Moifaa was known not for his steeplechasing exploits but for his unorthodox arrival in 1903 from his native New Zealand, when he was found by fishermen running loose on the beach after being shipwrecked off the Irish coast.]

BIG RACE RESULTS

2,000 Guineas	St Amant	K Cannon	11-4f
1,000 Guineas	Pretty Polly	W Lane	1-4f
Derby	St Amant	K Cannon	5-1
Oaks	Pretty Polly	W Lane	8-100f
St Leger	Pretty Polly	W Lane	2-5f
Grand National	Moifaa	A Birch	25-1

Valentine Steeplechase Aintree: 12 November

Injury to Manifesto

From HOTSPUR

The breakdown of Manifesto in the Valentine Steeplechase struck quite a pathetic note, for the hope was cherished that the gallant old horse would on the scene of his former triumphs end his racing career by scoring one more success. The fates decreed otherwise, and the veteran, who broke a small bone at the back of the knee, hobbled back to the paddock ingloriously to arouse the sympathy of hundreds of his admirers.

It is doubtful if a more popular animal has ever crossed this Aintree country, where his exploits have been unique. For many years he was rarely absent from the Grand National field, and his

attempts to win the race for the third time under seemingly hopeless weights has engendered some remarkable outbursts of enthusiasm. He was a wonderfully safe jumper, and it is said that he has only fallen in a steeplechase once in his life, and that was in the Grand National of 1896, when he was really knocked over.

In eight attempts, he won twice, was third three times and fourth once. He will now be allowed to end his days in peace at Mr Moore's place, but a halo of sentiment will always cling round the name of the horse whose record in connection with the time-honoured steeplechase may never be approached.

1905

1 Feb The Duke of Portland's 19-y-o stallion Donovan, Derby and St Leger winner in 1889, when he set a world record career earnings of £55,443 having won 18 and been placed in the other 3 of his races, is destroyed as a result of injuries sustained two days ago when he got loose and dashed head first into a tree.

18 Feb The King's 11-y-o chaser, Ambush II, National winner in 1900, suddenly drops dead while being exercised in a long gallop at the Curragh.

10 May There are only 3 runners in the Kentucky Derby, won by Agile (1-3f).

31 May G.Evans, Sam Loates's apprentice, meets with fatal injuries while riding Braw Lass filly in the Juvenile Plate at Epsom on Derby day, his mount slipping at the first tan road.

The Grand National Aintree: 31 March

King's new chaser disappoints

From HOTSPUR

This year's Grand National was associated with incidents which may in a measure be regarded as unique, for, in the first place, the sudden death of Ambush II, and the subsequent purchase of Moifaa by the King, are items which have hardly any parallel in connection with national sport. It is almost needless to say that seldom has disappointment been so plainly expressed as it was today when Moifaa (4-1f) egregiously failed to bear the Royal colours with the credit which might reasonably have been expected. Perhaps never before has a horse been backed with such blind confidence and loyal enthusiasm as was the New Zealand-bred gelding.

In points of looks, Kirkland appeared to much better advantage than he has ever done before, his substance and immense quarters contrasting curiously with Moifaa, who beat him last year.

At the water the first time, Ranunculus led from Timothy Titus and Moifaa. The latter was jumping in his customary inimitable style, but was even thus early labouring, and he eventually came to grief at Becher's Brook, to the general disappointment. After jumping Valentine's Brook the second time there were few left standing with anything like flattering chances.

Ranunculus was at this point leading, but he gave way to Kirkland immediately they entered the racecourse. Kirkland (6-1) ran on in dogged style, and though impeded by two loose horses, he came on, and won cleverly by three lengths from Napper Tandy (25-1), with the little-fancied Buckaway II (100-1) third and Ranunculus (7-1) fourth, only seven completing the course. There was great cheering when Kirkland returned to the paddock, as he is owned by a local businessman, Frank Bibby, and Frank Mason, his rider, is a native of the Cheshire side of the Mersey.

[Mason, who rode Kirkland into 2nd place last year, was paid £300 not to ride for two weeks before the race to ensure his availability.]

BIG RACE RESULTS

2,000 Guineas	Vedas	H Jones	11-2
1,000 Guineas	Cherry Lass	G McCall	5-4f
Derby	Cicero	D Maher	4-11f
Oaks	Cherry Lass	H Jones	4-5f
St Leger	Challacombe	O Madden	100-6
Grand National	Kirkland	F Mason	6-1

CHAMPIONS

Jockey	Elijah Wheatley	124
Leading Trainer	WT Robinson	£34,466
Leading Owner	Col W Hall Walker	£23,687
Horse	Cherry Lass (3)	£13,119

Coronation Cup Epsom: 1 June

Pretty Polly's brilliant performance

From HOTSPUR

The field for the Coronation Cup may not have been commensurate with the intrinsic value of the prize, but this could scarcely be expected with such equine giants as Pretty Polly and Zinfandel entering the lists.

An international flavour was imparted to the race by the presence of the French horse Caius (100-15), the only other runner. A great, fine horse, standing over a lot of ground, he yet lacks the exquisite quality of Pretty Polly (4-9f), who stripped a perfect picture. She has grown into one of the handsomest mares ever seen on a racecourse. Zinfandel (7-2), as usual, was the beau ideal of a well-trained muscular horse.

The most sanguine hopes were, I believe, cherished that he would repeat his victory of last year, but in Pretty Polly, who had finished in front of him in the now notorious Grand Prix de Municipal in Paris, he again met a filly who has had few if any superiors during the last half-century. How she came to be beaten by an animal like Presto II will ever remain an unsolved mystery, for she today accomplished a performance which places her far ahead even of the average of most Derby winners.

She not only won in smashing style, fairly smothering Zinfandel at the bottom of the hill when asked for an effort, but she beat the record time made in the Blue Riband by no less than six seconds, and was not in the least distressed after her three-length victory.

Gold Cup Ascot: 22 June

Zinfandel's Gold Cup

A brilliant scene

From HOTSPUR

It is an unwritten though well inspired racing law that no animal has set the seal on its fame until it has claimed the distinction of winning the Ascot Cup. Pretty Polly, but for an untoward accident, would assuredly have crowned her laurels by winning the race today, and the statement is more than ever prompted by the easy victory of Zinfandel, for at Epsom Gallinule's lovely daughter had defeated the handsome son of Persimmon with consummate ease.

Morny Cannon, profiting by the somewhat bitter experience of twelve months ago, when Zinfandel was beaten by the older Throwaway, evidently intended to leave nothing to chance, for he sent Zinfandel along and drew into second place in the Swinley Bottom. When fairly in the Old Course the son of Persimmon was taken to the front, and he came into the straight with clear lead of Chatsworth. For some distance afterwards the latter looked like being second, but he tired rapidly, and at the Spagnoletti board Maximum II (10-1) passed him. The efforts of the latter to reach Zinfandel (2-5f), however, were absolutely fruitless, and Lord Howard de Walden's horse won in a canter by three lengths, in record time for the race, with Throwaway (11-2) a further two lengths back.

One naturally begins to wonder what sort of a mare Pretty Polly is, seeing how she beat Zinfandel at Epsom, and though, as a rule, little faith is attached to the time test, it is more than ever palpable that Major Eustace Loder's mare is the most remarkable filly seen for many decades.

The American invasion

A number of American jockeys came over to England in the late 1800s and transformed English racing. They revolutionised the style and tactics of race riding and enjoyed considerable success. But some brought with them the sleazy elements of American racing – the gamblers, crooks and dopers for whom racing was not a sport but a way of making a dishonest living.

The greatest influence on riders and riding was the diminutive Tod Sloan, and perhaps the most successful of the Americans was Lester Reiff, but both of these jockeys had their English careers cut short by the Stewards of the Jockey Club.

Monkey on the stick

The Americans adopted a forward-leaning, crouching attitude, using short reins and shortened stirrup leathers, designed to shift the centre of gravity forward and produce a streamlined shape that reduced the air resistance. Said to have been copied from the American Indians, this style was soon dubbed "monkey on the stick".

Although it was Sloan who first popularised the style on British racecourses, it was originally introduced by Willie Simms, a black jockey who had two Belmont Stakes to his credit and who was derided and scoffed at when he first appeared on an English racecourse in 1895 to take part in Newmarket's Crawfurd Plate. But he had the last laugh as he rode Eau Gallie to victory with his monkey crouch, leaving the top English jockeys struggling in his wake.

Simms, however, found it difficult to obtain rides, and he returned to America. But the following year Lester Reiff and then, in 1897, Tod Sloan came over and demanded respect as they recorded win after win and established themselves among the leading jockeys.

On his Tod

Sloan was born at Bunker Hill, Indiana, in 1874, and was nicknamed "Toad" (hence "Tod") as a boy because of his short, stumpy legs. He left an indelible mark not only on racing but also, through Cockney rhyming slang, on the English language, "on one's tod" coming to mean "on one's own".

When Sloan first arrived in England to ride for the American Mr James R.Keene, he was soon disputing the judge's decision after losing by a head in the Cambridgeshire, demonstrating a disregard for officialdom that was to be his downfall. The impact he made on his second visit, the following autumn, was of a different kind altogether, with 12 winners in 16 rides over the four days of the Newmarket October meeting.

From that moment, he was rarely out of the public eye. And his short-reined style – crouching low over the horse's neck, his hands within a few inches of the bridle rings – could not be ridiculed, as his predecessor Simms' was, because of his remarkable and continuing success. He had many imitators, but the man was a genius, and would have succeeded with whatever style of riding he chose.

Sloan enjoyed a wonderful rapport with horses and appeared to inspire many of his mounts to victory. He was also a remarkable judge of pace. When asked why he would gallop his mounts at top speed for a furlong or so when taking them down to the post, he explained that it would tell him how fast he

Tod Sloan, most famous and infamous of the American invaders

could expect them to be able to go in the last stages of a race.

Aggressive tactics

It was not just the American seat that had such a profound effect on British racing, but also the aggressive tactics employed by the "invaders". Sloan, indeed, made his English counterparts look silly. Where they would take the traditional "pull" at the start, preserving their horses for the celebrated Chifney "rush", he burst out of the gate and raced the whole distance, and still kept enough in hand for a sprint at the finish.

Soon, it was a case of "if you can't beat 'em, join 'em", as many leading home jockeys began to adopt these foreign tactics. A notable effect was the improvement in race times – by an average of some four seconds in the Derby, for example, and 14 in the Ascot Gold Cup.

Sloan enjoyed the patronage of Lord William Beresford, who also employed an American trainer, John Huggins, and raced mostly American-bred horses. Sadly for Sloan, as brilliant as he was on the racecourse, his genius was not apparent off it. He made a fortune, but gambled it away playing cards in his expensive suite of hotel rooms with the shady American characters he kept company with.

In the end, gambling was his downfall – combined with the arrogance of a prima donna. Smoking a large cigar as he left the jockeys' room to converse with his patron in the paddock was one thing, but organising a coup together with his cronies by virtually fixing a race was another kettle of fish and understandably quite unacceptable.

The focus of the coup was his mount, Codoman, in the Cambridgeshire. His "gang" went to extraordinary lengths to ensure that he would win, buying off jockeys and somehow arranging for them to ride the other favoured horses. But one rival proved incorruptible, the Irish champion John Thompson; nor could his ride, Berrill, be nobbled.

And, as luck would have it, Berrill beat Codoman by three lengths. In the jockeys' room afterwards, the furious Sloan cursed the Irishman roundly, accusing him of having cost him a fortune. An official overheard the row, and the next day Sloan was summoned before the stewards. He freely admitted betting on the race – and standing to win £60,000 – naïvely asserting that it was quite legal to back his own mount. Of course, it was not, and he was suitably reprimanded. And if he thought he had got off lightly, he was in for a rude awakening when the Stewards of the Jockey Club later informed him that he need not reapply for a licence to ride.

As a result, Sloan missed riding what would have been his first Derby winner, Volodyovski, in 1901. Nor would he ever become champion jockey, for he reapplied for his licence for the next 15 years to no avail.

Of the other American jockeys of their dominant period, Martin and Maher enjoyed relatively unblemished reputations, and the latter won the jockeys' title in 1908. Then, to compound the discomfiture of the home riders, the Australian "wonderboy" Frank Wootton annexed it four years running, before Maher's second championship in 1913.

It was 1914 before the public could acknowledge another British champion, Steve Donoghue, who became the most popular jockey since Fred Archer. Ironically, as a youth, Donoghue idolised Tod Sloan. A genius in his own right and a master horseman, Donoghue nevertheless learned much from the wayward American, with whom he shared a love and supreme understanding of horses.

Sloan, 'on his tod', walks out to mount Holocauste in the 1899 Derby. His mount fell in the straight while disputing the lead with eventual winner Flying Fox and had to be put down. Sloan never rode a Derby winner.

Donoghue rode six Derby winners, including four out of five in the early twenties, and he remained the darling of the British racegoer until he retired in 1937. For ten years, he sat proudly at the top of the jockeys table, and, with the advent of Gordon Richards, the most prolific winner in the history of British racing, it would not be until 1957 that the title went abroad again.

His best year had been 1899, when he finished fifth, with 108 winners from 345 rides, a remarkable proportion of successes compared with the figures of Sam Loates, who won the title with 160 wins from more than twice as many rides. Such had been Sloan's ascendancy that in 1898, when he rode five winners and a second at Newmarket, bookies almost unanimously took the unprecedented step of deducting five percent from future Sloan winners.

American domination

Despite the absence of Sloan. the American domination of the English Turf continued. In 1900, five of the first 10 in the jockeys table were Transatlantic invaders, the championship being won for the first time by an American, Lester Reiff, with 143 winners. In that year, Royal Ascot was a débâcle as far as home riders were concerned, 17 of the 28 races going to the Americans.

And it was Lester Reiff who enjoyed the Derby victory on Volodyovski in 1901, followed by J.H. "Skeets" Martin on the great Ard Patrick (1902), Danny Maher on Rock Sand (1903), Cicero (1905) and Spearmint (1906), Lester's brother Johnny on Orby (1907) and Tagalie (1912), and Matt McGee on Durbar (1914).

Lester Reiff's success was also short-lived, however, for he was to fall foul of the Jockey Club and was warned off in 1901 for his riding of Dr Lacy in a minor race at Manchester, where he was beaten a short head by his brother on Minnie Dee. Some thought his punishment too harsh, but this was not an isolated incident and his dishonesty and his involvement with American gambling syndicates were well known. Johnny, a lightweight with a great record in the big handicaps, realised the Jockey Club meant business and diplomatically moved to France, although he returned for his Epsom triumphs and was deprived of his third Derby only by Craganour's controversial disqualification in 1913.

Steve Donoghue (left), who gave the British public a hero to applaud after the long period of American domination, with American jockey Frank O'Neill, whose Derby victory on Spion Kop in 1920 was the last American riding success in the great Classic until Steve Cauthen launched his own mini-invasion in 1985.

1906

30 Mar The Grand National is won by Ascetic's Silver (20-1), a riderless "1st" last year and half-brother to two previous winners, Cloister and Drumcree, the latter coming 8th (33-1). The winner is one of three runners owned by international sportsman Prince Franz Hatzfeldt, and is trained and ridden by the Hon Aubrey Hastings. The hot favourite John M.P. (7-2), unbeaten in his 5 races this season but new to the National, is disturbed by the noise of spectators at the Canal Turn and falls into the wings of the obstacle.

22 Jun An unusual show of generosity by the bookies at Royal Ascot sees all 3 runners in the King's Stand Stakes start as 2-1 joint favourites.

24 Oct Bought last month by Mr Solly Joel for 4,200gns notwithstanding his lack of form, the 4-y-o Polymelus brings off a famous ante-post betting coup for his owner, easily winning the Cambridgeshire after being backed down to 11-10 favourite, despite a 10lb penalty for winning a handicap at Kempton and the Champion Stakes at Newmarket in the intervening weeks. [Between 1914 and 1921, Polymelus becomes leading sire 5 times, with 8 Classics to his credit including 3 Derbys.]

26 Oct The Stewards of the Irish Turf Club warn off a trainer, Mr McAuliffe, for instructing his jockey not to win a race at Baldoyle, while the Newmarket stewards suspend jockey Frank Wootton, not yet 13, for 10 days for unnecessary use of his whip, having cautioned him for a similar offence last week.

New York: 17 June

Death of Sysonby

FROM OUR OWN CORRESPONDENT

It is no exaggeration to say that all sporting America mourns the death of Mr James Keene's Sysonby, America's great thoroughbred, which died yesterday night at Sheepshead Bay, Long Island, in the presence of his owner, who was much attached to the animal.

Sysonby had been suffering constantly during the last two months, and the poor animal was in great agony for hours before he passed away. He died from the worse form of septic poisoning. The veterinary surgeons found that Sysonby's lungs and kidneys were twice as large as those of an ordinary racehorse, and this explains the stamina and courage that marked his running.

Sysonby was suffering from an incurable blood disease that had been communicated to the unfortunate beast by an attendant who, in rubbing the animal's mouth with a sponge, had introduced the poison into the wound.

Sysonby was a bay colt four years old, by Melton-Optime, by Orme, and was imported from England with his dam while still unborn. He was foaled at the Castleton stud in 1902. The horse had a career of but two years, and started fifteen times, winning fourteen races and coming in third once.

Ascot Gold Cup: 21 June

Pretty Polly beaten

From HOTSPUR

All sorts of sensational rumours were afloat about Pretty Polly, and it was currently reported that she would not run for the Gold Cup. It appears that a few days ago she experienced some inconveniences from a wart which had formed under her body. The excrescence developed a certain amount of humour, and had to be lanced by Mr Livock, the well-known veterinary surgeon. Mr Livock informed me, just prior to racing, that he considered the mare was little the worse. But it must be confessed that she did not, in the paddock, create such a favourable impression as usual.

That Pretty Polly would have secured the coveted prize twelve months ago had she been able to run has always been accepted as certain, though doubtless the view may be modified after today's sensational race, when the Cup furnished one of those remarkable surprises which have from time to time distinguished it.

Everybody seemed to be stupefied to realise that a catastrophe had somehow occurred. This expression is permissible where Pretty Polly is concerned, for she had never

The Derby Epsom: 30 May

Victory of Spearmint

From HOTSPUR

There were no equine giants in the field to compare with Ormonde, Isinglass, or even Rock Sand, but the unusually open character of the Derby engendered a certain amount of excitement, and the anticipations of a huge crowd were realised to the letter. The winner, Spearmint (6-1), had not appeared in public this season before yesterday, and for his jockey, Danny Maher, it was a third Derby win in four years.

The favourite, Lally (4-1), began slowly and was never on fighting terms with the leaders. As they rounded Tattenham Corner, Spearmint improved his position at a great pace, and though Picton and Troutbeck were closely followed into the straight by His Eminence and Radium, Spearmint, on the outside, quickly closed up the gap, and, heading Picton (18-1) below the distance, won very comfortably by a length and a half, with Mr Dugdale's colt well clear of Troutbeck (33-1), who ran surprisingly well.

Mr Gilpin's experience in having in his stable two animals capable of winning

Mr Eustace Loader leads Spearmint in

the Derby is probably unique. It is an open secret that he fully expected to secure the race with Flair, the One Thousand Guineas winner, who went amiss. Then Spearmint was suddenly protruded as a colt likely to secure the spoils for the Clarehaven Lodge establishment, but people were naturally incredulous. But on the strength of having acquitted himself so well with Pretty Polly in the home trial, he was backed to win a large stake.

previously been beaten in this country, having achieved a triumphant and unbroken series of successes extending over three seasons.

The race was run at a tremendous pace, with Bachelor's Button waiting behind Pretty Polly at the back of the five runners. After passing the brick-kilns, Achilles deprived St Denis of the lead, and was followed into the straight by Bachelor's Button and Pretty Polly. A quarter of a mile from home Achilles was done with, and excitement reached a high point as the favourite made her effort to overhaul Bachelor's Button.

For a few strides it looked as though she would win easily, and then Dillon had suddenly to take up his whip. It was at once seen that the mare was in difficulties, and with Bachelor's Button struggling on in the most dogged style he won by a length.

People seemed too disappointed at the result to make any demonstration. But to give honour where honour is due, Bachelor's Button has now unquestionably shown himself to be about the best stayer in training.

1907

19 Mar A record 118 runners take part in the 6 races on the Lincoln card, including 24 in the Lincolnshire Handicap and 28 in the Lincoln Plate for 2-yr-olds, of which a quarter are unnamed.

1 Apr Grand National winner Eremon makes light of a 12lb penalty 10 days later to thrill his connections with an easy win in the Lancashire Chase at Manchester, but the 7-y-o gelding's promising career is cut short soon afterwards, when he escapes his handlers on the gallops, injures himself badly, and has to be put down.

CHAMPIONS

Jockey	Billy Higgs	146
Leading Trainer	A Taylor	£24,708
Leading Owner	Col W Hall Walker	£17,910
Horse	Lally (4)	£11,555

Lincolnshire Handicap Lincoln: 19 March

Ob's double victory

From HOTSPUR

For the first time in the history of the race, the same horse has won the Lincolnshire Handicap twice. The French-trained Ob, carrying 10lb more than last year, was victorious again, ridden by George Stern who came over from France.

The handsomest horse in the paddock was undoubtedly second favourite Bill of the Play (15-2), who is a typical Bill of Portland. He is a beautifully moulded horse and his black coat shone like satin. On the other hand, Ob (25-1), if lacking the quality of Bill of the Play, was undoubtedly the fittest animal in the race. He walked about in a cool, business-like way, which gained him many friends. Still, few thought him good enough to win again, with 8st 10lb on his back.

There was a long and tedious delay before the barrier was raised, Bill of the Play behaving like a mad horse and lashing out on all sides. But he got well off, much to the relief of his many backers, and he set a strong pace.

Ob was on the extreme outside but one. He nevertheless always held a nice place, and had taken up the running below the distance. When Bill of the Play compounded a quarter of a mile from home, Athi looked dangerous for a few strides, but immediately Stern dashed Ob to the front the affair was virtually over. The French horse drew right away, followed by Kaffir Chief (100-7), and won in a canter by five lengths.

It was a smashing and impressive victory and it is now clear that the winner is a much better horse than he was thought to be twelve months ago, when he only just scrambled home.

The Grand National Aintree: 22 March

Eremon's popular victory

From HOTSPUR

It is questionable if a more moderate lot of animals have ever gone to the post for a Grand National, and it is pretty certain that the field contained nothing which for the moment could compare with such animals as Cloister and Manifesto. But the race was a remarkable one in many respects, not least for the display of the winner, Eremon, whose rider, Alfred Newey, broke a leather at the second fence, and thereafter only had the use of one iron. The circumstance that Eremon continued to jump sideways is therefore explained. His performance was one of the most extraordinary in the history of the race, and Newey is deserving of the utmost praise for his coolness and pluck under exceptionally trying circumstances.

In addition, Rathvale, who fell at the second fence, galloped on riderless, and completed the full course, finishing second. He seriously interfered with several of the candidates, notably Extravagance, whom he caused to fall at the water, and continued to hamper Eremon throughout the race.

Timothy Titus and Drumcree fell pretty early on, and so did Centre Board, and for all practical purposes the issue may be said to have been confined to Eremon (8-1) and Tom West (100-6). For the greater part of the journey Eremon led the field a merry dance, and, jumping perfectly throughout, was really never headed.

Tom West was running on most gallantly, and though he once looked like getting on equitable terms with the leader, Eremon came away again on the flat, and won in a canter by half a dozen lengths, the pair being a long way ahead of the others, of whom only eight completed the course.

Eremon's owner, Mr Stanley Howard, is a young gentleman who has only recently become associated with the Turf – yet he has secured the blue riband of cross-country sport at the very first attempt. Eremon is the only animal in his possession and was purchased for £400 from Mr James Daly, of Dublin. The horse had been regularly hunted for a couple of seasons before being put into training last year with the former football player, Tom Coulthwaite, at Hednesford, and had shown such brilliant fencing capacity and fine staying powers at home that his success, with only 10st 1lb to carry, was anticipated with the greatest confidence.

BIG RACE RESULTS

2,000 Guineas	Slieve Gallion	W Higgs	4-11f
1,000 Guineas	Witch Elm	B Lynham	4-1f
Derby	Orby	J Reiff	100-9
Oaks	Glass Doll	H Randall	25-1
St Leger	Wool Winder	W Halsey	11-10f
Grand National	Eremon	A Newey	8-1

The Derby Epsom: 5 June

Orby is Ireland's first triumph in Derby

From HOTSPUR

The victory of Orby in the Derby was a popular one, for whereas public opinion ranged itself on the side of the favourite, Slieve Gallion, the open policy pursued by Mr Croker, the winner's owner, was much appreciated. He made no secret of his faith in his splendid colt, and it was freely stated that he had shown himself to be more than two stone in front of Hayden in home gallops. Though this seemed almost too good to be true, results have shown that every justification existed for the gratuitous statement.

Orby (100-9), who was walking just behind Slieve Gallion in the paddock, made the 13-8 on favourite look almost undersized. The son of Orme and Rhoda B is a tremendously big colt, standing fully 16 hands 2 inches.

The pace was by no means a strong one, and after going half a mile Slieve Gallion took up the running. But the favourite did not seem to be able to act down the incline, and he ran very wide coming round the fateful Tattenham Corner, letting up Orby on the inside.

Orby appeared to be only cantering, and he won comfortably by two lengths from Wool Winder, who came up with an electric rush to take second place by half a length from the favourite.

In every way it was an unqualified triumph for Ireland, where Orby was both bred and trained, and the Irish brigade, who were on Orby to a man, could not restrain their enthusiasm.

1908

15 Jan The King's famous stallion Persimmon, Derby and St Leger winner in 1896 and winner of the Ascot Gold Cup and Eclipse Stakes in 1897, fractures a pelvis and is put down four days later. He sired a host of winners including the quadruple Classic winner Sceptre and Zinfandel, winner of the Coronation Cup and Ascot Gold Cup.

24 Mar One of the great patrons of horse racing, the Duke of Devonshire, dies at the age of 74 in Cannes, where he was convalescing, having been taken ill at Ascot races last year. His only Classic success (as Lord Hartington) was the 1,000 Guineas with Belphoebe in 1877, yet the money he must have spent in entrance fees and forfeits was truly enormous. A former cabinet minister, he once declined an offer by the Queen to form an Administration, and will be remembered for his famous apology to the House of Commons for yawning while delivering an official statement because he found it "so inordinately dull".

5 Jun Signoretta, shock 100-1 winner of the Derby, is drawn No.13 again two days later in the Oaks, and this time starting at 3-1 becomes only the 3rd horse to complete this remarkable double, the 6-4 favourite Rhodora being brought down by a fallen horse. [National winner Rubio was also drawn No.13.]

The Grand National Aintree: 27 March

Victory of an outsider: American-bred winner

From HOTSPUR

Not only was the result of the Grand National totally unexpected, but even in such a moderate field the prospects of the ultimate winner, Rubio (66-1), were lightly esteemed by his immediate connections. He took charge of his field at the fence after Becher's the second time around. He jumped superbly throughout, and won in a canter by ten lengths from Mattie Macgregor (25-1), Kirkland (13-2f) having fallen at the last fence.

Rubio is an American-bred horse, a son of Star Ruby, who was a half-brother to Sceptre. His history is a curious one. As a yearling he was sent over to this country with a consignment of bloodstock bred by Mr J.B.Haggin in the United States. Submitted at the Newmarket Sales, he was knocked down to a farmer and dealer named Septimus Clarke for 15gns. At the age of four years he was sold to his present owner, Major Douglas-Pennant, for 95gns. After being hunted he broke down, and with a view to getting his legs callous, he was sent to the proprietor of a hotel at Towcester, and this gentleman ran him in a 'bus!

---

2 April

Death of St Simon
A famous sire

The career of one of the most famous sires of all time was terminated yesterday morning as the Duke of Portland's St Simon, who appeared to be in the best of health and spirits, suddenly dropped dead while returning from exercise at Hunciecroft, Welbeck Abbey.

St Simon was foaled in 1881, a brown horse by Galopin-St Angela, standing 16 1/2 hands high. He was bred by Prince Batthyany, who died without seeing him race. St Simon went up for sale as a two-year-old with the rest of Prince Batthyany's horses. The late Matt Dawson bought him on behalf of the Duke of Portland for 1,600 gns, this proving the greatest bargain ever made in the history of the Turf, for in stud fees alone he earned for his owner about £250,000.

The total amount he won in stakes was £4,678, a mere bagatelle to what it would have been had not his breeder's death invalidated his engagements. Had he been able to compete for the Derby he would undoubtedly have won, and to give an idea of what sort of horse he was it may be mentioned that in 1884 he proved himself in a home gallop over 2st the superior of The Lambkin, who went on to win the St Leger that year. Later, in the Goodwood Cup, which closed his active career on the Turf, he beat 1883 St Leger winner Ossian by twenty lengths.

It would be unfair to say that St Simon was a better racehorse than Ormonde, as no just comparison can be made of their respective merits, but it is pretty certain that no other horses have been bred as good as this illustrious pair.

St Simon sired only two Derby winners, Persimmon and Diamond Jubilee, but his grandsons, Volodyovski, Ard Patrick, and St Amant, are also numbered among the Blue Riband heroes, and he sired five winners of the Oaks.

BIG RACE RESULTS

2,000 Guineas	Norman	O Madden	25-1
1,000 Guineas	Rhodora	L Lyne	100-8
Derby	Signorinetta	W Bullock	100-1
Oaks	Signorinetta	W Bullock	3-1
St Leger	Your Majesty	Wal Griggs	11-8f
Grand National	Rubio	H Bletsoe	66-1

CHAMPIONS

Jockey	Danny Maher	139
Leading Trainer	C Morton	£26,431
Leading Owner	Mr JB Joel	£26,246
Horse	Your Majesty (3)	£19,286

The Derby Epsom: 3 June

Another great surprise: Outsider's victory

From HOTSPUR

The present season has been one of startling surprises so far as the leading three-year-old races are concerned, and the crowning sensation came today, when the Derby was won by an animal whose chance was considered so utterly obscure that it was allowed to start at the forlorn odds of 100 to 1. Moreover, the triumphs of fillies in the Blue Riband have been of such rare occurrence that the victory of Signorinetta will remain memorable. In fact, quite a romantic story could be written around the daughter of Chaleureux and Signorina and her veteran owner.

Mountain Apple (11-2jf) took up the running after going about three-quarters of a mile and he came into the straight almost clear of White Eagle, Sir Archibald, Primer and Signorinetta. He appeared to have the full measure of his field, but below the distance he was joined by Primer (40-1), and then began to stop to nothing. All in an instant Signorinetta, on the outside, came with an electrifying rush and settled the pretensions of the other pair in a few strides. She sailed past the post the easiest of winners by two lengths, while Primer just kept Llangwm (100-8), who was finishing fast, out of second berth.

The owner of Signorinetta is the aged Italian sportsman Chevalier Ginistrelli, who owned that peerless mare Signorina, for whom he refused £20,000 at a time when such prices were regarded as ridiculously excessive. His loyalty to the old mare has now been amply repaid. It seems very fitting that in the autumn of her days she should earn undying distinction through one of her daughters.

Signorinetta was also trained by Chevalier Ginistrelli and his son at Newmarket, and is engaged in the Oaks on Friday.

1909

26 Mar The French-bred and owned 5-y-o Lutteur III (100-9jf) wins the Grand National, masterfully ridden by French jockey Georges Parfrement, but trained at Lewes by Harry Escott. [No 5-y-o has won since.]

19 Apr Ernest Williams, a well-known steeplechase jockey in Scotland, is killed during a 'chase at Kelso when his mount is balked by a loose horse and his neck is broken.

2 Jul The Stewards of the Jockey Club, investigating the poor showing of Sir Harry in the Ascot Stakes prior to a comprehensive victory in the Northumberland plate, severely reprimand his jockey Madden, strongly cautioning him as to his future conduct. They do not accept his explanation that he was tied down with waiting orders, preferring to believe the assertion of trainer Dobson Peacock and owner Mr Jardine that they were dissatisfied with the way the horse was ridden in the Ascot Stakes.

The Derby Epsom: 26 May

The King's Derby – Minoru's brilliant victory

From HOTSPUR

Jones urges Minoru home by a head

Never in the history of Epsom or the Derby has such a thrilling scene been witnessed on the famous Downs as that which was associated with the triumph of Minoru in the Blue Riband today. The bubbling enthusiasm which permeated the huge crowd bursting with loyalty and the love of a splendid sport was a sight which will never fade from the memory of those who were fortunate enough to witness it. It was a Royal victory in every sense of the word.

In the preliminary canter nothing went better than Minoru (7-2), who is a particularly light-actioned horse, with a beautiful low sweeping stride. Both Sir Martin (3-1f) and Bayardo (9-2) moved well.

About half-way down the hill, and just before reaching Tattenham Corner, there was a lot of bunching together. In the scrimmaging Sir Martin fell, his rider J.H.Martin having a miraculous escape from serious injury. At this point, Louviers (9-1) had taken up the running from Minoru, and immediately the line for home was entered, Minoru closed with Louviers, whom he headed a few strides later. Then ensued a struggle as desperate and thrilling as anything which has ever been seen on a racecourse.

Both horses ran on in the gamest possible way. In the dip Minoru appeared to falter slightly, and for a moment it seemed as though he would succumb to Mr Raphael's colt. Both Stern and Herbert Jones rode magnificently. Responding to the latter's call in the most indomitable way, Minoru put forth a fresh effort, and, amidst a scene of unparalleled enthusiasm, won by a head.

His Majesty, followed by the Prince of Wales, came on to the course amidst the frantically cheering crowd. The police were powerless to keep them back, and as he waited for Minoru to return, many of the spectators endeavoured to shake his Majesty by the hand. He accepted the humour of the situation in the good-natured way so splendidly characteristic of the finest sportsman in the land. Probably it was one of the happiest moments of his life. The cheering increased in volume as his Majesty personally led his gallant horse back to the enclosure, and perhaps future historians may have to write of today's celebration of the Derby as the greatest of all time.

The St Leger Doncaster: 8 September

Victory of Bayardo

From HOTSPUR

If the result of the St Leger was a disappointment to the vast concourse of people who assembled on the Town Moor in the hope of being able to give expression to their enthusiasm and vociferously cheer a Royal victory, it was satisfactory to know that the famous "Sellinger" had at least been won by a good horse. Bayardo has now thoroughly vindicated his juvenile excellence and shown himself to be the best three-year-old in training.

As the winner of the Two Thousand Guineas and Derby, it was of course, regrettable that Minoru should have given what can only be described as a poor display, but it is now abundantly clear that he is deficient in stamina. It will doubtless be urged that he was fortunate to win the Derby.

It was not a fast-run race.

At the bend Minoru was in difficulties, but Bayardo (10-11f) was running very smoothly, and when Maher asked him for the final effort he shot out in fine style and scored a decisive victory by a length and a half from Valens (100-8). Minoru (7-4) was only fourth, six lengths behind the winner.

There was hardly any cheering, but, putting all royal sentiment aside, the victory was a popular one, and thousands of people profited by the victory of Bay Ronald's gallant son. In the overwhelming hour of his triumph, his trainer Alec Taylor should not be forgotten. He had his many anxious moments, and, a pastmaster in the art of preparing and developing stayers, he deserves the utmost credit for the way he has nursed Bayardo back to his best form.

Free Handicap Sweepstakes Newmarket: 28 October

A Royal Victory: Picturesque incident

From HOTSPUR

The outstanding feature of the afternoon's racing was the victory of the Derby winner, Minoru, in the Free Handicap Sweepstakes, which he only won after a magnificent and strenuous finish.

Herbert Jones, the stable jockey, had been so badly injured as the result of his fall the previous day that his services were not available. Maher had been engaged for St Victrix, but Mr Fenwick readily agreed to the release of that fine horseman to ride Minoru.

Minoru had to concede a lot of weight to his three opponents, of whom Cattaro was in receipt of no less than 16lb. In the Abingdon Mile Bottom, Minoru appeared to be beaten. Then it was that Maher displayed his superb horsemanship. The jockey rode the race of his life. Spectators were absolutely thrilled as Minoru, distressed as he was, responded with courage to the calls of his rider, and shook off the splendid challenge of Electra to win by a neck.

Minoru's victory not only furnished the opportunity for a loyal demonstration of enthusiasm such as is rarely witnessed on a racecourse, but it also provided the setting for a pretty incident. His Majesty came from the Jockey Club enclosure to congratulate Maher upon riding a wonderful race. It was probably the proudest and most memorable moment of the jockey's life.

The 1910s

L ike every other facet of civilian life, racing in the second decade of the 20th century was overshadowed by the Great War. In May 1915, with the exception of Newmarket, racing was abandoned for the duration of the war, so it was 1919 before the sport got back to anything like normal again.

The decade had only just got under way when racing – and the whole of the country – was under a cloud, losing its greatest patron with the death of King Edward VII in May 1910. George V surprised many by taking over the royal horses with as much enthusiasm for the sport as his father. But in 1913, there was a portent of things to come, as the most extraordinary Derby in the history of the Blue Riband unfolded. A suffragette, Miss Emily Davison, threw herself in front of the King's horse, Anmer, at Tattenham Corner. The horse was unhurt, the jockey recovered, but the poor woman died for her cause. There was a further sensation, however, when the favourite, first past the post, was disqualified, and the race awarded to the 100-1 shot Aboyeur.

The year 1913 also saw the Jersey Act, a protectionist measure that virtually prohibited American thoroughbreds – so the owners took their horses to France. Also that year, the Jockey Club made 5 furlongs the minimum distance for racing, and proclaimed that no horses over two years old could race unnamed.

The Classics continued to be run during the war, but all five at Newmarket (and a substitute Grand National was staged at Gatwick). Consequently, the Triple Crowns accomplished by Pommern (1915), Gay Crusader (1917) and Gainsborough (1918) and the Derby-Oaks double by Fifinella (1916) are historically devalued. Notwithstanding these feats, the horse widely acknowledged to have been the best of the war years was late developer Hurry On, the St Leger winner of 1916. But before the war came the classic duels of Swynford and Lemberg, and the unique feat in 1912 of the filly Tagalie, who brought off a 282-1 double with victories in the 1,000 Guineas and the Derby.

American jockey John Reiff pilots Tagalie to victory in the 1912 Derby

1910

18 Mar The 7-y-o Jerry M (6-1f), carrying top weight of 12st 7lb, just fails to give 13lb to the Grand National field, losing by 3 lengths to 9-y-o Jenkinstown, who is receiving 30lb, with the 100-1 shot Odor, receiving 41lb, 3 lengths further back in 3rd place. There are no previous National winners in the 25 starters, and only 5 finish. It is a second National winner for Tom Coulthwaite, who saddled Eremon in 1907, also owned by Mr Stanley Howard. The race is a disaster for Mr Frank Bibby, whose unfancied Wickham (66-1) brings down his other two runners, Caubeen (8-1) and Glenside (25-1).

19 Jun In winning the Grande Steeplechase de Paris, Jerry M sustains an injury that is to keep him out of next year's Grand National.

7 Sep Swynford (9-2), a late developer who was unplaced in the Derby, wins the St Leger, beating Derby winner Lemberg (4-5f), who also thrashed him at Ascot, into 3rd place.

2 Oct The first meeting at Laurel, Maryland, is held.

Ascot: 14 June

"Black Ascot" – A sombre opening

From HOTSPUR

A "Black Ascot" is really the expression most suited to this year's celebration of the world-famous meeting. It was not in the least like the brilliant Ascots of tradition. The splendours and brightness which have ever been its most striking asset were missing and the scene was curiously sombre and subdued. An air of sadness seemed to permeate everything, and even the high-class racing did not arouse the enthusiasm it has been accustomed to do in what may be described as "normal" years.

In the Royal enclosure, which usually furnishes such a gorgeous colour-picture, everybody wore deep mourning *[for King Edward VII, who died on 6 May]*, and the singularly funereal aspect was unrelieved except by the emerald green of the grass and the pink roses which clustered round the closed Royal pavilion.

Ascot Gold Cup: 16 June

A double for Manton

Bayardo's fine performance

From HOTSPUR

The field of 13 for the Ascot Gold Cup was the largest which has ever gone to the post, and included Bachelor's Double, who had gained such a decisive victory in the Royal Hunt Cup the previous day.

Bayardo's easy victory

It was satisfactory to see a couple of French representatives in the field. Our Gallic neighbours have always exhibited a strong penchant for the race, not surprising in that much more pains are taken to develop staying talent in France than is the case in this country, which is essentially the home of the thoroughbred.

The trainer of Sea Sick II was heard to express the view that he was only afraid of Bayardo, last year's St Leger winner. Mr Vanderbilt's horse is known to be one of the best stayers in France, and his sire, Elf, won the Ascot Gold Cup in 1898.

On all public form, Bayardo appeared to dominate the situation, but many professed to doubt his staying capacity. It was also argued that he had not made any improvement. But he looked splendid, and I think Alec Taylor was satisfied that the son of Bay Ronald had never been better.

Southannan set a capital pace and settled down with a clear lead of Sea Sick II, with Bayardo and Bachelor's Double near the back. About six furlongs from home, Bayardo, in a few strides, rushed from about seventh position into second place. He almost immediately headed Southannan, and entered the line for home in advance of Sea Sick II and Bachelor's Double.

As this point it was seen that the race was virtually over, for Bayardo (7-4f) strode along and won in a hack canter by four lengths, Sea Sick II (6-1) just beating the easing-up Bachelor's Double (7-1) on the post for second place.

Before to-day's race, Alec Taylor is understood to have expressed the opinion that Bayardo was the best horse in the world. I don't think that he would now find many people to contradict the assertion.

After Bayardo's gallant display, it only remained for his half-brother Lemberg (1-8f) to win the St James's Palace Stakes for the Manton stable with equal facility. There was an idea that Swynford, in receipt of 7lb, might bustle him up; but, on the contrary, the Derby winner, whose action is no less convincing than that of Bayardo, practically won with his head in his chest, by five lengths from Prince Rupert (25-1), with Swynford (10-1) another length away third.

Goodwood Cup: 28 July

Bayardo beaten

Remarkable Goodwood Cup

What may be regarded as the sensational feature of the present racing season occurred yesterday at Goodwood when Mr "Fairie's" Bayardo, the champion racehorse of his day, was most unexpectedly defeated in a field of three for the historic Goodwood Cup race. To show the public confidence in the horse in his attempt to concede as much as 36lb to Mr Beddington's Magic (20-1) and 34lb to Mr James de Rothschild's Bud (66-1), both three-year-olds, the long odds of 20 to 1 were betted on Bayardo.

Apparently there was not the slightest fear that he would fail, for his form this year, especially at Ascot, where he won the Gold Cup, suggested that this would be a comparatively easy task. But it is always the unexpected which is happening on the Turf, and, to the consternation of all onlookers, he was beaten. A quarter of a mile from home when Maher, on the favourite, moved up to Magic, who up to that point had made all the running, it was thought that the crack had won once more. Then, however, it was noticed that the younger horse was gradually forging ahead again, and though Maher rode with all his skill and resolution, Bayardo could do no more, and was beaten by a neck, with Bud a bad third. The big difference in weight told, and the horse was defeated after a long and splendid series of fifteen wins.

Only twice before had Bayardo been beaten in his brilliant career – in the Two Thousand Guineas and Derby last year. He was never beaten as a two-year-old, and has won the immense sum of £44,534 in stakes.

1911

15 Jun The 4-y-o Willonyx, a late developer and a lazy horse, shows his true greatness for, having destroyed the field in the Ascot Stakes at 9-2, he follows up with a hard-fought neck victory (at 5-4f) over Charles O'Malley in the Gold Cup – a tribute to his trainer, Sam Darling, who bought him as a yearling and after several setbacks produced a champion for owner Mr Charles Howard, and his jockey, Billy Higgs, who discovered the secret was not to allow the colt to "go to sleep" when in the lead. (He proceeded to win the Cesarewitch at 9-2, carrying a record 9st 5lb, and the Jockey Club Cup at 20-75 by 20 lengths from Martingale II, the only horse left in to oppose him.)

Nov Frank Wootton completes a hat-trick of jockeys' titles with 187 winners, the most since Tom Loates in 1893.

BIG RACE RESULTS

2,000 Guineas	Sunstar	G Stern	5-1
1,000 Guineas	Atmah	F Fox	7-1
Derby	Sunstar	G Stern	13-8f
Oaks	Cherimoya	F Winter	25-1
St Leger	Prince Palatine	F O'Neill	100-30
Grand National	Glenside	Mr J Anthony	20-1

CHAMPIONS

Jockey	Frank Wootton	187
Leading Trainer	Hon G Lambton	£49,769
Leading Owner	Lord Derby	£42,781
Horse	Stedfast (3)	£16,079

The Derby Epsom: 31 May

Coronation Derby: Sunstar's gallant victory

From HOTSPUR

The Coronation Derby, as it has been termed, ended in a complete and unqualified triumph for the favourite Sunstar. The pleasure for the owner, Mr J.B.Joel, was increased tenfold by the circumstance that not only did he breed Sunstar himself but he had the satisfaction of knowing that the open policy pursued throughout the piece caused thousands of the little public to support the colt, even in the face of the somewhat restricted odds laid against him. Mr Joel had for weeks publicly expressed his entire confidence in the son of Sundridge, notwithstanding sinister rumours and the absurd suggestion that there was a conspiracy amongst certain jockeys to unduly interfere with his chance in the race.

On public form Sunstar (13-8) stood out boldly as the best horse in the race. His brilliant victories in the Two Thousand Guineas and the Newmarket Stakes made a profound impression upon all who witnessed them. There was an idea that the stock of Sundridge were deficient in stamina. This view must surely be modified if not exploded altogether by the magnificent performance of Sunstar to-day.

Sunstar practically won the race on three legs, to use a colloquialism well understood on the Turf, as he broke down coming round Tattenham Corner. The race was run at a very fast pace. The moment they had entered the line for home Sunstar closed with Bannockburn, and soon afterwards drew out with a clear lead to win comfortably by two lengths from Lord Derby's colt Stedfast (100-8).

It was a fine victory, but unfortunately it was discovered that Sunstar's breakdown had been so bad that he may not be able to run again.

Eclipse Stakes Sandown Park: 14 July

Swynford again beats Lemberg

From HOTSPUR

Now that the Eclipse Stakes is over it has been made pretty clear that Swynford is, after all, a better horse than Lemberg. It is evident that whereas Swynford has been coming on every day since Epsom, Lemberg has practically stood still, and so feeble was his attempt to tackle his rival in the line for home that it was difficult to reconcile his listless exhibition with the overwhelming form he displayed in the Coronation Cup. The horses have now met six times, each having won thrice.

There was an immense crowd to witness another struggle between the two celebrities, winners of last year's Derby and St Leger respectively. Some very thrilling contests have been witnessed for the Eclipse Stakes, not least last year's desperate finish between Lemberg and Neil Gow, which resulted in a dead-heat. Those who anticipated a similarly exciting contest today were doomed to disappointment. Swynford's triumph was thorough and complete.

Swynford (10-11f) led entering the straight, travelling very smoothly, and increased his advantage to several lengths. Then Lemberg (9-4) began to make an effort to close the gap, with Dillon sitting bolt upright like a trooper. This contrasted curiously with Wootton's essentially Yankee seat. But Lemberg appeared to put little heart into his work, and Swynford, striding along, won very decisively indeed by four lengths.

The Grand National Aintree: 24 March

A remarkable race at Aintree: Glenside's victory

From HOTSPUR

Never in its lengthy history has the Grand National provided a lamer race or ended in such an extraordinary and unsatisfactory way as it did this afternoon.

Of the twenty-six starters only one, Glenside, actually completed the course without mishap, and he had been amiss and was so hopelessly beaten when he was left all alone in his glory that his rider had to use his greatest powers of persuasion to get the old fellow over the last three fences. He blundered at the final obstacle but happily kept his balance.

It was nevertheless far from an edifying spectacle to see Glenside, full of distress, crawling along to achieve the greatest triumph which falls to the share of any steeplechase horse. The nine-year-old gelding, who has only one eye, could scarcely stand when he was pulled up.

There were two past National winners in the field in Lutteur III (7-2f) and Jenkinstown (100-7), and the first sensational incident was the downfall of the heavily weighted (12st 3lb) favourite at the fence after Becher's. It appears that Lutteur III, in trying to avoid a loose horse, took off too soon and landed in the middle of the fence, where he was hung up until his jockey could extricate him. Two fences before reaching the water Jenkinstown came to grief, and at the water Rathnally blundered so badly that he shot Chadwick on to his neck. The jockey made a wonderful recovery.

Caubeen (8-1), who was jumping well, continued to lead, but at the obstacle after Becher's he ran clean into the fence and in doing so baulked Rathnally, who this time shot Chadwick out of the saddle on the opposite side of the obstacle. The jockey had to run round to catch the horse and remount. He then followed on at a respectful distance.

Glenside (20-1) had established such a long lead that he managed to struggle on and win. For his rider, Mr Anthony, 21, one of the family of celebrated jockeys, it was an eventful introduction to the National.

Rathnally (8-1) finished second, twenty lengths adrift, and the only other finishers, both remounted, were Shady Girl (33-1) and Foolhardy (50-1).

1912

1 May Mr J.B.Joel's White Star, full brother to last year's Derby winner Sunstar and a very confident evens favourite, is beaten into 4th place in the 2,000 Guineas, the winner, American-bred Sweeper II (6-1), having his first outing of the season.

3 May There's another surprise at Epsom, where it's 20-1 bar three for the 1,000 Guineas, and only one of those three, the hitherto unbeaten 7-4 favourite Belleisle, is placed, coming 3rd to the grey filly Tagalie, who made all the running.

Taking Becher's in the National

The Grand National Aintree: 29 March

Jerry M's popular win

From HOTSPUR

The Grand National day was a brilliant success after all, despite the chaos created by the coal strike. The cross-country Derby, as it is popularly termed, is without doubt the most sporting event of the year, and notwithstanding the pessimistical views which were expressed when the conditions of this year's race were so drastically changed, the policy pursued by Messrs Topham has been thoroughly justified by the gratifying results achieved to-day. On Tuesday it was doubtful whether the meeting would be held at all; but there was not the semblance of a hitch.

Jerry M, despite carrying top weight of 12st-7, wound up equal favourite with Rathnally at 4-1, and so far as looks were concerned,

the runners-up in the last two Nationals quite bore away the palm.

Caubeen, Bloodstone and Ballyhackle were the leaders for a long way. Jenkinstown was always jumping in difficulty, and it transpired that he hurt his stifle and was pulled up at the fence before Becher's Brook the second time round. Caubeen led over the water and stayed in front until falling four fences from home. With two fences to go, Bloodstone jumped across Jerry M, and appeared to hamper him; but Piggott rode a very cool race and, taking the top weight to the front after clearing the last fence, he won in splendid style by six lengths from Bloodstone (40-1), with Axle Pin (20-1) third.

BIG RACE RESULTS

2,000 Guineas	Sweeper II	D Maher	6-1
1,000 Guineas	Tagalie	L Hewitt	20-1
Derby	Tagalie	J Reiff	100-8
Oaks	Mirska	J Childs	33-1
St Leger	Tracery	G Bellhouse	8-1
Grand National	Jerry M	E Piggott	4-1jf

CHAMPIONS

Jockey	Frank Wootton	118
Leading Trainer	Hon G Lambton	£22,884
Leading Owner	Mr T Pilkington	£20,822
Horse	Prince Palatine(4)	£20,730

The Derby Epsom: 15 June

Defeat of the favourite: Filly's popular Derby victory

From HOTSPUR

Owing to the tangle of three-year-old form, the Derby was regarded as one of the most perplexing and remarkable witnessed for many years. But it ended in a complete and overwhelming triumph for the One Thousand Guineas winner, Tagalie, who thus joins the small and select band of fillies that have secured the Blue Riband of the Turf.

She may, of course, have been fortunate to compete for a Derby in such a year as this; but it would be an unthankful task to attempt to depreciate the merits of her decisive victory. She has beaten the Two Thousand Guineas winner, Sweeper II, amongst others, and she stands as a good game filly.

The field was not so large as expected, after all. Still, it numbered a score, but on the whole the majority of the runners were moderate to compete for a Derby, and would not have been started in an ordinary year. Sweeper II bore evidence of having done a great deal of work since the Two Thousand Guineas and started at 2 to 1, a wide gap separating him from Jaeger (8-1) and White Star (10-1), and then came Pintadeau and Tagalie, both on 100-8.

The race admits of little description, as Tagalie practically made all the running and won by four lengths from Jaeger, who became second at the mile-post and never afterwards lost that position. White Star and Sweeper II were done with a quarter of a mile from home, when the former appeared to turn it up and stop with startling suddenness. The favourite simply failed to stay, like so many American-bred horses before him.

Mr Raphael received a flattering reception when he led back his victorious filly, his satisfaction being more pronounced from the circumstances that he bred her himself. The success of a grey in the Derby is sufficiently notable, more especially of a grey filly. And no One Thousand Guineas winner has ever before gone on to win the Derby.

1913

6 Jun The 1,000 Guineas winner Jest, starting at the extraordinarily generous price of 8-1, easily wins the Oaks in a record 2min 37 3/5sec, the same time as disqualified Derby 1st Craganour took two days ago. It is another triumph for owner-breeder Mr J.B.Joel, and the bay half-sister of 1911 Derby winner Sunstar is further proof of their sire Sundridge's capacity to produce stayers.

The Grand National Aintree: 4 April

An amazing race: 22 starters – 20 fall

From HOTSPUR

As a race and a contest, the Grand National was a hollow farce. How could it be otherwise with only two horses standing up out of twenty-two starters, and only three passing the judge at the finish? It made one recall Glenside's Grand National two years ago, when only that horse went round without accident.

What is the expectation? Probably we shall hear again the cry which was loudly raised in 1911 that the fences are so big as to be unfair. Or it will be argued that the old type of good steeplechaser has become extinct, and our jockeys are not what they were. Perhaps a little of each of these things contributes to the melancholy fiascos which now seem to be part of every Grand National that comes. I suggest that much of the grief is due to the presence of horses that have not a thousand to one chance of completing the course, to say nothing of winning at any weight.

The point where the winner, Covertcoat (100-9,) settled the question was between the first two fences going into the country the second time. He went right to the front and was never afterwards headed, beating Irish Mail (25-1) by a distance.

Emily Davison makes her tragic protest in front of the King's horse during the running of the Derby

The Derby Epsom: 4 June

Sensational race for the Derby

Disqualification of Craganour: King's horse thrown in suffragist incident: 100-1 winner

By "HOTSPUR"

The most sensational and lamentable Derby in the history of the race was added to the records at Epsom yesterday. The horse to finish first was the favourite, Mr C.Bower Ismay's Craganour. He passed the judge a head in front of the extreme outsider Aboyeur, while a neck away was Louvois. But after a stewards' objection, Craganour was disqualified and the race awarded to Aboyeur.

Half a mile from the finish a dreadful thing happened. A woman by deliberate design flung herself at Anmer, the horse carrying the colours of his Majesty the King, who, with her Majesty, was looking on. The result of the tragic incident is described elsewhere, but let me return to the finish of the race.

As Craganour's number was hoisted in the frame there was plenty of cheering, and Mr Ismay, obviously influenced by the overwhelming excitement of the moment, went out to meet his horse and returned leading him in. There were cheers, too, for Johnny Reiff, the jockey. Suddenly there occurred a distinct lull in the buzz of conversation. We who had been in a position to see had noticed some scrimmaging and squeezing among the leaders, but any thoughts of an objection in the Derby were instantly banished.

There appeared to be an all-clear, and the winner was just on the point of passing out of the gate when there was a sharp and authoritative shout, "Stop! Bring the horse back!" The "All right" was all wrong, so far as the officials were concerned.

At the end of half an hour of intolerable suspense, the stewards, who had objected to the winner for jostling the second horse, announced the disqualification of Craganour for not keeping a straight course and for interference, and awarded the race to Aboyeur.

What a sensation! The general rejoicing was swiftly turned to bitter lamentation. A raging hot favourite, a popular horse with the people, had won the Derby at 6 to 4 against, and here he was deprived of honour, and instead the one enthroned in his place was an animal whose starting price was 100 to 1. The public are poorer and the bookmakers are indeed richer.

Epsom: 5 June

Outrageous act of a suffragist

Jockey seriously hurt – woman in hospital

Yesterday's Derby was made tragically historical by the perpetration of a daring and dastardly suffragist outrage. Whilst the great race was in progress a woman, afterwards identified as Miss Emily Wilding Davison, a well-known militant, rushed on to the course in front of the King's horse, Anmer, ridden by Herbert Jones. Horse, rider and woman fell in a tangled heap. The woman was seriously injured and the jockey, too, was badly hurt. Both lay prostrate on the ground. Anmer, apparently unscathed, got to his feet.

It was as the horses were galloping past Tattenham Corner that the mad act was committed. Here there are double rails and the woman dashed under both. According to Earl, who was riding Agadir, she deliberately threw herself in front of Anmer with the result that the horse rode into her, knocking her senseless to the ground.

Mrs P. Lawrence's views: "It is a very extraordinary action," said Mrs Pethick Lawrence to an interviewer, "and it shows the immense pitch of desperation to which women have been driven by the trickery and chicanery with which their question has been dealt with in the House of Commons. The plan was well thought out on the part of Miss Davison, and carried through with amazing coolness and resource and almost superhuman courage. There is not the smallest doubt that she deliberately laid down her life with the idea that by this action she would call the attention of the world to the exclusion of women from any political status."

National Breeders' Produce Stakes Sandown Park: 19 July

The Tetrarch wins: A phenomenal horse

From HOTSPUR

The Tetrarch is still unbeaten. On Saturday he won the National Breeders' Produce Stakes, the most valuable race for two-year-olds in the calendar, and this made his fourth win, including his successful debut at Newmarket on April 17 last. His victory was taken for granted by the public, and certainly by owners having horses engaged in the race, as many of them forbore to embark on the apparently hopeless task of laying low this Goliath.

Yet The Tetrarch (12-100f) did not win by half a furlong this time. The judge declared the margin in his favour to be a neck over Calandria (50-1), who received 17lb, but it was an easy one, and might have been extended had Donoghue cared to press the colt. But he was on a horse that had not got well away and with 9st-5 on his back there was no need to make a "gallery" show.

He is quite the most remarkable two-year-old there has been since Pretty Polly, and perhaps it would not be an exaggeration to say that there is an even bigger margin separating him and his contemporaries.

[Because of bad visibility, what Hotspur and most of the spectators did not see was how much The Tetrarch lost at the start, in which he collided with the tapes, and was left several lengths. He gained 3 more wins in effortless fashion, including a 6-length victory over Princess Dorrie, next year's 1,000 Guineas winner, but a rapped fetlock resulted in a premature end to his season, and a repeat of the injury, to his career, so he never raced as a 3-y-o.]

BIG RACE RESULTS

2,000 Guineas	Louvois	J Reiff	25-1
1,000 Guineas	Jest	F Rickaby Jr	9-1
Derby	Aboyeur	E Piper	100-1
Oaks	Jest	F Rickaby Jr	8-1
St Leger	Night Hawk	E Wheatley	50-1
Grand National	Covertcoat	P Woodland	100-9

CHAMPIONS

Jockey	Danny Maher	115
Leading Trainer	R Wootton	£28,284
Leading Owner	Mr JB Joel	£25,430
Horse	Jest (3)	£11,350

1914-18

26 Mar 1914 Lady Nelson is the first woman owner to be successful over Aintree fences when her 5-y-o gelding Ally Sloper wins the Stanley Steeplechase.

9 May 1914 Old Rosebud (17-20f) wins the Kentucky Derby in a record time of 2min 3 2/5sec.

13 May 1914 Trainer Atty Persse makes the sad announcement that Capt McCalmont's The Tetrarch, unbeaten in 7 races as a 2-y-o and 10lb better than the next horse in the Free Handicap, will be scratched from the Derby.

Dec 1914 Aintree is handed over to the War Office.

BIG RACE RESULTS 1914

2,000 Guineas	Kennymore	G Stern	2-1f
1,000 Guineas	Princess Dorrie	W Huxley	100-9
Derby	Durbar II	M MacGee	20-1
Oaks	Princess Dorrie	W Huxley	11-4f
St Leger	Black Jester	Wal Griggs	10-1
Grand National	Sunloch	W Smith	100-6

CHAMPIONS 1914

Jockey	Steve Donoghue	129
Leading Trainer	A Taylor	£52,052
Leading Owner	Mr JB Joel	£30,724
Horse	Black Jester (3)	£11,008

The Derby Epsom: 27 May 1914

Favourites left at start of Derby: Fiasco at Epsom: French horse's 20-1 triumph

By HOTSPUR

The bare facts of the Epsom Derby are that it was won by the French-trained Durbar II (20-1) by three lengths from Hapsburg (33-1), with Peter the Hermit (100-1) one and a half lengths away third. Now let me say what should have won the Derby. Not the 9-4 favourite Kennymore, because he lost the race when he lost his temper at the post. No, the horse that in my opinion should have won was Brakespear (100-8) for the King. The fact that he did not do so is simply tragic.

The start was a fiasco. I do not blame Mr Willoughby. He had to perform an impossible task in getting away thirty highly strung thoroughbreds on level terms. Some of them were lashing themselves into a hopeless state of fury, rioting and upsetting their neighbours. Kennymore was the worst culprit, and, when, after 15 minutes, the cry of "They are off," was finally heard, another no sooner went up, "The favourite's left!" What a world of dreadful meaning was conveyed by those shouted words.

But Brakespear also was left. He had not begun to move when those first away were a hundred yards in front. From the mile post, Jones, his jockey, had to thread him in and out among hopeless animals that had no pretensions to be where they were, except that they were eligible through the mere fact of entry. A quarter of a mile from home, he finally realised the hopelessness of it.

Thus this Derby will go into history as one of the most unsatisfactory and disappointing on record. There was no cheering as the winner passed the post, but some was heard as Mr Duryea led in his horse.

The Grand National Aintree: 27 March 1914

Success of Sunloch: Small owner's triumph

From HOTSPUR

In splendid weather and before a huge gathering, the Grand National Steeplechase has this afternoon been won by the lightly weighted Sunloch (100-6), owned and trained by Mr Tom Tyler, a Leicestershire farmer, and ridden by a jockey named Bill Smith. The French horses, Trianon III (100-8) and Lutteur III (10-1), were second and third respectively, the distances being eight lengths and eight, with Covertcoat (7-1f) the last of the eight finishers.

A little while ago, Sunloch was at 40 to 1 in the betting. But his odds came down because, no doubt, it was recognised that he was the best public performer of the light-weights. He carried the minimum 9st-7, more than 2st less than the other placed horses.

Sunloch's performance was astonishing from the fact that he must have covered far more ground than any other in the race. This he did by jumping wide to the right at every fence, and thus having to be brought in to meet every new fence in turn. But it made no matter at all. He kept up a rare gallop, with just a prodigious appetite for getting the job over with the least possible delay and interference from fences. I have never seen a National won in this way.

Few that saw him go out into the country for the second time with a long lead expected the horse to last. But the astonishment grew, for his lead increased rather than decreased. Before Valentine's Brook, it was seen that the other jockeys were at last becoming aware that Sunloch was not likely to be caught. Mr Whitaker, in particular, on Rory O'Moore, called on his gallant horse to pull out his best effort, and at last Alec Carter began to improve his position on Lutteur III.

But there was no catching Sunloch, although his backers must have been given a fright as he pecked badly on landing over the last fence. The roar of cheering that went up when he was seen to be safely over was repeated again and again as he passed the winning post. And after making every yard of the running, he passed the judge the freshest Grand National winner I have ever seen.

The Grand National Aintree: 26 March 1915

How Ally Sloper won

From HOTSPUR

A game and courageous horse won the Grand National today – Lady Nelson's Ally Sloper (100-8), splendidly ridden by Mr Jack Anthony, and trained by the Hon Aubrey Hastings, who himself rode the winner, Ascetic's Silver, in 1906. Jacobus (25-1) was second beaten two lengths, and the third, eight lengths away, was Father Confessor (10-1).

The race was decided before a gathering which seemed very little below that of normal years. Lord Derby's stand was closed, except for that reserved portion of the top which was occupied by officers of the Liverpool "Pals" Battalion. Most of the men in the paddock and in the county stand were officers in uniform, and they included a fair sprinkling of members of the Naval Service.

My friend, Mr Anthony, had two bad moments, described best in his own words: "It was the nearest thing in the world I did not come to grief at the second fence, but fortunately my horse bumped against Ilston, ridden by my brother Ivor, and this kept him on his legs. And when he took off too soon at the canal turn, I lost both irons and my reins, but got going again all right. After that the horse jumped perfectly."

1914-18

8 May 1915 Regret is the first filly to win the Kentucky Derby (and the last for 65 years).

15 Sep 1915 Mr S.B.Joel's Pommern (1-3f) wins the September Stakes, the substitute St Leger, by 2 lengths from the 20-1 Oaks winner Snow Marten (2-1) in a 7-horse field to complete the wartime Triple Crown at Newmarket, partnered again by Steve Donoghue.

24 Mar 1916 The Racecourse Association Steeplechase, intended as a substitute Grand National but bearing little resemblance to Aintree's blue riband, is held at Gatwick over 4mi 856yd and won by Mr P.F.Heybourne's 6-y-o gelding Vermouth (100-8) from 20 other runners, including 1915 National winner Ally Sloper (9-2f), who is 8th; there is only one faller.

20 May 1915

Racing abandoned for duration of war
Newmarket excepted

The following letter was sent yesterday by Mr Runciman, President of the Board of Trade, to the Jockey Club on the subject of race meetings in war time:

May 19, 1915
Dear Captain Greer – The Government have ascertained and appreciated the motives actuating the Stewards of the Jockey Club in continuing to give their sanction to those of the race meetings which have taken place since the outbreak of war, and we have been fully conscious of your desire to protect the interests of those persons who are dependent upon horse racing and horse breeding for their livelihood. The general feeling on both sides of the House of Commons is, however, so strongly against the meetings being continued that the Government have felt the present moment opportune for a fuller consideration of the subject.

I have to inform you that, owing to the circumstances of the war, and in particular the necessity for keeping the whole of our British railway system free from congestion at any time for the rapid and unimpeded transit of troops and munitions, and the special condition of the munition areas, we think it necessary to ask the Stewards of the Jockey Club to suspend all race meetings in Great Britain after this week for the duration of the war.

The only exception to this general suspension should be at Newmarket, the peculiar circumstances and industries of which, dependent as they are entirely on racing, combine to make this exception expedient.-

Yours very truly,
WALTER RUNCIMAN.

It followed, of course, that the Jockey Club would comply with the Government's request; in fact, Mr Runciman himself announced at a public dinner in London last night that they had already done so. With the solitary exception of Newmarket, they would not sanction any race meeting until peace was declared. That was, he said, a striking instance of the sacrifice people at home were prepared to make while the younger generation were doing their work at the front.

WARTIME WINNERS

Derby*
1915	Pommern	S Donoghue	10-11f
1916	Fifinella	J Childs	11-2
1917	Gay Crusader	S Donoghue	7-4f
1918	Gainsborough	J Childs	8-13f

Grand National
1915	Ally Sloper	Mr J Anthony	100-8
1916†	Vermouth	J Reardon	100-8
1917†	Ballymacad	E Driscoll	100-9
1918†	Poethlyn	E Piggott	5-1jf

All run at Newmarket. †Run at Gatwick.

The War Derby Newmarket: 15 June 1915

Success of Pommern
From HOTSPUR

To-day Newmarket provided an episode unique in the annals of English horseracing. On what would ordinarily have been the opening day of the Ascot Meeting was run at Newmarket the substitute for the Epsom Derby. Not in the memory of the oldest racegoer has there been such an overturning of tradition and of environment.

In place of the metropolitan, nay, cosmopolitan, crowd which swarm over Epsom Downs was to be seen a discreet assemblage distinguished pre-eminently by its obvious devotion to racing as a business, even more than as a pleasure.

But the attendance was not only composed of such. It comprised a large gathering of those who assuredly best deserved to be there for pleasure, and who were the most welcome. I refer, of course, to the soldiers, and these included not a few gallant warriors "winged" in the trenches, while others were limping along as best they might from stand to paddock.

Well, the War Derby has been won for one of the leading breeders of this or any country in Mr S.B.Joel, and the hero was Pommern, who gained a very popular and easy victory by two lengths.

CHAMPION JOCKEYS
1915	Steve Donoghue	62
1916	Steve Donoghue	43
1917	Steve Donoghue	42
1918	Steve Donoghue	66

The New Derby Newmarket: 30 May 1916

New Derby won by Fifinella
From HOTSPUR

The New Derby of 1916 – the second of the war Derbies, and may it be the last! – was to-day won at Newmarket by Mr Hulton's Fifinella (11-2), who defeated Kwang Su (3-1f) by a neck. Mr John Sanford's Nassovian (11-2) was a head away third. So Fifinella joins the small and remarkable band of mares that have won the Derby.

The general public were present in large numbers, and conspicuous were officers of all ranks, while many of the rank and file stationed locally and a large company of convalescent wounded made a khaki and blue border to the rails on either side of the course for some distance.

The race was exciting, and, in one phase of it, most extraordinary. As it was run, the wonder is that Fifinella won. That she did so proves what a good one she is, and what she must have had in hand. As they advanced across the flat towards the rails parallel with the plantation all the runners seemed to be bunched together, in spite of the great width of the course. Fifinella was tucked away towards the rear. On they came, and as the front rank held their places Fifinella did not find an opening.

They had left the Dip, and were breasting the gradient to the finish, and still Fifinella was baulked, though it was clear she was far from being beaten. I had given her up as hopeless, and was watching the struggle between Kwang Su and Nassovian.

Then in a flash Fifinella had shot up to them, Childs sandwiching her between the pair. It seemed impossible that she could make up the ground, but the mare's rush was irresistible, while probably the other two were slightly tiring. Amid this tremendous excitement she snatched the verdict, and Judge Robinson had her number up in a twinkling as the winner. It was an electrical performance.

[Two days later, Fifinella (8-13f) won the 7-horse New Oaks in a canter by 5 lengths, and so joined the select band of fillies who have accomplished the "double" – Eleanor (1801), Blink Bonny (1857) and Signorinetta (1908).]

1914-18

Mar 1917 The substitute Grand National at Gatwick, now called the War National Steeplechase, throws up a portent of 1956 and Devon Loch when Limerock, with the race virtually won, collapses and falls within yards of the winning post, leaving the race to Ballymacad (100-9).

12 May 1917 Omar Khayyam, foaled in England, is the first foreign-bred colt to win the Kentucky Derby.

29 May 1917 Philanthropist Mr Leopold de Rothschild, famous owner-breeder and member of the Jockey Club since 1891, dies at the age of 71. He was the "Mr Acton" whose colt Sir Bevys won the Derby in 1879, and his several Classic successes included another Derby winner, St Amant, in 1904.

Mar 1918 Poethlyn (5-1jf), ridden by Ernie Piggott, becomes the third bay gelding to win the wartime substitute National at Gatwick.

Obituary 10 November 1916

Death of Danny Maher

By HOTSPUR

The big world of racing, and many apart from it, will learn with deep regret of the death, which took place in a London nursing home early yesterday morning, of Daniel Aloysius ("Danny") Maher (*pictured*), the greatest jockey of his day. He has died at the age of 35, having been born at Hartford, Connecticut, U.S.A., in 1881.

The illness which brought about his death began even when he was at the zenith of his fame as a jockey, seven or eight years ago. At the end of the 1913 season, he was forced to stop riding, and he eventually went to South Africa, where his lungs seemed to recover their strength. But his longing for England, his adopted country by naturalisation, led him to return last summer.

Maher won the jockey's championship in 1908 and 1913, and enjoyed nine successes in the classics, including three Derbys – on Rock Sand, Cicero and Spearmint in the space of four years.

In 1910 he won the Two Thousand Guineas on Neil Gow, beating by a few inches Mr Fairie's Lemberg. That was a brilliant piece of race-riding, but perhaps those who were privileged to see it will say that his greatest triumph was when he dead-heated on Neil Gow with Lemberg for the Eclipse Stakes, the decider in a great rivalry after the latter had turned the tables on him in the Derby. Any other jockey would surely have been beaten on Neil Gow that day.

Stories of his loyalty and his decency abound. He rode Prue for Lord Rosebery, who had long retained his services, in the 1913 Derby, even though Lord Rosebery had offered to release him to ride Craganour, the hot favourite. But let Steve Donoghue, his close friend, have the last word. "A straighter, cleaner man and a better jockey never lived," said Donoghue. "He was loved and respected by all jockeys, because he would never stoop to take a mean advantage in a race." One cannot say more than that.

Jockey Club Cup Newmarket: 2 November 1916

Surprise result

From HOTSPUR

There was an astonishing result in the Dewhurst Plate at Newmarket to-day, when the odds-on favourite North Star and the second favourite, Athdara, were beaten by Telephus, one of the four outsiders that went to complete the small field.

Yet just to show that there can be such a thing as a certainty in racing Mr Buchanan's unbeaten three-year-old Hurry On duly won the Jockey Club Cup, for which the trifling odds of 25 to 1 were betted on. He won, pulling up, by ten lengths, this being the sixth race of his career and his sixth victory. He is undoubtedly a very fine racehorse, and though he has never opposed Fifinella, winner of the New Derby and New Oaks, I do not hesitate to suggest that were such an event to come about he would be made favourite and would, moreover, win.

Hurry On is a big horse of power and capacity, and with it he has splendid stamina and grand speed. Providing all goes well with him he ought never to experience defeat. Fred Darling, as trainer, is much to be congratulated on his important share in the notable sequence of wins.

[Hurry On, who stood 17 hands and was a late developer, had not raced as a two-year-old nor been entered in the Derby, but he had won the Newmarket St Leger (11-10f). Sam Darling went to war, and Hurry On never raced again, but he sired three Derby winners in the 1920s.]

September Stakes (St Leger) Newmarket: 12 September 1917

Gay Crusader's triumph

By OUR SPECIAL CORRESPONDENT

The field for the September Stakes, the substitute for the St Leger, from one cause and another, dwindled down to three, the smallest on record. So great was the superiority shown in the New Derby over his rivals by Mr Fairie's good colt, Gay Crusader, that it was not altogether surprising to find only two others saddled in opposition to the crack.

Odds of 11 to 2 were laid on the Derby winner at the start, and he won by six lengths pulling up. The only surprise was that the outsider, Kingston Black (33-1), finished second, with Dansellon (100-15) a poor last. Mr Fairie was sufficiently well to be present to witness the success of the son of Bayardo and Gay Laura, who thus takes rank as a winner of the triple crown – although the New Derby and September Stakes are only war-time substitutes for the Derby and Leger.

New Derby Newmarket: 4 June 1918

Triumph of Gainsborough

From OUR SPECIAL CORRESPONDENT

For the first time in the long history of the Derby it has fallen to a colt bred and owned by a lady. That Gainsborough (8-13f) would win, bar accident, for Lady James Douglas was foreshadowed by his victory in the Two Thousand Guineas.

He always had a good position in the race, and won cleverly by a length and a half from his stable-companion, Blink (100-8). It is evident that Gainsborough, trained at Manton by Alec Taylor, has inherited to the full all the staying properties of his sire Bayardo and his dam Rosedrop, winners respectively of the St Leger and the Oaks.

[Gainsborough emulated Pommern and Gay Crusader to become the third winner of the war-time "triple crown", starting an 11-4 on favourite in a 5-strong September Stakes field and winning by an easy 3 lengths.]

1919

28 Mar The Grand National returns to Aintree and is won by the hot favourite (11-4) and top weight (12st-7) 9-y-o gelding Poethlyn, who beats Ballyboggan by 8 lengths and provides Ernie Piggott with his second success. French rider T.Williams on All White (66-1) has an unusual hard-luck story: having wasted to make the weight when the horse's regular rider was injured, he injudiciously samples the wares of a racecourse seafood stall before the race and has to pull up after jumping Becher's for the second time to be violently sick, ruining his chances when in a challenging position, but still finishing 8th.

20 Jun The popular Lord Glanely – "Old Guts and Gaiters" – has a double at Royal Ascot to bring his tally for the meeting to 7, which, after his Derby success, goes a long way to clinching his place as leading owner.

The Derby Epsom: 4 June

Victory Derby: Great race won by an outsider

By HOTSPUR

The best feature of Victory Derby Day was the roar of prolonged cheering which greeted the win of his Majesty's horse Viceroy in the race for the Stewards' Handicap. It was a fine and exhilarating spectacle as the King and Queen, with the Prince of Wales, Prince Albert, and Princess Mary, stood at the front of the Royal box smiling their pleasure. The worst feature was the dramatic failure of the Derby favourite, The Panther (6-5), who could not even get a place.

No one could have expected the Two Thousand Guineas winner to suddenly develop extraordinary excitement and temper at the starting-post, and then, as the outcome, lose several lengths at the start. The best horse conceivable cannot overcome such a handicap the way races are run these days, and his failure leaves me dissatisfied and unconvinced.

Meanwhile Lord Glanely has won the Victory Derby with his second string, Grand Parade (33-1), who beat Buchan (7-1) in a strenuous finish by half a length. The market had implied the winner was inferior to his stable-companion Dominion (100-9), the stable jockey A.Smith had elected to ride the latter, and both Lord Glanely and his trainer F.B.Barling had concluded that Dominion was now the superior horse. Well, if owner, trainer, and jockey can be so misled, what chance has the looker-on?

Royal Hunt Cup Ascot: 18 June

Record for Irish Elegance

From HOTSPUR

The second day of the Ascot Meeting, on which the Royal Hunt Cup race is the outstanding feature, was marked by the triumph of a great horse, and all else that happened to-day is commonplace by comparison. Irish Elegance created a new record for the race by winning under the big burden of 9st-11. It was a thrilling performance, and the people cheered the hero of it. When the horse returned to the paddock to be unsaddled the traditional decorum of Ascot was momentarily broken. Well-known people were so moved to enthusiasm that they applauded, and there were cries of "Bravo!", "Well done!".

It was indeed well done. History has no parallel for it. Collingwood, a six-year-old, won under 9st-7 as long ago as 1849 – seventy years since! I cannot imagine that what we saw the four-year-old Irish Elegance do to-day will ever be equalled. I wrote with enthusiasm of his chance on the morning of the race, and suggested that he would surely gain a place. I thought it was scarcely possible that he could give 34lb to a horse of his own age in Jutland, with whom he shared favouritism at 7-1. But Irish Elegance was to remind us once again that no one can really gauge the limits of a good big horse when it really runs into the top of its form.

My impression is that Irish Elegance was never headed from start to finish, which is the biggest tribute of all to his wonderful speed. He tore along inexorably, and half a mile from home his jockey was sitting perfectly still and leaving it all to the horse. Arion made his effort two furlongs out, and it was quite a game one, but the big horse had merely to be shaken up to throw off the danger thus momentarily threatened. And so he came on to win quite comfortably by a length and a half, untouched by whip or spur.

Middle Park Plate Newmarket: 17 October

Tetratema wins again: A brilliant performance

From HOTSPUR

The hard going did not deter Mr Persse from producing the champion two-year-old Tetratema to run for the six-furlong Middle Park Plate. Sir Abe Bailey resolved to have another cut at the crack with Southern, even though his good-looking Sunstar colt had been badly beaten at Doncaster for the Champagne Stakes. Southern got an even bigger trouncing this time. Swynburn, the big Swynford colt that had won earlier in the week in good style, was also in opposition.

Tetratema's display was perfectly brilliant, the most impressive the unbeaten grey has given since he first appeared on a racecourse at Sandown Park in midsummer. Not only did he win easily, but he paralysed his four opponents from the moment the start took place in a manner irresistibly reminiscent of his wonderful sire. It was the first time, indeed, that I have seen him race in similar fashion to The Tetrarch, who used to have his opponents utterly beaten and sprawling in the first furlong or two of his races.

In his four previous races, Tetratema had merely drawn out towards the end and won in the style of a really good colt. This afternoon Carslake must have wished to give a spectacular show, for he was away in a flash, and at once drew a length or so ahead. Two furlongs from home all except Tetratema (1-4f) were racing under pressure. The champion proceeded to draw away without any apparent effort, and so, galloping well within himself, he strode up the hill to the winning post an extremely easy winner by half a dozen lengths from Southern (100-7).

The 1920s

In the wake of The Great War, the twenties ushered in an age of increased sporting activity, with huge crowds attending the great events. The public, forever in search of heroes to applaud, had one in Steve Donoghue, who, although he won the last of his ten consecutive jockeys' titles in 1923, when he shared the title with Charlie Elliott, continued to be the popular favourite. "Come on, Steve" was a familiar cry on racecourses up and down the country, especially at Epsom, where he completed an unprecedented hat-trick of Derby winners in 1923 and made it four out of five with Manna in 1925.

By the end of the decade, there was a new young champion, Gordon Richards having already accumulated four titles. And behind the scenes, Alec Taylor completed his seventh successive season as leading trainer in 1923.

The twenties saw the first Prix de l'Arc de Triomphe and the first Cheltenham Gold Cup and Champion Hurdle, although none of these races yet enjoyed the prestige they would later earn. The Kentucky Derby was first broadcast in 1925, followed in England by the Grand National and the Derby two years later.

Betting grabbed the limelight in the latter twenties, with the introduction of a betting tax by Mr Churchill in 1926, and the establishment in 1929 of the "Tote".

Grand National fields increased despite Topham's efforts to reverse the trend, culminating in a record 66 starters in 1929. There was the usual "grief", and in both 1921 and 1928 only one horse completed the Aintree course without falling.

Spion Kop broke the Derby time record in 1920, and in 1924 Sansovino was the first success for a Lord Derby in 137 years. But the monopoly of the English aristocracy and landed gentry as patrons of horse racing was broken for the first time, when the fame won by the "flying filly" Mumtaz Mahal heralded a new, legendary owner – the Aga Khan – who was to be an important influence on the British racing scene for many years to come.

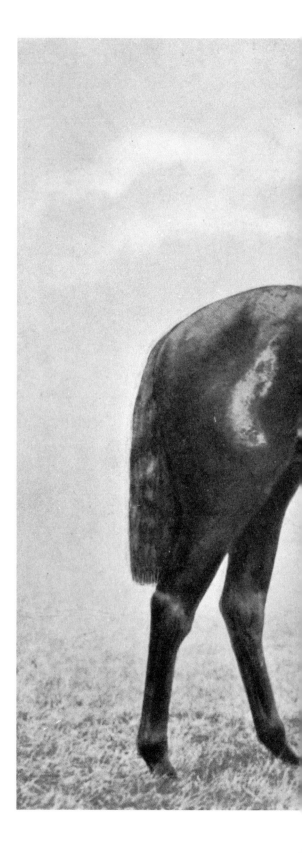

Steve Donoghue with Papyrus, the horse on which he completed a Derby hat-trick in 1923

1920

26 Mar Jack Anthony pilots his third Grand National winner for Ireland, the popular 7-y-o Troytown (6-1), who makes all the running and wins by 12 lengths from The Turk II (66-1), while hot favourite Poethlyn (3-1), with a run of 11 straight wins behind him, falls at the very first fence, and only 5 finish in the treacherously muddy conditions.

2 Jun Champion jockey Steve Donoghue rides a treble (including a dead-heat) at Epsom, two of his wins coming after his alarming fall on Abbot's Trace in the Derby.

27 Jun National winner Troytown, having tragically been put down after breaking a leg at Auteuil two days ago, is buried at the animals' cemetery at Asnières, the first racehorse to be interred there. The great Irish gelding, 3rd in an attempt to repeat last year's success in the Grande Steeplechase, came to grief 6 days' later in the Prix des Drags.

12 Oct The great American champion Man o' War, or "Big Red," as he is known, wins the last race of his 2-year career, a special match over 1mi 2f at Kenilworth Park, Canada, in which he beats the 4-y-o Sir Barton by 7 lengths

and lowers the track record by 6sec. He retires with 7 world or American speed track records to his credit, beaten only once, when he lost several lengths at the start, having won his other 20 races, never starting at odds against, and 3 times starting at 100-1 on.

Jack Anthony on Grand National winner Troytown, tragically killed 3 months later.

BIG RACE RESULTS

2,000 Guineas	Tetratema	B Carslake	2-1f
1,000 Guineas	Cinna	Wm Griggs	4-1
Derby	Spion Kop	F O'Neill	100-6
Oaks	Charlebelle	A Whalley	7-2
St Leger	Caligula	A Smith	100-6
Grand National	Troytown	Mr J Anthony	6-1

CHAMPIONS

Jockey	Steve Donoghue	143
Leading Trainer	Alec Taylor Jr	£35,907
Leading Owner	Sir Robert Jardine	£19,385
Horse	Cinna (3)	£8,529

The 2,000 Guineas Newmarket: 28 April

Great "2,000" race – How Tetratema won
From HOTSPUR

A great crowd was present at Newmarket to-day and witnessed the victory of Major Dermot McCalmont's Tetratema (2-1f) in the Two Thousand Guineas. The grey was never headed throughout.

As they were coming down the hill, Allenby (100-7) came swinging along after the favourite. He got to Tetratema's girths in the Abingdon Bottom, where the grey gallantly shook him off, Carslake riding with all his strength and using his whip. Coming up the rise to the winning-post, Allenby pressed forward again, but the grey held him at bay to win all out by half a length.

In my opinion, Tetratema had pulled out every ounce of his reserve to win by the margin stated, and from now onwards I prophesy a raging controversy as to whether he will stay the mile and a half of the Derby course.

Grand Prix de Paris Longchamp: 27 June

English victory in the Grand Prix de Paris: Comrade wins
By HOTSPUR

France's premier race, the Grand Prix de Paris, was this afternoon won by the English horse Comrade, owned jointly by the French sportsman M de St Alary and the Newmarket trainer Mr Peter Purcell Gilpin. Our Derby winner, Spion Kop, who with the French Derby winner Sourbier was heavily backed at the pari-mutuel booths, was a disappointing fifth.

There were at least two breaks away, but at last they were sent off to a fair start, the horses cantering up to the starter as is the fashion here. As they made the last turn into the rather short straight for home, Spion Kop was badly placed on the outside. Donoghue had been made to come wide in order to escape interference. The French horse Embry was then in the lead on the rails, but Joe Childs on Sourbier was hot in pursuit, and then came Comrade.

A furlong from home, however, it did not seem possible that the English horse could get up and win. But Bullock rode a magnificent finish, gaining steadily until one great effort from horse and rider enabled the black horse to get up in the last stride.

This is the horse that cost Mr Gilpin £25 as a yearling, and now, as winner of this magnificent stake, beating the English and French Derby and Oaks winners and still remaining unbeaten, he must go into history as the most remarkable bargain ever made in bloodstock.

The Derby Epsom: 2 June

A record Derby: Spion Kop's victory
The favourite unplaced
By HOTSPUR

The race for the 1920 Derby was decided at Epsom yesterday in front of a gathering which for size broke all records. Major Giles Loder's Spion Kop (100-6), after taking the lead fully three furlongs from home, carried on to win easily in a new record time of 2min 34 4/5sec

The people's favourite, Tetratema, was overthrown, finishing nearer last than first. Lord Dewar's Abbot's Trace, with Donoghue in the saddle, fell within a furlong of the winning-post. And Allenby, the second favourite, broke a blood-vessel and had to be pulled up.

Tetratema, early put to rights by Mr Persse, looked no different from the day he won the Two Thousand Guineas. To-day, this horse, which has been so much talked and written about, may scarcely have looked a champion, but that is because he can never be the fine, commanding, and impressive horse his great sire The Tetrarch was.

Spion Kop was naturally a horse of much general interest as being one of Mr Gilpin's pair. He has many of the characteristics of his sire, Spearmint, but is not quite as big.

The first to show in front was the ever-alert Donoghue on Abbot's Trace. They had not gone far when he was three lengths or so clear of Tetratema, and then came Sarchedon, with Spion

Spion Kop: surprise winner

Kop in close attendance. As they bowled round Tattenham Corner, Abbot's Trace still led from the favourite, with Spion Kop drawing up. That was the last I saw of Tetratema. Seldom has such a great Derby favourite been beaten so far from home.

Abbot's Trace continued to lead into the straight, but Spion Kop was at once sent up to him, responding with wonderful speed. Finding him so full of running, O'Neill did not hesitate to send him to the front. From that point he never looked like being beaten, and finally went past the judge the winner by a couple of lengths from the fast-finishing Archaic (10-1).

1921

18 Mar Capt G.H.Bennet remounts Turkey Buzzard three times to claim 4th place in the Grand National, and is chased round the paddock for his trouble by owner Mrs Hollins with her umbrella for subjecting her horse to unnecessary hardship.

1 Jun A case in the Lord Chief Justice's court develops into a farce as a messenger brings in a piece of paper announcing Humorist's Derby victory, which is passed from Press box to judge, to counsel and then round the members of the jury, before the witness in the box is told the news and then proceeds with his interrupted testimony!

27 Jun Epsom Derby 3rd Lemonora, trained at Manton by Alec Taylor, wins the Grand Prix de Paris, starting at the generous odds of about 13-2 on the pari-mutuel.

The Grand National Aintree: 18 March

Dramatic "National": Shaun Spadah's victory

From HOTSPUR

Their Majesties the King and Queen to-day witnessed the Grand National Steeplechase from the roof of Lord Derby's private stand, which adjoins the Press stand. In order to follow the progress of the immense field, they stood near the Pressmen, and listened to the reading of the race by Mr Meyrick Good. They listened to an amazing tale of woe.

Of the thirty-five starters, all but one fell. That distinction belonged to Shaun Spadah (100-9). He won by a distance from The Bore (9-1f), who fell two fences from home and was remounted by his plucky owner Mr Harry Brown.

This incident in itself was absolutely dramatic, for in falling Mr Brown broke his collar-bone and one rein was torn off. While still dazed, he was lifted into the saddle, and with only the near-side rein to guide his mount he got the gallant old horse over the last fence and then cantered on to claim second place. Also remounted to finish were All White (33-1), a bad third, and Turkey Buzzard (100-9).

Shaun Spadah jumped perfectly, except for pecking badly on landing over the water jump – at this stage there were only six still in the race. By the time the Canal turn was reached, he was going much better than the only other survivor, The Bore, and the latter's fall left him to come home in a canter.

The Derby Epsom: 1 June

How Humorist won: Victory by a neck

By HOTSPUR

A great triumph has been achieved for one of the leading owner-breeders associated with the English Turf, as for the second time in his career Mr J.B.Joel lived those glorious moments in which a man may lead back the winner of the Derby. He repeated his success with Sunstar ten years ago, when Humorist, third in the "Guineas", won at Epsom yesterday. Son of Mr Joel's great sire Polymelus and of Jest, who won the Oaks for him eight years ago, Humorist will carry on the name of the mare, who died this year.

Humorist (6-1) beat Guineas winner Craig an Eran (5-1) by a neck, with Guineas second Lemonora three lengths away third. The 7-2 favourite, Leighton, was fifth.

Alan Breck was the first to show in the lead, and he was still surging along in front as they swung round Tattenham Corner. Entering the straight, Leighton was already being hailed the winner as he threatened to pass the leader, but

Newmarket: 29 April

Unique meeting: Both "Guineas" held on same day

From HOTSPUR

The races took place this afternoon at Newmarket for both the Two Thousand Guineas and the One Thousand Guineas. The occasion, as everyone knows, was unique, and we may hope that the circumstances attending it may never recur. Here were the two classic races of the first half of the season, one confined to fillies, brought to an issue as a result of the policy by which they were saved from the wreckage and devastation caused through the complete cancellation of racing by the miners' strike. A few minor races helped to make up a programme of seven events, each contested by big fields, for owners and trainers were keen to take any and every chance, however apparently forlorn.

Humorist, the 3-1 favourite for the "2,000", was out in lead leaving the Bushes. How easily was he going to win! Not often do you see a horse at Newmarket out so clear and looking every inch a winner that does not win. There was apparently no danger. Donoghue was sitting still with a firm hold of his head, suggesting that the horse was still running with plenty in reserve.

Then, as they came out of the dip to meet the rising ground to the winning post, Craig an Eran (100-6) was seen to be closing the gap. Humorist's stride was beginning to shorten, as is the way with the non-stayer. Craig an Eran got to his head. Donoghue asked for a big effort, and the horse was game, but a better had come up against him. That was the truth.

Lord Astor's horse forged ahead, stride by stride until, as he passed the judge, only hand and heel ridden, he had three-parts of a length to spare of his own stable-companion, Lemonora (100-7), who had also profited by the favourite's lack of stamina to go on and beat him by three-parts of a length for second place.

The winner's owner, Lord Astor, was too unwell to attend Newmarket, and in the One Thousand Guineas, which followed immediately, his filly Pompadour (7-1) found two too good for her in the rank 33-1 outsiders Bettina and Petrea.

suddenly there was a dramatic change as he faltered and moved away from the rails.

Steve Donoghue darted Humorist into the opening in pursuit of Alan Breck. And as the leader, too, heeled slightly away from the rails, Donoghue, realising Craig an Eran was coming along on the outside, brilliantly moved his mount inside Alan Breck and daringly urged him into the lead. Craig an Eran put in a splendid effort, but Donoghue, amid tremendous excitement and served by the most powerful finish he may ever have ridden, got to the goal in time, with the Derby won. He had won War Derbys at Newmarket on Pommern and Gay Crusader, but this was the real thing at last.

[Less than a month later, Humorist tragically died of a haemorrhage to the lungs, a reason apparently explaining why he stopped so suddenly with the 2,000 Guineas at his mercy.]

1922

24 Mar Inspection of the Grand National horses in the paddock is made easier by the printing of their names on large saddle-sheets, but more carnage in the race brings the first protests from the RSPCA, as only 3 of the 32 finish without a fall, and one of those on three legs.

15 Jun Two days after winning the Ascot Gold Vase (2mi), Golden Myth (8-1) completes a rare double by taking the Gold Cup against a field described by HOTSPUR of The Daily Telegraph as the equivalent of a "good-class long-distance handicap". His opponents include last year's St Leger winner Polemarch ("deteriorated"), the Coronation Cup winner ("a much shorter distance"), and winners of a Cambridgeshire, a Cesarewitch, and a Manchester Cup. HOTSPUR does, however, praise Golden Myth's young Newmarket trainer, Jack Jarvis, and points out that the time of 4min 17sec indicates a "remarkably fast-run race".

BIG RACE RESULTS

2,000 Guineas	St Louis	G Archibald	6-1
1,000 Guineas	Silver Urn	B Carslake	10-1
Derby	Captain Cuttle	S Donoghue	10-1
Oaks	Pogrom	E Gardner	5-4f
St Leger	Royal Lancer	RA Jones	33-1
Grand National	Music Hall	LB Rees	100-9

CHAMPIONS

Jockey	Steve Donoghue	102
Leading Trainer	Alec Taylor Jr	£52,059
Leading Owner	Lord Woolavington	£32,090
Horse	Royal Lancer (3)	£14,522

The Derby Epsom: 31 May

A great Derby: The victory of Captain Cuttle

By HOTSPUR

The race for the 1922 Derby was won to-day for Lord Woolavington by Captain Cuttle (10-1), ridden by the leading jockey, Stephen Donoghue. Second was Lord Astor's Tamar (10-1), ridden by Frank Bullock and beaten by four lengths. Three lengths further way, third, was Mr Barclay Walker's Craigangower (20-1), ridden by Michael Beary, and the judge officially placed the favourite, St Louis (4-1), fourth.

Captain Cuttle was the first to leave the barrier. Jacquot and another then headed him, and so, in a rapidly lengthening line, they streamed up that first three or four furlongs of gradient. Beginning the descent of Tattenham Corner, Captain Cuttle was still "there", St Louis lying about sixth. As they made the last curve of the famous Corner into the straight for home, Jacquot was still in front, but it was Donoghue's race even then. He must have moved hand and heel, that signal which the good horse can respond to, for he went racing, almost flying, as it seemed, into the lead, and began instantly to draw away. Tamar flung out a challenge of sorts, but could make no impression.

Congratulations are due to Lord Woolavington, the winning owner, who is also the breeder of Captain Cuttle, and to his trainer, Fred Darling, for no more magnificent-looking horse has won the Derby for years past.

Donoghue could have had one of a half a dozen or more mounts, but he waited until last Friday evening, and when he was approached on behalf of Lord Woolavington he accepted what has given him his second Derby winner at Epsom.

The Grand National Aintree: 4 March

Dramatic "National": How Music Hall won: Only five horses finish

From HOTSPUR

A lasting impression with me from Liverpool is that, however game a large number of candidates may have been, they nevertheless had no pretensions to be in a Grand National field. One can only suppose that they were there out of their owners' vanity to have their colours carried on an occasion such as this. No wonder only five horses finished. It was not the big fences that primarily brought about the grief, but rather hopeless inefficients getting in one another's way, and by falling doing tremendous damage to the good horses.

What, for instance, could be more flabbergasting than to see Southampton (100-12) and Shaun Spadah (100-8) fall at the first fence – the favourite and the winner of last year! At the Canal turn, a dreadful contretemps occurred, the cause of all the trouble being Sergeant Murphy, who slipped on taking off and baulked no fewer than eight or nine horses. Hawkins took Sergeant Murphy back and got him over the fence, but there were now only five others surviving.

Music Hall went on with a slight lead into the country for the second time. At Becher's, Arravale was most unluckily brought down, getting entangled on landing with a dead horse still lying where it had fallen.

From this point the race became confined to Music Hall (100-9) and the lightly weighted Drifter (18-1). But the latter was struggling, with one hoof virtually hanging off, and on three legs he was outpaced by Music Hall, who won by twelve lengths.

Eclipse Stakes Newmarket: 14 July

Thrilling "Eclipse" race: Golden Myth's triumph

By HOTSPUR

The "Eclipse" was run at Sandown Park during one of the brief, infrequent intervals when heavy rain did not fall. Tamar, the favourite, looked to have done well since the Derby. Golden Myth (8-1), however, is far more commanding, even allowing for the fact that a four-year-old must show evidence of maturity, although he was almost slouching round the ring.

Always with the leaders, Tamar seemed about to take charge two furlongs from home. Frank Bullock was able to take the rails position, which left him in front, with Golden Myth coming along, hand over hand, as it were, on his outside.

There was no mistaking the seriousness of the challenge. Bullock realised it, but before he could get an extra effort out of his horse Golden Myth had drawn half a length in front, with less than a furlong to go. The whip was drawn on Tamar, and Bullock rode one of the best finishes he may ever have shown. One wondered whether the weight would tell on the four-year-old, but the young Charlie Elliott kept Golden Myth going to win by a head. Thus was the hot favourite beaten in a race which will long be recalled.

Golden Myth has done a very wonderful thing in my opinion – to win both the Gold Vase and Gold Cup at Ascot and then come on to win the Eclipse Stakes over a much shorter course and after a comparatively short interval. He must be something of a phenomenon, for there is a great deal of difference in the training of a Cup

Golden Myth: triumphant season

horse and of a mile-and-a-quarter horse in the highest company. Which all goes to show how immensely he has improved. And to think that at the beginning of the season he could only just win from Trespasser when receiving 20lb in the Queen's Prize race at Kempton Park. He could not get within four lengths of Chivalrous at Manchester just before Ascot. What a transformation since then!

He has finished with racing now, and certainly no horse could pass from the racecourse in more brilliant circumstances.

1923

23 Mar The 13-y-o Sergeant Murphy (100-6) is the first American-owned winner of the Grand National, beating 1921 winner and top weight Shaun Spadah (20-1), who was giving him 18lb, by 3 lengths. The winner, bred in Ireland, is owned by Mr Stephen Sanford and trained at Newmarket by George Blackwell, who saddled Rock Sand to win the 1903 Derby and thus completes a unique double. [Sergeant Murphy's jockey, Capt "Tuppy" Bennet, goes on to lead the gentleman riders' list before receiving fatal injuries in a fall at Wolverhampton on 27 Dec.]

20 Jun The King (George V), having enjoyed success yesterday with Knight of the Garter (5-4f) in the Coventry Stakes (2-y-o), brings off a popular Royal Ascot double with a 20-1 winner, when his 4-y-o colt Weathervane, a son of Lemberg, carries a mere 6st-12 to victory in the Royal Hunt Cup.

29 Aug The 6-y-o gelding Flint Jack (10-1) becomes the first horse to win the Ebor Handicap twice, carrying 8st-12 to victory at York, 3lb more than last year when he won at 5-1. On the same card, Derby winner Papyrus (85-40), conceding 20lb, is beaten a short head by Craig Eleyr (100-8) in the 1 1/4mi Duke of York Stakes (3-y-o), but is placed 1st after an objection, with Concertina (8-13f) placed 2nd in the 4-horse field.

12 Sep Lord Derby's 1,000 Guineas winner Tranquil (100-9) pulls off a shock win in the St Leger, beating Derby winner Papyrus (15-8f) by 2 lengths.

21 Sep The Royal Borough 3-y-o Handicap of 1 1/4 miles at Windsor produces a triple dead-heat for 1st place between Dumas (2-1f) and Dinkie (6-1), both carrying 8st, and Marvex (8-1), with 9st.

20 Oct Derby winner Papyrus, who embarked for the USA on 21 Sep, is beaten 5 lengths by Kentucky Derby winner Zev (4-5f) in a $110,000 match at Belmont Park.

Sergeant Murphy

Queen Mary Stakes Ascot: 19 June

A phenomenal filly

By HOTSPUR

On the first day of Royal Ascot, the racing was that which only Ascot can produce, for the winners included the King's most promising two-year-old colt Knight of the Garter, the best filly probably known to the present generation in Mumtaz Mahal, and the winner of the Two Thousand Guineas, Ellangowan.

I fancied I said all there was to say about the Aga Khan's now famous grey filly, Mumtaz Mahal, when she came out as a débutante at Newmarket a little while ago, and spreadeagled a field of smart ones in record time. Here she made her second appearance to win the Queen Mary Stakes by a long ten lengths. And what a smashing, amazing show she gave!

She stood perfectly still behind the tapes while others, with no pretensions to be in her world, were making a fuss. Then, when the tapes went up, she was into her stride in a flash, away out in front, just as her great sire, The Tetrarch, did before her on the same course. On she came, lengthening the gap at every stride, and so far was she in front as the winning-post was reached that her jockey, Hulme, took a long look back, to assure himself, I suppose, that there had been no false start.

I think the spectacle really eclipsed what I recall happening ten years ago, when her sire came in literally alone for the Coventry Stakes. I am glad she was not in Knight of the Garter's race. He is a good horse, probably in what we regard as the first class. But Mumtaz Mahal is a phenomenon, and such defy classification.

The Derby Epsom: 6 June

Donoghue's triumph in the Derby: Third successive win

By HOTSPUR

The race for the Derby was decided at Epsom yesterday in favour of Mr Ben Irish's Papyrus (100-15), who beat Lord Derby's Pharos by a length. It was a triumph for Stephen Donoghue, who for the third year in succession rode the Derby winner, and so created a record which is not likely to be surpassed in our time.

For once the highest honours of the Turf have not been given to the patrician owners and breeders. They find themselves overlooked in favour of the "small" owner, an owner moreover with but a single horse. Mr Irish was for most of his life a farmer in the Fen country, and only comparatively late in life yielded to the glitter and allurements of ownership on the Turf. He has simply stormed his way to the summit of all owner's ambitions, while others, like Lord Derby, whose third runner-up Pharos is in thirteen years, spend their lifetimes in vain endeavour.

But, of course, this is not the first success for Mr Irish. Five years ago, he gave a matter of 300gns for a yearling colt by Radium, which he named Periosteum, and won the Ascot Gold Cup with him in 1921. With the proceeds, he invested 3,500gns in another colt at the Doncaster yearling sales, this one by Tracery from a mare named Miss Mattie, and he duly called it Papyrus.

Not the least amazing thing of the parade before the start was the spectacle of the favourite, Town Guard (5-1), under an escort of detectives. It was like an illustration from a super-film or a hair-raising melodrama. It was plain they were there for the purpose of guarding him against possible attack. I have never before seen such elaborate precautions taken. There must have been exceptional reasons, but at present I am in ignorance of their precise nature.

The misty conditions made it difficult to pick out the colours at the start, but Knockando took the lead and was still in front as they approached Tattenham Corner. Papyrus took it up as they turned the Corner, but in a few strides Pharos loomed into the picture. Gardner

Owner Mr B. Irish leads in the winner

brought him almost level with Papyrus, and for a moment it looked as if he might go on and win for Lord Derby, before Donoghue called for an extra effort and Papyrus forged ahead again to win comfortably. Parth (33-1), who had lost several lengths at the start, came with a late run to snatch third place, a length and a half further back.

1924

12 Mar There are 8 starters for the first running of the Cheltenham Gold Cup, in which, according to "Hotspur" of The Daily Telegraph, "the onlookers were treated to a very fine and most instructive steeplechase of three miles and a quarter". It is won by the 5-y-o gelding Red Splash (5-1), who is running only because the last-minute withdrawal of favourite Alcazar releases jockey Dick Rees, by a head and a neck from Conjuror II (7-1) and Gerald L (5-1). After the race, the winner is recognised as a "potential" champion, as the Gold Cup will not for some time be regarded as a race for the championship.

28 Mar The 5-2 National favourite Conjuror II, a 12-y-o gelding who has never fallen, is sent sprawling by a loose horse when jumping Becher's first time round. Another jockey, Bill O'Neill, having parted company with his own mount, Libretto, catches Conjuror, catches up with Libretto and switches horses – all to no avail, when he falls again.

9 May The Aga Khan's "flying filly", Mumtaz Mahal (6-5f), just fails to stay the 1,000 Guineas mile and is beaten half a length by Lord Rosebery's Plack (8-1).

BIG RACE RESULTS

2,000 Guineas	Diophon	G Hulme	11-2
1,000 Guineas	Plack	EC Elliott	8-1
Derby	Sansovino	T Weston	9-2f
Oaks	Straitlace	F O'Neill	100-30
St Leger	Salmon-Trout	B Carslake	6-1
Cheltenham Gold Cup	Red Splash	F Rees	5-1
Grand National	Master Robert	R Trudgill	25-1

CHAMPIONS

Jockey	Charlie Elliott	106
Leading Trainer	RC Dawson	£48,857
Leading Owner	HH Aga Khan	£44,367
Horse	Straitlace (3)	17,958

Obituary: 13 January

Death of Capt. Bennet: Brilliant amateur rider

"Hotspur" writes: The death of Captain Harbord Bennet, the winning rider in last year's Grand National, occurred yesterday, seventeen days after he received an injury to his head through falling in the Oteley Steeplechase at Wolverhampton on Dec.27. There has not been an amateur rider so brilliant and at the same time so popular for years.

Captain Bennet was born at East Barton, Bury St Edmunds, only 29 years ago, and was by profession a veterinary surgeon at Newmarket. On the outbreak of war he served with the colours both in France and Egypt, and on returning to England commenced steeplechase riding with such success that on the day he met with his accident he was level with Fred Rees and Hogan, Jun, at the head of the winning jockey list, with sixty-two victories.

The Derby Epsom: 4 June

Sansovino a popular victor in great Classic race: Lord Derby wins at last

By HOTSPUR

To Lord Derby go the honours of the Derby of 1924. His colours were carried to easy victory by the 9-2 favourite Sansovino *(pictured)*, ridden by T.Weston and trained by the Hon George Lambton. After years of patient endeavour and many disappointments, Lord Derby has succeeded, and so the long span of 137 years since a Lord Derby won the race has at last been bridged.

It was not the best Derby start we have had in recent years, and Salmon Trout must have been twenty lengths behind in the first furlong. They had barely turned at the top of the hill for the descent of Tattenham Corner when Sansovino went into the lead. In the heavy going, his jockey never gave way an inch. The colt might have been trained all his life to go round the famous Corner, so close did he race to the rails.

Weston did the right thing in leaving nothing to chance. He rode hard with his hands, keeping his willing and courageous horse sternly to his task until at last the goal had been reached. A furlong from home his victory was assured. Not for many years has there been such an easy winner of the Derby, a full six lengths to the good.

At last Lord Derby found himself about to lead in his first Derby winner and overwhelmed on all sides with congratulations. Need it be added that Sansovino was of his own breeding, a son of that gallant racehorse and sire – which he also bred – Swynford (who also sired the 100-7 runner-up, St Germans). Lord Derby must have felt very rewarded for all the years of striving in the captivating cause of the thoroughbred.

Irish Derby The Curragh: 25 June

Irish Derby record: English horses dead heat

By HOTSPUR

After many postponements the writer has at last seen a race for the Irish Derby, and an amazing, thrilling one, too, with a sequel worthy in every way of the country in which the race took place.

Except for the straight, which is railed off, the course on the spacious plain of the Curragh is merely marked out at intervals, but it is a very fine racecourse all the same, even though the length of straight from the turn to the winning post is less than three furlongs.

I found those two men who are the backbone of racing in this country lamenting the dearth of good three-year-olds, with consequent inability to take their own part yesterday. Well, if they will sell their best horses to England and abroad, they obviously cannot have them bidding for a prize of approximately £5,000.

There were only seven starters and three had been sent over specially from England – Haine (1-1f), winner of the Bessboro' Stakes at Ascot last week, Zodiac (3-1), second to Polyphontes for the Ascot Derby, and Bucks Yeoman (7-1).

They did not do a good gallop by any means, and it was left to Haine's rider to make the pace. When Haine was headed by Zodiac (3-1) not far from home, it appeared as if the hot favourite would be beaten, but he rallied and got up on the post to make a dead-heat, with Illyrian (10-1) three parts of a length third.

The objection which followed was truly astonishing. Mr Peard, Illyrian's trainer, objected to Haine on the ground that Mrs Davis, wife of the horse's trainer, C.Davis, was a disqualified person and resided with him. Under what rule it was brought I am unable to say. Even in Ireland such a thing should have been impossible. It was not even funny, which excuses so much here, so it was highly salutary when the Stewards marked their sense of its frivolous nature by overruling the objection and fining Mr Peard £25.

I am glad I undertook this hasty visit, and desire to acknowledge the courtesy of the Irish racing authorities. I enjoyed a delightful afternoon's racing, managed to see some interesting bloodstock at the stud, and witnessed the only dead heat that has occurred in the history of the Irish Derby.

1925

16 May The Kentucky Derby is broadcast for the first time on network radio, from Louisville, and is won by Flying Ebony.

9 Sep Solario (7-2jf), unlucky in the Derby when he got caught up in the starting tapes, wins the St Leger by 3 lengths from Zambo (6-1), with Derby

winner Manna (7-2jf) not only beaten for the first time but beaten out of sight.

28 Nov In his first season as a fully fledged jockey, 21-yr-old Gordon Richards, weighing in at 6st-11, becomes Champion Jockey for the first time, with 118 winners.

BIG RACE RESULTS

2,000 Guineas	Manna	S Donoghue	100-8
1,000 Guineas	Saucy Sue	F Bullock	1-4f
Derby	Manna	S Donoghue	9-1
Oaks	Saucy Sue	F Bullock	30-100f
St Leger	Solario	J Childs	7-2jf
Cheltenham Gold Cup	Ballinode	TE leader	3-1
Grand National	Double Chance	Maj J Wilson	100-9

CHAMPIONS

Jockey	Gordon Richards	118
Leading Trainer	Alec Taylor Jr	£56,570
Leading Owner	Lord Astor	£35,723
Horse	Saucy Sue (3)	£22,155

The Grand National Aintree: 27 March

Double Chance's popular National

By HOTSPUR

In magnificent weather conditions the Grand National was won in great style by Double Chance (100-9), ridden by Major Wilson and owned in partnership by Mr D.Goold and Fred Archer, the young Newmarket trainer, for whom, from first to last, this was a most memorable triumph.

It was a splendid start, which, no doubt, was due to the starting gate being in use for the first time. As the runners arrived at Becher's, they were well strung out. At the Canal Turn, Winnall swerved and caused the veteran Sergeant Murphy, now fifteen, to crash into the wing. Double Chance made a magnificent leap at Valentine's to lead by a very small margin from Drifter, and he was still just in front at Becher's the second time around.

Double Chance made a mistake three fences from home, but was still very much alive. Between the last two fences the favourite, Old Tay Bridge (9-1) was actually leading, and when Jack Anthony felt confident to take

a look back he must have had an idea that he was going on to win. The last fence was crossed all right, and the many supporters of this gallant horse were just beginning to cheer when suddenly Double Chance began to develop an extraordinary turn of speed. He came along with an irresistible burst to master Old Tay Bridge, who was very tired and at the end of his resources. It was astonishing to see a National won by such a comparatively fresh horse. The margin was four lengths.

The winner and his gallant jockey, Major Wilson, were given a splendid reception, for Mr Goold is a Liverpool man, a former cotton broker. Major Wilson used to be in a cavalry regiment, from which he transferred into the Air Force, where a crash had such consequences that his hair turned white in a night. No man could have ridden better or with more enterprise. The way he and his horse went over Valentine's both times I shall never forget.

The Oaks Epsom: 29 May

Supremacy of Saucy Sue: Brilliant Oaks triumph

By HOTSPUR

With the Oaks victory yesterday of Lord Astor's great filly, Saucy Sue, the glory of Manna's Derby achievement for the time being was slightly dimmed. It is not possible to concentrate at the same moment on two events in the racing history of the year quite so captivating and illuminating. Saucy Sue, having wòn the Oaks by eight lengths, not only retains her unbeaten record, but has still never been properly extended.

It is a long time since the

same filly won both the One Thousand Guineas and the Oaks, just as we have to go back to 1911 for an instance of the winner of the Two Thousand Guineas and the Derby. Manna and Saucy Sue have shown by their recent triumphs that consistency is not yet a lost possession with our high-class horses. In all the circumstances, the starting price of Saucy Sue for the Oaks – 100 to 30 on – was a wonderfully good one.

Frank Bullock let Saucy Sue have her way shortly

The Derby Epsom: 27 May

Manna's Derby: Donoghue's victory in runaway race: "The Epsom Wizard"

By HOTSPUR

The Derby victory of Manna, with the great little Epsom wizard Steve Donoghue on his back, was a most gratifying result for tens of thousands of people who permitted themselves to have some financial interest in the result of the long-debated race. Awful rain and a gale of wind lashed the Downs and turned the great picnic into something approaching disaster.

Fred Darling, the trainer of Manna, was not worried half as much as other people. He philosophically summed it up by remarking that it would be no worse for Manna than others. He even suggested that a horse of his beautiful action would get better through it than the big horses. He was right.

The people who were wrong were the bookmakers, who kept on extending the odds against the Two Thousand Guineas winner as if his chance had already been cut by half. So from being at about 5 to 1 at the weekend,

we now had him returned at 9 to 1.

It was just as they came to the six-furlong post that Donoghue let Manna go into the lead. It seemed a long way from home for him to begin displaying such supreme faith in his mount, but he said afterwards that he was confident he had got the race won even at that early stage. Cheered home by the soaking multitude on the rails side of the course, the Manna-Donoghue combination triumphed in astonishingly easy style by what the judge assessed at eight lengths from Zionist (10-1), with The Sirdar (50-1) filling third place.

This was Donoghue's fourth Derby success at Epsom, added to a couple of War Derby wins. Fred Darling is far younger than most other trainers today, and this was his second Derby winner at Epsom, after Captain Cuttle in 1922, and in 1916 he trained what was probably the best of his age in Hurry On, who was never beaten.

after the mile and a quarter post had been passed. From that point she was set with a very lonely furrow to plough. She just "loped" along in her irresistible way. And when Bullock glanced over his shoulder, he could see only Miss Gadabout (100-8) next in attendance, with Donoghue urging Riding Light (20-1) so as to make sure of third place.

Counting two New Oaks triumphs in the war period, this was Alec Taylor's seventh winner of the major fillies' classic.

Saucy Sue: in a canter

1926

1 Feb The famous mare Sceptre, who won 4 of the 5 Classics in 1902, dies at Lord Glanely's stud near Newmarket.

19 Apr For the second time in three years, the winning Grand National jockey dies from a fall – the Tasmanian-born William Watkinson, who piloted Jack Horner to victory at Aintree on Mar.26, fails to recover from injuries sustained in the Montgomerie Steeplechase at Bogside two days ago.

2 Jun Coronach (11-2) wins a rain-soaked Derby, leading all the way, by 5 lengths from Lancegaye (40-1), who was left several lengths at the start but catches Colorado (2-1f) at the post for 2nd place. Unluckiest horse is perhaps 4th-placed Swift and Sure (9-2), who was going well and moving up to the leaders when a dog ran into his path and nearly brought him down.

16 Jul Coronach (2-5f) becomes the first Derby winner to win the Eclipse in the same year since Diamond Jubilee in 1900 (Lemberg dead-heated in 1910), and he later goes on to crown a splendid season by winning the St Leger.

6 Aug Chepstow racecourse is opened, and the first race, a 2-y-o seller, won by Lord Harewood's colt Conca D'Oro (7-4f).

Coronach, the 1926 Champion

---

6 February

The betting tax: A case for legislation

By A.P.Herbert

If an apology is needed for returning to this subject, it is to be found in a newspaper report that the Treasury are opposed to a betting tax on the ground of its "difficulties". If this is so, it may be well to recall that the Select Committee presided over by the then Mr H.S. Cautley in 1923 concluded, after an exhaustive inquiry, that the thing was "practicable", and only by 11 votes to 7 decided to leave out the words "desirable".

The tax is "undesirable" (so the moralists say) because thus we should legalise, recognise, condone, encourage, and increase a harmful practice. But – it cannot too often be repeated – is this the effect of the liqour taxes? Has the whisky-duty made intemperance respectable, or increased the excesses of the poor? Do life-long teetotallers flock to the public-houses on the information that the beer duty has gone up? The evidence, on the whole, is quite the other way.

Moreover, so far as the contribution of revenue can give a moral cachet to a vice, the mischief in this case is already done. For the State is not ashamed to exact income-tax, super-tax, and death duties from the abandoned bookmaker, illegal or not. But it would in this pious land be immoral to register or license him, or put a twopenny stamp on a betting ticket, as they do in our corrupt Dominions. One would expect to hear in those benighted countries the whole moral tone of the populace has taken a tumble since the institution of a tax on betting. What one does hear, in fact, is that in Australia, where the bookmaker is licensed, registered, taxed, and disciplined, there are no "welshers" or disorderly racecourse gangs. Here, where betting is legally neither fish nor fowl, it cannot be controlled, or its worst evils (such as the employment and corruption of children) diminished.

In short, this objection is twaddle. The present condition of the law is a nasty compound of hypocrisy and injustice. The rich can bet freely, on credit, through the King's mails, or over the King's telephones. The poor man and his ready-money bookmaker are hounded along the back street, reluctantly, by the King's police. That bookmaker is compelled to employ a cloud of scouts, runners, and spies, including many children, who grow up masters of subterfuge and devoted gamblers; while he, his staff, his clients, and his neigbours, daily looking on or assisting at the successful evasion of the law, can scarcely be blamed if they learn to despise it for its impotence as much as they detest it for its inequalities. The registered betting office, for rich and poor alike, might put an end to all this; but it would be "immoral".

[The Chancellor of the Exchequer, Mr Winston Churchill, in his April 26 budget, instituted a 5% betting tax on every stake on a racecourse or with a credit bookmaker, to take effect from Nov.1, the bookie to recover it from his public "by the simple device of shortening the odds".]

Coronation Cup Epsom: 3 June

Solario's Coronation Cup: A great horse

By HOTSPUR

Solario is not only the best horse in this country, but it cannot be doubted that he is the best horse in the world. Such a brilliant and impressive display as he gave yesterday at Epsom when winning the Coronation Cup has never been seen in this country since, say, Bayardo and Persimmon won the Ascot Gold Cups in their respective years.

Sir John Rutherford was quickly on the course to lead in his champion. Turning to the writer, he remarked, "What I am so glad about is that he has won a race at Epsom." I know what he had in his mind. He was thinking of last year's Derby, when Solario never had a chance through getting hung up in the tapes at the starting-post and being practically pulled up.

Opposed to Solario were Zambo and Warden of the Marches, who had filled the minor places behind him for the St Leger last year, but whose connections appeared to be almost confident of overthrowing him now. The betting told an amazing tale. Instead of Solario being an odds-on chance, as he was entitled to be, there was a decided reaction in the market against him, so that his price dropped from 11 to 10 against to 2 to 1.

Solario did not take close order with the leaders until, with six or seven furlongs to go, he flashed up the field. Zambo (9-4) led while making Tattenham Corner, but the way Solario then proceeded to blot him out of the picture was simply wonderful. Zambo might have been tethered in the mud, for Sir John Rutherford's great horse just seemed to float past him with no apparent effort. Without being in the slightest degree pressed, but always galloping freely on the bit, Solario came in literally alone to win by a margin of fifteen lengths.

1927

1 Feb The 13-y-o gelding Old Tay Bridge, allotted top weight for next month's National, drops dead at exercise. In the last two Nationals, ridden by Jack Anthony, he was beaten into 2nd place on the run-in.

25 Mar Favourite for the second year running, Sprig (8-1) just holds off 100-1 shot Bovril III by a length in the first Grand National to be broadcast. The runner-up has only one eye,

which is apparently why his rider, Mr G.W.Pennington, takes him the long way round.

1 Jun The first Derby to be broadcast is a "two-horse race" in the running as well as the betting, as Call Boy (4-1f) beats Hot Night (9-2) by 2 lengths in a new record time of 2min 34 2/5sec, with Shian Mor (22-1) 8 lengths away 3rd. Parker and Stampede both start at 1,000-1.

BIG RACE RESULTS

2,000 Guineas	Adam'a Apple	J Leach	20-1
1,000 Guineas	Cresta Run	A Balding	10-1
Derby	Call Boy	EC Elliott	4-1f
Oaks	Beam	T Weston	4-1
St Leger	Book Law	H Jelliss	7-4f
Champion Hurdle	Blaris	G Duller	11-10f
Cheltenham Gold Cup	Thrown In	Hon H Grosvenor	10-1
Grand National	Sprig	T Leader	8-1f

CHAMPIONS

Jockey	Gordon Richards	164
Leading Trainer	Frank Butters	£57,468
Leading Owner	Lord Derby	£40,355
Horse	Booklaw (3)	£27,745

Champion Hurdle Challenge Cup Cheltenham: 9 March

Blaris as Champion Hurdler

By HOTSPUR

The very interesting meeting between Blaris, Boddam, and Harpist for the Champion Hurdle Challenge Cup followed immediately after the big steeplechase [*National Hunt Steeplechase*]. It did, at least, mark the first success at the meeting of a favourite, as Blaris (11-10) pulled through in the style of an undoubted champion.

The race, until he made his winning effort, was always between him and Boddam (7-2). Harpist (9-4) obviously could do nothing

in the deep ground. The other two, therefore, kept close company until approaching the bend to the finish. At that point Duller asked Blaris to spurt ahead. The right answer was forthcoming, and this strong and bold horse went on to win amid cheering by eight lengths.

[*This meagre description of the first Champion Hurdle, a 4-horse race with a prize to the winner of £365, was indicative of the standing of hurdle racing at this time.*]

Cambridgeshire Stakes Newmarket: 26 October

Cambridgeshire dead-heat

A disputed verdict: Did third horse win?

By HOTSPUR

The race for the Cambridgeshire of 1927 will long be remembered. It was not only remarkable for the fact that the result was a dead-heat, but because of a widespread opinion that the judge did not award the race to the actual winner.

As the result stands, Medal (20-1) and Niantic (25-1) dead-heated a length in front of Insight II (100-6), the winner of a year ago. Most onlookers, and especially those in the vicinity of the finish, including some of those in the Jockey Club stand, were under the impression that Insight II was a clear winner. The jockey of that horse, Thwaites, declared that he was confident he had won by half a length. One has always been taught to be loyal to the judge's decisions on a racecourse, and an honest endeavour has been made

here to pass on the teaching, but I should not be a faithful recorder of facts did I not stress the almost unanimous disagreement with the decision, especially, too, as Insight II was placed as far back as a length behind the dead-heaters.

To come to the actual race, it should be understood that they ran in two groups – one a big one on the stand side, the other a small one led by Insight II – racing very wide of each other. Soon after the start, Insight II and Orbindos on the far side ran as if they were engaging in a match, with the former always having just the better of it. As the last crucial stage was being entered upon, Insight II continued to shape like the winner.

Meanwhile, on the stand side, Medal was crowding on all sail, with the lightly

Princess of Wales's Stakes Newmarket: 30 June

Coronach v. Colorado
Surprise of the season

By HOTSPUR

The King was present at Newmarket yesterday, and was a witness of the overthrow of Lord Woolavington's 7-2 on favourite Coronach for the Princess of Wales's Stakes of a mile and a half.

His conqueror was Lord Derby's well-known horse Colorado (4-1). It involved the pricking of a somewhat gigantic bubble. This must be the case when a horse which has been exalted and elevated to the pinnacle of "horse of the century" is overthrown. The result is not unduly magnified if alluded to by that much-abused word – sensation.

To appreciate this it is only necessary to point to the brilliant career of the 1926 Derby winner Coronach. Not since Colorado had trounced him by five lengths for the Two Thousand Guineas had he known defeat. He had taken an ample revenge on Lord Derby's colt in the Derby, and his every engagement since he had won easily, including the St Leger. Once this year he was made to gallop, and that was when Embargo stretched him for the Coronation Cup at Epsom.

He afterwards gave a spectacular display at Ascot, and now came to

take on his old opponent and contest the rubber with Colorado. With most people there was supreme confidence in him, and yet, among some who were not wholly convinced, there was a belief that Colorado would not easily be disposed of.

Colorado's career I have referred to. He finished up his three-year-old days under a cloud; his ills varying between lameness and a choking habit, each being equally mysterious and still apparent. He returned to high favour by reason of a fluent winning performance at Ascot and a brilliant win of the Newbury Summer Cup a week ago. It was, nevertheless, believed that Coronach would demonstrate the truth of the old adage that a good big one would always beat a good little one. But this was an exception.

And what is the result of it all? What is the effect of Colorado's triumph with eight lengths to spare? It means that Coronach has been exposed and revealed as by no means a super-horse. On the other hand, the value of Colorado has been advanced by ten, twenty or thirty thousand pounds.

weighted Niantic close on his heels and being cleverly held together and urged on by the sixteen-year-old apprentice Stephenson. This four-year-old must have got up literally on the post to make the dead-heat.

The judge paused before

ordering the numbers into the frame, but still the backers of Insight II were not anxious. Rather were they curious to discover the placings. Then came the enlightenment and, for some people, the painful disillusionment.

1928

6 Jun Derby favourite Fairway (3-1), excited in the parade before the start, is inexplicably beaten after six furlongs, while Harry Wragg demonstrates why he is known as the "Head Waiter", pouncing on Felstead (33-1) after Charlie Elliott on Flamingo (2nd, 9-2) and Gordon Richards on Sunny Trace (5-1) destroy each other's chances at the front. [Fairway later wins the St Leger.]

9 Nov The former Newmarket trainer Mr P.V.Gilpin, 70, dies at his home in Co.Kildare. He saddled two Derby winners, Spearmint (1906) and Spion Kop (1920), but is best known for the brilliant filly Pretty Polly.

BIG RACE RESULTS

2,000 Guineas	Flamingo	EC Elliott	5-1
1,000 Guineas	Scuttle	J Childs	15-8f
Derby	Felstead	H Wragg	33-1
Oaks	Toboggan	T Weston	100-15
St Leger	Fairway	T Weston	7-4f
Champion Hurdle	Brown Jack	L Rees	4-1
Cheltenham Gold Cup	Patron Saint	F Rees	7-2
Grand National	Tipperary Tim	Mr W Dutton	100-1

CHAMPIONS

Jockey	Gordon Richards	148
Leading Trainer	Frank Butters	£67,539
Leading Owner	Lord Derby	£65,603
Horse	Fairway (3)	£29,707

The Grand National Aintree: 30 March

100 to 1 winner of the National

Amazing race won by Tipperary Tim

By HOTSPUR

Something awful was bound to happen. Forty-two horses went to the post for the Grand National Steeplechase at Liverpool and only one stood up to the end. That horse, of course, was the winner. Yesterday morning Mr H.S.Kenyon's Tipperary Tim was practically unheard of. In the afternoon he became world famous. He came in alone for a steeplechase worth over £11,000. Only one other, the American Billy Barton (33-1), was placed by the judge, and that after the horse had been on the ground through falling at the last fence when holding a short lead.

A great massacre had occurred during the race. Fiction cannot compete with the cold facts of this latest celebration of burlesque steeplechasing, for the winner of so much money would scarcely be ranked as a humble selling plater elsewhere. Need it be added that his starting price was 100 to 1.

The holocaust happened at the Canal Turn, which makes a sharp left-handed move necessary. Almost invariably it is the scene of alarming trouble, but nothing to compare with what happened now. The mischief-maker was the £7,000 horse, Easter Hero.

I have written on previous occasions how this horse has jumped awkwardly to the right at these National fences. It was for this reason that I would never entertain his chance of winning, notwithstanding Mr Loewenstein's ideas when he gave that extraordinary price for him. Anyhow, he distinguished himself now by jumping on to the top of the fence, and there he remained until finally he fell back into the ditch. Meanwhile, in a few seconds there was a crowd of our much-discussed National horses baulked and prevented from getting on with their business.

Yet it says something for the sportsmanship of our people when, though they had lost their money on others, they rushed to the paddock to give a rousing cheer to horse and rider for what, after all, had been a gallant display .

The One Thousand Guineas Newmarket: 4 May

King's first classic winner

By HOTSPUR

I have had no more pleasant duty to perform, and certainly none which will live longer in the memory, than to tell the story of how, at Newmarket, yesterday, his Majesty achieved his first classic race triumph. Scuttle (15-8f), bearing the Royal colours, won the One Thousand Guineas by a length from Lord Dewar's Jurisdiction (100-8). Third, six lengths further away, was Lord Derby's Toboggan (11-2).

The crowning glory of the victory, which means so much for the good of the Turf in this country, was that the King was a witness, and was therefore able to engage in the thrills of what was quite a dramatic race.

The betting suggested that the issue might be awaited with the utmost confidence, but the favourite became unsettled at the post; indeed, she was seriously ill-behaved, and when the tape eventually shot upwards and the race had begun, it was evident that she must have lost three or four lengths. I must say at this moment I came near to abandoning hope. So very seldom do you see horses capable of giving away so much distance.

Even at half-way I did not give her a chance. It was when the leaders were leaving the Bushes that the situation underwent a dramatic change. We saw Childs ask the filly to pull out more; she responded, and he drove her up to Jurisdiction. Just before entering the Dip the Royal victory began to assume definite shape. And despite losing a length in the Dip when she swerved, Childs got her beautifully balanced again and urged her forward by a touch from the whip. Scuttle raced like a piece of machinery up the hill, with the cheering already breaking out, and it grew in volume when it was realised that Jurisdiction was held and beaten.

Jockey Club Inquiry: 7 September

Jockey's license withdrawn: Smirke and the Stewards

The Stewards of the Jockey Club have withdrawn the licence of the well-known jockey, Charles Smirke *(pictured)*.

This drastic action is the sequel to a race at Gatwick on Friday of last week, in which Smirke rode Welcome Gift. The horse was a hot favourite (4-11) for the Home-Bred Two-Year-Old Plate, and was left at the post. The Gatwick Stewards were unable to accept Smirke's explanation of what occurred, and reported him to the Stewards of the Jockey Club.

Yesterday the Stewards of the Jockey Club met in London. After hearing statements from Smirke; Captain H.Allison, the starter; Walter Nightingall, the trainer of Welcome Gift; and K.Robertson, who rode in the race, they issued a statement that they "were of the opinion that Smirke made no effort to start his horse, and withdrew his license".

Smirke, who is 22, has been prominently before the racing public since the time S.Wootton brought him out as an exceptionally promising apprentice. Last year he was first jockey for the Aga Khan, and this season has been attached to the Clarehaven Lodge stable at Newmarket, and came third in the Derby on Black Watch.

[It was 5 years before Smirke was allowed back in the saddle, to resume his brilliant, maverick career, and he continued to rub many people up the wrong way with his gamesmanship and cockiness. But it was ironic that he had been suspended for making, according to the starter, "no attempt to start", on a horse that had hitherto given no trouble, but which later, in India, earned a reputation for refusing at the tapes and eventually had to be destroyed for jumping some running rails.]

1929

22 Mar A record 66 runners turn out for the Grand National, including some, according to "Hotspur" of The Daily Telegraph, "exciting nothing but derision... at least one lame horse" and two or three others that "would have discredited a decayed-looking cab". With the Canal Turn ditch filled in, top weight Easter Hero (9-1f), fresh from his success in the Cheltenham Gold Cup, stands up this time, but spreads a plate when well to the fore and is beaten 6 lengths by his half-brother, the 7-y-o gelding Gregalach (100-1), with Richmond II (40-1) a bad 3rd, 10 finishing.

5 Jun Another outsider wins the Derby, Irish-bred Trigo (33-1) beating Walter Gay (100-8) by 1 1/2 lengths, with Brienz (50-1) 3rd, as the fancied horses are again routed. The winning jockey, J.Marshall, 20, is still serving his apprenticeship.

30 Nov Coole, the 100-8 winner of the Saturday Selling Handicap Hurdle at Haydock, returns a record Tote dividend of £341 2s 6p to a 2s stake, representing odds of 3,410-1. The winning ticket is worth more than twice the sum realised by the sale of the winning horse!

Newmarket: 2 July

First impressions of the "Tote": How it worked

By HOTSPUR

The great adventure in racing was duly embarked upon at Newmarket today. The totalisator method of betting, from which a golden future for the Turf in this country is to come, was set in operation, and, with the exception of that section whose identity is too obvious to need naming, there was general satisfaction with what happened on this momentous first day, on which more than £12,000 was placed with the totalisator.

It required little search to find the low wooden buildings which served as offices. There was one in the paddock, another in the members' enclosure on the plantation side, still another for members on the opposite or stands side; and the main structure, on which was displayed the progress of the pools and the dividends, divided Tattersall's and the cheaper enclosure.

I don't think it would be quite fair to criticise too seriously this first attempt, but there are one or two points where I believe the "Tote" authorities have gone wrong. For instance, I heard loud complaints over the absence of a ten-shilling window. The units are two shillings and a pound. If an individual wished to have a ten-shilling bet, he had to stand in the bigger two-shilling queue and take five tickets. Then, if the individual had one pound win and place, and the horse won, he had to join in two queues, one to receive the win money and another to get his place winnings.

The great joke of the day was when the bookmakers returned the winner of the first race, a selling plate which had only seven runners, at 33 to 1 against. This, then, was their first gesture against the "Tote". But instead of impressing by its magnificence, it merely created hilarity among those who interpreted it as a confession that not until today have fair odds against a winning outsider been forthcoming. It has been the custom in the past for such a winner to be returned among the 10 to 1 or 100 to 8 "others". Yet here we had this splendid bouquet thrown to the betting world at the very outset and before even the "Tote" mathematicians could get out their figures.

Mr Guy Hargreaves, who had the distinction of winning this historic first race with an unknown named Huncoat, had, I believe, £5 invested with a bookmaker and £5 on the "Tote". The latter could still beat the books, as the starting-price amounted to 39 1/4 to 1.

On the two odds-on winners, the starting-prices did beat the "Tote", and this will generally be the case, as I have pointed out before, because the bookmakers gamble against hot favourites, while the "Tote" bets never to lose.

The "Tote" today taught us in that respect no more than we already knew, namely that the prices of favourites, as a rule, will be better with the bookmakers, and the winners over about 7 or 8 to 1 will be better with the "Tote".

Channel Selling Plate Brighton: 6 August

Depressing day for racers at Brighton

By HOTSPUR

Those who had the misfortune to be of the crowd on Brighton racecourse this afternoon for the opening of the August three-day fixture had to pay some attention to weathering a fearful storm of wind and rain. The task so occupied them as to make any propositions concerned with the racing quite a subsidiary matter. Anything more un-Augustlike could not well be imagined. To all who were thoroughly soaked to the skin I may say that the rainfall did much good to the course.

I am assured there have been worse experiences in the past at Brighton in August, but the trouble today was that the racing was so disappointing and extremely unpretentious that it did not permit one for a moment to forget the malevolence of this particularly pernicious and successful demonstration of drought-breaking.

They must have been a class "C" lot of two-year-olds that competed for the Channel Selling Plate, for I do not recollect seeing a worse looking sample. A favourite was found in the Sonoma colt, who may have the distinction of being a stable companion of Diolite, but also happens to be almost bobtailed, narrow and split up, and something of a clever caricature of what a racehorse should be. Yet it is also true that they race in all shapes, for this nameless one beat all but the 10 to 1 chance, Broken Tendril gelding, who appeared to make the whole of the running and lasted home to win by a head. The Nattering Nan gelding, narrow and sweating, filled third place, three lengths behind the pair that made of the race a match.

[Perhaps the gale was blowing the horses down the Brighton slope, but what Hotspur omitted to say was that the unnamed gelding who beat the unnamed 'caricature of what a racehorse should be' by a head in this 'class C lot of two-year-olds' on this day of 'extremely unpretentious' racing recorded a time of 1min 6 1/5sec, a world record for 6 furlongs – and one that still stands today!]

BIG RACE RESULTS

2,000 Guineas	Mr Jinks	H Beasley	5-2f
1,000 Guineas	Taj Mah	W Sibbritt	33-1
Derby	Trigo	J Marshall	33-1
Oaks	Pennycomequick	H Jelliss	11-10f
St Leger	Trigo	M Beary	5-1
Champion Hurdle	Royal Falcon	F Rees	11-2
Cheltenham Gold Cup	Easter Hero	F Rees	7-4f
Grand National	Gregalach	R Everett	100-1

CHAMPIONS

Jockey	Gordon Richards	135
Leading Trainer	RC Dawson	£74,754
Leading Owner	HH Aga Khan	£39,886
Horse	Trigo (3)	£23,690

The 1930s

T here was a sharp downward curve in the bloodstock market after the boom in the twenties, but the trend reversed, and the mid-thirties was a time of prosperity for horseracing in Britain. In France, however, the sport seemed to be going downhill. Important French owners began to send their yearlings over the Channel to be trained in greater numbers than before. The Deauville yearling sales stood still, while Newmarket flourished, and it was a sign of the times when the Aga Khan began to favour the latter.

The Aga Khan became the biggest owner to race in Britain, winning the Derby three times – with Blenheim (1930), Bahram (1935) and Mahmoud (1936), and finishing leading owner on five occasions. Mahmoud set a Derby time record that remained unsurpassed until 1995, and Bahram was the only horse in the thirties to achieve the Triple Crown, although Blue Peter in 1939 was deprived by the outbreak of World War II of his favourite's chance of doing so.

Gordon Richards lost his jockeys' title to Fred Fox in 1930 and then proceeded to monopolise it for the rest of the decade. In 1933, he broke Fred Archer's long-standing record of winners for the season, and at one stage rode 12 consecutive winners, an achievement that remains unequalled in any major racing nation. The much loved Steve Donoghue, another racing legend, retired in 1937, but not before he had chalked up another two Classics after a long gap without such success. Meanwhile, the Derby was fast becoming a holy grail for Richards, who three times rode the runner-up, while Fox succeeded twice – as did Charlie Smirke, after his enforced five-year absence from "Newmarket Heath".

The name that dominated steeplechasing in the decade was that of Miss Dorothy Paget's Golden Miller, whose feats of winning the Cheltenham Gold Cup five years in succession and winning that trophy and the Grand National in the same season have stood the test of time.

Mahmoud's Derby, 1936: Charlie Smirke brought the Aga Khan's colt home in a record time which stood for nigh-on 60 years, before being beaten by Lammtarra in 1995.

1930

17 May A starting machine is used for the first time to get the 15 runners off in the Kentucky Derby, won by Gallant Fox to register the first leg of the American Triple Crown. One horse, Sir Barton in 1919, had accomplished the feat before – winning the Derby, the Preakness and Belmont Stakes – but it is while covering Gallant Fox's victories that sportswriter Charles Hatton first uses the old-established English term for the three races.

30 Jun The patrol camera is used for the first time on a British course, at Newmarket.

4 Nov The 4-y-o New Zealand-bred chestnut gelding Phar Lap *(pictured right)* – the name is Sinhalese for "lightning", but he was nicknamed "The Red Terror" for his exploits in Australia last season – starting at 11-8 on favourite and carrying 9st-12, wins the Melbourne Cup.

CHAMPIONS

Jockey (Flat)	Freddy Fox	129
Jockey (NH)	Billy Stott	77
Leading Trainer	HS Persse	£49,487
Leading Owner	HH Aga Khan	£46,259
Leading Money Winner	Rustom Pasha	£13,933

Gold Cup and Champion Hurdle Cheltenham: 11 March

Double for J. Anthony at Cheltenham: Easter Hero and Brown Tony carry off principal events

By HOTSPUR

The National Hunt festival at Cheltenham has been given a brilliant send-off. When the sun forced a way through the rolling banks of heavy cloud all was well. The attendance was a wonderfully big one, the chief attraction of course, being the meeting of Easter Hero (8-11f) and Gib (13-8).

For the second year in succession Easter Hero is the winner of the Cheltenham Gold Cup, but as a great match between him and Gib the affair was a profound disappointment. How could it be otherwise when Gib should have done the last thing expected of such a brilliant jumper? He fell two fences from home just as he was drawing alongside his rival to battle out what remained of the distance. The other two runners had been utterly negligible.

Whether Gib went unbalanced into the fence, or the effort took the last out of him, I do not know. I believe Easter Hero would have won anyway, for there were reserves in him still untouched, while Gib had to be put under strong pressure. Gib was remounted to finish third behind Grakle, who was beaten twenty lengths.

It is impossible to convey in print the immense thrill created by the finish for the Champion Hurdle Challenge Cup. Here were in opposition five of the best hurdlers of the day, and four of them seriously fancied. Through the race one could see the young horse, Brown Tony, pulling hard. It possibly indicated a moderate pace, but they certainly touched full pressure through the last half-mile. Peertoi was going the best at the last hurdle. Then there began an epic struggle up the hill, and just as Clear Cash was getting his nose in front Brown Tony came with a dramatic burst to snatch the verdict in the last two strides. It left onlookers positively bewildered for the time being. And it completed a memorable double for the trainer Jack Anthony and jockey Tommy Cullinan.

The Grand National Aintree: 28 March

Thrilling finish for the "National"

How Shaun Goilin beat Melleray's Belle by a neck

By HOTSPUR

History may not hold a parallel to the magnificent finish for the Grand National today. It will live for all time in the memory of those who saw it. Shaun Goilin (100-8) won by a neck from Melleray's Belle (20-1), with Sir Lindsay (100-7) only a length and a half away in third place.

Of the forty-one starters only six finished, but the usual low percentage did not seem to matter on this occasion. The big thrill of the finish alone stirred the emotions as they may never have been stirred before.

Something big seemed to be happening every moment, and always the field was being steadily thinned. Every one of the starters passed safely over the first fence. Becher's took toll, but not as severely as usual; indeed, it was surprising to see so many still alive and heading for the Canal turn. But from that point up to the next half-mile the grief really set in. Gregalach had been going well when he appeared to stop at the formidable ditch-fence beyond Valentine's, where Grakle (100-12f) also went out.

Soon afterwards I noticed Sir Lindsay make another mistake which, coming on top of two others, would have stopped most horses, but he rallied again with surprising stoutness and began to close up with Glangesia, Melleray's Belle, and Shaun Goilin. These were the four left definitely in the picture as they came on to the racecourse for the last time, with only two fences remaining.

As they came charging to the last fence, I really thought Sir Lindsay was going to win. I am sure he was travelling the strongest, just in front of Melleray's Belle. Shaun Goilin would be less than a length behind them at the take-off, with Sir Lindsay on the outside. It transpired that the latter's jockey lost an iron hereabouts, which explains why he began to bore out of the direct line for home and thereby sacrificed precious ground.

The mare from Yorkshire kept plugging on, Sir Lindsay continued to come wide and Shaun Goilin, splendidly assisted by his jockey, crept up inch by inch until, thirty yards from home, he had drawn level with the mare. The next stride or two carried him definitely into the lead, and, amid great excitement, he held on to win the big prize.

Tommy Cullinan, his jockey, was the lucky man of the moment. He was to have ridden Easter Hero. But when that horse finally broke down, he was at once secured for Shaun Goilin, and so added the National to his great Cheltenham double.

NATIONAL HUNT

Champion Hurdle	Brown Tony	T Cullinan	7-2
Cheltenham Gold Cup	Easter Hero	T Cullinan	8-11f
Grand National	Shaun Gollin	T Cullinan	100-8

The Derby Epsom: 4 June

The Aga Khan wins his first Derby: Blenheim surprises his stable

By HOTSPUR

In the great surge of victory, the emotions of the winning owner are no aid to coherent articulation. It may be that the first words uttered by his Highness the Aga Khan, after he had escorted his hero into the unsaddling enclosure for the winner were, "Well, I've won the Derby at last!"

In those words were epitomised his ten years or so of endeavour on the most elaborate lines and the consummation of immense planning, expenditure of money, and personal ambition. Blenheim, the bearer of an honoured name, brought the long sought-for award to-day, and the Aga Khan was made an intensely happy man.

Blenheim (18-1) was the neglected rather than the selected of the stable. If the obvious thing had happened here, Rustom Pasha, the second favourite, carrying the Aga Khan's first colours, would have finished in front of Blenheim, and Diolite (11-

4f), who had finished well in front of Blenheim for the Two Thousand Guineas, would have won.

Diolite, indeed, was in the lead as they entered the straight, having fought off all challenges. But after a long struggle, he succumbed to Iliad (25-1), who looked to have the race won.

Then, inside the distance, say just over a furlong from the finish, Blenheim was brought up on the outside with a most menacing challenge. Every stride he gained ground until he was level, and then he gradually forged ahead, answering with the greatest pluck the strong hand-riding of his jockey, and so he gained his meritorious victory by a length and a half.

The "wrong one" in the Aga Khan's colours had won, yet there were some who could remember to cheer home the effort of a game colt and the fine judgment of his jockey, Harry Wragg. The "Head Waiter" had done it again.

ENGLISH CLASSICS

2,000 Guineas	Diolite	F Fox	10-1
1,000 Guineas	Fair Isle	T Weston	7-4f
Derby	Blenheim	H Wragg	18-1
Oaks	Rose of England	G Richards	7-1
St Leger	Singapore	G Richards	4-1jf

Berks Selling Handicap Newbury: 25 June

Newbury dead-heat

First case of a run-off at a tote meeting

The first instance of a dead-heat being run off at a meeting where the totalisator was in operation occurred at Newbury yesterday.

Ruby's Love and Walloon dead-heated for first place in the Berks Selling Handicap, and it was decided to run off for first place. Ruby's Love won. Before the totalisator was introduced, backers to win of the horse beaten in the run-off lost their money, but under the new rules of betting, in the event of a dead-heat the bets go to the horses as officially shown on the

number board, and no subsequent decider disturbs the destination of such bets. The decider constitutes a separate race.

This also applies to totalisator betting, so that backers of both Ruby's Love and Walloon at either bookmakers' or totalisator odds are entitled to receive. Backers to win at bookmakers' prices lose half their stake, and receive full odds to the other half.

[This was the last time a dead-heat was run off in Britain.]

Ascot: 18 June

Violent storm floods Ascot course:
Stewards forced to postpone five events

By HOTSPUR

Ordinary language will not convey the faintest understanding of the disastrous thunder and rainstorm which devastated Ascot today, killed a bookmaker in Tattersall's enclosure, half-drowned thousands, turned parts of the paddock and course into broad ribbons and patches of water, and brought about a thing unprecedented in the long history of racing at Ascot – the abandonment for the day of the remaining five races.

The race for the Royal Hunt Cup had just been run in fairly heavy rain, when suddenly the heavens seemed to burst open with an appalling crash of thunder. No other warning was given. Instantly the rain came with a fury of a waterspout. A matter

of seconds sufficed to drench to the skin people not already in shelter. At rapid intervals the steaming, tense atmosphere was lit up by vivid zigzags of forked lightning. It was terrifying and appalling as the thunder crashed immediately overhead. As the fierce storm proceeded, the approaches to the enclosures and buildings were turned into spates of rushing waters, and cascades fell from roofs to add to the general confusion.

A thin trickle across the course rapidly assumed the width of a broad canal, then a river, which came into existence as if by magic. It was running directly across the course, and made abandonment of further racing for the day a formality.

OTHER MAJOR RACES

Arc de Triomphe	Motrico	M Fruhinsholtz	83-10
Kentucky Derby	Gallant Fox	E Sande	119-100f
Melbourne Cup	Phar Lap	JE Pike	8-11f

Manchester: 22 November

How Fox beat Richards for riding honours

By HOTSPUR

The great race for the jockeys' championship, which ended in a one-point victory for the senior, Freddy Fox, and the consequent dethronement of Gordon Richards, created an astonishing amount of speculation and interest at Manchester on the last day of Flat racing. Not until Fox won the last race but one of the season was it decided.

Who could have imagined that in 1930, Fox, a greatly respected jockey in his 40's, would have overthrown an exceptionally formidable rival and claimed the head of the table? I am delighted he has succeeded.

Fox's championship has come to him late in his riding life, but it comes as the just reward of hard work, of a high level of consistency and skill, and of all-round ability.

If brotherly love and solicitude could have worked the oracle, then Clifford Richards would have made his brother champion jockey once more. He surrendered a

winning mount in his interest at Warwick, and a second one here to-day. One appropriately named Rivalry (and by Chivalrous, too!) was to have been ridden in the first race, for the Farewell Handicap, by Clifford. He asked to stand down in favour of Gordon, who won on the 3-1 favourite by ten lengths. He was leaving nothing to chance.

Fox, having no such obliging brother, received no help of the kind. He even saw the race for the November Handicap from the stands, and was a witness of the win of Glorious Devon, a 25-1 shot which for the first time put his rival one in front. The very next race Fox won on Landsong (5-1f), which made them all square. This race for the Last Selling Handicap brought the champion's riding career to an end for 1930. It was his turn to go into the stand and see Fox win the Worsley Nursery on the 6-5 on favourite Isthmus.

That was the end. Neither had a ride in the last race.

1931

5 Jun In the Acorn Plate at Epsom, a race for fillies run on Oaks day, Lady Trace (7-1) clocks 55¹/₅sec, a new 2-y-o record.

18 Sep The Windsor stewards fine the handicapper, Mr Kenneth Gibson, £10, after he admits a mistake in the weights for tomorrow's Ivor Nursery. Lord Ellesmere had complained that his horse Attractive had been set to give 29lb to Wantalot, who had beaten him earlier this month by half a length when receiving 13lb, a result the handicapper had apparently ignored.

5 Dec The Newbury stewards disqualify Golden Miller, winner of yesterday's Moderate Steeplechase, after establishing that he had not carried the 7lb extra required by the conditions of the race, and fine his trainer, A.B.Briscoe, £50. Bets are not affected.

The Grand National Aintree: 27 March

T.Coulthwaite gains notable National triumph with Grakle
Popular local victory in record time
By HOTSPUR

The great race for the Grand National Steeplechase was won this afternoon for Mr Cecil Taylor, a Liverpool business man, by his horse Grakle (100-6). Second, beaten a length and a half, was Gregalach (25-1), the winner of two years ago, carrying the colours of Mrs Gemmell, and third was Lady Glenapp's Annandale (100-1). The most perfect weather conditions for Aintree in living memory helped to produce a new time record for the race.

As they became strung out, with the length of a fence between first and last, it was seen that Easter Hero was holding the expected prominent place. His progress was being watched with breathless attention, for he had come down to a very short price (5-1f). As they streamed away into the country again, Gregalach seemed to be going well, and one marvelled at the transformation in a horse that had been distressed beyond words on more than one occasion this year. While others were dropping out, either from falls, refusals, interference or fatigue, Mrs Gemmell's horse was shaping like the winner. Then, in colours very similar to those carried by Gregalach, one's attention was compelled by Grakle. Here was one that had failed time after time, now galloping and jumping as if his big day had at last arrived.

As the field became more and more thinned out, the two horses in similar colours began to monopolise our attention. Few on the stands would know it at the time, but Easter Hero was stopped for good at that fateful Becher's Brook in the course of this second circuit. He may have been horribly unlucky, for as he was landing he appears to have trodden on a fallen horse.

Gregalach and Grakle began to draw out as they raced for the second fence from home. Both horses rose at it and jumped cleanly, and then one noted the first signs of weakening in Gregalach. First over the last fence, and with cheering already beginning to break out, was Grakle. But Gregalach was not yet done with. Both horses were tiring and fading out fast. Grakle and his rider, however, stuck it out grimly to win by one and a half lengths.

There was much satisfaction that that great trainer of jumpers, Tom Coulthwaite, had at last been vindicated in his faith that Grakle would one day win a Grand National.

CHAMPIONS

Jockey (Flat)	Gordon Richards	145
Jockey (NH)	Billy Stott	81
Leading Trainer	J Lawson	£93,899
Leading Owner	JA Dewar	£39,034
Leading Money Winner	Cameronian	£29,484

NATIONAL HUNT

Champion Hurdle	No race (frost)		
Cheltenham Gold Cup	No race (frost)		
Grand National	Grakle	R Lyall	100-6

The Derby Epsom: 3 June

How Cameronian gained a great triumph
F.Darling's fourth Derby winner since the war
By HOTSPUR

The perfect Derby. Good weather, a fair race, victory for the favourite, and well-backed horses second and third. Mr Arthur Dewar's Cameronian (7-2) won by three-parts of a length from Sir John Rutherford's Orpen (9-1), with Lord Rosebery's Sandwich (8-1), a similar distance behind, third.

I was delighted to be able to say before the race that I liked none better than Cameronian. I had not set eyes on him since his win of the Two Thousand Guineas. Fred Darling has done fine things in his time, and now he has won four Derbys since the war, but he has never been paid such a tribute to his ability as was given him to-day by Cameronian.

The great thrill began soon after the leaders were fairly headed for their goal. Gallini held on for a while, but I could see that Fox was riding as if supremely confident that he held the Yorkshire horse safe. He must have been aware that Orpen was coming up on his right hand, for now he had to sit down and ride in earnest. That was what Bobby Jones on Orpen was doing.

Then did Fox draw his whip and call on the favourite to produce what he might have in reserve. Being a generous and willing horse, it was immediately forthcoming. A touch of the whip – and he seemed to extend his stride. Gallini had fallen back. Orpen's gallant effort was over, too. And so, with Fox riding with all his strength, Cameronian was driven home to his gallant victory.

Now I come to Sandwich. It was a long time before H. Wragg managed to thread his way into the race proper. What Sandwich did after that was truly prodigious. I am sure he was the unlucky horse of the race, and equally I am sure he will, in due time, furnish solid evidence of the fact.

Race seen at home: Television success.

Many people saw the thrills of the Derby on the Televisor in the comfort of their own homes.

It was the first television of the race, and was done by the Baird Television Co, in co-operation with the B.B.C.

Fifteen miles from the course, in the company's studio at Longacre, all the Derby scenes were easily discernible – the parade of the horses, the enormous Epsom crowd, and the dramatic flash past at the winning post.

After the transmission Mr Baird said that he was quite satisfied with the experiment:

Cameronian wins from Orpen

"This marks the entry of television into the outdoor field, and should be the prelude to televising outdoor topical events."

The Oaks Epsom: 5 June

French triumph in fillies' classic

Four Course beaten by Brulette after thrilling duel

By HOTSPUR

The powerful challenge launched in the Oaks on behalf of the French filly Brulette (7-2jf) could not be resisted. She made up a tremendous lot of ground to win a great race by a length from the Classic winner Four Course (6-1), in Lord Ellesmere's colours. Mr W.M.G. Singer's Links Tor (10-1) finished third, three-parts of a length behind the second. The three were well clear of the rest, and may be said to have entirely monopolised interest in what was a

more dramatic finish even than that seen for the Derby.

Owned by an Englishman in Col.Birkin, trained by an Englishman in Frank Carter, and ridden by an Englishman in Charles Elliott, the victory in that sense was made to bear an international character. France claims the real right of the triumph by reason of the filly having been bred and raced there. She had, indeed, never set foot in this country until brought here a few days ago.

The "Don Pat" Libel Case: 1 December

£16,000 damages award for trainer

Damages of £16,000 were awarded yesterday to Mr Charles Chapman, racehorse trainer, of Shifnal Cottage, Lavant, Sussex, in his libel action in the King's Bench Division.

The defendants were the Earl of Ellesmere, the Earl of Harewood, and the Earl of Rosebery, Stewards of the Jockey Club, Weatherby and Sons, of Cavendish Square, London, and the "Times" newspaper.

Mr Chapman claimed damages in respect of the publication of a decision of the Jockey Club Stewards warning him off Newmarket Heath and disqualifying Don Pat, which he had trained, for the Bedfont High-Weight Handicap at Kempton Park Summer Meeting in 1930.

He complained that the publication had injured him in his character, credit, and reputation on the Turf. The defence was a plea of privilege and justification.

The special jury assessed damages as follows: £3,000 for publication to the news agencies, £3,000 for publication to the "Times", and £10,000 for publication to the Racing Calendar.

Mr Justice Horridge entered judgment against the Stewards and Weatherby's for £13,000, with costs, and against all the defendants for a further £3,000, with costs.

Mr Pritt, K.C. said Mr Chapman had suffered very grievously, and, except in a menial occupation, had been unable to earn anything for over a year. He would not have been able to bring the action but for the help of friends.

Summing up, Mr Justice Horridge said that the question for the jury was: Are the words in their ordinary meaning true? The jury must ask themselves whether a reasonably minded person, reading the notice, would say: "Well, he must have been warned off for doping, because that is the only thing they have been inquiring about."

As to the question of damages, his lordship said that the Stewards were put in their position to do their duty. They might have made a wrong statement in the newspapers. If that were so, they had to pay for it, and the jury had to say whether their conduct subsequent to publishing that statement was in any way such as to aggravate the damages they ought to pay.

[Later, a Court of Appeal ruled that the Jockey Club and Weatherby's had been protected by privilege, and although the sympathy was with Chapman it didn't bring him back his licence.]

The St Leger Doncaster: 9 September

Veterinary examination of beaten Leger favourite

Sandwich the most convincing winner for years

By HOTSPUR

The St Leger victory of Sandwich (9-1), in Lord Rosebery's colours, this afternoon, is in no sense astounding. It was written very clearly that this colt had a great chance in the event of the favourite, Cameronian (5-6), not being good enough. But what was astounding was the utter and inglorious defeat of Mr Dewar's colt. It was not a defeat, but a rout, and so complete as to leave no sort of doubt that it was ridiculously wrong.

The light was too bad to see much of the race in its middle stages, but I could see one of my place selections, Sir Andrew, making the running, while the other one, Sandwich, was about sixth. Slightly better placed at that point was Cameronian.

They had a long way to go yet. One picked them up again as they turned into the straight, and Sir Andrew was still leading. However, he had to surrender first to Orpen, hard on whose heels came Sandwich.

One could see Harry Wragg on Lord Rosebery's colt sitting perfectly still, the embodiment of confidence and just waiting to launch a challenge. When it did come it was devastating. In a few telling strides he had got the better of Orpen (11-2), and then he put in such a powerful finish that Orpen appeared to be standing still. It was the most emphatic St Leger win we have seen for years.

What, meanwhile, of Cameronian? He was left to finish last of all, beaten even by the pace-making Birthday Book. Professor Reynolds, the well-known veterinary surgeon, supplied the explanation. Fred Darling immediately requested him to make an examination and he found the colt with a temperature of 103. It shows that the colt was ill. His jockey, Fox, reported that he never for a moment settled down.

[The widely held suspicion was that Cameronian had been got at, but it was never proved.]

Edinburgh: 22 September

Remarkable riding feat by W Nevett

By HOTSPUR

If honours could be shaped in such a way, then a special medal should be struck for presentation to the Yorkshire jockey W.Nevett, to commemorate three wonderful days of riding. On Saturday, at Bogside, he scored a hat-trick of three winners; he repeated the feat at Edinburgh on Monday; and yesterday he went one better. He rode four of the

half-dozen winners at Edinburgh and brought his total of successes to ten out of sixteen rides.

The achievement is quite remarkable, and can only be qualified to the extent of remembering that the opposition at those two Scottish meetings has not been what it is practically every day on English racecourses, especially in the south.

1932

16 Jun On an interesting day at Ascot, the 6-y-o Trimdon (15-2) wins the Gold Cup

for the second year running, with last year's St Leger winner Sandwich (100-9) unplaced, and last year's Derby winner Cameronian (8-13f) is only 3rd in the Ribblesdale Stakes. [Notching his first win, in the 5f New Stakes, is a Gainsborough colt called Hyperion (6-1), owned by Lord Derby.]

7 Sep The Aga Khan's 4 St Leger horses finish in the first 5. His chestnut colt Firdaussi (20 to 1) beats his first hope, Dastur (6-1), by a neck. Third, 4 lengths back, is Silvermere (33-1), owned by Mrs C.Rich, and 4th, beaten a head for third place, is the Aga Khan's filly Udaipur (9-1), with Kaj Tasra (40-1) 3 lengths away 5th. Derby winner April the Fifth (100-6) comes 13th, and 2,000 Guineas winner Orwell (4-1f), the beaten Derby favourite, is 7th.

28 Sep At Kempton Park, the members' stand, Royal box and telegraph offices are destroyed by fire, the second in a month at the racecourse. Arson is suspected.

Cheltenham Gold Cup: 1 March

National favourite's bad luck at Cheltenham

Brought down in race for Gold Cup: Golden Miller wins

By HOTSPUR

The prospect of having a good story to tell of the race for the Cheltenham Gold Cup was dashed when the three most interesting horses in the small field of half a dozen came to grief in circumstances that were most deplorable, at any rate, in the case of the favourite, Grakle (10-11), who, as the world knows, is favourite for the Grand National. He was brought down by Kingsford's fall at a plain fence after covering rather more than half the distance.

In that instant all the bottom seemed to go out of what should have been an interesting and instructive affair. One badly wanted to see how Grakle would acquit himself in this company, and then there was Kingsford (3-1), to whom many gave a very

live chance. Gib (100-8) fell at the second fence, and so there were only three left in it. Golden Miller (13-2) had made more than one bad mistake when he, Inverse (8-1) and Aruntius (20-1) were left as the survivors. He not only ignored that blunder, but another one soon afterwards, and yet was able to take the lead off Inverse and win with four lengths to spare.

As Insurance (4-5f) won the Champion Hurdle Challenge Cup by twelve lengths from Song of Essex (5-4) at level weights, he is entitled to rank as the season's hurdling champion. So did Miss Dorothy Paget bring off a very notable double event, bringing her two cups, nearly £2,000 in prize money, and any proceeds from exchanges with the layers.

CHAMPIONS

Jockey (Flat)	Gordon Richards	190
Jockey (NH)	Billy Stott	77
Leading Trainer	Frank Butters	£72,436
Leading Owner	HH AgaKhan	£57,778
Leading Money Winner	Firdaussi	£17,441

The Grand National Aintree: 18 March

National favourites routed

Forbra wins at his first attempt

By HOTSPUR

Drama most vivid makes up the story of still another amazing Grand National. The great steeplechase was won by the 50 to 1 chance Forbra, owned by W.Parsonage, who was at one time a starting-price bookmaker at Ludlow.

Second was Mrs Ireland's Egremont (33-1), ridden by Mr E.C.Paget, beaten only three lengths, but easily at that, while third was Shaun Goilin (40-1), the hero of three years ago. Behind this brief synopsis is a story even more astonishing than usual of disaster to all the fancied horses in the very firm going.

At Becher's a number were left behind, but they did not include the cracks at the top of the handicap. Their supporters found relief for a few more moments. It was at the second fence beyond Valentine's that a riderless horse ran across the fence and prevented several horses jumping. One of them was Grakle (100-12f), who at the time was a dozen lengths behind. His rider had to pull him round and set him at the

fence again, and he finally refused, as did several others, at the fence just before the water.

Gregalach (100-9) fell at the last fence before the racecourse is re-entered. There were not many survivors as they came to the water jump, and even there K.C.B. (50-1) broke a shoulder and had to be destroyed.

So they went away on the second circuit, and a long way from home there were only two in it, and one could see that, bar a fall, they would be first and second. It was also as clear as the day that Forbra was going the stronger, and he came away from Egremont at the last fence and went past the post with his ears pricked.

Thus it happened again that though so many (36) started only two gave the National the dignity of a race. Not the least astonishing thing about this National is the fact of the winner being absolutely new to the course. Indeed, he is one of the season's recruits to steeplechasing, and is only seven years old.

NATIONAL HUNT

Champion Hurdle	Insurance	T Leader	4-5f
Cheltenham Gold Cup	Golden Miller	T Leader	13-2
Grand National	Forbra	J Hamey	50-1

Agua Caliente Handicap Tanforan: 20 March

The wonderful Phar Lap

By HOTSPUR

In future the great stake winner, Phar Lap, who at the week-end won the big race at Agua Caliente in Mexico, must not be referred to as an Australian horse, as is stated in the cables from America. He was bred in New Zealand, and an ardent New Zealander who holds a highly responsible position in this country sends me this letter:

"Why, oh why, are you persisting in calling the wonderful horse, Phar Lap, an Australian racehorse? I did think you would watch our interest and see that he was duly described as born in New Zealand, reared in New

Zealand on New Zealand grasses, the rich land that produces the wonderful meat, butter and cheese that we send you...Carbine, born and bred in our country, is constantly described as an Australian horse. I notice Jerome Fandor, the winner of the Lincolnshire, had Spearmint and Carbine on the dam's side."

[There was no report of the race, staged just over the California border because of betting restrictions, but Phar Lap (3-2f), carrying 9st-3 and giving away 9-39lb to the others, won the 10f race easily in a new course record.]

ENGLISH CLASSICS

2,000 Guineas	Orwell	RA Jones	1-1f
1,000 Guineas	Kandy	EC Elliott	33-1
Derby	April the Fifth	F Lane	100-6
Oaks	Udaipur	M Beary	10-1
St Leger	Firdaussi	F Fox	20-1

OTHER MAJOR RACES

Arc de Triomphe	Motrico	CH Semblat	38-10f
Kentucky Derby	Burgoo King	E James	893-100
Melbourne Cup	Peter Pan	W Duncan	4-1f

California: 5 April

Phar Lap dead: "Wonder Horse" that cost 100 guineas: Won £66,450

Phar Lap, the "wonder horse" of New Zealand and Australia, has died of colic at the E.D.Perry Stock Farm, in California. The big chestnut gelding was taken ill yesterday morning, says an Exchange message, and the illness developed so rapidly that the veterinary surgeons were helpless.

The horse died at 2.20 p.m. but the news was kept secret for some time while efforts were made to communicate with the owner, Mr David Davis, who was flying to Los Angeles.

With the death of Phar Lap passes one of the greatest racehorses of all time. Bred in New Zealand from an English-bred sire, Night Raid, from a New Zealand mare, Entreaty, Phar Lap was bought as a yearling by Mr Davis, at Wellington, for 100 guineas.

He was afterwards sent to Australia, and won every honour on the Turf that country had to offer. Mr Davis intended to send the horse to England this year to run in some of our big handicaps, such as the Cesarewitch and Cambridgeshire. He has won over all distances from six furlongs to two miles.

Only last month Phar Lap carried off one of the richest prizes on the American Turf, the Agua Caliente Handicap, worth £10,000. His winnings in stake money amounted to £66,450, a total which has been surpassed by only one other, the American horse Sun Beau, who won nearly £75,000.

Phar Lap's victory in the Agua Caliente Handicap may have led indirectly to his death. After the race he was being garlanded. He took fright at this, stamped on a concrete step and injured a foot. The injury, however, was stated to be not serious, and he afterwards wore a special shoe.

[It was at first thought that Phar Lap died from eating plants that had been sprayed with poison. Later, an autopsy performed in Sydney on his heart suggested arsenic poisoning, but the mystery was never solved.]

The Derby Epsom: 1 June

Epsom-trained April the Fifth triumphs in Derby
Downfall of a great favourite
By HOTSPUR

Their Majesties, the King and Queen, with all the members of their family, were present at Epsom today, and witnessed the Derby triumph of April the Fifth in the colours of Mr Tom Walls. The winner (100-6), ridden by F.Lane, and trained by his owner on Epsom Downs, passed the post three-parts of a length in front of the second, the Aga Khan's Dastur (18-1), Lord Rosebery's Miracle (100-9) being only a short head away in third place. The great favourite, Orwell (5-4), who had been thought unbeatable, finished no nearer than ninth.

They had gone little more than a furlong when Orwell was behind the first half of the field. As they began the descent of Tattenham Corner, he was in front of April the Fifth, but still no better than ninth. They were half-way home in the straight when Dastur came through, moving easily. But the rising ground found out the weakness in Dastur and the strength in the long-striding, staying April the Fifth. Never have I seen a Derby winner come from behind as he did to make up so much ground and deliver such a forceful storming challenge. It was simply irresistible. It carried him with a sweep up to Miracle, who had been the first to threaten danger to Dastur, and then past the pair of them to gain his most deserved victory.

After nearly a hundred years it has been demonstrated that a Derby winner can be trained at Epsom. For until April the Fifth came – he was practically unheard of little more than a month ago - the only Epsom trained winner was Amato, in 1838. And only once before has an owner-trainer won the Derby, in 1908, when the filly Signorinetta won at 100 to 1 for the Chevalier Ginistrelli. Thank goodness the world has much more cause for rejoicing over the result today.

Newbury Spring Cup: 9 April

Abbots Worthy an astonishing winner: Caught and remounted to win after covering 4 miles
By HOTSPUR

Every horse competing for the Spring Cup race at Newbury on Saturday had to cover the mile from the paddock to the starting post and then the mile of the race. The first mile could be covered at leisure according to the mood of the horse or the will of the jockey. Abbots Worthy, who won the cup for Mr V.T.Thompson, covered four miles.

While the large crowd in the stands and enclosures were waiting for the race to start, with Abbots Worthy filling the part of favourite, or nearly so, that horse was suddenly seen to be riderless and making for the stands, two miles away. This posed two or three questions: Would he be caught? And, if so, would his jockey be able to come back to the stands and get him back to the starting post in time. And, most important of all, where was the jockey?

As the horse slowed up near the paddock gate, someone caught him, and a motor-car was seen coming down the course. Gordon Richards hopped out of it, ran towards Abbots Worthy, regained the saddle, and proceeded back to the starting-post at a smart canter.

Nevertheless, it seemed any odds against Abbots Worthy now, and they began to lengthen until they reached 8 to 1. I had made the horse my star selection, and I confess I was resigned to seeing him come in with the tail-end of the field.

Then came the amazing sequel. Always he was in the front line. At the half-distance he was well there. A quarter of a mile from home he astonished me as I saw him still prominent and going smoothly. As they entered the last hundred yards, Abbots Worthy was now definitely in command, and was being driven home to his victory with all the concentrated power of Gordon Richards.

What the horse proved capable of was remarkable. Yet it would not have been demonstrated at all but for the quick thinking and determination of Gordon Richards and the kindly action of the starter, Major Kenneth Robertson, not only in waiting for the horse to return, but in offering his car for "retrieving" purposes.

April the Fifth leads the field home at Epsom

1933

8 Mar Golden Miller *(pictured below)* and Insurance again provide a Cheltenham double in the Gold Cup and Champion Hurdle, respectively, for Mrs Dorothy Paget and trainer Basil Briscoe.

20 Apr The King watches his colt The Abbot (5-2jf) dead-heat in the Nonsuch Plate at Epsom with trainer Stanley Wootton's Jim Thomas (5-2jf), named after Mr J.H.Thomas, the Secretary of State for the Dominions, who is also present.

26 Sep After losing on the favourite in the first race at Newmarket and then riding two fancied winners, champion jockey Gordon Richards completes his hat-trick and rides his 200th winner of the season on Nevertheless, a 20-1 shot in the Abingdon Mile Nursery.

NATIONAL HUNT

Champion Hurdle	Insurance	W Stott	10-11f
Cheltenham Gold Cup	Golden Miller	W Stott	4-7f
Grand National	Kellsboro' Jack	D Williams	25-1

CHAMPIONS

Jockey (Flat)	Gordon Richards	259
Jockey (NH)	Gerry Wilson	61
Leading Trainer	F Darling	£44,276
Leading Owner	Lord Derby	£27,559
Leading Money Winner	Hyperion	£23,179

The Grand National Aintree: 24 March

Kellsboro' Jack's victory in record time: Golden Miller comes to grief

By HOTSPUR

An American woman owner, Mrs F.Ambrose Clark, today won the Grand National in record time with her seven-year-old gelding Kellsboro' Jack (25-1), ridden by Dudley Williams and trained by Ivor Anthony at Wroughton. The winner finished three lengths in front of Really True (66-1), with Slater (50-1) a neck back in third. Then came sixteen more to complete the course, a number which has never been equalled in my time.

Although the field of 34 were very soon strung out, which inevitably happens in every Grand National, there was astonishingly little grief throughout the first circuit. No fewer than 27 came safely over the water.

By the time they had come to Becher's the second time round, it was seen that top weight Gregalach (10-1) was labouring heavily, and he was mercifully pulled up at the canal turn, having broken a blood vessel. The blunder of 9-1 favourite Golden Miller at Becher's was just the prelude to his final exit at the canal turn – a thoroughly beaten and distressed horse.

Dudley Williams, the successful rider, said that his horse seemed to gain a length or two on any other at every fence, so splendid was his jumping. He was never out of the first three, and he took up the running three fences from home. But there was drama at the last fence, where Pelorus Jack fell when he seemed to have just as good a chance as the winner.

The Derby Epsom: 31 May

Hyperion wins the Derby by four lengths in record time

By HOTSPUR

Beyond any shadow of doubt, the best horse won the 1933 Derby, which is precisely as it should be. Hyperion (6-1f), carrying the first colours of Lord Derby, was an amazingly easy winner by four lengths. It seemed nearer twice that margin. He covered the distance in 2min 34sec, two-fifths of a second inside the previous record shared by the 1927 and 1928 winners, Call Boy and Felstead.

Hyperion did not actually make all the running, but he was always the winner from the moment they were sent on their way by the starter. He left nothing to the narrator to tell. Tommy Weston, Hyperion's jockey, was delightfully contemptuous of those he left behind him in the so-called race. "I only saw three horses from start to finish," he said to me.

If Hyperion was capable of making such sparkling history, his chief contemporary of last year, Manitoba (13-2), was an abject loser. Gordon Richards, in his own words, said that the colt went only for five furlongs or so and then was hopeless.

It was as they came into full view in the straight that Donoghue on Thrapston, in Lord Derby's second colours, opened out to let Hyperion through on the inside. The Derby was all over so far away. The further they came the more the grand little horse increased his lead. Talk about not being able to act on firm ground! Such may have been the case last year.

He is now the exemplification of the really good horse that can go on any sort of going. The cheering had started before he reached the winning-post. And as the runner-up, King Salmon (7-1), was about the best-backed horse in the race each way, I do not need to be told that the bookmakers must have been considerable losers over the result.

It was a splendid victory because it was so clear cut and beyond the vestige of criticism. And the winner's breeding stands for all that is best in the stud book, by Gainsborough, a great sire of brilliant horses, from one of his owner's best mares, Selene, a daughter of a Derby winner in Minoru.

Queen Alexandra Stakes Ascot: 16 June

Brown Jack's Ascot record

By HOTSPUR

One-year-old history was repeated at Ascot yesterday in a remarkable way. Twelve months ago his Majesty's Limelight, Sir H.Cunliffe-Owen's Concerto, and Sir Harold Wernher's Brown Jack were winners on the last day of the meeting. All three won again yesterday.

A year ago Limelight won the Jersey Stakes. Yesterday he scored in the Hardwicke Stakes, an event of more importance and of considerably more value. Concerto took the Wokingham Stakes for the second year in succession. But the palm must go to Brown Jack, who performed his usual task of winning the Queen Alexandra Stakes and created a record which may never be beaten. The grand old horse won the race for the fifth consecutive time.

The winning jockeys were the same – case Joe Childs in the King's colours, Harry Wragg succeeding again on Concerto, and Steve Donoghue as usual partnering Brown Jack.

Brown Jack had to battle for his victory, but as he excels in battling he put all his heart and strength into his task. The betting of 5 to 1 on suggested that he was virtually walking over, and that his three opponents did not count. Yet one of them, Corn Belt (10-1), put him very much on the stretch, so that Donoghue had to sit down and ride him with all his strength and artistry to get him home by a length and a half before the cheering could really break forth. There is no reason now why he should not make five consecutive wins into six. *[He does.]*

The St Leger Doncaster: 13 September

Hyperion proves himself a true champion by easy St Leger win

By HOTSPUR

Hyperion gained a glorious St Leger victory here today in the colours of his breeder and owner, Lord Derby. The 6-4 favourite won by three lengths, without being pressed, from the Aga Khan's Felicitation (22-1), who gained rapidly on Scarlet Tiger (100-8) to deprive Lord Durham's colt of second place by a neck.

The crowd round were, indeed, already cheering the gallant winner's entry when Lord Derby, hampered by an injured foot, came on the scene, and then they gave the owner, for whom the public have a very real affection, a rousing cheer, followed by more for the worthy trainer, the Hon.George Lambton.

One of the first things Lord Derby did, with the horse still in the enclosure, was to enter the weighing room to thank his jockey, Weston, and have a chat with him. The modest and cool Weston, ever the little man for the big occasion, was able to tell Lord Derby that Hyperion was never off the bit and could be said to have made the whole of the running.

For, though Sans Peine and Raymond kept close company for a long way, the chestnut had pulled his way to the front well before the turn into the long straight had been reached. There was no change after that except among those following.

On came Hyperion, galloping with all that zest and keenness we had seen at Epsom. The winning margin was not so big, but Weston was content to let him stay where he was, showing the way and making the others look so common by comparison.

ENGLISH CLASSICS

2,000 Guineas	Rodosto	R Brethès	9-1
1,000 Guineas	Brown Betty	J Childs	8-1
Derby	Hyperion	T Weston	6-1f
Oaks	Chatelaine	S Wragg	25-1
St Leger	Hyperion	T Weston	6-4f

Liverpool: 8 November

Richards gets his record: 247th winner at Liverpool

By winning the first race, on Golden King (4-11f), at Liverpool yesterday, Gordon Richards broke Fred Archer's 48-year-old record of 246 winners in a single season.

News of the champion jockey's success was telephoned to Buckingham Palace, and a few minutes later Richards received a telegram from the King.

It can now be revealed that up to last Wednesday Richards went around telling his friends that he did not believe he could beat the record. "The luck won't hold," he said, over and over again. His nerves were reaching breaking point. To the public, however, he showed the same outward imperturbability which has never deserted him.

His young wife felt the strain, too. He allowed her to go to his meetings for several days. Still the record escaped his grasp and yesterday he implored her to stay at home.

It was characteristic of the man that his first thought, when he came into the weighing room with the cheers of 15,000 people ringing in his ears, was for his wife at Marlborough. He asked that a telegram should be sent telling her the news.

He looked round at his fellow-jockeys who surrounded him in honest boisterous enthusiasm. His boyish face beamed – the first time probably that Richards had smiled with real happiness for weeks.

Later, after riding another winner, he made perhaps one of the shortest speeches on record to the "talkie" camera. It was just this: "I am delighted to have broken the record and to know that it is all over."

[Later that evening, the humble champion jockey made a nervous broadcast from the Adelphi Hotel, in which he paid tribute to Fred Archer, coincidentally on the 47th anniversary of his death. He presented the whip he was carrying during this historic season to Hotspur of The Daily Telegraph.]

Chepstow: 5 October

Great feat by Richards
Twelve winners in succession

FROM OUR SPECIAL CORRESPONDENT

Gordon Richards, champion jockey and smasher of records, completed a winning sequence today which will probably stand for all time. Riding the winners of the first five races – he was beaten in the sixth on a 3 to 1 on chance – he set up the amazing record of twelve consecutive successes. Here is the "score card":

Tuesday (at Nottingham): Barnby 11 to 2.

Wednesday (at Chepstow): Manner 6-4 on, Brush Past Evens, Miss B 7-4, Arcona 6-4 on, Red Horizon 7-4, Delicia 5 to 4 on.

Thursday (at Chepstow): The Covenanter Evens, Kirrimuir 6-4 on, June Rose 9-4, Montrose 7-4 on, Lady Swift filly Evens.

A great number of people made the journey here specially to back Richards' mounts. One wildly excited backer drawing his winnings for the fourth time loudly exclaimed, "Gordon is the greatest public benefactor the world has ever known." "All we had to do the last two days," said another, "has been to hand our money to the bookmakers, mention Gordon's name and draw our winnings!"

When Richards went past the winning post on Lady Swift filly, his fifth winner of the day, a white-haired man in Tattersall's ring solemnly laid his race-glasses on the ground, took off his hat, and, facing the crowded stand, called for "Three cheers for Gordon!"

The golden spell was broken in the last race of all. Richards rode like a man possessed to keep his mount, Eagleray, in front a hundred yards from home, and the crowd urged him on as one man, but he could finish no nearer than third.

So ended a memorable meeting for Gordon Richards. The last I saw of him was a half-clothed figure dashing from the weighing-room to catch a train to take him to Haydock Park, where he rides several much fancied horses tomorrow.

So alarmed have the bookmakers become over the continued successes of Richards that as a defensive measure they are reducing the odds on offer against his mounts.

Richards has now ridden 217 winners, and there are 39 racing days left in which he can ride the 30 winners needed to beat Archer's 1885 record of 246.

OTHER MAJOR RACES

Arc de Triomphe	Crapom	P Caprioli	22-10
Kentucky Derby	Brokers Tip	D Meade	893-100
Melbourne Cup	Hall Mark	J O'Sullivan	4-1

Richards the record-breaker

1934

6 Mar Golden Miller (6-5f) chalks up his third successive Cheltenham Gold Cup, beating the 5-y-o Avenger (6-1) by 6 lengths, with last year's National winner Kellsboro' Jack (10-1) the same distance away 3rd. Inverse breaks a leg and has to be destroyed.

7 Mar In a day of carnage at Cheltenham, Mr A.C.Heber-Percy, 27, a lieutenant in the Welsh Guards, is killed when his horse falls in the National Hunt Steeplechase – the "amateur riders' Grand National" – while three professional jockeys are hurt and two horses killed. Mr Heber-Percy is the third NH rider to be killed in races this season. (A fourth horse is killed next day.)

21 Jun The Aga Khan's 4-y-o colt Felicitation (9-2), ridden by Gordon Richards, having cantered home yesterday by 10 lengths in the Churchill Stakes, beats French horse Thor II (100-7) by 8 lengths to win the Ascot Gold Cup, with last year's Derby hero Hyperion (8-11f) 1 1/2 lengths back in 3rd, finding the 2 1/2 miles beyond him.

22 Jun The Aga Khan, after a disastrous no-winner Royal Ascot last year, finishes with 7 in 1934 as his second string Theft (20-1) wins the 2-y-o Windsor Castle Stakes, also providing Newmarket trainer Frank Butters with his 9th winner of the meeting.

1 Dec In a speech at the Gimcrack Club dinner, the Aga Khan highlights the shortage of top-class jockeys and suggests ways of encouraging "first-class jockeyship".

Windsor Lad, the Derby winner

CHAMPIONS

Jockey (Flat)	Gordon Richards	212
Jockey (NH)	Gerry Wilson	56
Leading Trainer	Frank Butters	£88,844
Leading Owner	HH Aga Khan	£64,897
Leading Money Winner	Windsor Lad	£24,903

The Derby Epsom: 6 June

Windsor Lad equals Hyperion's record time in the Derby
By HOTSPUR

Windsor Lad, ridden by Charles Smirke and trained by Marcus Marsh, won the Derby yesterday for the Maharaja of Rajpipla. Second, beaten a length, was Lord Woolavington's Easton, ridden by Gordon Richards, and third was the hot favourite, Colombo, in Lord Glanely's colours, a neck further back. The winner covered the mile and a half in 2min 34sec, which equals the record set up by Hyperion a year ago.

Really the only horses that interested the critics and the public generally were the unbeaten Colombo (11-8f), Windsor Lad (15-2), Easton (100-9), Umidwar (7-1) and Tiberius (18-1). Four of them were in the first four positions. Only Umidwar ran below expectations, to be placed seventh.

The story of the race might have had to be written differently had Colombo not been so tucked up close to the rails that he found himself pocketed as they came round Tattenham Corner. Meanwhile, Tiberius had gone to the front, and was being followed into the straight by Windsor Lad. When, soon afterwards, Windsor Lad took the lead from Tiberius, the race was won for the Maharaja's colt. Gordon Richards was able to get a clear run on Easton on the outside, but did not really challenge the leader. Colombo finally came with a storming finish, but it was too late.

The right thing in the circumstances is to give a great measure of credit to Windsor Lad and to say that he won without leaving the slightest doubt as to his stamina, his speed and his courage.

The Maharaja of Rajpipla bought him as a yearling because he was a son of Blandford, whose stock were winning the big races. Blandford, indeed, has now sired three Derby winners – Trigo, Blenheim and Windsor Lad.

We must not forget the big parts played by the trainer and jockey. If only the late Richard Marsh could have been spared to witness the success of a Derby winner trained by his son! The King's late trainer himself saddled the Derby winners Jeddah, Persimmon, Diamond Jubilee and Minoru. The jockey, Charles Smirke, was unable to ride for five years because of the displeasure of the Jockey Club, but he came back last autumn, and has taken his great chance with coolness, fine judgment and skill, and is now re-established in the best sense.

The Grand National Aintree: 23 March

Golden Miller wins the National in record time
By HOTSPUR

The most popular winner of the Grand National Steeplechase for many years is Golden Miller, who, in the colours of Miss Dorothy Paget, went to a smashing victory this afternoon by five lengths, and in the wonderful time of 9min 20 2/5sec, which breaks last year's record by just on eight seconds.

Second was Delaneige, and five lengths further away, in third place, was Thomond II. Forbra, the hero of two years ago, was quite a good fourth, after making a valiant show for four miles or more.

The great thrill developed when the five or six horses forming the leading party swung left-handed after clearing the canal turn and were heading for home for the last time. Forbra (100-8) was in front, jumping splendidly, with Delaneige (100-7), Golden Miller (8-1), Really True (7-1f) and Thomond II (18-1) some lengths behind. The rest of the thirty starters seemed to be definitely out of it. Scarcely had the position been understood than the favourite fell at the fence just beyond Valentine's.

Now there were four left, and they stood up to the end. Forbra began to weaken just before reaching the racecourse, leaving Delaneige and Golden Miller to draw ahead. At the same time one looked back to see Thomond II making up ground.

Coming to the second fence from home there were actually two in it, Delaneige and Golden Miller. Which would win? I looked for the proved fine speed of Golden Miller now to determine the issue, having got so far. Delaneige put up a game response to the limits of his endurance, but Golden Miller came galloping home like the champion he is.

Once over the last fence, his success was never in doubt. Having won the Cheltenham Gold Cup for the third time earlier this month, Golden Miller becomes the first horse to win the National as well.

NATIONAL HUNT

Champion Hurdle	Chenango	D Morgan	4-9f
Cheltenham Gold Cup	Golden Miller	G Wilson	6-5f
Grand National	Golden Miller	G Wilson	8-1

Queen Alexandra Stakes Ascot: 22 June

Brown Jack's sixth victory at Ascot
Crowd's ovation a fitting tribute to "Old Man"

By HOTSPUR

The gates closed on Royal Ascot for another year soon after five o'clock yesterday when the four days' racing festival ended. Brown Jack, for the sixth year in succession, was the bright particular star of the racing on the last day. He and his jockey, Steve Donoghue, who have never been separated during the six anniversaries, were given a great ovation such as Ascot has rarely, if ever, known.

Brown Jack set the great crowd cheering when, halfway up the straight, it was seen there was no danger and that he was really going to win the Queen Alexandra Stakes once again. It was a thrilling spectacle.

There had been ranged against the 6-4 favourite a notable staying mare in Nitsichin (13-2); Harinero (4-1), who was quite seriously fancied because of a belief that he had unlimited stamina; and Loosestrife (100-30), one of the best of long-distance handicappers. Also in the field of nine was Solatium (100-8), who, however, had completely failed when so much fancied for the Ascot Stakes on the opening day, but who in the end ran Brown Jack to two lengths.

The grand old horse and his famous jockey came in for a rapturous reception. We knew there would be a great ovation but what happened exceeded everything that has gone before in the six years' history-making of the horse in regard to the longest distance race of the season.

There was the evidence that at ten years of age Brown Jack can still defy all that are made to take him on. There was the knowledge that there had been nothing like such a string of unbroken victories over as many as six years, and that we may never look on his like again. So everyone, whether they had backed him or not, saluted the "Old Man" as he is affectionately called, in order that a fitting tribute should be paid to him.

Belvoir 'Chase Leicester: 3 December

Reynoldstown a 40 lengths winner

By HOTSPUR

One of the winners at Leicester yesterday, Reynoldstown, was officially declared to have won a steeplechase by as much as 40 lengths. This is by way of variation of the familiar intimation of winning by a "distance", which I always look upon as something rather too long for the judge to measure up in lengths.

Reynoldstown is no newcomer to fame as a jumper. He has won long-distance hurdle races for Major Furlong, who did the right thing when he took the word of the horse's breeder, Mr Richard Ball, whose place is named Reynoldstown, that he was sure he had got a prospect-ive winner in this brown gelding. He was bred right – by My Prince, sire of Easter Hero and Gregalach – had ample size, and the intelli-gence to make a reliable jumper.

No doubt Reynoldstown had very little to do yesterday. Certainly no other gave the impression of being seriously fancied to beat him. The point is that if all goes well he will show himself to be a high-class 'chaser, although I am not certain that he will belong to the Grand National class. That point will doubtless be cleared up before the end of this season. He is "getting on". Such can be truthfully said of a horse that is rising eight years old.

Grand Prix de Paris Longchamp: 24 June

Donoghue wins Grand Prix on chance mount: Horse that was last in the Derby

By HOTSPUR

Steve Donoghue has had many amazing experiences in the course of his full and varied fifty years. Today one of the greatest stokes of luck came his way. He flew over to France on a busman's holiday to watch the race for the Grand Prix de Paris – the most import-ant race of the year on the Continent. He had no mount in the race. But after watching two races from the stands, he was asked to replace an apprentice on Admiral Drake in the Grand Prix – the horse that had finished absolutely last in our Derby a little more than a fortnight ago. And Admiral Drake won!

Donoghue rode a great race. As the field was strung out on the rising ground, Admiral Drake was one of the last two or three. When they reached the short run-in, Gordon Richards had Easton in front. But Donoghue brought Admiral Drake through with a splendid run to pass the Derby runner-up and win by a length and a half.

ENGLISH CLASSICS

2,000 Guineas	Colombo	WR Johnstone	2-7f
1,000 Guineas	Campanula	H Wragg	2-5f
Derby	Windsor Lad	C Smirke	15-2
Oaks	Light Brocade	B Carslake	7-4f
St Leger	Windsor Lad	C Smirke	4-9f

George Thursby Welter Plate Salisbury: 2 July

Another riding success for Prince Aly Khan
Pegomas clever dual winner at the Bibury Club meeting

By HOTSPUR

Prince Aly Khan carried off the amateur riding honours at the Bibury Club meeting which ended yesterday at Salisbury. He was the only rider to have more than one success. Both his wins, with a day's interval between them, were scored on his French purchase, Pegomas. Yesterday the prize won was the George Thursby Welter Plate.

The owner of Pegomas has reminded us again of his cleverness in buying what he wants and what he thinks will improve. He found Pegomas in the stable of his father's late trainer in France, and though he once thought of returning the horse to race in France, that idea has since been dropped. The dual winner was now penalised, so that he had to give as much as 17lb to Sunderland, who, as I anticipated, was very much fancied and started a short-priced favourite.

Pegomas readily gave the weight. He made the whole of the running, and when Jack and Sunderland looked like drawing up to him to challenge, Prince Aly had no more to do than shake him up to come away for another readily gained win.

OTHER MAJOR RACES

Arc de Triomphe	Brantôme	C Bouillon	21-20f
Kentucky Derby	Cavalcade	M Garner	6-4f
Melbourne Cup	Peter Pan	D Munro	14-1

1935

8 Jun Omaha wins the Belmont Stakes to clinch the American Triple Crown, ridden again by Willie Saunders.

10 Jun Harry Beasley, who trained and rode Come Away to victory in the 1891

Grand National and one of four famous Irish brothers, amateur riders of the late 1800s, rides his last race at the age of nearly 83, finishing unplaced on Mollie at Baldoyle (Flat) in the Corinthian Plate.

10 Sep Freddie Fox is injured in a fall at Doncaster and will miss tomorrow's St Leger and the chance to gain the Triple Crown on hot favourite Barham. The ride goes to Charlie Smirke.

Major Noel Furlong leads in the winner

The Grand National Aintree: 29 March

Reynoldstown's family triumph in Grand National

Golden Miller refuses and throws his jockey: Thomond II third again

By HOTSPUR

The story of the Grand National to-day is the story of the eclipse of the favourites. Golden Miller, who started at 2 to 1, went out first time round at the fence after Valentine's Brook, and Thomond II (9-2) finished third, beaten three lengths and eight lengths by Reynoldstown (22-1) and Blue Prince (40-1).

I will deal first with Golden Miller. He lay well up in the first half-mile, and then, when Castle Irwell took a clear lead after jumping Becher's, Wilson took him into second place. He was then jumping with his usual ease and appeared to be going well. He cleared the plain fence after the Canal turn and the more formidable Valentine's, but at the fence after that, according to Wilson, he stuck his toes in,

made no effort to jump and threw his jockey over his head.

At the fence before Becher's Mr Furlong decided to push Reynoldstown along, and he took up the running, followed by Thomond II. There was casualty after casualty at the succeeding fences, and coming on to the racecourse the only effective horses in the race were the three that I selected to be first, second and third – Thomond II, Reynoldstown, and Blue Prince.

Reynoldstown jumped the last fence in front, but Blue Prince was gaining ground, and headed Thomond II. But he could not quite get to Reynoldstown, who won with something in hand and knocked one-fifth of a second off the record set by Golden

Miller last year.

It was probably the most striking family success that has ever been gained in the Grand National. The winning owner, Major Noel Furlong, an Irishman who left County Cork some years ago and settled at Skeffington Hall, in Leicestershire, trains Reynoldstown and a few other horses there with the help of his wife. Reynoldstown was ridden by their son, Mr Frank Furlong, a subaltern of the 9th Lancers. He finished second to Kellsboro' Jack on his father's horse, Really True, two years ago, rode him again last year, but to-day was on their "second string".

Cheltenham Gold Cup: 14 March

Golden Miller wins in record time

Thomond II gallant second in race for Gold Cup

By HOTSPUR

It was Golden Miller's day here today in the widest sense. Miss Paget's remarkable horse won his fourth Cheltenham Gold Cup, and won it in the record time of 6min 30sec by three-parts of a length from Thomond II. And he won it amid scenes the like of which have never been seen on this course since the National Hunt meeting was established at Cheltenham.

Golden Miller (1-2f) is always a draw, even if he has nothing to run against. The presence of a formidable rival like Thomond II (5-2) made the race doubly attractive. Miss Paget, who has been in Germany since last summer, came by aeroplane across the Channel, stopped for the necessary formalities at Croydon, and flew to the course, where she arrived half an hour before the Gold Cup, to be greeted by her father, Lord Queenborough.

It was a moot point which horse would be in front, but Fawcus had no doubts on the matter. He sent Southern Hero ahead at once, and he settled down in front followed by Thomond II and Golden Miller.

It was at the third fence from home that Southern

Hero shot his bolt. Golden Miller then took a slight lead of Thomond II, and the crowd, now hushed, prepared themselves for a great finish.

Over the last fence but one they raced, with Golden Miller still holding to his slight lead and under no pressure from Wilson, who was sitting still and leaving it all to his horse. Coming to the last fence, Speck was more active. He drew his whip and pushed Thomond II. The response was the sort that is always expected from this courageous little horse.

Golden Miller had not yet won. Thomond II landed over the last fence less than a length behind, and then began a terrific race between them. But Golden Miller was always holding his rival and, without having to be put under severe pressure, he won amid a tornado of enthusiasm. Kellsboro' Jack (100-7) ran on to beat Avenger (20-1) for third place, with Southern Hero (20-1) last of the five runners.

Now comes the problem of the Grand National, in which Golden Miller has to give Thomond II 8lb. I will only say this at present, that he did not give Mr Whitney's horse an 8lb beating today.

NATIONAL HUNT			
Champion Hurdle	Lion Courage	G Wilson	100-8
Cheltenham Gold Cup	Golden Miller	G Wilson	1-2f
Grand National	Reynoldstown	Mr F Furlong	22-1

The regrettable thing of the race was the default of Golden Miller. Horses do astonishing things at times, and this has been Golden Miller's one lapse in a highly spectacular career. As he is none the worse and has hardly had a race, it may be decided tomorrow morning to start him in the Champion 'Chase.

[Starting evens favourite in the Champion 'Chase, Golden Miller sensationally made another blunder, hitting the relatively easy first fence hard and putting Wilson down, but again not falling himself. Miss Paget blamed Basil Briscoe for the whole débâcle and removed all her horses from his yard.]

Bahram passes the post with two lengths to spare

ENGLISH CLASSICS

2,000 Guineas	Bahram	F Fox	7-2
1,000 Guineas	Mesa	WR Johnstone	8-1
Derby	Bahram	F Fox	5-4f
Oaks	Quashed	H Jelliss	33-1
St Leger	Bahram	C Smirke	4-11f

The Derby Epsom: 5 June

Bahram's flawless Derby triumph
By HOTSPUR

The Derby is over, and Bahram is still unbeaten. The Aga Khan's colt, the 5-4 favourite, won his second and greatest classic race yesterday by two lengths and half a length from Sir Abe Bailey's Robin Goodfellow (50-1), and Lord Astor's Field Trial (9-1).

These are the facts and the figures, but they give no adequate impression of the ease with which Bahram won. In the field that he raced against he was Olympian – unchallenged and unchallengeable.

One might say, and probably with some truth, that it was a miscellaneous field, but the best way to judge a good colt is not by the standard of what he beats but by the style in which he wins. And Bahram's manner of winning the Derby of 1935 was without flaw.

At any time his jockey wished Bahram could have gone to the front, and when Fox decided that it was time to give the others a taste of his mount's mettle, the Derby was won.

Actually, it was about a quarter of a mile from the winning-post when Bahram took the lead from Field Trial. When he did so Lord Astor's colt could not live with him, nor had Robin Goodfellow, excellent race as this outsider ran, any chance of reaching him.

When Fox had weighed-in after riding the winner, he had, like the Needy Knife-grinder, "no story" to tell. For him it was roses all the way. He had never been out of the first half-dozen. He made every move how and when he wished, and won without having to ask the colt for an extra effort.

It is the second time the Aga Khan has won the Derby, but this is a sweeter victory than that of Blenheim, for he bred Bahram himself at his stud in Co.Kildare. The Aga Khan's great hope now is that Bahram will never be beaten, and that he will be numbered with Ormonde among the immortal winners of the Derby.

Irish Derby The Curragh: 26 June

Donoghue's Irish Derby
By HOTSPUR

When Steve Donoghue won the Irish Derby yesterday on Sir Victor Sassoon's Museum it must have brought back many memories to him, for a quarter of a century ago, after a period of hardship in France searching the small meetings at Marseilles and around the Midi for chance rides, he landed in Ireland, poor and unknown, in the hope of getting some of the riding that was denied to him in England.

It was in Ireland that he first made his reputation, and when he came back to England and rode for the Chattis Hill stable he was an established jockey. It is a long time now since he rode a winner at The Curragh, and

the Irish people, who claim him as one of their own, although he was born in Warrington, gave him a tremendous reception.

Museum, who belongs to Sir Victor Sassoon, is the colt that started at 100 to 1 when he won the Irish Two Thousand. Sir Victor keeps a few mares in Ireland, and is in the habit of sending some of the foals from his stud at Newmarket to be kept there for a time.

Museum, who started at 100 to 8, was one of four of the eight starters trained by J.T.Rogers at The Curragh. Rogers supplied the favourite in Mr R.J.Duggan's filly, Smokeless, who was a 5 to 4 chance. She finished third.

The Oaks Epsom: 7 June

Lord Stanley wins the Oaks with 33 to 1 chance Quashed
Favourite Mesa is third
By HOTSPUR

Lord Stanley's filly Quashed (33-1) won the Oaks yesterday by a short head and a length from Ankaret (100-6) and Mesa (5-4f). Lord Derby was hoping to win the Oaks with Coronal (7-2), who finished fifth. But what the fates took away with one sweep they gave back with another, for it was his son's filly who got up on the post to snatch the spoils from Ankaret. The race for the Derby was humdrum. This contest for the Oaks was full of drama.

It was the first success Lord Stanley has gained in a classic race. Indeed, his adventures in ownership have been strictly limited. Quashed he has on lease from her breeder, Lady Barbara Smith, to whom her dam, that very great mare Verdict, who is not in the Stud book, was bequeathed by her father, Lord Coventry.

Quashed had never run in public up to the form she showed yesterday, and she had never shown her trainer, Colledge Leader, at home what she showed in the race.

CHAMPIONS

Jockey (Flat)	Gordon Richards	210
Jockey (NH)	Gerry Wilson	73
Leading Trainer	Frank Butters	£59,687
Leading Owner	HH Aga Khan	£49,201
Leading Money Winner	Bahram	£31,328

St Leger Doncaster: 11 September

Triple Crown triumph for Bahram
Retiring unbeaten after St Leger victory
By HOTSPUR

No smoother or more effortless victory has ever been gained in the St Leger than that of this afternoon by the favourite, Bahram. There was never a thrill, never a moment of suspense. Everything worked like a piece of machinery.

Bahram (4-11f) dominated the situation throughout, from the moment he jumped off until he had passed the judge, five lengths in front of Solar Ray (100-6), who was again three lengths in front of Buckleigh (25-1). It was the apex, as it was the end, of the racing career of a remarkable colt who has never been beaten and can now retire from the Turf as the first Triple Crown winner since Rock Sand 32 years ago.

I have said that everything went smoothly – everything, that is, except the regrettable accident to F.Fox yesterday, which deprived him of the distinction of having ridden Bahram in the three classic races which he has won. Smirke, however, rode the colt admirably, and this jockey has now the distinction of having ridden the winner of the St Leger in two consecutive years.

The Aga Khan, who is in Geneva, was not present to see his horse run, but there is no likelihood of his changing his intention to retire him now, and Bahram will go to the stud at a fee of 500 guineas, at which he is full for the next three years.

OTHER MAJOR RACES

Arc de Triomphe	Samos	W Sibbritt	20-1
Kentucky Derby	Omaha	W Saunders	4-1
Melbourne Cup	Marabou	K Voitre	9-2f

1936

16 Jun Rhodes Scholar *(pictured below being led in by his owner Lord Astor)*, having missed the Derby because hard ground prevented his being properly trained, shows what might have been by beating the speedy Derby winner Mahmoud by 5 lengths in the St James's Palace Stakes (1m) at Royal Ascot.

14 Oct Near Relation, at 22-1 the same price as last year, is within a neck of becoming the first horse to win the greatest long-distance handicap of the season, the Cesarewitch, twice in succession, beaten by the 5-y-o grey gelding Fet (10-1), carrying 6st-12, who only last August Bank Holiday was bought in for 200gns after winning a seller.

CHAMPIONS

Jockey (Flat)	Gordon Richards	177
Jockey (NH)	Gerry Wilson	57
Leading Trainer	J Lawson	£61,775
Leading Owner	Lord Astor	£38,131
Leading Money Winner	Rhodes Scholar	£12,466

The Grand National: 27 March

Reynoldstown triumphs again

Davy Jones runs out at last fence when leading: Golden Miller down at first jump

By HOTSPUR

Amid tumultuous scenes of enthusiasm, Reynoldstown (10-1) won the Grand National this afternoon for the second year in succession, and equalled a record that has stood for 66 years.

It was as thrilling a National as has ever been seen. At the first fence, Golden Miller (5-1) jumped on to a fallen horse and came down. Then the favourite, Avenger, who started at 100 to 30, fell at the first fence in the country when they were going round the second time. He broke his neck. And as a climax to all this drama, a tubed horse, Davy Jones (100-1), after making all the running, ran out when still leading at the last fence of all.

I have never seen such a thing in the Grand National as the disappearance of Davy Jones when the only danger that threatened him was from Reynoldstown, who was lying about two lengths behind him. Davy Jones was a useful horse on the flat once, but had to be tubed, and had been running in selling plates for the Winchester trainer Rayson. Lord Mildmay of Flete wanted a horse for his son, the Hon.Anthony Mildmay, to ride in the Grand National, so he bought Davy Jones a few months ago.

To-day the horse set off in front and when they were going past the stands the second time he was still in front and going strongly. We had expected to see him disappear when they went off into the country again – but not so. He came on the racecourse again leading and in such a strong position that if he stood up he had every chance of beating Reynoldstown.

When they came to the second last fence, Davy Jones reached for it. The reins slipped through Mr Mildmay's hands, the buckle broke, and, with his rider having no means of controlling him, the horse, when they approached the last jump, ducked away to the right and ran out.

I have not even read of such a thing happening before. As for a horse running out of the National when he came to the last fence with the lead, it must surely be one of the most unhappy occurrences in the history of the race. It is a delicate point whether Davy Jones would have won. He was certainly going strongly and had the advantage, but Reynoldstown was also going well. Between them it would assuredly have been a great race.

And now for Golden Miller. His jockey, E.Williams, had set off towards the outside of the field and rose boldly at the first fence. There was a gasp from the crowd when he was missing as the field went on. The disaster was the fault of the French runner, Oeil de Boeuf, who had fallen where he landed, and there is no blame attaching to Miss Paget's horse. Williams remounted and set off in pursuit. Golden Miller jumped 10 fences well, but when he came to the open ditch, that is the second after Valentine's, three horses had fallen in it. He was baulked and pulled up. Thus ended his part in the race. He had provided still another sensation.

Cheltenham Gold Cup: 12 March

Fifth successive Gold Cup win for Golden Miller – with new jockey riding

By HOTSPUR

Golden Miller vindicated himself this afternoon by a glorious victory in the Cheltenham Gold Cup, and for the fifth year in succession brought the trophy to Miss Paget, a record that may never be beaten, unless he beats it himself by winning again next season. He finished a dozen lengths in front of Royal Mail.

Everything was in his favour except, perhaps, the ground, which had been a good deal cut into. The opposition was as weak as, or weaker than, he has ever faced in this event. He did nothing better than he had done before. His jumping, if not orthodox – and such as would almost inevitably bring him to grief at Liverpool – was a delight to watch, for he flicked over each fence, gaining ground every time and giving his new jockey, Evan Williams, something to do to keep him under restraint.

When he came away up the hill alone there was a hurricane of cheering, for he is still the most popular steeplechaser in training. There had been strong hostility displayed in the betting towards his chance, however, for he opened at evens and at the close was 21 to 20 against – a remarkably good price, considering that there was only one serious lapse on the part of the horse himself to be forgiven, his refusal at Newbury. The runner-up, Royal Mail, was 5-1 joint second favourite and Kellsboro' Jack (10-1) finished third, two lengths further back.

NATIONAL HUNT

Champion Hurdle	Victor Norman	H Nicholson	4-1
Cheltenham Gold Cup	Golden Miller	E Williams	21-20f
Grand National	Reynoldstown	Mr F Walwyn	10-1

The Derby Epsom: 27 May

Aga Khan's third Derby triumph
Mahmoud beats Taj Akbar in record time
By HOTSPUR

For the second year in succession and the third time in seven years, the Aga Khan has won the Derby. Not only did his grey colt, Mahmoud (100-8), win it yesterday, but his Taj Akbar (6-1) was second.

Mahmoud beat his stable-companion with consummate ease by three lengths and in the record time of 2min 33 4/5sec, knocking one-fifth of a second off the new record. His performance was an astonishing one, for when Thankerton (33-1), who eventually finished third, three-parts of a length behind Taj Akbar, shot away down the hill with a long lead, he must have been eight to ten lengths in front of the winner. Yet so great was the speed shown by Mahmoud after making the turn, that he caught the Northern colt two furlongs out and then ran right away from him.

Smirke, his jockey, who now has the enviable record of having ridden two

winners of the Derby and two of the St Leger in the last three years, said to me after the race that Mahmoud was so full of running he could have gone another two furlongs at least without being troubled. And this is the colt that so many people had put down as unlikely to stay the distance!

Indeed, an original idea was to run him for the Two Thousand (in which he finished second to yesterday's 5-1 favourite Pay Up), miss the Derby with him, and keep him for one of the valuable mile races at Ascot.

Steve Donoghue, who rode Mahmoud in the Guineas, gave his owner's son Prince Aly Khan, and the trainer, Frank Butters, his opinion that the colt stayed well and that he ought to run at Epsom. As Donoghue was not asked to ride him in the Derby, he was naturally entitled to be registering vexation after the race yesterday.

ENGLISH CLASSICS

2,000 Guineas	Pay Up	R Dick	11-2
1,000 Guineas	Tide-way	R Perryman	100-30
Derby	Mahmoud	C Smirke	100-8
Oaks	Lovely Rosa	T Weston	33-1
St Leger	Boswell	P Beasley	20-1

6 July

French mass attack on English prizes:
Plans to send stables en bloc to this country
By HOTSPUR

It is likely that, unless there is a rapid improvement in internal conditions in France, there will be a further large influx of French horses into this country. I hear of several prominent French owners who are making plans to send their stables en bloc to England, not with any fixed idea of racing permanently here, but to run their horses out in their races and then try to sell them on their English form.

These plans show what a gloomy view of the future of French racing is taken by those immediately concerned with it. It has been languishing for some time past, and the outlook grows darker instead of brighter.

It was a sign of the times when the Aga Khan, who has been a vendor in Normandy for some years, sent a few of his surplus yearlings to be sold at Newmarket last year, and sent them all there for disposal last week.

If racing were going through a bad time in England, this French competition in our bloodstock market would be having a serious effect, and possibly some people would be demanding a quota. But fortunately racing is so prosperous in England at the present time, and the bloodstock market is so strong and so resilient, that we have been able to absorb all the importations without prices here having been affected.

A close Anglo-American finish

Ascot Gold Cup: 18 June

Quashed's Gold Cup triumph
American champion beaten by short head
By HOTSPUR

In as great a struggle as has ever been seen for the Ascot Gold Cup, the English filly Quashed (3-1), in the colours of Lord Stanley, yesterday beat the American challenger Omaha (11-8f) by a short head.

Knowing the reputations and the performances of this very good filly and this very good colt, one had anticipated a struggle that would be epic, and that might occupy for ever a supreme place in the records of International racing. And it was epic, magnificent, for the pair had drawn clear away after the turn into the straight – three furlongs from the winning-post.

The others might not have been there, so hopelessly outclassed were they. The pair locked together and the crowd watched the contest with a breathless interest, for until the judge gave his decision no one could tell which had won. I venture the opinion that, had not Omaha

hung just a little as they were close home, the verdict might have been a dead-heat.

As it was, there could not have been a more satisfactory result. Omaha has proved himself a great colt, and has entirely vindicated the judgement of his owner in deciding to pit him against the best that England could produce. And the Cup has been kept in the country, so that there is no loss of prestige to English breeding.

While giving every credit to Quashed, I will venture to say that she may have been a little lucky to have found the American colt on a day that may not have been his best.

The three French horses in the field were outclassed, Bokbul (100-6) doing best by finishing third. But he was beaten off by five lengths, and none of them, either French or English, was ever able to get near enough to challenge the leading pair.

Eclipse Stakes Sandown Park: 16 July

Lord Astor wins his fifth Eclipse
Rhodes Scholar first – the rest nowhere
By HOTSPUR

The Eclipse Stakes yesterday was most easily won by Lord Astor's Rhodes Scholar (8-11f), who beat two of his own age, His Grace (100-7) and Fairey (8-1), by six lengths and four lengths. It was a smashing performance by the colt that had beaten the Derby winner Mahmoud so easily at Ascot, and Rhodes Scholar is now a short-priced favourite for the St Leger.

The outstanding superiority of Rhodes Scholar to the eight others made the race seem a little tame. His pace-

maker, Portfolio, went into the lead at once, and Rhodes Scholar settled down second. When they had come about a furlong in the straight, R.Dick took him to the front and he just strolled home.

Had Rhodes Scholar been able to run for the Derby, it is not too certain that a colt of his conformation would have come down the hill well.

[Rhodes Scholar (6-4f) did not stay the St Leger trip, the race being won by outsider Boswell, with Mahmoud (5-1) third.]

OTHER MAJOR RACES

Arc de Triomphe	Corrida	EC Elliott	4-5f
Kentucky Derby	Bold Venture	I Hanford	205-10
Melbourne Cup	Wotan	O Phillips	100-1

1937

11 Mar Rain and snow causes the abandonment of the already once postponed National Hunt festival and so denies Golden Miller the chance to make it six Cheltenham Gold Cups in succession, but he is backed down to 100-12 favouritism for next week's National.

9 May War Admiral (5-2f), after giving trouble and delaying the start 4 minutes, leads all the way to win the Kentucky Derby by 2 lengths from Pompoon (15-2). [He goes on to become the 4th horse to achieve the US Triple Crown.]

4 Jun Exhibitionnist is again faster than the colts when she adds the Oaks to her 1,000 Guineas victory, this time beating the time of her Derby-winning half-brother (Solario was their sire) Mid-day Sun by 3/5sec. It is Steve Donoghue's 14th Classic victory, having earlier won the "1,000" for the first time, his first Classic success for 12 years.

16 Jun The day's takings on the Tote at Royal Ascot reach a new record, £144,029, largely owing to the 33-runner Royal Hunt Cup, won by the 4-y-o colt Fairplay (18-1).

23 Jun Young Irish jockey Peter Maher guides former French horse Nectar II (100-8) to a short-head victory in the Northumberland Plate at Newcastle to continue his extraordinary run of successes in big handicaps this season, having won the Victoria Cup at Hurst Park, the Chester Cup, the Penrhyn Cup, also at Hurst Park, the Queen Elizabeth Cup (dead-heat) at Lingfield, and the Royal Hunt Cup and Bessborough Stakes at Ascot last week.

Champion Hurdle Cup Cheltenham: 9 March

Free Fare proves himself champion in big hurdle race at Cheltenham

By HOTSPUR

Mr Ben Warner's nine-year-old gelding Free Fare (2-1f), proved himself a real champion here to-day when he won the Champion Hurdle Challenge Cup in storming fashion.

At the finish he led by two lengths from Our Hope(100-8), who finished very fast to beat Menton (11-2) on the post for second place, with Citadel (7-2) inches behind Menton.

The weather for the first day of the National Hunt meeting was fine and not particularly cold. The going had dried up well and was in very much better condition than might have been expected. There was, however, not nearly so large a crowd as is usually associated with Champion Cup day.

As is his custom, Victor Norman (9-2) tried to make the running in the big race of the afternoon, but Menton kept with him. They were still in front approaching the bend into the straight, but shortly afterwards Free Fare was sent into the lead and jumped the last hurdles with his race won.

CHAMPIONS

Jockey (Flat)	Gordon Richards	214
Jockey (NH)	Gerry Wilson	45
Leading Trainer	Cecil Boyd-Rochfort	£61,212
Leading Owner	HH Aga Khan	£30,655
Leading Money Winner	Mid-day Sun	£15,273

NATIONAL HUNT

Champion Hurdle	Free Fare	G Pellerin	2-1f
Cheltenham Gold Cup	No race (snow)		
Grand National	Royal Mail	E Williams	100-6

Poule d'Essai des Poulains Longchamp: 16 May

Le Ksar beaten in French 2,000 Guineas

By HOTSPUR

The Derby situation, more intriguing than ever after last week's racing at Newmarket, was further complicated yesterday when the Two Thousand Guineas winner, Le Ksar, was beaten in the Poule d'Essai des Poulains, the French equivalent to our "Two Thousand", at Longchamp.

There were only four runners, and Drap d'Or, owned by M Jean Pratt, took the lead at the start, followed by Le Ksar. The former was several lengths in front entering the straight, and although Le Ksar made up ground, he was still a length behind when the winning-post was reached.

The French Two Thousand is run over 1,600 metres, approximately a mile. The result bears out my contention that Le Ksar was as fit as hands could make him at Newmarket last month, and I shall be surprised if his price at the call-over tomorrow does not lengthen.

ENGLISH CLASSICS

2,000 Guineas	Le Ksar	CH Semblat	20-1
1,000 Guineas	Exhibitionnist	S Donoghue	10-1
Derby	Mid-day Sun	M Beary	100-7
Oaks	Exhibitionnist	S Donoghue	3-1f
St Leger	Chulmleigh	G Richards	18-1

OTHER MAJOR RACES

Arc de Triomphe	Corrida	EC Elliott	1-1f
Kentucky Derby	War Admiral	C Kurtsinger	5-2f
Melbourne Cup	The Trump	A Reed	11-2cf

The Grand National Aintree: 19 March

Royal Mail's "National" triumph

Golden Miller refuses at same fence again

By HOTSPUR

Another Grand National has gone to Ivor Anthony's famous Wroughton stable. Mr H.Lloyd Thomas's eight-year-old gelding Royal Mail (100-6), ridden by Evan Williams, won the centenary race here this afternoon by three lengths from the mare Cooleen (33-1), with another mare, Pucka Belle (100-6), a further 10 lengths away third.

Golden Miller, who was favourite at 8 to 1, once more failed. He jumped nine fences and then refused at the first after Valentine's – the same one he refused at two years ago when starting at 2 to 1, the hottest favourite on record.

Only seven of the 33 starters completed the course. The much fancied Ego (10-1) was fourth, Crown Prince (50-1) fifth, Pencraik (25-1) sixth and Don Bradman (100-8), who was remounted after falling, came in last. Four of the seven finishers were ridden by amateurs.

My faith in Royal Mail never wavered and his victory is most gratifying. There was no last-minute sensation. The parade passed off without incident, and I thought the three best movers on the way to the post were Golden Miller who strode out magnificently, Royal Mail and Milk Punch.

Don Bradman, usually a safe jumper, was knocked over at the first jump. He was remounted and finished the course without ever having a chance of success. Golden Miller and Ready Cash were soon leading the field, but the favourite then showed his dislike for Aintree, refusing just as Royal Mail and Pucka Belle were moving up to the leaders. Ready Cash also disappeared, and there were not many of the field standing up at the end of the first circuit.

Going to Becher's the second time round, Royal Mail was in grave danger of interference from loose horses, and Williams cleverly avoided trouble. Royal Mail led round the canal turn, and soon afterwards it was obvious that he had a real chance except for a fall. He held on grimly, however, to beat the unlucky Cooleen, who had nearly been savaged by the riderless Drim.

Before this, Cooleen had made a sensational leap, jumping Dawmar as well as a fence. Dawmar had tried to refuse and was left half over the obstacle. Cooleen was unable to check herself and cleared everything that was in her way. She was showing no signs of weakening in the run home.

Mid-day Sun finishes ahead of the strung-out field

The Derby Epsom: 2 June

Woman makes history in Derby: Mrs G.B.Miller's Mid-day Sun beats 100 to 1 chance

By HOTSPUR

For the first time in the history of the race, that is since 1780, a woman has won the Derby. By a length and a half, Mrs G.B.Miller's colt Mid-day Sun (100-7) beat a 100 to 1 chance, Sandsprite, also owned by a woman (Mrs F. Nagle), with the Aga Khan's Le Grand Duc (100-9) third, a further length and a half back.

Thus the Coronation Derby made history with a vengeance. Mrs Miller seldom goes racing and is a comparative newcomer to the Turf. She owns Mid-day Sun in partnership with her mother, Mrs Talbot. Mrs Miller has owned only four racehorses, one of the other three being Ankaret, who finished second to Quashed in the Oaks of 1935. She was left a fortune the previous year by her great uncle, Colonel Brocklehurst, a silk manufacturer of Macclesfield.

Michael Beary, who rode Mid-day Sun, had never won the Derby before, though he was unlucky not to have done so, twice choosing the wrong horse. It was the first classic winner for Fred Butters, the Kingsclere trainer and younger brother of Frank Butters, who saddled Le Grand Duc.

Scarlet Plume was not too well away, but Sandsprite and Snowfall lost even more ground than he did. As the field approached the top of the hill leading down to Tattenham Corner, Sandsprite was last of all, but he made up a lot of ground coming down the hill.

For a moment it looked as if Goya II and Le Grand Duc would fight out the finish, but neither could withstand the challenge of Sandsprite, who himself was unable to hold off the perfectly timed run of Michael Beary on Mid-day Sun.

There was no excuse for the more fancied colts like 7-1 joint favourites Cash Book and Perifox, who came fourth, and Le Ksar (9-1), or for the filly Gainsborough Lass (100-7).

Mid-day Sun won the Free Handicap at Newmarket in April from Exhibitionnist, who went on to win the One Thousand Guineas. He was afterwards third in the Two Thousand, and then won the Derby Trial Stakes at Lingfield.

The Oaks Epsom: 4 June

Steve Donoghue's triumph in Oaks: Exhibitionnist wins by three lengths

By HOTSPUR

The King and Queen saw the race for the Oaks at Epsom yesterday, when Sir Victor Sassoon's filly Exhibitionnist, ridden by Steve Donoghue, gained an easy victory. The most popular jockey of all time was given a great reception on his return to the unsaddling enclosure. It was the first occasion in his long career that he had won this popular classic at Epsom – he was successful in the war-time substitute at Newmarket on My Dear in 1918.

Donoghue, who is in his 53rd year, is riding as well as ever. He won the One Thousand Guineas on Exhibitionnist – Sir Victor Sassoon's first classic success – and is enjoying a wonderful last season in the saddle.

Unless he changes his plans – and it will be a big wrench for him to give up riding – Donoghue intends to take up training next year. He has been riding for more than 30 years and included in his 14 classic victories are six Derby winners.

The winner, who started as 3-1 favourite, is trained at Manton by J.Lawson, who saddled Lord Astor's Penny-comequick when she won the Oaks in 1929.

There was never any doubt about Exhibitionnist's victory. As soon as the field settled down, she was second to Burlington Lass, and they increased their lead approaching Tattenham Corner. Donoghue sent his mount to the front immediately on reaching the straight.

From that point there was no danger, and the roar of "Come on, Steve" rivalled that of one of the biggest Yorkshire crowds. Steve "came on" to such good purpose that he had three lengths to spare passing the post from the rank outsider Sweet Content (33-1), who showed great improvement on her One Thousand running. Sculpture (20-1), Lord Astor's second string, was beaten only a head for second place.

Final "Welter" Plate Manchester: 27 November

Steve chose the wrong horse
Last race drama at Manchester

By WATCHMAN

Steve Donoghue had set his heart on winding up his career as a jockey with a winning ride. In the Final Plate at Manchester he had been offered the mount on Pegomas, the gelding who won the corresponding race last season, when Highlander had been a bad third. On that occasion the two horses were at even weights, whereas Highlander was receiving 10lb on Saturday.

This caused Steve to suppose that Lord Derby's gelding had the better chance of success. Lord Derby's jockey, Dick Perryman, kindly soul that he is, said he would gladly stand aside to help Donoghue ride his last winner.

And so all was fixed up. Donoghue rode out happily. The bookmakers asked odds (4-5) about his mount, and the great crowd prepared to give Steve a tumultuous reception.

Then came the anti-climax. Highlander was again beaten into third place by Pegomas. Donoghue had him beautifully balanced for his culminating run, and the familiar shout "Come on, Steve!" went up from all the enclosures. But Highlander's effort did not suffice to get him on terms with the leader, and a few yards from the post Donoghue drew rein, and lost second place.

It was characteristic of Donoghue that while intensely anxious to win he refrained from giving Highlander a punishing race. He will always be remembered as a great jockey who was never hard on his horses. It was the irony of fate that he should have chosen the wrong horse for his last mount, and his face was a study in seriousness as he rode into the unsaddling enclosure.

Never mind, Steve. The incident was comparatively unimportant and will soon fade into insignificance compared with the great achievements of a marvellous riding career.

Opinions will naturally differ as to the best races ever ridden by Donoghue. I have seen him win nearly all his chief races, and my view is that his achievement on Humorist in the Derby was the best example of dashing horsemanship given by him or by any other jockey.

1938

15 Jun Guineas and Oaks winner Rockfel,

6-4 favourite for the Coronation Stakes (1m) for 3-y-o fillies at Royal Ascot, is unplaced, failing to give a stone all round, the race going to Solar Flower (100-9), who was 3rd behind Rockfel in both Classics.

1 Nov The 5-y-o late developer Seabiscuit

(11-5), leading money-winner in the US last year, takes on War Admiral (1-4), last year's US Triple Crown winner, in a match – the Pimlico Special – at Pimlico, Baltimore, and reverses their usual roles by leading all the way to inflict a rare defeat on the champion son of Man O'War by 4 lengths.

2 Nov Champion steeplechase jockey Gerald Wilson, on Prince Memnon, a chance ride in the last race of the day, the Cowley Hurdle, at Cheltenham, his home course, falls and breaks two ribs, causing him to miss tonight's dinner being given in his honour by the directors of the Cheltenham Steeplechase Co.

CHAMPIONS

Jockey (Flat)	Gordon Richards	206
Jockey (NH)	Gerry Wilson	59
Leading Trainer	Cecil Boyd-Rochfort	£51,350
Leading Owner	Lord Derby	£34,434
Leading Money Winner	Rockfel	£22,094

Cheltenham Gold Cup: 10 March

Golden Miller second in the Gold Cup: Beaten by Morse Code after gallant effort to record sixth win

By HOTSPUR

Golden Miller (7-4f) made a great effort to win his sixth Gold Cup here this afternoon, but found one too good for him in Morse Code (13-2) who, if the book of form is worth anything, did not seem to have much chance of beating Miss Dorothy Paget's grand old horse – or Airgead Sios (7-2) or Macaulay (3-1).

It is sad to have to write that a great horse is not so good as he was, but I fear Golden Miller, who will always be regarded with affection by everyone interested in racing, has passed his best. His indomitable spirit was evident as usual, but where the spirit was willing the flesh was weak. When I say weak I mean not quite strong enough, for Golden Miller met his Waterloo gallantly.

Airgead Sios, as is his custom, made the running. Golden Miller joined him on the bend approaching the straight, and Morse Code moved up on the outside, Southern Hero being beaten and Red Hillman tailed off. At the second last fence Golden Miller, Airgead Sios and Morse Code jumped almost together, Airgead Sios blundering and putting himself out of the race to all intents and purposes.

As the two leaders came to the last fence, the huge crowd, obviously longing to cheer home their old champion, Golden Miller, became almost silent when it was apparent that Morse Code had his measure. And so it proved, Golden Miller, gallantly as he fought on, having to admit defeat by a couple of lengths, with Macaulay three lengths behind him.

NATIONAL HUNT

Champion Hurdle	Our Hope	Capt R Harding	5-1
Cheltenham Gold Cup	Morse Code	D Morgan	13-2
Grand National	Battleship	B Hobbs	40-1

ENGLISH CLASSICS

2,000 Guineas	Pasch	G Richards	5-2f
1,000 Guineas	Rockfel	S Wragg	8-1
Derby	Bois Roussel	EC Elliott	20-1
Oaks	Rockfel	H Wragg	3-1f
St Leger	Scottish Union	B Carslake	7-1

OTHER MAJOR RACES

Arc de Triomphe	Eclair au Chocolat	C Bouillon	26-10
Kentucky Derby	Lawrin	E Arcaro	86-10
Melbourne Cup	Catalogue	F Shean	25-1

The Grand National Aintree: 25 March

17-year-old boy's National triumph at Aintree

Bruce Hobbs' great riding on Battleship to beat Royal Danieli by head in terrific finish

By HOTSPUR

To an American, Mrs Marion Scott, fell the distinction of owning the winner of the Grand National here this afternoon. Her eleven-year-old horse Battleship gained a thrilling victory by a head from the Irish gelding Royal Danieli. Another Irishman, Workman, was third, and altogether 13 of the 36 starters completed the course.

Battleship, winner of the American Grand National four years ago, was ridden by the 17-year-old Bruce Hobbs, and is trained by his father, Reg, at Lambourn. Mrs Scott is a member of the syndicate which bought Blenheim from the Aga Khan for £50,000.

Battleship started at 40 to 1, Royal Danieli at 18 to 1 and Workman at 28 to 1, all the best fancied horses, therefore, failing to reach the first three. Nevertheless, it was a great race and never have I seen a better or a closer finish.

Trouble started early in the race, but Airgead Sios was jumping in front in his usual fluent manner before hitting the top of the fence after Valentine's, and that was the end of him. This left Royal Danieli in the lead. Royal Mail made a mistake at the famous "chair" fence, which could not have done him any good, and at the water Delachance joined Royal Danieli.

Going into the country the second time, Lough Cottage took a slight lead of Dunhill Castle and Delachance, Royal Danieli having dropped back a little. By this time the weight was beginning to tell on Royal Mail.

Royal Danieli and Battleship were just in front of Delachance when Becher's was reached, and at the Canal turn Royal Mail broke a blood vessel and Evan Williams had to pull him up. I did not notice Cooleen until the field were approaching the racecourse again, and she was then too far behind the leaders to have any chance.

Workman, who had moved up to Royal Danieli and Battleship after jumping Valentine's, then became a fighting factor for the first time, and soon afterwards it was obvious that one of the three would win, providing they stood up.

Two fences from home, Workman was just in front of Royal Danieli, with Battleship a couple of lengths behind, but Workman made a bad mistake there and nearly came down. A loose horse – Takvor Pacha – nearly caused Royal Danieli to run out at the last fence, but Moore avoided him cleverly and landed on the flat just ahead of Battleship.

It seemed that the thousands of Irishmen present would indeed have something to shout about, but Bruce Hobbs, riding a great finish, crept up inch by inch – the run-in is nearly 500 yards – and overhauled Royal Danieli in the last few strides to score by a head.

The two finished on opposite sides of the course, Battleship being on the stands side, and it was almost impossible to say from the stands which had won. Workman was a poor third, with Cooleen (8-1jf) fourth and Delachance (100-9) fifth.

Mr Beatty leads in his bargain Derby winner

The Derby Epsom: 1 June

Bois Roussel only stayer in Derby
Scottish Union and Pasch easily beaten
By HOTSPUR

Bois Roussel (20-1), the French-bred colt owned by the Hon.Peter Beatty and ridden by C.Elliott, gained a spectacular triumph in the Derby this afternoon, winning by four lengths from Scottish Union (8-1), with Pasch, the 9 to 4 favourite, two lengths further away, third.

After the victory of Bois Roussel, it is almost possible to believe in fairy stories. Mr Beatty bought the colt in France less than a couple of months ago for £8,000, and this was the first time the winner had seen an English racecourse. It seems incredible that such luck is possible – and it is only two or three days ago that Mr Beatty was lamenting to me the fact that the only classic engagement his horse held was the Derby! The story is well worth telling.

Mr Beatty happened to mention to Prince Aly Khan that he wanted to buy a good horse, and said he was prepared to go to £3,000. Prince Aly Khan, who had seen Bois Roussel, then the property of M Volterra, in France, suggested the purchase of the colt, but told Mr Beatty he would cost £8,000.

Offers were made to M Volterra, who, however, stuck out for his price, and

eventually Mr Beatty and Fred Darling crossed the Channel to see Bois Roussel race. He won his race at Longchamp, and the deal was immediately closed with what happy result the whole world now knows.

To say that Bois Roussel won easily is understating the case. Elliott brought him with one long run from the distance and, shooting past Pasch and Scottish Union without any effort at all, the French-bred colt passed the post, cantering.

Bois Roussel had been trained for the race by Darling, who was also responsible for Pasch and Troon, and it seems hard luck on Gordon Richards, first jockey to the Beckhampton stable, that he should have been on Pasch and not on the winner.

Pasch was beaten because he did not stay; in fact Bois Roussel looked the only true stayer in the field, which is an unpleasant reflection on the English three-year-olds.

Darling has now turned out five winners of the big Epsom classic since the war.

[With the Derby winner not entered, Scottish Union (7-1) won the St Leger, leaving Pasch (6-5f) trailing four lengths away in third place.]

The Oaks Epsom: 3 June

Rockfel leads all the way to win Oaks
By HOTSPUR

The 3-1 favourite Rockfel this afternoon gained an easy victory in the Oaks by four lengths from Radiant (100-7), who beat Solar Flower (100-9) by a length and a half for second place.

The race requires little description, as Rockfel led from start to finish. A better idea of her achievement can perhaps be obtained from the fact that she won in nearly two seconds faster time than it took Bois Roussel to win the

Derby on Wednesday.

Sir Hugo Cunliffe-Owen told me that his filly's success delighted him chiefly because he had bred her from his Derby winner, Felstead.

It is a curious coincidence that neither the Derby nor the Oaks winner is engaged in the St Leger, which must perforce remain an exceedingly open proposition. I would dearly love to have seen them in opposition at Doncaster in September.

Grand Prix de Paris Longchamp: 26 June

How Nearco won Grand Prix: Triumph of unbeaten Italian horse
By WATCHMAN

This afternoon, Nearco became the first Italian horse to win the Grand Prix de Paris. A year ago Donatello II had come very close, and now Nearco (29-10) has taken ample revenge for his former stable companion's reverse.

Is to-day's winner one of the best horses seen in our generation? This was his 14th race, and he has never been beaten. Nearco's owner, Signor Frederico Tesio, has bred about a dozen winners of the Italian Derby, and is one of the greatest students of pedigree in the world. Later, I had the opportunity of a long chat with him. He said that before the race he had not been quite certain whether Nearco was merely the best of a moderate lot of horses in Italy or whether he was a real champion. There is no doubt on that point now.

No fault could be found

with the appearance on parade of either Bois Roussel or Legend of France, who had temporarily returned from England to their native land in an endeavour to win the highest honours of French racing.

For Legend of France I have no excuse. Bois Roussel, on the other hand, may have been an unlucky loser. Gordon Richards rode a perfect race on him until they reached the top of the hill, but then took him to the inside, with the unhappy result that the Derby winner was bumped and baulked, and was unable to put in his run until it was all too late.

After always holding a good position, Nearco made his culminating effort as soon as he was in the line for home, and won by a length and a half from Canot, who kept Bois Roussel out of second place by half a length.

Newmarket: 29 June

£60,000 paid for unbeaten Italian colt: Nearco secured for British stud
From WATCHMAN

Nearco, the unbeaten Italian colt who on Sunday won the Grand Prix de Paris, was to-day purchased for £60,000 by Mr Martin H. Benson, who owns the Beech House Stud at Cheveley, Newmarket. The price equals the record paid by the late Sir H.Mallaby-Deeley for the 1927 Derby winner, Call Boy.

For the most part, Nearco is of English blood. His sire was Lord Derby's Pharos, runner-up in the 1923 Derby. The dam is by the Italian-bred Havresac.

Mr Benson, who is also the

owner of Derby winner Windsor Lad, whom he bought from the Maharaja of Rajpipla for £50,000 in 1934, told me the colt will join Windsor Lad at stud.

Signor Tesio had to receive the permission of Signor Mussolini before he sold Nearco, as the colt was considered a valuable asset to Italian breeding. He will hand over the sterling received for Nearco to the Minister for Foreign Exchange and Currency, and will receive the equivalent either in Italian currency or in state bonds.

1939

9 Aug The last ever race meeting at Derby is marked, appropriately enough, by apathy, which drastically affects the Hartington High-weight Handicap, none of the 19 owners and trainers who nominated entries at £3 each bothering to turn up. So the race is declared void and the £300 prize goes begging – a lot of money in these hard times.

18 Oct A large crowd at Newmarket enjoy the first day's racing since the start of the war, and see Gyroscope (100-6) and Orichalque (25-1) win the two races, each with 27 runners, that make up the Cambridgeshire. The bookies also enjoy themselves, with not a single successful favourite in the 7 races (169 runners).

CHAMPIONS

Jockey (Flat)	Gordon Richards	155
Jockey (NH)	Fred Rimell	61
Leading Trainer	JL Jarvis	£56,219
Leading Owner	Lord Rosebery	£38,464
Leading Money Winner	Blue Peter	£31,964

The Grand National Aintree: 24 March

Workman scores all-Irish triumph: Kilstar third after bad blunder

By HOTSPUR

It was a complete triumph for the Irish in the Grand National here to-day, which was won by Workman, a nine-year-old gelding belonging to Sir Alexander Maguire, a wealthy Dublin and Belfast match manufacturer. The winner was trained and ridden by Irishmen – John Ruttle and Tim Hyde, respectively – and was backed by practically everyone in Navan, the owner's home in County Meath, with a population of about 10,000.

Workman, who is the first Irish horse to win the Grand National since Troytown in 1920, was bought as a two-year-old for 40 guineas. He has already won more than £10,000 in prize money.

The success was well merited, but the hard luck story of the race comes from Jack Moloney, the veteran rider of Black Hawk. He said: "Black Hawk was travelling so well that I felt certain my turn to win had come at last. But three fences out, Workman collided with him. My horse lost his hind legs and tossed me out of the saddle."

When the racecourse was reached the second time it was obvious that Workman or MacMoffat would win. Kilstar had taken too much out of himself when he blundered, Royal Mail faded out when the weight began to tell on him, and Inversible came down at the last fence when lying fourth.

Workman (100-8) had a lead of a couple of lengths from MacMoffat (25-1) at the final obstacle and increased it to three by the finish, with Kilstar (8-1f) 15 lengths further back in third place.

NATIONAL HUNT

Champion Hurdle	African Sister	K Piggott	10-1
Cheltenham Gold Cup	Brendan's Cottage	G Owen	8-1
Grand National	Workman	T Hyde	100-8

The Oaks Epsom: 26 May

Galatea II wins the Oaks by head
Fine finish by White Fox after mishap

By HOTSPUR

Galatea II, at 11-10 on, the hottest favourite for the race since Saucy Sue was successful 14 years ago, won the Oaks this afternoon, but may have been lucky to do so. A furlong from the finish, Galatea II had a clear lead, but White Fox (9-1) put in a late challenge that failed only by a head.

If White Fox had not been impeded when Curtain Call fell coming down the hill to Tattenham Corner, she might well have won. Curtain Call struck into the heels of the filly ahead of her, and came down just in front of White Fox, who had to be snatched up.

E.C.Elliott, who rode White Fox, told me he thought his mount was unlucky. "I lost quite three lengths through the accident to Curtain Call," he said, "but we made up ground at a great pace in the straight." Nevett, fortunately, was thrown clear when Curtain Call fell, and was little the worse for his unpleasant experience.

Galatea II was ridden by R.A.Jones, who won the race on Short Story in 1926. Jones did not think his mount lucky, and thought he could have won more easily. "Though I won by only a head," he told

They're off: the tapes rise for the start of the Derby

The Derby Epsom: 24 May

Blue Peter's spectacular triumph: Derby won by four lengths from Fox Cub

By HOTSPUR

Blue Peter, 7 to 2 favourite, gained a most spectacular triumph in the Derby this afternoon, drawing away from his rivals a couple of furlongs from home and going on to win easily by four lengths from Fox Cub (100-6), who beat Heliopolis (100-9) by three lengths for second place.

Lord Rosebery, Blue Peter's owner, was overwhelmed with congratulations on achieving his first success in the great race, as were Jack Jarvis, who had not previously trained a winner, and Eph Smith, whose first classic victory was on Blue Peter in the Two Thousand Guineas a month ago.

The result was one of the most popular in the history of the race. Lord Rosebery has been racing for more than 30 years and has been a member of the Jockey Club since 1924.

No-one has worked harder than he in the best interest of the Turf. His father won the Derby three times – with Ladas, Sir Visto and Cicero.

In the midst of Blue Peter's great triumph, I felt real sympathy for Gordon Richards, who has now been runner-up in the Derby three times, without yet tasting victory.

The favourite came down the hill looking all over a winner, and approaching Tattenham Corner had taken third place to Larchfield and Heliopolis. Richards on Fox Cub suddenly loomed up on the outside, and looked very dangerous, but rather more than two furlongs from home Smith decided to say good-bye to his rivals. And the moment Blue Peter was asked for his effort, his stride lengthened with devastating effect, and he strolled away from the opposition.

me, "I was never in danger of defeat. When White Fox drew up to me, Galatea II saw her shadow and did all I asked of her."

J.Lawson, who trains Galatea II for the American Mr R.S.Clark, was of the same opinion. "She is inclined to stop when she gets in front," he said, "and that is the reason White Fox was able to get so close."

Doncaster: 4 September

Doncaster races abandoned

No triple crown for Blue Peter

By Hotspur

As we expected, the Doncaster Race Committee have abandoned the four days' meeting which should have started tomorrow. I learn that the Stewards of the Jockey Club and the National Hunt Committee will meet later in the week to decide as to the future of racing.

The St Leger being "off", we shall not see the race of the century between the Derby winner Blue Peter and Pharis II, whose successes in the French Derby and the Grand Prix have stamped him as champion of France.

Blue Peter is the greatest three-year-old I have ever seen, and there has never been the slightest doubt in my mind that he would have won the Triple Crown. The St Leger was instituted in 1776 and, except during the last war, when it was decided at Newmarket on four occasions, has been run at Doncaster without interruption ever since.

Paris: 17 September

Interned on Paris racecourse: Horse-box bedrooms

From Our Own Correspondent

The picturesque racecourse at Maison Laffitte, a few miles from Paris, has been turned into an internment camp for Germans and Austrians, like the Sports Stadium at Colombes, where 10,000 are already interned.

Maison Laffitte at present houses only about 300, who are accommodated in horseboxes. Most of the Germans are Jewish refugees. They have quarters on the paddock side of the racecourse.

The Austrians are accommodated in the popular enclosure, where they are sleeping in the totalisator.

The camp is fed from French Army field kitchens and is guarded by a battalion of French Territorials, nearly all of whom are veterans of the last war.

Obituary: 20 October

Mr H.Beasley: "Grand old man of the Turf"

Mr Harry Beasley, after a remarkable racing career, died yesterday at Eyrefield Lodge, The Curragh, at the age of 87.

"Hotspur" writes: He was the unchallenged "Grand Old Man" of the Turf. With the exception of his brother Tom, he was the finest amateur steeplechase rider of the eighties and nineties, and rode in 13 Grand Nationals. He rode and trained the winner in 1891 with Come Away, was second on three occasions and third once.

No man who had ridden so long as he had remained so long able to ride. He rode a winner over the severe Punchestown course when he was 65, incidentally beating his son Willie. He continued to race on occasions until he was well over 80 years of age.

The Beasleys were a remarkable family, for there were four brothers who were first-class horsemen, and it was not unusual to see three at least of them riding in the same Grand National. Tom was perhaps the most brilliant, and he rode in 12 Nationals, winning three and being second twice.

After he had given up riding in the big races, Harry still continued to train at The Curragh, and was sending out winners of steeplechases and flat races until only a few years ago.

Horsemanship is hereditary in the Beasley family, for two of his sons, Harry and Patrick, have been successful jockeys for some years, and another, Willie, was a successful steeplechase rider in Ireland.

---

11 September

Trainers selling horses: Government pay £60 for Marshwood

By HOTSPUR

There are no signs yet even of a partial resumption of racing, but the position may be clarified to some extent after the special meetings of the Jockey Club and the National Hunt Committee on Wednesday.

In the meantime, more and more horses are being turned out of training, and others are being sold to the Government as remounts. During the week-end, I visited a number of Berkshire stables, and the story was very much the same wherever I went.

Hubert Hartigan, the owner-trainer of East Hendred, near Wantage, told me that five of his horses have been taken over by the Government. He was paid £60 each for Marshwood, a five-year-old mare who had won five races this season, and Kuadza, winner of three races, and £30 for Gipsy Lad, a nine-year-old with many successes to his credit.

Hartigan invested £4,000 in yearlings purchased at the Newmarket Sales and in Ireland during the summer. He is not the only one who will get a poor return, if any at all, for his money.

Steve Donoghue, who trains at nearby Blewbury, has 56 horses at his quarters. Ten of them are being turned out. He took me round his yard to see Pharis II, the French colt who came to this country a day or two before the war for the St Leger.

Pharis II is a grand-looking horse, and Donoghue is keeping him fit in the hope that we may yet run a substitute St Leger before the season ends.

Several famous steeplechase jockeys and ex-jockeys, including Evan Williams, Danny Morgan, Tommy Morgan and Sean Magee, have joined the Royal Artillery as gunners and are stationed not far away.

Obituary: 8 October

Mr R.S Sievier: Turf gambler who owned Sceptre

Mr Robert Standish Sievier, who has died at the age of 79, had over a period of many years enjoyed a highly spectacular career on the Turf.

He was, in his early years, a soldier, and after serving in the Zulu War and other campaigns became an actor in England. Then he went to Australia, where he established himself as a leading bookmaker, and he returned to England some time before the outbreak of the South African War.

His betting luck was extraordinary; with it he possessed exceptional intelligence and judgment and a remarkable knowledge of racing. At one time he was credited with a fortune of at least £250,000.

In 1900 he astonished the racing world by paying what was then by far the highest price that had ever been given for a yearling – 10,000 guineas for a daughter of Persimmon and Ornament at the sale of the late Duke of Westminster's bloodstock.

This yearling, which was afterwards named Sceptre, was probably the greatest bargain ever acquired in a sale ring. She proved to be the greatest mare of her time, perhaps of all time.

In 1902, Sievier decided to train his horses himself, and he sent out Sceptre to win four classic races outright, a unique achievement in the history of the Turf.

The 1940s

With World War II dominating the first half of the decade, racing struggled along as best it could. Newmarket, as in the first war, continued to function and staged the Derby and Oaks throughout the conflict. The St Leger, having been the first casualty of the war, when it was lost completely in 1939, was shunted from pillar to post – Thirsk (as the Yorkshire St Leger), Manchester, Newmarket (1942-44) and finally York. Gordon Richards won three of these substitute runnings, twice for the Aga Khan and once for the King.

But the champion jockey, who retained his title throughout the forties apart from when he broke his leg in 1941, still could not manage to notch his first Derby, and it was Billy Nevett who won three of the Newmarket runnings. Richards, however, became the world's leading jockey in 1947, and broke his own seasonal record of winners.

The Aga Khan spent the war in neutral Switzerland, but his horses continued to run in England and he was leading owner in 1944, a position he regained at the end of the war and held to the end of the decade. However, he controversially sold his England-based stallions Bahram and Mahmoud to American studs at the beginning of the war, and he was never as popular again.

National Hunt racing suffered more than the Flat, losing two complete seasons mid-war, and there was no Grand National from 1941 to 1945.

The post-war boom in sport was shared by racing, and as the crowds flocked to the racecourses betting also flourished. But British bloodstock was in for a shock as French raiders, led by textile millionaire M Marcel Boussac, began to make English Classic and Cup contenders look second rate. The French enjoyed particular success in the Ascot Gold Cup until that great stayer Alycidon restored English pride in 1949.

The photo-finish and evening meetings were introduced to Britain in the forties, both in 1947.

Crowds flocked to sporting events after the war: here packed grandstands overlook the water jump at the 1946 Grand National, as a riderless horse shows the way.

1940 – 1945

12 Jun 1940 Trainer Fred Darling sends out his own Pont l'Eveque (10-1) to win the first wartime Derby by 3 lengths from the Aga Khan's Turkhan (100-7). The race is held at Newmarket, having originally been scheduled for Newbury.

7 Sep 1940 British bloodstock receives another blow when it is announced that, having sold Bahram last month to an American stud for £40,000, the Aga Khan has now exported his other great Derby-winning stallion, Mahmoud, to the USA.

8 May 1941 A mishap at Salisbury, in which he is kicked by a filly at the start and suffers a broken leg, keeps champion jockey Gordon Richards out for the rest of the season, the only one in 23 years (1931-53) when he does not win the title.

18 Jun 1941 Fred Darling saddles his 7th Derby winner, his 3rd in 4 years, when Mrs Macdonald Buchanan's Owen Tudor (25-1) beats Morogoro (11-2), also trained by Darling.

21 Mar 1942 Lord Sefton's gelding Médoc II (9-2) wins the last Cheltenham Gold Cup

of the war by 8 lengths from Red Rower (3-1f) in thick fog (a fact not mentioned by radio commentator Raymond Glendenning to avoid giving weather information to "the enemy"). For Red Rower's jockey, Danny Morgan, in what is his last Gold Cup, it is a 7th consecutive placing in the first 3, including his win when Morse Code beat Golden Miller in 1938.

25 Jun 1942 Windsor Slipper (2-7f) wins Irish Derby in record time, 2min 35sec.

10 Sep 1942 Steeplechasing is discontinued for the duration of the war.

---

7 February 1940

No Ascot races this year: Heavy blow to owners

By Hotspur

Ascot races, which were fixed to begin on June 18 this year, will not be held.

The announcement, made yesterday, that the meeting has been abandoned, does not come as a surprise. There was no racing at Ascot in the years 1914-18, and substitute races for the Gold Cup and other big events may be run.

The abandonment of Ascot, following the news that there will be no racing this year at Epsom, is another heavy blow to owners. The prizes to be won there, in the aggregate, are the most valuable of any meeting. Last year the owners of the winners of the 28 races decided shared £67,870 in stake money.

His Majesty the King leads in Sun Chariot after the Oaks

The Grand National Aintree: 5 April 1940

Bogskar wins National
MacMoffat finishes second again

By HOTSPUR

Bogskar (25-1), owned and trained by Lord Stalbridge, a steward of the National Hunt Committee, and ridden by M.A.Jones, won a thrilling Grand National this afternoon by four lengths from MacMoffat (8-1), with Gold Arrow (50-1) six lengths away third.

MacMoffat and his rider, Ian Alder, thus had the mortification of having to play the part of runner-up for the second year in succession. Seventeen – an unusually large number – of the field of 30 completed the course, and Bogskar's time, 9min 20 3/5sec, was only two-fifths of a second outside the record.

"Bogskar gave me a wonderful ride," said Mervyn Jones to me after the race. "He never put a foot wrong." Jones, a sergeant in the Royal Air Force, is a nephew of

the Anthony brothers, who have such a famous record in the National.

Passing the stands, MacMoffat led top weight Royal Danieli (4-1f), and I have seldom, if ever, seen so many horses standing up as the field went out into the country for the second time. MacMoffat was jumping beautifully in the lead, and looked all over a winner.

Approaching Valentine's, Bogskar was noticed for the first time, and shortly afterwards he moved up into second place, with Gold Arrow close up, Royal Danieli by this time beginning to tire. Two fences from home Bogskar joined MacMoffat, and they came to the final obstacle together, Bogskar landing on the flat a fraction of a second in front and increasing his lead all the way up to the finish.

New St Leger Newmarket: 12 September 1942

Sun Chariot a great filly
Richards hails 'best ever'

By HOTSPUR

Gordon Richards' tribute to Sun Chariot after her brilliant triumph in the St Leger was that she is the "best ever".

There has never been an easier St Leger winner, and, strong though the belief in Sun Chariot (9-4) was all along, the emphatic margin of the victory astonished everyone. Only a really great filly could have beaten Watling Street (2-1f), the Derby winner, by as much as three lengths.

Gordon Richards did not have a moment's anxiety. He told me that the filly

wanted to go with the leaders, Solway and Ujiji, in the first quarter of a mile, but he pulled her back and settled her down last of all. He moved up gradually and half a mile from home was trailing Watling Street. When a furlong and a half out, he called on Sun Chariot for her effort, and she went right away from the Derby winner with a brilliant burst of finishing speed.

[This completed the fillies' Triple Crown, Sun Chariot being only the fifth to achieve it.]

10 Sep 1942 The Newmarket Sales, over two days, realise £84,544. A war-time record price of 8,200gns for a yearling is paid by the Aga Khan for a bay colt by Hyperion-Eclair.

4 Apr 1943 Racing goes on at Longchamp in Occupied France despite a British bombing raid prior to the meeting.

1 May 1943 Johnny Longden rides Count Fleet (2-5f) to victory in the Kentucky Derby on his way to the US Triple Crown and the emulation of Eddie Arcaro's feat on Whirlaway in 1941.

22 Dec 1943 Registering a new company, Jockey Club Racecourse Ltd, with the Stewards as directors, the Jockey Club is set to buy up all the racecourse it needs from existing private companies on an agreed basis.

13 Apr 1944 Lord Lonsdale, 87, "The Sporting Earl" and a familiar and popular figure on English racecourses, dies at his home in Rutland. He won the St Leger in 1922 with Royal Lancer.

6 Jan 1945 After a void of nearly three years, National Hunt racing resumes in Britain, at Cheltenham.

24 Apr 1945 Gordon Richards displays a masterly piece of horsemanship in Division I of the Barrow Stakes at Newmarket when, with his mount Leventina 200 yards from the winning post, his saddle slips from under him and his stirrups go flying. Riding bare-backed, he gets his filly home two lengths ahead of the odds-on favourite Goodasgold.

23 Jul 1945 The Hon.George Lambton, 84, a leading trainer for over 50 years, who retired only two days ago, dies at his home in Newmarket. He saddled the winners of 13 Classics, including the Derby twice, with Sansovino (1924) and Hyperion (1933).

8 Dec 1945 Irish jump jockey John Lynn, 38, dies from injuries sustained in a fall yesterday at Southwell.

12 Dec 1945 Freddy Fox, the 1930 champion jockey, 57, is killed in a car accident. He won the Derby on Bahram in 1935, retiring the following year.

MAJOR WARTIME RESULTS

Grand National

1940	Bogskar	M Jones	25-1

Derby (at Newmarket)

1940	Pont l'Evêque	S Wragg	10-1
1941	Owen Tudor	W Nevett	25-1
1942	Watling Street	H Wragg	6-1
1943	Straight Deal	T Carey	100-6
1944	Ocean Swell	W Nevett	28-1
1945	Dante	W Nevett	100-30f

New St Leger Newmarket: 18 September 1943

Lord Derby's 17th Classic win

By HOTSPUR

The 1943 racing season will be remembered for the gallant but unsuccessful efforts of Lord Rosebery's filly Ribbon to win a classic race. Her sequence of narrow defeats in the One Thousand Guineas (neck), Oaks (neck) and St Leger (short head) can have few parallels. She went under in the last two strides in a dramatic St Leger at New-market on Saturday to Lord Derby's Herringbone, who in May snatched the One Thousand Guineas spoils from her.

A quarter of a mile from home, Ribbon (10-1) was involved in some scrimmag-ing with Why Hurry and Umiddad and, in my opinion, the bump she received cost her the race. Regaining her balance, Ribbon tackled the rise to the winning post in rare courage, but Herring-bone (100-6), finding a clear opening, began rapidly to overhaul her. Harry Wragg timed his effort to a split second and Lord Derby's filly won on the post.

The Derby winner, Straight Deal (100-30f), was third, three-quarters of a length behind the two fillies. Kings-way and Why Hurry, winners of the 2,000 Guineas and Oaks, respectively, finished way down the field.

Herringbone, a beautifully made filly by King Salmon-Schiaparelli, is Lord Derby's 17th Classic winner. He has now won the St Leger six times.

New 2,000 Guineas Newmarket: 17 May 1944

Filly wins 2,000 Guineas

By HOTSPUR

For the first time in 42 years a filly proved superior to the colts in the 2,000 Guineas at Newmarket yesterday, when Lord Derby's Garden Path (5-1) beat Growing Confidence (20-1) in a thrilling head finish, with Tehran (50-1) a length and a half farther away, third. Only six fillies have won the race since its inception in 1809.

It was by far the most popular victory in the war-time classics. Many good judges backed Garden Path at long odds – she was once a 50-1 chance – and the public, admiring Lord Derby's bold decision to challenge the colts, supported the filly strongly. Indeed, there was so much money for her towards the close of the wagering that she deposed Orestes as favourite.

She is Lord Derby's 19th classic winner and the fourth Harry Wragg has ridden in the famous black jacket and white cap in the last two years.

CHAMPIONS

1940	Gordon Richards	68 wins
1941	Harry Wragg	71 wins
1942	Gordon Richards	67 wins
1943	Gordon Richards	65 wins
1944	Gordon Richards	88 wins
1945	Gordon Richards	104 wins

Obituary: 24 March 1945

Steve Donoghue

Racing has lost its biggest personality by the sudden death of Steve Donoghue, who was 60, in London early yesterday morn-ing, *writes Hotspur*. No jockey of this century rode so many famous horses. None was more admired by the experts for brilliant horsemanship or more beloved by the general public, whose idol he was for 20 years. His fame and popularity were world-wide.

Donoghue rode six Derby winners, beginning with Pommern and Gay Crusader in substitute races at Newmarket in the last war. Then, in the twenties, came a wonderful Epsom hat trick on Humorist, Captain Cuttle and Papyrus, followed by Manna.

But of all the horses he rode, Steve's favourite was old Brown Jack. They formed a wonderful partnership. Brown Jack won the Queen Alexandra Stakes at Ascot, the longest race run under Jockey Club rules, six times in succession. Steve rode him in 14 of his winning races, which produced £23,500 in prize money for the owner Sir Harold Wernher.

Describing the horses he had ridden, Steve once said that Brown Jack was his favourite, Humorist the gamest, Gay Crusader the best, The Tetrarch the fastest and Tishy the slowest.

Donoghue was a fearless rider as well as a superb judge of pace. That is why the Epsom course was his happiest hunting ground. Horses with Steve up used to come bowling down the hill and round Tattenham Corner like a cricket ball. He won every race of importance in England and had ridden for nearly all the leading owners of the last quarter of a century.

Steve took out a trainer's licence in 1938 and met with a fair measure of success.

The 1,000 Guineas Newmarket: 8 May 1945

Lord Derby's classic again

From HOTSPUR

With a record war-time *[it happens to be VE Day]* Guineas crowd filling the enclosures and lining the rails ten deep on the far side of the July course, Lord Derby's filly Sun Stream (5-2f) gained a most popular victory today in the 1,000 Guineas. She won in unmistakably easy style by three lengths from Blue Smoke (25-1), with Mrs Feather (4-1) third, two lengths behind the second.

What a pity it was that Lord Derby, who recently celebrat-ed his 80th birthday, could not be present to see his famous colours triumph in the race for the seventh time.

Sun Stream is a very beautiful-looking Hyperion filly out of Drift, and is, of course, home-bred. I am not exaggerating when I say she outclassed today's field, and I have rarely seen Harry Wragg ride such a confident race.

Icklingham Stakes Newmarket: 31 October 1945

Gordon's 3,000th winner

From HOTSPUR

Gordon Richards rode his 3,000th winner on Exotic who, giving weight all round, beat Highland Division by a head in a thrilling finish for the Icklingham Stakes. The popu-lar little champion was given a great reception on returning to scale. His wonderful record will stand for all time.

1946

21 Jun French horses fill the first 3 places in the Ascot Gold Cup, M Marcel Boussac's 4-y-o colt Caracalla II (4-9f) winning by 2 lengths and 5 from Chanteur II (33-1) and Basileus (15-2).

12 Oct In the inaugural running of the King George VI Stakes at Ascot, Derby winner Airborne (4-5f) is beaten 5 lengths and a short head by the French horse Souverain (11-2), with Bright News 2nd.

16 Nov The "Head Waiter" to the last, Harry Wragg goes out with a flourish, riding 3 winners on his final day as a jockey, including Las Vegas (20-1) in the Manchester November Handicap to complete a 201-1 treble. Champion jockey in 1941 and rider of 13 Classic winners, including 3 Derbys and the last 2 Oaks, he is setting up as a trainer at Newmarket.

Champion Hurdle Challenge Cup Cheltenham: 12 March

Miss Paget lands Irish treble at Cheltenham

From HOTSPUR

Miss Dorothy Paget had a great day here this afternoon, Distel winning the Champion Hurdle, Dunshaughlin the National Hunt Handicap 'Chase and Loyal King the Grand Annual 'Chase. Her three winners all came from Ireland.

Distel proved himself a champion indeed when he gained a convincing and clear-cut victory over Carnival Boy in the Champion Hurdle. A shade of odds had to be laid on Distel (4-5), who took the lead at the last bend from The Diver, with Carnival Boy (7-2) moving up. Two hurdles from home it was obvious that the Irish-trained favourite had the race in safe keeping, and he went on to win by four lengths.

In the National Hunt Handicap 'Chase, Dunshaughlin (7-1) was still well handicapped despite a 5lb penalty for a recent win a Windsor. He was not, however, nearly as well backed as African Collection, another Irish invader, who started a good favourite. Dunshaughlin, like Distel, was most capably ridden by Bobby O'Ryan, and beat Silver Fame (100-9) into second place.

Miss Paget's third winner, Loyal King (7-2), defied a 10lb penalty in the Grand Annual 'Chase to beat another Irish horse, Keep Faith, by a couple of lengths.

CHAMPIONS

Jockey (Flat)	Gordon Richards	212
Jockey (NH)	Fred Rimell	54
Leading Trainer	Frank Butters	£56,140
Leading Owner	HH Aga Khan III	£24,118
Leading Money Winner	Airborne	£20,345

NATIONAL HUNT

Champion Hurdle	Distel	R O'Ryan	4-5f
Cheltenham Gold Cup	Prince Regent	T Hyde	4-7f
Grand National	Lovely Cottage	Capt R Petre	25-1

ENGLISH CLASSICS

2,000 Guineas	Happy Knight	T Weston	28-1
1,000 Guineas	Hypericum	D Smith	100-6
Derby	Airborne	T Lowrey	50-1
Oaks	Steady Aim	H Wragg	7-1
St Leger	Airborne	T Lowrey	3-1f

OTHER MAJOR RACES

Irish Derby	Bright News	M Wing	100-8
Arc de Triomphe	Caracalla II	EC Elliott	3-10f
Kentucky Derby	Assault	W Mehrtens	82-10
Melbourne Cup	Russia	D Munro	16-1

The Grand National Aintree: 5 April

Prince Regent crawls into third place in National

From HOTSPUR

One of the most amazing Grand Nationals of all time ended this afternoon in a four lengths' victory for Mr J.Morant's 25 to 1 outsider, Lovely Cottage, over Jack Finlay, a 100 to 1 chance, with the hot favourite, Prince Regent, three lengths farther back third.

An amazing race because of the dramatic climax which in a matter of seconds turned what had seemed certain victory for the favourite into defeat, with the sudden prospect of a 100 to 1 outsider in Jack Finlay coming to the rescue of the bookmakers, who stood to lose fortunes if Prince Regent had completed the thousands of doubles in which the Lincolnshire winner, Langton Abbot, was coupled.

A surprise prior to racing was the manner in which Prince Regent, trained in Ireland by Tom Dreaper, reacted in the market. Backed at 9-4 overnight, it was generally supposed that the 11-year-old Cheltenham Gold Cup winner would start at the shortest price in the history of the race. Instead, "The Prince" drifted out, perhaps because he had not tackled the Aintree fences before, and finally started at 3 to 1. (Golden Miller was 2 to 1 when he failed in the 1935 race.)

The race was run in most perfect conditions. Every incident could be easily followed from the stands, and when Hyde sent Prince Regent into the lead after passing Valentine's second time round, I thought the favourite would come home alone. He was striding out in grand style, full of running and, over the last fence but one, must have been the best part of 20 lengths ahead.

Surely nothing could catch the leader if he cleared the 30th and last jump of all? Then, for the first time, I saw Lovely Cottage as a possible danger. Between the last two fences he was travelling faster than the favourite, but when Prince Regent took the final obstacle two lengths clear it seemed all over.

But the weight was taking full toll on the gallant top weight. Though hampered by several loose horses, Lovely Cottage, with nearly 2 stone less in the saddle than Prince Regent, got in a strong and determined challenge, and in a flash the whole picture changed.

Whereas Prince Regent's stride shortened from sheer tiredness, Lovely Cottage strode out full of running. The "Prince" finished at a crawl, and was beaten for second place by the outsider Jack Finlay, who, I thought, finished the gruelling course the freshest of the three and may have been an unlucky loser.

Housewarmer, another 100-1 chance, proved the best of Miss Paget's runners, and finished fourth. Gallant old Schubert (100-7), outpaced, but a fine jumper to the end, was fifth, and Limestone Edward was the only other to finish among the 34 starters.

Lovely Cottage, ridden by Capt.Robert Petre, was bought for £2,000 last December with a contingency of an extra £1,000 if he won the National. He is trained by Tom Rayson, who left Aintree on the eve of the National owing to illness, and spent today in bed at the house of a friend in Yorkshire.

After the race Capt.Petre said: "I had a very good ride all the way round. Between the last two fences I suddenly realised that Prince Regent had nothing left, so I set Lovely Cottage 'alight', and he went on then to win." Tim Hyde, rider of Prince Regent, said that he was hampered by three loose horses in the last mile, and in consequence had to go to the front earlier than he had wished.

Although there were 28 casualties in the race, the majority of fallen jockeys suffered little more than cuts and bruises. But Symbole, one of the two French horses was killed when he fell.

Leading in Mr Ferguson's 50-1 winner, Airborne

The Derby Epsom: 5 June

King and Queen see exciting Derby finish: Longest-priced winner since 1913

By DOUGLAS WILLIAMS

In one of the most thrilling and unexpected finishes the classic race has ever produced, Airborne, a 50-1 outsider owned by Mr J.E.Ferguson, a plastics manufacturer of Godalming, yesterday won the 167th Derby, run at Epsom for the first time since the war.

The Earl of Derby's Gulf Stream, ridden by H.Wragg, which was heavily backed at 7-1, looked a certain winner a furlong from home, and was already being greeted with roars of cheering from the excited spectators massed along the rails, when the almost unknown grey horse, Airborne, suddenly emerged and, with a magnificent spurt of tremendous speed, flashed past the post a length ahead.

Radiotherapy was placed third at 8-1, after an original error by the judges giving third place to Fast and Fair had been corrected. Happy Knight, the favourite at 5-1, was unplaced.

Airborne, numbered 13 on the card and the first horse the owner had ever entered in a classic, was trained by R.Perryman. By a freak typical of racing luck, he was bought for Mr Ferguson at 3,300 guineas by Walter Earl, who trained Gulf Stream. Airborne had won only one race previously – an event for three-year-olds at Newmarket last month. His value has of course risen tremendously – a horse worth, say, 2,000 guineas before the race would be worth at least 50,000 guineas immediately he was first past the post in the Derby.

Airborne's starting price was the highest recorded for a Derby winner since the sensational success of Aboyeur, who was placed first in 1913 at 100-1 after Craganour had been disqualified. But his victory was highly popular with the veterans of Arnhem, hundreds of whom had backed him in memory of their dramatic invasion of Holland two years ago.

July Cup Newmarket: 4 July

The Bug beats Honeyway in July Cup

By HOTSPUR

Half an hour after Airborne's triumph today, the onlookers had another thrill, the gallant but unsuccessful effort of Honeyway (2-1) to concede 18lb to The Bug (8-11f) in the July Cup. It was a wonderful duel between two great sprinters – Honeyway, the five-year-old champion who won last year's race, and the three-year-old "pretender" from reland, who had arrived at the course only just in time.

The 1,000 Guineas Newmarket: 3 May

Hypericum's Royal success in 1,000 Guineas

From HOTSPUR

The King's good filly, Hypericum (100-6), bred at the Royal stud at Sandringham, won a fine race for the One Thousand Guineas today by one and a half lengths from Neolight (4-6f), with Iona (9-1) three-quarters of a length farther away third. The winner had been a good second favourite until she threw her jockey at the start and bolted off to the car park, where she was caught.

Neolight, on whom Gordon Richards rode a perfect waiting race, palpably failed to stay home up the hill, though she was handicapped by being drawn on the far side of the course.

Quite unperturbed by his mishap at the starting gate, Doug Smith rode a splendid race to gain his first classic success. Boyd-Rochfort has trained the winner of the One Thousand once before, and that was 13 years ago, when Brown Betty gained the day.

Hypericum is a half-sister to yesterday's royal winner, Kingstone. Whereas Kingstone is by King Salmon, Hypericum is by Hyperion. She is out of Feola, who finished third in the Oaks in 1936.

A mile and a half should be well within the compass of Hypericum, who has sound prospects of winning the Oaks for the King, but she will have nothing in hand on Iona, who ran a splendid race and was unlucky in the running.

The escapade of Hypericum before the race brings back memories of other similar incidents. How many people remember the day at Sandown Park some 30 years ago, when Frank Wootton was riding Royal Escort for King Edward VII? The horse bolted, went right round the course, started in the race and led from pillar to post. There was another occurrence somewhat similar to Hypericum's at Newbury in 1932, when Abbot's Worthy, after unshipping Gordon Richards and galloping the length of the course, was taken back to the start and won his race.

Princess of Wales's Stakes Newmarket: 4 July

Airborne wins in fine style: Now 3-1 favourite for St Leger

From HOTSPUR

The prestige of the British thoroughbred, somewhat damaged by the successes of the French invaders of Ascot, was restored today when Airborne (9-4), the Derby winner, won the Princess of Wales's Stakes in storming style from Paper Weight, with Royal Commission half a length farther behind third, and the French horse, Priam II (5-6f) last.

Though there were only four runners, it was an engrossing contest, and the instant it was realised that Lowrey had the race in safe keeping on Airborne the crowd began to roar its delight. The cheering started as Airborne, Paper Weight and Priam II, closely bunched on the stands side, came out of the Dip.

Paper Weight was then being pressed to maintain his slight lead, and Elliott was also at work on the Frenchman. Lowrey, on the inside, was sitting still on Airborne. As they struck the foot of the hill Airborne was given his head, and the Derby winner then made his long stride tell effectively.

Immediately after the race Airborne was made a 3-1 favourite for the St Leger.

When they had gone half a mile, The Bug was running unevenly and Smirke wisely gave him a chance to find his balance. Honeyway, in the meanwhile, went slightly ahead. Immediately The Bug was racing smoothly again, Smirke challenged, and the weight told, as it was bound to. Honeyway was beaten, but not disgraced, by three-quarters of a length.

1947

24 Feb The first call-over is held at the Victoria Club, for the Lincolnshire, in which the 13 declared French horses are lumped together at 5-1. [The race eventually has 46 starters, and is won by 100-1 shot 5-y-o Jockey Treble, carrying 6st and ridden by E.Mercer.]

29 Mar The Grand National is held on a Saturday (instead of Friday) by request of Prime Minister Clement Attlee, "in the interests of British industry".

22 Apr The photo-finish makes its first appearance on a British racecourse, at Epsom.

7 Jun The Derby is run on a Saturday for the first time, except during the two world wars.

18 Jul Tudor Minstrel (1-2f) fails again, decisively outstayed in the Eclipse over 1 1/4 miles by the Aga Khan's Migoli (7-2) after leading by six lengths coming into the straight. The result shows conclusively that Tudor Minstrel is only a brilliant miler and, however he would have been ridden, he would not have won the Derby.

18 Jul Hamilton Park stages Britain's first evening meeting.

24 Oct The Beachfield Handicap Plate at Doncaster provides the first dead-heat recorded by the photo-finish camera in Britain, Resistance and Phantom Bridge being the two inseparable protagonists.

The Grand National Aintree: 29 March

New scheme to stop big "National" fields

By HOTSPUR

The Grand National of 1947, which was contested by 57 horses, will probably be the last one with a mammoth field. I understand that conditions for next year's race are to be altered to prevent very moderate horses from cluttering up the field. Horses considered entitled to carry less than the minimum of 10 stone will not be allowed to compete.

Mr J.J.McDowell's Caughoo, Saturday's 100-1 winner, would have been a border-line case under the new conditions suggested, but having won the Ulster National Handicap 'Chase twice, he would not, I imagine, have been debarred from running. He is only the third horse to win the National with the minimum weight (10st) this century.

The race itself was most disappointing as a spectacle. Visibility was so poor that the runners could only be made out with certainty at the first three fences and the last four.

Caughoo was out on his own coming on to the racecourse, and he won unchallenged by 20 lengths from the tiring Lough Conn (33-1), with Kami (33-1) four lengths farther away third.

The 8-1 favourite, a very gallant but exceedingly weary Prince Regent carrying the top weight of 12st-7, came in fourth.

The winner's owner is a Dublin jeweller. His brother, Mr Herbert McDowell, a veterinary surgeon, has trained the horse on the sands at Portmarnock. The horse is stabled at Sutton, a small place seven miles from the centre of Dublin.

Mr McDowell bought Caughoo, the first racehorse he has owned, for 50 guineas at Ballsbridge Sales as a two-year-old, and he called him after his old homestead in Co.Cavan. Caughoo's strange colours are those of the local rugger club at Sutton, of which Mr McDowell is chairman. It was all, in fact, very much a family affair.

The man who rode Caughoo, Eddie Dempsey, had never been in England before. He is now a farmer and only rides occasionally in public, but is the jockey who first schooled Prince Regent over fences and first rode him in a 'chase. Caughoo, needless to say, was bred in Ireland, by a Co.Wexford farmer, Mr John Power.

CHAMPIONS

Jockey (Flat)	Gordon Richards	269
Jockey (NH)	Jack Dowdeswell	58
Leading Trainer	Fred Darling	£65,313
Leading Owner	HH Aga Khan III	£44,020
Leading Money Winner	Migoli	£17,215

Worcester: 19 May

Gordon's world record

Gordon Richards made history at Worcester yesterday when he set up a new world record of winning rides, beating the previous record of 3,260 held by Sam Heapy, British-born jockey, who rode in Belgium.

The champion jockey passed Heapy's figures by winning on Le Bosc Giard, and brought his total up to 3,262 when he won the last race on Overcast.

Tudor Minstrel wins by a street at Newmarket

The 2,000 Guineas Newmarket: 30 April

Tudor Minstrel scatters Guineas field

From HOTSPUR

Tudor Minstrel, the 11-8 favourite, won the Two Thousand Guineas to-day in devastating style. I have never seen a classic race won more easily. It is not often a horse palpably has the Two Thousand in his pocket before the Bushes, and though it was a procession over the last two furlongs it was a very thrilling procession.

Tudor Minstrel – perhaps the horse of the century – was followed home by 14 other three-year-olds, with Saravan (25-1) second, eight lengths behind the winner, and Sayajirao (33-1) a short head further away third.

A year ago at Hurst Park, Gordon Richards told a friend of mine that he was riding a two-year-old at Bath called Tudor Minstrel who would probably never be beaten. I thought the champion jockey would be proved wrong today, but I am delighted I was wrong when a horse wins the Guineas as Tudor Minstrel did.

Gordon Richards sailed into the Dip far in front, and as he did so there was a roar of cheering. The champion jockey probably then had a moment of anxiety, thinking perhaps the roar was a warning something was coming out of the blue to challenge him.

There was no possible danger. The crowd were cheering him home – acknowledging a most dazzling performance. I have never known a Guineas winner finish to the accompaniment of more applause.

The pace which Tudor Minstrel set had the majority of the field in trouble three furlongs from the finish. First Petition and Kingsclere were beaten and then Goldsborough and Nebuchadnezzar.

As these weakened, Saravan and Sayajirao improved, and both finished strongly up the hill without making any impression on Tudor Minstrel, who continued at his ease in the lead to win in a common canter.

Tudor Minstrel will start one of the hottest Derby favourites of the past quarter of a century. As soon as he passed the post, full of running and with Gordon Richards patting his neck, the bookmakers cut the colt's Derby odds from 8-1 before the race to 6-4. It is impossible to see what is going to beat Tudor Minstrel at Epsom.

At long last it seems that Gordon Richards will, in 1947, achieve a lifetime's ambition and ride the winner of the Derby.

The Derby Epsom: 7 June

British humiliation in the Derby: Why French horses keep on winning

By HOTSPUR

The result of the Derby of 1947 is the most staggering I have known and the most humiliating for those who take an interest in and follow with some pride the fortunes of the British thoroughbred.

Our French correspondent gave only very remote chances to the three French runners, Pearl Diver, Cadir and Parisien, because on all known form they were well behind the best of their age in France.

And yet Pearl Diver (40-1), beaten in two out of his three races in France this year, wins the Derby not by a short head in a desperate finish but easily by four lengths from Migoli (20-1), with Sayajirao (13-2) three-quarters of a length further away third and Tudor Minstrel, the 7-4 on favourite, fourth.

The results of the Derby, the Oaks and the Coronation Cup – all won by French horses – point to the fact that at the moment the best of the French three-year-olds and older middle-distance horses are at least a stone superior to the best we can put in the field.

Now that neither Airborne nor Look Ahead can run in the Ascot Gold Cup next week, it seems long odds on the French occupying first, second and third places, as was the case last year.

It is not reasonable to blame the war for the present sorry state of affairs. French breeders on the whole suffered worse in the war years than we did. Baron G de Waldner, owner and breeder of Pearl Diver, lost several of his brood mares. M Pierre Corbiere, breeder of Imprudence, lost many mares, and the Rothschild studs were scattered to the winds.

The chief reason for the present debacle is in my view the fact that for a long time we have laid far too much emphasis on five-furlong scurries for two-year-olds. As a result, breeders, who have to earn their keep, have been sending good mares to sprinting sires of the type of Denturius and Panorama, who cannot by the wildest stretch of imagination toughen or improve our breed and, in fact, are steadily having the reverse effect.

To return to the Derby. The moderate Blue Coral was the one to make the running, with Tudor Minstrel, Sayajirao, Pearl Diver and Cadir lying well up, and Migoli and Grand Weather two of the backmarkers. As they neared the top of the hill, Tudor Minstrel was fighting fiercely for his head and refusing to settle down. Blue Coral dropped out as they turned towards Tattenham Corner and Migoli began to make up ground. Britt was riding a beautiful race on Sayajirao, hugging the rails and coming the shortest way home.

Coming into the straight, Sayajirao was lying third to Tudor Minstrel and Pearl Diver, the favourite still running all too freely. Tudor Minstrel took up the running in the straight. If he had the stamina there was nothing to prevent him winning, but, alas, at 1 1/4 miles he was a beaten horse. Pearl Diver challenged and went by him.

NATIONAL HUNT

Champion Hurdle	National Spirit	D Morgan	7-1
Cheltenham Gold Cup	Fortina	Mr R Black	8-1
Grand National	Caughoo	E Dempsey	100-1

ENGLISH CLASSICS

2,000 Guineas	Tudor Minstrel	G Richards	8-11f
1,000 Guineas	Imprudence	WR Johnstone	4-1f
Derby	Pearl Diver	G Bridgland	40-1
Oaks	Imprudencee	WR Johnstone	7-4f
St Leger	Sayajirao	E Britt	9-2

Irish Derby The Curragh: 25 June

Sayajirao has easy win in Irish Derby

By HOTSPUR

Sayajirao, for whom the Maharaja of Baroda gave 28,000 guineas as a yearling, was a worthy winner of the Irish Derby at The Curragh yesterday. His owner will decide whether to send his good horse by air to run in the International race in America next month when it is known whether Sayajirao is any the worse for yesterday's race.

Sayajirao, starting an even-money favourite, won by 1 1/2 lengths from the second favourite, Grand Weather. Britt rode Sayajirao, who at Epsom was considerably further ahead of Grand Weather at the finish than was the case yesterday.

Sayajirao was bred at the Friar Ings Stud by Sir Eric Ohlson, who won the Derby with Sayajirao's full brother, Dante. It is comparatively rare for full brothers to be of great racing merit. It was the Irish Derby winner's ninth race and his third victory. He has never failed to finish out of the first three.

OTHER MAJOR RACES

Irish Derby	Sayajirao	E Britt	1-1f
Arc de Triomphe	Le Paillon	F Rochetti	23-2
Kentucky Derby	Jet Pilot	E Guerin	54-10
Melbourne Cup	Hiraji	J Purtell	12-1

Leicester: 10 November

Gordon Richards breaks the record: Short head victory in last race

From HOTSPUR

On the course on which he rode his first winner in an apprentice race 26 years ago, Gordon Richards to-day broke his own record of 259 winners in a season.

He had to wait until the last race of the afternoon before the record he set up in 1933 was beaten. After two reverses, including a head defeat on Lugano, he got the favourite, Twenty Twenty, home by a short head in the Stoughton Plate amid scenes of tremendous enthusiasm.

As Gordon came to win his race, hats went into the air. Some present remembered a quarter of a century ago when, a boy of 16 apprenticed to Martin Hartigan, he rode his first winner at Leicester on Gay Lord, owned by the late Mr James White.

While the jockeys were changing after the last race to-day, a crowd gathered and chanted: "We want Gordon." But the modest little champion did not face them. He arranged for a car to meet him at the back of the stands and tried to slip unnoticed through a window in the weighing room.

The ruse nearly came off, but not quite. As he neared his car he was mobbed, and then willingly signed over 100 racecards before driving away.

Neither Gordon Richards's wife nor his family saw him ride to-day, but he remarked after the race: "I know they will all be listening to the six o'clock news to hear how I got on."

What was not realised by the majority of the enthusiastic crowd was that the champion jockey's record this season is much more brilliant than in 1933, when he beat Fred Archer's 1885 total of 246 winners. In 1933 Richards had no fewer than 975 mounts of which 259 won, 163 were second, 113 third and 440 unplaced. This year he has so far ridden in 792 races, of which he has won 260, finished second in 163, third in 106 and unplaced in only 263.

1948

2 Mar The 7-y-o National Spirit is the first horse since Insurance in 1933 to win the Champion Hurdle twice running, and the

first hurdler to capture the public imagination.

13 Mar The Lincolnshire Handicap, with a British record of 58 runners for a Flat race, is won by Commissar (33-1), ridden by Bill Rickaby, who beats the favourite, Clarion III, by 2 lengths.

12 Jun Citation wins the Belmont Stakes to become the fourth horse to achieve the

US Triple Crown in the 1940s but only the eighth of all time. For jockey Eddie Arcaro, it is an unprecedented second Triple Crown (after Whirlaway in 1941). *[Arcaro later clinches his third season as top jockey, while Citation, with 19 wins in 20 starts, creates a record $709,470 earnings in one season.]*

18 Aug The first race at Haydock, the Wigan Lane Selling Plate, is won by a 10-1

chance, The Chase, partnered by a 12-year-old apprentice riding his first winner; the name of the boy – Lester Piggott.

3 Oct The Aga Khan's 4-y-o colt Migoli (101-10), trained by Frank Butters and ridden by Charlie Smirke, strikes a counter-blow for English horses with a successful raid on the Prix de l'Arc de Triomphe.

Obituary: 4 February

Death of the Earl of Derby: King's condolences

The Earl of Derby died at his home, Knowsley, Prescot, Lancs, yesterday. He was 82. On Tuesday night his heart began to fail, and he died in his sleep at 2 a.m. Lady Derby and Lord Stanley, his grandson and heir, were at his bedside. The King and Queen and Princess Elizabeth sent private messages of sympathy to Lady Derby.

The Earl of Rosebery, Senior Steward of the Jockey Club, in a tribute said, "Lord Derby was by far the greatest influence in racing, not only in this generation but in its history. He stood for all that was best in racing, and built up his stud with such care and success that the blood of his racehorses is the backbone of thoroughbred racing not only in this country but throughout the world."

Sir Oliver Harvey, British Ambassador in Paris, stated: "Right up to his death Lord Derby maintained his keen interest in French affairs and followed them very closely. Britain has lost a great man and France a great friend."

HOTSPUR writes: Lord Derby was the foremost owner and breeder of racehorses of his time. He

won every race of importance in England. In 30 years, horses of his breeding won more than 800 races on the Flat with more than £800,000 in stake money.

He headed the list of winning owners seven times, his highest total being £65,603 in 1928. Ten times he was leading breeder of the year. His best, £64,994, was also in 1928.

The famous colours – black jacket and white cap – triumphed in 20 classic races, but it was not until 1924 that Sansovino won for Lord Derby his first Derby. Nine years later he won it again with Hyperion, and a third time in 1942 with Watling Street. The St Leger was his luckiest race. He won it six times – first with Swynford in 1910 and finally with Herringbone in 1943.

In the breeding world, Lord Derby's influence was world-wide. His most famous stallions were Swynford, Phalaris, Pharos, Fairway and Hyperion. During the past 27 years there were 13 occasions when one of his sires headed the winning list.

Lord Derby was elected a member of the Jockey Club in 1905.

CHAMPIONS

Jockey (Flat)	Gordon Richards	224
Jockey (NH)	Bryan Marshall	66
Leading Trainer	Noel Murless	£66,542
Leading Owner	HH Aga Khan III	£46,393
Leading Money Winner	Black Tarquin	£21,423

The Grand National Aintree: 20 March

Stewards may act over "National" blunder: Order to mark all courses

By HOTSPUR

The National Hunt Stewards are likely to issue an instruction very shortly that "dolls" should be placed on all tracks where riders might easily mistake the proper course. Once again in the Grand National we had a horse running off the proper course after jumping the last but one fence and holding a winning chance. The horse was the 100 to 1 outsider Zahia.

In 1936 – Reynoldstown's second year – Davy Jones was out in front when the reins broke and the horse ran out. In Zahia's case, however, it was the jockey's mistake. Reavy mistook the course, and he could not get the mare back in time to jump the last fence.

Zahia was then lying third, but one cannot be certain that she would have won. She seemed to be going better than First of the Dandies at the time, but she might not have been able to hold the challenge of the winner, Sheila's Cottage – the only other mare in the race.

It would certainly have been very remarkable if the only two mares in a field of 43 – both daughters of the great sire of chasers, Cottage – had finished first and second. As it is, the nine-year-old Sheila's Cottage has broken the hoodoo which seemed to prevent mares winning the National. Shannon Lass was

the last to do so, in 1902.

Sheila's Cottage is not in the Stud Book. She was hunted in Ireland and was then bought two years ago for 350 guineas by Sir Harvey Bruce, who resold her on New Year's Day to Mr J.Procter for 3,500 guineas. Mr Procter has succeeded in the National at the first attempt when others have been striving for many years.

Three weeks ago Sheila's Cottage was lame. At the beginning of the week there was still a doubt whether she would run, but the rain came and it was decided to risk her. Her trainer Neville Crump said after the race she might not run again.

It was a wonderful National to watch. First of the Dandies (25-1) led over the water, was momentarily headed by Zahia coming to the second last fence, and first over the last was beaten by Sheila's Cottage (50-1) in the last 100 yards.

Walwyn's pair, Happy Home and Rowland Roy, both ran great races, but faded in the last half mile. Cromwell (33-1) was a worthy third. His gallant rider, Lord Mildmay – the unlucky jockey in 1936 – ricked his neck after the Canal Turn the second time round, and could not raise his head high enough at the last two fences to see them. He took them virtually blind.

NATIONAL HUNT

Champion Hurdle	National Spirit	R Smyth	6-4f
Cheltenham Gold Cup	Cottage Rake	A Brabazon	10-1
Grand National	Sheila's Cottage	A Thompson	50-1

ENGLISH CLASSICS

2,000 Guineas	My Babu	C Smirke	2-1f
1,000 Guineas	Queenpot	G Richards	6-1
Derby	My Love	WR Johnstone	100-9
Oaks	Masaka	W Nevett	7-1
St Leger	Black Tarquin	E Britt	15-2

OTHER MAJOR RACES

Irish Derby	Nathoo	WR Johnstone	7-2
Arc de Triomphe	Migoli	C Smirke	10-1
Kentucky Derby	Citation	E Arcaro	2-5f
Melbourne Cup	Rimfire	R Neville	66-1

Irish Derby The Curragh: 23 June

Record riding treble: Johnstone's three Derby winners
By HOTSPUR

Rae Johnstone, an Australian who has done most of his race riding in France, won his third Derby of the season yesterday when the Aga Khan's Nathoo (7-2) easily defeated the Maharaja of Baroda's Star of Gujrath in the Irish Derby at the Curragh.

Johnstone is the first jockey to win the Epsom Derby, the French Derby and the Irish Derby in one year, and he is now hopeful of bringing off a remarkable quadruple by winning the Grand Prix de Paris on Sunday on our Derby winner, My Love (100-9). It was on My Love's stable companion, Bey (39-2), that he won the French Derby 10 days ago.

Our French correspondent informs me that Bey went better than My Love in a gallop yesterday, but both were beaten by a three-year-old called Espace Vitale, a son of Oleander and foaled in Germany. Espace Vitale is not in the Grand Prix.

It will be remembered that before the Epsom Derby Royal Drake showed superior form at home to My Love. Evidently My Love reserves his best for the racecourse.

Northumberland Plate Newcastle: 23 June

Top weights fight out Pitmen's Derby
BY HOTSPUR

There was a tremendous finish to the Northumberland Plate at Newcastle yesterday between the top weight Pappatea and two others of the 9st division, Billet and Urgay. Blackshaw, who won the Ascot Stakes on No Orchids last week, forced Pappatea (20-1) up on the post to win by a short head. Never before have the top weights had the finish to themselves in the Pitmen's Derby.

Pappatea is owned by an Edinburgh chartered accountant, Mr R.G.Simpson, and is trained in Scotland by George Boyd. He was bought in Ireland as a three-year-old for 2,000gns.

Folkestone: 29 September

Five-timer for Paget-Walwyn-Marshall combination

The combination of owner Miss Dorothy Paget, trainer Fulke Walwyn and champion jump jockey Bryan Marshall monopolised the National Hunt meeting at Folkestone yesterday, winning the first five races and coming second in the last.

Langis Son (10-11f) won the 1.30 by 12 lengths and then Loyal King walked over. The next three races were won by Endless (7-4jf) by a length, Jack Tatters (11-10f) by a neck and Legal Joy (Evens F) by 10 lengths, before Loyal Monarch (3-1jf) went down by 5 lengths to Civvy Street (3-1jf) in the last race.

Johnstone is all smiles as My Love passes the post

The Derby Epsom: 5 June

The Aga Khan's Epsom triumphs: £20,664 in Stakes
By HOTSPUR

The Aga Khan becomes the third man in the past 50 years to win both the Derby and the Oaks in the same season. His victory with My Love in the Derby on Saturday follows the success of his filly Masaka in the Oaks on Thursday.

The two previous owners to bring off the Derby-Oaks double were Chevalier O.Ginistrelli, who won both races with his filly Signorinetta in 1908, and Sir Edward Hulton, who as Mr Hulton won the two substitute races with Fifinella at Newmarket in 1916.

In addition to his two main successes at the Epsom meeting, the Aga Khan won three other races. His total winnings for the week in stake money alone amount to £20,664, of which the Oaks brought in £10,680 and a half-share of the Derby £6,492. M L.Volterra, the French owner-breeder, is the holder of the other half-share

The 1948 Derby was an even greater French triumph than last year, when Pearl Diver carried Baron G.de Waldner's colours to success. Both the first and the second, Royal Drake, were bred by M Volterra and trained by Carver.

My Love (100-9) ran in the Aga Khan's second colours, Royal Drake (25-1) in M Volterra's. But for a late run by Noor (22-1), in the Aga Khan's first colours, all the first three would have been French-bred, as the favourite, My Babu (4-1), a son, like the heavily backed Djeddah, of Djebel, finished fourth.

Sixty-four-year-old Dick Carver, who has trained winners of all the French classics except the Two Thousand Guineas, still would not have it after the race that My Love was the best three-year-old in his stable. That honour he accords to Turmoil, who he expects to win the French Derby next week.

Saturday's race was most dramatic. Royal Drake, having shaken off Tormie and Djeddah a furlong after rounding Tattenham Corner, looked all over a winner. A furlong later he had beaten off the gallant run by My Babu, and then My Love came for him.

Doyasbere, on Royal Drake, had the advantage of the rails. As My Love began to gain rapidly he sensed the danger in good time and drew his whip with a furlong to go. Royal Drake ran on but could not quicken, and in the last 100 yards My Love swept past him at a great pace to win by 1 1/2 lengths. Noor, also finishing fast, flashed past My Babu, but was four lengths behind Royal Drake at the post.

Both Noor and My Love were among the back markers in the first half-mile. My Love was brilliantly ridden by the Australian, W.R.Johnstone.

1949

5 Jun M Leon Volterra, 61, owner of yesterday's Derby runner-up Amour Drake, who has been ill for some time, dies of a heart-attack having listened to the race on the radio from his sick-bed.

6 Jun All 6 races at Yarmouth are won by

fillies, Eastern Secret (13-8f), Treachery (15-8f), Scamper (7-4f), Jane Craig (6-1), Peroration (11-10f) and La Pomponette (11-4).

29 Jun Narrowly beaten 2,000 Guineas favourite Abernant shows he has the sprinting blood of his great-grandmother Mumtaz Mahal, the "flying filly" of the twenties, as he slams the opposition in the July Cup and receives the accolade from his jockey, Gordon Richards: "This is the best sprinter I have ever ridden."

The exciting three-way photo-finish to the Derby

The Derby Epsom: 4 June

Split-second decision loses Derby: Johnstone went wrong way

By HOTSPUR

A split-second decision – and the wrong one – cost Amour Drake the Derby on Saturday.

His Australian jockey, W.Johnstone, instead of continuing the challenge on the outside, checked his horse 100 yards from home and went for an opening on the far rails.

Amour Drake should have won by at least half a length. In a photo-finish, desperately and tensely exciting – he lost by a head to the game Two Thousand Guineas winner, Nimbus.

I have never before seen so thrilling a Derby finish. All the way up what seemed an eternally long straight from Tattenham Corner, Elliott on Nimbus and D.Smith on Swallow Tail fought a desperate and long-drawn-out struggle, with first one and then the other apparently going the better.

Royal Forest looked the only danger to them until, less than a quarter of a mile from home, we saw Amour Drake and Johnstone, in the cherry and white Volterra jacket, making up ground rapidly on the outside.

As they came to the foot of the hill, Nimbus and Swallow Tail were two gallant but very tired horses. I thought then that Swallow Tail would wear the Guineas winner down on the final rise. They both began to hang towards the stands side and gradually edged into the middle of the course.

As they met the rise, Nimbus bumped Swallow Tail, though in the excitement of the race Elliott did not afterwards realise he had done so. It was, however, quite clear from my position on the stands.

The bump meant that Swallow Tail – with Nimbus near him – came still farther towards the stands side, and Johnstone, on Amour Drake, coming up hand over fist, was suddenly faced with the alternative of being perhaps impeded by Swallow Tail, as he hung under pressure, or of switching Amour Drake to the inside.

I think there is no doubt that Amour Drake would have won had he been allowed to continue his run, for he had sufficient in hand of the other two to make light of possible interference from Swallow Tail.

Amour Drake (10-1), though checked and taken behind Swallow Tail (100-8) and Nimbus (7-1), got going again so well in the last 50 yards that he very nearly caught Nimbus on the post. The photograph showed that Amour Drake had been beaten a good head. With a couple of yards more to go he would surely have won.

If Amour Drake had not been there, the Stewards would have been faced with the difficult decision of whether to disqualify Nimbus

The Grand National Aintree: 26 March

Russian Hero was hunter: National triumph for farmer

From HOTSPUR

Against the advice of trainer and jockey, Mr W.F.Williamson ran his horse, the rank outsider Russian Hero (66-1), in the Grand National and won decisively from the top weight, Roimond (22-1), with Royal Mount (18-1) third, and the favourite, Cromwell (6-1), fourth.

George Owen, the trainer, a good Cheshire cross-country rider, and Irish jockey L.McMorrow thought Russian Hero had no chance of staying four and a half miles. Owen begged Mr Williamson to start Russian Hero in the 2 1/2 miles Topham Trophy last Wednesday and not for the National, but Mr Williamson, who refused 4,500 gns for his horse a fortnight ago, stuck to his guns.

He bought Logique, his only brood mare and Russian Hero's dam, for 25gns at Newmarket sales and has had 11 foals from her – including twins – in 10 years. The service fee of Russian Hero's sire, Peter the Great, who was killed by a bomb, was the princely one of 3gns!

For the fourth successive National, the bookmakers have won handsomely. The Totalisator's 200-1 was a far truer estimate of Russian Hero's expectations.

Though only 11 of the 43 runners completed the course, I have rarely seen more with a chance of going to Becher's the second time round. The pace, still a snorter, now began to tell. Royal Cottage refused, Monaveen, Bricett and Southborough fell, Happy Home blundered, and coming to Valentine's Royal Mount was leading from Roimond, Russian Hero, Cromwell, Astra and Gallery.

Three fences from home a loose horse impeded Roimond and in jumping sideways he brought down Astra and Gallery. Cromwell was also having a difficult passage with loose horses and was beginning to tire.

Approaching the last fence but one the race lay between Royal Mount, Russian Hero and Roimond. Here Royal Mount blundered, and his rider, Paddy Doyle, thinks it cost him the race. I am not so sure.

Anyway, Russian Hero came away in the long run-in to win by eight lengths from Roimond, who passed the tiring Royal Mount close home. Cromwell was a good fourth, then came a long gap to Flaming Steel, who was staked during the race.

NATIONAL HUNT			
Champion Hurdle	Hatton's Grace	A Brabazon	100-7
Cheltenham Gold Cup	Cottage Rake	A Brabazon	4-6f
Grand National	Russian Hero	L McMorrow	66-1

Nimbus leads from Swallow Tail at Tattenham Corner

and award the race to Swallow Tail. W.Earl, trainer of Swallow Tail, told me, however, that he considered Swallow Tail a beaten horse at the time he was bumped. This may have been so; but Swallow Tail, a smaller horse than the Guineas winner, though put out of his stride, still finished within two heads of Nimbus.

It was a pity that there could not have been a triple dead-heat. Each would have been a worthy winner.

Ascot Gold Cup: 16 June

Alycidon wins Gold Cup by 5 lengths: Fine double for Lord Derby

From HOTSPUR

Amid much cheering and enthusiasm Lord Derby's Alycidon decisively outstayed the St Leger winner, the American-bred Black Tarquin, in the Gold Cup to-day. He beat him by five lengths, reversing their placings at Doncaster last September. It was good to see an English horse win this great race after horses bred in France or Belgium had filled the first three places for three long years.

Lord Derby's two pacemakers, Stockbridge and Benny Lynch, played their part in Alycidon's triumph to perfection. At the end of nine furlongs Benny Lynch passed Stockbridge, and Alycidon went up second. With a mile to go, D.Smith on Alycidon was beginning to move up to Benny Lynch and soon afterwards he took the lead, with Black Tarquin and Vic Day on his heels.

As they came to the final bend, Alycidon (5-4) and Black Tarquin (11-10f) had drawn right away and the race was between them. Alycidon came into the straight leading Black Tarquin by two lengths with both going well.

With a quarter of a mile to go Britt asked Black Tarquin to go up to Alycidon. For a moment the St Leger winner promised to do so, but in the final furlong he was a beaten horse and Alycidon, galloping on relentlessly, drew away to win.

Doncaster Cup: 8 September

Alycidon's big Cup treble equals record

From HOTSPUR

Alycidon, with odds of 7 to 2 laid on him, won the Doncaster Cup in impeccable style here to-day by eight lengths from the handicapper Aldborough and Harlech. Lord Derby's great horse thus equalled Isonomy's 70-year-old record of winning the Ascot Gold Cup, the Goodwood Cup and the Doncaster Cup in the same season, and he retires to the stud with full honours. His time, 3min 57 1/5 sec, was, I think, a record for the race.

In the absence of Alycidon's usual pacemakers, Benny Lynch and Stockbridge, the three-year-old Amiris made the running, with Aldborough lying third and Harlech fourth and last. Neither the Frenchman Alindrake nor the much-travelled Spam were saddled.

It was feared that Amiris might not be up to the occasion but, in fact, he did his work as a pacemaker well, was going quite a good gallop as the four passed the stands, and continued to lead all round the far side of the course until the field approached the bend into the straight.

Harlech, lying last, was then being driven and clearly had no chance, and as they came to the turn Alycidon had taken over from Amiris and was soon well clear.

D.Smith kept Alycidon going to the end to prove once again the big gap there is between a classic or a good Cup horse and a top-class handicapper. Despite the watered course, Alycidon's time was 12 seconds faster than Auralia's last year.

Royal Commission: 10 September

Race bets average 2s a household: Prize money cut by taxes

DAILY TELEGRAPH REPORTER

Figures were given in evidence before the Royal Commission on Betting, Lotteries and Gaming in London yesterday to show the extent of betting in Britain.

It was stated by Maj. J.R.Chambers, a former secretary of the Racecourse Betting Control Board, that one of the largest and most reputable bookmaking firms had a gross turnover of £2 million to £3 million a year. The average sum spent in betting on horses per household for every working day was 2s.

Viscount Allendale, Senior Steward of the Jockey Club, told the Commission that in 1948 Britain exported about 1,000 thoroughbred horses, worth between £500,000 and £1 million. The cost to an owner of running and training a racehorse would now be not less than £600 a year.

The Jockey Club, in a summary of evidence, said that owing to present high taxation and wages, and the greatly increased cost of policing racecourses on race days and of maintaining courses and buildings, it was exceedingly difficult for racecourse companies to maintain prize money at the high level necessary to ensure that they attracted the best horses.

Entertainment duty also militated against the racecourse. It was imposed at the maximum rate of 9s 2d in the pound, against 3s 2d in the pound for cricket, football, swimming, boxing, theatres and other living performances.

Lord Allendale said that the cost of racing to the owner was going up considerably, and it would become increasingly difficult to carry on flat racing without further aid. The money received by racecourse companies was less than before the war because of the 48 per cent entertainment tax, which had also led to a drop in attendance at race meetings.

A member of the Commission, Sir Eric Mieville, pointed out that at a meeting at Longchamp on Sunday the stakes for the Prix de l'Arc de Triomphe were about £38,000, with £30,000 for the winner. That was at least twice as much as we gave for any of our races. "If French prizes are so much greater than ours," he asked, "are we not in danger of having our best three-year-olds running in French classics rather than our own?" Lord Allendale said that he thought it might be a great temptation.

Chichester 'Chase Fontwell Park: 10 September

Princess sees her horse win

From Our SPECIAL CORRESPONDENT

Princess Elizabeth saw her racing colours carried to victory for the first time here this afternoon. The eight-year-old 'chaser Monaveen, which she owns in partnership with the Queen, won the Chichester 'Chase by 15 lengths.

Though Monaveen was a convincing winner in the end, there was an anxious moment after the three runners had covered the first mile of the 3 1/4 miles course. Getting too close to a plain fence, Monaveen pecked on landing, but the jockey, A.Grantham, quickly had his mount balanced again.

Princess Elizabeth, who was wearing a beige costume and dark brown hat, was delighted with the result of the race, which she followed closely through binoculars.

The 1950s

F rench horses continued to plunder the big British races – to the extent that thirty percent of the English Classics in the 1950s went to raiders from across the Channel. It was the Boyd-Rochfort-trained Meld, however, arguably one of the fillies of the century, who brought off the fillies' Triple Crown (1955) and took her trainer's record career-winnings past the £1m mark.

The most popular Classic win of all was Pinza's victory in 1953, which gave the newly knighted Sir Gordon Richards his Derby win at last and a happy retirement. The new "king", Lester Piggott, did not have to wait long for success in the Blue Riband, winning on Never Say Die in 1954 and notching four more Classics by the end of a decade in which he was rarely out of the headlines – not always for the best reasons. But it was Doug Smith who took up Gordon's reins in the jockeys' championship, winning it five times after the great man's retirement.

On the National Hunt scene, famous hat-tricks, or the completion of them, were performed by Cottage Rake in the Gold Cup and Hatton's Grace and Sir Ken in the Champion Hurdle, the first two of these trained in Ireland by Vincent O'Brien, who then proceeded to pull off an unprecedented hat-trick of Grand Nationals (1953-55). But it was the 1956 National that will forever be remembered – for the "disaster" that overtook the Queen Mother's Devon Loch.

Two major international races were introduced in the fifties, Ascot's King George VI and Queen Elizabeth Stakes and the somewhat gimmicky Washington International. And if an Irishman, O'Brien, was the trainer of the decade, making his mark on the Flat with the likes of Ballymoss (King George, St Leger and Arc) and Gladness (Ascot Gold Cup) after dominating the jumps, then it was an Italian colt who was the horse of the decade, perhaps of the century – Ribot, unbeaten in 16 races, including two Arcs and a King George.

Sir Gordon at last: at the 28th attempt, Richards wins the Coronation Derby on Pinza in 1953.

1950

25 Mar Yorkshire-trained horses fill the first 3 places in the Grand National, Freebooter (10-1jf) winning by 15 and 10 lengths from Wot No Sun (100-7) and

Acthon Major (33-1). Monaveen (100-7), who comes 5th, is jointly owned by the Queen and Princess Elizabeth, and the first royal competitor in the National for 42 years.

4 May Gordon Richards rides his 4,000th winner the day before his 46th birthday, when one of his all-time favourite horses, the grey Abernant, wins the Lubbock Sprint at Sandown.

26 May Derby favourite Prince Simon, his trainer Capt.Boyd-Rochfort and his jockey W.Carr have a narrow escape when a runaway hack ridden by an apprentice gallops out of hand into Epsom's paddock and just misses them.

3 Jun Citation, 1948 US Triple Crown winner, takes his career winnings past Stymie's world record of $918,485 with a success at Albany.

20 Sep Lester Piggott, 14, loses his claiming allowance when he rides Zina to victory in the Brighton Autumn Cup, his 40th success in races not confined to apprentices, and is already being spoken of as a possible successor to Gordon Richards.

8 Oct St Leger winner Scratch II is beaten into 4th place in the Prix de l'Arc de Triomphe, won by Tantième.

CHAMPIONS

Jockey (Flat)	Gordon Richards	201
Jockey (NH)	Tim Molony	95
Leading Trainer	Charles Semblat (Fra)	£57,044
Leading Owner	Marcel Boussac	£57,044
Leading Money Winner	Palestine	£21,583

Holbeton, S.Devon: 12 May

Sea and air search for Lord Mildmay

Clothes found after bathe: Footprints on Beach

From our SPECIAL CORRESPONDENT

Lord Mildmay of Flete, 41, the 6ft 4in amateur steeplechase jockey, was missing late tonight after failing to return from an early morning bathe in the sea here today. When darkness fell and the search was abandoned, little hope was entertained for his safety.

Lord Mildmay had gone for his usual morning swim from the private beach of Mothecombe House, where he lived. It was his practice to swim out to a rock a mile from the shore every day.

Small naval craft from Plymouth and Otter aircraft of the Fleet Air Arm, which took part with other vessels in the search, were recalled tonight. The area of the Channel outside Mothecombe had been covered. Also recalled were the Plymouth lifeboat and an RAF sea-rescue launch.

He left the house at 8.30 taking with him a bucket of fresh water for a wash-down after his bathe. When he had not returned shortly after nine o'clock an immediate search was made.

A pile of clothing, the bucket of fresh water and a trail of footprints across the otherwise unmarked sand leading into the sea were all the searchers found. There

were no returning footprints.

Lord Mildmay is the second holder of the title and is unmarried. In the event of his death the title would become extinct. He succeeded on the death of his father in 1947, inheriting £180,000 and estates in Devon and Kent. He was educated at Eton and Trinity College, Cambridge.

Despite his height, he is one of the most successful, as well as most popular, amateur riders. He is a member of the Jockey Club and a steward of the National Hunt Committee. He is also an underwriting member of Lloyds.

During his riding, he has hurt himself many times, his injuries including three fractured ribs, a fractured arm and a severely bruised thumb and collar-bone.

His life's ambition is to win the Grand National. Fate has been against him. He would have won the race in 1936 on Davy Jones but the reins broke and the horse ran off the course. When he ricked his neck on his own horse, Cromwell, he jumped the last three fences blindly, yet finished third. He has ridden in the race six times.

In 1946-7 he was leading amateur steeplechase jockey, with 32 winners, and last season rode 30.

NATIONAL HUNT

Champion Hurdle	Hatton's Grace	A Brabazon	5-2f
Cheltenham Gold Cup	Cottage Rake	A Brabazon	5-6f
Grand National	Freebooter	J Power	10-1jf

Cheltenham Gold Cup: 9 March

Cottage Rake lands Gold Cup hat-trick

Beats Finnure by 10 lengths

From HOTSPUR

Cottage Rake to-day joined Golden Miller as the second horse to win the Cheltenham Gold Cup three years in succession. Thanks partly to the brilliant opportunism of his jockey, Aubrey Brabazon, Cottage Rake (5-6f) won very easily by 10 lengths from Finnure (5-4). It was the easiest Gold Cup victory since the days of Golden Miller.

It is a pity Cottage Rake has not yet been allowed to take his chance in the Grand National. He stays so well I think he would acquit himself with credit. A National triumph would entitle him to be considered on the same plane as The Miller.

Brabazon showed once again that he is a great man for the

big occasion. It was a very poor gallop for the first mile and a half, and contrary to expectation Brabazon took Cottage Rake to the front with the other five bunched close up.

Going away from the stands again, Cottage Rake was asked to quicken, and he went into a six lengths lead. Making the final turn for home, he was about four lengths clear, but Brabazon slipped his field directly he rounded the bend and came to the next fence at least a dozen lengths in front of Finnure – with his race won.

It was rather a sad anti-climax. Nevertheless, all honour to Cottage Rake for a smashing performance; to his jockey, winner of the last two Champion Hurdles and Gold Cups; and to his trainer, Vincent O'Brien, who has saddled these.

Brabazon and Cottage Rake take the last fence to win the Gold Cup for a third time

The Derby Epsom: 27 May

M Boussac lands Oaks-Derby double

Fading Galcador hangs on to win by a head

By HOTSPUR

For the first time since the Italian Chevalier E.Ginistrelli won both the Derby and the Oaks with his filly Signorinetta 42 years ago, the same owner, trainer and jockey have brought off the double at Epsom. M Marcel Boussac, who won the Oaks with Asmena, landed the Derby with Galcador, ridden by Asmena's jockey, W. Johnstone, and trained by C.H. Semblat in France. Galcador

(100-9) beat the favourite Prince Simon (2-1) by a head.

The defeat of Mr Woodward's colt was a great disappointment to many. I had hoped to be able to say today that Prince Simon was probably a great horse. He is not. He is a very good horse, but no more. He had his race as good as won at 10 furlongs and again 10 feet past the post, but not at the place which mattered.

St Leger Doncaster: 9 September

Scratch II brings Boussac winnings to £47,732: Another classic triumph for Johnstone

By HOTSPUR

For the first time since the St Leger was founded 174 years ago, a colt trained in France won the last classic race of the season at Doncaster on Saturday. The winner, Scratch II, is owned and was bred by M M.Boussac, and is trained for him in France by the former jockey, Charles Semblat. The only two French-bred winners of the past were Comte F. de Lagrange's pair Gladiateur (1865) and Rayon d'Or (1879), both trained by Tom Jennings at Newmarket.

This has been a wonderful season for M Boussac, who is now leading owner and breeder in this country with £47,732 for five races won, including Galcador's Derby (£17,010), Asmena's Oaks (£13,508) and now Scratch's St Leger (£13,959).

It has been a record season for his jockey too, the Australian Rae Johnstone, who, in addition to those three classics, also won the 1,000 Guineas on Camarée.

What of Saturday's race? Without detracting from the courage and ability of Scratch, I must report that I think Johnstone's skill probably made all the difference.

As seemed probable on form, the St Leger was, in effect, a duel between Scratch (9-2) and Vieux Manoir (7-4f) in the last quarter of a mile. Vieux Manoir moved smoothly into the lead with fully three furlongs to go, with Scratch about five lengths behind. But Johnstone did not become flurried, and slowly closed with the favourite until Scratch won an exciting race by a length.

Jockey Club Cup Newmarket: 26 October

Colonist II brings 1950 winnings to £7,202
Slams French pair to win 6th in a row
From HOTSPUR

From the jockey prodigy Lester Piggott and the gallant filly Zina, so narrowly beaten in the Cambridgeshire yesterday, the scene shifted this afternoon to Mr Churchill, another of racing's "new boys", and his equally gallant grey Colonist II, who set the seal on a memorable 1950 record by winning the Jockey Club Cup from his two French-trained rivals Pas de Calais and Miel Rosa.

Colonist II and Mr Churchill will go down in racing history as a unique partnership. Mr Churchill had never owned a racehorse in his life until 15 months ago, when Colonist II, bred in France, was bought for him for 1,500gns.

No one took the venture very seriously, but this remarkable colt started by winning a small race in Mr Churchill's colours at Salisbury in August last year and his only occasionally stopped winning since.

He wound up 1949 with three wins, and this year Colonist II has won eight of his 11 races – the last six in succession. His winning stake money for 1950 totals £7,202. He is surely the bargain horse of the year, perhaps of 10 years. Colonist II has taken on Brown Jack's mantle and is

just as popular as that grand stayer of the 1930's.

Mr Churchill has enjoyed the thrill of watching Colonist II in nearly all his races. He flew in from Northolt this afternoon just in time to see his horse saddled. The race for the Jockey Club Cup is run over the full Cesarewitch Course of 2¼ miles and it is not until the field has turned well into the straight, a mile out, that the colours can be picked up.

Gordon Richards, on Baron Guy de Rothschild's three-year-old Miel Rosa, who was receiving 12lb from Colonist II, was making the running on the outside when my glasses picked up the three starters. More than a quarter of a mile from home Gosling had Colonist II go, and once again we had the gripping spectacle of this grey and gallant horse, flaxen tail flowing in the wind, plugging along in front. He finished a length and a half ahead of Pas de Calais with Miel Rosa eight lengths behind the second.

There followed the ringing cheers and the familiar scene of hundreds of happy people scampering to the unsaddling enclosure to acclaim horse and owner. Never, surely, has there been a racing partnership the equal of this.

Cambridgeshire Handicap Newmarket: 25 October

Kelling first in exciting photo-finish
Disappointment for Piggott
From HOTSPUR

After one of the most exciting photo-finishes on record, the Cambridgeshire was won here this afternoon by Mr C.Jarvis's colt Kelling. The camera showed he had beaten Lady Isabel Guinness's filly Zina by a neck, with Mr L.Redfern's Valdesco a head away third.

Only those standing dead in line with the winning post knew which of the three had gained the day when the loudspeaker announced a photo-finish, but young Lester Piggott, who was making a forced farewell appearance for the season by edict of the Jockey Club, seemed to harbour no doubts. He rode Zina confidently into the enclosure reserved for the winner. Douglas Smith took Kelling into the place allotted to the second horse.

Excitement was tense as Lady Guinness rushed to congratulate Piggott. Kelling's

The 14-year-old Piggott (right)

owner also felt sure that Zina had won, and there was a cry of surprise from the huge crowd when Kelling was declared the winner.

I have no doubt the best horse won at the weights. Kelling overcame the handicap of having to race on his own in the centre of the course. He took the lead going into the Dip and from that point was never headed.

Wimbledon Handicap 'Chase Kempton Park: 24 November

Manicou easy winner in the Queen's colours
Possible beaten by eight lengths
From HOTSPUR

Very happy racing history was made here this afternoon when the Queen's colours – blue, buff strips, blue sleeves, black cap and gold tassel – were successful for the first time. Her Majesty and Princess Elizabeth were present to see the five-year-old chaser Manicou win the Wimbledon Handicap 'Chase by eight lengths from the Duchess of Norfolk's Possible and five other rivals.

Manicou jumped faultlessly and Grantham, his rider,

never had a moment's anxiety about the outcome. Cheering, increasing in volume, began when Manicou went to the front entering the straight, to which point Possible, winner of the Molyneux 'Chase at Aintree a fortnight ago, had made the running. These two were well clear of the rest of the field, and Manicou jumped slightly ahead at the last fence. Taking this in his stride, the Queen's horse sprinted away on the flat to win handsomely.

1951

9 Jan Middleham trainer Neville Crump saddles his 7th consecutive winner, at Leicester, the first having been sent out at Birmingham on 12 Dec.

5 May Champion jockey Gordon Richards celebrates his 47th birthday with a hat-trick at Newbury, following a 4-timer yesterday at Newmarket.

13 Jun Val d'Assa (100-6) is the first filly to win Ascot's Royal Hunt Cup since Gratitude in 1865, and her Australian jockey N.Sellwood, in his first season over here, also steers Proud Scot (100-6) home in the Bessborough Stakes.

14 Jul 6-y-o Citation becomes the first "dollar millionaire" when winning the Hollywood Gold Cup in California, having been kept in training, despite injury problems, solely to achieve this target, an ambition of his late owner, Warren Wright; he is retired forthwith, having amassed $1,085,760 in prize money, with 32 wins, 10 2nds and 2 3rds in 45 starts.

25 Aug Lester Piggott, 15, who last month won the Eclipse on French horse Mystery IX, breaks a leg and collar bone when his mount No Light is brought down by Persian Wood (Eph Smith) at Lingfield and is out for the rest of the season; Smith also breaks a collar-bone.

31 Oct At Newmarket, the Cambridgeshire Handicap, with a field of 44, beating by one a record that has stood since 1862, is won by 5-y-o Fleeting Moment (28-1).

CHAMPIONS

Jockey (Flat)	Gordon Richards	227
Jockey (NH)	Tim Molony	83
Leading Trainer	Jack Jarvis	£56,397
Leading Owner	Marcel Boussac	£39,339
Leading Money Winner	Supreme Court	£36,016

Grand National Aintree: 7 April

National debacle stuns Aintree crowd

29 crash in first quarter of race

By HOTSPUR

After a race reminiscent of the fiasco of Tipperary Tim's year, three out of 36 horses finished the Grand National course on Saturday. The only two who remained standing were the winner Nickel Coin (40-1) and the runner-up Royal Tan (22-1). Derrinstown (66-1), brought down at Becher's second time round, was remounted and finished third, long after Nickel Coin had passed the post.

After such high hopes of a thrilling race, it was desperately disappointing to see only a handful of horses still on their feet after Valentine's first time round. All the giants were gone – Finnure and Land Fort with nine others at the first, Freebooter at the second, Shagreen (a victim of his own carelessness) at the fifth, 8-1 favourite Arctic Gold (his attention distracted by a loose horse) at the Canal Turn when leading, where Armoured Knight, Cloncarrig and Price Brownie also met their fates, and finally Roimond at Valentine's.

The perfect light one sometimes gets after rain, the reasonable going and the best National field since the war, all pointed to a thrilling tussle. Who could have expected 29 victims in the first quarter of the race?

It was so staggering that the crowd was silent as the seven survivors came on to the racecourse for the first time, Russian Hero leading and jumping like a stag, and apparently going best of the lot. But loose horses badly hampered him at the Chair, and the 1949 National winner hit the top and came down – as for the same reason did his stable companion Dog Watch.

Now there were only five standing. Gay Heather went at Becher's bringing down Derrinstown, Broomfield at the next, and that left only Nickel Coin and Royal Tan to fight it out.

A good race between the two it certainly was. There was nothing to choose between them coming to the last fence, with Royal Tan, if anything, going the better. But it was Royal Tan and not the gallant little mare who hit the fence, and it was then "all Nickel Coin to a China orange".

All praise to Nickel Coin's Staffordshire rider, John Bullock, former paratrooper, captured at Arnhem, and now in his middle thirties. It was his first Grand National ride and only the second time he had ridden over fences at Aintree. Full marks also to Royal Tan's rider, Mr A. O'Brien, younger brother of the horse's trainer, Vincent, riding at Aintree for the first time.

NATIONAL HUNT

Champion Hurdle	Hatton's Grace	A Brabazon	4-1
Cheltenham Gold Cup	Silver Fame	M Molony	6-4f
Grand National	Nickel Coin	JA Bullock	40-1

Champion Hurdle Cheltenham: 6 March

Hatton's Grace makes Cheltenham history

Pulls off Champion Hurdle hat-trick

From HOTSPUR

The Old Guard showed themselves far superior to their younger rivals in the Champion Hurdle to-day, for National Spirit and Hatton's Grace came to the last hurdle almost together and with the race between them. National Spirit fell, leaving Hatton's Grace to win on his own from the French pair, Pyrrhus III and Prince Hindou.

Hatton's Grace (4-1) thus becomes the first horse to win the Champion Hurdle three times, and what is more he has achieved the feat in successive years. He is no beauty but he has great courage, and handsome is as handsome does.

Poor old National Spirit! He is the finest hurdler I have ever seen and with any luck at all would have won not two Champion Hurdles but five. He has not the finishing speed of Hatton's Grace, but as a hurdler pure and simple he is the best for many years.

His fall at the last is almost too sad to write about. If he had stood up I think there would have been a great finish between the two old warriors. National Spirit held a slight lead at the time, but Hatton's Grace seemed to be going the better of the two. It is a question about which people will argue for a long time to come.

It was Tim Molony's first success in the Champion Hurdle and a lucky chance ride for him, for his brother, Martin, would have ridden the 11-year-old gelding had he not been laid up with measles.

Cheltenham Gold Cup: 25 April

Silver Fame's Gold Cup in record time

By a SPECIAL CORRESPONDENT

In brilliantly fine weather the postponed race for the Cheltenham Gold Cup was won here this afternoon after a thrilling finish by Lord Bicester's Silver Fame, who defeated Mr J.V.Rank's Greenogue by a short head, with Mr L.B.Chugg's Mighty Fine two lengths away third.

Only six went to the post, but the race, which was worth £2,783 to the winning owner, has not produced such cheering by the excited onlookers since the epic struggle of 1933 when Golden Miller beat Thomond.

Martin Molony has never ridden a better-judged race or a finer finish. He kept Silver Fame, the 6-4 favourite, well in the rear while Greenogue (25-2) and Lockerbie (3-1) made the running. Silver Fame joined the leaders three fences out and they were level at the last fence.

Lockerbie faded on landing, and responding to Molony's efforts Silver Fame got up to beat Greenogue in the last stride.

Horse and rider were given a tremendous ovation and Lord Bicester was almost overwhelmed with congratulations.

Silver Fame has for long been one of the most popular 'chasers in training and to-day's triumph crowns a great record at Cheltenham, where he has won nine times. The firm going was all in Silver Fame's favour and the race was run in the record time of 6min 23.4sec.

The Derby Epsom: 30 May

Arctic Prince slams his rivals by six lengths

French challenge a complete failure

From HOTSPUR

For the first time for five years the French challenge in the Derby failed completely. The race – the richest ever run in this country – was won with great ease by Arctic Prince (28-1), winner by six lengths from Sybil's Nephew (50-1) and Signal Box (20-1), who were divided by a head in a photo-finish for second place. It was the easiest Derby victory since pre-war days.

Arctic Prince was ridden by 32-year-old C.Spares, stable jockey to W.Stephenson, who trains at Royston, in Hertfordshire. It was Spares's first ride in the Derby. Gordon Richards, taking part in the race for the 26th time, never looked like being concerned in the finish. Such is the luck of racing!

The winner is owned and was bred in Ireland by Mr J.McGrath, who took a prominent part in Irish politics after the first world war, and started the Irish Hospital Sweepstakes. He is a Dublin man by birth.

As they came to Tattenham Corner, Mystery IX was leading from Raincheck, with Arctic Prince and Crocodile on his heels. With three furlongs to go Spares took Arctic Prince to the front. I did not at this stage notice Sybil's Nephew, and when I did the race was over, such was the superiority of the winner.

King George VI and Queen Elizabeth Festival of Britain Stakes Ascot: 21 July

Supreme Court probably best 3-year-old in Europe

By HOTSPUR

Supreme Court, turned down in his younger days by two of England's leading trainers, won the Festival of Britain Stakes at Ascot on Saturday by three-quarters of a length to show himself the best three-year-old in the country – and probably in Europe.

Zucchero, the runner-up, gave Supreme Court a good race, but Tantième, principal hope of the French, only just scrambled into third place at the expense of Colonist II, finishing six lengths behind Zucchero.

When the Festival race was first projected last year, there were some who said it would be foolish to run it over a mile and a half, for it would be at the mercy of the French. Fortunately, such faint-hearted counsel did not prevail, and the race was run as such a race should be run, over the full Derby distance.

After the many reverses we have had since the war at the hands of the French, it is pleasant to be able to record that both first and second in the Festival race are British bred.

Mr T.Lilley paid 8,100gns for Supreme Court's dam, Forecourt, and gave Supreme Court to his wife as a present. As a result of the colt's successes, Mrs Lilley is now the season's leading owner. It was because of his lack of promise in his yearling days that Supreme Court was not entered in any of the classic races. In winning the Festival Stakes, Supreme Court broke the course record for the distance, his time being 2min 29.4sec.

Light was shed yesterday upon the failure of Arctic Prince, the Derby winner, by his trainer, W.Stephenson, who announced that the horse had been found to be lame when he returned to Royston.

[Supreme Court was retired to stud without racing again, his 3-y-o winnings of £36,016 only £3,556 short of Coronach's 1926 record. 'Festival of Britain' was subsequently dropped from the race title.]

ENGLISH CLASSICS			
2,000 Guineas	Ki Ming	A Breaseley	100-8
1,000 Guineas	Belle of All	G Richards	4-1f
Derby	Arctic Prince	C Spares	28-1
Oaks	Neasham Belle	T Clayton	33-1
St Leger	Talma	WR Johnstone	7-1

OTHER MAJOR RACES			
Irish Derby	Fraise du Bois	C Smirke	5-2jf
Arc de Triomphe	Tantième	J Doyasbère	17-10f
Kentucky Derby	Count Turf	C McCreary	146-10
Melbourne Cup	Delta	N Sellwood	10-1

Prix de l'Arc de Triomphe Longchamp: 7 October

Tantième brings off big French race double

English trio fail to gain a place

By HOTSPUR

M F.Dupré's Tantième, the favourite, won the Prix de l'Arc de Triomphe decisively for the second year in succession at Longchamp yesterday. He won by two lengths from the Italian colt Nuccio, who has been trained in France since the early summer, with Le Tyrol a length farther away third.

None of the three English-trained runners, Fraise du Bois II, Le Sage or Saturn were concerned in the finish, though Festival Stakes form at Ascot is a pointer to the fact that if Supreme Court had been in the field he would have been a comfortable winner.

At Ascot, over yesterday's distance of a mile and a half at weight-for-age, Supreme Court defeated Tantième by an official margin on 6 3/4 lengths. Even allowing for the fact that Tantième is a bad traveller and is therefore a better horse on home ground, it is still reasonable to suppose that Supreme Court would have won comfortably had his owner let this lightly raced three-year-old take his chance.

Vauxhall Novices' Hurdle Kempton Park: 21 November

Devon Loch is 'chaser in the making – well beaten but still backward

From HOTSPUR

The Queen has a promising 'chaser in the making in her five-year-old Devon Loch, who, though still a bit backward, finished second to the more experienced Rahshas in the Vauxhall Novices' Hurdle here to-day.

Devon Loch has the stamp of a 'chaser rather than a hurdler, and it is at steeplechasing that he should shine. The Queen and Princess Elizabeth both came so see him run.

At the bottom end of the course Rahshas and Devon Loch had drawn clear with the race between them. Devon Loch could not quicken in the run-in and Rahshas won decisively by eight lengths.

Devon Loch should be the better for the experience of to-day's race, and it will be disappointing if he does not win a hurdle race for the Queen shortly.

1952

6 Mar With the Champion Hurdle won by Sir Ken, Mont Tremblant's victory in the Gold Cup means that the two big Cheltenham races have been won for the first time in the same season by horses bred in France.

5 Apr A copyright dispute between Aintree owners Tophams Ltd and the BBC deprives listeners of their usual excellent radio coverage of the Grand National, and a last-minute compromise by Tophams with their own team backfires when their commentator gives Teal as a faller at the first fence. Teal wins!

3 May Hill Gail is the 5th Kentucky Derby winner for jockey Eddie Arcaro, the 6th for trainer Ben Jones, both two more than than the next best records in the race.

19 Jul With his victory at Ascot in the "King George", Derby hero Tulyar brings his grand total of stake money won to £60,956, beating the previous highest aggregate for a racehorse in Britain, the £58,655 won by Isinglass from 1882 to 1885. The King George, at £23,302 bringing nearly £3,000 more prize money than the Derby, takes Tulyar's seasonal earnings to £59,351 and beats the record set by Coronach (£39,624) in 1926.

CHAMPIONS

Jockey (Flat)	Gordon Richards	231
Jockey (NH)	Tim Molony	99
Leading Trainer	Marcus Marsh	£92,093
Leading Owner	HH Aga Khan III	£92,518
Leading Money Winner	Tulyar	£75,173

Cheltenham Gold Cup: 6 March

Mont Tremblant slams Gold Cup rivals

Freebooter falls: Shaef unlucky

From HOTSPUR

Miss Dorothy Paget won her seventh Cheltenham Gold Cup today with her six-year-old Mont Tremblant. The finish was tame, but it would certainly not have been so had not Knock Hard fallen two fences from home when lying second and going, in my opinion, better than the winner.

A race which had looked reasonably certain to end in a close finish failed to do so through various incidents. Shaef finished second in spite of almost losing his bridle at the water first time round.

Freebooter (7-2f) fell on the first circuit on his unlucky course. ESB (8-1) was lying second but a beaten horse when he came down at the last fence, but there was no excuse for last year's winner Silver Fame (6-1), who, on the soggy ground, ran like a light of former days.

Mont Tremblant was bought in France as a four-year-old for Miss Paget by Mr Michael Stacpoole, formerly leading amateur rider on the Continent. In France the horse won once on the flat and twice over hurdles.

Two fences from home Mont Tremblant (8-1) was still nearly two lengths in front of Knock Hard (5-1), who was steadily catching Miss Paget's six-year-old. I thought then that Knock Hard's speed would prove decisive in the run-in, as on more than one occasion it had done with his stable companion Cottage Rake. It was not to be. Knock Hard got too close to the fence and came down, leaving Mont Tremblant clear of a tiring ESB.

As Mont Tremblant came to the last he had his race won barring a fall. He blundered at it but stood up and a beaten ESB came down, leaving the gallant Shaef (7-1) to finish second and Galloway Braes (66-1) third.

Mont Tremblant was well ridden by D.V.Dick and looked a credit to his trainer, F.Walwyn, whose first Gold Cup winner this was.

NATIONAL HUNT

Champion Hurdle	Sir Ken	T Molony	3-1f
Cheltenham Gold Cup	Mont Tremblant	DV Dick	8-1
Grand National	Teal	AP Thompson	100-7

OTHER MAJOR RACES

Irish Derby	Thirteen of Diamonds	J Mullane	10-1
Arc de Triomphe	Nuccio	R Poincelet	74-10
Kentucky Derby	Hill Gail	E Arcaro	11-10f
Melbourne Cup	Dalray	W Williamson	5-1f

Grand National Aintree: 5 April

Ex-hack lands National gamble of century

Teal joins ranks of the immortals

By HOTSPUR

Mr H.Lane, 52-year-old Stockton-on-Tees engineering contractor, whose Barnes Park won the Lincolnshire Handicap last year, refused an American offer of £20,000 for his ex-hunter 'chaser Teal after the 10-year-old second favourite had triumphed in the Grand National on Saturday.

The race was worth £9,268 in stake money to Mr Lane, who, I believe, also brought off the biggest Grand National betting coup of the century (his win is thought to run well into five figures), besides having the superb thrill of winning the Lincoln and National in successive year.

Teal, who was point-to-pointing last year, has, like many National winners of the past, had an extremely varied career. His Irish breeder, Mr G.Carroll, of Clonmel, once offered him for sale for £2 10s - with no takers - and later sold him with another horse for £38 the pair.

Mr Lane bought Teal for £2,000 last May after he had won the United Border 'Chase at Kelso for his then owner-rider Mr Ridley Lamb, of Thornaby, a hunting farmer.

It was Mr Ridley Lamb who first realised Teal's possibilities. Before be bought him, Teal had been used as a ladies' hack, had been owned by an Army officer at Catterick Camp, and by Mr John Patterson, a Northallerton farmer who gave 36gns for him but found him a bit of a handful.

Bad visibility marred the race. After a false start and 10 minutes delay due to the tapes being broken, the field were well away. The first fence took heavy toll but was not so disastrous as last year. Ten of the 47 went here, including the 1949 winner Russian Hero (50-1), who fell.

Soon after Valentine's Wot No Sun (33-1), who had never made the semblance of a mistake, began to tire, and Legal Joy (100-6), Teal (100-7) and Royal Tan (22-1) drew away with the race between them. Two fences from home, Teal and Legal Joy were racing neck-and-neck with Royal Tan just behind.

At the last, Legal Joy, on the rails, and Teal jumped almost together. Royal Tan hit the fence, as he had done last year, and crumpled up on landing. It was desperately bad luck on his rider, Mr A.S.O'Brien, but I thought he was beaten at the time.

In the long run-in to the finishing post, Teal had more in reserve and drew away to win by five lengths in very fast time - only one-fifth of a second outside Golden Miller's record. A weary Wot No Sun finished a bad third.

ENGLISH CLASSICS

2,000 Guineas	Thunderhead	R Poincelet	100-7
1,000 Guineas	Zabara	K Gethin	7-1
Derby	Tulyar	C Smirke	11-2f
Oaks	Frieze	E Britt	100-7
St Leger	Tulyar	C Smirke	10-11f

Tulyar storms home to beat Gay Time in a tight Derby finish, with French challenger Faubourg II third

The Derby Epsom: 25 May

Tulyar gives Aga Khan fifth Derby triumph

Gay Time unlucky, but a gallant second

From HOTSPUR

In winning his fifth Derby with Tulyar today, the Aga Khan equalled the 126-year-old record of Lord Egremont, the only other owner to have won five Derbys in the long history of the race. Tulyar (11-2f) won by three-quarters of a length from Gay Time (25-1), with Faubourg II (100-6), the best of the French colts, a length away third.

Tulyar, in the leading six throughout, spread a plate during the race, which probably caused him to hang in the closing stages. In doing so he may have slightly interfered with the run of leading apprentice Lester Piggott on Gay Time.

After the race, Piggott wished to object to the winner. The Stewards asked Noel Cannon, trainer of Gay Time, if he wanted to lodge an objection. Neither Cannon nor Gay Time's owner Mrs J.V.Rank wished to, so none was made.

The decision was the sequel to a tense half-hour which followed the race, for after passing the winning post, Gay Time threw Piggott near the entrance to the paddock, eluded a gateman and made off towards the town.

Piggott arrived back at the unsaddling enclosure minus horse and saddle, and on the orders of the Stewards weighed in as he was. The Stewards hurriedly met to consider the position, but fortunately at 3.55 - 25 minutes after the start of the race - Gay Time was returned to the unsaddling enclosure, and Piggott, who had changed into different colours for the next race, weighed in officially. Then came the matter of the "objection", so it was not until 4.10, when the next race was due to start, that the "all right" was hoisted.

Tulyar was without doubt a worthy winner, but Gay Time's luck was certainly out. He spread a plate in the paddock and did not take part in the parade. Then he was bumped at the start and was soon at the tail end of the field. With two furlongs to go, Tulyar was in the lead. When Gay Time came to challenge, I noticed Tulyar edging to his right, but I did not see him interfere with Gay Time.

It was Tulyar's fourth successive victory this season and he remains unbeaten as a three-year-old.

[Tulyar set the seal on his fame at Ascot by winning the King George VI and Queen Elizabeth Stakes clearly on merit, holding off Gay Time by a neck in a tremendous finish, and went on to capture the St Leger, too.]

Aureole's impressive win for the Queen

From HOTSPUR

The Queen may well have in Aureole a colt good enough to carry her colours in the Coronation Derby next year. Though "green" and not seriously fancied by his stable, Aureole won the Acomb Stakes to-day from a useful field. As the colt was at least 10 lengths behind the leaders at one stage, his performance was considerably better than it appears on paper.

Capt.Charles Moore, the Queen's racing manager, hopes and believes that Aureole is a high-class colt in the making. By Hyperion out of Angelola, who won the Yorkshire Oaks for King George VI, Aureole is a bright chestnut with rather a lot of white about him. He is inclined to be flashy, and I confess I did not like him much in the parade ring beforehand. But in the race he ran home as true as a die.

With a furlong to go, the race looked to be between Brolly and North Light, with Aureole making up ground steadily. Brolly mastered North Light, but Aureole came through to challenge like an old hand.

Carr had strict orders not to show Aureole the whip, but it was not necessary, for Aureole ran on well to win by a head in a photo-finish, with North Light one and a half lengths further away third.

Carr told me after the race that Aureole was well away, but that he purposely tucked him in behind other horses to teach him to race, and the colt was thus left with a lot of ground to make up. Carr was extremely pleased with Aureole's running, as was Capt.C.Boyd-Rochfort, his trainer.

Wilwyn's triumph was course record

By HOTSPUR

In spite of the sharp course and the long air journey, Mr R.C.Boucher's Wilwyn surprised American experts by winning the international race over one-and-a-half miles at Laurel Park, Maryland, on Saturday in the course-record time of 2min 30.8sec.

Wilwyn, who paid 13-2 on the Tote, won by one-and-a-half lengths from an American horse, Ruhe, with Britain's other representative, the temperamental Zucchero, a neck further behind, third. The rest of the field comprised two other American horses, a German and a Canadian horse.

Wilwyn's victory is extremely good news for British breeders, who were feeling somewhat discomfited by the poor prices realised at the Newmarket Sales last week. Mr Boucher, a fruit farmer, bred Wilwyn at his own Kentish stud.

Since the war, French and Irish breeders have gone out of their way to boost their stock. It is therefore pleasant that a small English breeder should succeed in the first international race run in America.

In this country, Wilwyn has never been considered quite in the top class. At the end of his three-year-old days, the Jockey Club handicapper rated him 15lb inferior to last year's Derby winner Arctic Prince and 8lb behind Zucchero.

No one really knows how good a four-year-old Wilwyn now is, for he has been brilliantly placed by his Newmarket trainer, George Colling, to win 10 races off the reel in this country - almost always against non-classic horses. After this American triumph, however, one is left wondering what would have happened had Wilwyn taken part in the King George VI and Queen Elizabeth Stakes at Ascot against Tulyar and company.

The English jockeys, E.Mercer, on Wilwyn, and C.Smirke, on Zucchero, received high praise from their American counterparts. Eddie Arcaro, acknowledged as America's foremost jockey, who rode the unplaced 6-5 favourite Greek Ship, said he had been tremendously impressed by the cool way his British rivals had ridden their mounts, and how they had stayed close to the rails throughout and timed their finishing efforts perfectly.

1953

28 Feb Jump jockey Tim Molony rides 5 winners and a 4th at Haydock Park.

1 Jun Champion jockey Gordon Richards, 49, is knighted in the combined Coronation and Birthday Honours List, the first professional jockey so honoured.

24 June In the first photo-finish in the Irish Derby, Premonition (2-1) edges a head verdict over Chamier (5-4f) but the 2nd's trainer, Vincent O'Brien, lodges an objection and Premonition is disqualified.

6 Jul The 20-1 on favourite Galloping Gold, ridden by G.Lewis, is beaten in the Elvaston Apprentice Stakes at Nottingham – by a distance – by the only other runner, Priory Paul (20-1), who gives owner-breeder Miss P.M.Judson her first winner.

11 Jul Billy Nevett is successful with all 5 of his mounts at Newcastle.

1 Sep Doug Smith is successful with all 5 of his mounts at Birmingham.

4 Oct It's more bad luck for St Leger winner Premonition, who is struck into while challenging the leaders in the Arc and finishes sixth, sustaining a gashed leg that threatens to end his career. The race is a remarkable triumph for M.Duboscq and his Chantilly trainer Etienne Pollet, who saddles the first two, the 3-year-old filly La Sorellina and, beaten by a head, her half-brother Silnet.

24 Oct After 17 consecutive wins (including one on the Flat), Champion Hurdler Sir Ken's streak comes to an ignominious end in a weight-for-age event at Uttoxeter when, starting at 7-1 on, he is beaten into 3rd place by outsider Impney.

CHAMPIONS

Jockey (Flat)	Sir Gordon Richards	191
Jockey (NH)	Fred Winter	121
Leading Trainer	Jack Jarvis	£71,546
Leading Owner	Sir Victor Sassoon	£58,579
Leading Money Winner	Pinza	£44,101

NATIONAL HUNT

Champion Hurdle	Sir Ken	T Molony	2-5f
Cheltenham Gold Cup	Knock Hard	T Molony	11-2
Grand National	Early Mist	B Marshall	20-1

Grand National Aintree: 28 March

Marshall was superb on Early Mist: National a triumph for the Irish

By HOTSPUR

Early Mist, bought by Mr J.V.Rank as a yearling with the object of winning the Grand National and sold to Mr J.H.Griffin of Dublin for 5,300 guineas at the Rank dispersal sales, was the easiest winner of this famous steeplechase since the war.

The eight-year-old's victory by 20 lengths from the courageous Mont Tremblant was a complete triumph for his owner, who came near to winning the race two seasons ago with Royal Tan, his brilliant young trainer, Vincent O'Brien, and his jockey, Bryan Marshall.

O'Brien, who trains in Co.Tipperary, is in his middle thirties, and has easily the most outstanding record of any National Hunt trainer in these islands. In the last six years he has saddled the winners of four Cheltenham Gold Cups, three Champion Hurdles, and now the supreme triumph – the National.

Of Marshall, another Irishman in the top rank of his profession, one can only say that no man since the war has been more deserving of the highest honours. He has had some terrible falls in the past two seasons, yet his nerve remains unshaken. His riding and judgment on Saturday were beyond praise.

The Irish cannot claim the National as a total Irish success, however, for Early Mist, though Irish owned, trained and ridden, was bred in England. His breeder was Mr D.J.Wrinch, of Shotley Hall, near Ipswich, who bought Early Mist's dam, Sudden Dawn, for only 27 guineas in 1938.

It was not until the fifth fence that the first really well-fancied horse went out. This was Cardinal Error, who got too close to it and, sad to say, broke his back.

At Becher's first time round Ordnance was in front, bowling merrily along and taking his fences in his stride. At the Canal Turn he had quite a long lead. There was plenty of grief here, Parasol II, lying second, came down and was unfortunately killed. She brought down Whispering Steel who, according to his rider, had been jumping superbly.

There was still more grief, and when the field came on to the racecourse for the first time, Ordnance held a clear lead of Mont Tremblant, Little Yid, Armoured Knight and Early Mist. Ordnance dragged his hind legs through the Chair fence, but got over and passed the stands well clear of the other four. Even at this, the half-way stage, no other horse looked to have a chance.

Going away from the stands for the second time, Armoured Knight went, and Ordnance got too close to a fence shortly before Becher's. This left Early Mist, who had moved up second, to take the lead from Mont Tremblant and Little Yid.

Little Yid (7-1f), whose jumping had been superb, began to tire after Becher's, and at the Canal Turn the race was reduced to a duel between Early Mist (20-1) and Mont Tremblant (18-1), who was conceding 17lb.

Early Mist led Mont Tremblant by about two lengths as they came on to the racecourse, and despite making a slight mistake at the second last, he came right away in the long run-in to win unchallenged by 20 lengths.

Mont Tremblant ran on to finish second, four lengths in front of Irish Lizard (33-1), who managed to make up a considerable amount of ground after being badly baulked.

Open Handicap 'Chase Sandown: 14 March

Winter makes it 101 for season

From HOTSPUR

A feature of the racing at Sandown on Saturday was a double for F. Winter (*pictured right*) who thus rode his 100th winner of the season after having been for a week on the 99 mark, which equalled the record set last season by Tim Molony.

Winter's 100th success came on Air Wedding, who won a thrilling race for the Open Handicap 'Chase by a short head from the favourite, Whispering Steel. His 101st winner came in the Lilac Open Hurdle, in which he rode a dashing race on Father Thames. He was later presented to the Queen and the Queen Mother.

When the jump jockey's championship was decided over the calendar year (pre-1925/26), F.B.Rees and Eric Foster each rode 108 winners under National Hunt rules. If he avoids injury, Winter should break this record.

ENGLISH CLASSICS

2,000 Guineas	Nearula	E Britt	2-1f
1,000 Guineas	Happy Laughter	E Mercer	10-1
Derby	Pinza	Sir G Richards	5-1jf
Oaks	Ambiguity	J Mercer	18-1
St Leger	Premonition	E Smith	10-1

OTHER MAJOR RACES

Irish Derby	Chamier	W Rickaby	5-4f
Arc de Triomphe	La Sorellina	M Larraun	163-10
Kentucky Derby	Dark Star	H Moreno	249-10
Melbourne Cup	Wodalla	J Purtell	14-1

The Derby Epsom: 6 June

Gordon Richards ends Derby hoodoo on Pinza

Game Aureole not quite good enough

By HOTSPUR

The crowd rises to greet Sir Gordon Richards on Pinza as he approaches the winning post for one of the most popular Derby victories of all time

If the Queen's colt, Aureole, could not win the Derby on Saturday, as would certainly have been a fitting climax to Coronation Week, then a victory for Pinza, ridden by the newly knighted Gordon Richards, owned by Sir Victor Sassoon, bred by Mr Fred Darling and trained by Darling's former head lad, N.Bertie, was the second best result.

It was Gordon Richards's first victory in the race at his 28th attempt, and now, having fulfilled a life-long ambition, it may be that Pinza will prove his last Derby mount.

Sir Victor Sassoon was also gaining his first Derby triumph. This staunch supporter of racing, who won the 1,000 Guineas and the Oaks with Exhibitionnist in 1937, has thoroughly deserved his success.

For Mr Darling, trainer of a succession of Derby winners, Pinza's victory completes the chapter. Yet once again the Derby illustrated the glorious uncertainty of racing, for Pinza was bought by Sir Victor Sassoon against the advice of Mr Darling, who sent up three yearlings to the Newmarket July Sales in 1951 and told Sir Victor which one he thought most promising. It was not Pinza, who was sold for only 1,500gns.

Aureole was inclined to play up in the parade, but by the time he had got to the starting post he was quiet again and did not take much out of himself.

Coming to the top of the hill, Pinza was tucked in on the rails in a group behind the leader, Shikampur. Richards was lucky to get a clear run as the pace increased approaching Tattenham Corner, and emerged some four lengths behind Shikampur but clear of the remainder.

The positions were the same going into the straight, with Pinza, in turn, four or five lengths ahead of a group. A furlong later, Richards was almost on the tail of Shikampur, waiting for the moment to challenge. The champion jockey asked Pinza to win his race about a quarter of a mile from home. The colt drew up to Shikampur without ado, and with more than a furlong to go took a clear lead.

The only danger now was Aureole, whom Carr brought to challenge wide of Pinza. Aureole (9-1) ran on well, but was not quite good enough to put in a challenge, and Pinza (5-1jf) won decisively by four lengths, with the fast-finishing Pink Horse (33-1) snatching third place from a dying Shikampur.

Obituary: 10 June

Mr F.Darling – greatest trainer of his generation

Three days after Pinza, whom he bred, had won the Derby, Fred Darling, the outstanding trainer of his generation, died at Beckhampton yesterday after a long illness, **writes HOTSPUR**. He was 69.

Darling saddled three Derby winners in the 1920s, before he was 40, and in all trained seven. No other trainer in the 20th century has a comparable record. His father, Sam Darling, who had himself sent out two Derby winners, was the creator of the great Beckhampton stable, which he handed on to his son.

Fred started as a lightweight jockey, but soon grew too heavy for riding, and when he was only just turned 20 was appointed private trainer to Lady De Bathe (Mrs Langtry). He later enjoyed a successful spell in Germany as trainer to the brothers von Weinberg, before returning to assist his father and then take over at Beckhampton.

In the years immediately after the first war, success followed success, and his establishment was easily the strongest in the country, his patrons including Lord Woolavington, Lord Dewar and Mr H.E.Morriss.

During the war, Lord Woolavington, then Mr James Buchanan, had bought a 500 guineas yearling by Marcovil, who was named Hurry On, was never beaten and won a substitute St Leger. Great as he was as a racehorse, he was even better as a sire. It was with the stock of Hurry On that Fred Darling achieved some of his greatest successes.

Darling was leading trainer six times between 1926 and 1947, when he retired owing to ill-health, to be succeeded at Beckhampton by Noel Murless.

In 1942 Darling saddled Big Game and Sun Chariot to win four of the five classic races for King George VI. Sun Chariot won the fillies Triple Crown, and Fred considered her the best filly he had ever trained.

No trainer turned out his horses better than Darling – the "Beckhampton bloom" has for long been a by-word in racing – and few trainers were better judges of a horse.

---

19 July

Horse that won at 10-1 found

Another also taken away: Bets firm named

DAILY TELEGRAPH REPORTER

There were three developments yesterday in the investigations into the attempted betting coup at Bath races on Thursday, when the telephone cable to the racecourse was cut, "isolating" it for half an hour before the first race.

The first was that Francasal, 10-1 French winner of the Spa Selling Plate, was traced to Carters Barn, Sonning Common, near Henley-on-Thames, Oxon. Scotland Yard officers there supervised the loading of it and another horse of similar colour and markings into a horse box. Both were taken to Epsom.

At Carters Barn, Francasal was in the care of Mr Zicky G Webster, a horse carrier. Mr Webster was out for the day, but his wife said that he had received a telephone call asking if he would look after two horses for a day or two. They arrived on Saturday.

Meanwhile Mr A.Harrison Ford, secretary of the National Turf Protection Society, named a firm of bookmakers which he said had placed "a substantial commission for the horse."

Thirdly, a man who may be able to help the police in their inquiries was questioned at Bracknell police station, Berks, late last night about the betting coup.

It is now thought that there may have been a "switch" without the knowledge of the owner, trainer or jockey. On Friday, Francasal was driven back to a farm at Burnham and collected from there early on Saturday morning.

The former owner of Francasal, M Chatain, a Frenchman, said yesterday that he sold it a fortnight ago for £300. It was good for nothing as a racer.

The general public is not deeply involved. But the attempted coup threatens to cost bookmakers thousands of pounds. The National Sporting League advised members who accepted large bets on the horse shortly before the race to send covering cheques to the League. It will hold the money until inquiries are ended.

1954

1 Jan The new National Hunt rule comes into force in which a disqualified horse may now be downgraded rather than disqualified.

18 Jun The Queen enjoys a double on the last day of Royal Ascot when Landau leads from start to finish in the Rous Memorial Stakes and then Coronation Cup winner Aureole holds off Janitor to win the Hardwicke Stakes in the most thrilling race of the meeting.

3 Oct Rae Johnstone, 49, wins his second Arc, on French-trained favourite Sica Boy, having previously won on Nikellora in 1945.

13 Oct The new experimental hurdle, effectively a smaller version of a regular steeplechase fence, built of birch, well sloped, and tightly packed into a low wooden frame, is put to use for the first time in a race at Cheltenham. The new development is approved by the majority of riders.

CHAMPIONS

Jockey (Flat)	Doug Smith	129
Jockey (NH)	Dick Francis	76
Leading Trainer	Cecil Boyd-Rochfort	£65,326
Leading Owner	HM The Queen	£40,993
Leading Money Winner	Never Say Die	30,332

Grand National Aintree: 27 March

Marshall's tactics paid in Irish triumph: National double on Royal Tan

By HOTSPUR

When Mr J.H.Griffin's Royal Tan, in the hands of Bryan Marshall, hung on by the skin of his teeth on Saturday to win the most thrilling Grand National since the war, it was the third time in the long history of the race that an owner and rider had won the greatest of 'chases in two successive years with different horses.

Marshall thus joins the great George Stevens, who brought it off on Lord Coventry's Emblem (1863) and Emblematic, and Mr J.M. Richardson, who repeated the feat on Captain Machell's Disturbance (1873) and Reugny.

Royal Tan's trainer, Vincent O'Brien, the outstanding Irish National Hunt trainer since the war, saddled three other winners at the meeting.

It seems to have been the fashion in recent months to belittle the National. Those at Aintree on Saturday will perhaps revise their views. The National is, and I hope always will remain, the greatest of 'chases. It is a very severe test for horse and rider, but it is a perfectly fair test. The pace at which the race is run, coupled with the fact that riders are "strung up" for the big occasion and horses are used to making blunders and getting away with them on park courses, brings the casualties.

Bryan Marshall deliberately went on a wide outside course in the early stages of the race and rode a waiting race in the real George Stevens tradition, laying out of his ground for the first two miles and making it up on the second circuit. Marshall showed that it is not essential to lie up with the leaders from the start. If more jockeys follow these tactics in the future, the casualties in the race will be fewer.

Coming on to the racecourse for the last time there were five still in it with a winning chance – Tudor Line, the stablemates Churchtown and Royal Tan, and Irish Lizard and Sanperion. Churchtown made a bad mistake at the second last and the race lay between Royal Tan (8-1), Tudor Line (10-1) and the gallant Irish Lizard (15-2f).

At the last fence Royal Tan was about a length in front of Tudor Line, who screwed badly to his right, losing three or four lengths. Marshall, on the stand side, drew clear away at the beginning of the run-in and thus was able to take the inside at the bend 200 yards from home. This made the difference between victory and defeat.

G.Slack, on Tudor Line, began to catch the leader rapidly in the last 300 yards. But he had to challenge on Royal Tan's outside, and the winning post came 10 yards too soon for him. He was still a neck behind as the post was reached, with both horses and riders giving all they had. Irish Lizard was a well-beaten third.

NATIONAL HUNT

Champion Hurdle	Sir Ken	T Molony	4-9f
Cheltenham Gold Cup	Four Ten	T Cusack	100-6
Grand National	Royal Tan	B Marshall	8-1

The Derby Epsom: 2 June

Never Say Die (33-1) and Piggott romp home

American-bred colt lands the Derby

From HOTSPUR

Three weeks ago veteran American owner Mr R.S. Clark received a cable from his English racing manager, Mr Gerald McElligott, saying that Never Say Die had no chance in the Derby and seeking permission to scratch the horse from the race.

To-day Never Say Die (33-1), ridden by the apprentice Lester Piggott, who is still in his teens, won by two lengths from Arabian Night (33-1), a doubtful runner last week, with the 2,000 Guineas winner Darius (7-1) a further neck away third. Rowston Manor, who started joint favourite with Ferriol, was seventh after leading round Tattenham Corner.

Piggott was 18 years old on Nov.5 – Guy Fawkes day. He is certainly the youngest jockey to win the Derby in my time, and for all I know in the history of the race. As a boy of 16 he was second on Gay Time to the 1952 winner Tulyar.

By contrast, Mr Robert Sterling Clark, owner and breeder of Never Say Die, is 78 years old and was not present to see his colt win today. Joe Lawson, the colt's trainer, is 73 and was saddling a Derby winner for the first time.

Owing to a mix-up, Never Say Die was nearly scratched after he finished third to Elopement in the Newmarket Stakes on May 12. Piggott, who should have ridden the colt, had begged to be excused as he had more promising mounts at Bath on the same afternoon. E.Mercer, who rode Never Say Die that day, reported that the colt hung badly. It was thought by Mr McElligott that Never Say Die hung to his right and would therefore be ill-suited by Epsom and have no chance in the Derby.

Mr Clark wrote to Mr McElligott, accepting his decision to scratch the colt, but just after posting the letter he had another cable from England, saying that Never Say Die was, in fact, inclined to hang to his left, that there had been a misunderstanding, and that the horse was being left in the race.

Rowston Manor (on the rails) led round Tattenham Corner with Landau second and Darius third, followed by Blue Sail and Never Say Die. Rowston Manor had run much too freely, and with a quarter of a mile to go he and Landau were beaten. Darius then took the lead, with Never Say Die moving up to challenge.

With a furlong to go Piggott sent Never Say Die into a clear lead and, with Darius now fading, Arabian Night took second place from the 2,000 Guineas winner in the last few strides.

ENGLISH CLASSICS

2,000 Guineas	Darius	E Mercer	8-1
1,000 Guineas	Festoon	A Breasley	9-2
Derby	Never Say Die	L Piggott	33-1
Oaks	Sun Cap	WR Johnstone	100-8
St Leger	Never Say Die	C Smirke	100-30f

Never Say Die in the winner's enclosure after the Derby

The Oaks Epsom: 4 June

Johnstone gets Sun Cap home by six lengths: All-French triumph in the Oaks

From HOTSPUR

For the first time in the history of the Oaks, French fillies finished first, second and third – the winner, the grey Sun Cap (100-8); the runner-up, the Boussac filly Altana (8-1jf); and the third, Philante (20-1). Sun Cap was ridden by Rae Johnstone, gaining his 26th classic success in England, France and Ireland, easily the outstanding record among the present generation of jockeys.

Owned by Mme R.Forget, wife of a French industrialist, Sun Cap was the only grey in the field of 21. She is the first of that colour to win the Oaks in the 20th century, and indeed in the last 75 years.

In her final gallop last weekend, Sun Cap finished last, and her owner told Johnstone that she wondered if it was worth sending her across the Channel. Johnstone replied: "I do not believe in gallops."

Johnstone said after the race that he had had a very lucky passage, for nearing the top of the hill he found four fillies beside him and wondered how he was going to get near the rails for the run down to Tattenham Corner. Two of them then obligingly went on, two fell back, and he was on the rails as he came round the bend into the straight.

He said that he gave Sun Cap plenty of time after coming into the straight before he made his challenge, but throughout the last half-mile Sun Cap was going so well that he felt he could ask her to win her race when he wanted to. She won it by six lengths.

13 November

The Queen is season's leading owner

By HOTSPUR

Chief features of the 1954 flat-racing season which ended at Lingfield on Saturday were the successes of the Queen, who heads the winning owners' list, the retirement of Sir Gordon Richards from race riding and the successes of Doug Smith, who succeeds Sir Gordon as champion jockey.

The Queen owes her position as leading owner largely to Aureole, whose four victories included the King George VI and Queen Elizabeth Stakes and the Coronation Cup, and, in a lesser degree, to Landau and winning two-year-olds such as Corporal.

It is the second time that the reigning monarch has headed the list of winning owners. King George VI did so in 1942, when Big Game and Sun Chariot, which he leased from the National Stud, won four of the five classic races.

Racing has seemed to lack something since Sir Gordon Richards retired from the saddle. His successor as champion jockey, D.Smith, is undoubtedly riding better now than at any time in his career. As he has no weight difficulties, I think he will continue as champion jockey for many more seasons.

Jockey Club Inquiry: 18 June

Piggott loses licence for six months

By HOTSPUR

Lester Piggott, 18, the apprentice who won the Derby on Never Say Die, will not ride under Jockey Club rules again this season. The Stewards of the Jockey Club yesterday decided to withdraw his licence to ride.

The Stewards made their decision before racing began as a result of a report by the Ascot Stewards on the King Edward VII Stakes on Thursday when Piggott rode Never Say Die.

At the moment Piggott is attached to his father's stable at Lambourn, Berks, and lives at home. I understand that Piggott is now required to attach himself to another stable. There is no question of him being allowed to ride again for six months after new arrangements have been made. He will miss the St Leger at Doncaster in September at which he was to have ridden Never Say Die.

I understand the offence for which Piggott has been suspended took place before the scrimmaging between Rashleigh, Garter and Never Say Die. In evidence, Piggott, I believe, said that he had been unable to prevent Never Say Die hanging to the left at one period. Unlike Epsom, Ascot is a right-handed course, and J.Lawson, Never Say Die's trainer, was apprehensive whether the colt would be all right there.

[On 24 August, the Stewards of the Jockey Club gave a severe warning to Piggott as a result of their inquiry at Ascot, in which they told him that "they had taken notice of his dangerous and erratic riding, both this season and in previous seasons, and that, in their opinion, in spite of numerous warnings, he continued to show complete disregard for the Rules of Racing and the safety of other jockeys.]

11 August

Sir Gordon Richards quits the saddle: Plan to train at Beckhampton

By HOTSPUR

Sir Gordon Richards, 50, champion jockey on 26 occasions, has retired from the saddle. He will train at Beckhampton, Wilts, at a 30-horse stable built by the late Fred Darling.

He announced his retirement last night at his bungalow at Worthing, Sussex, where he is recuperating from his accident at Sandown Park on July 10. A bone in his pelvis was fractured when the Queen's filly Abergeldie unseated him and rolled on him.

"I have talked the matter over with Mr Noel Murless, the trainer, and all concerned, and everything is now settled," he stated. "I shall not ride again in public.

"After 34 years as a jockey, every minute of which I have enjoyed, it is naturally with no little regret that I make this announcement. I wish I could see the season out, for I shall miss the familiar racing scene and the thrills a jockey gets when a vast and enthusiastic racing public share his triumphs."

Sir Gordon won practically all the principal flat races. In 1933 he passed Fred Archer's seasons's record of winners with a total of 259, and in 1947 broke his own record with 269. Archer's total of 2,749 winners was eclipsed by Sir Gordon in 1943. His riding record is 21,834 mounts, 4,870 winners.

In the days of Steve Donoghue, the most popular racecourse cry was "Come on Steve!" In Gordon Richards's day, it has been "Come on Gordon!" and it has been shouted now with immense fervour by a large number of Englishmen for close on a quarter of a century. The sport will not be the same without him.

OTHER MAJOR RACES

Irish Derby	Zarathustra	P Powell Jr	50-1
Arc de Triomphe	Sica Boy	WR Johnstone	41-10f
Kentucky Derby	Determine	R York	43-10
Melbourne Cup	Rising Fast	J Purtell	5-2f

1955

26 Mar Vincent O'Brien's outstanding feat of saddling his third Grand National winner in succession goes unrecorded in The Telegraph because of a strike. This time it is Quare Times (100-9) who obliges, as Tudor Line comes 2nd again, 12 lengths adrift.

9 May Sir Gordon Richards sends out a winner at his first attempt as a trainer, the 2-y-o The Saint at Windsor, ridden by stable jockey J.Wilson and owned by Miss Dorothy Paget.

23 May The first evening meeting takes place in London, at Alexandra Palace, several jockeys arriving by plane from the Leicester afternoon meeting.

27 May Lady Zia Wernher's Meld (7-4f) adds the Oaks to her 1,000 Guineas success with a comprehensive 6 lengths win over Ark Royal (8-1) at Epsom.

30 May With 2 winners at Towcester, Tim Molony pips Fred Winter for the 1954-55 NH Jockey's Championship, both having started with 65 winners on the last day,

16 Jul Derby winner Phil Drake (8-11f) suffers a shock defeat, coming 6th of 9 in the "King George" at Ascot, but the big race still has its first French winner, the 3-y-o Vimy (10-1) winning a head.

26 Oct Lester Piggott, 19, becomes the youngest jockey to ride 100 winners in a season in this country for over 40 years.

Dec US champion 3-y-o Nashua, who won both the Preakness and Belmont Stakes, is sold to Mr Leslie Combs, of the appropriately named Spendthrift Farm, Lexington, Kentucky, for $1,251,200 (£446,785).

CHAMPIONS

Jockey (Flat)	Doug Smith	168
Jockey (NH)	Tim Molony	67
Leading Trainer	Cecil Boyd-Rochfort	£74,424
Leading Owner	Lady Zia Wernher	£46,345
Leading Money Winner	Meld	£42,562

Cheltenham Gold Cup 10 March

Gay Donald 33-1 shock Gold Cup winner
From HOTSPUR

Gay Donald, the outsider of nine, and in the opinion of many people the one horse with no chance on form, won the Cheltenham Gold Cup this afternoon on merit by 10 lengths from Halloween.

Starting at 33-1 (Tote odds were more than 50's), Gay Donald is the longest priced winner and certainly the biggest surprise in the history of the race. His trainer, J.Ford, has only seven horses in training, not counting the young stock, in his stable at Cholderton, in Wiltshire.

The race was run at a great pace from the start, with Gay Donald making the running, followed by Halloween, and the remainder bunched up close. At half-way Gay Donald led from Halloween and last year's winner, Four Ten.

As they turned for home for the last time, I thought that Halloween would win. But Gay Donald, instead of coming back to his field as everyone expected, in fact increased his lead. Two fences from home he was 10 lengths in front. He jumped the last fence competently and won challenged from Halloween (7-2), with Four Ten (3-1f) third and Early Mist (5-1), who had been unable to go the pace, a moderate fourth.

NATIONAL HUNT

Champion Hurdle	Clair Soleil	F Winter	5-2f
Cheltenham Gold Cup	Gay Donald	A Grantham	33-1
Grand National	Quare Times	P Taaffe	100-9

Ascot 14 July

Ascot crowd hit by lightning
Woman dies, 46 people injured
DAILY TELEGRAPH REPORTER

Lightning struck a wire fence and went to ground in the midst of a crowd on Royal Ascot racecourse yesterday. A woman was killed and 46 people were injured. The incident happened a short distance from the Royal Box. The Queen, who was not present, sent a message of sympathy to the Duke of Norfolk, her representative at Ascot.

Over a wide area temperatures remained in the eighties, making it the hottest day of the heatwave. Thunderstorms, mainly in the south, caused widespread damage by flooding and lightning.

The people affected at Ascot were on the "popular" side of the course, opposite the Royal Box, sheltering from a thunderstorm. The storm broke, with tropical intensity, just before 4 p.m.

Many people in the Royal Enclosure saw the vivid flash at 4.10. It appeared first to strike the wire fence round No.2 enclosure and then go to ground where a group of about 100 people were sheltering under the lee of a tea tent.

In the words of one witness, "people were thrown around like ninepins, and in a fraction of a second a fairly lighthearted scene became one of horror and confusion."

The woman who was killed, Mrs Barbara Batt, 28, of Caroline Street, Reading, was an expectant mother. Her husband, Mr Ronald Batt, was seriously injured and was taken to Heatherwood Hospital, Ascot.

When the extent of the incident became apparent, the Stewards conferred hurriedly and then announced the abandonment of racing for the day.

The Derby Epsom: 25 May

Phil Drake wins Derby for France
Late run and last-minute switch beats 100-1 chance
From HOTSPUR

Mme Suzy Volterra to-day became the third woman to win the Derby. Her Phil Drake, 18th of the 23 at Tattenham Corner, came with one of the most thrilling late runs in the history of the race to take the lead less than 100 yards from home from the rank outsider Panaslipper, and yet win by 1½ lengths.

Fred Palmer, who was winning the Derby for the first time, is English by blood, but French by birth and domicile. He was formerly a leading steeplechase rider, and has the reputation of being the man for the big occasion.

Phil Drake's trainer is F.Mathet, for 16 years a French cavalryman, and since the war a most successful trainer at Chantilly. Phil Drake was his third Derby runner.

To-day's race reminded me of that first photo-finish Derby six years ago between Nimbus, the late M Leon Volterra's Amour Drake, and Swallow Tail. Just as Phil Drake swooped from behind today, so in 1949 Rae Johnstone brought Amour Drake with a thrilling late challenge. And just as Amour Drake was switched by Johnstone to the rails in the final furlong, so was Phil Drake in the same colours today.

The Irish-trained Panaslipper was in front with his race apparently won a furlong from home when he began to hang to his right. Palmer brought Phil Drake to challenge and had to make a split-second decision to go between Panaslipper and the far rails. In Johnstone's case the Amour Drake switch unluckily failed. Today it came off. It was history repeating itself – with a difference.

But for Phil Drake (100-8), there would have been the biggest surprise in the Derby since the 100-1 chance Aboyeur was awarded the race in 1913. Panaslipper, the 100-1 runner up, was not in the first eight in the Irish 2,000 Guineas a week ago. Today he beat the 11-4 favourite Acropolis into third place by three lengths.

ENGLISH CLASSICS

2,000 Guineas	Our Babu	D Smith	13-2
1,000 Guineas	Meld	WH Carr	11-4f
Derby	Phil Drake	F Palmer	100-8
Oaks	Meld	WH Carr	7-4f
St Leger	Meld	WH Carr	10-11f

Voltigeur Stakes York: 24 August

Princess Royal's colt disqualified in Voltigeur Stakes

From HOTSPUR

Acropolis, joint favourite for the St Leger with Meld at last Monday's call-over, was beaten half a length by the Princess Royal's Va Presto in the Voltigeur Stakes today and was then awarded the race on an objection.

It appeared from the stands that Va Presto was hanging in the last quarter of a mile, and the stewards, who are in an exceptionally good position to see interference in the straight, objected to the winner for bumping and boring. The objection was sustained.

This was a sad end to an exciting race, and one's sympathy goes to the Princess Royal, a keen supporter of racing, who has not had much luck recently. To lose a race in this way at her home meeting must have been a bitter blow, particularly as I think that at the difference in the weights of a stone, Va Presto showed himself the better horse.

Acropolis will have gained few friends for the St Leger. He did not reproduce Ascot form, changed his legs in the straight, possibly after being bumped, but did not quicken in the last hundred yards as one expects a top-class horse to do. If all goes well with her, Meld will be my selection for the St Leger.

Doncaster Cup: 9 September

Favourite breaks down in Doncaster Cup: Race goes to Entente Cordiale

From HOTSPUR

George Colling, who had such bad luck in his St Leger hope Acropolis, received some compensation when saddling the winners of the two big races on the final day of the meeting – Entente Cordiale in the Doncaster Cup and Ark Royal in the Park Hill Stakes.

The Doncaster Cup, for which there was only a field of four, was marred by the fact that the 7-4 favourite Double Bore, winner of the Goodwood Cup, broke down badly during the race. Entente Cordiale won, but it was only in the final furlong that he caught the 66-1 chance Naucetra, who led by more than 20 lengths at half-way. For champion jockey Doug Smith, it was his fifth Doncaster Cup win in six attempts.

Prix de l'Arc de Triomphe Longchamp: 9 October

Unbeaten Ribot wins big French race for Italy

By HOTSPUR

Ribot, unbeaten Italian three-year-old, won the £39,000 Prix de l'Arc de Triomphe at Longchamp yesterday, the second time since the war that an Italian-bred colt has taken the race. The other was Nuccio in 1952.

Ribot, bred by the late Signor F.Tesia and carrying the colours of the Marchese Incisa della Rocchetta, was a convincing winner in the hands of the veteran Italian rider E.Camici, who won the Ascot Gold Cup on Botticelli in the same colours.

Sad to relate, Elopement, the only English runner, and the Irish Hugh Lupus both failed badly. Second place went to the St Leger third, Beau Prince II, and the outsider Picounda was third.

Ribot, by the Goodwood Cup winner Tenerani, who now stands at the National Stud, was taken out of the Italian classics because of an injury.

A record crowd of over 100,000 watched yesterday's race on going which was good. Coming round the final bend into the straight, Ribot took the lead followed by Beau Prince II, and went on to win decisively by three lengths.

The running of Beau Prince, who finished well behind Meld in the St Leger on going firmer than he likes, suggests that Meld is probably better than Ribot.

[Two weeks later Ribot won the Milan Jockey Club Grand Prix by 15 lengths.]

Meld hangs on for her record-breaking win

The St Leger Doncaster: 7 September

Meld coughs, wins and survives Piggott objection

Fillies' Triple Crown

From HOTSPUR

In spite of being a victim of the coughing bug, Meld won the St Leger to-day, not as I feel certain she would have done had she been at her best, but hard pressed, by three-quarters of a length from Nucleus.

L.Piggott, rider of Nucleus, objected to Meld for crossing. But the stewards overruled the protest and ordered Piggott to forfeit his £10 deposit as they were of the opinion that there were "no good and reasonable grounds" for the objection.

Meld coughed more than once this morning, but she had no temperature, so it was reasonable to let her take her chance in what was almost certain to be her final appearance.

By the success of Meld, Cecil Boyd-Rochfort becomes the first trainer to top £1m in prize money in England.

Meld is the sixth filly to win the St Leger at Doncaster in the 20th century, joining those great race mares Sceptre (1902) and Pretty Polly (1904) in achieving the fillies' Triple Crown of 1,000 Guineas, Oaks and St Leger. Sun Chariot also brought off this treble, for King George VI, in substitute races at Newmarket in the war.

Meld's winnings for the season now total over £43,000

– an all-time record for an English filly.

The race was full of incident, though, owing to the coughing, it was a sub-standard field of eight. Soon after they had turned for home, Boullenger sent Beau Prince up to Daemon, who was racing on the rails. Meld was on the outside of these two with a clear run, and at least 2 1/2 furlongs from home her jockey Carr began to move forward. He struck the front with a quarter of a mile to go.

Piggott brought Nucleus out to challenge Meld on the outside, and seemed to be going the better of the two, but when Piggott showed him the whip he appeared to resent it and ducked behind Meld. Piggott had to switch inside. There was then plenty of room between Meld and the far rails, but Meld was gradually edging over towards them. And when Piggott, having balanced Nucleus again, tried to come through, Carr edged Meld over.

Piggott appeared to have to snatch up Nucleus and challenged again on the outside, but Meld, though tiring, hung on to win. A further three lengths away came the one-paced Beau Prince II.

OTHER MAJOR RACES

Race	Horse	Jockey	Odds
Irish Derby	Panaslipper	J Eddery	4-1
Arc de Triomphe	Ribot	E Camici	88-10
Kentucky Derby	Swaps	W Shoemaker	28-10
Melbourne Cup	Toparoa	N Sellwood	6-1

1956

30 Jan Three-times Champion Hurdler Sir Ken, in the hands of Tim Molony, wins the Elvaston 'Chase at Nottingham under 12st 8lb.

21 Mar Three Star II (40-1) wins the "Lincoln", his first success in 37 starts since 1951, when he had two wins.

9 May Harry Wragg sends out 3 winners for total prize money of £6,686: Lucero in the Irish 2,000 Guineas, Golovine in the Chester Cup, and Bedser in the Great Cheshire Stakes.

13 Oct Nashua, who had already overtaken Citation's record career earnings, wins his last race, the $50,000 Jockey Club Gold Cup at Belmont Park, New York, his 22nd success in 30 starts, to take his total prize money to $1,288,565.

17 Nov Billy Nevett, long-time champion jockey of the North, retires after thirty three years with a win at Manchester in the last race of the season.

17 Nov Jump jockey Pat Taaffe, having taken another toss 3 days ago at Navan on his return after 2 1/2 months out of the saddle, is back at Manchester winning both the 'chases for Tom Dreaper's stable.

Devon Loch comes to a mysterious halt with victory in sight

Grand National Aintree: 24 March

Unsolved mystery of Devon Loch

Unluckiest National loser of all time: Royal 'chaser, out clear, stops 55 yards from winning post

By HOTSPUR

With 55 yards to go and the Grand National at his mercy, Queen Elizabeth the Queen Mother's Devon Loch, clear of all opponents, stumbled, skidded, tried to keep his legs and stopped at Aintree on Saturday. It was, I think, the saddest and most dramatic event I have ever seen on a racecourse.

So ESB (100-7), ridden by D.V.Dick, strode on past him to win by 10 lengths from the mare Gentle Moya (22-1), with the 1954 National winner Royal Tan (28-1) a further 10 lengths away third.

It is unlikely that anyone will ever really know exactly what happened to Devon Loch. It was all over in a matter of seconds and occurred on the run-in from the last fence to the winning post, exactly opposite the water jump.

Some held that Devon Loch might have run into a patch of false-going, I do not think so. My impression was that the horse was in pain. One of the racecourse vets who examined Devon Loch immediately after the race thought he might have had a sudden attack of cramp. Another felt his behaviour might have been due to a small blood clot in a hind leg.

Though the result cannot show it, this was in all but name Devon Loch's National, and one cannot but feel extreme sympathy for his owner, his rider Dick Francis, and his trainer Peter Cazalet.

I can think of only two other National incidents of a comparable nature. One was in 1936 when Cazalet's great friend, the late Lord Mildmay, appeared to have the race won on Davy Jones two fences from home when the reins broke and the horse ran out; the other when Reavey took the wrong course from the last fence on Zahia in 1948. There is no doubt, however, that Devon Loch was the unluckiest loser in the 120 years' history of the race.

I shall long remember the picture of the Queen Mother, as ESB was being led triumphantly in, going quietly towards the racecourse stables with a smile on her face, to see if her horse was all right. A few minutes later, after the vets had examined Devon Loch, the Queen and

The 2,000 Guineas Newmarket: 2 May

Barlow wins Guineas on Gilles de Retz (50-1) – then fractures rib in mix-up.

From HOTSPUR

Less than two hours after winning the 2,000 Guineas on Mr A.G.Samuel's 50-1 outsider Gilles de Retz, former Manchester pageboy Frank Barlow was taken to hospital with a cracked rib. He was hurt at the start of the last race, when half the field of eight charged into the starting gate.

Gilles de Retz gave the 27-year-old Barlow his first success in a classic race. Mr Samuel, who bred the colt, and Mrs Gordon Johnson Houghton, who trains it in association with Charles Jerdein (official holder of the licence) at Blewbury, were also winning a classic for the first time.

Gilles de Retz ran unaccountably badly in the Greenham Stakes at Newbury last month behind Ratification, and it was touch and go whether he would be allowed to take his chance in the Guineas.

To-day he ran quite unfancied, for in his final gallop at the week-end he went most disappointingly. The well-known jockey who rode Gilles de Retz in this gallop said to Barlow before today's race: "Frank, I bet you a large gin and tonic that you finish in the last four. Gilles de Retz went like a crab on Saturday." Barlow, knowing that Gilles de Retz is apt to be lazy at home, accepted the bet!

Running on the stands side, Gilles de Retz took the lead with about two furlongs to go and was nearly two lengths in front of Chantelsey (10-1). I thought that Chantelsey might catch Gilles de Retz, but Mr Samuel's colt ran on gallantly under pressure to hold the northerner by a length. Buisson Ardent (201-), finishing well, was a further one and a half lengths away third.

the Queen Mother were congratulating Mr and Mrs Leonard Carver, owners of ESB, his rider Dick, and his trainer Fred Rimell, on their victory. It was just as if nothing untoward had happened.

Though Devon Loch's fantastically bad luck blighted the race, ESB's victory was that of a game, thoroughly exposed horse, now the winner of 17 'chases out of the 56 races he has run.

At the second last, Devon Loch, on the inside, Eagle Lodge and ESB jumped almost in line and it seemed that Devon Loch was going the best. As they came to the last,

the race lay between Devon Loch and ESB.

Devon Loch took it well (about a length in front), and so did ESB. At the "elbow" in the long run-in, Devon Loch had increased his lead over ESB and 100 yards from the post Dick had accepted defeat and was looking round. Francis was riding Devon Loch out with hands and heels, all set for victory, when the unbelievable happened.

It remains to add that ESB's time was only 4/5ths of a second outside the record of 9min 20 1/5sec set up by Reynoldstown in 1935. Devon Loch, had all gone well, would certainly have beaten it.

The Derby Epsom: 6 June

English colts routed in Derby
Lavandin is Johnstone's 30th Classic win
From HOTSPUR

For the first time since the Derby was founded in 1780 no English-trained horse finished in the first three to-day. The winner was the French-trained favourite Lavandin (7-1), the second the French-trained outsider Montaval (40-1), and the third the Irish-trained Roistar (22-1).

This was the fifth victory of a French colt in the Derby since the race returned to Epsom after the war, and the score is now only six-five in favour of England.

Lavandin belongs to M. Pierre Wertheimer, the "Scent King" of Europe, an owner for 48 years, and the winner of the 1,000 Guineas with Mesa exactly 21 years ago. Mesa was ridden, as was Lavandin to-day, by the imperturbable Australian Rae Johnstone.

No other jockey of his generation has a record in big races comparable with Johnstone. It was his third victory in the Derby, and he already has three Oaks to his credit. His successes in the classic races of England, France and Ireland now number 30 – a record which fills one with the greatest admiration.

He rode with supreme confidence to-day, taking the lead from the fading Monterey just over a furlong from home, and riding as if he had something up his sleeve. In fact, he did not see Montaval coming with a desperate late run in the middle of the course, and Lavandin had only a neck to spare at the finish.

King George VI and Queen Elizabeth Stakes Ascot: 21 July

Italian champion Ribot beats Queen's High Veldt in King George
By HOTSPUR

The unbeaten Ribot won his 14th and, according to present plans, his last race at Ascot on Saturday, when he defeated the Queen's High Veldt decisively by five lengths in the King George VI and Queen Elizabeth Stakes.

Two lengths further behind came the Belgian three-year-old Todrai, who just beat the Boussac four-year-old Kurun for third place, Kurun finishing roughly eight lengths behind Ribot as he had done when fourth in the Prix de l'Arc de Triomphe at Longchamp last autumn.

Those who laid the odds of 5-2 on Ribot must have been uneasy when they saw his rider Camici niggling at him at the end of half a mile, asking him to keep with the leaders. Camici continued to ask Ribot to lie up with the pacemaker, Todrai, to the final bend, and it was only in the last two furlongs that the favourite showed his real worth.

Those watching Ribot for the first time would hardly consider that he won like a great horse. He had a hard race and did not seem to act well on the soft going – a fact which was corroborated by his rider. But he won like a nailing good horse.

OTHER MAJOR RACES

Irish Derby	Talgo	E Mercer	9-2
Arc de Triomphe	Ribot	E Camici	3-5f
Kentucky Derby	Needles	D Erb	8-5f
Melbourne Cup	Evening Peal	G Podmore	15-1

Del Mar, California: 3 September

Longden beats Sir Gordon's record
By HOTSPUR

Sir Gordon Richards was one of the first to cable congratulations yesterday to American jockey Johnny Longden, who broke Sir Gordon's world riding record of 4,870 winners at Del Mar, California, on Monday. Sir Gordon commented: "I hope to see Johnny at Doncaster next week. I think he has put up a remarkable performance. Racing in America is a young man's game."

Longden, who is 46, is due to ride Irish trainer P.J.Prendergast's Calgary Court – a 50-1 chance – in the St Leger.

Irish Derby The Curragh: 27 June

Talgo romps away with Irish Derby
Another blow to English Classic form
By HOTSPUR

The Derby form was further discredited at The Curragh yesterday when the English-trained Talgo was much too good for Roistar in the Irish Derby, winning unchallenged by no less than six lengths, with No Comment third. Talgo was not entered in either the 2,000 Guineas or the Derby.

In the Derby, Lavandin defeated Montaval by a neck with Roistar a further two lengths away third, so it is reasonable to think that Talgo is one of the best three-year-olds in England and that he would have run extremely well in the Derby had he taken part.

The first six in the Derby have now all been beaten in the last 10 days. It must be many years since the Derby form has been discredited so quickly and so thoroughly.

ENGLISH CLASSICS

2,000 Guineas	Gilles de Retz	F Barlow	50-1
1,000 Guineas	Honeylight	E Britt	100-6
Derby	Lavandin	WR Johnstone	7-1f
Oaks	Sicarelle	F Palmer	3-1f
St Leger	Cambremer	F Palmer	8-1

Prix de l'Arc de Triomphe Longchamp: 7 October

Ribot romps away with £43,000 French race
Owner rejects £400,000 American offer for wonder horse
From HOTSPUR

Odds-on favourite in a 20-strong field, the unbeaten Italian-trained Ribot won Europe's richest race, the £43,000 Prix de l'Arc de Triomphe, like a great racehorse today, defeating the English-owned and trained Talgo by a very long six lengths, with the French-trained Tanerko third and the American Career Boy fourth.

I do not believe in using the adjective "great" to describe a racehorse unless I am certain that it is well and truly earned. Ribot, who has run his last race, to my mind now joins the small band of truly great horses – the St Simons and the Sceptres of racing. Undefeated in 16 races, Ribot has won well over £100,000 in stake money and must be the biggest stake-winner in the history of European racing.

After he had won the King George at Ascot in July from High Veldt and Todrai, I did not feel Ribot was more than a top-class racehorse. It was a very different Ribot we saw today.

He was never out of the first three, always on the bit, and when his Italian rider, Camici, asked him to win his race three furlongs from home he left the remainder standing and finished full of running.

The bare verdict gives little idea of the brilliant way in which Ribot won. The crowd – one and all – rose to him when he came back to him in the unsaddling enclosure. The Marchese Incisa della Rochetta, joint owner of Ribot with Donna Lydia Tesio, said after the race that Ribot will now go to stud – either in Italy or, if negotiations are successful, at Lord Derby's stud at Newmarket.

After Ribot had won the Prix de l'Arc de Triomphe last year, an American owner gave a blank cheque to the Marchese in an attempt to buy the Italian champion, but Ribot was not for sale. Today the Marchese was reported to have rejected an American offer of £400,000 for the horse.

1957

12 May Merry Deal (28-1), a Dorothy Paget cast-off owned and trained by Shropshire farmer Arthur Jones, who bought him for £160, springs the biggest Champion Hurdle surprise in the history of the race, beating Irish-trained Quita Que

(2nd last year) and the French challenger Tout ou Rien 5 and 5 lengths, with hot favourite Clair Soleil 7th.

10 Jun Ryan Price saddles 3 winners at Fontwell Park to beat his own NH training record of 72, set in 1952-53 (and finishes the season with 79).

19 Jul A.J.Russell rides all 6 winners at Bogside – Double Up (2-5), Cligarry (2-1), Wage Claim (100-8), Courtlier (8-1), Newton (8-13) and Roseline (11-8) – a 1,956-1 accumulator.

19 Jul Maj-Gen David Dawnay, Ascot's clerk of the course, narrowly escapes serious injury when the 3-stone zoom lens from a BBC TV camera falls 40ft from the top of a stand and strikes him a glancing blow on the shoulder.

8 Aug With Candytuft's success in the Alfriston Stakes at Brighton, Noel Murless takes his 1957 prize money to £94,080, beating the record set in 1931 by Joe Lawson.

11 Sep Irish Derby winner Ballymoss (8-

1) is the first Irish-trained horse to win the St Leger in its 181-year history, beating Court Harwell (100-8) by a length to give all-conquering jump trainer Vincent O'Brien his first English Classic success.

6 Oct French-trained Oroso (50-1) is a shock "Arc" winner, with English hopes Talgo and Pipe of Peace and Irish filly Gladness out of the first 10.

6 Oct Unbeaten 2-y-o French filly Texana wins the Prix l'Abbaye at Longchamp, her 11th straight success.

CHAMPIONS

Jockey (Flat)	Scobie Breasley	173
Jockey (NH)	Fred Winter	80
Leading Trainer	Noel Murless	£116,898
Leading Owner	HM The Queen	£62,211
Leading Money Winner	Crepello	£32,257

30 January

Dick Francis has ridden his last race: Queen Mother's jockey retires at 36 "before going down scale"

By HOTSPUR

Dick Francis, one of the best steeplechase riders since the war – and one of the most courageous – has decided to retire from race-riding at the age of 36. Francis, who rode as first jockey to Queen Elizabeth the Queen Mother, said yesterday:

"It was a terrible decision to have to make, but I wanted to stop before I began going rapidly down the scale."

He added that his decision was precipitated by the Queen Mother's Devon Loch breaking down at Sandown and being taken out of training. "I had

been looking forward to another ride on him in the Grand National," he said. Francis's name will always be associated with Devon Loch on whom he all but won last year's race.

Champion National Hunt rider in the 1953-54 season, Francis had his first ride an an amateur in October 1946 and turned professional 18 months later. He came second in the 1949 National on Lord Bicester's Roimond.

[Francis turned his hand to writing, and became a huge best seller with his racing thrillers.]

Grand National Aintree: 29 March

Third time lucky for gallant Sundew

From HOTSPUR

It was third time lucky for Mr and Mrs Geoffrey Kohn, of Henley-in-Arden, Warwickshire, when Sundew, a 20-1 chance, ridden by champion jockey Fred Winter, romped home an eight lengths

Sundew (right) leads at the water jump

winner of the Grand National from Wyndburgh (25-1) and the unconsidered Tiberetta (66-1).

Sundew was the third horse the Kohn's have purchased in Ireland with the sole object of winning the world's greatest steeplechase – Quite Naturally and Churchtown were the others – and he triumphed at the third attempt.

Mr Kohn, a stockbroker, bought Sundew on the eve of the Grand National in 1955. The horse led approaching Becher's in that year but fell four fences from the finish. He tried again 12 months ago and came down at Becher's the second time round when lying second.

That he should succeed at the third attempt, and after making practically all the running, is the more credit to him. Yet when he was offered for sale at Newmarket in December there was not one bid! An attempt to sell him

afterwards at £2,500 also produced no takers.

The winning owners have a farm adjoining the gallops of Sundew's trainer, Frank Hudson. Hudson has been a trainer for 30 years, and now has the distinction of having won, within a short period, the longest race on the flat – the Queen Alexandra Stakes with Bitter Sweet – and the longest steeplechase, the National. Sundew, strangely enough, is the only 'chaser in his 10-horse stable.

Fred Winter has had few chances to shine in steeple-chases at Aintree because he rides for Capt H.R.Price, who concentrates on hurdlers. Today's race was his first steeplechase victory at Aintree and he was riding in his fourth National. There is no more popular rider under National Hunt rules and he was given a great reception when Sundew returned to the unsaddling enclosure.

NATIONAL HUNT

Champion Hurdle	Merry Deal	G Underwood	28-1
Cheltenham Gold Cup	Linwell	M Scudamore	100-9
Grand National	Sundew	F Winter	20-1

The Derby Epsom: 5 June

Piggott times run on Crepello to perfection: French colts eclipsed

From HOTSPUR

Sir Victor Sassoon's Crepello (6-4f) came home a clear winner of the Derby today from the Irish-trained Ballymoss (33-1) and Pipe of Peace (100-8). For only the fourth time since the war there was no French-trained runner in the first three.

Competently and coolly ridden by Lester Piggott, Crepello won by one and a half lengths and did an

exceptionally good time – 2min 35.4sec, the fastest since Mahmoud set the record with 2 min 33.8sec in 1936.

In winning the Derby with Crepello, Sir Victor Sassoon was gaining his second success in the race as an owner and his first as a breeder. When Pinza won for him in 1953, he started joint favourite at 5-1. Crepello was the shortest priced winning

favourite since unbeaten Bahram in 1935.

Sir Victor has now won six classic races. The imperturbable Piggott has added a second Derby to his name, and Noel Murless, Crepello's trainer, had saddled his first Derby winner.

Throughout the last three furlongs of the race Crepello always looked like justifying the faith Murless has had in

him since his early days. Though Crepello had a clear run, at least half a dozen of his fancied opponents did not.

Rarely have I heard such a tale of woe after a big race, but the most unlucky horse was undoubtedly the second favourite, the Aga Khan's Prince Taj, who lost at least 15 lengths at the start. However, I shall be very surprised if the best horse did not win.

Ladies' Day at Epsom sees the Queen congratulating her Oaks heroine Carrozza, with the Queen Mother and Princess Margaret joining the party

The Oaks Epsom: 7 June

Carrozza gives Queen 1st Classic triumph: Piggott rides super-finish

From HOTSPUR

Amid scenes of tremendous enthusiasm the Queen, looking radiantly happy, led in her first classic winner today – not Mulberry Harbour, generally considered her principal hope in the Oaks, but Carrozza, a 100-8 chance, trained like Crepello by Noel Murless and ridden like the Derby winner by Lester Piggott.

It was one of the most exciting finishes I have ever seen. At the distance, Piggott had Carrozza out in front on the rails. The Irish filly Silken Glider (20-1), ridden by J.Eddery, was closing with her, and the favourite, Rose Royale II (11-10), was in trouble after looking the winner.

Throughout the last desperate 100 yards it seemed as if Silken Glider would prevail, but neither Piggott nor Carrozza would give in. Piggott reminded his mount of her responsibilities, then sat still.

But in the last 20 yards, with hopes of victory fading, he rode like a man inspired, almost willing Carrozza to win. Brownie Carslake in his heyday could not have squeezed more out of the filly.

Carrozza and Silken Glider flashed past the post together. There was a momentary silence. I thought Carrozza had hung on to win by inches – a colleague on my right favoured Silken Glider's chance. The majority of people hoped for the best but feared the worst.

It seemed a long time before the loudspeaker announcement of the result of the photograph. When it came, a mighty cheer went up and out came the Queen to lead in her winner. The photo showed clearly that Carrozza had won by about nine inches.

It was the first Royal victory in an Epsom Oaks since the race was founded in 1781, though King George VI won a substitute Oaks at Newmarket with Sun Chariot in 1942. The last Royal victory in a Classic race at Epsom was in 1909, when Minoru won the Derby for King Edward VII.

ENGLISH CLASSICS

2,000 Guineas	Crepello	L Piggott	7-2
1,000 Guineas	Rose Royale II	C Smirke	6-1
Derby	Crepello	L Piggott	6-4f
Oaks	Carrozza	L Piggott	100-8
St Leger	Ballymoss	TP Burns	8-1

OTHER MAJOR RACES

Irish Derby	Ballymoss	TP Burns	4-9f
Arc de Triomphe	Oroso	S Boullenger	512-10
Kentucky Derby	Iron Liege	W Hartack	84-10
Melbourne Cup	Straight Draw	N McGrowdie	13-2

Obituary Geneva: 11 July

The Aga Khan dies in his 80th year: One of racing's "greats"

FROM OUR OWN CORRESPONDENT

The Aga Khan, whom millions of Ismaili Moslems the world over looked to as their head, died near here of heart failure at 12.30 today. He was in his 80th year.

Hotspur writes: With the death of the Aga Khan, there passes the outstanding owner-breeder of his time, and certainly one of the great figures in the long history of the Turf.

Fortunately, his son, Aly Khan, is also a racing enthusiast, and intends to carry on his father's studs in Ireland on the old scale, and to have a large number of horses in training in France.

The Aga Khan was unfairly criticised by many people for transferring his horses in training from England to France a few years ago. He made the move primarily because it is possible in France for a successful non-betting owner almost to make

both ends meet, whereas in England prize money bears no relation to the costs of training. In addition, for the aging Aga Khan, who lived in France, he could more easily see his horses run there.

I think the only criticism that can fairly be made of the Aga Khan was that he was inclined to retire some of his top-class horses to stud at the end of their three-year-old days.

The Aga Khan has also been criticised for selling his three Derby winners – Bahram, Mahmoud and Blenheim – to the United States in the early part of the war. However, he first offered them to the National Stud at a price well below their true value, and in spite of the efforts of the then Minister of Agriculture, the Treasury [with more pressing demands on its resources, no doubt] could not be persuaded to put up the money.

King George VI and Queen Elizabeth Stakes Ascot: 20 July

Crepello decision was fully justified: King George goes to Montaval

By HOTSPUR

With a downpour of almost tropical intensity before racing, the 2,000 Guineas and Derby winner Crepello was not risked in the King George on Saturday, and the race went to last year's Derby runner-up, Montaval, who had been well beaten by Arctic Explorer in the Eclipse nine days ago.

Montaval (20-1) won by inches in an all French triumph from Al Mabsoot (100-7), with Tribord (100-7) third. Talgo (9-1), last year's "Arc" runner-up, was fifth, the best of the English-trained horses. The Italian four-year-old Tissot (5-2f) finished 10th of the 12 runners.

Crepello's owner and breed-er, Sir Victor Sasson, and his trainer, Noel Murless, came in for some harsh criticism for deciding at the last moment not to run the colt. I think this was unjustified. Naturally, they want Crepello, above all else, to join the small band who have won the Triple Crown.

Murless considered that a hard race for Crepello on testing going seven weeks before the St Leger would be to the detriment of his horse's prospects at Doncaster.

[Crepello broke down and did not run again. The 2,000 Guineas and Derby had been his only races as a 3-year-old.]

Hennessy Gold Cup Cheltenham: 16 November

Mandarin wins despite last-fence mistake

By MARLBOROUGH

Few who were at Cheltenham on Saturday will forget the heart-stopping finish in which Mandarin (8-1) beat Linwell and won this inaugural Gold Cup for Mme K.Hennessy.

The race developed into a duel as Linwell, conceding 16lb to Mandarin, jumped level with the six-year-old at

the second last. Mandarin hit the last fence hard, and halfway up the hill it looked like another triumph for the Cheltenham Gold Cup winner.

But Madden found the last ounce of Mandarin's stamina and drove him past and up the hill to win an unforgettable race by three lengths.

1958

30 Apr The Queen enjoys her second Classic triumph (after Carrozza's Oaks success last year) when Doug Smith rides 20-1 shot Pall Mall, already winner of two Classic trials, to victory in the 2,000 Guineas. (The colt misses his later engagements through an attack of heel bug.)

1 Jun Hot ante-post Derby favourite Alcide, trained by Cecil Boyd-Rochfort, is scratched from the race. He won the Lingfield Derby Trial by 12 lengths, but a few days later was found in his box in pain. Now, 3 days before the race, having shown "no life at all" during home canters, he has to be withdrawn. (The whispers of nobbling never die out.)

4 Jun Hard Ridden (18-1) is the first Irish-trained horse to win the Derby since Orby in 1907 and, bought at 270gns as a yearling by Sir Victor Sassoon, is the cheapest Derby winner acquired at public auction this century. For jockey Charlie Smirke, 51, it is a 4th Derby triumph and, he announces, his last ride in the Derby before retirement at the end of the season.

16 Oct French filly Bella Paola (4-1) lands the Champion Stakes at Newmarket, her third victory in three visits to England this season, after her successes in the 1,000 Guineas and Oaks - a total of over £35,000 in prize-money for her owner-breeder, French hotelier M F.Dupré. She is only the fourth filly to win the Champion in the last 20 years, all of them Classic winners.

CHAMPIONS

Jockey (Flat)	Doug Smith	165
Jockey (NH)	Fred Winter	82
Leading Trainer	Cecil Boyd-Rochfort	£84,186
Leading Owner	John McShain	£63,264
Leading Money Winner	Ballymoss	£38,686

Lincolnshire Handicap Lincoln: 26 March

Gallant Babur repeats "Lincoln" triumph: Storms home under top weight

From HOTSPUR

Babur, owned by Capt S.Riley Lord, trained by Capt C.Elsey at Malton, in Yorkshire, and ridden by the Australian E.Britt, put up an outstanding performance in winning the Lincolnshire Handicap for the second year in succession today from 36 opponents.

Under top weight of 9st and in holding going, Babur, a 25-1 chance, defeated Who You (28-1) by one and a half lengths, with Statfold (28-1) a further three lengths away third and Chief Barker, whose chance was destroyed by being badly drawn, fourth.

Only once before since the Lincolnshire Handicap was first run in 1853 has a horse won the race twice in successive years. This was Ob, successful in 1906 and 1907.

Babur is the first horse to win with 9st or more since Flamenco carried 9st to victory in 1935. The only other to win with 9st in the last 30 years was the mare Dorigen (9st 1lb) in 1933.

Grand National Aintree: 29 March

Cramp nearly robbed Freeman of race: National winner's jockey "wasted" in trying to make the weight

By HOTSPUR

A violent attack of cramp, induced by fasting, nearly robbed Arthur Freeman of his triumph on the Irish-trained Mr What in the Grand National at Aintree on Saturday.

It struck Freeman between the last two fences, but in spite of being in considerable pain he sat tight when Mr What made his almost fatal blunder at the last, got him going again and held on as the eight-year-old finished all too strongly for the gallant mare Tiberetta.

As Mr What passed the post a long 30 lengths ahead of Mr E.R.Courage's mare, Freeman was doubled up in pain and only just managed to stagger from the unsaddling enclosure to the scales to weigh in.

If the cramp had struck Freeman a few minutes earlier, there would probably have been a different tale to tell this morning. But it would have been an injustice, for his success was well deserved. In spite of his efforts at wasting, he still had to put up 6lb overweight on Mr What, whom he was engaged to ride only at the beginning of the week.

Mr What was bred near Mullingar in Co.Westmeath, by Mrs Arthur O'Neill, who did not know what to call him – hence the name.

It is the fourth time in the last six years that horses trained in Ireland have won the National, but Mr What must be the first National winner for many years who has started the season as a novice 'chaser.

Cheltenham Gold Cup 13 March

Kerstin lands Gold Cup for the North

From HOTSPUR

For only the second time a mare won the Cheltenham Gold Cup when Kerstin (7-1), owned by Mr G.H.Moore, a retired Northumbrian businessman, trained by C.Bewicke in Northumberland and ridden by S.Hayhurst, also a Northumbrian, got the better of a long duel with Polar Flight (11-2) by half a length.

Both Mandarin (9-4) and Linwell (100-30), first and second favourites, made mistakes and got rid of their riders at the 13th fence, and the finish concerned only the first two. Gay Donald (13-2), the old man of the party, was a bad third.

The Gold Cup was Kerstin's 10th victory. Last year she won only once, but was placed in five other races including her second to Linwell in the Gold Cup, so that if luck was on her side today she certainly deserved it.

She never made a mistake throughout, and though one or two of her opponents might have beaten her for finishing speed if all had remained standing, quite rightly it is jumping which counts, or rather should count, in steeplechasing, and Kerstin was a most worthy winner.

The only other mare to have won the Gold Cup was Ballinode, successful in 1925 when the race was run for the second time.

NATIONAL HUNT

Champion Hurdle	Bandalore	G Slack	20-1
Cheltenham Gold Cup	Kerstin	S Hayhurst	7-1
Grand National	Mr What	A Freeman	18-1

ENGLISH CLASSICS

2,000 Guineas	Pall Mall	D Smith	20-1
1,000 Guineas	Bella Paola	S Boullenger	8-11f
Derby	Hard Ridden	C Smirke	18-1
Oaks	Bella Paola	M Garcia	6-4f
St Leger	Alcide	WH Carr	4-9f

St Leger Doncaster: 13 September

It was Alcide's St Leger two furlongs out

By HOTSPUR

By his effortless victory in the St Leger on Saturday, Sir Humphrey de Trafford's home-bred colt Alcide showed clearly that he is far and away the best staying three-year-old trained in England this year, and also that with reasonable luck in running he would have won the Derby had he been able to take part. I certainly think he would have outstayed Hard Ridden.

Alcide is the sixth St Leger winner sent out by Captain C.Boyd-Rochfort, and the Newmarket trainer has now surpassed the feats of Alec Taylor of Manton and Frank Butters, who each trained five winners of the season's last classic.

A quarter of a mile from home Alcide (4-9f) was in front, and Carr kept him going to the finish to win by eight lengths from None Nicer (10-1), who just got the better of a long duel with Nagami (100-8), beaten three-quarters of a length for second place.

Ballymoss triumphs for Ireland in the Arc, two lengths in front of French horse Fric

Prix de l'Arc de Triomphe Longchamp: 5 October

Ballymoss romps home in Longchamp mud

From HOTSPUR

Ballymoss, with conditions all against him, stormed home in the Longchamp mud to win the Prix de l'Arc de Triomphe clearly on merit today by two lengths from the French-trained Fric, with another French horse, Cherasco, a further two and a half lengths away third.

The colt thus becomes the biggest money-spinner ever trained in the British Isles. To-day's race was worth £37,925 to the winner, and in England, France and Ireland Ballymoss has now won £98,650 in prize money, thus surpassing the record set up by Tulyar in 1951-52 by £22,233.

The race was another triumph for his Irish trainer Vincent O'Brien, who has had a staggering run of successes this season with Ballymoss and the Ascot Gold Cup winner Gladness.

It is the first time since the victory of the Aga Khan's Migoli in 1948 that a horse of British blood has won the Prix de l'Arc de Triomphe, and it is the first time in the history of the race that an Irish-trained runner has been successful.

It rained hard at Longchamp in the early hours yesterday, but the course dried quickly and before the first race this afternoon it seemed that the going would

Cesarewitch Newmarket: 15 October

Morecambe romps home on his own
Defies weight to become easiest Cesarewitch winner in memory
From HOTSPUR

Morecambe, with 9st 1lb on his back, put up the best weight-carrying performance in the Cesarewitch for nearly 50 years when he won today by 10 lengths from Predominate. Excluding war-time substitutes on a shortened course, it is only the third time in 119 years that a horse has carried over 9st to victory in the race.

I rate Morecambe's victory this afternoon, with his ears pricked, just as good a performance as Gladness's in the Ebor, for weight counts for much more over the 2¼ miles of the Cesarewitch than in the Ebor (1¾ miles), and Morecambe, on this showing,

must be considered up to Cup standard.

In spite of the weight, Morecambe (15-2), to the horror of most of his supporters, took up the running more than five furlongs from home. But after Sacarole had come at him and been beaten off before the Bushes, no one else looked like getting near him.

Predominate came from behind to pass the fading Sacarole, Kubba, and Hollyhock going down into the Dip, but he never got in a challenge, and Morecambe who won more easily than any Cesarewitch winner within memory.

be reasonable. It was coming down in buckets as the horses paraded for the big race, however, and there was talk that O'Brien was considering withdrawing Ballymoss at the last moment.

Fortunately, he wisely decided to let his four-year-old take his chance, and as usual the colt was completely unconcerned, both in the parade ring and in the parade in front of the stands.

I believe Bella Paola was interfered with, but I doubt if

it made any difference to the result, for Ballymoss was going exceptionally well and with more than a furlong to go took a clear lead from Fric.

Ballymoss did not quite win like Ribot won in 1956. Ribot's victory as a four-year-old was the most impressive of any horse I have seen in a top-class race, and I cannot quite rate Ballymoss in the same category. He has, however, now proved himself a smashing good horse, both on top of the ground and in the mud.

Washington International Laurel Park, Maryland: 11 November

US race sensation
Sailor's Guide wins on objection, Ballymoss third
FROM OUR OWN CORRESPONDENT

Sailor's Guide, the Australian champion, won the £35,700 Washington International here today after a sensational race in which he finished second and was then awarded the premier prize on an objection.

Ex-English-trained Tudor Era, now American-owned, finished first by 3 1/2 lengths from Sailor's Guide, with the Irish-trained Ballymoss third. But Howard Grant, who rode Sailor's Guide, objected to the winner for "crowding on the first turn" and the judges upheld the objection, awarding the race to Sailor's Guide and placing Tudor Era second.

Pandemonium broke out among the crowd when it became known that the objection had been sustained,

and there was continuous booing.

The race was crammed with drama from the moment the 10 runners began walking behind the man with the red flag towards the start. There were no fewer than half a dozen false starts, mostly provoked by the temperamental Argentine horse, Escribano, and even when they did get away Zaryad, the best of the two Russians, was badly left.

As the field came back to the enclosure after the race, Zaryad's jockey, Viktor Kovalov, could be seen making angry gestures to the Russian trainer Gottlieb, and was obviously complaining fiercely. He said later: "Zaryad wanted to go but someone

kept hold of the reins and we were held back."

Kovalov was obviously unfamiliar with the technique of a walk-up start. Judging by his actions and the torrent of Russian that came from his lips afterwards, he had a good deal more to say than the official quotation and translation.

It was a bitterly disappointing result for the British contingent present, for Ballymoss, the favourite, finished only a head behind Sailor's Guide in a photo-finish.

It was clear, even from the Press box, that the race was no gentlemanly affair, and this was borne out by the jockeys' comments afterwards. A.Breasley, the Australian, who rode Ballymoss, said: "The track

was a bit sharp with its turns, and we met interference a couple of times. But Ballymoss ran very well considering the circumstances."

Grant was, of course, vehement: "I got bothered every inch of the way," he said, "I got badly knocked at the head of the stretch."

One thing was certain, Tudor Era got off to a wonderful start and held his lead all the way though closely challenged by Sailor's Guide at the head of the stretch where the foul occurred. After this unhappy episode, Tudor Era forged ahead again, and nothing ever looked like catching him.

Sailor's Guide was substantially backed, and paid over 8-1 on the Tote.

OTHER MAJOR RACES

Irish Derby	Sindon	L Ward	100-8
Arc de Triomphe	Ballymoss	A Breasley	39-10
Kentucky Derby	Tim Tam	I Valenzuela	21-10jf
Melbourne Cup	Baystone	M Schumacher	10-1

1959

2 May A triumphant season ends on a disastrous note for new champion jump

jockey Tim Brookshaw, who is persuaded to take a spare ride on Turnstone in the Tiverton Handicap Chase at Taunton and breaks a leg in a fall. Ironically, Brookshaw only became certain of his title a short time ago when a fractured skull prevented rival Fred Winter riding again this season.

2 May Tomy Lee (37-10) beats Sword

Dancer by a nose and survives an objection to give jockey Willie Shoemaker his 2nd Kentucky Derby, in a temperature of 94°F.

30 Sep Jump jockey Johnny Gilbert rides two more winners at Fontwell Park before his fabulous run comes to an end, but his 10 wins on the trot, dating back to 8 September, is a National Hunt record, as

is his 13 wins from 14 rides.

3 Oct Aly Khan's Saint Crespin III, ridden by George Moore, is the 17-1 winner of the Arc, at Longchamp, despite dead-heating with Midnight Sun, who is demoted to 2nd place after the first two object to each other. The English colt Primera is 5th, less than half a length behind the winner.

CHAMPIONS

Jockey (Flat)	Doug Smith	157
Jockey (NH)	Tim Brookshaw	83
Leading Trainer	Noel Murless	£145,727
Leading Owner	Prince Aly Khan	£100,668
Leading Money Winner	Petite Etoile	£55,487

Coombe Stakes Sandown Park: 16 May

Bali Ha'i III springs big surprise, upsets long odds on Vacarme

By MARLBOROUGH

The book of form was torn to shreds at Sandown on Saturday afternoon when Vacarme, conqueror of the mighty Alcide, was beaten fair and square by the Queen Mother's Bali Ha'i, the horse presented to her on her tour of New Zealand.

Odds of 8-1 were laid on Vacarme, but he never really looked likely to land them. Bali Ha'i (10-1) hit the front early in the straight and was not fully extended to hold off

the favourite by three-quarters of a length.

The result will cause great pleasure in New Zealand, and I must humbly apologise to the people of that country for suggesting, after Bali Ha'i's last race at Chester, that his best chances of success lay under National Hunt rules.

It is some consolation that Capt Boyd-Rochfort was as surprised as anyone by Bali Ha'i's performance.

NATIONAL HUNT

Champion Hurdle	Fare Time	F Winter	13-2
Cheltenham Gold Cup	Roddy Owen	H Beasley	5-1
Grand National	Oxo	M Scudamore	8-1

ENGLISH CLASSICS

2,000 Guineas	Taboun	G Moore	5-2f
1,000 Guineas	Petite Etoile	D Smith	8-1
Derby	Parthia	WH Carr	10-1
Oaks	Petite Etoile	L Piggott	11-2
St Leger	Cantelo	E Hide	100-7

Grand National Aintree 21 March

Oxo & Scudamore hold on to win National
Luck of the Irish runs out
By HOTSPUR

Willie Stephenson, son of a Durham farmer and formerly a competent flat-race jockey, became the third trainer to saddle both a Derby and a Grand National winner when Oxo (8-1), in the colours of Bedfordshire farmer Mr J.E.Bigg, won the National on Saturday from the proven Aintree horses Wyndburgh (10-1), Mr Watt (6-1f) and the gallant mare Tiberetta (20-1). Eight years ago Stephenson won the Derby with Arctic Prince.

Although the going was perfect on Saturday, only those four of the 34 finished, Becher's claiming the majority of the fallers – eight first time round, six the second. Most of the grief there on the first circuit was caused by two of the early leaders falling and bringing down several of those following.

At Becher's the second time Tim Brookshaw, riding Wyndburgh, broke a stirrup. He kicked his foot out of the other iron to give him better balance for the rest of the race. In spite of his rider's

great handicap, Wyndburgh was beaten by only one and half lengths and would probably have won in another hundred yards – a great performance.

Michael Scudamore, who rode Oxo, had twice come second in the National, on Legal Joy in 1952 and Irish Lizard in 1954.

Coming on to the racecourse for the last time, Oxo held a clear lead, and Mr What, now third, appeared to be going better than Wyndburgh. Oxo jumped the second last brilliantly, gained ground on both his rivals, and must have been nearly six lengths clear of Wyndburgh coming to the last. He hit it hard, but Scudamore sat tight. Nevertheless, Oxo was a tired horse in the long run-in.

Afterwards I learned that Mr What had lost a plate during the race. It must have affected his chances a bit, for he walked feelingly from the unsaddling enclosure. The luck of the Irish, so prominent in Nationals in recent years, had deserted them at last.

The Derby Epsom: 3 June

Parthia and Fidalgo shatter the French
From HOTSPUR

Father and son-in-law fought out the finish of the Derby today, 42-year-old Harry Carr on Parthia (10-1) defeating his 24-year-old son-in-law Joe Mercer on Fidalgo (10-1) by one and a half lengths after a tense duel over the final three furlongs. Unlucky Shantung (11-2f), badly balked in running, came from last at Tattenham Corner to finish third. It was Carr's 13th ride in the Derby and his first success.

Parthia is owned and was bred by Sir Humphrey de Trafford, who rode as an amateur as a young man. It

was his first success in the Derby, and a success long overdue for his trainer, Capt C.Boyd-Rochfort, who now has all five classic races to his credit.

The pace after three furlongs seemed definitely on the slow side for a Derby, and there was a good deal of bunching as the course begins to swing to the left. Piggott sent Carnoustie for an opening and badly interfered with Above Suspicion. Moore, on Princillon, had to snatch up his colt, and Palmer, who had perhaps unwisely been making up ground on the

inside, could not prevent Shantung striking into him. Shantung fell back quickly, and Palmer was on the point of pulling him up altogether when he began to go better again.

Soon after turning into the straight, Mercer brought Fidalgo out to make sure of a clear run, and with three furlongs to go he had taken a clear lead. Carr, however, had been biding his time on Parthia, and a quarter of a mile from home he joined Fidalgo.

For the next furlong it was difficult to say which of the

two would gain the day, but Parthia gradually began to wear down his rival and in the last furlong went clear to win by one and a half lengths.

Shantung, coming with a long run on the outside, passed horse after horse in the straight and snatched third place on the post from Saint Crespin III, one and a half lengths behind Fidalgo. He never looked like getting to the first two, but from the amount of ground he made up in the last half mile it is reasonable to think he would have gone very near winning with a clear run.

The Oaks Epsom: 5 June

Petite Etoile makes it a Guineas-Oaks double

Murless fillies 1, 3 and 4

From HOTSPUR

Aly Khan won his fifth classic race of the season today when Petite Etoile (11-2) decisively beat Cantelo (7-4f) in the Oaks. He had previously won the 1,000 Guineas with Petite Etoile, the 2,000 Guineas with Taboun, the French 1,000 Guineas with Ginetta and the Irish 1,000 Guineas with Fiorentina.

I had thought that Petite Etoile, being by the Fair Trial horse Petition, would be most unlikely to stay the Oaks distance, but Piggott was able to ride a waiting race and

Petite Etoile came from behind to win clearly on merit by three lengths.

Lester Piggott was winning the Oaks for the second time. He looked to have a lot up his sleeve as he waited to pounce on Cantelo as the two drew away from the rest in the straight.

The race was certainly a triumph for Noel Murless. Besides Petite Etoile, who beat the northern-trained Cantelo, Murless saddled the third and fourth, Rose of Medina and Collyria.

---

9 June

Piggott accused by US turf writer

Undisciplined behaviour alleged in Laurel Park International

By HOTSPUR

Lester Piggott, suspended by the Nottingham stewards last night for "rough riding" on Astrador, and in trouble at Chantilly on Sunday, has also come in for searing criticism from a leading American racing journalist, Frank Talmadge Phelps, because of his conduct at Laurel Park last year.

Phelps, in the new edition of the Bloodstock Breeders' Review, says: "Had American riders conducted themselves as Piggott and the Russian Kovalev did at the start of the Washington International, they would have been suspended on the spot."

According to Phelps, Piggott behave badly at the "walk-up" start, and for this race because visiting horses are not used to the American-type starting gate. There were seven false starts. The chief offenders were Escribane, from Venezuela, the Russian horse Zaryad, ridden by Kovalev, and the German Derby winner Orsini II, ridden by Piggott.

Phelps says "Orsini kicked and stomped about and his jockey appeared unable or unwilling to control him. Finally the German colt was removed from the next-to-inside post position and placed on the extreme outside, where he could do less damage with his lashing heels – but every time the starter looked away, Piggott tried to edge towards the inside.

The Russian delegation protested after the race, Kovalev saying that Zaryad's reins had been held too long at the start. When the patrol film failed to substantiate this charge, the entire Soviet group denied that it had ever been made!

The ruling body at Laurel Park could have reported Piggott to the Jockey Club, but apparently did not think his behaviour at the start warranted this. It seems that the American starter to some extent lost control of the field, and I hope and think Phelps must have exaggerated Piggott's behaviour.

OTHER MAJOR RACES

Irish Derby	Fidalgo	J Mercer	1-2f
Arc de Triomphe	Saint Crespin	G Moore	169-10
Kentucky Derby	Tomy Lee	W Shoemaker	37-10
Melbourne Cup	Macdougal	TP Glennon	8-1

King George VI and Queen Elizabeth Stakes Ascot: 18 July

Alcide triumphant in farewell race: International rivals well beaten

By HOTSPUR

Alcide (2-1f) gained an overwhelming victory for Britain in an international field for the King George VI and Queen Elizabeth Stakes (£23,642) at Ascot on Saturday, and will now be retired to stud and syndicated. The syndication figure will be around £200,000 and I think this resolute horse will be an outstanding success as a sire.

Alcide won eight races and over £56,000 in stakes. But for injuries I have no doubt he would have won last year's Derby and this year's Ascot Gold Cup. After Parthia had

won the Derby, I asked Sir Humphrey de Trafford which he considered the better of his two great horses. His opinion, without hesitation, favoured Alcide.

The "King George" was an intensely exciting race, for after Chief III had led into the straight, the German horse Orsini, then the French Balbo, then the Irish mare Gladness all looked likely winners until Alcide came onto the scene. He won by two lengths from Gladness (9-2), with Balbo (33-1) third and Cantelo (6-1) fourth.

Ascot: 26 September

Manny Mercer killed

From HOTSPUR

Emmanuel Mercer, known to all racegoers as Manny Mercer and one of the best of the post-war generation of flat race jockeys, was killed instantaneously at Ascot on Saturday when his mount in the fifth race whipped round on the way to the post, unseated him and then kicked him in the face as he lay on the ground.

The meeting was abandoned and the horse, Priddy Fair, will not be raced again.

Marlborough writes: A tragic shadow was cast at Ascot on Saturday over the entire fabric of British racing. Racegoers everywhere heard with incredulous dismay that Manny Mercer was dead.

To many thousands more who had never seen him in the flesh, this cheerful, smiling little man had long been a familiar, much-respected friend. Only a name in their morning papers, perhaps, but a name that could be trusted day in, day out, to do a difficult job as well as any man.

It is 12 years now since a tiny 17-year-old apprentice won the Lincolnshire Handicap on a 100-1 chance called Jockey Treble, carrying 6st. There were 46 runners that day, and the track was a quagmire. Faced in the last furlong by a wall of horses and a barrage of flying mud, Mercer got through to win because, in the words of an astonished senior jockey, "he went for a gap that simply wasn't there."

In the years that followed, it

quickly became evident that there was much more to Manny Mercer than just the courage that goes with youth. One had only to watch Mercer cantering to the post – as he was when tragedy overtook him on Saturday – to know that this was that precious rarity, a horseman as well as a jockey.

The angle of the body, the easy confident length of rein, and the horse itself obviously at peace with the world – these were the trademarks of Manny Mercer, and few men now riding have brought them to such perfection.

Strong in a finish, nerveless in the big field, and capable of fitting his tactics to the special needs of the hour, he had carved himself a secure niche very close to the top of the tree, and would no doubt have retained it for many years to come.

Great jockeys are rare enough, but those that command and keep the respect and liking of the entire racing world must in their way be great men as well. Manny Mercer was one of these.

The 1960s

A number of technical and administrative innovations introduced in the sixties contributed to the smoother, fairer running of the sport in Britain. The patrol camera arrived in 1960, overnight declarations a year later, and starting stalls in 1965, a couple of years after they first appeared on French racecourses.

The Horserace Betting Levy Board was established in 1961, and betting shops were legalised in Britain, a boon for the punter diluted five years later by the introduction of a ten percent off-course betting tax. In 1962, sponsorship of the Irish Derby by the Irish Hospitals' Trust transformed it from obscurity into a major international race.

Women had won the right to vote five years after a suffragette threw herself in front of the King's horse in the 1913 Derby, but it was not until 1966 that they were reluctantly allowed to hold a training licence by the Jockey Club.

Lester Piggott won his first jockeys' championship in 1960 and, after a popular hat-trick of titles went to the Australian Scobie Breasley, he monopolised it for the rest of the decade, despite controversially ending a highly successful partnership with Newmarket trainer Noel Murless in 1966 to go freelance.

The sixties will be remembered for two pile-ups – in the 1962 Derby, when seven horses came down on Tattenham Hill, and the 1967 Grand National, in which the whole field were stopped at the fence after Becher's except for 100-1 shot Foinavon, who was still negotiating the "Brook" at the time and then plodded through the carnage to win the race.

The greatest equine performances of the decade include the 10-lengths Oaks victory in 1963 by the Irish filly Noblesse, the awesome triumphs in the 1965 Derby and Arc of the French colt Sea Bird II, and above all every race run by the charismatic Irish steeplechaser Arkle, surely the most beloved horse in the history of the sport.

The great Sea Bird II, ears pricked, romps home from Meadow Court and I Say in the 1965 Derby.

1960

12 May The Churches' Council on Gambling "reluctantly acquiesces" in the setting up of betting shops as provided in the Betting and Gaming Bill now before Parliament, but it is still fighting against the right to advertise such shops and would like the hours of opening reduced.

2 Jun The 4-y-o colt Indigenous, carrying 9st 5lb and ridden by Lester Piggott, wins the Tadworth Handicap at Epsom in 53.6sec (hand-timed) to set a new British 5-furlong record and so become the "fastest horse" – averaging 41.98 mph.

30 Jun Shamrock Star, the third of an Edward Hide 4-timer at the Liverpool night meeting, lands his third course record in 24 days, covering the 6f of the Merseyside Handicap in 1min 12.6sec, following up his success in the 5f Redcar Champion Sprint and the 5f Gosforth Park Cup at Newcastle.

4 Aug Anne, Duchess of Westminster pays farmer's wife Mrs Henry Baker 1,150gns for a 3-y-o that will turn out to be arguably the greatest steeplechaser of all time – Arkle.

CHAMPIONS

Jockey (Flat)	Lester Piggott	170
Jockey (NH)	Stan Mellor	68
Leading Trainer	Noel Murless	£118,327
Leading Owner	Sir Victor Sassoon	£90,069
Leading Money Winner	St Paddy	£71,256

Grand National Aintree: 26 March

£470 ex-hunter wins the Grand National

Scottish-bred Merryman II triumphs for woman owner

By HOTSPUR

For the first time in the history of the race a horse bred in Scotland won the Grand National on Saturday, Merryman II, beautifully ridden by G. Scott, beating Badanloch by 15 lengths with Clear Profit a further 12 lengths away third.

Merryman was bred at Hopetoun, near Edinburgh, by the late Marquess of Linlithgow and was sold by the present Lord Linlithgow at a bargain price of £470 to a friend of the family, Miss Winifred Wallace, in whose colours Merryman won Saturday's great race.

To Miss Wallace, one of the best woman riders in Scotland, must go much of the credit for the victory of Merryman, for she hunted him regularly and won three point-to-points on him. In February last year Miss Wallace brought him south to Leicester to run in a hunter's race and he was just beaten. Neville Crump, much impressed by the horse, persuaded Miss Wallace to send him to his Middleham stable to be put into training, and before the end of last season he had won both the Liverpool Foxhunters' and the Scottish Grand National.

He is now the third Crump-trained winner of the National, following in the footsteps of Sheila's Cottage (1948) and Teal (1952), who had a similar point-to-point background to that of Merryman.

The field of 26 was the smallest since Troytown won 40 years ago and Merryman (13-2) was the first outright favourite to succeed in the race since Sprig in 1927. He is, in fact, only the fourth clear favourite to win the race this century.

In view of the grief in steeplechases in the two previous days, Lord Sefton, the senior steward of the meeting, spoke to the National jockeys before the race, which was run at a much more sensible pace for the first circuit of the course than had been the case in several recent years. As a result more than half the field were standing after the water.

As they went away from the stands for the second time, Tea Fiend was leading with Scott biding his time on Merryman, and Badanloch, Eagle Lodge, Mr.What and Cannobie Lee among those going well close behind. But by the time they came to Valentine's again, Merryman and Badanloch (100-7) had drawn clear of Tea Fiend and throughout the last mile it was a duel between the two. Merryman was about four lengths clear over the last and drew right away in the long run-in.

NATIONAL HUNT

Champion Hurdle	Another Flash	H Beasley	11-4f
Cheltenham Gold Cup	Pas Seul	W Rees	6-1
Grand National	Merriman II	G Scott	13-2f

Obituary: 9 February

Miss Dorothy Paget dies in her sleep

Daily Telegraph Reporter

Miss Paget with Golden Miller

Miss Dorothy Paget, the racehorse owner, died in her sleep early yesterday at her home at Chalfont St Giles, Bucks. She was 54 and had been in poor health for some years.

Miss Paget owned more racehorses than any other woman in the history of British racing. She had over 50 horses in training in England and Ireland, and has been a great supporter of the turf for a quarter of a century. It is estimated that she spent during her racing career nearly £3 million on the sport.

Miss Paget's death is a great blow to Sir Gordon Richards, who trained his first winner in Miss Paget's colours and has 36 horses in training for her at his stables near Marlborough, more than half his string. Sir Gordon said yesterday: "She was the best loser I have ever known and a wonderful person to train and ride for."

Hotspur writes: The death of Miss Dorothy Paget, for a quarter of a century one of the leading owner breeders of the British turf and famous as the owner of the most brilliant chaser of all time, Golden Miller, is a severe blow to racing.

Miss Paget was equally well known on the flat and in steeplechasing. But there is little doubt that over the years she was more successful as an owner of jumpers, although she won a wartime Derby with Straight Deal which was bred at Elsenham, her stud in Essex.

Miss Paget, who as a girl was extremely good on a horse, first came into racing under National Hunt Rules when she had a few humble horses in training with Alec Law, at Findon. She then sent her horses to be trained by Basil Briscoe at Newmarket. Her name became well known when Briscoe bought, on her behalf, Golden Miller, who won five Cheltenham Gold Cups in succession for Miss Paget and the 1934 Grand National in record time.

Miss Paget gave 6,000 gns for Golden Miller and in the same period 4,000gns for Insurance, with which she won the Champion Hurdle.

Nearly all Miss Paget's jumpers were home-bred but Mont Tremblant was one of the exceptions. He was bought in France and won the 1952 Cheltenham Gold Cup as a six-year old. Her other horse to win the Gold Cup was Roman Hackle in 1940.

Miss Paget, with her large figure and old-fashioned clothes, was known by sight by everybody who went racing, but she was shy and usually spoke only to her immediate entourage and her trainers. She undoubtedly enjoyed her racing thoroughly, loved to have a tilt at the Ring and trembled with excitement while watching her horses doing battle.

Obituary Paris: 12 May

Aly Khan dies in Paris car collision

From Our Own Correspondent

Aly Khan, racehorse owner and diplomat, died in hospital after a car crash tonight in the Paris suburb of Suresnes. He was 48. His friend, Bettina, the former model whose real name is Simone Bodin, was in the car with him and suffered injuries, but was allowed to leave hospital after the wounds had been stitched.

In 1958, Aly Khan, son of the late Aga Khan, was appointed head of the Pakistan delegation to the United Nations. Yesterday it was announced that his appointment as Ambassador to Argentina had been approved, and he intended to go to Buenos Aires within a fortnight.

His first wife was Mrs Loel Guinness, the former Hon. Joan Yarde-Buller. Their elder son, Karim, is the present Aga Khan and leader of the Ismaili Moslem sect. His second wife was Rita Hayworth, the film actress, whom he married in 1949. They had a daughter, Yasmin. The marriage was dissolved in 1953.

Marlborough writes: Since his boyhood, much of which was spent in Ireland, the racing and breeding of thoroughbred horses was the abiding interest and passion of Aly Khan's life. And after his father's death he was himself entirely responsible for the organisation and planning of one of the biggest and most successful stables in the history of racing.

Aly Khan leads in one of his great horses, Petite Etoile (Piggott up), after last year's Oaks

Last season, Aly Khan and his trainers Alec Head and Noel Murless had a fantastic run of success in France, England and Ireland which may never by equalled. They won the English 2,000 Guineas with Taboun, the English 1,000 Guineas and Oaks with Petite Etoile, the Irish 1,000 Guineas with Florentina, the French 1,000 Guineas with Ginetta, and finally the Eclipse Stakes and the Prix de l'Arc with St Crespin III.

Since well before the war, when he used to ride with considerable dash and success as an amateur, Aly Khan had been a popular and widely known figure on English racecourses.

Irish Derby The Curragh: 22 June

Dope case horse wins Irish Derby

By HOTSPUR

Amid scenes of great enthusiasm, Chamour, trained by A.S.O'Brien, won the Irish Derby at The Curragh yesterday by one length from the 3-1 on favourite Alcaeus, runner-up to St Paddy in the Derby at Epsom. Chamour (3-1) won clearly on merit and his stable companion, Prince Chamier, was third.

Chamour is the colt over which his then trainer, Vincent O'Brien, lost his licence after winning the £202 Ballysax Plate at The Curragh, on April 20.

It is the custom in Ireland on the Flat for a sweat and saliva test to be carried out on one winner a day, and it is said that after the test on Chamour traces of a stimulant were found. Despite police investigation the person who administered the dope has not yet been found. In view of Chamour's victory yesterday, to dope him would seem to have been a singularly unnecessary action, for he would certainly have won that £202 plate without any artificial encouragement.

OTHER MAJOR RACES

Irish Derby	Chamour	G Bougoure	3-1
Arc de Triomphe	Puissant Chef	M Garcia	14-1
Kentucky Derby	Venetian Way	W Hartack	63-10
Melbourne Cup	Hi Jin	WA Smith	50-1

The Derby Epsom: 1 June

£100,000 favourite hurt in Derby and shot
St Paddy's 3-length win

Daily Telegraph Reporter

Thousands of people cheering the 1960 Derby winner, St Paddy, as he passed the winning post at Epsom yesterday, and millions more watching the race on television, knew nothing of the tragedy which struck down the favourite, Angers. The French horse, a 2-1 chance, broke his near foreleg as he came down the hill two furlongs before reaching Tattenham Corner. He was destroyed by a veterinary surgeon following immediately behind in a car, even before Lester Piggott got St Paddy past the post. It is estimated that, before the Derby, the value of Angers was about £100,000.

St Paddy (7-1) finished three lengths in front of the Irish trained Alcaeus (10-1), ridden by A. Breasley. This was Sir Victor Sassoon's fourth Derby winner in eight seasons, and Piggott's third. Kythnos (7-1) was third and Auroy fourth. All four were bred in England.

The death of the favourite was a final stroke of ill-luck in the 1960 Derby. On Tuesday, another Derby runner, Exchange Student, broke a fetlock while working on the course and had to be destroyed. Then, barely six hours before the race, Sir Winston Churchill's well-backed Vienna was withdrawn after a nail pierced a foot of the horse while be was being plated at the Derby stables.

Only a small section of the crowd lining the rails above Tattenham Corner knew of the drama that was taking place as the horses thundered past. Angers, fourth from last, suddenly stopped. His French jockey, Gerrard Thiboeuf, having his second Derby ride, heard the horse's foreleg snap.

Ron Hutchinson, who tracked the winner into the straight on Kythnos, said that St Paddy was always going far better than any of his rivals, and Lester Piggott, who had once more ridden a flawless race, considers that this, his third Derby victory, was more easily gained than either of the other two – on Never Say Die and Crepello.

ENGLISH CLASSICS

2,000 Guineas	Martial	R Hutchinson	18-1
1,000 Guineas	Never Too Late	R Poincelet	8-11f
Derby	St Paddy	L Piggott	7-1
Oaks	Never Too Late	R Poincelet	6-5f
St Leger	St Paddy	L Piggott	4-6f

King George & Queen Elizabeth Stakes Ascot: 17 July

Piggott erred – but the better horse won

By MARLBOROUGH

It is my considered opinion that Petite Etoile was beaten at Ascot on Saturday because in the soft going she did not stay the mile and a half quite as well as Aggressor. Lester Piggott did not ride his usual perfect race, but I do not believe that tactics affected the result.

Instead of coming wide into the straight, he seemed for a moment to be attempting a passage on the rails – a passage fraught with hazard. For Jimmy Lindley on Aggressor, the chance came off and Piggott now wishes he had tracked the winner through. Instead, he changed his mind, pulled out across Kythnos, and may have sustained a slight bump in the process.

Nevertheless, Petite Etoile, with a furlong to go, was not more than two lengths behind Aggressor. She was, moreover, still on the bit and if the old spectacular burst of speed had been forthcoming, would still have won.

Let us rather rejoice that Aggressor has now proved himself a horse of the very highest class. If the race were run again on the same ground next week, I would back him cheerfully – and 100-8, I fancy, would not be available.

1961

8 Mar The BBC announce that henceforth they will give all starting prices with racing results.

1 May Betting shops become legal in the UK.

20 May Trainer Noel Murless announces from Newmarket that 5-1 Derby favourite Pinturischio will not run in the Classic at the end of the month owing to a recurrence of his stomach upset. *[This is the last straw in Pinturischio's interrupted preparation and there are strong rumours that the colt has been "got at". Professional ante-post punters are supposed to have lost a fortune, but it is never proved. Pinturischio never races again.]*

1 Sep Horse Race Betting Levy Board and

Horserace Totalisator Board created.

8 Oct For the third time in seven years the Italians win the Prix de l'Arc de Triomphe as the colt Molvedo, a son of Ribot ridden by E.Camici, beats the French Derby winner Right Royal V by two lengths

11 Nov Edward Hide, who rode Henry the Seventh (100-8) to dead-heat for 1st place in the Cambridgeshire, completes a remarkable double when landing that horse's brother, Henry's Choice (100-8), first home in the Manchester November

Handicap.

11 Nov The flat season closes with Noel Murless leading trainer for the fourth time in five years, while Bill Elsey's 74 winners is an unprecedented feat for a trainer in his first season. The competition for leading owner has never been greater, with Major Lionel Holliday (£39,227) emerging just £73 ahead of Lady Sassoon and the late Sir Victor, and three women owners following – Mrs Vera Lilley, Mrs S.M.Costello and Mrs Arpad Plesch – all with over £35,000

CHAMPIONS

Jockey (Flat)	Scobie Breasley	171
Jockey (NH)	Stan Mellor	118
Leading Trainer	Noel Murless	£95,972
Leading Owner	Maj Lionel Holliday	£39,227
Leading Money Winner	Sweet Solera	£36,988

Grand National Aintree: 25 March

It's Nicolaus Silver as weight tells on Merryman II

By HOTSPUR (B.W.R.Curling)

Nicolaus Silver leads Merryman II over the last at Aintree

To Merryman II belongs most of the honours but not the final victory in the 1961 Grand National. Although badly kicked at the post he was never out of the first six, jumped magnificently, and just failed to give 25lb to Nicolaus Silver – the first grey to win the National for 90 years.

Fourteen out of the field of 35 completed the course on Saturday. Nineteen – more than half – were still in the race jumping the water first time round. Imposant, Oxo and Penny Feather were pulled up on the second circuit when their chance had gone.

So, in fact, about half the field fell and the rest either got round or were pulled up. There is no doubt at all that

the modifications to the fences have been a success. The Aintree fences will always be tough and formidable, but they are fair. Several of those who fell, including Taxidermist, did so because loose horses interfered with them at the critical moment.

The National has sometimes been under fierce attack in the last few years. With the changes made, I hope criticism will now die. Those lucky enough to see the great race on Saturday could not but be thrilled.

The National was a triumph for two famous racing families – the Beasleys and the Rimells. Bobby Beasley, who rode Nicolaus Silver, is the son of Harry

The 2,000 Guineas Newmarket: 26 April

Rockavon upsets form book in '2,000'

66-1 chances finish 1st and 2nd

From HOTSPUR (B.W.R.Curling)

Unplaced in the Northern Free Handicap at Newcastle three weeks ago, the rank outsider Rockavon, trained in Scotland by George Boyd, won the 2,000 Guineas today by two lengths from another outsider, Prince Tudor. It was the most staggering result in the history of the race.

First and second both started at 66-1 with the bookmakers, but the Tote starting price for the winner was 105-1, which more correctly represented Rockavon's chance on form. The Irish-trained Time Greine, a 25-1 chance, finished third, a short head away, just in front of the hot favourite Pinturischio.

Rockavon, Scotland's first-ever classic winner, is owned by Mr T.C.Yuill, a dairy farmer with pedigree Ayrshires, from Strathavon, in Lanarkshire. Mr Yuill has one brood mare, and Rockavon is only the third horse to carry his colours. All

three have been winners.

Bought as a yearling at the Newmarket October Sales for 2,300gns, Rockavon was bred by Mr T.R.Badger at the Biddlesden Park Stud, near Brackley, Northants. Mrs. Badger offered him for sale as a foal, and he was knocked down for only 410gns to an Irishman, Mr R.J.Donworth, who bought him as a speculation and resold him at a handsome profit as a yearling.

George Boyd did not see Rockavon win. He missed his plane this morning, so Epsom trainer D.Whelan took his place and saddled the winner. The winning jockey, N.Stirk, was riding in the 2,000 Guineas for the first time, but he is no stranger to Newmarket, for he won the 1959 Cambridgeshire on Rexequus, also trained by Boyd. Stirk, in fact, has had eight rides at Newmarket and has now won on four of them.

NATIONAL HUNT

Champion Hurdle	Eberneezer	F Winter	4-1
Cheltenham Gold Cup	Saffron Tartan	F Winter	2-1f
Grand National	Nicolaus Silver	H Beasley	28-1

Beasley, for many years stable jockey to another Irishman, Atty Persse, and successful on Mr Jinks in the 2,000 Guineas of 1929.

Fred Rimell, trainer of Nicolaus Silver, was a top-class rider under National Hunt rules in his day, rode the brilliant Avenger when he was much fancied to win the National, and won the Champion Hurdle on Brains Trust. This was Rimell's second National winner, for he saddled ESB five years ago. His father, Tom, won it with Forbra (1932) in the colours of Mr W. Parsonage.

As was generally expected, the two Russian horses were completely outclassed. They

appeared to be almost the last two coming to Becher's first time round. Grifel fell here and was remounted, his rider, Prakhov, going round in cold blood a quarter of a mile behind the rest of the field to complete a circuit of the course. Reljef was out of the race soon after Becher's first time round.

There was not much to choose between Merryman (8-1) and Nicolaus Silver (28-1) at the last two fences, and although Merryman had the advantage of the rails, it was clear soon after jumping the last fence that the weight was telling on him, and the grey had his race won before the bend on the long run in.

The Derby Epsom: 31 May

Rank outsider Psidium romps home in Derby

Piggott was offered the ride – and rejected it!

From HOTSPUR (B.W.R. Curling)

In hushed silence the rank outsider Psidium won the Derby today by two lengths from Dicta Drake, Pardao and Sovrango. The winner and fourth are both trained at Newmarket by Harry Wragg. Psidium, starting at odds of nearly 90-1 on the Tote and 66-1 with the bookmakers, is the longest-priced winner of the Derby since Aboyeur, a 100-1 chance, in 1913. The runner-up, Dicta Drake, started at 100-1.

The first three to finish are all owned by women, Psidium by Mrs Arpad Plesch, a Hungarian now living in the south of France, Dicta Drake by Mme Leon Volterra, and Pardao by the gallant American octogenarian Mrs C.O. Iselin, from Long Island.

A fortnight ago Lester Piggott, who had dubbed Psidium a miler after he had finished fourth to Moutiers over 10½ furlongs in France, was approached by Mr and Mrs Arpad Plesch to ride Psidium, if not required for Murless's stable. Piggott rejected the offer and shortly afterwards the Plesch's booked Roger Poincelet, who rides regularly for them in France.

Mrs Plesch, thrilled at being received and congratulated by the Queen, told me how they bought Psidium's Italian dam Dinarella, who came from the same female line as Donatello II, from French breeder Mme J. Couturie for nearly £3,000. "Dinarella was our very first mare," she said, "and her first foal, Thymus, won the French 2,000 Guineas for us, and now her third foal has won the Derby."

For Harry Wragg, it was a first Derby success as a trainer, although in his riding days he won it twice at Epsom, on Felstead and Blenheim.

It is really due to Wragg that Psidium was trained for the Derby at all, for after Piggott had advised that Psidium was a non-stayer the colt was started in the 2,000 Guineas and ran badly. It was only after a long discussion that Wragg's view, that Psidium would stay, prevailed and it was decided to train him for Epsom.

Lambourn training grounds: 16 July

Pandofell's trainer calls in police

SUNDAY TELEGRAPH REPORTER

Only a few hours before he was due to run in the Sunninghill Park Stakes at Ascot yesterday, Pandofell, winner of the Ascot Gold Cup and overnight favourite for the race, was found in his box, dazed, bruised and bleeding from the head, probably as the result of knocking himself when not fully conscious of what he was doing.

Pandofell would have been a hot favourite for the Sunninghill Park Stakes at Ascot on Saturday. Lester Piggott, who won the Ascot Gold Cup on the horse, was to have ridden him again. It is probable that, as a result of his injuries, Pandofell will not be able to run again this season.

His trainer, Farnham Maxwell, who has done outstandingly well with his horses this season, reported the incident to the Berkshire police. Still looking shocked and distressed, he said: "From his condition, I have grounds for believing that Pandofell has been interfered with. I have put the matter in the hands of the police, which is what I understand the Jockey Club wish trainers to do in these circumstances."

[A dope test proved that phenobarbitone had been administered, but the perpetrators were never found. Pandofell missed the Goodwood Cup, but recovered in time to win the Doncaster Cup in September.]

Cambridgeshire Stakes Newmarket: 27 October

Dead-heat in Cambridgeshire

By HOTSPUR

The finish of the Cambridgeshire: Henry the Seventh (left) and Violetta III (right) dead heat for first place

Saturday's Cambridgeshire was an even more thrilling race than the Cesarewitch and produced the first dead-heat for 34 years.

The camera on Saturday showed clearly that Henry the Seventh (100-8) and Violetta III (33-1), both racing on the far side of the course, were inseparable, with Miss Biffin (22-1), on the stands side, a neck away third.

Midsummer Night II, who finished eighth, was just over three lengths behind the winner which gives some idea of the excitement of the race.

Without any doubt Violetta III would have won in another stride, for she was catching the fading Henry the Seventh very fast indeed as they came to the winning post.

Paris: 10 October

Drugs set problem in international races

By HOTSPUR

The Jockey Clubs of Great Britain, France, America and Ireland met in Paris last week-end, under the chairmanship of M. Boussac, President of the French Jockey Club, to discuss the development of international racing and, in particular, the adjustment of dates for big races.

This meeting, the first of its kind, augurs well for the future. International racing is certain to continue to develop as a result of air transport and it is important that the leading racing authorities should be fully conversant with each other's thoughts and ideas on racing problems.

The introduction of the long-range camera in England, France and Ireland means that the stewards of the day should well be able to cope with objections and dubious riding in the chief races in these countries.

The biggest problem in international racing, however, is doping. The English are not in a position to give a lead in this matter, through lack of experience. In America, different racing authorities apparently interpret the doping to win rule with a different degree of severity. In other words a certain drug may be permissible in one state and not in another. This, I think, is one of the most important problems to be settled by racing authorities in the next decade.

1962

19 Mar The Finn crashes through the first fence in the Monaveen 'Chase at Hurst Park, unseating Derek Ancil, and then gallops loose, only to fall again at the second. Ancil, who also trains The Finn, is convinced the horse was got at, this following the nobbling of another hot favourite, Another Flash, beaten into third place last week behind Anzio in the Champion Hurdle.

5 May In winning the Kentucky Derby, Decidedly sets a new track record of 2min 0.4sec for the 1 1/4 miles.

9 Jun Finishing 4th in a selling 'chase at Cartmel, Creggmore Boy, at 22, is the oldest runner yet known.

21 Jul Match II, French-owned, bred, trained and ridden, defeats home-trained Aurelius by three-quarters of a length at Ascot to take the King George VI and Queen Elizabeth Stakes, the last of the four principal mile-and-a-half races in England, all of which have now gone to horses trained outside England – and to add insult to injury the only three English jockeys in this 11-horse race finish 9th, 10th and 11th!

21 Jul Wolverhampton stages Britain's first Saturday evening meeting

30 Sep French jockey Georges Chancelier, due to ride Val de Loir in the Arc next week, is killed in a motor accident. *[His intended mount is placed third.]*

7 Oct As the Prix de l'Arc is won by the 3-y-o Soltikoff, a 40-1 outsider, with English hope Aurelius last but one of the 24 runners, Romulus saves the day for English pride by taking the Prix du Moulin to prove himself the outstanding miler in Europe.

22 Dec Racing in Britain is abandoned owing to severe conditions of ice and snow.

CHAMPIONS

Jockey (Flat)	Scobie Breasley	179
Jockey (NH)	Stan Mellor	80
Leading Trainer	Dick Hern	£70,26
Leading Owner	Maj Lionel Holliday	£70,206
Leading Money Winner	Hethersett	£38,497

Riseholme Selling Plate Lincoln: 30 May

Piggott suspended by Lincoln stewards: Sequel to riding of Ione

From a special correspondent

Lester Piggott was suspended for the remainder of the Lincoln meeting after he had finished second on Ione in this evening's Riseholme Selling Plate. The winner of the race, Polly Macaw, and Ione are both trained by R.Ward at Hednesford. Their running was referred to the stewards of the Jockey Club.

Polly Macaw, who led from halfway, opened at 5-2 but started an even money favourite, while Ione eased from 11-8 on to 11-8 against.

Trainer Ward said to me after the race: "I backed both of them. They are a very moderate pair and ran on their merits. Polly Macaw does better with blinkers and she carried them to-night."

[The Jockey Club suspended Piggott until 28 July for making "no effort to win", and trainer Ward had his licence withdrawn.]

The Derby Epsom: 6 June

No cheers for Larkspur in chaotic Derby

Debacle on the hill shocks crowd to stunned silence

From HOTSPUR (B.W.R.Curling)

The Derby, run in perfect June weather, was wrecked to-day by the falls of seven horses on the long hill down to Tattenham Corner. Victory among the survivors – and it seemed rather a hollow one – went to Larkspur, owned by the American Mr Raymond Guest, ridden by the Australian Neville Sellwood, and trained in Ireland by Vincent O'Brien.

Larkspur, a 22-1 chance and the outsider of O'Brien's two runners, was out clear a furlong from home and won comfortably by two lengths from the Boussac colt Arcor, who came from almost last to take second place close home from the fading Le Cantilien, with Escort fourth.

The sight of six riderless horses passing the stands stunned most of the vast crowd to silence, and there was more concern for the missing jockeys, lying perhaps seriously injured on the course out of view of the stands, than excitement over the winner.

It seems probable, but by no means certain, that Romulus, runner-up in the 2,000 Guineas, struck into the heels of a horse in front of him, bringing down Crossen. The favourite, Hethersett, was certainly brought down by the prostrate Romulus, and Pindaric in turn by Hethersett. The others to fall were the rank outsiders Changing Times, Persian Fantasy and King Canute II, who broke a leg and had to be destroyed on the spot.

Six of the jockeys were taken to the local hospital, and four were kept there, including W.H.Carr, rider of Hethersett, and W.Swinburn, who rode Romulus.

Of the survivors, there can be do doubt that Larkspur won on merit, and it is clear that it was only very quick avoiding action by Sellwood, and some luck, that enabled

Grand National Aintree: 31 March

Kilmore's victory stirs Brown Jack memory

Twelve-year-olds take first three places in National

By Hotspur (B.W.R.Curling)

Memories of Brown Jack came flooding back at Aintree on Saturday when Kilmore (28-1), who is closely related on his dam's side to the great stayer, won the Grand National in the hands of Fred Winter. Kilmore, bred in Ireland by Mr G.S.Webb, is out of the mare Brown Image, whose second dam was Querquidella, dam of Brown Jack, winner of 18 races under Jockey Club Rules.

Brown Jack, who won the Queen Alexandra Stakes six times and also the 1928 Champion Hurdle at Cheltenham, kept his zest for racing for an extraordinarily long time, and it seems that Kilmore is one of those who keep their form over the years.

Few horses have won the National after having reached the age of 12. The last to do so was Sergeant Murphy in 1923, and he, in fact, scored in his fifth Grand National at the age of 13.

Sergeant Murphy won from the then 12-year-old Shaun Spadah and the 11-year-old Conjuror II. Their combined ages were thus 36 years, and that was the total for the first three on Saturday, Kilmore, Wyndburgh (45-1) and Mr What (22-1) – all 12-year-olds.

There is a further similarity in that in each case a previous winner of the race was concerned in the finish – Shaun Spadah in 1923 and Mr What on Saturday.

The victory of Kilmore was another triumph for Fred Winter, who had the nerve to ride a waiting race and did not come to the front until between the last two fences though he could have done so earlier. Winter's list of important successes now includes two Grand Nationals, three Champion Hurdles and two Cheltenham Gold Cups.

For Kilmore's trainer, Ryan Price, this was a first Grand National victory. He has previously been regarded as a brilliant trainer of hurdlers rather than as an outstanding trainer of steeplechasers. His Champion Hurdle winners have been Clair Soleil in 1955, Fare Time in 1959 and Eborneezer last year.

NATIONAL HUNT

Champion Hurdle	Anzio	GW Robinson	11-2
Cheltenham Gold Cup	Mandarin	F Winter	7-2
Grand National	Kilmore	F Winter	28-1

Derby disaster: more like Aintree than Epsom

him to steer clear of trouble.

Larkspur is one of the smallest Derby winners in recent years. He stands 15 hands 2 1/2in. and was bought as a yearling by his trainer, O'Brien, at Ballsbridge sales for 12,200 gns.

Grand Steeplechase de Paris Auteuil: 17 June

Heroic Mandarin gains greatest triumph

Bit breaks and Winter rides three miles without bridle

From MARLBOROUGH

Without a bridle – with only his own great heart and Fred Winter's matchless strength to keep him going – Madame K.Hennessy's Mandarin this afternoon became the first English-trained horse to win the Grand Steeplechase de Paris since Silvo in 1925.

The bit broke in Mandarin's mouth after only three fences, and for three twisting, hazardous miles Fred Winter had neither brakes nor steering. So when in the end, unbelievably, Mandarin thrust his head across the line in front, we who were here knew beyond doubt we had seen a feat of courage, skill and horsemanship never excelled on this or any other racecourse.

For a few dreadful moments, however – staggering, dazed and hoarse from the stands – we did not know if this was victory or just a bitter heroic defeat. A photo had been called for. Then the right number was in the frame, and as Winter and Mandarin pushed their way back through the wondering crowd a cheer went up – from French throats as well as English – that would have made the Irish yell at Cheltenham sound like a feeble whimper.

But once more this was Mandarin's day, and as he bounded past the stands, a gay, determined bundle of fire and muscle, already up in front and pulling Winter's arms out, there was no hint of the drama to come.

The little horse was wearing his usual bridle, the one with a rubber-covered bit in which he won both the Hennessy and the Cheltenham Gold Cup last season. But going to the fourth (a privet fence nearly 6ft high), some hidden fault appeared and the bit parted – and Winter found the reins loose and useless in his hands. "What could I do?" he said afterwards to Bryan Marshall. "I couldn't steer him, I couldn't stop – and I was much too frightened to jump off!"

In fact, of course, the thought of giving up occurred neither to horse nor jockey. On they went, pitching dangerously over the big water, and it was not till the second circuit that we in the stands realised the desperate situation they were in.

Desperate indeed it was! Quite apart from the near impossibility of steering without reins round this tortuous figure-of-eight, Mandarin, a horse who always leans hard on his bridle, must have felt horribly ill at ease and out of balance. As for Winter, his task defies description.

Round most of the bends Winter managed to keep a horse or two outside him, and the French champion Daumas, upsides on Taillefer when the bit broke, did his best to help.

Coming to the turn, Mandarin almost ran out the wrong side of a marker flag. The hesitation cost precious lengths, and round the last bend he was only fifth, six lengths behind the leader. But with all the stops pulled fully out and answering Winter's every demand, the little hero was actually in front by the last fence.

He made no mistake and landed perhaps a length clear. But up the long run-in, hard and brilliantly though Winter rode, like a man sculling without oars, Mandarin was tiring. Inch by inch Lumino crept up, and at the line not one of us could really be sure.

But all was well. And as Mandarin walked away, dog-tired but sound, his faithful attendants quite speechless with delight, the dreams of his owner, Madame Hennessy, had been realised. At an age when many jumpers are past their best, and after many hardships, her wonderful horse had come back to triumph in the land of his birth – to a triumph even finer than any in his long career.

I never expect to be more moved by a man and a horse than I was by Winter and Mandarin this afternoon. Separately, they have always been superb. Together, to-day, taking disaster by the throat and turning it to victory, they have surely earned a place of honour that will be secure as long as men talk, or read, or think of horses.

ENGLISH CLASSICS

2,000 Guineas	Privy Councillor	W Rickaby	100-6
1,000 Guineas	Abermaid	W Williamson	100-6
Derby	Larkspur	N Sellwood	22-1
Oaks	Monade	Y Saint-Martin	7-1
St Leger	Hethersett	WH Carr	100-8

Irish Derby The Curragh: 30 June

Poincelet's master move wins Irish Derby

By HOTSPUR

Tambourine II, American-owned and French-trained, just held on to win the £50,000 Irish Derby in the record time for the course of 2min 28.8sec at The Curragh on Saturday. In another stride he would have been beaten by the Irish 2,000 Guineas winner Arctic Storm, whose late run came just too late.

Before an enormous crowd on a warm June day and on very fast going, this first running of the Irish Sweeps Derby could not have produced a more thrilling finish.

The disappointment was the failure of Larkspur (9-4f).

One likes to see a good horse going on winning, and I have no doubt that Larkspur did not reproduce the form he had shown at Epsom.

In the Derby he was much too good for his stable-companion Sebring, whereas on Saturday he finished about two lengths behind Sebring (6-1), who was third, with Larkspur a well-beaten fourth.

The fact remains, however, that Tambourine (15-2) and Arctic Storm (15-2) came right away from the remainder in the final quarter of a mile, and these two had the finish to themselves.

7 November

Neville Sellwood killed in French race

By HOTSPUR

Neville Sellwood's tragic end after a racing fall in France yesterday is a sad blow for European racing. Quiet and friendly, a first-class jockey and, like all the leading Australians, a fine judge of pace. Sellwood first came to England in 1951 to ride for the late Atty Persse.

He made his mark straight away and a victory on the unpredictable Val d'Assa in the Royal Hunt Cup was among his notable successes that season. But Sellwood became homesick and returned to Australia the same year.

He did not come back to Europe again until Alec Head, with the approval of the Aga Khan, persuaded him to do so last year. Sellwood was unlucky not to find a champion among the stable's horses. But his chance came unexpectedly in this year's Derby when Vincent O'Brien engaged him to ride the American-owned Larkspur. He only just escaped the trouble that caused several horses to fall and then came with a long run to win decisively.

Sellwood was a good loser and a modest winner – two likeable attributes that are not always evident in front-rank jockeys. He will be very much missed.

OTHER MAJOR RACES

Irish Derby	Tambourine II	R Poincelet	15-2
Arc de Triomphe	Soltikoff	M Depalmas	40-1
Kentucky Derby	Decidedly	W Hartack	87-10
Melbourne Cup	Even Stevens	L Coles	3-1

1963

8 Mar Racing resumes after a harsh winter in which there has been only one meeting, at Ayr on **5 Jan**, since 21 Dec.

1 Apr Responsibility for the National Stud is transferred from the Ministry of Agriculture to the Horserace Betting Levy Board.

29 May French jockey Yves Saint-Martin, 21, adds the Derby to last year's triumphs in the Coronation Cup and Oaks, when Relko (5-1f) cruises home at Epsom by 6 lengths from Merchant Venturer (18-1), with Ragusa (25-1) a further 3 lengths away 3rd. It is a first Derby for septuagenarian owner-breeder M F.Dupre.

4 Dec In the Holly Handicap Hurdle at Liverpool, ex-champion Tim Brookshaw, 34, fractures his spine in a fall from Lucky Dora, who has to be destroyed.

a Paris hotelier, the second for trainer F.Mathet, and the first for France since 1956.

CHAMPIONS

Jockey (Flat)	Scobie Breasley	176
Jockey (NH)	Josh Gifford	70
Leading Trainer	Paddy Prendergast (Ire)	£125,294
Leading Owner	Jim Mullion	£68,882
Leading Money Winner	Ragusa	£66,011

Grand National Aintree: 30 March

Horse nobody wanted triumphs in National

Ayala, once sold for 40gns, snatches victory in desperate finish

By HOTSPUR (B.W.R.Curling)

Ayala (66-1), sold as an unwanted two-year-old at Newmarket December sales for a humble 40gns and now owned in partnership by the London hairstylist Mr P.B.Raymond and his trainer Keith Piggott, just outstayed Carrickbeg (20-1) in Saturday's £21,315 Grand National to win an agonisingly thrilling race by three-quarters of a length.

Mr John Lawrence rode a brilliant race on Carrickbeg and it was cruel luck that the horse he owns in partnership with Mr G.Kindersley should "die under him" in the last 100 yards of that long run-in from the final fence to the winning post. It was, perhaps, 20 yards from the post that Ayala caught Carrickbeg and took the lead – definitely finishing the more strongly.

Ayala, being by the Ascot Gold Cup winner Supertello, is the stouter-bred horse on his sire's side and it was his bottomless stamina that just turned the day.

As a foal and in all his early days, Ayala was an unwanted ugly duckling. Bred by Mr J.P.Philipps at the Dalham Hall Stud, near Newmarket, he was a big, rangy colt with bad forelegs, and at the Newmarket December sales of 1954 Mr Philipps decided to weed him out. He was sold to Major G.Mostyn Owen for 400 gns – the highest price he has reached in his life.

Ayala went into training with H.Jelliss, but at the end of his two-year-old days was

weeded out again and knocked down to Mr.N.Smith. Jelliss considered that he was "too slow as a flat racer to win a donkey race".

The following year Mr John Chapman, a patron of Keith Piggott, heard that there was a horse to be sold in Epping Forest, and his wife, on the way back from a Newmarket meeting, looked in to see this three-year-old. She took a liking to him and bought him for a song as a potential hunter.

Ayala was such a bad hunter that it was decided to send him to Piggott to see if he could make anything of him as a hurdler. He ran two or three times, but as his owner had a more promising horse in training at the time he decided that he could not afford Ayala as well and sent him up to the Epsom sales in November 1959, where he was knocked down to Mr Raymond for 250gns.

Piggott felt Ayala might make a 'chaser if he stood training and in the 1960-61 season Ayala won three 'chases like a useful horse, but last season had leg trouble and had to be pin-fired. Thus, although he is a nine-year-old he has had comparatively little racing and his chance on Saturday was, in the eyes of the majority, represented by his Tote starting price of 141-1.

Bargain horses have won the National before, but I can think of none who was culled by so many people before landing the prize.

The Oaks Epsom: 31 May

Brilliant Noblesse

Irish filly's 10-length victory not matched at Epsom this century
From HOTSPUR (B.W.R.Curling)

Noblesse won the Oaks to-day like a champion to crown a memorable Epsom meeting. Relko dominated the Derby on Wednesday, Exbury won yesterday's Coronation Cup brilliantly, and last, but certainly not least, Noblesse came home alone in the Oaks.

Ridden with supreme confidence by the Australian G.Bougoure, Noblesse (4-11f) won by no less than 10 lengths from the 1,000 Guineas runner-up Spree (100-7), who just lasted long enough to keep the fast-finishing Pouponne (33-1) out of second

place by a neck.

This is the first time this century that either the Derby or the Oaks has been won by such a wide margin. Manna won the 1925 Derby by eight lengths, and the same year Saucy Sue won the Oaks by a similar margin. Meld (1952), who took the fillies' Triple Crown, won by six lengths and Petite Etoile (1959) by three from the subsequent St Leger winner Cantelo. Petite Etoile was undoubtedly a brilliant filly, but I rather wonder if she was as good as Noblesse.

ENGLISH CLASSICS

2,000 Guineas	Only for Life	J Lindley	33-1
1,000 Guineas	Hula Dancer	R Poincelet	1-2f
Derby	Relko	Y Saint-Martin	5-1f
Oaks	Noblesse	G Bougoure	4-11f
St Leger	Ragusa	G Bougoure	2-5f

Ascot: 19 June

Lester Piggott's day in Ascot drizzle
From MARLBOROUGH

It was Lester Piggott's day to-day and, by way of a change, the English jockeys had all six winners to themselves. Piggott, who had wasted down to his "minimum" to win the Hunt Cup on Spaniards Close, had an armchair ride on The Creditor and rounded off his treble when, with a brilliant mixture of strength and timing, he nursed Raccolto home in the Bessborough Stakes.

A miserable drizzling rain kept the umbrellas sprouting throughout the afternoon, and even so, many a cherished hat will

never be the same again. By a quarter to five the ground had got really soft, and Raccolto's somewhat doubtful stamina (he is by the sprinter Como) was put to a pretty searching test.

But Piggott shot him past the leader, Dahabeah, a furlong out, and the advantage he poached, though dwindling fast towards the end, was just enough to hold the desperate challenge of the favourite, Voivode.

[Piggott went on to claim the riding honours at the Royal Ascot meeting with six winners.]

NATIONAL HUNT

Champion Hurdle	Winning Fair	Mr A Lillingston	100-9
Cheltenham Gold Cup	Mill House	GW Robinson	7-2f
Grand National	Ayala	P Buckley	66-1

Queen Alexandra Stakes Ascot: 21 June

Trelawny lands great staying double: Breasley's superb judgement of pace

From MARLBOROUGH

Welcomed home as few, if any, horses have been at Royal Ascot since Brown Jack's final bow in 1934, Trelawny won his second Queen Alexandra Stakes to-day, and for the second time brought off a glorious double at the meeting. The seven-year-old is better now than ever before and would, in my opinion, have gone very close indeed to winning the Gold Cup itself had he been eligible to run.

This unique triumph (no horse has ever done the double two years running) was of course gained largely by Trelawny's own great heart and bottomless stamina.

Victory for Trelawny in the Ascot Stakes, first leg of the double

But a share of credit is due also to the superbly accurate clock in Scobie Breasley's head – and to the skill of George Todd who, though himself reluctant to run again to-day, had got the old horse in such tremendous form that Tuesday's wonderful effort in the Ascot Stakes under a record 10st had served merely to warm him up.

Breasley in fact says that, whereas last year Trelawny gave him one of his hardest ever rides, this time there was never an anxious moment. Nevertheless to take the lead after seven furlongs was a bold decision based on superlative judgment of pace.

Trelawny, who seemed to enjoy the change, strode gaily along in front until Sannazaro passed him going down to Swinley Bottom – and here once again Breasley's timing came into play. Quite undisturbed, he let the leader go six lengths clear, waited calmly until he collapsed and then swept by to turn for home with Grey of Falloden the only remaining danger.

Just for a moment, three furlongs out, that danger looked a real one – but gallantly though Grey of Falloden struggled, there was no chink in his rival's impregnable armour. And so, with ladies running helter-skelter across the Royal lawn to watch him, with the top hats waving as if for a Royal triumph, Trelawny galloped relentlessly into the history books.

Hennessy Gold Cup Newbury: 29 November

Mill House has proved himself a champion: Best 'chasing display since the war

By HOTSPUR

Mill House, who in winning the £5,000 Hennessy Gold Cup at Newbury on Saturday put up the finest display of jumping seen in England since the war, will not clash again with his beaten Irish-trained rival Arkle until the Cheltenham Gold Cup.

Saturday's race drew an enormous crowd, but the expected duel between these two fine 'chasers never really materialised. Mill House finished on his own after Arkle had made a bad mistake three fences from home when lying second to the Cheltenham Gold Cup winner.

Though Arkle's error destroyed any chance of a spectacular finish, my opinion is that Mill House was going better at the time. He was jumping superbly and gaining at practically every fence, whereas Arkle's jumping was competent but not brilliant.

A colleague at the third last fence told me that Mill House put in a prodigious leap there and this probably caused

OTHER MAJOR RACES

Irish Derby	Ragusa	G Bougoure	100-7
Arc de Triomphe	Exbury	J Deforge	36-10
Kentucky Derby	Chateaugay	B Baeza	94-10
Melbourne Cup	Gatum Gatun	J Johnson	25-1

Irish Derby The Curragh: 29 June

Ragusa triumphs after Relko's shock exit

By HOTSPUR

Paddy Prendergast added the £49,000 Irish Sweeps Derby to the three classics he had already won this season when Ragusa, bred by the American Mr H.F.Guggenheim and owned by Mr J.R.Mullion, won decisively at The Curragh on Saturday in the last-minute absence of the unsound odds-on favourite Relko (8-11).

The shock withdrawal of Relko completely spoilt the race. The favourite looked hard-trained in the paddock and, I thought, not quite so well as on Derby Day at Epsom. He lashed out once or twice but seemed perfectly sound as he walked round the parade ring.

By the time he got to the post Relko was clearly lame, and because of language difficulties there was some delay while his jockey, Saint-Martin, made it clear to the starter that he wished to ask the permission of trainer Mathet to withdraw the colt.

As a result there was a delay of a quarter of an hour before the race got under way. It needs little description for, despite being struck into and losing a plate, Ragusa (100-7) won easily from Vic Mo Chroi (28-1), Tiger (18-1) and Tarqogan (20-1).

Tarqogan apparently failed to act in the holding going. He finished about six lengths behind Ragusa compared with the half-length that divided them at Epsom.

In the Derby, Relko beat Ragusa by nine lengths, but it looks as if Ragusa had probably improved, which was the opinion of his trainer before the race.

[As Relko did not come under starter's orders, 10/- in £1 was deducted from winning SP bets.]

Racing Calendar: 3 October

Relko keeps Derby: Seven dope cases closed

From HOTSPUR

The Relko affair was concluded to-day with an announcement from the Jockey Club stewards which officially confirms M F.Dupre's high-class colt as the 1963 Derby winner. It was also revealed that the £35,338 prize money was paid over in June.

The Jockey Club stewards, together with those of the National Hunt committee, have dropped investigations into the cases of Relko and six other horses on whom routine dope tests were alleged to have revealed a substance other than a normal nutrient.

The mystery of the drug found in these seven instances in the spring and early summer is still unsolved, but the stewards have decided to close the cases. They could find no evidence to justify the disqualification of the winners concerned.

The findings will be received with relief throughout the racing world. An even more encouraging feature of the Racing Calendar announcement is the disclosure that there have been no positive findings in routine tests made since the Derby on May 29.

As no confirmed cases of nobbling have been reported by trainers this season (although one or two have been suspected), it would appear that the clouds of suspicion and doubt surrounding the sport are now lifting.

Arkle to take off too soon. At any rate the Irish horse appeared to brush through the top of it, slipped on landing and was almost down.

This settled the race. As the result of Arkle's mistake Happy Spring went past him to finish second, eight long lengths behind Mill House, who was eased in the last 50 yards.

P.Taaffe, rider of Arkle, said afterwards that he thought Arkle might well have beaten Mill House. This certainly appeared unlikely from the stands. Mill House is certainly a real champion. Wherever he goes I am quite sure the crowds will follow. One probably sees a 'chaser of his calibre only two or three times in a lifetime.

1964

12 May Canadian-bred Northern Dancer (3-1) wins the Kentucky Derby by a neck from the favourite, Hill Rise, in a race worth £40,700.

21 May Last meeting at Lincoln; it has been announced that the Lincolnshire

Handicap will in future be run at Doncaster.

18 June Royal Ascot races abandoned when torrential rain saturates the course.

13 July Lester Piggott is the first English

jockey to ride winners in two countries on the same day, landing a shade of odds on 2-year-old Mexico II in the afternoon on a flying visit to St-Cloud, and turning up at Birmingham in the evening to win the first race on Prince of Norway and complete the treble later on First Prize.

CHAMPIONS

Jockey (Flat)	Lester Piggott	140
Jockey (NH)	Josh Gifford	94
Leading Trainer	Paddy Prendergast (Ire)	£128,102
Leading Owner	Mrs Howell Jackson	£98,270
Leading Money Winner	Santa Claus	£72,067

Cheltenham Gold Cup: 7 March

Arkle settles a thousand arguments, and does it in record time

From John Lawrence

Arkle jumps ahead of Mill House

Our wildest dreams came true this afternoon as, with the Cheltenham Gold Cup between them, Mill House and Arkle rose together at the second last. Then, as Arkle swept irresistibly away, a thousand arguments were settled – and we who watched stood hats in hand, lifted clean out of ourselves by the finest racing spectacle I ever saw or hoped to see.

A few breathtaking seconds earlier as Mill House turned downhill towards the last three fences anything seemed possible. For Arkle had moved up easily a length behind him and, hearing him come, Willie Robinson must have known the chips were well and truly down.

Three fences out, with Arkle at his quarters, Mill House threw one final, almost despairing, leap, but it gained him not one yard, and in a dozen strides the "challenger" was level.

Long before this, cheering broke out all over the stands. Now, as the Irish saw the prize within their grasp, it rose to an awesome yell of triumph.

And suddenly, going to the last, as Robinson drew his whip, it was all over. With the burst of speed about which we all had talked and wondered

for so long, Arkle rocketed clear, swept up and over, silky-smooth – and on to victory in record time.

Mill House never faltered, never gave up. Forced by circumstances to lead from the start, he was simply beaten by a faster horse, but both winner and victim covered themselves with glory. Both are great chasers – perhaps, no almost certainly, the greatest of all time.

Trotting serenely down towards the start, Mill House (8-13f) looked invincible – ears cocked and shooting out his toes, a ballet dancer with the power of a tank. Beside him Arkle (7-4) looked almost small – but hard as nails and superbly fit.

From the start Willie Robinson sailed into the front and what looked an easy pace – but must have been a fast one. Arkle, pulling hard, disputed second place with Pas Seul ahead of King's Nephew – and jumped the first few fences, like all the rest, with an ideal blend of accuracy and boldness.

Mill House, by contrast, "fiddled" more than once, and after the first full circuit drew an agonised gasp from the crowd by getting right under the open ditch in front of the stands. But then, as if to

---

Grand National Aintree: 21 March

Team Spirit's victory makes it a Grand inter-National

From John Lawrence (as seen from the saddle)

For the second year running, 494 yards of flat, featureless turf decided the Grand National. This time it was poor Johnny Kenneally, on Purple Silk (100-6), who saw the prize snatched cruelly away – and Willie Robinson, riding the marvellous little 12-year-old Team Spirit (18-1), in his fifth consecutive National, who caught and beat them two agonising heartbeats from the line.

Throughout the final half mile, Kenneally, as he told me later, "was going so well I could hardly believe it". Too well, indeed – for Purple Silk must not be left in front too long, and as Peacetown (3rd, 40-1) ran down to the last fence there was no choice but to set sail for home.

Behind them as they started up the long run-in, history was again being repeated. Team Spirit, jumping the last in third place, was perhaps four

lengths behind (a little further than Ayala 12 months ago) – and Willie Robinson, though hopeful, "never really thought I'd catch him until I actually did." Coming on to the racecourse, Eternal (4th, 66-1) actually overtook Team Spirit – but from there the little horse's bottomless stamina was always steadily closing the gap.

To me, on my 35th birthday, as Crobeg scrambled, tired but game, over the second last, none of this was visible. All my strength, and mind, were concentrated on finishing the course – and we did it too, ninth of the 14 survivors.

Team Spirit's trainer Fulke Walwyn won the National himself on Reynoldstown. Team Spirit was bred in Ireland by Mr P.J.Coonan, is owned by an Anglo-American syndicate and was ridden by an Irish jockey.

NATIONAL HUNT

Champion Hurdle	Magic Court	P McCarron	100-6
Cheltenham Gold Cup	Arkle	P Taaffe	7-4
Grand National	Team Spirit	GW Robinson	18-1

reassure us, he stormed off down the hill opening up a six-length gap from his pursuers.

For just a moment it seemed the race might be decided there and then. Could any horse alive, we wondered, find the speed to match those giant strides?

But, turning past the farm, Pat Taaffe and Arkle gave their answer. It echoed load and clear across the course and already a mile from home the crowd's murmur became a roar as the Duchess of Westminster's yellow jacket drew closer stride by stride.

"I was never worried at any stage," said Pat Taaffe later. "This is by far the best horse I ever rode."

Well, a great horse deserves a great jockey, and Arkle got one today. He was ridden

throughout with supreme confidence and perfect timing – the tactical plan of using one decisive burst carried out to the letter.

Poor Willie Robinson, bitterly disappointed, felt that Mill House had not jumped as well as he can. Possibly this was caused by lack of company and, with a pacemaker, Willie feels that there would still be hope. "He beat me fair and square today," he said sadly, "but I can't believe it's right."

I have never seen at Cheltenham, or anywhere else, enthusiasm to equal the welcome Arkle got today. Mobbed, patted and pushed on every side, he walked calmly through the milling, cheering crowd – and found the winner's enclosure almost too full to allow him to enter.

The Derby Epsom: 3 June

Santa Claus swoops to Derby triumph

By HOTSPUR (B.W.R.Curling)

Scobie Breasley, at the 13th time of asking and at the age of 50, won the Derby to-day on the 15-8 favourite Santa Claus. The winner was sold as a foal for only 800gns and resold as a yearling for 400gns more.

Like another celebrated champion jockey, Sir Gordon Richards, Breasley has taken a long time to win the Derby. To-day, as many expected, he rode a waiting race and came from a long way beck to catch and beat the Chester Vase winner Indiana (30-1) in the last 50 yards.

The winning margin was a length. The 100-1 chances Dilettante II (a further two lengths away) and Anselmo, both prepared for the race in Ireland by Paddy Prendergast, were third and fourth, with Crete, the Prendergast first-string, sixth.

After the 2,000 Guineas it was good to see a colt English-bred and English-owned winning the most valuable race ever run in Europe. Santa Claus's breeder, Dr F.A.Smorfitt, lives in Warwickshire, acts as a course doctor at two or three Midlands meetings and has always been keen on hunting and horses. His trainer, Mickie Rogers, is one of the few Englishmen training in Ireland – there are many Irishmen training in England!

The winner's joint-owners are Mr J.Ismay, an owner-breeder for many years and owner of the Winter Paddocks Stud in Norfolk, and Mrs Darby Rogers, mother of the trainer.

ENGLISH CLASSICS

2,000 Guineas	Baldric	W Pyers	20-1
1,000 Guineas	Pourparler	G Bougoure	11-2
Derby	Santa Claus	A Breasley	15-8f
Oaks	Homeward Bound	G Starkey	100-7
St Leger	Indiana	J Lindley	100-7

King George VI & Queen Elizabeth Stakes Ascot: 18 July

Santa Claus way below form against Nasram II

By HOTSPUR

Santa Claus, asked for the first time to race on going baked fairly hard by a hot summer sun, was beaten by the outsider Nasram II in Saturday's King George VI and Queen Elizabeth Stakes at Ascot.

This was certainly one of the biggest shocks of the season, for Santa Claus started at 13-2 on. No-one likes to see a Derby winner beaten, but the Irish colt failed to show his usual brilliance and was clearly ill-suited by the conditions.

Santa Clause has not the best of forelegs and I think they let him down on the hard ground. He seemed to me to come back to the unsaddling enclosure feeling them.

The surprise winner, the four-year-old Nasram II (100-7), though bred by his owners, Mr and Mrs E.Howell Jackson, at their stud in Virginia, is a horse entirely of European blood. He is by the British-bred Nasrullah out of the French-bred La Mirambule, a top-class racemare bought by the British Bloodstock Agency for Mrs Howell Jackson for about £30,000.

[Santa Claus is later beaten three-quarters of a length by Prince Royal II in the Arc de Triomphe.]

OTHER MAJOR RACES

Irish Derby	Santa Claus	W Burke	4-7f
Arc de Triomphe	Prince Royal II	R Poincelet	158-10
Kentucky Derby	Northern Dancer	W Hartack	3-1
Melbourne Cup	Polo Prince	R Taylor	12-1

1 July

Last 'National' at Aintree in 1965
Property company buys course for housing
DAILY TELEGRAPH REPORTER

Next year's Grand National steeplechase will be the last to be run at Aintree. The famous Liverpool course and motor racing circuit is to be sold to a development company.

Mrs Mirabel Topham, managing director of the lessees of the course, said last night that houses will probably be built on the 270-acre course if planning permission is granted. The Grand National is likely to be transferred to another course. Mrs Topham said she would like to see it go to Ascot.

Mr Leslie Marler, chairman of the Capital and Counties Property Company, said 15,000 people would be housed on the course. The closure was a question of priorities. Homes were badly needed in the Liverpool area. Mr Marler added that his firm had paid a "fair figure" for the land and did not expect much change out of £1 million.

The news was received with shock by racegoers, jockeys and owners. "This is the most staggering piece of news I have ever heard," said the Earl of Derby. "I understand that Mrs Topham said everyone knows that racing is in rather a sorry state. I think this is the most utter nonsense I have ever heard."

HOTSPUR writes: The racing authorities will do all they can to save Aintree from the property developers. No doubt the House of Commons, also, will not want to see the course given up.

Only this year the Betting Levy Board decided to sponsor the Grand National for the first time. The race dwarfs in value any other steeplechase run in this country.

JOHN LAWRENCE (Marlborough of THE DAILY TELEGRAPH, who rode Carrickbeg to second place in the 1963 Grand National) writes: There was nothing like it and nothing can ever take its place. That I'm afraid will be the first sad bitter reaction from all of those for whom, like me, the Liverpool Grand National has been so long something to dream about and live for.

Washington International Laurel Park, Maryland: 11 November

Kelso sets record and survives objection
By Edwin Tetlow

Kelso, the favourite, won today's 13th running of the Washington International and then survived an objection. His fellow-American horse and close market rival Gun Bow was second, four and a half lengths behind.

The Russian horse Anilin, who had not been greatly favoured because of an ankle injury in training, put up a wonderful performance to finish third.

Kelso's time was 2min 23 4/5sec, a record for the course. Ten minutes after the race finished the objection flag was raised, but the objection, by Gun Bow's jockey Walter Blum, who claimed that Kelso had crossed in front of him half-way up the straight, was overruled.

The announcement that the objection had been overruled was welcomed by a massive roar from the crowd of nearly 40,000. Kelso was undoubtedly the most popular horse of the race and had been ridden beautifully by Ismael Valenzuela.

Piggott's mount, the French filly Belle Sicambre, obviously disliked the hard going, was fretful in the parade and after showing early speed in the race gradually dropped back.

Biscayne, the Irish horse ridden by W.Williamson, finished fourth, Belle Sicambre fifth, Primordial (Venezuela) sixth and Veronese (Italy) seventh.

Half an hour after dismounting from Belle Sicambre, Lester Piggott rode the winner of the next race. On Lucky Turn, he came brilliantly to challenge and beat the favourite by a head. Lucky Turn's time of 1min 41 1/5sec, was a record for the one mile and one-sixteenth stretch.

1965

13 Feb NH jockey Trevor Pink, 34, dies from injuries sustained when Balus Boy falls in a novices' chase at Taunton.

2 Jun The Derby prize goes to an overseas stable for the 10th time in 20 years – and France scores her seventh victory in that period – as M. Jean Ternynck's Sea Bird II coasts home from Irish-trained Meadow Court. The French colt starts as the hottest favourite since Crepello in 1957.

8 Jul Newmarket's Chesterfield Stakes is first English race to be started from stalls.

1 Sep The Duke of Norfolk's Committee publishes its report on the future pattern of racing, recommending more races for the better types of horse, fewer handicaps (and none for maidens) and a reallocation of prize money for prestige events.

1 Sep Two horses die from heart failure in the same race, a selling handicap hurdle at Devon & Exeter, collapsing a few yards after the winning post – odds-on favourite Galatea, who had thrown its rider at the last flight, and 20-1 winner Jungle Student. Another favourite, Templeorum, collapses after finishing last in a later race, and his owner calls for a private dope test.

20 Nov Whisky firm James Buchanan Ltd provide all the added money for Ascot Heath's 'Black and White Day', over £10,000

14 February

'Prince' Ras Monolulu dies at 84

DAILY TELEGRAPH REPORTER

The racing tipster Prince Ras Monolulu, self-styled chief of the Falasha tribe of Abyssinia, famous for his magnificent costume and raucous cry of "I gotta horse", died yesterday in Middlesex Hospital, London, aged 84.

He was born in Abyssinia, went to America as a young man and arrived in England in 1902. After a period on the Continent and in Russia, he returned to Britain in 1919.

In the book of his life story, "I Gotta Horse", published in 1950, he said he made and lost from £100,000 to £150,000 on the Turf between 1919 and 1950.

He came, according to himself, by the regal title by which he was known to millions when he was "shanghaied" aboard an America-bound ship. Having been told that "princes were great men in other lands," he announced himself as Prince Ras Monolulu.

Among jobs he said he had done at one time or another were: fire-eater in a circus, artists' model in Munich, and

'I gotta horse!'

peddling tooth-paste "as used by King Tutankhamen". It was mostly chalk.

After spending the 1914-18 war years in a German prison camp he returned to England. As a tipster his biggest coup, the one that made him known overnight among racing people, was tipping and backing Spion Kop to win the 1920 Derby. He made £8,000.

Cheltenham Gold Cup: 11 March

Arkle runs away from gallant Mill House: 20 lengths to spare in second Gold Cup

By HOTSPUR (Peter Scott)

Anne, Duchess of Westminster's Arkle broke one record, equalled another and set a time that seemingly only he can better, when winning his second Cheltenham Gold Cup with complete authority here this afternoon. Arkle's 20-length margin over Mill House has been equalled in this race only by Easter Hero, both in 1929 and 1930, but Easter Hero had no rival of Mill House's calibre to beat.

Arkle's earnings, from 19 steeplechase and hurdle victories, now stand at £36,818. Team Spirit's old record of £29,495 for English and Irish National Hunt racing is thus eclipsed. Arkle returned 6min 41 1/5 sec against 6min 45 3/5 sec a year ago when he had 75 yards farther to run. Jockey Pat Taaffe believes he is a much better horse now, and few will quarrel with that.

Poor Mill House – so much superior to any other long-distance 'chaser yet fated to compete with a superb racing machine, invincible on anything like fair and level terms.

Between the final two fences Taaffe decided that the "match" had lasted long enough and Arkle accelerated into a lead of some eight lengths as they came into the last. Here, said Taaffe, he made his biggest leap of the whole race and the gap back to Mill House more than doubled at the run-in as Arkle galloped mercilessly on.

Thirty lengths behind Mill House came the Australian farmer Mr Bill Roycroft on his Tokyo Olympic Games eventer Stoney Crossing. It was Stoney Crossing's first steeplechase anywhere and he fully earned cheers that eclipsed those for many of the meeting's winners.

Grand National Aintree: 27 March

American triumph in Grand National: Freddie "trumped" on line

From W.D.Tadd

Twice up the long gruelling run-in that makes the final and supreme demand on horse and rider, Mr Tom Smith almost lost the strength he needed to drive Jay Trump (100-6) to victory in the richest Grand National of all time. With the 7-2 favourite, Freddie, at his girth and Pat McCarron getting every ounce out of the gallant ex-hunter, it looked odds-on that the experience and stamina of the professional would wear down the guts and determination of the amateur.

But Freddie could not find that last vestige of extra speed which means the difference between immortality as the winner of perhaps the last Grand National and sympathy for being narrowly beaten by three-quarters of a length.

After the race, a tired but jubilant Mr Smith said: "It was bedlam. I have never ridden in a race like it." This was a pretty accurate assessment, for only 15 of the 47 starters finished, and Becher's took a heavy toll on both circuits.

Perhaps in years to come the 1965 Grand National will be remembered as the amateurs' year. For on Mr Jones (50-1), in third place, was 25-year-old Mr Christopher Collins who has never won a race under rules and had never ridden at Aintree before.

Ascot: 30 April

Ascot 'chasing course passes first test

By MARLBOROUGH

Ascot's new jumping course passed its first, most searching trial with flying colours here to-day. Of 18 runners in the Kennel Gate Handicap 'Chase, won by Another Scot, four horses pulled up and one refused but, almost unbelievably, there was not a single faller.

The brand new fences, though beautifully built, looked big, stiff and altogether formidable. But the acid test of any course is not how it looks but how it rides. And with a few minor reservations (notably the water-jump!), the jockeys' reaction was almost entirely favourable.

ENGLISH CLASSICS

2,000 Guineas	Niksar	D Keith	100-8
1,000 Guineas	Night Off	W Williamson	9-2f
Derby	Sea Bird II	TP Glennon	7-4f
Oaks	Long Look	J Purtell	100-7
St Leger	Provoke	J Mercer	28-1

OTHER MAJOR RACES

Irish Derby	Meadow Court	L Piggott	11-10f
Arc de Triomphe	Sea Bird II	P Glennon	6-5f
Kentucky Derby	Lucky Debonair	W Shoemaker	43-10
Melbourne Cup	Light Fingers	R Higgins	15-1

Prix de l'Arc de Triomphe Longchamp: 3 October

Sea Bird's Arc rivals routed as record goes

By HOTSPUR (Peter Scott)

Champion, not only of Europe but also surely of the whole world, Sea Bird II gave a magnificent farewell performance in slamming M Dupre's hitherto unbeaten Reliance II by six lengths in the Prix de l'Arc de Triomphe here this afternoon.

Five lengths behind Reliance II, Baron Guy de Rothschild's pair Diatome II and Free Ride fought out third place, which just went to Diatome, the younger horse. Russia's Anilin was fifth, after showing prominently throughout, and the American star Tom Rolfe sixth.

Neither of our own hopes, Oncidium and Soderini, ever promised to be concerned with the finish. Oncidium was one of the last away, after being reluctant to enter the starting stalls.

The Prix de l'Arc de Triomphe has not been won by such a margin since Ribot's victory in 1956. Today Sea Bird II showed himself almost certainly the best horse to have run in Europe since Ribot retired.

Sea Bird II will not run again. He goes to Kentucky on a five-year lease to Mr John Galbraith, with record European stakes earnings of over £200,000, together with a racing record of seven wins and a second in eight starts. Exbury, with £156,211 from eight successes was the previous record holder.

Sea Bird II took a position close behind the leaders. Reliance II tracked him, and Meadow Court was in fourth place turning for home behind Anilia, but the Russian could not sustain his tremendous early effort.

No sooner had the straight been reached than Sea Bird II made his thrust, with Reliance II coming after him. But expectations of a close battle between them were quickly dispelled. Reliance simply could not match Sea Bird's superb acceleration.

The Derby winner, with his beautiful flowing action, strode clear, and his winning margin would have been still wider but for his shying slightly at the cheers which greeted this magnificent performance.

Irish Derby The Curragh: 26 June

Meadow Court earns solo from Mr Crosby

From John Lawrence

The Irish Sweeps Derby unfolded here today with the relentless precision of a well-rehearsed dramatic spectacle. Far from home, Lester Piggott and Meadow Court had already taken the centre of the stage and, winning in the end by a comfortable two lengths from the gallant Convamore, they never looked like relaxing their grip.

So the merit of Sea Bird's Derby is gloriously confirmed and, watching Meadow Court storm home untiring this afternoon, it was hard to remember the disdain with which the great French colt treated him at Epsom.

The real star was absent, but the understudy did him proud – and was rewarded in the winner's enclosure with a solo rendering of "Irish Eyes Are Smiling" from his famous part-owner Mr Crosby.

There had never really been much doubt about Meadow Court's stamina and clearly Lester Piggott felt none today. After half a mile he moved into fourth place. He may have given Meadow Court just one reminder, but it was hardly needed, for inside the last furlong the battle was over. This was not a victory as effortless as that of Santa Claus 12 months ago, but it was, nevertheless, entirely decisive.

Gallaher Gold Cup Sandown Park: 6 November

Arkle makes nonsense of all handicaps

Sandown speed record set under 12st 7lb

By HOTSPUR

After the peerless Arkle's record-breaking triumph in Saturday's £5,000 Gallaher Gold Cup, surely the most brilliant steeplechasing feat of the century, he is now quoted at 5-1 on for both the Hennessy Gold Cup, later this month, and the Cheltenham Gold Cup next March.

Since Arkle is also to be aimed at Kempton Park's King George VI 'Chase on Boxing Day, it follows that bookmakers will ask for similar long odds. From a purely competitive point of view Arkle seems to have destroyed these three big races.

The big problem now facing the respective authorities is that of persuading owners to pit their horses against Arkle for the doubtful reward of picking up place money.

Can Mr W.H.Gollings, for instance, be fairly asked to risk another drubbing for the stout-hearted Mill House? The Arkle-Mill House score now stands at 4-1.

Arkle, in taking Saturday's prize, brought his stakes-winning tally to more than £50,000, easily a record for a steeplechaser. He carried 12st 7lb, the absolute maximum under the new handicap rules, and lowered the course record for three miles by 11 seconds.

Now, if Arkle (4-9f) can do this – he won by 20 lengths and four lengths from Rondetto (9-1) and Mill House (7-2), and returned looking completely unruffled – it is clear that all the accepted theories regarding handicapping cannot apply in his case.

His measure of superiority is so great that it seems safe to assume that Mill House, Rondetto, The Rip and Co could hardly have done better if they had been weighted from 9st 7lb downwards.

Of the Hennessy, King George VI and Cheltenham Gold Cup, only the first is run on handicap terms, and since Arkle incurs no penalty he can meet Mill House on exactly the same terms as at Sandown Park. Yet I feel sure that if only two or three turn out against the great Irish champion in any of these races, the crowds will still throng just to see his effortless and magnificent jumping. With all respect of Golden Miller, there never was a 'chaser such as this.

29 October, Orly Airport, Paris: Sea Bird II doesn't seem to like the idea of boarding the plane to America despite the best efforts of his handler. The famous French racehorse has been hired out to a wealthy US breeder for five years.

1966

16 Mar Snowdra Queen wins the United Hunts Challenge Cup at Cheltenham to make her owner, Mrs Jackie Brutton, the first officially recognised woman trainer to saddle a National Hunt winner.

27 Jun Lester Piggott captures his 3rd Oaks an Valoris (11-10f), trained in Ireland and owned by Mr Charles Clore.

3 Aug Pat, ridden by Scobie Breasley in the South Coast Stakes at Brighton, is the

first Flat winner saddled by an officially recognised woman trainer, Miss Norah Wilmot.

5 Sep Piggott rides the first 5 winners at Warwick but fails on his last mount.

CHAMPIONS

Jockey (Flat)	Lester Piggott	191
Jockey (NH)	Terry Biddlecombe	102
Racehorse of the Year	Charlottown	3-y-o
NH Champion of the Year	Arkle	9-y-o
Leading Trainer	Vincent O'Brien (Ire)	£123,848
Leading Owner	Lady Zia Wernher	£78,075
Leading Money Winner	Charlottown	£78,075

Grand National Aintree:26 March

Anglo rescues bookmakers in National

By HOTSPUR (Peter Scott)

There will always be an Anglo, it seems, whenever the bookmakers' need is greatest. Saturday's 50-1 Grand National winner rescued them with a vengeance as he galloped home, ears pricked, 20 lengths ahead of the luckless Freddie.

Backed down to 11-4 as money poured in on him in the last few minutes, Freddie started the hottest Grand National favourite since Golden Miller (2-1) and Gerry Wilson parted company at Valentine's Brook in 1935.

Freddie would have cost the books a fortune, while other leading fancies were also heavily coupled in doubles with the Lincoln Handicap winner Riot Act (8-1).

Anglo, the fourth successive Grand National winner trained in Lambourn, was no such bookmaker's bogy, and Fred Winter saddled him with only the

mildest hopes of repeating Jay Trump's victory.

Anglo's past form earned him only 9st 6lb in the original Grand National assessments, this being raised to the 10 stone starting minimum. Saturday showed him a far better horse at four and a half miles than shorter distances. Rarely has a Grand National winner finished so fresh. Anglo jumped well throughout and entered the race as a major threat with just over a mile to go. He took the second fence from home on terms with Forest Prince (100-7) and was clearly going the better.

Tim Norman sent Anglo into a decisive lead before the last, which he jumped in style. From that point his advantage widened without Norman needing to feel for the whip, and Anglo just coasted in. Freddie passed the tiring Forest Prince on the run-in.

The Derby Epsom: 25 May

English colts triumph in richest Derby: Pretendre worn down by Charlottown

By HOTSPUR (Peter Scott)

English-trained horses were triumphant – magnificently so – in the Derby here today. Charlottown (5-1) and Pretendre (9-2jf) drew out in the last two furlongs and fought like heroes for the richest prize in British Turf history.

It was Charlottown's race by a neck, but how sad that one of them had to lose. Scobie Breasley, with a veteran's skill, and Paul Cook, with the dash of youth, rode races worthy of their mounts.

Black Prince II (20-1), briefly in front after Right

Noble and St Puckle had weakened early in the straight, finished five lengths away third.

Sodium, prominent all the way, ran on to be fourth. Whatever the private dope test taken on him afterwards may show, Sodium was far from disgraced.

This is more than can be said for your shamefaced correspondent, who had feared a clean sweep by the Irish horses. Right Noble (9-2jf), the only one of their seven who ever promised to win, finished ninth.

Cheltenham Gold Cup: 17 March

Arkle strolls home in third Gold Cup: 30 lengths to spare despite blunder

By HOTSPUR (Peter Scott)

Arkle, a spray of shamrock in his browband for luck on St Patrick's Day, survived an 11th-fence blunder with complete nonchalance and won his third Cheltenham Gold Cup here this afternoon by a strolling 30 lengths.

The widest winning margin in Gold Cup history could have been trebled at least had jockey Pat Taaffe wished. Never was Arkle remotely at full stretch.

The champion hacked along for the first mile, allowing Dormant and Snaigow to lead. At the eighth fence he jumped his way to the front of the five-strong field.

Arkle's error at the end of the first full circuit was probably a lapse in concentration. He hit the fence hard, but imperturbable Taaffe hardly shifted in the saddle. As if to atone, Arkle stood well back at the following jump – a ditch – and cleared it with plenty to spare.

Dormant (2nd, 20-1) and Snaigow (3rd, 100-7) were allowed to keep within reasonable touch until racing down towards the third fence from home. Arkle (1-10f), still on a tight rein, accelerated clear and from that point defeat was as probable as racing tomorrow at Hurst Park.

NATIONAL HUNT

Champion Hurdle	Salmon Spray	J Haine	4-1
Cheltenham Gold Cup	Arkle	P Taaffe	1-10f
Grand National	Anglo	T Norman	50-1

Irish Derby The Curragh: 2 July

Sodium has revenge for Epsom defeat

From John Lawrence

A hard luck story became a fairytale this afternoon when Mr R.J. Sigtia's Sodium won the Irish Sweeps Derby by a length from Charlottown. "Never make excuses," they say – but George Todd trusted the evidence of his eyes at Epsom, and today, turning the tables with vengeance, Sodium proved him absolutely right.

Fifty years ago, Todd was an infantry soldier at the Somme. Acquiring from that experience a lasting distaste for foreign travel, he has never been abroad since, and was not here today to witness the greatest triumph of his long career.

And what a triumph it was both for Todd himself and for Sodium's rider Frankie Durr, who like the trainer has always been convinced that Mr Sigtia's colt failed to give his true running at Epsom.

Now Sodium improved on that form to the tune of more than seven lengths, and there can be little doubt that something – probably an abscess developing in his foot

– upset him on Derby day.

But this time too, the luck which had so favoured Charlottown at Epsom was all on Sodium's side. In a fast-run race both horses lay well back early on, but turning down hill for home Durr went for, and found, an opening near the rails, while Breasley, some way behind him, had to come round the wide outside.

It may well be that Charlottown could not go the early pace or that, as in the Lingfield Derby Trial, he hung fire for a moment when first asked to improve. Whatever the reason, as Paveh took over the lead from Busted on the turn, the favourite was at least a dozen lengths back.

Finding a trouble-free passage through beaten horses, Sodium (13-2) stormed past Paveh two furlongs out. Behind him, Charlottown overtook the weakening Crozier and Paveh, but Breasley's whip was out, and the gap was only closing inch by inch. With a furlong to go there was just the one to beat, but that one wasn't stopping.

28 July

Woman wins right to trainer's licence

DAILY TELEGRAPH REPORTER

Mrs Florence Nagle, 70, won her 20-year fight against the Jockey Club Stewards yesterday and became the first woman in Britain to be granted a licence to train racehorses for Flat racing.

Her challenge to the unwritten rule of the male-controlled Jockey Club that no woman should hold a trainer's licence ended in the High Court, after she had been granted leave to appeal an earlier decision. The Jockey Club agreed to grant her a trainer's licence, provided she expressly acknowledged that the licence was granted in the exercise of the Stewards' "absolute and unfettered discretion".

Mrs Nagle, who trains horses near Petworth, Sussex, sued Viscount Allendale, of Hexham, Northumberland, and Sir Randle Guy Feilden of Minster Lovell, Oxon, on their own behalf and on behalf of the Stewards and all other members of the Jockey Club.

Outside the court, Mrs Nagle said: "I am very happy. It is not a glamorous profession for a woman. There are more knocks than anything else. But there was a principle involved in my fight. I am a feminist and believe that things should be decided on ability and not sex."

For more than 20 years, Mrs Nagle has trained a stable of about 14 horses, with her head lad holding the trainer's licence.

ENGLISH CLASSICS

2,000 Guineas	Kashmir	J Lindley	7-1
1,000 Guineas	Glad Rags	P Cook	100-6
Derby	Charlottown	A Breasley	5-1
Oaks	Valoris	L Piggott	11-10f
St Leger	Sodium	F Durr	7-1

Hennessy Gold Cup Newbury: 27 November

Beaten! But Arkle still wears the crown

From John Lawrence

It had to happen some time and the manner of its happening today was wonderful as well as sad. For Arkle, though robbed of his third Hennessy Gold Cup by the rank outsider Stalbridge Colonist (25-1), has never run a finer race. Giving away 35lb, he went down fighting as a champion should, and the steeplechasers' crown is as firm as over on his head.

While Arkle paraded this afternoon – proud as a peacock and hard as nails – the bookmakers, shutting their eyes to his evident well-being, began to wager fiercely against him. They allowed the Pride of Ireland to start at 6-4 on, a price which many here found irresistible.

Nor for nine-tenths of the race was there the slightest evidence that these odds would be upset. At the very first fence Arkle sailed past Freddie to take the lead, and there he remained – till the last dramatic act – serene in solitary glory.

This in itself was, of course, a crushing disadvantage leaving Arkle to do the others' work for three and a quarter miles. For a horse with 12st 7lb on his back, having his first race for more than eight months, it added dreadfully to an already Herculean task.

But this is hindsight. At the time, as Arkle floated across the water, he looked capable of anything. And, welcomed over the second last with a tremendous cheer, he still looked sure to win – even to Stan Mellor – a bare length behind on Stalbridge Colonist. But only for a moment. The weight had begun to tell now, and launching Stalbridge Colonist at the last fence with his own inimitable flourish, Stan drew from the little grey a leap that even Arkle could not match. It gained him half a length and, more important, a yard or so of extra impetus.

Yet for a couple of heartbeats halfway up the straight the gallant champion seemed to be gaining once more. Perhaps with the advantage of a previous race he would just have pulled it off.

But it was not by standing still that Stalbridge Colonist won eight races in 11 tries last season, and it was not by losing chances such as this that Stan Mellor won two jockeys' championships. So now together they struggled on to hold the greatest of them all by half a length.

Cesarewitch Newmarket: 1 October

Age and experience decide Cesarewitch

From John Lawrence

Age and experience were triumphant here today when Doug Smith, the oldest jockey in the field, and Persian Lancer, the oldest horse, defied their years to win the 1966 Cesarewitch from the rank outsider C.E.D. It was Doug's sixth victory in this great handicap, and neither he nor anyone else has ever ridden a better or a cooler race.

Almost unbelievably, Persian Lancer had not won a race of any sort for five seasons. Ryan Price, who trains him for Lord Belper, won with Utrillo in 1963 – his only other Cesarewitch runner.

The stamina needed for this unique marathon is a rare commodity indeed these days, and there were really only ever three horses in with a serious winning chance. The 7-1 favourite Miss Dawn, third in the end, led till three furlongs from home, and thereafter C.E.D. (66-1) and Persian Lancer (100-7) had it to themselves.

Smith, 49 next month and barely recovered from the injured rib that robbed him of two winners on Thursday, found a dreamlike passage for the eight-year-old. Well behind early on, he dodged smoothly through into second place as C.E.D. took over the lead.

C.E.D. was wandering slightly under pressure and Doug must have been in two minds over which side to make his challenge. With the icy confidence of a jockey who rode his first Cesarewitch winner in 1939, he waited until the post was little more than a 100 yards away. Then "go on old man" – and Persian Lancer went.

OTHER MAJOR RACES

Irish Derby	Sodium	F Durr	13-2
Arc de Triomphe	Bon Mot III	F Head	11-2
Kentucky Derby	Kauai King	D Brumfield	24-10f
Melbourne Cup	Galilee	J Miller	11-2

King George VI 'Chase Kempton Park: 27 December

Arkle beaten on three sound legs
Tragic sequel to shock defeat by Dormant
By HOTSPUR (Peter Scott)

Arkle was beaten one length by Dormant in a stunning and tragic race for the King George VI 'Chase here today. Palpably lame afterwards, this great horse was found to have fractured the main bone of his off-fore hoof.

Arkle's bright chance of eclipsing Golden Miller's sequence of five Cheltenham Gold Cup triumphs is extinguished. He will be unable to bid for a fourth next March. Indeed, it is no more than even money whether Arkle can ever race again.

Pat Taaffe, associated with the champion in today's tragedy as in so many past triumphs, thought Arkle might have injured himself by hitting the guard rail of some fence. Correct or not, Arkle never seemed to be racing with his usual freedom, and when he blundered badly at the 14th jump an upset was very much on the cards.

Woodland Venture was still with him when they entered the straight and seemed to be going better than Arkle when he hit the second fence from

Arkle's owner, Anne, Duchess of Westminster, studies an X-ray of her champion's hoof

home and came down. Arkle, who started at 9-2 on, was left with a clear lead, but even this proved insufficient.

Dormant, a 10-1 chance, made a determined challenge from the last jump, and with Arkle stopping fast, Mrs Wells-Kendrew's horse snatched a dramatic win close home.

[Arkle never raced again.]

1967

27 Jan Having his first run over hurdles, Mr I.Kirman's Sirius III, ridden by David Mould, wins Div.II of the Combermere Novices' Hurdle at Windsor. Trained by Peter Cazalet, Sirius was bought by Mr Kirman from the Soviet government, and is thought to be the first Soviet-bred winner on the British Turf.

8 Apr One of the two loose horses that cause 26 horses to be brought down or to a halt at the 23rd fence in the Grand National is appropriately called Popham Down. Foinavon, the first blinkered National winner since Battleship in 1938, had not managed to win any of his 23 races in the past two seasons.

1 Jul Lester Piggott follows up his Irish Derby win on Ribocco yesterday with victory in the German Derby at Hamburg on the Belgian-trained favourite Luciano. The total value of the race is £8,800 compared with Ribocco's £57,610 first prize.

14 Aug Leading jockey Joe Mercer is out for the season with serious back injuries after a fall from Native Copper in the last race at Folkestone. The horse has to be destroyed.

8 Oct The Prix de l'Arc goes to an 80-1 chance, Mme Volterra's Topyo, who hangs on to take the £81,000 first prize by a fast-dwindling neck from English challengers Salvo and Ribocco.

CHAMPIONS

Jockey (Flat)	Lester Piggott	117
Jockey (NH)	Josh Gifford	122
Racehorse of the Year	Busted	4-y-o
NH Champion of the Year	Mill House	10-y-o
Leading Trainer	Noel Murless	£256,899
Leading Owner	Jim Joel	£120,925
Leading Money Winner	Royal Palace	£92,998

Grand National Aintree: 8 April

Foinavon escapes National pile-up

From W.D.Tadd

Foinavon, the 100 to 1 chance, who was left a fence in front after a tremendous pile-up at the 23rd obstacle, went on to gain a shock victory in the £17,630 Grand National at Liverpool yesterday. Trained by John Kempton and ridden by John Buckingham, Foinavon kept going strongly to foil a gamble on Ryan Price's Honey End (15-2f), who was brought by Josh Gifford with a strong run to finish second.

Third was Red Alligator (30-1), with Terry Biddlecombe's mount, Greek Scholar (20-1), fourth. Eighteen of the 44 runners eventually finished.

The pile-up at the 23rd, the fence after Becher's, was the worst in the Grand National for years, with horses refusing and falling all over the place, causing the departure of many of the leading fancies.

The bemused but delighted John Buckingham, telling his story of the Grand National, admitted frankly that at the time of the fiasco he was nearly a fence behind, having just landed over Becher's.

"As I came away from Becher's I saw horses stopping at the next fence, others hitting into them and more galloping back towards me. I was very lucky. Josh was right on the inside of the course, and I was in the middle. I pulled to the outside and two loose horses came galloping straight towards me. I nearly had to pull up, but avoided them and I just managed to hop over the fence.

"I was so far behind when it all happened that I was not sure whether anyone had got over safely in front of me, and it was not until the Canal Turn that I saw there was no one ahead. I took a quick look back and discovered there was nobody immediately behind me either."

After the race, the stewards took the unusual step of making an announcement over the public address system to explain what had happened. The statement was: "The stewards want the racing public to know that in the Grand National two loose horses in the lead at the fence after Becher's refused. They balked or brought down the majority of the field."

NATIONAL HUNT

Champion Hurdle	Saucy Kit	R Edwards	100-6
Cheltenham Gold Cup	Woodland Venture	TW Biddlecombe	100-8
Grand National	Foinavon	J Buckingham	100-1

ENGLISH CLASSICS

2,000 Guineas	Royal Palace	G Moore	100-30jf
1,000 Guineas	Fleet	G Moore	11-2
Derby	Royal Palace	G Moore	7-4f
Oaks	Pia	E Hide	100-7
St Leger	Ribocco	L Piggott	7-2jf

The Derby Epsom: 7 June

Royal Palace sweeps to superb Derby victory

By HOTSPUR (Peter Scott)

Mr H.J.Joel's Royal Palace proved a most worthy Derby favourite here today, achieving his owner-breeder's lifetime ambition after a fairly run race in which two other English-trained horses, Ribocco and Dart Board, chased him home.

Royal Palace (7-4f) went into a clear lead with more than two furlongs to run and from that point only Ribocco (22-1) offered the slightest danger. The pair of them had been Derby favourites when betting opened last autumn.

Ribocco, redeeming himself after three disappointing spring races, came wide for his challenge and drew almost level with about a furlong left. Then George Moore produced the whip on Royal Palace, and Lester Piggott, riding Ribocco, saw the mount who might have

The first ever stalls start in the Derby

been his pull away once more to give Moore his greatest-ever triumph and his third successive English classic.

Piggott resisted the temptation to drive Ribocco for all he was worth and Ribocco, who has shown marked dislike for such forcing tactics, returned the kindness by giving all he had.

It was not enough. In Royal Palace he met an emphatically better horse and one who is surely destined now, barring accidents, to win the Triple Crown.

Ashbourne 'Chase Uttoxeter: 15 June

Josh Gifford sets up NH record

BY A SPECIAL CORRESPONDENT

Josh Gifford broke Fred Winter's 14-year-old record of 121 winners in the National Hunt season when landing a treble at Uttoxeter last night.

The last meeting of the season, Uttoxeter gave Gifford an all-or-nothing chance and provided an exciting finale for the large crowd who thronged the course.

"I never thought I'd do it," said Gifford. "At this time of year I would have considered myself lucky to have ridden one winner, let alone three.

"I haven't been chasing the records. I wanted to ride 100 winners and I was quite happy with that. It's only now that I realise how much it means to me. I feel absolutely marvellous."

His three winners were Stealthy Approach, Jolly Signal and Red Flush, and none was an easy ride.

Stealthy Approach made all the running in the Swadlincote 'Chase, upsetting the odds of 9-4 laid on Vulmidas, to win by a length.

Gifford used different tactics on Jolly Signal in the Chesterfield Hurdle. This time he waited until inside the final furlong before making his move, but the result was the same, and Winter's record had been equalled.

Then came the big moment, when Red Flush and Gifford passed the post 10 lengths clear in the Ashbourne 'Chase. The record was broken and racegoers gave the champion a tumultuous reception in the winner's enclosure.

Irish Derby The Curragh: 1 July

Ribocco ends nightmare for Piggott

From John Lawrence

Lester Piggott's long nightmare came to an end at last this afternoon when, riding a supremely artistic race, he won the Irish Sweeps Derby on Mr Charles Engelhard's Ribocco. This time, for a change, it was George Moore on Sucaryl who had to resign himself to second place – and with Dart Board third and Gay Garland fourth the English had it properly to themselves.

There was, alas, one tragedy to spoil this eminently satisfactory result, for Royal Sword, the principal hope of Ireland, fell seven furlongs from home, broke a leg and had to be destroyed.

This was the first time in 1967 that Ribocco has looked more than a shadow of his two-year-old self. At Epsom his coat still had a wintry, moth-eaten appearance, but now the shine was back and with it the spring in Ribocco's step.

Over two furlongs from home, just as he had on Royal Palace at Epsom, George Moore sent Sucaryl (8-1) smoothly past Sovereign Slipper and into the lead. But while at Epsom Ribocco (5-2f) gave the winner many lengths start from Tattenham Corner, this time he was glued like a little bay shadow to Sucaryl's tail.

For a moment Piggott was in two minds which side of the leader to challenge, but then switching to the left he set Ribocco alight without so much as feeling for his whip.

The little horse quickened explosively, swept past Sucaryl in a dozen strides, and won going away by a length in a style which makes nonsense of any doubt about his stamina.

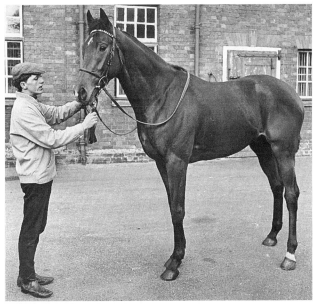

Newmarket Sales: 7 December

Vaguely Noble brings record 136,000gns

By HOTSPUR

The hammer fell at 136,000 guineas on Vaguely Noble's record sale here tonight. Two minutes and 12 seconds of auction time was dominated by the US dollar, but this colt *(above)* probably goes to be trained in Ireland by Paddy Prendergast.

Vaguely Noble's new owners are Dr and Mrs Robert Alan Franklyn, who live at Hidden Valley, California. They entered racing only four months ago with the purchase of five foals and seven yearlings. So far their racing colours have not even been registered let alone carried. Dr Franklyn is a plastic surgeon noted for his work on Hollywood film stars.

The previous record price paid for a horse at any English public auction was 47,000gns given in 1932 for Solario, then a 10-year-old stallion.

8 August

Happy end to painful Hill House case

By MARLBOROUGH

Born six months ago in a storm of angry boos and biased bitterness, the Hill House case was laid to rest yesterday in a very different atmosphere of common sense and justice. And no lover of National Hunt racing in his senses can but rejoice at this happy sending to a sad affair.

Two separate inquiries ended yesterday, and to the first – the question of Hill House's alleged "abnormal improvement" between Feb.11 at Sandown Park and Feb.18 at Newbury – there could never have been any other outcome.

The TV film of the Sandown race – a slow-run contest in which Hill House made two serious mistakes – shows him there with every chance at the second-last flight. Having his first run for three months, he could only stay on at one pace thereafter and was beaten for speed by faster horses.

The Schweppes, a week later, was run by contrast at a furious gallop, and Josh Gifford, realising this, dropped Hill House right out early on. He was, as a result, the only horse galloping at the finish, and Gifford, far from deserving the shameful boos which greeted him, should have been cheered to the echo for riding a brilliant race.

As to the second part of the inquiry, the Racing Calendar will no doubt explain tomorrow how the stewards (advised by a panel of scientific experts) satisfied themselves that the "drug" found in Hill House's system at Newbury was naturally and innocently produced.

All I would like to add is that anyone who, remembering the rumours and publicity focused around Hill House before the Schweppes, seriously supposes Ryan Price capable of doping him, must also suppose that this brilliant and experienced trainer is a raving lunatic. For of all horses in the race this one, win or lose, was the most likely to be tested.

I am convinced, therefore, that any result other than the complete exoneration accorded yesterday to all concerned would have been a disastrous injustice.

25 November

Axe may fall on racing till Christmas

By Lionel Hampton

With the spread of foot-and-mouth disease showing no sign of abating, the National Farmers' Union yesterday appealed to the Ministry of Agriculture to put a ban on all racing in Britain until the epidemic ends.

The NFU pointed out that a lot of people and vehicles may frequently go through infected areas to race meetings.

In a joint statement, the Ministry and the stewards of the National Hunt Committee said that any meeting may be cancelled if it involved a risk of spreading the disease.

Several meetings have been abandoned already, including those at Leicester tomorrow and Tuesday, leaving these both blank days. But unless the number of new cases abates rapidly it may well be considered that this piece-meal defence is insufficient in the face of such a virulent onslaught.

The Ministry have no legal powers to stop racing, but the National Hunt Committee have cooperated fully with their every request to abandon a meeting and would certainly also accede to one for a 'blanket' stoppage.

The next four weeks are not the busiest, nor the most important, for racing, and if a complete break were made now it would presumably be possible to resume with the eight meetings scheduled for Boxing Day.

OTHER MAJOR RACES			
Irish Derby	Ribocco	L Piggott	5-2f
Arc de Triomphe	Topyo	W Pyers	80-1
Kentucky Derby	Proud Clarion	R Ussery	301-10
Melbourne Cup	Red Handed	R Higgins	4-1

1968

30 Mar Red Alligator, owned by Mr John Manners and trained by Denys Smith at Bishop Auckland, storms home with 20 lengths to spare in the Grand National. The 17-2 favourite, Different Class, carrying the colours of actor Gregory Peck, finishes third. Mr Tim Durant, 68-year-old American owner-rider of Highlandie, determined to finish the race, remounts the 11-y-o to take 15th place of the 17 finishers (45 ran) and collect a case of champagne from the bookmakers as well as a £500 donation to the Injured Jockeys' Fund.

6 Jul Mr Jim Joel's decision to keep Royal Palace (9-4) in training is brilliantly justified as last year's Derby winner gets up on the line to snatch a desperate short-head victory from old rival Taj Dewan in the Eclipse Stakes at Sandown, with this year's Derby winner Sir Ivor, only a week after his shock defeat at the Curragh, three-quarters of a length behind.

12 Dec The Jockey Club, which has governed Flat racing for nearly 200 years, and the National Hunt Committee, whose centenary as the supreme power of steeplechasing and hurdle racing was celebrated in 1966, amalgamate into one body, the full title of which is the Jockey Club (Incorporating the National Hunt Committee) but which will be known simply as the Jockey Club.

CHAMPIONS

Jockey (Flat)	Lester Piggott	139
Jockey (NH)	Josh Gifford	82
Racehorse of the Year	Sir Ivor	3-y-o
NH Champion of the Year	Persian War	5-y-o
Leading Trainer	Noel Murless	£141,508
Leading Owner	Raymond Guest	£97,075
Leading Money Winner	Sir Ivor	£97,075

Lincolnshire Handicap Doncaster: 27 March

Frankincense does it with record 9st 5lb

Waterloo Place beaten in fine Lincoln finish

By HOTSPUR (Peter Scott)

Lady Halifax's four-year-old Frankincense carried the highest winning Lincoln Handicap weight in its 115-year history when he defied 9st 5lb to beat Waterloo Place by half a length in a fine finish here this afternoon.

Norton Priory was two lengths away third. A couple more lengths further behind him came last year's winner Ben Novus, who finished fast to beat Copper's Evidence and Petros, by inches for fourth money. Bluerullah, who started 10-1 favourite despite being worst drawn of all, finished last but one.

Irish Derby The Curragh: 29 June

Ribero slams Sir Ivor

From John Lawrence

Two furlongs from home in the Irish Sweeps Derby here today Lester Piggott glanced sideways. He was looking at Sir Ivor – in his own words the best horse he has ever ridden – and a couple of heartbeats later, moving his hands on Ribero's neck, he scattered those words and a million others across the sunlit Curragh.

For in those few seconds we saw the impossible happen. Stepping gracefully into the footsteps of his full brother Ribocco, Ribero (100-6) strode irresistibly away to win by two very comfortable lengths.

That Sir Ivor (1-3f) should be beaten at all was hard enough to believe; that he should be beaten like this –

treated almost contemptuously by a horse who last time out finished a dozen lengths behind Connaught at Ascot – was as strange and inexplicable as anything ever seen in a classic race.

My first reaction to it is a feeling of heartfelt sympathy for Liam Ward, who had taken Piggott's place today, as was his right on his home track before an adoring Irish crowd.

Ward's only consolation must be that he rode the favourite flawlessly. Sir Ivor suffered no interference, was given every conceivable chance. He was beaten fair and square and no one who saw him at Epsom can believe they were watching the same horse this afternoon.

19 March

Double duty on betting

DAILY TELEGRAPH REPORTER

Gamblers took a hard knock in the Budget, which doubles the betting duty to 1s in the £, and raises the duty on football pools and fixed odds to a third of stakes.

William Hill, the bookmaker, said that the five per cent tax on horse racing and greyhound betting would have to be passed on to the public. Sir Alexander Sim, chairman of the Horserace Totalisator Board, said: "The Tote was set up for making money for racing but is fast becoming a revenue-raising instrument." Joe Coral's thought that the increase could lead to a decrease in betting and a consequent drop in revenue.

Generally it was felt that the punter will find his winnings for place results reduced by off-course bookmakers, with on-course bookmakers increasing to one shilling the deduction of 6d from every £1 paid to winning punters.

The Derby Epsom: 29 May

Sir Ivor's brilliant speed irresistible

By HOTSPUR (Peter Scott)

Sir Ivor, with a turn of speed that puts him in the Sea Bird II class among post-war Derby winners, split open all defences when Lester Piggott set him alight here this afternoon and he beat Connaught running away. Piggott, riding his fourth Derby winner, handled Sir Ivor with even more audacious confidence than he had done in the 2,000 Guineas, and was in no way flurried when Connaught opened up a lead that had his admirers counting their spoils.

Sixth as they entered the straight, Piggott did not shake up the favourite until a furlong and a half out.

Lengthening his stride – and what a picture he makes in full flow – Sir Ivor (4-5f) skimmed past Remand (4th, 4-1) and slashed down Connaught's (100-9) lead that had once been four lengths. Sir Ivor's head was in front only 100 yards from home, yet he won by a length and a half. Mount Athos (45-1) was third, another two and a half lengths back.

The time of 2min 38.73sec testifies to a truly run race. Sir Ivor stayed the distance all right and will undoubtedly stay further if he is ever required to.

Sir Ivor (left) becomes the second Derby winner for owner Raymond Guest and trainer Vincent O'Brien

NATIONAL HUNT

Champion Hurdle	Persian War	J Uttley	4-1
Cheltenham Gold Cup	Fort Leney	P Taaffe	11-2
Grand National	Red Alligator	B Fletcher	100-7

King George VI & Queen Elizabeth Stakes Ascot: 27 July

Gallant Royal Palace

From John Lawrence

Mr Jim Joel's Royal Palace set a sad but unforgettable seal on his glorious racing career this afternoon. It was only by a rapidly dwindling half length that he scrambled home to win the King George VI and Queen Elizabeth Stakes, but as he walked back lame we learnt the explanation – a badly torn suspensory ligament in his off-fore leg.

So this, which would in any case have been Royal Palace's last race, was also his bravest, and perhaps his best. Sandy Barclay said afterwards that he felt the leg go nearly a furlong from home and in those circumstances only a very gallant horse indeed could have kept going long enough to hold the furious challenges of the French pair Felicio II and Topyo.

But the race had started with a knockabout farce. For Ribero swerved sharply cantering past the stands and Lester Piggott, poised in his usual lofty precarious perch, was shot off like a ping-pong ball. Riderless but apparently quite undisturbed, Ribero galloped down into Swinley Bottom where he began to graze hungrily, behaviour that may conceivably have been his undoing, for even a small snack of grass is inadvisable when a horse has to race flat out for a mile and a half.

But eventually, reunited with Piggott, Ribero trotted back calmly enough and they were off. The Italian pacemaker Golden Fizz II set out in front at a tremendous pace. Piggott moved Ribero up second ahead of Royal Palace, and Roger Poincelet, adopting the tactics for which he is famous or infamous depending on your point of view, settled Felicio II last of all.

Golden Fizz II did his job well, so the stage was set for the duel we all expected, and for a hundred yards in the straight Ribero seemed to be holding his great opponent. Then suddenly he cracked in half a dozen strides and a great roar of welcome greeted Royal Palace (4-7f) as Sandy Barclay drove him clear.

Had all been well, he would very likely have won unchallenged. But when he faltered, Topyo began to gain, and a far greater danger appeared as Poincelet, giving his celebrated imitation of a demented windmill, drove Felicio up the far rail. For an awful moment the gap seemed to be closing too fast, but Barclay called for a last effort – the final effort Royal Palace will ever be asked to make – and it was enough.

For Noel Murless, this was, after Aunt Edith and Busted, a wonderful third consecutive King George.

Prix de l'Arc de Triomphe Longchamp: 6 October

Superb 'Arc' triumph for Vaguely Noble

Gallant Sir Ivor beaten three lengths

By HOTSPUR

Vaguely Noble brushed aside Sir Ivor and the rest of today's star-studded 'Arc' field with a superb exhibition of thoroughbred class that won him Europe's richest race by three lengths.

Sir Ivor, giving the best performance of his career in Lester Piggott's opinion, finished another four lengths ahead of the unconsidered Carmarthen, who made a late challenge that deprived Roselière of third place. Among the disappointments were Ribero – badly kicked before the start – and Luciano, who refused to settle down early.

Vaguely Noble was ridden with great confidence by Bill Williamson, who never even felt for his whip as the winner strode home a true champion.

Well in touch racing down the hill, Vaguely Noble burst through a gap between the two leaders, Luthier and Roselière, entering the straight. Sir Ivor, who had been near the inside from his favourable draw most of the way, gave chase, but Vaguely Noble was two lengths ahead almost immediately after striking the front and, although Piggott rode his hardest, Sir Ivor could not prevent Vaguely Noble increasing that lead.

ENGLISH CLASSICS

2,000 Guineas	Sir Ivor	L Piggott	11-8f
1,000 Guineas	Caergwrle	A Barclay	4-1f
Derby	Sir Ivor	L Piggott	4-5f
Oaks	La Lagune	G Thiboeuf	11-8f
St Leger	Ribero	L Piggott	100-30

OTHER MAJOR RACES

Irish Derby	Ribero	L Piggott	100-6
Arc de Triomphe	Vaguely Noble	W Williamson	5-2f
Kentucky Derby	Forward Pass	I Valenzuela	36-10
Melbourne Cup	Rain Lover	J Johnson	7-1

---

9 October

Arkle's racing career has ended

By HOTSPUR

Arkle will race no more. Anne, Duchess of Westminster, who owns perhaps the greatest steeplechaser in Turf history, announced this sad news from Ireland yesterday and added that Arkle would spend his retirement on her estate in Co.Kildare.

Since Arkle fractured the pedal-bone of his off-fore foot at Kempton Park's 1966 Christmas meeting, his countless admirers have hoped for a comeback – but nobody would wish to see just the shadow of a true champion.

There had been tentative plans for a return race in late December, but Arkle will be officially 12 years old on Jan.1 and this is not an age at which steeplechasers easily recover championship form after so long away.

The owner took her decision in collaboration with Arkle's trainer, Tom Dreaper, and Mr Max Cosgrove, the veterinary surgeon who looked after him with such skill. The great horse's injury has healed and there is every hope that he will enjoy a long, happy retirement.

Arkle's 26 jumping wins, which included three Cheltenham Gold Cups, made him easily the record National Hunt stakes earner. His class was such that he could give lumps of weight and a thrashing to horses of normal championship standard. Arkle added much to the golden moments he gave us by so obviously enjoying them himself.

Washington International Laurel Park, Maryland: 11 November

Sir Ivor crowns career with Laurel triumph

By HOTSPUR (Peter Scott)

Sir Ivor – by three-quarters of a length! Mr Raymond Guest's Derby winner saved probably his most momentous triumph for his last race when surging to the front 100 yards from home in the £62,500 Washington DC International.

Czar Alexander and Fort Marcy, the two American hopes, were fighting it out when Lester Piggott roused Sir Ivor for his last decisive run, and they could not match the Irish colt's acceleration.

Along the back straight Sir Ivor's progress was continually blocked out, but he found room to move up on the final bend and gained ground quickly. There was a bad moment a furlong from home when Lester Piggott showed Sir Ivor the whip and he did not immediately respond. Possibly it was the soft ground that stopped him quickening at once. At any rate, when Sir Ivor really got going his class asserted itself.

American backers once again displayed their preference for backing horses they know best. Hefty support for Czar Alexander and Fort Marcy from the 30,000 crowd enabled Sir Ivor to start at the remarkably good odds of 19-10, a fractional favourite over Czar Alexander.

1969

4 Jun On his first Derby mount, 21-year-old jockey Ernie Johnson rides a masterly race at Epsom to come through on the inside and steer Blakeney (15-2) to victory, on only the colt's fourth racecourse outing, by a length from Shoemaker (25-1). The win is a personal triumph for Arthur Budget, who bred, trains and owns (half-share) Blakeney, an achievement accomplished only three times before in the Derby's 189-year history, by William l'Anson, with both Blink Bonny (1857) and Blair Athol (1864), and the Italian Chevalier Ginistrelli with Signorinetta (1908).

5 Jun Lester Piggott scores his fifth Coronation Cup victory, on 5-y-o Park Top (11-4); Ribero refuses to enter the stalls and takes no part.

20 Jul Jockey Derick Stansfield, 39, dies after a fall at Hamilton on Friday (18th) from High Daddy, brought down by another horse in the Blantyre Stakes. It is the first fatality on the Flat since Manny Mercer's death 10 years ago. Originally apprenticed to Capt. Charles Elsey at Malton, Stansfield did much of his riding in East Africa and Scandinavia before returning to join Frank Carr's stable.

10 Sep Piggott is criticised for a "badly misjudged" ride on St Leger favourite Ribofilio (11-10) at Doncaster, as Ron Hutchinson keeps Intermezzo (7-1) ahead to win by a length and a half, with Derby winner Blakeney, interfered with more than once, back in 5th place. It would have been a Leger hat-trick in successive years for Piggott, and for The Daily Telegraph's Hotspur (Peter Scott) a 2,346-1 six-timer at Doncaster!

4 Nov Rain Lover, who set a record of 3min 19.1sec for the 2-mile Melbourne Cup last year, becomes the first horse to win the race in successive years since Archer in 1861-62.

CHAMPIONS

Jockey (Flat)	Lester Piggott	163
Jockey (NH)	Bob Davies	
	Terry Biddlecombe	77
Racehorse of the Year	Park Top	5-y-o
NH Champion of the Year	Persian War	6-y-o
Leading Trainer	Arthur Budgett	£105,349
Leading Owner	David Robinson	£92,553
Leading Money Winner	Blakeney	£63,108

Champion Hurdle Cheltenham: 19 March

Brave Persian War battles on to retain his title
By MARLBOROUGH (John Lawrence)

Persian War about to catch Drumikill at the last

"He's beat." Between the last two flights in yesterday's Champion Hurdle at Cheltenham the same thought must have been in many minds. But it was not in Persian War's, and, a moment later, storming back past Drumikill, he had proved himself not just the greatest champion since Sir Ken, but also the bravest.

To Jimmy Uttley, the spectre of defeat had appeared – though not for long. Going on from Supermaster at the top of the hill, Uttley was reluctant to make his final move. "I sat as long as I dared," he said afterwards.

"Then, suddenly, there was Brogan beside me with both hands full".

To us in the stands, at that moment the odds on Drumikill looked as long as his journey back to Hawick. Barry Brogan had not meant to strike the front so soon, but jumped the second last too well to wait any longer. And in any case, no tactics could have altered the result.

For now, with the sight of a rival to spur him on, Persian War had all sail set. And although he was still half a length behind as they rose at the last, the race was over as they landed.

2 May

Ribofilio's Guineas flop shakes Derby market
By HOTSPUR (Peter Scott)

Ribofilio, whose complete and bewildering 2,000 Guineas failure caused "dope" and cardiograph tests to be taken on this hot favourite (15-8), was not the only casualty in Wednesday's classic won by Right Tack. The French colt Yelapa finished lame.

Before the 2,000 Guineas, Ribofilio and Yelapa had been first and second favourites for the Derby on June 4. Now Hill Run has been promoted 12-1 favourite in a shaky market. Maurice Zilber, Yelapa's trainer, reckons it very doubtful whether his colt can run.

Neither Lester Piggott, who rode Ribofilio, nor the colt's trainer, Fulke Johnson Houghton, could account for his poor running when asked by the stewards. Ribofilio was going so badly that Piggott almost pulled him up three furlongs out.

Cheltenham Gold Cup: 20 March

What a Myth ends his career with Gold Cup triumph
By HOTSPUR

Jumping and stamina earned What a Myth the Cheltenham Gold Cup yesterday. Lady Weir quickly decided this was the moment to retire her gallant 12-year-old, who had just joined Silver Fame as the oldest winner in Gold Cup history.

What a Myth and Domacorn fought out the finish on deep, testing ground, and once again Domacorn paid a severe penalty for faulty jumping. He was close up behind What a Myth when hitting the second fence from home really hard.

Terry Biddlecombe, shooting up in the air, miraculously stayed on board, but lost his whip, and Domacorn's momentum was seriously checked. What a Myth, with priceless ground gained, thus came into the last fence with a lead of nearly two lengths.

Domacorn (7-2jf) staged a fine rally and halfway up the run-in he had drawn almost level. But Mr Jenks's horse could not sustain that effort and What a Myth (8-1), fighting dourly, drew out once more to win by a length and a half.

Grand National Aintree: 29 March

Highland Wedding streaks home in National
By John Lawrence

Age and experience swept the board at Aintree yesterday. Running in his third Grand National and superbly ridden by Eddie Harty (31), the father of three, Mr Thomas McKoy's 12-year-old Highland Wedding (100-9) beat two equally seasoned veterans – the 11-year-old Steel Bridge (50-1), who was 10th last year and 13th in 1967, and the year older Rondetto (25-1), who had already come three times heartbreakingly close to victory at Liverpool.

Three years ago "thrown in" in the National handicap with only 10st, Highland Wedding, then in the prime of life, had what looked a golden opportunity. Only eighth to Anglo that year, he was found afterwards to have spread a plate – but to many that sounded just another of the hard luck stories that Nationals always produce.

And in any case, although the great race history is studded with tragic near misses, only very very few of them ever get a second chance. Highland Wedding's seemed to have come and gone last year, when, apparently with every chance again, he could trail in only seventh. His trainer, Toby Balding, was one of the few who never lost faith, and this year, producing the big brown horse better than ever, he has made his opinion stick in the only way that counts.

1,000 Guineas Newmarket: 1 May

Patrol film showed Full Dress II a worthy winner

By MARLBOROUGH (John Lawrence)

Five minutes after Mr R.B.Moller's Full Dress II won the 1,000 Guineas at Newmarket yesterday, odds of 11-10 were still being laid against her. But this time the bookies were wrong. The objection lodged by Lester Piggott, on Hecuba, was overruled, and Full Dress kept a race she would have been desperately unlucky to lose.

The value of the patrol camera was never more clearly demonstrated, for without it justice might easily not have been done. Many experienced observers, including several of the beaten jockeys, were convinced that the winner would be disqualified. Only after seeing the film was all doubt removed.

For although Full Dress (7-1) did hang violently towards her rival in the last 20 yards, the race was already decided when it happened. Caught and passed 50 yards from home, Lester Piggott had given Hecuba (100-7) a last despairing slap and then accepted defeat.

A split second later, in the last strides of all, seeing Full Dress hang across, he quite justifiably took avoiding action – and if his gestures were slightly exaggerated for the benefit of the audience, do you wonder? If this had been a football match, after all, the losers would still be screaming.

But Rule 153 states clearly that a horse is liable to be disqualified "if he crosses another so as to interfere with that horse's chance". When Full Dress crossed Hecuba yesterday, the French filly had no chance. So that, according to both law and common sense, was that.

NATIONAL HUNT

Champion Hurdle	Persian War	J Uttley	6-4f
Cheltenham Gold Cup	What a Myth	P Kelleway	8-1
Grand National	Highland Wedding	EP Harty	100-9

Prix de l'Arc de Triomphe Longchamp: 5 October

Park Top beaten by Levmoss in Arc

By HOTSPUR (Peter Scott)

Levmoss, setting a Longchamp time record with his 51-1 Prix de l'Arc de Triomphe victory, and Lester Piggott, with four successes – on Tower Walk, Shaft, Vela and Habitat – dominated an afternoon of summit-class international racing there yesterday.

Park Top so nearly made it a Piggott five-timer in the big race. Piggott blamed himself for challenging too late, but no hard-luck stories can detract from the laurels so worthily won by Levmoss, Ireland's tough and versatile hero.

Already crowned the long-distance champion of Europe, Levmoss now became the first Ascot Gold Cup winner to be successful in the Prix de l'Arc de Triomphe since Caracalla II 23 years ago.

Bill Williamson wisely utilised Levmoss's stamina by a forcing race from the outset. He took up a good position straight away and went into the lead from Chaparral as they entered the straight.

Levmoss had the rails and quickly opened up a clear lead from the hard-ridden Grandier, who was now second but making no impression. Park Top, on whom Piggott had ridden his usual waiting race, then emerged from the pack. She passed horse after horse as if they were standing still but Levmoss was one too many for her.

A hundred yards out it still seemed that Park Top's run might prevail, but near home she was gaining no more. Levmoss, his head thrust forward with the last gasp of physical effort, held her by three-quarters of a length.

The three-year-olds were badly eclipsed and made to look a very moderate bunch. Prince Regent confirmed himself as the best of them in finishing fifth. Blakeney and Ribofilio were drawn on the extreme wings of the field and finished out of the first seven.

Cambridgeshire Handicap Newmarket: 4 October

Cambridgeshire so easy for Prince de Galles

By Robert Glendinning

Prince de Galles landed the ante-post coup of the season and at the same time turned the Cambridgeshire, first leg of the Autumn Double, into a handicapper's nightmare when romping home four lengths clear of his nearest rival, Grandrew, at Newmarket on Saturday.

The winner, who started at 5-2, the shortest-priced Cambridgeshire favourite for 63 years, was a 40-1 chance before the weights were published on Aug.28. Two days later he ran the good-class colt Welsh Pageant to less than a length over a mile at Newcastle.

This clearly underlined his big race chance with only 7st 12lb, but the gamble really started when Prince de Galles went on to land Newmarket's Norwich Handicap by 10 lengths, smashing the time record for the Cambridgeshire course in the process.

Frank Durr always had him well placed on the stand side as Kamundu, the top weight, led a small group on the far rails. Lester Piggott got maximum response from Kamundu, who ran a magnificent race, but at least three furlongs out it became obvious that the favourite was going to win.

Mastering Foggy Bell, the stands-side leader, before the two-furlong marker, Prince de Galles stormed up the hill to a great burst of cheering. Grandrew, a 40-1 chance, took second place close home and was two lengths ahead of Kamundu.

ENGLISH CLASSICS

2,000 Guineas	Right Tack	G Lewis	15-2
1,000 Guineas	Full Dress	R Hutchinson	7-1
Derby	Blakeney	E Johnson	15-2
Oaks	Sleeping Partner	J Gorton	100-6
St Leger	Intermezzo	R Hutchinson	7-1

OTHER MAJOR RACES

Irish Derby	Prince Regent	G Lewis	7-2
Arc de Triomphe	Levmoss	W Williamson	515-10
Kentucky Derby	Majestic Prince	W Hartack	7-5f
Melbourne Cup	Rain Lover	J Johnson	8-1

Washington International Laurel Park: 12 November

Karabas gives Pigott second Laurel triumph

By Richard Beeston

Karabas, trained at Newmarket by Bernard van Cutsem, gave Lester Piggott his second successive victory in the Washington DC International at Laurel yesterday and became the first English horse to land this prize since Wilwyn took the first running 17 years ago.

Karabas (18-5) won by one and a quarter lengths from the American horse Hawaii, with Czar Alexander, Irish-bred but also representing America, half a length away third. The German horse Hitchcock finished fourth of the seven runners.

Piggott rode a magnificent and confident race, staying coolly close to the rail all the way until the final bend, when the field opened out for him and he finished with an irresistible burst.

A photograph was needed to determine that Hitchcock, ridden by Jimmy Lindley, had beaten the Brazilian challenger Sabinus for fourth place. Don Florestan (Venezuela) was sixth, ahead of Japanese hope Takashiba-0.

Karabas is the first winner of the Washington International bred by a previous winner of this race – Worden II (1953).

The 1970s

T he seventies was a decade when the ladies flourished – equine as well as human. The Jockey Club permitted races for women riders, the first of which was won in May 1972 by Meriel Tufnell. Linda Goodwill was the first to beat male jockeys, in 1974, and 1976 saw women competing, and winning, under National Hunt rules. Then, in 1977, the Jockey Club lifted its 225-year ban on women members.

The French filly Dahlia became the first dual winner of the "King George" (1973-74), and another, Oaks winner Pawneese, won it in 1976. But perhaps the best of the French fillies was Allez France, who won the Arc in 1974 and always seemed to have the beating of Dahlia.

All this, however, came after a period of superiority enjoyed by some of the best colts of the century. In 1970, the O'Brien-trained Nijinsky, ridden by Lester Piggott, became the first horse since Bahram in 1935 to bring off the Triple Crown, including a Derby in the best time since Mahmoud's record of 1936. Two English colts then bestrode the stage – Mill Reef, who won the Derby, King George and Arc in 1971, and Brigadier Gerard, one of the all-time great milers, who beat Mill Reef in the Guineas and ran up an unbeaten string of 15 races. Across the Atlantic, in 1973, Secretariat not only became the first US Triple Crown winner in 25 years, but broke the track record in both the Kentucky Derby and the Belmont Stakes, which he won by a gargantuan 31 lengths. The finest long-distance stayer of the period was French horse Sagaro, the first ever to win three Ascot Gold Cups (1975-77), all under Lester Piggott, who claimed a fourth in 1979 on Le Moss.

Another great steeplechaser captured the public imagination in the seventies, Red Rum, who became the first horse to win the National three times, and L'Escargot won two Cheltenham Gold Cups as well as a National.

Inset: Lester Piggott rides the great Nijinsky to victory in the last leg of the Triple Crown.

Main picture: Pat Eddery on Grundy after their famous battle with Bustino in the 1975 "King George"

1970

4 Apr Grand National winner Gay Trip chalks up his first victory over more than 2 1/2 miles, carrying top weight of 11st

5lb, 6lb more than the next horse. Only 7 of the 28 runners finish. It is an Irish triumph, for although Gay Trip is trained in Worcestershire by Fred Rimell he was bred in Ireland; the second and third, Vulture and Miss Hunter, are trained there; and the first five jockeys home have Irish blood in their veins.

2 May Diane Crump is the first female

jockey to ride in the Kentucky Derby, finishing 15th of 17 on Fathom.

25 Jul The performance of the still undefeated Nijinsky (40-85f) in the King George VI & Queen Elizabeth Stakes at Ascot when he beats Blakeney by an effortless 2 lengths, earns jockey Lester Piggott's accolade as the best horse he has ever ridden, and this, his 10th victory,

takes his earnings to £201,633.

7 Sep American jockey Willie Shoemaker rides his 6,033rd winner, at Del Mar, to pass fellow-American Johnny Longden's world record.

8 Sep London's Alexander Park stages its last meeting.

Champion Hurdle Cheltenham: 18 March

Persian War joins the immortals

By MARLBOROUGH (John Lawrence)

Finally and indisputably Persian War joined the immortals yesterday. In front throughout the final mile, he won his third Champion Hurdle the hard way, and as he beat off challenge after challenge there was no longer any shadow of a doubt about his claim to rank with the greatest hurdlers of all time.

Nor, if a horse's popularity can be measured in decibels, is there any doubt that he is the best-loved champion seen at Cheltenham since Arkle.

The racing public admires courage even more than glittering brilliance, and to come back victorious as Persian War has after seven

straight defeats takes a heart as big as all outdoors.

But yesterday's unforgettable race had another hero, too, and the length and a half which separated Persian War (5-4f) and Major Rose proved how, between horses of almost equal excellence, jumping is, as it should be, the decisive factor.

How magnificently in this, his last Champion Hurdle, Josh Gifford rode Major Rose. Just for a moment, as they landed on the flat, it seemed that he and trainer Ryan Price might end their uniquely successful partnership in triumph. But Persian War was not to be denied.

31 May

Arkle, mightiest of 'chasers, is dead

By HOTSPUR

Arkle, almost certainly the greatest steeplechaser of all time, was put down in Ireland yesterday at the age of 13.

He had been living in honoured retirement on his owner, Anne, Duchess of Westminster's estate at Maynooth, Co.Kildare, since the attempt to continue training him was finally abandoned in October 1968.

"Over the last few weeks Arkle had progressive arthritic lesions developing in both hind feet. As these became worse he was in a certain amount of pain," said his owner, last night.

She added: "All known drugs and antibiotics were used. In spite of this no improvement was achieved. In the opinion of my veterinary advisers, his condition was incurable and, rather than have him suffer, I had him put to sleep this afternoon."

Three Cheltenham Gold

Cup victories and at least one success in almost every other steeplechase of consequence except the Grand National were among Arkle's 26 jumping wins worth a National Hunt record of £74,920 stake money. He also won on the Flat.

Arkle's brilliant pace, intelligence, superb jumping, courage under crushing handicap weights and the fact that he never ran a bad race, nor ever fell, made this gentle-mannered champion the idol of racing men, and a household name.

Arkle was foaled on April 19, 1957, at the Ballymacoll stud in Co.Meath and was bought as a three-year-old by Anne, Duchess of Westminster, for only 1,150gns. He was trained throughout his career by Tom Dreaper and was generally ridden by Pat Taaffe (*in picture above*). Arkle was buried yesterday in the garden of his owner's estate.

Grand National Aintree: 4 April

Gay Trip romps home from Vulture

By John Lawrence

Life they say begins at 40, and yesterday at Aintree, coolly steering Mr A.J.Chambers's eight-year-old gelding Gay Trip around the course he knows as well as any man alive, Pat Taaffe gave the old words a new and glorious meaning. Arkle would have been proud of his old friend, and millions of middle-aged sportsmen will salute him.

A superb spectacle, run in perfect conditions, the 1970 National disposed forever of the chairborne "experts" who claim the race has gone soft since the fences were rebuilt. Only 12 horses completed the first circuit, and one fence – the third, an open ditch – was in my considered opinion as fearsome as any obstacle ever jumped at Aintree.

Walking round beforehand, I noticed it towered well above my head – higher than The Chair and all of 5½ feet high. The fence is supposed to be only 4ft 8in high and I

honestly do not believe it had been correctly measured.

Five horses had fallen there in the Topham on Thursday, and in repairing the damage, the course builders had conceived a monstrous hazard. The National claimed another eight, including Two Springs, the 13-2 favourite and poor Racoon, who broke his neck.

Out into the country second time the same fatal open ditch accounted for All Glory, and coming to Becher's Taaffe calmly pulled Gay Trip out towards the centre.

A blunder by Villay left Gay Trip in the lead. As they came on to the racecourse, to us in the stands it looked as though Gay Trip (15-1) had sprouted a pair of wings, for suddenly going to the second last he was out on his own. He jumped the last two as gaily and perfectly as he had done all the rest, and romped home to win by 20 lengths from his half-brother Vulture (15-1).

The Derby Epsom: 3 June

Nijinsky fastest Derby winner since Mahmoud

By HOTSPUR (Peter Scott)

Nijinsky, running Epsom's mile and a half faster than any Derby winner since Mahmoud in 1936, stretched his unbeaten record to eight races yesterday with a display of sheer brilliance. For the first time in his life, Nijinsky (11-8f) started at odds against.

Mr Charles Engelhard's colt, the third Derby winner for his Irish trainer, Vincent O'Brien, and Lester Piggott's fifth, won by a completely decisive two and a half lengths from Gyr (100-30), with Stintino (7-1), another French challenger, three lengths behind in third place.

Approval, regarded as the main English hope, totally failed to act on these gradients and the firm going. He was beaten at halfway and finished a poor seventh. Great Wall was the home-trained hero. This colt, the first Derby runner from Scobie Breasley's Epsom stable, was fourth despite interference.

Nijinsky, taught by skilled training and jockeyship to conserve his brilliant speed, settled down in the middle of the field. He was, in fact, running lazily and Lester Piggott had to produce the whip to rouse him up.

Once that happened, Nijinsky's great stride took him past Gyr just over a furlong from home. Then the gap between an excellent horse and a really outstanding champion rapidly widened.

Mr Charles Engelhard, Nijinsky's American owner, had never seen his colt run until yesterday. He intimated that Nijinsky will retire to stud at the end of the season. Canadian-bred, Nijinsky was bought as a yearling by Vincent O'Brien on Mr Engelhard's behalf for £35,000.

The St Leger Doncaster: 12 September

Triple Crown for Nijinsky

Effortless win in St Leger

By John Lawrence

Without fuss or frills or false dramatics, Nijinsky duly collected the Triple Crown at Doncaster yesterday. Neither he nor Lester Piggott expended an ounce of unnecessary energy in the process, and between them they made the 1970 St Leger look even easier than the 2,000 Guineas or the Derby.

Nijinsky wins the Leger

This was Nijinsky's 11th successive victory and the £37,082 prize brought the colt's winnings to £238,715 14s. It was the first Triple Crown since Bahram's in 1935.

Nijinsky (2-7f) cantered down – with a large green patch on the celebrated bottom perched high above his withers. The big boy stayed much cooler than usual during the preliminaries, and went into the stalls like the mildest sort of lamb. As always he had dwarfed his opponents in the paddock and, settling down calmly last but one, managed to give from start to finish an impression of totally relaxed superiority.

And no one, with the possible exception of Lester Piggott, could accurately measure just how easily this race was won. Without coming off the bit, with Piggott's hands just barely moving on his neck, Nijinsky strolled past Politico. Well before the end he was back on a tight rein easing up and it was only for this reason that Meadowville (20-1) was able to get within a length.

Politico (20-1) was half a length away, third, Charlton (10-1) fourth and the rest of the nine runners so utterly outclassed as not to matter.

So what else is there to say? The Triple Crown is won for the 12th and, who knows, perhaps for the last time. Vincent O'Brien, who confirms that Nijinsky is growing progressively more relaxed and calm with age, says he will run next as expected in the Arc de Triomphe.

OTHER MAJOR RACES

Irish Derby	Nijinsky	L Ward	4-11f
Arc de Triomphe	Sassafras	Y Saint-Martin	19-1
Kentucky Derby	Dust Commander	M Manganello	153-10
Melbourne Cup	Baghdad Note	EJ Didham	25-1

Prix de l'Arc de Triomphe Longchamp: 4 October

Nijinsky beaten: Sassafras takes 'Arc' by head

By HOTSPUR (Peter Scott)

Nijinsky met his first defeat in 12 races at Longchamp yesterday when he lost the Prix de l'Arc de Triomphe by a head to Mr Arpad Plesch's French Derby winner Sassafras.

Sassafras was never out of the first four, whereas Nijinsky, waiting among the backmarkers, gave him at least eight lengths start. Nijinsky forced his head in front near home, but then hung to the left as Piggott whipped him right-handed.

Nijinsky made a quick start but was eased back. He had to be switched outside several horses for his final run. Lester Piggott was criticised for waiting too long on Park Top in this race last year. His ultra-patient tactics yesterday on a horse who stayed well enough to win the St Leger were even more questionable.

Vincent O'Brien, Nijinsky's bitterly disappointed trainer, contented himself with saying that the horse was "given a lot to do". Whether Mr Charles Engelhard's Triple Crown hero runs again before his retirement to stud in Kentucky has yet to be settled.

"Never in my wildest dreams did I think Sassafras would beat Nijinsky," said Mrs Arpad Plesch, whose husband bred and owns the winner. Their trainer, François Mathet, had been more optimistic.

Sassafras was Mathet's third Arc winner. The colt does not run again this season, but will remain in training as a four-year-old.

Blakeney, last year's Derby winner and the only English-trained runner, finished fifth, having run prominently throughout. The ground was not really soft enough for him, but Blakeney still showed himself the best older horse in this great international field.

[Nijinsky did run once more, starting 4-11 favourite in the Champion Stakes at Newmarket on Oct.17, but was defeated again, 1½ lengths by English 5-year-old Lorenzaccio (100-7).]

5 October

Trainer Kane is banned for life

By HOTSPUR

Michael Kane, 50, the Scottish racehorse trainer, had his licence withdrawn by the Stewards of the Jockey Club at an inquiry in London yesterday and was told that he would never be granted another licence to train.

His son, Michael, 25, his assistant trainer, was declared a disqualified person for 10 years.

The inquiry followed Jockey Club investigations into three horses that won flat races this year. Kane and his son were "asked to explain" the wins of Golden Duck (5-2) at Hamilton Park on May 11, Jynxy (11-2) at Ayr on May 29, and Sontana (100-8) at Teesside Park on Aug. 11. The charges against both related to doping.

Kane, a war-time RAF pilot and now managing director of a Glasgow engineering firm, has been training about 25 horses at Howwood, Renfrewshire.

1971

17 Mar Bula (15-8f) shows no mercy to triple champion Persian War (9-2) in the Champion Hurdle at Cheltenham, winning by 4 lengths, his 12th race unbeaten.

5 Jun Oaks winner Altesse Royale (6-4f) records the fastest time since Petite Etoile

in 1959, and is a fifth of a second faster than Mill Reef in the Derby, albeit on much firmer ground. Her victory completes a remarkable Epsom treble for jockey Geoff Lewis, after the Derby and Coronation Cup (Lupe).

5 Jun Venezuelan horse Canonero II fails to bring off the US Triple Crown, finishing 4th to Pass Catcher (35-1) in the Belmont Stakes.

26 Jun Linden Tree (7-4f) is sensationally left in the Irish Derby, won by French-

trained Irish Ball (7-2), who had finished behind him at Epsom.

3 Jul Mill Reef (5-4f) leaves Caro and Welsh Pageant, two of the best older horses in Europe, floundering as he runs away with the 84th Eclipse Stakes in record time at Sandown. Beating Connaught's record by 3/5sec, he has an easy 4 lengths to spare over 4-y-o French champion Caro, who had just broken the Prix Ganay record.

24 Jul Mill Reef (8-13f) wins the "King

George" at Ascot by a record 6 lengths (Ribot won by 5 in 1956) from 4-y-o Ortis (11-1), with Irish Derby winner Irish Ball nowhere.

15 Oct A Native Prince colt (out of Review) fetches a European record for a yearling of 117,000gns at Newmarket in the Houghton Yearling Sales, paid by the Curragh Bloodstock Agency for Sir Douglas and Lady Clague after a sustained duel with Lady Beaverbrook, who minutes earlier had herself paid a new record price of 81,000gns for a Sir Ivor colt.

CHAMPIONS

Jockey (Flat)	Lester Piggott	162
Jockey (NH)	Graham Thorner	74
Racehorse of the Year	Mill Reef	3-y-o
NH Champion of the Year	Bula	6-y-o
Leading Trainer	Ian Balding	£157,488
Leading Owner	Paul Mellon	£138,786
Leading Money Winner	Mill Reef	£121,913

NATIONAL HUNT

Champion Hurdle	Bula	P Kelleway	15-8f
Cheltenham Gold Cup	L'Escargot	T Carberry	7-2
Grand National	Specify	J Cook	28-1

The 2,000 Guineas Newmarket: 1 May

It's Brigadier Gerard

By John Lawrence

Flat racing often seems a cold and heartless business in which pounds and pence count more than flesh and blood. But yesterday that image was dealt a memorable blow as Mrs John Hislop's Brigadier Gerard stormed irresistibly home to win the 2,000 Guineas.

For this was not just the victory of a handsome, well-bred colt, superbly trained and ridden. What Brigadier Gerard carried on his back was the belief that racing CAN still be a sport, and his name will always henceforth stand as a reminder that the joy of owning a really good horse may, for some people, have a value which cannot be expressed in money terms.

In this, surely the supreme moment of his long and eventful racing career, John Hislop, who bred Brigadier Gerard and owns him in partnership with his wife Jean, remained as calm as he used to be when the chips were down in an amateur race.

Asked in the winners' enclosure how he felt now about refusing the bid of £250,000 made for his colt last year, he answered quietly: "We didn't really refuse it. The horse was never for sale." Brigadier Gerard is now at a very conservative estimate worth all of a million pounds.

For yesterday there was no trace of doubt or fluke about

his superiority. Three furlongs from home Geoff Lewis on Mill Reef had just begun to feel really confident. "I knew I had My Swallow beat," he said later, "But the moment Joe appeared it was all over,"

And so it was, for while the long-awaited battle between the two favourites was being fought and won, Joe Mercer had calmly bided his time on Brigadier Gerard (11-2).

Racing wide in the middle of the course, My Swallow (2-1) had led to halfway, but Mill Reef (6-4f) was never more than a length behind him, and they came together with three furlongs left to go.

But behind them, the Brigadier – named after Conan Doyle's second most favourite character, the brave but braggart French cavalryman – was poised to deliver a charge of which the Hussars would have been proud. He took a moment to find his full stride and Mercer tapped him once. But the response was more than he or anyone can have expected. For in a 100 yards, racing down the hill into the dip, Brigadier Gerard brushed aside the two colts who last year dominated European two-year-old racing.

They finished together far ahead of the others, but he was three lengths clear and going away, as decisive and brilliant a winner of the 2,000 Guineas as has ever been seen.

Cheltenham Gold Cup 18 March

L'Escargot leaves Gold Cup rivals floundering

By HOTSPUR (Peter Scott)

L'Escargot won his second Cheltenham Gold Cup yesterday. He galloped doggedly home through deep mud to finish well clear of five opponents who passed the post as weary as survivors picked up from a shipwreck.

Yesterday's race, like that of 1970, was followed by arguments as to whether L'Escargot would have beaten the horse who fell when leading three fences from home. Last year it was Kinloch Brae. Yesterday Glencaraig Lady crumpled on landing. Tommy Carberry, Escargot's rider on both

occasions, believes that his mount would have won each time in any case.

L'Escargot (7-2jf) escaped interference from Glencaraig Lady's fall, but Leap Frog (7-2jf) and The Dikler (15-2) were not so lucky. The Dikler had to check and swerve to avoid her.

Carberry had hoped L'Escargot would not be left in front so far from home and when L'Escargot slowed up approaching the last fence it still seemed that Leap Frog might catch him. Leap Frog, however, was very tired and L'Escargot forged clear again to win by 10 lengths.

The favourite, Mill Reef, is a comfortable Derby winner

The Derby Epsom: 3 June

Mill Reef romps home in Derby to confound his detractors

By HOTSPUR (Peter Scott)

Mill Reef, confounding those who doubted his stamina, outclassed and outpaced his 20 Derby rivals at Epsom yesterday. The result was a foregone conclusion well before he overtook Linden Tree, about 350 yards from home.

Mill Reef follows Sir Ivor and Nijinsky as the third Derby winner in four years to have been bred on the American continent. He has, like them, maintained consistently high-class form throughout his career.

The standard of this seasons's three-year-olds has

been much belittled, but Mill Reef and his 2,000 Guineas conqueror, Brigadier Gerard, are good classic winners by any yardstick.

Linden Tree (12-1) led as they rounded the last stage of Tattenham Corner. Mill Reef (100-30f) turned for home in fourth place and cruised up to him without Lewis having felt for his whip. Lewis finally produced it to ride out Mill Reef in the closing stages and his lead increased to a couple of lengths. Irish Ball (25-1) was a fast-finishing third, two and a half lengths further back.

Park Lodge Maiden Stakes Newmarket: 21 August

Prince loses his crown

By John Lawrence

With a pop that may well have been clearly audible in Kentucky, the Crowned Prince bubble was exploded at Newmarket yesterday. Watched by his breeder, his three joint owners and a large expectant crowd, the world's most expensive two-year-old trailed home a very ordinary sixth in the Park Lodge Maiden Stakes and for the time being at £212,000 looks, to put it politely, a trifle expensive.

He jumped off well enough, but Lester Piggott's bottom was never really at the high port, his hands were always busy and, as he himself confirmed afterwards, the 7-2 on favourite was really never going.

For just a moment, two furlongs out, he looked like getting into the race. But then – and this to me was the most ominous sign of all – a final slap from Piggott's whip caused him to go backwards instead of forwards.

So that was that. Jeune Premier (33-1) held on admirably, ridden by Mick Kettle, to beat Sleat (8-1) – and the racing world was left to conduct its agonised post-mortem. This disastrous display, taken with stoic sportsmanship by all concerned, bears no resemblance whatever to the brilliance Crowned Prince had been showing against older horses at home.

His trainer Bernard van Cutsem thinks that in the long run, if not the short, blinkers may be the answer, and certainly Crowned Prince looked in need of an alarm clock yesterday. But then he did have Piggott to wake him up, and since the champion failed it must be questionable whether anything or anyone else will succeed.

[Crowned Prince finished the season as champion 2-y-o, with 9st 7lb in the Free Handicap, having won the Champagne Stakes at York and the Dewhurst at Newmarket, but a soft-palate problem as a 3-y-o led to an early retirement and a disappointing stud career.]

OTHER MAJOR RACES

Irish Derby	Irish Ball	A Gibert	7-2
Arc de Triomphe	Mill Reef	G Lewis	7-10f
Kentucky Derby	Canonero II	G Avila	87-10
Melbourne Cup	Silver Knight	RB Marsh	10-1

Prix de l'Arc de Triomphe Longchamp: 3 October

Mill Reef sets new record in superb 'Arc' triumph

By HOTSPUR (Peter Scott)

Mill Reef, ridden in copybook style by Geoff Lewis, set a new time record for Longchamp's mile and a half when winning the Prix de l'Arc de Triomphe yesterday by three lengths from Pistol Packer.

Mill Reef has now won 10 of his 12 races and a European record of £256,000 in first prize money, but yesterday provided his finest hour and emphatically placed Mr Paul Mellon's tough little bay colt among the great horses of modern times.

Ian Balding, his trainer, had hoped for good going and a draw in the middle of the field. Both wishes were fulfilled. Baking sun dried the course and Mill Reef was drawn No.7 in the 18-horse field.

Mill Reef (7-10f) was never out of the first six and never more than four lengths behind the leader. Ossian, pace-making for Ramsin, was soon in front, and Mill Reef established a position on the rails. He did not leave it until approaching the straight, when Lewis pulled out a little and found a gap between Ortis and Hallez.

Lester Piggott on Hallez had held a brief lead, but the older horse possessed no answer to Mill Reef's acceleration. Mill Reef struck the front just under two furlongs from home. Pistol Packer then made her challenge and got to within a length of Mill Reef, but the favourite then drew steadily clear again. Lewis rode him right out to win in a time which beat by 7/10ths of a second the record set by Levmoss in this race two years ago.

Rock Roi Inquiry: 27 August

Walwyn fined £100 but acquitted of all blame

By MARLBOROUGH (John Lawrence)

Nearly three months after they were administered, two grammes of a drug called Equipalazone had their last, most baleful effect in London yesterday when Col.F.R.Hue-Williams's Rock Roi was deprived under Rule 180 (ii) of the £12,429 Ascot Gold Cup.

Mrs G.S.Benskin's Random Shot, whom Rock Roi beat by four lengths at Ascot, now becomes the 1971 Gold Cup winner. Mrs Benskin said at her home last night: "I never wanted to win the race like this."

While disqualifying Rock Roi and fining his trainer Peter Walwyn £100, the stewards of the Jockey Club completely exonerated both Walwyn and his head lad, Ray Laing, of all blame and acquitted them both of any corrupt practice or intent. They accepted that Walwyn had followed his vet's instructions in treating Rock Roi, but found that the minute trace of oxyphenbutazone (a product of Equipalazone) that showed up in a routine post-race test constitutes a substance "other than a normal nutrient *which could alter its (the horse's) performance at the time of racing.*"

The italicised words (taken from Rule 180) are, of course, the crux of this whole regrettable and complex affair. And, in deciding as they did, the stewards have clearly interpreted the words "could alter its performance" in their widest possible sense.

ENGLISH CLASSICS

2,000 Guineas	Brigadier Gerard	J Mercer	11-2
1,000 Guineas	Altesse Royale	Y Saint-Martin	25-1
Derby	Mill Reef	G Lewis	100-30f
Oaks	Altesse Royale	G Lewis	6-4f
St Leger	Athens Wood	L Piggott	5-2

Newmarket: 15 October

William Hill, the bookmaker, dies at Newmarket

DAILY TELEGRAPH REPORTER

Mr William Hill, 68, who built up the world's biggest bookmaking empire over 40 years, died yesterday at an hotel in Newmarket, where he was attending the yearling sales.

Although his name was synonymous with book-making, Mr Hill was also one of this country's best-known breeders of horses, and a keen farmer.

Born in Birmingham, Mr Hill left school at 12 to take a job as a farmer's boy at 2s 6d a week. At 18 be began collecting bets using an old motorcycle, and later opened a small office in that city. But office betting was too slow, although he admitted that the first time he went on a racecourse he was "fleeced".

He moved to London in 1929, opening a small office in Jermyn Street shortly afterwards. His name was then best known at greyhound and pony racing tracks.

The racing boom in the immediate post-war years put the name of the William Hill Organisation firmly on the map. His business, which now included football interests, mushroomed to an extent that in the mid-1950s Holders Investment Trust took over all the operations of the former Hill Organisation for a reputed £1,500,000.

Mr Hill's stud achievements included breeding 1949 Derby winner Nimbus and 1959 St Leger winner Cantelo.

Hotspur writes: William Hill had appeared in great spirits when chatting with friends in his Newmarket hotel on Thursday night and his death came as a great shock.

He was the last and probably the greatest of those racecourse bookmakers who would stand up and bet in tens of thousands. But he gave this up some years ago, and the racecourse market weakened considerably after his departure.

1972

13 Jan The Jockey Club announce that by 1973 all handicaps may be compiled centrally rather than as at present by a single individual. They are convinced that centralised and therefore faster handicapping will enable the period between entry and running for any given race to be cut by half – from the present month to 14 days.

6 May Miss Meriel Tufnell, on her mother's 5-y-o mare Scorched Earth (50-1), wins the first ladies's race under Jockey Club rules, beating 20 others in the 1m 1f Goya Stakes at Kempton.

1 Jul Epsom apparently takes its toll on Derby winner Roberto, the 15-8 favourite of the Irish counterpart finishing only 12th of 14 at the Curragh to Steel Pulse (10-1), who was a good 5 lengths behind Brigadier Gerard at Royal Ascot in the Prince of Wales Stakes.

22 Jul In the continued absence of the virus-stricken Mill House, Brigadier Gerard (8-13f) stretches his unbeaten record to 15 wins with a resounding triumph in the "King George" at Ascot.

16 Sep Meriel Tufnell, 23, clinches the first lady jockeys title with her third victory, on Hard Slipper (10-1) at Newbury in the 11th of the 12 ladies' races.

24 Nov Denys Smith's young claiming rider Michael Eddery, brother of Pat, breaks his leg in a fall from Grimsby Town in a novices' hurdle at Newcastle, an injury that later tragically necessitates amputation.

CHAMPIONS

Jockey (Flat)	Willie Carson	132
Jockey (NH)	Bob Davies	89
Racehorse of the Year	Brigadier Gerard	4-y-o
NH Champion of the Year	Bula	7-y-o
Leading Trainer	Dick Hern	£206,767
Leading Owner	Mrs Jean Hislop	£155,190
Leading Money Winner	Brigadier Gerard	£151,213

12 January

Kempton to stage first women's race on Cup Final day

By HOTSPUR

Twelve dates were announced yesterday for the Jockey Club's much-discussed experimental series of ladies' Flat races. The first will be at Kempton Park on May 6 – a meeting held in the morning because of the FA Cup Final.

All 12 races (twice the number originally suggested) will be additional to the normal six-race programmes, and the stewards have stressed that they must not be substituted for existing apprentice or male amateur races.

Geographically, they have been well spaced out, from Folkestone to Ayr, and, where possible, holiday meetings have been chosen.

No ladies' race will be shorter than one mile or longer than a mile and a half. They will all be started from stalls.

A detail of considerably more interest for would-be female Lester Piggotts is that the basic weight will be 9 stone and the age limit 18. No doubt this, like all other features of the enterprise, will be reconsidered in the light of experience, and I fancy that a lower age limit and a higher weight may eventually prove more satisfactory.

The normal strict rules concerning amateur status for male jockeys will not apply. In fact, the only ladies not eligible to ride are those who have either held professional licenses abroad or have actually been paid for riding in a race. But they will require certificates of competence from two licensed Flat-race trainers.

So there it is, the stage is set, and all we need now are a few actresses.

Prix du Cadran Longchamp: 21 May

Rock Roi, Parnell outclass French

By HOTSPUR (Peter Scott)

Rock Roi beat Parnell by a length for yesterday's Prix du Cadran at Longchamp. The two crack English stayers completely outclassed all their French opponents in this race, which has equivalent status to the Ascot Gold Cup.

Rock Roi started at 2-1, with Parnell the 6-4 favourite. Rock Roi went ahead early in the straight and, although Parnell looked very dangerous a furlong out, Rock Roi resolutely withstood his challenge. Le Chouan was six lengths away third.

Rock Roi finished second in the Prix du Cadran last year. His easy Ascot Gold Cup win a month later was followed by disqualification because of an irregular substance in his routine dope test sample.

It seems as if Rock Roi is better than ever this season. He is the first English-trained horse to score a Prix du Cadran victory since the war.

"Never a Quarrel" Ladies' Race Folkestone: 24 May

Miss Tufnell makes it a double

By MARLBOROUGH (John Oaksey)

There was absolutely nothing "gimmicky" or frivolous about the "Never a Quarrel" Ladies' Race at Folkestone yesterday – won, as its prototype had been, by Miss Meriel Tufnell on her mother's Scorched Earth (5-1). For this, let there be no mistake, was a highly competitive, genuinely exciting horserace. The form worked out, the best horse won.

And many a man has ridden assiduously for years without ever achieving the quiet effectiveness with which Miss Tufnell rode home to beat her old rival Jennifer Barons on Headmaster (9-2f) by half a length and keep her own 100 per cent record.

These two had been first and second in the Goya Stakes at Kempton Park, but yesterday's finish, on faster ground and less tired horses, was an infinitely more convincing affair. This time Miss Tufnell did not claim to have shut her eyes at any stage and had, in fact, been perfectly placed close to the rail throughout.

Personally – though you may detect a note of jealousy here – I question her judgment in kissing the Times racing correspondent afterwards – but, at least, she probably made history as the first winning jockey ever to celebrate in this peculiar fashion.

In many other ways – not least the extremely generous starting prices – the race was a complete and happy success.

NATIONAL HUNT

Champion Hurdle	Bula	P Kelleway	8-11f
Cheltenham Gold Cup	Glencaraig Lady	F Berry	6-1
Grand National	Well To Do	G Thorner	14-1

The Derby Epsom: 7 June

Roberto wins it by a nose – and survives inquiry

By HOTSPUR (Peter Scott)

American breeding, Irish training and English jockeyship proved the successful combination for yet another Derby when Lester Piggott drove home Mr John Galbreath's Roberto to beat Rheingold by the tip of a nostril at Epsom yesterday.

Roberto was the eighth winning Derby favourite in 10 years, and four of the last five winners have been bred on the American continent. He is trained in Tipperary by Vincent O'Brien, as were Sir Ivor and Nijinsky. For Piggott, it was a record-equalling sixth Derby triumph.

Yesterday's desperate finish was followed by a lengthy stewards' inquiry into possible interference during the last two furlongs, and had Rheingold won, he might have been disqualified. He bumped Roberto as they passed the pacemaking Pentland Firth a furlong and a half out. Roberto was knocked on to Pentland Firth, who had just come away from the rails.

Ernie Johnson, whose only previous Derby mount was the 1969 winner Blakeney, found Rheingold so unbalanced on this course that he had to ride out the colt with hands and heels in case the whip would cause him to create further trouble.

Piggott, who rode one of his strongest finishes to force Roberto ahead in the last 100 yards, did not think he had won, and dismounted on the course instead of steering Roberto into the winner's enclosure.

Grand Prix de Saint-Cloud: 2 July

Rheingold routs French to land Saint-Cloud prize

By HOTSPUR (Peter Scott)

Rheingold, short-head loser of a desperate Derby finish with Roberto, staked a powerful claim to be regarded as Europe's top middle-distance three-year-old by slamming Arlequino and Hard to Beat in yesterday's Grand Prix de Saint-Cloud.

Rheingold's Derby defeat was caused by his becoming unbalanced on the Epsom undulations. The level Saint-Cloud course suited this long-striding colt admirably, and after Yves Saint-Martin had sent him ahead one and a half furlongs out, Rheingold drew steadily clear.

Hard to Beat, winner of the French Derby (Prix du Jockey Club) in record time, started at odds-on yesterday. He made the running from Arlequino and Rheingold. But once Rheingold challenged him, Hard to Beat had little more to offer. The older Arlequino, three lengths behind Rheingold at the post, steadily wore down Hard to Beat and finished half a length in front of him for second money.

"A left-handed course like Saint-Cloud does not suit Hard to Beat and I feared he night run below form," said the favourite's jockey, Lester Piggott.

Rheingold's £47,224 first prize yesterday gave Barry Hills his richest victory in a brief but most successful training career. Hills had him in magnificent shape after the colt's hard struggle at Epsom.

Mr H.R.K.Zeisel, proprietor of the Rheingold Club in London, is the principal shareholder in a six-man syndicate which owns yesterday's big winner, who returned pari-mutuel odds of 43-10.

30 August

Mill Reef breaks leg – may still be saved for stud career

By HOTSPUR (Peter Scott)

Mill Reef, whose near foreleg was fractured in four places by a freak and tragic accident at Kingsclere yesterday may undergo surgery in a attempt to save him for stud. Whether an operation takes place will be settled on Saturday.

Mr Paul Mellon's great four-year-old was being ridden in a canter by his regular work jockey, John Hallum, when the tragedy occurred. He was exercising on what trainer Ian Balding regards as the best strip of ground on Kingsclere Downs.

Mill Reef had to be loaded into a horsebox and taken back to his stable, where the damaged leg was put into plaster. The champion's sweet temperament and disposition were never more vividly revealed than by his perfect behaviour during this time of shock and pain.

Mill Reef, with the European record first-prize money earnings of £300,192 from 12 wins out of 14 races and an immense stud value, was being prepared for a repeat success in the Prix de l'Arc de Triomphe, which he won so decisively last October.

Only 48 hours before this tragic accident his owner had decided to race Mill Reef again in 1973, because virus and injury had so curtailed his programme this season.

Whatever decision is taken this weekend, Mill Reef has an honoured place among the great racehorses of modern times. His speed, courage and the spectacular manner of his wins made him a special favourite. Sympathy will go out to all connected with the colt.

[Mill Reef was saved and went on to a brilliant career at the National Stud, siring Derby winners Shirley Heights and Reference Point, and becoming champion sire in 1978 and 1987, a year after his death.]

OTHER MAJOR RACES

Irish Derby	Steel Pulse	W Williamson	16-1
Arc de Triomphe	San San	F Head	37-2
Kentucky Derby	Riva Ridge	R Turcotte	6-4f
Melbourne Cup	Piping Lane	J Letts	40-1

Benson & Hedges Gold Cup York: 15 August

The Brigadier fails to answer call to arms

By MARLBOROUGH (John Oaksey)

Roberto, superbly ridden and trained by two past masters of the art, won the first Benson & Hedges Gold Cup deservedly at York yesterday. But his victory cast a shadow across the sunlit Knavesmire, for behind him, a sight no one wanted to see, Brigadier Gerard had found his Waterloo at last.

Two furlongs from home, for the first time in his life, Mrs Hislop's great horse had failed to answer the call to arms. "It just wasn't there," Joe Mercer told his owners. "No excuses, it just wasn't there."

The obvious explanation is that a long, hard campaign has taken its toll. But that familiar gleaming coat and eager head gave us no warning sign and nothing in any case should detract from Roberto's achievement or that of his Panamanian rider. Crouched low on the Derby winner's neck – noticeably more streamlined than his English rivals – Braulio Baeza had jumped Roberto (12-1) off in front as though the Knavesmire was his own backyard.

Bright Beam (300-1) kept him company for half a mile, but round the turn he darted two lengths clear, and only a moment later Joe Mercer's hands began to move.

Of the others, Rheingold (7-2), tucked in undesirably on the rails, was getting nowhere. Gold Rod (33-1) was under pressure and Bright Beam out of the hunt.

So the stage was set, but still the star's appearance was delayed. And, suddenly, halfway up the straight, the record crowd knew with sinking hearts that it would never come.

Balanced and cool, a stylist to his fingertips, Baeza drove for home, and Roberto, his Epsom gruelling forgotten, answered like a hero. The Brigadier (1-3f) did not surrender, but at the line, with the course record smashed by more than a second, there were three sad lengths to spare.

Ten lengths further back, ominously true to last year's form, Gold Rod was third. And, two lengths behind him, Lester Piggott on Rheingold could scarcely see the gallant horse he had forsaken.

ENGLISH CLASSICS

2,000 Guineas	High Top	W Carson	85-40f
1,000 Guineas	Waterloo	E Hide	8-1
Derby	Roberto	L Piggott	3-1f
Oaks	Ginevra	A Murray	8-1
St Leger	Boucher	L Piggott	3-1

Champion Stakes Newmarket: 14 October

'Brig's' career ends on note of triumph

By HOTSPUR

Brigadier Gerard has never been busier than he was as a four-year-old. The Champion Stakes, which he won for the second time at Newmarket on Saturday, was his eighth race of the reason and the 18th of a career which has seen him beaten only once. He is now destined for Newmarket's Egerton Stud.

Judged strictly on the form book, Saturday's win was not one of Brigadier Gerard's best efforts. But it came at the end of a year which has seen his versatility, as well as his toughness, thoroughly tested. The colt's own fine constitution, backed by the training and riding skills of Dick Hern and Joe Mercer, closed his career on a note of triumph.

Brigadier Gerard (1-3f) never looked like being beaten

Joe Mercer on the 'Brig'

after going ahead well over two furlongs from home, but Mercer had to push him out to win by a length and a half from the French colt Riverman (6-1).

1973

3 May Jump jockey Doug Barrott, 26, dies

in hospital, having failed to regain consciousness following a heavy fall from French Colonist in the Whitbread Gold Cup at Newcastle on Saturday (28 April).

5 May Secretariat, ridden by Canadian Ron Turcotte, storms to a 2 1/2-length victory over Sham in the £99,400

Kentucky Derby at Churchill Downs. Secretariat covers the 10 furlongs in 1min 59.4seconds, breaking Northern Dancer's record 2minute time set in 1964.

28 Jul Caroline Blackwell wins Ascot's first ladies' race, the Cullinan Diamond Stakes, on her father's horse Hurdy Gurdy (12-1).

14 Nov On the day HRH Princess Anne and Captain Mark Phillips are married, a public holiday, the bookmakers at Wolverhampton take a hammering as Royal Mark (11-10f) is coincidentally victorious in the Royal Wedding Handicap 'Chase.

Grand National Aintree: 31 March

Red Rum restores prestige to National

By HOTSPUR (Peter Scott)

The Topham family's long association with Aintree and the Grand National was climaxed on Saturday by Red Rum's win from Crisp in a race that restored the prestige of this famous steeplechase to its highest point for some years. Mrs Topham had the additional pleasure of presenting the trophy to Red Rum's owner, Mr Noel Le Mare, a long-standing family friend.

Crisp's name will be remembered with such gallant Grand National losers as Prince Regent and Easter Hero. Red Rum sustained an overreach during the race, so amid sympathy for the heavily weighted Crisp must go credit to a winner possibly feeling some pain.

Fast ground and the presence of so many natural front-runners suggested a record time, but none could have anticipated that Saturday's winner would be almost 19 seconds inside the record set by Golden Miller 39 years earlier.

Grey Sombrero, last year's Whitbread Gold Cup winner, led until Becher's on the first circuit. Crisp then went ahead to dominate so much of the race with his speed and a boldness of jumping that made those great fences look easy. Grey Sombrero was about eight lengths behind him in second place when he fell and broke a shoulder at the Chair fence, and had to be destroyed.

Crisp increased his lead soon afterwards to be almost a fence in front. Red Rum was prominent towards the outside of the field, racing near his stable-companion Glenkiln until Glenkiln fell at the Chair.

Early on the second circuit, Red Rum moved up into second place, and by the

Canal Turn had drawn clear of the rest but was making no ground on Crisp. But Brian Fletcher's hopes of a second Grand National win rose between the last two fences, when Crisp, under 12 stone, started to tire and poor Richard Pitman looked back in apprehension.

Crisp jumped the last fence about eight lengths ahead, but his weary legs were carrying him slower and slower. Red Rum, receiving 23lb, went ahead less than 100 yards from home, and as the two 9-1 joint favourites raced for the line Red Rum prevailed by three-quarters of a length. L'Escargot (11-1), also carrying 12st, was third, 25 lengths further back.

Red Rum was bred at the Rossenarra Stud, Co Kilkenny, by Mr Martyn McEnery. Tim Molony, his first trainer, gave 400gns as a yearling for Red Rum, who dead-heated for a two-year-old selling plate at Aintree in 1967. He returned there 12 months later for a mile handicap on Grand National day. Lester Piggott rode him and was beaten by a short head, little more than an hour after Brian Fletcher had won his first Grand National, on Red Alligator.

Red Rum was later bought by Freebooter's owner, Mrs Brotherton, and carried her colours during four busy National Hunt seasons. His only fall was over hurdles at Wetherby in May 1970, but he was later brought down in a steeplechase.

Donald McCain improved Red Rum considerably after paying 6,000gns for him on Mr Le Mare's behalf last August. The eight-year-old's injury rules out any chance of his running again this season, but he will be back for another Grand National.

Crisp just fails to hold off Red Rum (left) as they knock 18 seconds off the record time for the National

CHAMPIONS		
Jockey (Flat)	Willie Carson	163
Jockey (NH)	Ron Barry	125
Racehorse of the Year	Dahlia	3-y-o
NH Champion of the Year	Pendil	8-y-o
Leading Trainer	Noel Murless	£132,984
Leading Owner	Nelson Bunker Hunt	£124,771
Leading Money Winner	Dahlia	£79,230

King George VI and Queen Elizabeth Stakes Ascot: 28 July

Brilliant Dahlia repays faith of owner and trainer

By HOTSPUR (Peter Scott)

Dahlia's magnificent win at Ascot on Saturday came only a week after this valuable filly's Irish Guinness Oaks victory. Dahlia repaid the faith of her Texas owner, Mr Bunker Hunt, and Chantilly trainer, Maurice Zilber, by demolishing her King George VI and Queen Elizabeth Stakes rivals in a time bettered only by the inaugural running of this race 22 years ago.

Bill Pyers, who had wasted hard to make Dahlia's weight of 8st 4lb, rightly calculated that the early leaders were going too fast for their own good. He dropped Dahlia back into last place, while Park Lawn set a furious gallop from Roberto, Weavers' Hall and Hard to Beat.

Dahlia began to move up approaching the straight, but then Pyers found himself in a pocket. He switched position, giving Parnell a bump, and Dahlia shot up to the struggling leaders.

Striking the front just under two furlongs from

home, she strode right away to equal the record six-length winning margin for this race set by Mill Reef in 1971.

Dahlia began her two-year-old career by setting a new all-aged time record for the Deauville five furlongs. Twice defeated by Allez France this year, albeit at distances short of a mile and a half, she will be rested until the Prix Vermeille at Longchamp on Sept.23 before tackling her rival again in the Arc.

Rheingold (13-8f), who found trouble going the early pace, was the first losing King George favourite since 1967, but still emerged as the best four-year-old. He outstayed everything else in the final furlong but was gaining no ground on Dahlia (10-1). Another four-year-old colt, Our Mirage (25-1), was third, two lengths back. The biggest disappointment was Roberto (3-1), who went ahead five furlongs from home, but tamely capitulated to tail off 11th of the 12 runners.

NATIONAL HUNT			
Champion Hurdle	Comedy of Errors	W Smith	8-1
Cheltenham Gold Cup	The Dikler	R Barry	9-1
Grand National	Red Rum	B Fletcher	9-1jf

Belmont Stakes: 9 June

Secretariat's Triple Crown

Reuter report

Secretariat became the first horse in 25 years to win the US Triple Crown when he scored a devastating victory in the Belmont Stakes at Belmont Park on Saturday. Citation, in 1948, was the last to capture the Kentucky Derby, Preakness Stakes and Belmont.

It was an incredible performance by Secretariat, who won by a staggering 31 lengths from Twice a Prince to break the mile and a half track record in 2min 24sec. The time was also a US record for 12 furlongs on a dirt track.

Ron Turcotte, Secretariat's French-Canadian jockey, said: "He's the complete horse." Many US experts now believe that Secretariat, who has won 12 of his 15 starts, might be greater than Citation and Count Fleet.

ENGLISH CLASSICS

2,000 Guineas	Mon Fils	F Durr	50-1
1,000 Guineas	Mysterious	G Lewis	11-1
Derby	Morston	E Hide	25-1
Oaks	Mysterious	G Lewis	13-8f
St Leger	Peleid	F Durr	28-1

Corinthian Amateur Riders' Maiden Stakes Warwick: 16 October

Victor, 67, fulfils his ambition

Victor Morley-Lawson, 67, rode his first winner in Division II of the Corinthian Amateur Riders' Maiden Stakes at Warwick yesterday, on his own horse Ocean King. It was the last event on a nine-race card, but a big crowd stayed on to give a rousing reception to the retired London solicitor, who lives at Epsom and rides out every day.

"My first winner after trying for 25 years," said Mr Morley-Lawson, who added, "I never really rode a horse until I was 37. I went into racing with four ambitions – to own, breed, train and ride a winner. The first three I achieved with Miss Popsi-Wopsi."

Mr Morley-Lawson, judging from his sprightly performance on Ocean King, will be riding again next year, although he admitted to having a little difficulty in obtaining a permit this season on account of his age. "But the stewards were very kind to me," he said.

"I must be the first Past Master of the City Livery Company to ride a winner," added Mr Morley-Lawson, who bought Ocean King three years ago.

He had the seven-year-old chestnut, who had been plagued by spinal trouble, in front almost from the start, and although headed by Mick Henderson, riding Moth, a furlong and a half out, Mr Morley-Lawson rallied 4-1 shot Ocean King near the line to win by three-quarters of a length.

19 November

'National' safe for at least five years: Buyer a well-kept secret

By HOTSPUR (Peter Scott)

The Walton Group's conditional £3 million acquisition of Aintree will legally safeguard the Grand National for another five years. News of a conditional sale had been expected, but the buyer's name was a well-kept secret. Even Lord Leverhulme, the senior Jockey Club steward, did not know it until he arrived at yesterday morning's press conference, called jointly by Topham's and the Walton Group.

Mr William Davies, the Walton Group's chairman, readily admits his racing knowledge to be superficial, but he will enjoy expert guidance from Major Peter Beckwith-Smith, Aintree's newly appointed clerk of the course.

Within hours of yesterday's announcement, a meeting was held at the Jockey Club's London headquarters to discuss conditions of the 1974 race.

The Jockey Club programme book, listing conditions of all races in this National Hunt season's second half, is in the last stages of preparation. Grand National entry forms are also soon required, so the meeting was one of urgency.

Grand National added money will remain at £30,000 in 1974, with the Levy Board again providing £10,000. The Walton Group will contribute the remainder, which came this year from Topham's and British Petroleum.

The Walton Group's long-term plan is to develop one-sixth of Aintree's 260 acres as a shopping centre, but the exact site of that development is not yet settled.

Mrs Topham, clearly relieved and happy with Aintree's proposed sale, has conducted discreet negotiations with the Walton Group for 19 months. I understand that the five-year Grand National guarantee has been worded in such legal terms that it cannot be broken.

Prix de l'Arc de Triomphe Longchamp: 7 October

Rheingold gives Piggott first 'Arc' victory after 21 years

By HOTSPUR (Peter Scott)

Lester Piggott, who rode in his first Prix de l'Arc de Triomphe 21 years ago, won the world's richest race at his 17th attempt when Rheingold gave the favourite Allez France a decisive two-and-a-half lengths beating at Longchamp yesterday.

Rheingold, from Barry Hills's Lambourn stable, was among three English-trained winners on this lavish programme. Sparkler, also ridden by Piggott, gained a Prix de Moulin victory over Kalamoun and the Prix de l'Abbaye proved Sandford Lad to be Europe's top sprinter.

Horses drawn near the inside dominated the 27-runner Arc, and of the first seven home only Card King, a fast-finishing fourth, was drawn higher than eight.

Rheingold, in close touch and going strongly through-out, was third into the straight. Piggott sent him past Authi to lead two furlongs from home. Allez France had a good run through on the inside for her challenge, and for a few strides early in the straight it looked as if this filly's speed would carry her up to Rheingold. But the leader was running with tremendous power and gave her no chance.

Dahlia made a brief forward move two furlongs from home, but it never carried her into a really threatening position. She weakened again to finish out of the first 10, and Bill Pyers thought her recent training interruption caused her to tire. She finished 16th.

Hard to Beat, running his last race before he goes to stud in Normandy, was with the leaders throughout and finished four lengths behind Allez France.

OTHER MAJOR RACES

Irish Derby	Weavers' Hall	G McGrath	33-1
Arc de Triomphe	Rheingold	L Piggott	17-10f
Kentucky Derby	Secretariat	R Turcotte	6-4f
Melbourne Cup	Gala Supreme	F Reys	9-1

Canadian International Championship Woodbine: 28 October

Secretariat goes out with a typical flourish

By HOTSPUR

Secretariat, whose stable declined an invitation to run him for the Washington International, at Laurel on Nov.10, has ended his racing career. He went out with a spectacular weekend victory in Canada.

Secretariat's record has been full of runaway wins and fast times. His final race was the 13-furlong Canadian International Championship at Woodbine, Toronto. The great American three-year-old finished it six and a half lengths ahead of Big Spruce.

Secretariat's Canadian victory puts him fourth in the all-time list of win and place prize-money earners worked out by an American racing magazine, the Blood Horse. Only Kelso, Buckpasser and Round Table, sire of Apalachee and Cellini, stand above Secretariat.

1974

16 Apr Mr Bill Davies announces that his Walton Group have completed the £3m deal for Aintree Racecourse.

5 May Allez France (3-5f) beats Dahlia (5th) in winning the Prix Ganay by 5 lengths from Tennyson at Longchamp and in so doing also eclipses Dahlia as the record stakes-earning filly in European Turf history. This also completes a notable weekend double for jockey Yves Saint-Martin, who steered Nonoalco to victory in the 2,000 Guineas on Saturday.

18 Jun After an objection to the 1st by the 2nd and the 2nd by the 4th, the first 3 in the Queen Anne Stakes, the opening race at Royal Ascot – the aptly named Confusion (20-1), Gloss (7-1) and Royal Prerogative (6-4f) – are all disqualified, and the race awarded to the original 4th-placed Brook (12-1), a colt owned and trained in Italy, who had finished 6 lengths behind the 3rd.

27 Aug Trainers Ryan Price and Michael Stoute are fined after their horses fail dope tests, the last such cases before the new Jockey Club rules come into force. These give stewards discretion to waive the fixed £100 minimum fines provided they are satisfied that the person administering the banned substance did so in ignorance and had taken all reasonable precautions to avoid a breach of the rules.

Red Rum clears Becher's in the lead

Grand National Aintree: 30 March

Red Rum – the equine Bill Shankly

By HOTSPUR (Peter Scott)

Liverpool now has an equine Bill Shankly to worship. If any horse can revive the football city's enthusiasm for racegoing at Aintree it is Red Rum, who so decisively won a second Grand National for his Southport stable on Saturday.

Assuming that Aintree is still operational next year, Red Rum will return to attempt the unprecedented feat of winning a third Grand National. Unless the rules are changed, he can be given no more than the 12 stone which he has already defied.

If Crisp can be made sound again, Red Rum could conceivably have less than 12 stone, because Crisp failed by only three-quarters of a length to concede him 23lb in 1973.

Local pride helped to swell the rapturous and richly deserved cheers that greeted Red Rum after Saturday's win. His fan club, now growing fast throughout the country, will gain particular strength in the Liverpool area and this enthusiasm could be vital in Aintree's fight for survival.

Brian Fletcher is only the seventh man to ride three or more Grand National winners. At Becher's second time round, with Red Rum only seventh from the front, he briefly feared that the top weight's effort might have been made too soon. Another anxious moment came when Red Rum made his only serious mistake five fences from home.

Trainer Donald McCain said his worst moment was when Red Rum came back onto the racecourse hotly pursued by L'Escargot, whose finishing speed he feared might prevail.

But Red Rum (11-1) was fully a match for the dual Cheltenham Gold Cup winner's challenge. He doubled his three-length advantage between the last two fences, and extended it to seven lengths at the winning-post. L'Escargot (17-2) only just kept Charles Dickens (50-1) out of second place.

CHAMPIONS

Jockey (Flat)	Pat Eddery	148
Jockey (NH)	Ron Barry	94
Racehorse of the Year	Dahlia	4-y-o
NH Champion of the Year	Red Rum	9-y-o
Leading Trainer	Peter Walwyn	£206,445
Leading Owner	Nelson Bunker Hunt	£147,244
Leading Money Winner	Dahlia	£120,771

Ladbroke Lads and Lassies Handicap Nottingham: 1 April

Linda dents male supremacy myth

By MARLBOROUGH (John Oaksey)

The shop-soiled myth of male supremacy acquired another dent at Nottingham yesterday when Miss Linda Goodwill and Pee Mai (4-1f) won the Ladbroke Lads and Lassies Handicap with a ruthless efficiency on which Queen Boadicea could scarcely have improved.

Not, I hasten to add, that Miss Goodwill needed either chariots or scythes to carve her male opponents up. She did it fair and square the hard way, storming off in front at a gallop none of us could equal.

Speaking as one of lads (sic) who trailed respectfully in behind her, I can only say that no one could ask for a nicer or more ladylike bunch to rub knees with. No unseemly jostling disfigured the first few furlongs, and the turn for home was smoothly negotiated without a word of disagreement, let alone invective.

It was a nice clean contest, and Mr Hugh Hodge, fourth on March Malona, was the only man who played even a supporting role. In this class Miss Goodwill and Pee Mai are a formidable team. In 17 rides Linda had won five times and finished second four.

It is obviously far too early to draw any firm conclusions about the future of mixed races or for that matter female jockeys. Clearly as far as competition with amateurs is concerned this season, the girls – or some of them – are well able to compete on equal terms.

But amateurs are one thing, professionals quite another, as anyone who watched the Emmeline Pankhurst Handicap and the Flora Drummond Plate could see with half an eye. These races were won respectively by Willie "I can't see it happening for a good few years yet" Carson, and Jimmy Lindley. Whether you share Carson's opinion or not, it will be some little time, I suspect, before we see a woman who can match the brand of style and strength these male supremacists deploy.

NATIONAL HUNT

Champion Hurdle	Lanzarote	R Pitman	7-4f
Cheltenham Gold Cup	Captain Christy	H Beasley	7-1
Grand National	Red Rum	B Fletcher	11-1

The 1,000 Guineas Epsom: 2 May

Highclere lands 1,000 Guineas for Queen

By HOTSPUR (Peter Scott)

The Queen, who owns and bred Highclere, was at Newmarket yesterday to see this filly win the 1,000 Guineas. Highclere, wearing blinkers for the first time, held off Polygamy by a short head, but Polygamy's strong challenge would have prevailed in a few more strides.

Highclere follows Carrozza (1957 Oaks) and Pall Mall (1958 2,000 Guineas) to provide the Queen's third success in an English classic.

Highclere (12-1) went ahead with a quarter of a mile left. Mrs Tiggywinkle (3rd, 11-1) looked a big danger a furlong from home, but her stamina then began to give out. She hung badly to the left under pressure, and hampered Polygamy (4-1f) just as that filly's challenge was gaining full momentum.

Dick Hern, Highclere's trainer, has now managed the fine achievement of winning both "Guineas" classics with horses that had not run since the previous autumn. Hern pursued this policy with Brigadier Gerard, who beat Mill Reef and My Swallow in that memorable 2,000 Guineas of 1971. Joe Mercer who rode Brigadier Gerard in all his races was at his stylish best on Highclere.

Kentucky Derby: 4 May

Cannonade is the hero

Mr John M. Olin's Cannonade stormed along the inside rail to land the 100th Kentucky Derby at Churchill Downs, Louisville, on Saturday. Watched by a record 163,628 crowd, including Princess Margaret and Lord Snowdon, Cannonade, ridden by Angel Cordero, finished two and three-quarter lengths ahead of Hudson County, with Agitate third.

The 23-horse field was the largest in the history of the race. The runners swung wide into the final turn and Cordero, who had been desperately looking for an opening, slipped through inside to overtake pacemaking Hudson County.

Cordero, like most others in the race, complained of the rough passage he had, having to work his way through from 12th to first to land the prize.

Irish Derby The Curragh: 29 June

Battle of the 'Princes'

Yves Saint-Martin scored a decisive Irish Sweeps Derby win on English Prince (8-1), going ahead before the straight, and winning by an easy length and a half from Imperial Prince (11-5f).

It was English Prince's fourth win from five starts, and much his most important. This Petingo colt is improving all the time and he will be a very tough opponent for Snow Knight if they meet in the St Leger.

English Prince is owned and was bred by Mrs Vera Hue-Williams, whose husband was second with Imperial Prince. There was no real excuse for Imperial Prince, but perhaps a mile and a half is just beyond this colt's best distance at present.

Mississippian (5-1), third past the post, was relegated to fourth place for bumping Sir Penfro (12-1), who finished three lengths behind him. The stewards fined Mississippian's rider, Freddie Head, £50 for making "insufficient effort" to keep a straight course.

Ascot Gold Cup: 20 June

Ragstone lands Gold Cup for Duke of Norfolk

By HOTSPUR (Peter Scott)

Ragstone, watched by the biggest Ascot crowd for 10 years, produced a perfect blend of stamina and finishing speed to triumph in yesterday's Gold Cup. A lifetime racing ambition was thus achieved for his owner, the Duke of Norfolk.

Lassalle, last year's winner, shot into the lead once the straight was reached, but Ragstone's jockey, Ron Hutchinson, kept the French favourite well within his sights. Ragstone (6-4) was level with Lassalle (5-4f) a furlong out and then quickened to go ahead.

Proverb (25-1), badly placed on the last bend, came with a powerful challenge that took him past Lassalle to earn second place, three-quarters of a length behind the winner.

Ragstone has now won all his seven races during the past two seasons. John Dunlop, who turned the colt out looking magnificent, may now train him for the Goodwood Cup.

[The Duke bred Ragstone himself.]

ENGLISH CLASSICS

2,000 Guineas	Nonoalco	Y Saint-Martin	19-2
1,000 Guineas	Highclere	J Mercer	12-1
Derby	Snow Knight	B Taylor	50-1
Oaks	Polygamy	P Eddery	3-1f
St Leger	Bustino	J Mercer	11-10f

King George VI and Queen Elizabeth Stakes Ascot: 27 July

Dahlia's £337,500 breaks that Mill Reef record

By Hotspur (Peter Scott)

Dahlia *(right)*, back to her 1973 brilliance and now the only horse ever to win Ascot's King George VI and Queen Elizabeth Stakes twice, has beaten Mill Reef's European record for first-prize money earnings. Her total stands at more than £337,500.

Mr Bunker Hunt, elated by Saturday's win, revealed that an autumn campaign in America was under consideration for his champion filly. I hope this idea is dropped and that the Prix de l'Arc de Triomphe is made Dahlia's next target. She still has a score to settle with Allez France, who has beaten her in all their six clashes so far. Tennyson has finished ahead of Dahlia in three of their four meetings.

Neither Allez France nor Tennyson ran at Ascot. Other notable absentees were English Prince and Dibidale, winners of the Irish Sweeps Derby and Irish Guinness Oaks. Snow Knight's failure will now cause many to consider English Prince as his superior among England's three-year-old colts.

The early pace was moderate, and Dahlia's time was almost three seconds slower than she returned in last year's race. Dankaro (3rd, 6-1) turned for home with only two behind him. Snow Knight (11-2) had a slight lead over Hippodamia entering the straight, with Buoy (7-1) third and Dahlia (15-8f) going easily in fourth place.

Hippodamia soon dropped back and, just as Buoy was mastering Snow Knight, Dahlia swept nonchalantly past both with that smooth flow of acceleration that stamps a really outstanding horse. Highclere (5-1), off the bit soon after halfway, struggled on tenaciously into second place, but the Queen's dual classic winner had no chance of achieving a further triumph.

OTHER MAJOR RACES

Irish Derby	English Prince	Y Saint-Martin	8-1
Arc de Triomphe	Allez France	Y Saint-Martin	1-2f
Kentucky Derby	Cannonade	A Cordero	6-4f
Melbourne Cup	Think Big	H White	12-1

Prix de l'Arc de Triomphe Longchamp: 6 October

Allez France beats Comtesse de Loir in 'Arc' thriller

By HOTSPUR (Peter Scott)

Yves Saint-Martin, who had a pain-killing injection half-an-hour before the race, rode M Daniel Wildenstein's brilliant filly Allez France to a head victory over Comtesse de Loir in the Prix de l'Arc de Triomphe at Longchamp yesterday.

This was Allez France's 10th win from 14 races over the last three seasons, and her first prize money earnings have rocketed to £387,850. She does not run again this autumn, but will stay in training next year.

Allez France, coupled with her stable companion Paulista, started at 2-1 on. Those odds would have been still more cramped but for Allez France's unfavourable draw. Not since Molvedo in 1961 has any Arc been won by a horse drawn higher than 15, which was Allez France's starting position.

Being forced to race near the outside did not stop her. She came rapidly from one of the rear positions to pass Riot in Paris more than two furlongs from home. Allez France then went clear and the race looked over.

Suddenly, the three-year-old filly Comtesse de Loir burst out of the pack, gaining with every stride under vigorous riding from Jean-Claude Desaint. Saint-Martin, by contrast, kept Allez France going with no more than hands and heels.

This was big-race jockeyship at its coolest and specially remarkable by one who had not ridden for 10 days because of injury. Saint-Martin's previous Arc winner was Sassafras, who narrowly beat Nijinsky in 1970.

Highclere, Proverb and Coupe de Feu, England's challengers, all finished out of the first 10. Highclere was beaten a long way from home and the Queen's dual classic winner now retires to stud, to be mated with Mill Reef next spring.

Beating the bookies

By Joe Saumarez Smith

In the endless battle between punter and bookmaker, there is little that sets the pulse racing faster than the landing of a well-planned coup. Few would dispute that in the long run the backer has scant chance of triumphing over the layers. But there is also little doubt that a series of well executed plots can severely shake the "old enemy".

The move in the last three decades towards the bookmaker acting as accountant rather than as "punter in reverse", as the late William Hill, founder of the eponymous firm, saw himself, has significantly weakened the bookmaking market. But it is still not impossible for enormous sums to be taken from their satchels.

Bookies beaten by a Furlong

That much has been proved in recent years as huge gambles have been attempted, perhaps most notably by Noel Furlong, the Irish carpet multi-millionaire, at the Cheltenham Festival of 1991. Furlong, a long-time owner in Ireland, planned one of the most audacious coups of modern time when entering two of his horses, Destriero and The Illiad, on the first day of the Festival. Destriero, running in the opening Trafalgar House Supreme Novices Hurdle, duly obliged at 6-1, landing his owner somewhere between £500,000 and £2.5 million, depending on whether one believes his account or that of the bookmakers.

While this was something of a shock to the rails layers who bore the brunt of the success, there was a far greater concern. Furlong had placed The Illiad, a one-time Ladbroke Hurdle winner on whom he had won an estimated £2 million the previous January, in a double with Destriero, taking a morning price of 25-1 about the former. The realisation that its victory would take around £13.5 million out of the betting ring saw rare scenes of panic among the bookies, and the horse's price plummeted to 11-2 at the off. Alas, Furlong had to be content with his earlier profit as The Illiad limped in considerably nearer last than first, never having looked a contender.

Historically such a punt would be considered "a good cop" but would hardly rate as a major coup on the scale of those regularly attempted throughout the eighteenth and nineteenth centuries.

Growth of betting

Until the latter part of the eighteenth century, races were almost always run as matches with bets struck between two individuals. While this inevitably means that many major wagers have not been preserved for posterity, a look through surviving match books of noblemen shows that sums of £5,000 were common stakes and that £20,000 would not have been considered unduly excessive (equivalent to £250,000 and £1 million today).

In those days betting was largely the preserve of the landed gentry, taking place either around the betting post on each racecourse or in the subscription rooms of coffee houses in cities (the former gave rise to the term "betting ante-post"). While others were involved in the practice, they came from the criminal element and were intent only on stealing and cheating from the aristocracy rather than making a book with them.

Only when, in 1776, Richard Tattersall, whose name on the Turf is preserved both by the Newmarket-based auctioneers and by the betting disputes arbitration committee that sits

The odds tumble (left) on Destriero at Cheltenham in 1991 and a concerned bookie (above) counts the cost

monthly at the Café Royal, opened his coffee house close to Hyde Park, did it become possible for a wider audience to become involved. For an annual subscription of two guineas, anyone could come and bet with like-minded punters. For a market to open it required that at least six people should be seated around the house's hexagonal table, a custom that gave rise to the term "betting ring".

The other great innovation in betting came from a Lancastrian bookmaker named Ogden. He was the first to accept bets on all runners in a race, breaking the system where the layer would offer "one horse against the field". While the initial reaction of his contemporaries was that Ogden would lose his fortune instantaneously, they soon discovered that the opposite was true and that their only hope of staying in business was to follow suit.

A national hobby

From the early 19th century onwards, betting as a pastime for all took off, so much so that it entrenched itself as a national hobby. In 1853 the government became so concerned about its influence that they passed an Act for the Suppression of Betting Houses. The preamble of the Act describes a kind of gaming "that has sprung up tending to the injury and demoralisation of improvident persons by the opening of places called Betting Houses or Offices and the receiving of money in advance..."

While this legislation limited the open display of betting odds it did little to curtail the scope of gambling, and, throughout the latter part of the century, horse racing and the attendant wagering continued to grow. Not unsurprisingly it was accompanied by a similar rise in skulduggery, led by owners, trainers and unscrupulous betters who discovered the effect of speed-enhancing drugs.

Little did it matter that a horse would give the appearance of being half mad, frothing at the mouth and eyes bulging; if the animal won, they were content. The Rules of Racing did not prevent use of the drugs, so they continued to use them, taking bookmakers for huge sums as a result. It was not until early this century that the Jockey Club banned drugs after an American team perfected the cocaine-based "speedball" leading to a serious undermining of public confidence in the integrity of the sport.

The Druid's Lodge Confederacy

Shortly before the turn of the century, perhaps the greatest ever syndicate for planning betting coups was put together. In 1895 five respected men joined together to form what became known as the Druid's Lodge Confederacy. Setting up their own stable, Druid's Lodge, on Salisbury Plain, they employed their own trainer and ran one of the strictest training yards ever, aimed at preventing any rumours about their runners leaking out.

While the stable enjoyed significant successes with their commissions in the initial years of operation, it was not until 1903 that the public became aware of the extent to which the stable were ahead of both the bookmakers and the handicapper.

In Kempton's Grand Jubilee Handicap of that year the stable entered Hackler's Pride and backed it from an ante-post price of 25-1 into 7-2 favouritism at the off. The horse duly obliged and the five picked up a payout equivalent to £4 million today.

That was only the start of their investments on Hackler's Pride. She was entered in that year's Cambridgeshire, but the five initially backed only the stable's other entries. As bookmakers started to believe that Hackler's Pride was not to be the subject of a second plunge, the odds lengthened. This was the signal for the confederates' contacts overseas to get to work betting the long odds available in foreign books.

Many small bets were struck at 25-1, and with a week to go towards the race the total amount bet on Hackler's Pride had reached the equivalent of £60,000, with a potential profit of £850,000. On the Tuesday before the race, they availed themselves of the odds again, striking one bet of £1,000 to £11,000 (equivalent to £43,000 to £473,000) and numerous smaller ones.

On course the horse was backed down from 8-1 to 6-1 and Hotspur's commentary in the following day's Daily Telegraph tells of the ease with which the gamble was landed: "The race was singularly devoid of incident for a Cambridgeshire, and is very easily described, as immediately they had settled down Hackler's Pride made the running... and was never headed, winning in a hack canter." He added, somewhat innocently: "In fact, it is doubtful if another 10lb would have stopped her, and it is certainly difficult to reconcile her previous form this season with such a smashing exhibition today. It would be an exaggeration to say that the victory was a popular one, for there was no enthusiasm as she returned to the Birdcage, and the only thing one can do is marvel at the astounding luck – I suppose astuteness would be the more appropriate term – of a stable which has during the past few years brought off an inordinate number of successful and profitable coups."

It was estimated that the Druid's Lodge team's finest hour had landed £250,000 profit, equivalent to £10.5 million today.

Heyday of betting

Perhaps the heyday of betting in Britain was between the end of the First World War and the legalisation of betting shops in 1961. While cash betting off-course was illegal, street bookies prospered, their operations more or less tolerated by the police.

Most were healthy operations, although shortly after the end of the Second World War many disappeared overnight owing to the 66-1 victory of Airborne in the 1946 Derby. As John Prendergast, a Glasgow street bookie at the time, later wrote: "Every bloody paratrooper that was ever at Eindhoven, Nijmegen or Arnhem – and their bloody mammies and grannies and aunties – must have backed that bloody horse yesterday."

The passing of the Betting and Gaming Act of 1961 saw the end of the street bookies and has been responsible for the present shape of the modern gambling industry. As more information becomes available to punters and bookmakers, the chances of pulling off massive coups have diminished, with the latter's network of contacts jokingly (but not entirely inaccurately) said to be better than those of MI5.

The Cartmel coup

It is unlikely that before 1961 a coup such as the Gay Future affair would have been exposed. At Cartmel, on August Bank Holiday Monday 1974, a horse named Gay Future was declared by his permit trainer Anthony Collins to run in a novice hurdle. On the morning of the race, the horse's connections went round the country placing bets of £5, £10 or £20 in doubles and trebles with two other of Collins's runners that day, Opera Cloak and Ankerwyke.

Bookmakers soon twigged that something was afoot but did not know which horse to be wary of. By midday all bets were being refused, and representatives had been sent to each

Laying the odds at Cheltenham

of the three courses the horses were meant to be running at to shorten their starting price.

The poor travel connections to Cartmel meant that the bookies arrived too late, discovering that Gay Future had hacked up by 15 lengths at the distinctly generous price of 10-1. The other horses had been declared non-runners – indeed they had not even set off to the courses they were supposedly running at – and it looked as though a remarkable gamble had been pulled off.

But the bookmakers called foul, and the perpetrators were tried for conspiracy to defraud, a charge they were found guilty of, although in his summing-up the trial judge said in mitigation: "On the facts of the case, the degree of dishonesty is in my assessment, although a conspiracy to defraud, very much at the bottom end of the scale."

The future

Where the future of betting coups remains is uncertain. There are many who believe that sports betting now offers more lucrative opportunities, especially where humans are the object of the gambler's attentions. But it would be naïve to suggest that horse racing gambles are dead, judging by the regularity with which some trainers seem to be able to manipulate the handicap system. Horses backed from 14-1 to 15-8 favourites in a maiden chase at Fakenham are not unusual, but you can be pretty sure that these days the gamble can be measured in monkeys (£500s) rather than being the product of an aristocrat wagering his last 20,000 acres.

The Trodmore Hunt sting

The card for the Trodmore Hunt, the race meeting that never was, was printed in The Sportsman on 1 August 1898. The editor had been asked to list runners and riders, and in good faith he did. Several bookmakers in the London area took bets on the "meeting", and the following day the "results" were published in The Sportsman.

Some of the bookies paid out on winning bets, but others decided to wait until the results were published in The Sporting Life. However, when they were, there was a discrepancy in the SP of one of the winners, necessitating an inquiry. As a result, it was found that no such place as Trodmore existed. The perpetrators were never discovered.

1975

20 Mar Having changed in the ambulance room, Jane McDonald, 21, is the first woman jockey to compete professionally against the men, in the 1m Crown Plus Two Apprentice Championship Handicap. Riding Royal Cadet (25-1), she leads for a furlong before her horse fades to finish 11th of 17.

1 Jun Allez France (1-10f) chalks up her 7th success on the trot when winning the Prix Dollar at Longchamp to take her first-prize money earnings to nearly £450,000.

29 Jun Europe has a new middle-distance champion as Grundy's brilliant Irish Derby triumph is followed the next day by the defeat of Allez France (1-5f) in the Prix d'Ispahan at Longchamp. Unbeaten since October 1973, the French filly finishes only 3rd to 4-y-o colt Ramirez (33-1), who breaks the course record for 1,850m (just over 9f).

5 Oct The 4-y-o Star Appeal (119-1), ridden by Greville Starkey, is the shock German winner of the Arc as the buffeted favourite Allez France finishes 5th.

1 Nov Elain Mellor is the leading lady jockey, having an unassailable lead of 69 points to Joy Gibson's 57 in the 1975 title race.

1 Nov Beaten by Rose Bowl in the Champion Stakes 2 weeks ago, travel-weary Allez France suffers another defeat, coming last of 11 in a 10f dirt-track

handicap at Santa Anita, California, in what turns out to be the last of her 21 races – she won 13.

8 Nov The 3-y-o filly Nobiliary (5-2) spearheads a French clean sweep in the Washington International at Laurel, Maryland, with Comtesse de Loir 2nd and On My Way 3rd.

11 Nov There are an unprecedented 7 joint favourites at 8-1 in the 22-runner Blackburn Nursery at Haydock Park, one of them, Hargrave Rogue, finishing 1st.

Grand National Aintree: 5 April

L'Escargot comprehensively foils Red Rum National hat-trick

By HOTSPUR (Peter Scott)

L'Escargot flew home to Ireland within hours of Saturday's News of the World Grand National triumph. His victory breakfast at Dan Moore's stable yesterday included champagne and a dozen eggs, while runner-up Red Rum took more normal nourishment in Don McCain's Southport yard.

Saturday's race was unique in Grand National history because never had the same horses taken first and second places two years running. The all-important difference of reversed positions was accepted with sportsmanship by Red Rum's stable. Dan Moore's attempts to ride or train a Grand National winner go back to Royal Danieli's head defeat by Battleship in 1938.

L'Escargot became the first Irish-trained Grand National winner since Mr What in 1958. Remarkably, they have the same breeder, Mrs Barbara O'Neill of Co Westmeath. What a Daisy, L'Escargot's dam, is a half-sister of Mr What. Mrs O'Neill sold L'Escargot as a foal. Three years later, still unnamed, he went up for sale again and Mr

Raymond Guest became his new owner at 3,000gns.

L'Escargot's Cheltenham Gold Cup triumphs of 1970 and 1971 have been followed by four Grand National appearances. Knocked over early in the 1972 race, he finished third and second in Red Rum's triumphant years before Saturday's well-deserved win.

Tommy Carberry, whose riding triumphs in the last month have included the Gold Cup, Irish Distillers Grand National and now the Grand National itself, had his worst moment on Saturday when L'Escargot blundered badly at the seventh fence. He soon worked back to a position near the leaders and three fences from home L'Escargot and Red Rum began to draw clear. They jumped the last just about level, but Carberry then shook up L'Escargot (13-2), who was receiving 11b, and the battle was over.

Red Rum (7-2f), though finishing 15 lengths behind L'Escargot, still beat Spanish Steps (20-1) by eight lengths for second place, meeting him on 20lb worse terms than in 1974.

CHAMPIONS

Jockey (Flat)	Pat Eddery	164
Jockey (NH)	Tommy Stack	82
Racehorse of the Year	Grundy	3-y-o
NH Champion of the Year	Comedy of Errors	8-y-o
Leading Trainer	Peter Walwyn	£382,527
Leading Owner	Dr Carlo Vittadini	£209,492
Leading Money Winner	Grundy	£188,375

NATIONAL HUNT

Champion Hurdle	Comedy of Errors	K White	11-8f
Cheltenham Gold Cup	Ten Up	T Carberry	2-1
Grand National	L'Escargot	T Carberry	13-2

The stable lads' protest that delayed the Guineas

The 1,000 Guineas Newmarket: 1 May

Nocturnal Spree snatches Guineas for Ireland

Race delayed by stable lads' strike

By HOTSPUR (Peter Scott)

Nocturnal Spree (14-1), trained in Ireland by Stuart Murless, younger brother of Noel, beat the French filly Girl Friend (13-1) by a head in yesterday's 1,000 Guineas. This classic and the three preceding races were delayed by demonstrators spreading themselves across the course.

About one-third of Newmarket's 638 stable lads are on strike over a wage claim. It had been feared that the disruption would spread to affect the racecourse's various technical services, but fortunately most of them were in operation. The photo-finish camera was especially welcome after the 1,000 Guineas because little more than a length separated the fist six.

The Queen's filly Joking Apart (25-1) finished a length behind Girl Friend. Rose Bowl (7-4f), Lighted Glory and

Carnauba, separated by a head in each case, followed Joking Apart home.

The Houghton-trained Rose Bowl may well have been an unlucky loser. The moderate pace left a string of horses still holding chances until the last furlong and Lester Piggott did not get a clear run on the favourite until much too late.

Joking Apart, hotly challenged by Nocturnal Spree, who was running only the third race of her life. went ahead one and a half furlongs from home. Just as Nocturnal Spree mastered Joking Apart, Girl Friend challenged on the outside to overtake both.

Girl Friend faltered close home and Johnny Roe gained his first success in an English Classic by forcing the grey Nocturnal Sprees in front again in the final strides.

ENGLISH CLASSICS

2,000 Guineas	Bolkonski	G Dettori	33-1
1,000 Guineas	Nocturnal Spree	J Roe	14-1
Derby	Grundy	Pat Eddery	5-1
Oaks	Juliette Marny	L Piggott	12-1
St Leger	Bruni	A Murray	9-1

The Derby Epsom: 4 June

Grundy a powerful Derby winner

By HOTSPUR (Peter Scott)

Grundy (5-1), confounding the doubt about his stamina, won yesterday's Derby with a smooth flow of power that took him past Anne's Pretender over a furlong out. He drew clear to win by three lengths from Nobiliary (20-1), the first filly to make a Derby challenge since 1944. Hunza Dancer (50-1) was third, another four lengths back.

Green Dancer (6-4f), the wretchedly disappointing French favourite, was under pressure before the straight. He finished sixth, about 10 lengths behind Grundy.

Peter Walwyn achieved his greatest ambition after saddling two of the six previous Derby seconds.

Prix de Diane Chantilly: 15 June

French Oaks off: Stable lads' demo

By HOTSPUR (Peter Scott)

Chantilly's Prix de Diane (French Oaks) meeting had to be called off yesterday following early afternoon demonstrations by local stable lads and then unsuccessful efforts by the French Turf authorities to restore harmony between lads and trainers.

Chantilly is the principal training centre in France, with a large stable labour force making it as vulnerable to disruptive action as Newmarket. At least Newmarket managed to stage both its "Guineas" classics last month after some delays.

Pickets are expected at Royal Ascot's opening afternoon tomorrow, but it does not seem the strikers' intention to prevent racing.

18 November

Hill's to take on 'Nunthorpe'

By HOTSPUR (Peter Scott)

The William Hill Organization's contribution to race sponsorship in 1976 has been raised to approximately £150,000 by news that they will take over York's Nunthorpe Stakes next August.

The Nunthorpe was once a selling race, but after the war this five-furlong test became established as one of the season's major sprints. It will become the William Hill Sprint Championship, with added money doubled to £20,000 and all given by the sponsor.

Top-class middle-distance horses compete for a great deal more money than leading sprinters, who well deserve this extra incentive. But I question whether the Turf Authorities should have allowed the word "Nunthorpe" to be dropped.

Commercial sponsorship cannot be guaranteed as a matter of permanence, but continuity of major Flat-race titles has international importance to the breeding world. The fairest compromise is to join a sponsor's name with at least part of what should be a permanent title.

22 December

Ladbrokes save the National for Aintree

By MARLBOROUGH (John Oaksey)

Barring yet another unforeseeable disaster, the Grand National was saved at the 11th hour last night. Ladbrokes have signed an agreement with the Walton Group to manage Aintree for the next seven years.

After more than eight hours of discussion yesterday, Ladbrokes' chairman, Mr Cyril Stein, appeared at a Press conference, together with Lord Wigg, who had been assisting throughout the long-drawn-out negotiation.

Mr Stein explained that, subject to the Jockey Club's approval, the great race is safe for at least two years. Under the agreement, Ladbrokes will still have the right to run the race that long, even if the Walton Group sells Aintree elsewhere.

All income from the course will go to Ladbrokes, but they will pay £200,000 for the first two years, £225,000 for the next two and £250,000 for the

King George VI and Queen Elizabeth Diamond Stakes Ascot: 26 July

It's Grundy again in record time

By John Oaksey

In a battle worth more than all the diamonds in the world, Grundy and Bustino combined to do British racing a signal honour at Ascot yesterday. Their record-breaking King George VI and Queen Elizabeth Diamond Stakes will never be forgotten by anyone fortunate enough to have seen it.

But although the credit for this superlative race was shared between the home-bred pair, it was Grundy who got home half a length in front. And if he retired to stud tomorrow no one can say any more that he has not been tested to the utmost – because, as in last year's St Leger, Bustino's owner Lady Beaverbrook was wonderfully served by her pacemakers. First Highest then Kinglet led the way according to plan, and when they tired, exactly half a mile from home, Joe Mercer asked Bustino to go and claim his place in the history books.

The big bay four-year-old quickened like a hero, but Patrick Eddery was very much on guard and had Grundy in second place like a flash. But even so Bustino galloped into the short straight with a clear three lengths advantage.

He fought for every inch of it too, and for a moment, with less than a quarter of a mile to go, all Grundy's admirers and connections (a phrase which includes every tax-payer in the British Isles) felt their confidence draining away.

If there had been even a shadow of weakness in the dual Derby winner's stamina or courage, the next hundred yards would infallibly have revealed it. But instead, down went his nose and with that blond tail flying like a comet he strained every nerve to answer Eddery's call.

If Bustino had been the one-paced stayer some of us thought him last season, the race would have been over there and then. But he, too, managed somehow to find some extra speed and for a few heartbeats they raced together head to head.

Bustino (4-1) never gave up even when Grundy (4-5f) had taken the half length by which in the end he won. That, in fact, was how they covered the last half furlong with a proud and delighted English crowd cheering them every yard of the way.

Having snatched his advantage, Grundy held it to the bitter end, and don't forget he had made up at least three lengths in the short Ascot straight at the end of a race run in 2min 26.98sec – more than two seconds faster than anything ever seen over a mile and a half on the royal heath.

Five lengths behind the two leaders, Dahlia (6-1), winner of the last two King Georges, did everything she could to make it three, and ran quite well enough in the process to suggest that she may be very nearly as good as ever.

OTHER MAJOR RACES

Irish Derby	Grundy	Pat Eddery	9-10f
Arc de Triomphe	Star Appeal	G Starkey	119-1
Kentucky Derby	Foolish Pleasure	J Vasquez	19-10f
Melbourne Cup	Think Big	H White	33-1

following three.

Earlier yesterday the Jockey Club had laid its cards on the table with a firm ultimatum to Mr Bill Davies and the Walton Group. Unless plans were approved by noon on Dec.29 to hold the Grand National at Aintree in 1976, an alternative race, to be called simply "The National 'Chase", would be run on April 3 at Doncaster.

The whole racing world will breathe a sigh of relief at the overdue attack of commonsense. Aintree hero Red Rum has already been installed favourite for the 1976 race. The dual National winner's trainer Donald McCain said last night: "I am over the moon – absolutely delighted. It would have been a tragedy if the race were run anywhere else. Let's face it, away from from Aintree the Grand National would be just another long-distance steeplechase."

1976

7 Feb Miss Diana Thorne is the first successful female jockey under National Hunt rules, riding Ben Ruler (9-1) to a neck victory over Air General (10-1), ridden by her father John, in the Nimrod Hunters' 'Chase for amateur riders at Stratford.

14 Feb Mrs Val Greaves is the first woman to compete against professionals over hurdles when she rides Silver Gal in the Brough Novices' Hurdle at Catterick.

1 May Bold Forbes, who began his racing career with a sequence of five runaway victories in Puerto Rico, defeats hot favourite Honest Pleasure by a length for the £90,000 first prize in the Kentucky Derby.

4 Jun French filly Pawneese (6-5f) coasts home by an easy 5 and 4 lengths in the Oaks from Roses for the Star (33-1) and African Dancer (15-2) at Epsom.

6 Jun Epsom Derby winner Empery's owner Mr Nelson Bunker Hunt and trainer Maurice Zilber complete a fine Derby double when Youth (39-20), who beat Empery in last month's Prix Lupin, wins the French Derby (Prix du Jockey Club) at Chantilly.

26 Jun Empery (4-5f) is beaten by another French-trained colt, Malacate (5-1), in the Irish Derby, which is the first Classic to have horses -Navarre and Riot Helmet – trained and ridden by women, Anne Brewster and Joanna Morgan, respectively.

5 Sep Lester Piggott lands a Longchamp treble, riding Youth (4-5f) to win the Prix Niel, replacing the colt's injured regular jockey, Freddie Head, as well as winning two 2-y-o races. Youth has Arctic Tern and Malacate behind him.

11 Sep Crow's bicentenary St Leger victory, after Flying Water (1,000 Guineas) and Pawneese (Oaks), enables owner M Daniel Wildenstein to match M Marcel Boussac's 1950 achievement of winning three English Classics in one season with different horses. Trainer Angel Penna and jockey Yves Saint-Martin share the triumph.

Spittal Hill Amateur Riders' Handicap 'Chase Ayr: 30 January

A clear round for debutante Muriel

Mrs Muriel Naughton duly made history by becoming the first woman to ride under National Hunt rules at Ayr yesterday. But she had only one man behind her at the finish of the amateur riders' 'chase as she passed the line a well-beaten sixth on her own horse, Ballycasey.

Mrs Naughton, 28, a mother of a five-year-old daughter, had to change in the ambulance room before weighing out on Ballycasey, who was prominent in the early stages.

Passing the stands at halfway, Ballycasey and his rider, who goes to scale at a trim eight stone, were disputing the lead, but turning into the back straight the horse began to weaken.

Muriel said: "He began to make the odd mistake. I was in two minds as to whether I should pull him up, but decided to press on." Ballycasey (33-1) was eventually beaten over 40 lengths.

Grand National Aintree: 3 April

Red Rum will be back for record

By W.D.Tadd

With the promise that both Red Rum and his vanquisher Rag Trade will be back to battle out next year's News of the World Grand National, it looks as though Aintree's dismal days of doubt are over.

Nearly 50,000 packed the course for yesterday's race, the biggest crowd for years, and the prospect of seeing these two great horses strain every nerve and muscle over the same 4 1/2 miles and 30 fences should bring every one of them back again – together with some of their friends.

Of course, National Hunt racing is a precarious sport that can upset the best-laid plans, but Fred Rimell, trainer of Rag Trade, and the owner, Mr Pierre "Teasy Weasy" Raymond, both declared that Rag Trade would put his title at stake.

Red Rum (10-1) might have achieved his record third win yesterday, so courageously did he respond to the roars of the crowd in the stands. For a moment he narrowed the gap between him and Rag Trade (14-1), but the winning jockey, John Burke said afterwards: "I knew I could hold on. I dared not look round although I knew Red Rum was answering to the crowd."

Until the leaders came to the last fence with the race clearly between them, the excitement had been sustained by a variety of leaders – first Money Market, then Nereo and then that great old horse The Dikler – before the greatest cheer went up as Red Rum, having worked his way quietly through the diminishing field, thrust his head in front with only three to jump.

He put his head down and stretched his legs a fraction further. But even he in the end had to concede to Rag Trade, who was receiving 12lb.

Eyecatcher (28-1) who was still in with a winning chance at the last, weakened to finish third, ahead of the favourite Barona (7-1). The winning distances were two, eight and three lengths.

CHAMPIONS

Jockey (Flat)	Pat Eddery	162
Jockey (NH)	John Francome	96
Racehorse of the Year	Pawneese	3-y-o
NH Champion of the Year	Night Nurse	5-y-o
Leading Trainer	Henry Cecil	£261,301
Leading Owner	Daniel Wildenstein	£244.500
Leading Money Winner	Wollow	£166,389

The Derby Epsom: 2 June

Empery makes it record seventh Piggott triumph

By HOTSPUR (Peter Scott)

Empery, who had managed only one win in six previous races and on recent form was not even the best three-year old in Maurice Zilber's Chantilly stable, gave Lester Pigott the all-time record of a seventh Derby-winning ride at Epsom yesterday. Empery is the first French-trained Derby winner since Sea Bird II in 1965.

Piggott had Mr Bunker Hunt's colt prominent throughout, and sent him past Relkino to lead a furlong from home. Wollow, starting at 11-10, became the shortest-priced losing Derby favourite since Tudor Minstrel in 1947. He finished fifth.

Hitherto unbeaten, Wollow ran a lustreless race and his inability to go the pace caused him to meet with some interference. He never made an effective challenge.

Gerard Rivases, riding not only in his first Derby but also in his first race at Epsom, sent Vitiges into an early lead and held it until passed by Relkino with two furlongs left. Piggott then switched Empery from his rails position to challenge outside the two leaders. Empery (10-1), responding to vigorous pressure, wore down Relkino (25-1) and then drew steadily clear to win by three lengths.

Oats (10-1) and the unconsidered Hawkberry were both under pressure early in the straight but stayed on to finish third and fourth. Wollow also passed the weakening Vitiges close home.

Mr Hunt had a half-share in Empery's sire Vaguely Noble when that horse won the 1968 Arc. Empery, whose only previous win was in the first of his three races as a two-year-old, provided Lester Piggott with his 22nd success in an English classic.

NATIONAL HUNT

Champion Hurdle	Night Nurse	P Broderick	2-1f
Cheltenham Gold Cup	Royal Frolic	J Burke	14-1
Grand National	Rag Trade	J Burke	14-1

ENGLISH CLASSICS

2,000 Guineas	Wollow	G Dettori	1-1f
1,000 Guineas	Flying Water	Y Saint-Martin	2-1f
Derby	Empery	L Piggott	10-1
Oaks	Pawneese	Y Saint-Martin	6-5f
St Leger	Crow	Y Saint-Martin	6-1jf

Pawneese (on rails) wins from Bruni (centre) and Orange Bay

King George VI and Queen Elizabeth Diamond Stakes Ascot: 24 July

Pawneese routs the colts

By HOTSPUR (Peter Scott)

The filly Pawneese won Saturday's King George VI and Queen Elizabeth Diamond Stakes to continue the domination by French-trained horses of this season's European racing. Even with Youth and Malacate running below expectation at Ascot, there was still no chance for England because Pawneese led from start to finish.

A repetition of last year's tremendous early speed, when Bustino's two pacemakers covered the first half-mile in 45sec, was never on the cards. But Pawneese took one second less than Grundy for the final two furlongs. Her overall time was 2.38sec slower than Grundy's track record.

Pawneese, a wonderful credit to trainer Angel Penna, has won all her six races

during 1976. M Daniel Wilden-stein's home-bred filly began her season at Saint-Cloud in March, nine days before the Champion Hurdle!

Winning the Oaks and Prix de Diane (French Oaks) little more than a week apart would alone ensure any filly an honoured place in Turf history. Now Pawneese has also beaten colts of three different generations.

When Youth (15-8f) swung very wide entering the straight and thus lost all chance, Malacate (13-2) looked the main threat to Pawneese (9-4), but he could never get within two lengths of her. Bruni (6-1), Orange Bay (10-1) and Dakota all overtook Malacate well inside the last furlong, relegating him to fifth place.

Goodwood: 31 July

Piggott hat-trick sharp reminder for the doubters

By HOTSPUR

Lester Piggott may no longer be a contender for championship honours – his total of mounts in England this season is approximately half those of Pat Eddery and Willie Carson – but when a touch of flair and showmanship is needed, the "long fellow" is still unequalled among his contemporaries.

Those with the temerity to cast doubts regarding Lester's skill and judgement as a result of his recent alleged "mishandling" of Bruni at Ascot and General Ironside at Goodwood had any such criticism cast back into their teeth as he brought off a

brilliant 771/2-1 hat-trick on the final day of the Goodwood meeting.

Piggott, who had landed a treble at Newmarket on Friday evening, made his Saturday Goodwood tally three from four rides when scoring on Paddington, Fool's Mate and Roussalka. He thus joined Joe Mercer as top jockey of the five-day meeting, each with five winning mounts.

Fool's Mate, who had won the opening race of the Goodwood meeting last Tuesday, defied a 3lb penalty with ease in the PTS Laurels Stakes to bring off a notable double.

Jockey Club Inquiry: 12 August

Boutin fined £1,250 and Trepan loses two big races

By HOTSPUR (Peter Scott)

Trepan was disqualified by the Jockey Club stewards late last night from his rich summer victories in the Prince of Wales Stakes at Royal Ascot and the Joe Coral Eclipse Stakes at Sandown Park. François Boutin, his Chantilly trainer, has been fined £1,250.

Trepan set 10-furlong time records in both those wins, but small traces of drugs were revealed in dope test samples taken from this French four-year-old on each occasion. Trepan is disqualified because the stewards feel these could have affected his performances.

The Jockey Club stewards followed a 12-hour inquiry attended by various legal, scientific and forensic experts, by stating they took a serious view of such rule breaches, and that Boutin's fine would have been more severe but for his own good record and the horse's disqualification. Any similar offences would be more harshly dealt with in future.

A small trace of caffeine was found in Trepan's dope test sample after Royal Ascot. Boutin attributed this to a diuretic given to his horse beforehand.

Boutin admits to treating a number of his overseas runners in this way, but says that a mistake by one of his stable staff resulted in Trepan's dose being administered 24 hours before the Prince of Wales Stakes, rather than the proposed three days. Gerard Fabien, the employee concerned, has been fined £100. Boutin has consistently maintained that Trepan received no further medication whatever during the two and a half weeks between Royal Ascot and the Eclipse Stakes, but a sample taken from the horse after the latter race revealed a small trace of theobromine.

Wollow, originally second in the Eclipse Stakes, has now been awarded this £38,258 first prize. Anne's Pretender will be given the Prince of Wales Stakes fist prize of £11,327.

Prix de l'Arc de Triomphe Longchamp: 3 October

Bruni fifth as Ivanjica cuts down Crow and Youth in 'Arc'

By HOTSPUR (Peter Scott)

M Jacques Wertheimer's four-year-old filly Ivanjica, trained by Alec Head and ridden by his son, Freddy, came from last place to beat the St Leger winner Crow by two lengths in yesterday's Prix de l'Arc de Triomphe at Longchamp.

Bruni, England's heavily backed main hope, made a quick start and was close up entering the straight, but then faded steadily into fifth place. He had run a similar type of race in last year's 'Arc'.

Kasteel led early from Pawneese, who went ahead approaching halfway. These two then went clear, but Pawneese weakened quickly in the last half-mile and

finished 11th. Kasteel, back in front for a few strides when Pawneese dropped out, was quickly challenged by Youth, Crow and Bruni.

Crow then forged ahead and looked an assured winner until Ivanjica unleashed her run. Noble Dancer, the Norwegian outsider, gave a fine performance to finish fourth, only a neck behind Youth.

Ivanjica's slow start helped her to overcome a moderate draw, because she was able to ease over to the inside. She was then fortunate to enjoy a remarkably good run through, never far from the rails. Her time was the slowest in the last 10 "Arc" runnings.

OTHER MAJOR RACES

Irish Derby	Malacate	P Paquet	5-1
Arc de Triomphe	Ivanjica	F Head	71-10
Kentucky Derby	Bold Forbes	A Cordero	3-1
Melbourne Cup	Van Der Hum	RJ Skelton	9-2f

1977

2 Feb Isle of Wight NH trainer Alan Aylett is banned for 2 years and fined £500 after a Jockey Club inquiry finds that his 12-y-o gelding Stand Clear, who won at Plumpton last October, was doped.

2 Apr In the race prior to the Grand National, the Templegate Hurdle, Champion Hurdler Night Nurse (4-5f) and Irish rival Monksfield (7-2) dead-heat for first place.

26 Aug A deputation of senior jockeys– Lester Piggott, Joe Mercer and Geoff Lewis– approach the Newmarket stewards after Ernie Johnson sustains a broken leg and other injuries owing to a crashing fall from Courjet in the Blue Peter Stakes. The filly, who was unhurt, had swerved and ducked off the course catapulting her rider into a post. The deputation suggest there should be running rails for at least the last 5f of 2-y-o races.

1 Nov Australian trainer Bart Cummings saddles a record 6th Melbourne Cup winner when the 5-y-o Gold and Black (7-2f) beats Reckless (11-2) by a length.

12 Dec The Jockey Club lift their 225-year ban and admit women members. The Countess of Halifax, Mrs Priscilla Hastings and Mrs Helen Johnson-Houghton are among 7 new members elected.

Cheltenham Gold Cup: 17 March

Davy Lad triumphs after Lanzarote's fatal mistake

By HOTSPUR (Peter Scott)

Lanzarote's death, an injury that has ended the veteran Summerville's career and mishaps to all the other leading fancies made yesterday's Piper Champagne Cheltenham Gold Cup a tale of woe. Davy Lad won it from another Irish outsider, Tied Cottage.

All Fred Winter's past training disappointments in what now seems more than ever his bogy race pale beside the stark tragedy of Lanzarote, who had to be put down after breaking his near hind leg at the ninth fence.

Lord Howard de Walden's 1974 Champion Hurdle winner had begun his steeplechasing career in such brilliant style this season that the highest honours seemed destined for him. These became so many shattered dreams when his hind legs gave way beneath

him two strides after the jump, and he slithered to the ground.

Lanzarote (7-2) held third place to Tied Cottage and Fort Devon when the tragedy occurred. He fell in the path of Bannow Rambler (11-4f), who unseated his rider. Summerville had just passed Fort Devon when the latter took off too soon six fences from home, failed to right himself on the sticky ground and fell.

Summerville overtook Tied Cottage with four fences left and appeared all set to win. He faltered suddenly between the last two jumps, but battled on to finish third before pulling up lame.

Tied Cottage (20-1) and Davy Lad (14-1) passed Summerville (15-1) approaching the last fence, where Davy Lad made a fine leap and drew steadily clear to win by six lengths.

CHAMPIONS

Jockey (Flat)	Pat Eddery	176
Jockey (NH)	Tommy Stack	97
Racehorse of the Year	The Minstrel	3-y-o
NH Champion of the Year	Night Nurse	6-y-o
Leading Trainer	Vincent O'Brien (Ire)	£439,124
Leading Owner	Robert Sangster	£348,023
Leading Money Winner	The Minstrel	£201,184

The Derby Epsom: 1 June

Piggott brings Derby tally to eight on The Minstrel

By HOTSPUR (Peter Scott)

Lester Piggott's eighth Derby victory, on The Minstrel at Epsom yesterday, meant success for a courageous horse, brilliantly ridden by a jockey who had influenced his Irish stable to run. The Minstrel (5-1) wore down Hot Grove (15-1) close home to win by a neck. French colt Blushing Groom (9-4f) faded in the last two furlongs to finish five lengths away third.

Hot Grove was the only English-trained colt to finish in the first seven.

Vincent O'Brien, who did so well to have The Minstrel

in peak form after two hard losing battles in the 2,000 Guineas and Irish 2,000 Guineas has now trained five Derby winners. After The Minstrel's short-head defeat by Pampapaul in the Irish 2,000 Guineas, O'Brien was undecided whether to let him join his stable's Derby challenge, but Piggott said he thought the colt had a great chance and would like to ride him.

Mr Robert Sangster, this Canadian-bred colt's owner, rejected £1 million for The Minstrel only a week ago.

Grand National Aintree: 2 April

Record third National for Red Rum: The day strong men wept

By HOTSPUR (Peter Scott)

Red Rum made National Hunt history at Aintree when winning the Grand National for a record third time and bringing his overall winnings total to £114,000– another jumping record.

Left in front after favourite Andy Pandy (15-2) had fallen at Becher's on the second circuit, Red Rum (9-1) never looked in danger and came home alone to a tumultuous reception 25 lengths ahead of Thursday's Topham winner Churchtown Boy (20-1), with Eyecatcher (18-1) again third and The Pilgaric (40-1) fourth.

Red Rum is now 12 and could have at least two more chances to improve what must now be reckoned the finest individual Grand National record. In five years, he has won three times and been twice second.

I cannot recall any Grand National winner showing less signs of fatigue after the race and the inevitable mobbing from his ecstatic admirers. It is said, with justification, that luck generally plays a bigger part in this race than any other, but Red Rum makes his own good luck. He nimbly

avoids trouble, measures each of those now familiar fences with precision and runs on with ever increasing power.

Christopher Wright writes: It was one of those days when the old cliché came true: strong men actually did weep, such was the emotional impact of Red Rum's historic achievement. Even before the Grand National record was in sight, the commentators' very mention of that magic name "Red Rum" brought waves of cheers from the 51,000 crowd, and when he went clear on the run-in pandemonium broke loose.

It was nearly all too much for jockey Tommy Stack. The winner's enclosure after the National is always mayhem, but on Saturday the place erupted with men and women laughing and shouting with tears in their eyes, proclaiming what had to be one of the greatest racing performances of all time.

[Charlotte Brew, the first woman ever to ride in the Grand National, made a gallant attempt to complete the course on Barony Fort but failed when her mount refused four fences from home.]

NATIONAL HUNT

Champion Hurdle	Night Nurse	P Broderick	15-2
Cheltenham Gold Cup	Davy Lad	DT Hughes	14-1
Grand National	Red Rum	T Stack	9-1

The Oaks Epsom: 4 June

Oaks celebration for the Queen

By HOTSPUR (Peter Scott)

The Queen's filly Dunfermline brought off the most popular classic victory for years when landing the Jubilee Oaks at Epsom on Saturday, setting aside much trouble in running to beat Freeze the Secret by three-quarters of a length.

Willie Carson, so narrowly beaten on Hot Grove in the Derby, brought Dunfermline (6-1) wide on the outside in the straight after being repeatedly balked on the run to Tattenham Corner. An Italian victory seemed certain as Vaguely Deb (14-1), in front almost from the start, was challenged by her stable-companion Freeze the Secret (7-1) with less than two furlongs to run.

Dunfermline, though, was now in top gear and with the Downs resounding to deafening cheers, she mastered the Luca Cumani-trained pair 100 yards from the line.

The classic had opened in sensational fashion when Lester Piggott, riding the favourite, Durtal, was lucky to escape with his life as she bolted and dragged him along at racing speed with one foot caught in an iron. His foot was finally released when she collided with a rail, but she spiked her leg and was withdrawn from the race without coming under starter's orders.

ENGLISH CLASSICS

2,000 Guineas	Nebbiolo	G Curran	20-1
1,000 Guineas	Mrs McArdy	E Hide	16-1
Derby	The Minstrel	L Piggott	5-1
Oaks	Dunfermline	W Carson	6-1
St Leger	Dunfermline	W Carson	10-1

Belmont Stakes: 11 June

Seattle Slew's Crown

Unbeaten Seattle Slew proved himself in the Secretariat class when taking the Belmont Stakes, third leg of the American Triple Crown, in brilliant style at Belmont Park, New York, on Saturday. No winner of the Triple Crown had ever before completed the hat-trick with an unbeaten record. Even Secretariat, the ninth horse to take all three classics in 1973, had one defeat in his previous performances.

Seattle Slew was in command of the eight-horse field from the start, bouncing out of the stalls under French-born Jean Cruguet, and was never headed throughout the mile and a half trip.

Entering the home straight, Seattle Slew had drawn four lengths clear of Run Dusty Run and Sanhedrin and he maintained that margin as the trio crossed the line.

The St Leger Doncaster: 10 September

Dunfermline's Jubilee toast

By HOTSPUR (Peter Scott)

The Queen's Oaks winner Dunfermline beat the favourite Alleged in a memorable Jubilee St Leger finish, but a stewards inquiry caused some 20 minutes' anxious delay between Dunfermline's passing the post and confirmation that she could retain her spoils.

My own reaction to viewing the head-on film patrol shots was one of surprise that the stewards should have kept not only Doncaster racegoers but countless off-course backers in suspense for so long.

Neither O'Brien nor Lester Piggott, who rode Alleged, lodged an objection. Piggott was able to keep his whip swinging regularly on Alleged until he accepted defeat close home. Alleged himself drifted slightly out from the rails. Dunfermline veered towards him when Willie Carson produced his whip in the last furlong, but there was no contact.

Gregarious had set a strong pace until early in the straight, where Alleged (4-7) went ahead. Dunfermline (10-1) soon gave chase and wrested the lead from him just over a furlong from home to win by a length and a half.

Ascot Gold Cup: 16 June

Sagaro makes Cup history and ends racing career

By HOTSPUR (Peter Scott)

Sagaro's third consecutive Ascot Gold Cup victory, a feat without precedent since the race was founded in 1807, was achieved yesterday with all the brilliance that has placed him among the greatest specialist stayers in Turf history.

The finishing speed which Mr Gerald Oldham's six-year-old combines with his stamina overwhelmed Sagaro's fellow French challenger, Buckskin. Lester Piggott, riding his eighth Ascot Gold Cup winner, allowed Sagaro to cruise home five lengths clear.

Citoyen, taking third place, made it a clean sweep for the French stayers. Bruni, England's chief hope, finished a tired and rather distressed fourth.

Mr Oldham had long envisaged yesterday's big race as the final appearance of Sagaro's distinguished career. Sagaro's £225,000 first prize money earnings from 10 wins are by far the biggest ever amassed by a specialist stayer.

King George VI and Queen Elizabeth Diamond Stakes Ascot: 23 July

The Minstrel's King George victory sets Vincent O'Brien 'Arc' problem

By HOTSPUR (Peter Scott)

The Minstrel, short-head winner of Saturday's King George VI and Queen Elizabeth Diamond Stakes, has fully earned the late-summer rest which is now due. Vincent O'Brien then faces the difficult decision whether to race him again. This gallant colt's £315,211 gives him the first-prize money earnings record for an English or Irish trained horse.

His magnificent courage and tough constitution have helped The Minstrel through some desperate battles, but there must be a limit even to his reserves, and O'Brien trains other "Arc" possibles, such as Meneval and Alleged.

The Minstrel's slow start and Pat Eddery's fine tactical jockeyship on Orange Bay made Saturday's race a very close call. The Minstrel (7-4f) finally struggled into the lead, but he began hanging to the right with fatigue, and Eddery conjured another effort from Orange Bay (20-1) that only just failed.

OTHER MAJOR RACES

Irish Derby	The Minstrel	L Piggott	11-10f
Arc de Triomphe	Alleged	L Piggott	39-10f
Kentucky Derby	Seattle Slew	J Cruguet	1-2f
Melbourne Cup	Gold and Black	J Duggan	7-2f

Prix de l'Arc Triomphe Longchamp: 2 October

Piggott triumphs on Alleged: Dunfermline 4th

By HOTSPUR (Peter Scott)

Alleged, taking command more than a mile from home, won yesterday's Prix de l'Arc Triomphe by one and a half lengths from Balmerino, with his St Leger conqueror Dunfermline fourth.

Alleged's victory crowned a record-breaking season for trainer Vincent O'Brien and Mr Robert Sangster, who now owns a majority share in the colt. Lester Piggott, successful on Rheingold in 1973, was riding his second Arc winner. O'Brien– previously successful with Ballymoss in 1958– said that Alleged would stay in training as a four-year-old.

Dunfermline, the only horse ever to beat Alleged, lost a hind plate in yesterday's race. She finished strongly and would have beaten Crystal Palace for third place in a few more strides. Willie Carson said that Dunfermline would have done still better with a stronger early pace. Yesterday's time of 2min 30.6sec compares favourably with most recent years, but seldom is the Arc run on such dry going. Alleged started favourite at 39-10

1978

8 Feb Jonjo O'Neill, 25, completes the fastest 100 winners in a National Hunt season when riding Sweet Millie to victory in a selling hurdle at Haydock.

1 Apr The late withdrawal of the injured ante-post National favourite Red Rum last night, and his subsequent retirement,

marks the end of an era, but with the first five covered by 3 lengths and the photo-finish equipment installed last year used for the first time, the great Aintree steeplechase provides its usual breathtaking spectacle. Last year's winner Rag Trade, the 8-1 favourite, is pulled up lame, and Lucius (14-1), trained by Gordon W.Richards, wins by half a length from Sebastian V (25-1) with Drumroan (50-1) a neck back in 3rd.

18 Apr 8-y-o Boldboy (11-10f), ridden by Willie Carson, wins his fourth Abernant Stakes (6f) at Newmarket in 5 years (he

was 2nd in 1975), bringing his first prize money earnings from 14 wins to over £93,000, more than double the total amassed by any other Flat-race gelding in British Turf history. Ubedizzy (20-1), beaten 2 lengths into 2nd place, stages a 'rodeo display' when being unsaddled and savages his lad's arm (he is subsequently banned from British racecourses).

10 Jun Graham Starkey completes an 80-1 Derby-Oaks double when he squeezes Fair Salinia home by a short-head from 2-1 favourite Dancing Maid in the fillies' Classic at Epsom after

Wednesday's Derby triumph on Shirley Heights, both horses starting at 8-1.

16 Aug Star Performance (4-1), saved from the knackers yard by Sally Masson, wife of the Lewes trainer, Mick, brings off a rare double when, after a successful first appearance over fences last week, he collects a 1m 2f amateur riders' handicap at Brighton for Brooke Sanders.

18 Aug Lorna Vincent is the first professional woman to win under NH rules when she steers Pretty Cute (25-1) to victory over 6 men at Devon.

Perth: 19 April

Five and record to O'Neill

Jonjo O'Neill (*above*) went to Perth yesterday needing one winner to equal and two to break Ron Barry's record of 125 in a National Hunt season – and he came away with five.

It is the first time a jockey has had five victories from five mounts since Barry Brogan at Wolverhampton on Nov.11, 1968. The only other race at Perth yesterday was

for amateur riders.

O'Neill's winners were Besciamella (7-2), Majetta Crescent (13-8f), Crofton Hall (7-2), Father Delaney (4-5f), and Tiger Feet (7-1), The accumulative odds were 764-1.

The Irishman has already achieved the fastest century in NH history and with six weeks of the season left now looks poised to pass the 150 mark.

CHAMPIONS

Jockey (Flat)	Willie Carson	182
Jockey (NH)	Jonjo O'Neill	149
Racehorse of the Year	Shirley Heights	3-y-o
NH Champion of the Year	Midnight Court	7-y-o
Leading Trainer	Henry Cecil	£382,812
Leading Owner	Robert Sangster	£160,405
Leading Money Winner	Ile de Bourbon	£136,012

Jockey Club Headquarters: 27 April

Gifford & Champion are exonerated

The long-running Nougat saga was finally concluded at Jockey Club headquarters in London yesterday when the horse's trainer and rider, Josh Gifford and Bob Champion, were cleared of any breach of the rules of racing.

The disciplinary committee exonerated the pair from allegations that Nougat had been "schooled in public" when finishing fourth at Leicester on Jan.10. Both men were legally represented.

Nougat, an eight-year-old, was having only his second run in 18 months, and the local Leicester stewards held an inquiry into the horse's running and recorded Gifford and Champion's explanations.

The gelding came out again at Kempton Park 11 days later to win the Lanzarote Handicap Hurdle after being backed from 14-1 to 8-1, and this time Josh's wife Althea was asked to explain the horse's "apparent

improvement compared with the Leicester race".

Mrs Gifford's account was accepted, but in the light of the Kempton victory, the Leicester stewards re-opened their examination and referred the matter to the Jockey Club.

At yesterday's eight-hour meeting, evidence was given on Gifford's behalf by several jockeys involved in the two races, among them Gerry Enright, who rode the horse to win at Kempton, and by Toby Balding, Nougat's former trainer.

Afterwards Gifford said: "I'm absolutely delighted but, to be honest, the result is nothing more than I expected." The Findon trainer, enjoying his best season, has turned out 78 winners, but Nougat will not boost that total. The son of Tapioca is being sent to the Ascot sales next month.

NATIONAL HUNT

Champion Hurdle	Monksfield	T Kinane	11-2
Cheltenham Gold Cup	Midnight Court	J Francome	5-2
Grand National	Lucius	BR Davies	14-1

Jockey Club Headquarters: 25 April

Bookie banned for 3 years

By Paul Potts

John Banks, the Scottish bookmaker, promised a major legal battle last night after being banned from racing for three years for breaches of Jockey Club rules.

At the same time, John Francome, former champion National Hunt jockey, was fined £750 and suspended from riding until June 3, the end of the season, for a breach of one rule.

After the hearing at the Jockey Club in Portman Square, Mr Banks, who was also fined a total of £2,500, said he would be in the High Court today to contest the disciplinary decision. He

described the day's events as a "Kangaroo court" and claimed the issue was a matter of the establishment against gamblers.

In a statement, the Jockey Club disciplinary committee said that the two men had committed breaches of the rule "in that Francome had supplied confidential information to Mr Banks, at Mr Banks's request, concerning horses in training and had received favours therefore".

Francome said he would consider an appeal and added: "I do not believe I have ever done anything wrong."

Kentucky Derby: 6 May

Affirmed lands Kentucky Derby

Steve Cauthen, the brilliant young jockey who broke all prize earnings records in the United States last year, continued his triumphant way when landing the Kentucky Derby on Saturday with Affirmed.

Top two-year-old in the United States last season, Affirmed was second favourite at 9-5.

Cauthen, 18, held Affirmed at the back of the field until about three furlongs from home, when

he gave the colt his head. Affirmed pulled smoothly away, led by three lengths a furlong out and passed the post a length clear. Alydar, the favourite, put in a late challenge to finish second, with Believe It third.

[Affirmed went on to complete the US Triple Crown, the 11th horse to do so, winning the Belmont Stakes on 10 June by a head from Alydar, who finished runner-up in all three classics.]

ENGLISH CLASSICS

2,000 Guineas	Roland Gardens	F Durr	28-1
1,000 Guineas	Enstone Park	E Johnson	35-1
Derby	Shirley Heights	G Starkey	8-1
Oaks	Fair Salinia	G Starkey	8-1
St Leger	Julio Mariner	E Hide	28-1

The Derby Epsom: 7 June

Starkey times it to perfection on Shirley Heights

By HOTSPUR (Peter Scott)

Shirley Heights, bred at the Yorkshire stud of Lord Halifax's family and trained at Arundel by John Dunlop, gave yesterday's Derby a welcoming English flavour after wins by Empery and The Minstrel in the previous two years.

Greville Starkey brought Shirley Heights swooping down close home to win by a head after Hawaiian Sound had looked as if he would give the American star Willie Shoemaker a Derby win on his first ride at Epsom – at the age of 46.

Shirley Heights completed a magnificent double for the National Stud stallion Mill Reef, who also sired Acamas, winner of Sunday's Prix du Jockey Club (French Derby). Shirley Heights may not have Mill Reef's brilliance, but Derby winners come no tougher. This was his fourth race of 1978, and none has been easy.

Lord Halifax owns this colt in partnership with his son Lord Irwin, and last month Shirley Heights realised a family ambition by winning the Mecca-Dante Stakes at York, where Lord Halifax is chairman of the Race Committee.

Shoemaker decided to take an early lead when finding the pace slower than he expected. Hawaiian Sound (25-1) beat off challenges from Julio Mariner, Remainder Man and Pyjama Hunt in the straight, but he drifted away from the rails near home and left a gap through which Starkey sent Shirley Heights (8-1).

Remainder Man (40-1) improved his fine record with a most creditable third, running on courageously to finish a length and a half behind Hawaiian Sound. The Vincent O'Brien-trained Inkerman (4-1), whose claims to favouritism had always looked fragile, finished with only four behind him, and Lester Piggott confirmed that his mount had no excuses as the race was run.

[Shirley Heights (5-4f) became the fifth English Derby winner to confirm his Epsom title in the Irish Sweeps equivalent, beating Exdirectory (8-1) and Hawaiian Sound (6-1) by a head and a neck, with Inkerman in 4th place.]

Jockey Club Inquiry: 5 December

Acamas ruled out from Ascot race: Trainer fined £250

By HOTSPUR (Peter Scott)

Acamas, second in Ascot's King George VI and Queen Elizabeth Diamond Stakes on July 22, has been disqualified because salicylic acid was found in his post-race urine sample. Guy Bonaventure, his trainer at that time, has been fined £250.

Bonaventure flew from Paris to attend yesterday's Jockey Club inquiry in London. His lawyer said after the hearing that traces of salicylic acid had derived from aspirins which Acamas was given some days before the big Ascot race. This is an officially prohibited substance, and once its presence was established, Acamas's disqualification became automatic.

Hawaiian Sound and Montcontour have been promoted to second and third place behind Ile de Bourbon, who beat Acamas by a length and a half.

Acamas won the Prix Lupin and the Prix du Jockey Club before carrying M Marcel Boussac's colours for the last time at Ascot. He was then bought by the Aga Khan and Irish breeder Capt.Tim Rogers and joined François Mathet's stable. After finishing 12th in the 'Arc', this Mill Reef colt was retired to the Ballymany Stud in Ireland and demand for his stallion services next spring is heavy.

19 July

Irate Walwyn asks Wildenstein to take horses away

By HOTSPUR (Peter Scott)

Peter Walwyn has asked M Daniel Wildenstein to remove the two dozen horses who joined his stable in February.

A rift between owner and trainer began to develop at Royal Ascot last month when M Wildenstein criticised Pat Eddery, Walwyn's jockey. Walwyn made it a clean break yesterday after learning from Weatherbys, the Jockey Club secretaries, that M Wildenstein had cancelled his "authority to act" as regards making entries, withdrawals, and other trainer's duties.

Walwyn and Eddery are a highly successful combination, whose intense mutual loyalty is apparent to all in the racing world. Walwyn quite rightly took the strongest exception to M Wildenstein's sour and ill-justified criticism of how Eddery rode Buckskin in the Ascot Gold Cup.

Buckskin suffers from foot corns and this problem interfered with his Gold Cup training. Eddery, England's champion jockey for the last four seasons, gave him every chance in the Gold Cup, but Buckskin weakened in the straight to finish fourth.

M Wildenstein openly expressed the view that Yves Saint-Martin or Lester Piggott would have done better. Had Walwyn attempted to prolong the Wildenstein association, he would have faced pressure to replace Eddery in important races with a rider of M Wildenstein's own choosing.

The Wildenstein horses have been very successful during their time with Walwyn. Crow has won the Coronation Cup and Ormonde Stakes, Leonardo da Vinci the White Rose Stakes, and Buckskin himself the Prix du Cadran, which is France's principal long-distance race for older horses.

OTHER MAJOR RACES

Irish Derby	Shirley Heights	G Starkey	5-4f
Arc de Triomphe	Alleged	L Piggott	14-10f
Kentucky Derby	Affirmed	S Cauthen	9-5
Melbourne Cup	Arwon	H White	5-1

Prix de l'Arc de Triomphe Longchamp: 1 October

Alleged and Piggott reign supreme in great 'Arc' double

By HOTSPUR (Peter Scott)

Alleged won his second Prix de l'Arc de Triomphe with minimum fuss at Longchamp yesterday. He beat Trillion by two lengths to provide both Lester Piggott and trainer Vincent O'Brien with their third victories in this race.

Mr Robert Sangster's brilliant four-year-old justified 14-10 favouritism with a predictable run. Never out of the fist four, he was shaken up two furlongs from home and quickened straight away to pass Dom Alaric and Frere Basile, who were fighting for the lead.

Willie Shoemaker switched Trillion out from the rails to challenge, but he could never close with Alleged. Dancing Maid was another two lengths behind Trillion in third place.

St Leger winner Julio Mariner and Exdirectory never got near the leaders, and both finished out of the first 10.

"Alleged is as good a horse as I have ridden, and Vincent O'Brien has done a marvellous job because this colt's illness had made him a doubtful runner until a few weeks ago," said Piggott.

While Piggott's handling of Alleged earned general acclaim, Trillion's trainer, Maurice Zilber, was not too happy with Shoemaker's jockeyship. Zilber considered that Shoemaker was too small to get the best out of this big filly and felt that in different circumstances Trillion would have given Alleged a much tougher fight.

Alleged has won nine of his 10 races, worth more than £300,000, and becomes the first dual Arc winner since his great-grandsire, Ribot, more than 20 years ago.

1979

22 Jan Mrs Linda Jones creates New Zealand racing history when she rides Holy Toledo to a head victory over Drum Short in the Wellington Derby at Trentham, the first success for a woman rider in a New Zealand classic – in the first season women jockeys have been allowed to ride.

16 Feb The Grundy colt, trained by Jeremy Tree for Mr Khaled Abdullah, whose 264,000gns purchase last October set a European yearling record has been named Mushoor - Arabic for "par excellence".

3 May Unbeaten One in a Million (1-1) justifies hot favouritism in the 1,000 Guineas to become the first English Classic winner owned by a business company for advertising purposes, Helena Springfield Ltd, a London-based firm.

28 Jun Appeals by trainer Harry Wragg against Buz Kashi's Coronation Stakes disqualification at Royal Ascot and the suspension of her jockey Paul Cook are dismissed. The body of opinion is that the rules need amending, in that the stewards, once they have satisfied themselves that a jockey is guilty of "careless riding", have no option but to disqualify her mount. Thus Buz Kashi (33-1), although acknowledged to have deservedly won by 1 1/2 lengths, is still disqualified.

1 Oct Greystoke trainer Gordon Richards sends 5 runners to local track Carlisle and all win, completing a 2,599-1 accumulator.

7 Oct Derby winner Troy is beaten into third place as the French filly Three Troikas wins the Prix de l'Arc de Triomphe at Longchamp. The win gives jockey Freddie Head the post-war riding record of four Arc victories.

Champion Hurdle Cheltenham: 14 March

Monksfield again a true champion

Sea Pigeon beaten for second time

By MARLBOROUGH (John Oaksey)

For the second year running Monksfield (9-4f) and Sea Pigeon (6-1) fought an epic duel for the Waterford Crystal Champion Hurdle at Cheltenham yesterday.

The result was the same, but this time there was real magic in the damp grey air. I never expect to see a finer hurdle race.

Forced to make almost all his own running and headed by Sea Pigeon before the last flight, Monksfield landed on the flat with his title apparently slipping away. But no horse ever refused more stubbornly to recognise defeat, and his fight-back up the hill for a three-quarter length victory brought tears to many an eye, English as well as Irish.

It was sad that there had to be a loser, and on ground far softer than he likes Sea Pigeon had probably never run a better race. The rapier of his speed blunted a little by the mud, was simply turned aside on the steel core which Monksfield uses for a heart.

Dessie Hughes took Monksfield straight to the front and steered him boldly wide in search of the best ground. Both Sea Pigeon and Kybo, who unluckily slipped on landing over the second-last fence, followed his lead, and those who unwisely took the conventional shorter route were all beaten a long way from home.

Monksfield gave a flawless exhibition of quick clean hurdling. Again and again he saved ground and energy in the air. As for those of us who dared suggest that the little stallion might be losing his enthusiasm, we can only hang our heads in respectful shame.

Grand National Aintree: 31 March

Rubstic the brave

By John Oaksey

The sun shone bright at Aintree yesterday, but as Mr John Douglas's Rubstic won the Colt Car Grand National for Scotland, the rest of the racing world felt more like tears than laughter.

For no less than 10 horses had either been knocked over or brought down at the Chair in the worst mass pile-up since Foinavon's year. And worse, far worse than that, the Gold Cup winner, Alverton, is dead, killed by the drop on the landing side of Becher's Brook, second time round.

Starting inevitably hot favourite (13-2), Alverton had miraculously got through the carnage in front of the stands with nothing worse than a violent bump and loss of half a dozen lengths.

So as Wagner led Zongalero and the other survivors down towards Becher's for the second time, poor Jonjo O'Neill must have felt that his Grand National luck had changed at last. A moment later he stood broken-hearted by the famous brook.

The only possible consolation is that Alverton died instantaneously, but this was the cruellest possible ending to a long, honourable and versatile career in which the Cheltenham Gold Cup was only the latest and greatest of his 22 victories on the Flat and over hurdles and fences.

Rubstic (25-1) had cannily avoided all the accidents and only Zongalero (20-1) was still with him when they reached the long run-in.

Zongalero's energy began to fade and Rubstic grew stronger as jockey Maurice Barnes called for his ultimate effort. It got him home, Scotland's first ever winner of the Grand National.

CHAMPIONS

Jockey (Flat)	Joe Mercer	164
Jockey (NH)	John Francome	95
Racehorse of the Year	Troy	3-y-o
NH Champion of the Year	Monksfield	7-y-o
Leading Trainer	Henry Cecil	£683,971
Leading Owner	Sir Michael Sobell	£339,751
Leading Money Winner	Troy	£310,359

Cheltenham Gold Cup: 15 March

Gallant Alverton may now tackle Grand National

By HOTSPUR (Peter Scott)

Alverton defied snow and mud to become yesterday's hero of the Piper Champagne Cheltenham Gold Cup. He won by 25 lengths, but Tied Cottage was putting up stern resistance when falling at the last fence.

Tied Cottage (12-1) had been in front from the start and at one stage held a long lead. The Irish horse retained a fractional advantage over Alverton (5-1jf) when his last-fence error ended their battle. Brown Lad, twice second in this race, started joint favourite with Alverton, but the Irish veteran reverted to his old habit of lagging far behind early on and never got on terms.

Peter Easterby, Alverton's trainer, favours tackling the Grand National next. Alverton has only 10st 13lb at Aintree, and as Easterby points out he will never be so favourably handicapped again.

NATIONAL HUNT

Champion Hurdle	Monksfield	DT Hughes	9-4f
Cheltenham Gold Cup	Alverton	JJ O'Neill	5-1jf
Grand National	Rubstic	M Barnes	25-1

ENGLISH CLASSICS

2,000 Guineas	Tap on Wood	S Cauthen	20-1
1,000 Guineas	One in a Million	J Mercer	1-1f
Derby	Troy	W Carson	6-1
Oaks	Scintillate	P Eddery	20-1
St Leger	Son of Love	A Lequeux	20-1

Troy romps home alone in the Derby

The Derby Epsom: 6 June

Troy's brilliant speed routs his Derby rivals

By HOTSPUR (Peter Scott)

Troy, a Derby winner of exceptional vintage, came from what looked a hopeless position to win yesterday's 200th running by a seven-length margin that has not been bettered since Manna's eight lengths victory in 1925.

Milford, the Queen's hope, whom Willie Carson proved so right in rejecting to ride Troy (6-1), finished only 10th. Dickens Hill (15-1), the Irish 2,000 Guineas winner, and the French outsider Northern Baby (66-1), were second and third.

Carson must have felt a worried man halfway through the race when Milford lay second and Troy was badly placed. Not only did the eventual winner appear to be struggling, but he had also lost ground when two others in front of him dropped back.

Lyphard's Wish, as expected, made the running. He had beaten off Milford's challenge with two furlongs to go, but then Dickens Hill came through to take a brief lead.

Troy, who had entered the straight with at least a dozen in front of him, was then switched from the rails and began to eat up ground. He passed Dickens Hill almost as if that horse was standing still and then drew right away.

Carson and Troy's trainer, Dick Hern, were both winning their first Derby. Sir Michael Sobell and his son-in-law, Sir Arnold Weinstock, are the joint owners of Troy, who was bred at the family's Ballymacoll stud in Ireland.

[Troy (4-9) goes on to outclass his rivals in a fast-run Irish Derby, having 4 lengths to spare over 2nd-placed Dickens Hill (9-2), and then coasts to an easy King George victory (2-5f) at Ascot, but the Arc proves a race too many.]

Queen Elizabeth II Stakes Ascot: 29 September

Golden Kris races on and on

By John Oaksey

Lord Howard de Walden's Kris gave us another golden moment at Ascot yesterday in the Queen Elizabeth II Stakes, bringing his score to a triumphant 10 wins from 11 races. It was sad, of course, that Tap on Wood, author of that one defeat, could not be present, but he would have needed every last ounce of his courage and speed to confirm the 2,000 Guineas result.

In a fast-run race, Joe Mercer left nothing to chance, and this time, unlike their last effort here,

Ascot Gold Cup: 21 June

Le Moss gallops to memorable Gold Cup triumph

By HOTSPUR (Peter Scott)

Le Moss emerged from the shadow of Buckskin with a magnificent performance in yesterday's Ascot Gold Cup. He beat his older stable-companion by seven lengths after a fast-run race that provided Lester Piggott's ninth Gold Cup victory.

Buckskin (10-11f), having his final race, finished leg-weary though not lame. Le Moss's high-class acceleration took him from third to first place in the 100 yards between entering the straight and passing the two-furlong pole. Le Moss (7-4) then drew steadily clear, looking as good as did his full-brother Levmoss when he won the Gold Cup in 1969.

Henry Cecil, accomplishing the fine performance of saddling first and second in this race, still admitted to finding it a bitter-sweet result. Buckskin, whose bravery had overcome persistent unsoundness, has a special place in Cecil's heart and was kept in training this year with the sole object of a Gold Cup triumph.

OTHER MAJOR RACES

Irish Derby	Troy	W Carson	4-9f
Arc de Triomphe	Three Troikas	F Head	88-10
Kentucky Derby	Spectacular Bid	RJ Franklin	3-5f
Melbourne Cup	Hyperno	H White	7-1

Tote-Ebor Handicap York: 22 August

Pure magic from old Sea Pigeon

By MARLBOROUGH (John Oaksey)

Sea Pigeon and Jonjo O'Neill together, by winning the Tote-Ebor by a couple of rapidly vanishing inches yesterday, gave York a moment of pure magic. Two moments to be exact, for after Jonjo had steered his old friend into the second's enclosure (not by design but because he lost his way!) the judge took some time to announce the result.

When he did so, two words, "No.1", produced perhaps the loudest cheer of even Sea Pigeon's fabulous career.

That career began with a victory, trained by Jeremy Tree as a two-year-old for Mr Jock Whitney, in the Duke of Edinburgh Stakes at Ascot. Two years later, Mr Muldoon bought Sea Pigeon for £10,000 – "including VAT," he says, "so the Government has a bit of him too."

Since that happy day, this incredible nine-year-old has earned £160,000 in win and place prize-money, a total of 11 victories on the Flat and 15 over hurdles.

Unlike Brown Jack, who won a Champion Hurdle before his Ebor, Sea Pigeon has of course so far missed the big one at Cheltenham. He is surely the greatest hurdler ever not to win a championship – but, who knows, that could still be put right.

After coming to pass Donegal Prince and win his race, Jonjo dropped his hands at least three strides too soon. Sea Pigeon (18-1), quite rightly thinking he had won, took this as a signal to down tools, and in one more stride Donegal Prince (33-1) would have got back in front. After showing Jonjo the film, the stewards gave him a friendly and unofficial caution.

everything went his and Kris's way. With Bolide trying to pull Willie Carson's arms out in front, Joe sat second from the start, and the moment they straightened out for home he sent Kris into his favourite position.

The only remaining question was the winning distance, and neither Kris (8-11f) nor his rider are in the habit of doing these things by halves. They did not relax the pressure and in the end Foveros (16-1) was beaten five lengths in very fast time.

The 1980s

Racing in the eighties became really big business. In 1980 an American colt was syndicated for over $22m, followed in 1983 by the sale of a yearling for $10m – and that was just the start. A "mega bucks" industry indeed. All the English Classics were sponsored in 1984. Arab owners began to dominate English racing, and the Maktoum family of Dubai had upwards of a thousand horses in training world-wide.

Two big international races were established in 1981 at opposite sides of the world, the Japan Cup (1¹/₂mi) in Tokyo and the Arlington Million (1¹/₄mi) in Chicago, both inviting the best middle-distance horses from around the globe. Among the winners of the latter, amazingly enough, was a five-year-old British gelding called Teleprompter, owned by Lord Derby. This victory in 1985 prompted the Jockey Club to open up several important races to geldings the following year, including the "King George" and the Ascot Gold Cup.

The decade was not short on sensations. The 1981 Derby winner, Shergar, was kidnapped in 1983 from the Aga Khan's stud in Ireland and never seen again. Then Lester Piggott, who set a new record for Classic winners before retiring from the saddle in 1985, was jailed for three years in 1987 for tax evasion.

Meanwhile a new name joined the jockeys' roll of honour: Steve Cauthen, who, as the youngest winner of the US Triple Crown (with Affirmed in 1978), came over from the States and won the fillies' Triple Crown on Oh So Sharp (1985), not to mention three jockeys' titles and two Derbys.

Record after record was broken in National Hunt racing by trainers Michael Dickinson and Martin Pipe and jockeys John Francome and Peter Scudamore. And jumpers provided some of the most wonderful moments of the racing decade – Bob Champion's poignant National victory on Aldaniti in 1981 and the thrilling exploits of Sea Pigeon, Dawn Run and the incomparable "Dessie".

There's nothing better for the sponsor than a tight finish: Secreto (20) shades El Gran Senor in the 1984 Ever Ready Derby

1980

12 Mar Spectacular Bid, the 1979 Kentucky Derby winner, is syndicated for stud duty at Claiborne Farm, Kentucky, for a record $22m (£10m), based on 40 shares of $550,000 (£250,000). The previous record was $16.5m (£7.5m) for Troy, last year's Derby and Irish Derby winner.

13 Mar A stewards' inspection finds parts of the Lingfield course waterlogged and tomorrow's programme becomes the 50th of the National Hunt season to be abandoned.

29 Mar Leading American amateur rider Charlie Fenwick wins his first English steeplechase – the Grand National, on Ben Nevis. His grandfather Howard Bruce owned Billy Barton, unluckily beaten in the 1928 National.

26 April Royal Mail, wearing a special bridle, wins the Whitbread Gold Cup at Sandown only 6 weeks after breaking his jaw in a crashing fall in the Cheltenham Gold Cup.

2 Jun Judge Graham Wemyss admits making a mistake in interpreting the photo of the finish to the Walmer Handicap at Folkestone and reverses his decision, placing King Hustler (12-1) 1st and Summary (9-4) 2nd, though bets on the race are decided on the original result.

8 Jun Willie Carson completes a remarkable 5-day treble, following his Derby and Oaks successes, by riding

Policeman (53-1) to victory at Chantilly in the Prix du Jockey Club, the French counterpart of the Derby.

31 July Muis Roberts, who rode 21 winners in England when attached to Gavin Hunter's stable in 1978, sets a South African record with 185 winners this season, beating Tiger Smith's score of 175 in 1950.

18 Aug George Duffield guides 2-y-o Spindrifter to his 11th win of the season at Leicester – in his only defeat of the season he was ridden by another jockey.

---

4 March

Wyatt attacks Sporting Life 'biased reporting'

By HOTSPUR (Peter Scott)

Mr Woodrow Wyatt's zest for a battle, spiced by the natural preference for a battle which he clearly regards as almost won, was reflected in a 25-minute speech by the Tote chairman concerning payout irregularities. Using offence as the best defence when speaking at the Tote's annual lunch in London, he savaged the Sporting Life for biased reporting of the whole case, which that daily racing paper originally exposed last July.

He drew a contrast with its relatively small coverage of Ladbrokes' withdrawn casino licences and Levy Board payment problems, and he stressed the speed with which he had asked the Home Secretary to set up an independent inquiry and the very small proportion of Tote bets involved.

The judicial findings were that improper reductions had been made not for personal gain but through misplaced enthusiasm by various Tote employees. Mr Aglionby, a Recorder of the Crown Court, conducted the five-month inquiry which found there had been improper reductions from 14 dual forecast dividends and from six win dividends.

The Tote chairman pointed out that 25,500 dividends from various pools were paid out last year and that the promise to meet all irregularity differences in full involved no more than £10,000. Tote turnover last year was £72 million.

The very low forecast payout on a Carlisle race won on 4 July by an 11-1 chance

from a 20-1 chance sparked off the Sporting Life investigations. The reason for it, said Mr Wyatt, was that a dual forecast bet of 50 10p units was mistakenly transmitted as a £50 bet.

The Sporting Life investigations then widened considerably, but Mr Wyatt seems less than fair in describing them as a "malevolent campaign to destroy the Tote" by a paper heavily dependent on bookmakers' advertisements. The Tote also advertises regularly with the Sporting Life.

Mr Wyatt, who has no intention of resigning, emphasised that no member of his board was aware of the irregular dealings, and said that there would not be a board left in England if mass resignations followed employees' abuse of their positions.

"I not only regretted the reduced dual forecast dividends, but they made me extremely angry," said Mr Wyatt. "I devised the present form of Tote dual forecast, first introduced in May 1977, and always hoped to promote them by spectacular dividends." He said that the Tote's soaring profits – £207,000 in his first year as chairman to £1,335,000 last year – still owed 60 percent to pool betting.

Mr William Whitelaw, Home Secretary, also spoke at the lunch. He strengthened Mr Wyatt's position by saying, after full investigations and the promise of tighter security in future, the whole case should be considered closed.

Plumpton: 4 March

Prince Charles is denied debut win

By MARLBOROUGH (John Oaksey)

Prince Charles's first active appearance on a racecourse was a mixture of success and disappointment as both he and a large, happy crowd enjoyed every moment of the Madhatters' Private Sweepstakes (2m flat). The only small blot on a golden afternoon was that one horse went slightly faster than the Prince's mount Long Wharf.

When I say "slight blot", I do not refer to the BBC's Derek Thompson, who fulfilled a lifelong ambition by winning on Classified. For a moment he was not the most popular man in the south of England. But in the end no one, least of all Prince Charles, held it against him.

"Next time I shall know a bit more about how to catch up," the Prince said afterwards. But apart from one moment, he had – as anyone who knows how

foolish racehorses can make a beginner look – acquitted himself with honour. That moment came halfway through the race, at the top of the Plumpton hill, when he let the two leading horses get away from him as they set off like mad down the slope.

Long Wharf (13-8f) failed to get up by two lengths and would have won in another 100 yards or so. His rider's only regret was on behalf of those whom he feared "might have put too much money on me".

[Prince Charles's first ride over fences was on the unplaced Sea Swell 4 days later at Sandown in the Duke of Gloucester Memorial Trophy, an amateur riders' 'chase over 3m 118yd, but he drew praise from jockey John Francome ("Very, very tidy") and trainer Fred Rimell ("A good style for a new boy").]

Waterford Crystal Champion Hurdle Cheltenham: 11 March

Sea Pigeon takes sweet revenge
By MARLBOROUGH (John Oaksey)

"He did just what he threatened to do to us last year." There was respect as well as sadness in the voice of Monksfield's rider Dessie Hughes as he described the triumph of Sea Pigeon *(right)* in the Champion Hurdle. Sad though it was to see the champion beaten, no one, not even Monksfield's most fervent admirer, could begrudge the winner his sweet, delayed revenge.

This was the sixth time the two had met, and the score, including three Champion Hurdles, was Monksfield five Sea Pigeon nil. But this time Pat Muldoon's great 10-year-old left no room for doubt. He and Jonjo O'Neill have given us many unforgettable moments, but now, for the first time, they got it absolutely right at Cheltenham.

The shorter course, and eight flights of hurdles instead of nine, probably told in Sea Pigeon's (13-2) favour. Certainly Monksfield (6-5f) used to love that steep climb past the stands first time round. But no one in the

loser's camp was offering any serious excuses. "If we had to be beaten, he was the only one to do it," they said of the horse that at the finish was going further ahead with every stride and won by seven lengths.

And, whatever his rank among Champion Hurdlers – he is the oldest winner for 30 years – Sea Pigeon, whose flat-race triumphs include the Chester Cup and the Ebor Handicap, can unquestionably claim to be one of the great all-rounders.

Cheltenham: 13 March

Whip controversy mars final day
By MARLBOROUGH (John Oaksey)

The whipping controversy raged again at Cheltenham when Joe Byrne – who is, they tell me, Ireland's champion jumping jockey – became the second of his countrymen to be reported to the Stewards of the Jockey Club for "excessive and improper use".

Unlike Tommy Ryan, Byrne did not even have victory to console him. Landing over the last flight in second place on Batista, he appeared to be handed the Daily Express Triumph Hurdle on a plate when the leader, Starfen, blundered and violently ejected Tommy Carmody. But Batista was desperately tired, and, instead of attempting to hold him together and help him up the hill, Byrne proceeded to give a painfully lifelike imitation of a man beating a carpet.

At the last Haydock meeting, he was fined £50 for

"excessive use", but the message clearly did not penetrate. As the race was run, any reasonably competent amateur prepared to sit still and push would have won on Batista – but he still would have been a doubly lucky winner. Heighlin, who got up to pip him in the last stride admirably ridden by Steve Jobar, had been stopped in his tracks by Starfen's blunder and actually had to jump Tommy Carmody before he could get going.

The stewards' first reaction to this hectic finish was no surprise – but it was not their last. After hearing a vet's report of marks on Andy Turnell's mount Hill of Slane (who finished third), they fined Andy £50. I have watched the film of the finish several times and can only totally disagree with the stewards' decision. Because, although Andy did slap Hill of

Cheltenham Gold Cup: 13 March

Brave 'Cottage' gives Carberry share in record
By HOTSPUR (Peter Scott)

Tied Cottage, leading throughout the Tote-sponsored Cheltenham Gold Cup to win by eight lengths, provided Tommy Carberry's fourth Gold Cup victory and enabled him to equal the race record now shared with his great Irish compatriot Pat Taaffe.

Second in 1977 and a last-fence faller when fighting for the lead with Alverton 12 months ago, Tied Cottage (13-2) finally went on the Gold Cup's winning roll with a display of stamina and sound jumping that proved too much for his weary opponents. Carberry sent him into a clear lead before Diamond Edge (5-2f) closed the gap with a mile to go, but the Irish veteran was merely taking a breather.

Diamond Edge suddenly ran out of steam racing down the hill, and Approaching then emerged as the likeliest danger. But Tied Cottage's gallop had worn him down entering the straight. Mac Vidi (66-1) kept on bravely, but the mudlark Master Smudge (14-1) came through to deprive him of second place.

[Tied Cottage was later one of three Irish-trained horses disqualified from their Cheltenham races after routine tests revealed an irregular substance thought to come from a consignment of equine nuts delivered to their stables in infected containers. No suspicion of malpractice was directed at the trainers, but this is irrelevant to the disqualification rules.]

2,000 Guineas Newmarket: 3 May

Guineas first Nureyev disqualified
By HOTSPUR (Peter Scott)

French-trained Nureyev, the 13-8 favourite, was disqualified at Newmarket after passing the post first in the 2,000 Guineas, and Known Fact (14-1), beaten a neck, promoted to first. Prompt action by the stewards saved Pat Eddery from having to lodge an objection to Nureyev for badly interfering with his mount Posse, who finished third, three-quarters of a length behind Known Fact, and was placed second.

The incident, missed by the television cameras but clearly shown up by the stewards' head-on patrol film, took place

about two furlongs from home. Nureyev and Posse went for the same gap. The French horse got there first but gave Posse a bad bump, knocking him right back. Eddery had to switch position and make up lengths at a crucial stage. He did well to finish such a close third.

Ideally Nureyev should have been placed third, but the rules do not permit this, and he was put back to last. His jockey Philippe Paquet was suspended for seven days. Nureyev is 6-1 favourite for the Derby, although his stamina cannot be guaranteed.

Slane seven or eight times after the last flight, "slap" is the word – not "hit". He never even "picked up" the whip, but held it throughout in the carrying position. It is a physical impossibility to hit a horse hard like that, and if Hill of Slane was marked, he must have an exceptionally thin skin.

I am fully aware, of course, that this will be regarded in some quarters as a grossly prejudiced Anglophile report. I can only reply that I have nothing but respect for top-class Irish jockeys like

Tommy Carberry and Dessie Hughes. But the riding of some of their lesser compatriots at this meeting has been unpleasant to watch – a disgrace to an honourable profession.

[Irish jockeys Joe Byrne and Tommy Ryan were both suspended for three months for their riding at Cheltenham. After a race at Liverpool a fortnight later, Turnell was charged again with excessive use and misuse of the whip on Hill of Slane, but completely exonerated by the Jockey Club disciplinary stewards.]

Derby Epsom: 4 June

Courageous Henbit's career may end with Derby triumph

By HOTSPUR (Peter Scott)

Henbit fractured a bone in his off-fore foot when winning the Derby in most heroic fashion and cannot run again this season. His stallion value having soared to at least £3 million, the chances are that Henbit's racing career is over.

The first sign that something was amiss came just after Henbit (7-1) had taken the lead from Rankin one and a half furlongs from home. He veered suddenly and sharply to his right, against the camber of the course. Master Willie (22-1) reduced Henbit's lead throughout the last furlong and finished second, three-quarters of a length behind, while Rankin (14-1) stayed on to finish third.

Yesterday's classic, condemned in advance as below normal Derby standard, was run in a time bettered only by the great Nijinsky in the post-war years, 2m 34.77s. It had another hero in Mister Willie, who contracted a throat infection two weeks ago which caused him to miss five days' exercise and, even more important, to go entirely off his feed for four days.

Willie Carson's main fear in preferring Henbit to Water Mill was that the descent to Tattenham Corner might upset his mount. Henbit in fact was labouring at that stage, but once in the straight he surged forward, while Water Mill, whose rider Tony Murray reported that he met with repeated interference, finished 10th. Nikoli, the disappointing Irish-trained 4-1 favourite, was cool enough beforehand, but the hill found him out, and he finished eighth.

Several of the 24 jockeys described it as a rough race, and blamed Philippe Paquet for some of the buffeting before halfway. His mount Garrido, was best of the French in fifth place.

Henbit's owner Mrs Arpad Plesch, who enjoyed a previous Derby triumph with Psidium in 1961, has followed her late husband's example in naming her horses after plants.

Oaks Epsom: 7 June

Bireme ends 29-year wait
By Tony Stafford

Bireme ended a 29-year wait for owner-breeder Mr Dick Hollingsworth at Epsom on Saturday, winning the Oaks to provide his Arches Hall Stud in Hertfordshire with its first Classic success. She also gave trainer Dick Hern and jockey Willie Carson their second Derby-Oaks double in successive years. Bireme (9-2) returned the fastest Oaks time, 2m 34.33s, since the record books began to list them in 1846.

King George VI & Queen Elizabeth Diamond Stakes Ascot: 26 July

Ela-Mana-Mou's 'King George' is echo of Grundy
By HOTSPUR (Peter Scott)

Memories of Grundy's epic struggle with Bustino five years earlier were revived in the King George VI and Queen Elizabeth Diamond Stakes when displays of class and courage by Ela-Mana-Mou and Mrs Penny provided another stirring finish.

Half a length separated Grundy and Bustino, while Ela-Mana-Mou (11-4) beat Mrs Penny (9-1) by three-quarters of a length, and in each of these splendid Ascot races the two principals drew five lengths clear of the opposition.

Dick Hern, Bustino's trainer, was this time on the winning side, and Ela-Mana-Mou's undefeated four-year-old campaign reflects the greatest credit on him. Willie Carson's determination matched that of his mount, whose maturity told near the finish after his younger rival had drawn almost level.

Mrs Penny and Lester Piggott also proved a formidable combination, although, with benefit of hindsight, Lester might have waited a little longer and challenged wider to avoid the protracted battle.

Goodwood Cup: 31 July

Le Moss courage clinches unique staying sequence
By HOTSPUR (Peter Scott)

Le Moss led throughout the Goodwood Cup to beat Ardross by a neck. Ardross's 2lb allowance enabled the gallant Irish colt to make a magnificent race a still closer struggle than was last month's Ascot Gold Cup.

Le Moss became the first horse in racing history to win both the Ascot Gold Cup and the Goodwood Cup in consecutive years. The Goodwood Cup was founded in 1812 and Le Moss is the eighth horse to win it twice running. The history of the Ascot Gold Cup, Europe's premier long-distance race, stretches back even further, to 1807. Le Moss is among the 12 horses to have won it in consecutive years, but Sagaro's hat-trick (1975-77) is unique.

Ardross (9-4) took second place three furlongs from home, and a furlong later was almost level with Le Moss (4-7f). But the courageous champion, brought to perfection by Henry Cecil despite his delicate training problems, refused to yield up his lead. He and Joe Mercer provided the perfect picture of resolution, rhythm and power. Ardross and Christy Roche lost nothing in defeat, but the five-year-old Le Moss is the more mature horse, with more than twice as many races under his belt.

While stars like these two are around to thrill and delight the race crowds, there is every justification for maintaining the long-distance cups in their present form. These heroes, like Sagaro and Buckskin before them, may not fatten the wallets of commercial breeders, but for that very reason they race longer and therefore take a firm hold on racegoers' hearts.

[Le Moss (4-6f) went on to beat Ardross (13-8) again by a neck in the Doncaster Cup to complete the supreme triple crown of long-distance cups for the second consecutive year.]

Yorkshire Handicap Ripon: 4 August

Red-flag blunder results in chaos over bets
By MARLBOROUGH (John Oaksey)

A red flag, waved by mistake at Ripon, set the local stewards on a collision course with the Sporting Life, the accepted arbiters of betting problems in this country. The first edition of the Yorkshire Handicap was spoiled – and in the stewards' opinion rendered null and void – by the inadvertent use of a red flag by an overzealous recall man. But as the starting stalls opened (quite normally), starting prices were (quite normally) returned for the 14 starters. And, according to Sporting Life, those, under Tattersalls rules, were the only starting prices that can count.

To the Ripon stewards, on the other hand, the most notable feature of this fiasco was that, while eight jockeys ignored the red flag and went on, six pulled up and went no further. In fairness to those six, the stewards declared the race void and reopened it an hour later.

When five horses turned out for the re-run – four who had pulled up plus the original winner, Wynburry – the usual betting-ring observers, including one from the Sporting Life, duly entered a starting price.

Not at all surprisingly, the second, re-run edition of the race was won by a horse who had taken no active part in the first, Swaying Tree, 4-1 originally, but now 6-5 favourite. He also had a different jockey, his original rider having been injured.

According to the stewards, betting should be settled on the re-run SP, with nine non-runners. The Sporting Life, on the other hand, insist that the Ripon stewards broke the Rules of Racing by declaring all bets on the first race void.

[Bookies were divided over the dispute. Some applied their own rules.]

Wetherby: 15 October

Easterby & O'Neill sweep the board

By Tony Stafford

Peter Easterby and Jonjo O'Neill, champion jump trainer and rider, gave notice at Wetherby that their titles will not be easily taken this season. They teamed up for four winners, Alick, Clayside, Davidoff and Selby, O'Neill having already won the first race with Jimmy Fitzgerald's Wyn-Bank. Then, in the bumper's event, Easterby's amateur son Tim partnered his father's Wink the Cop to victory.

Easterby has held a trainer's licence for 30 years, but for all his well-publicised achievements with Sea Pigeon, yesterday's feat was astonishing, for all five horses were making their seasonable debuts. The Easterby quintet paid 2,859-1, and O'Neill, whose other ride Andy Pandy was pulled up, landed a 4,399 nap hand.

OTHER MAJOR RACES

Irish Derby	Tyrnavos	A Murray	25-1
Arc de Triomphe	Detroit	P Eddery	67-10
Kentucky Derby	Genuine Risk	J Vasquez	133-10
Melbourne Cup	Beldale Ball	J Letts	11-1

Willie Shoemaker on Soaf shows Joe Mercer the way home

Chivas Regal Trophy Sandown Park: 22 October

Genius Shoemaker hands out lesson to locals

By MARLBOROUGH (John Oaksey)

Willie Shoemaker takes a size two in boots and weighs 6st 11lb in his colours. But at the age of 49 he taught British racing a salutary lesson at Sandown Park by winning the first Chivas Regal Trophy for the United States. Two victories out of three won him the individual prize by five points and, with his Panamanian team-mate Laffit Pincay in second place, the visitors beat the home team all ends up.

Pat Eddery finally saved us from a duck by winning the Chivas Regal Stayers' Handicap on Yellow Jersey (9-1). But he had to pull out all the stops – harried home by Messrs Cordero and Pincay. By that time, the legendary "Shoe" had already settled things and, in the process, brought his own all-time record lifelong total of winners to 7,907.

For those of us over-confident chauvinists who expected local conditions to tip the scales against America, the writing was on the wall. Soaf's (25-1) last winning form was back in May, but a high draw is a powerful advantage over Sandown's straight five furlongs on soft going, and, like his rival team captain Joe Mercer, Shoemaker used it to the full.

But the genius of this amazing little man was even more clearly demonstrated in the Chivas Regal Mile. His mount, Pelayo (14-1), was an outsider to begin with, and after two furlongs, as he trailed several lengths behind his nearest opponent, 100-1 would have looked a miserly offer. But 7,907 is an awful lot of winners, and no doubt quite a few of them were gained by making the best of a bad job. The fact that he appeared to have no chance did not disturb Willie Shoemaker in the slightest and, even more important, it did not make him forget Geoff Lewis's advice, given in the morning, that the fastest going is up the Grandstand rail.

So, after turning for home still well last, he took Pelayo across and quietly started creeping up. Another American, Pincay, was looking all over a winner on Seven Hearts (5-1), but despite ducking sideways at a path across the course Shoemaker caught him in plenty of time to win by half a length.

With characteristic charm and modesty, Shoemaker explained his two victories as follows: "I followed a good man (Joe Mercer) in the first," he said, "and did what another good man told me in the second."

Well, that may be, but pound for pound this is surely the greatest jockey in the world, and in the presence of both Sir Gordon Richards and Lester Piggott he proved it gloriously.

This does not seem at all likely to have been the last international contest of its kind. The weather, superb yesterday, played Sandown and Chivas Regal a dirty trick today, but, in spite of grey skies and rain, a crowd of 8,000 plus watched and was fascinated by the three Chivas races.

A similar, non-sponsored series is planned between American and European teams at Meadowlands in November, but Chivas Regal were delighted with the success of their experiment and, granted the Jockey Club's co-operation, which I cannot believe would be withheld, they fully intend to repeat it in some form next year.

King George VI 'Chase Kempton Park: 26 December

Silver Buck gives Carmody hat-trick in King George

By HOTSPUR (Peter Scott)

Tommy Carmody achieved the unprecedented feat of riding the King George VI 'Chase winner three years in succession when Silver Buck outjumped his old rival Night Nurse and outstayed Analog's Daughter at Kempton Park. Silver Buck's victory 12 months ago had provided the second leg of Carmody's King George VI 'Chase hat-trick, which was initiated by another of the Dickinson family's stables stars Gay Spartan in 1978.

Silver Buck, who has now won 16 of his 19 steeplechases, started 9-4 favourite. Diamond Edge (11-4) finished a rather disappointing third when receiving 3lb from the winner. A couple of mistakes did not help his chance, but Night Nurse's blunders were more spectacular.

Analog's Daughter (5-1) set off in front as usual and built up a long early lead. Silver Buck overtook the Irish mare four fences from home, at which stage they were clear. But Night Nurse (4-1), coming out of the pack, gave chase to such purpose that he was on terms and still going easily entering the straight. His first bad blunder came three fences from the finish. But he was back in challenging position approaching the last fence, which, however, he met all wrong and gave Alan Brown no chance of staying in the saddle. Analog's Daughter kept on gamely, but Silver Buck finished the stronger to beat her by five lengths. Diamond Edge was another five lengths away third, and the never-dangerous Chinrullah (11-2) was fourth, a similar distance behind.

1981

18 Mar Racing at Stockton is abandoned because of waterlogging, the 50th meeting lost this winter.

4 Jul Paul Cook rides a 91-1 treble – with winners on three different courses,

Princes Gate (6-1) the 2.15 at Sandown, Ramannolie (11-4) the 5.00 at Bath, and Pavilion (5-2f) the 7.50 at Nottingham.

16 Sep Lester Piggott rides 5 winners at Yarmouth in 6 races, 4 of them for Henry Cecil, the 5-timer including 3 odds-on favourites, with accumulative odds of nearly 40-1.

3 Oct Prince Charles had his first winner as an owner, 20-1 chance Good Prospect, ridden by Richard Linley at Chepstow.

28 Oct Maj-Gen Sir Randle Fielden, 77, chairman of the Turf Board since its inception in 1965, dies. He did more than most over the last 30 years to bring an up-to-date approach to racing and to the Jockey Club, of which he was senior steward for two terms (1954-57, 1965-73). The introduction of overnight declarations, 4-day declarations, starting stalls and overnight declaration of blinkers came during his spells in office, when racecourse security, with routine dope testing and camera patrol filming, was also

improved.

30 Oct Fulke Walwyn puts out 6 runners and saddles 6 winners, 4 at Kempton and 2 at Devon, a 3,875-1 accumulator.

8 Nov Tim Brookshaw, champion jump jockey in 1958-59, dies at 52 after a fall last week while exercising a horse on his Shropshire farm. In 1963 he broke his spine at Liverpool and doctors told him he would never ride again, but he was back in the saddle within 8 months.

Champion Hurdle Cheltenham: 17 March

Champion 'Pigeon' puts youngsters in their place

By HOTSPUR (Peter Scott)

Sea Pigeon, defying his years with elegant ease and treating his younger rivals with indulgent superiority, won his second Champion Hurdle in consecutive seasons. Pollardstown and Daring Run had no answer to the old horse's finishing speed, which remains razor sharp.

Sea Pigeon (7-4f) has now become the highest first-prize money earner under National Hunt rules, with a total of £130,395. He already holds the record for a flat-race gelding, with £96,985, and no-one watching him at Cheltenham could doubt there are further triumphs to come.

Peter Easterby, no stranger to records himself, has now achieved the unprecedented feat of training the Champion Hurdle winner five times, Night Nurse's double in 1976 and 1977 and Saucy Kit (1967) providing his earlier successes.

Sea Pigeon was close up with the leaders approaching the last flight, and Cheltenham racegoers, confident that their old favourite's finishing speed would prevail, had started to cheer as John Francome brought him through the field to pass Daring Run (8-1) and Pollardstown (9-1) on the flat and win by one-and-a-half lengths.

Cheltenham Gold Cup: 19 March

Records fall as Easterby lands Gold Cup one-two

Little Owl wins from stablemate

By HOTSPUR (Peter Scott)

Peter Easterby capped his magnificent achievement of adding the Tote Cheltenham Gold Cup to Sea Pigeon's Champion Hurdle triumph two days ago by saddling both first and second in the big race, Little Owl and Night Nurse, both 6-1 shots.

No other trainer during post-war years has accomplished this feat in the Gold Cup, and Easterby becomes the first to win both Cheltenham's major prizes in the same season since Fulke Walwyn landed that double with Anzio and Mandarin in 1962. And Mr Jim Wilson became the first amateur to ride the Gold Cup winner

since Mr Dickie Black on Fortina in 1947.

Mr Wilson owns Little Owl in partnership with his brother Robin. They were bequeathed today's big winner by their aunt, Mrs Bobby Gundry, who died 12 months ago. Third place also went to a Yorkshire stable. Silver Buck (7-2f), trained by Michael Dickinson, was handicapped by ground far too sticky for him, but he kept on well enough to withstand Spartan Missile's steady late challenge.

Little Owl has now won eight of his nine steeplechases, and interference contributed to his fall in the other.

Coral Golden Hurdle Cheltenham: 18 March

Echoes of Arkle as Willie strolls in

By MARLBOROUGH (John Oaksey)

Willie Wumpkins won the Coral Golden Hurdle Handicap Final for the third year running at Cheltenham. Like Arkle, he has won at four National Hunt Festivals, and, also like Arkle, he and his rider, Jim Wilson, were welcomed back like heroes.

Once again, they led more or less from start to finish, brusquely brushing aside challenge after challenge. Now in his 14th year, Willie Wumpkins was at least four years older than any of his opponents, and when he won the Aldsworth Hurdle here in 1973 only four of them were even born.

If any ill-natured spoilsport should ask Willie how he manages to time his rejuvenation quite so precisely year after year, he would be able to produce in reply some pretty convincing doctors' certificates. According to his devoted owner-trainer Mrs Jane Pilkington, his heart "sounds like the four o'clock train leaving Paddington", and the vets have twice despaired of his survival.

He also suffers from navicular, and no doubt it is this painful affliction of the feet which makes him so reluctant to perform on anything but soft ground. "He just stops himself most of the season," says Jim Wilson's wife Melinda, the owner's daughter.

Of course, it is possible to take a high-faluting moral view and complain that Willie Wumpkins has been given three rather special well-timed preparations for this valuable handicap. But the stewards, who asked no questions, clearly did not feel that any great harm had been done to the fabric of British racing – and I whole-heartedly agree.

Melinda Wilson says that neither her mother nor her husband take the slightest notice of what the other thinks. Jim warned that Willie should be retired last year, but happily he was overruled. Now everyone seems to agree that the old horse has run his last race. And whether you were on at 13-2 or not, any lover of a character will wish him a happy retirement.

Champion and Aldaniti take Becher's Brook

Grand National Aintree: 4 April

Bob Champion and Aldaniti: Two heroic fighters

By HOTSPUR (Peter Scott)

The Grand National blazed an example of courage and perseverance round the world when Aldaniti (10-1) and Bob Champion provided a miraculously triumphant ending to a tale of crippled horse and cancer victim. Aintree has not yet won its own battle to survive, but Saturday's heroism, added to so many played out on its historic turf, must strengthen the resolve not to let this hard-pressed warrior die a financial death.

Champion, 32, was given eight months to live when the doctors diagnosed cancer in July 1979. Two bouts of tendon trouble and a fractured hockbone made Aldaniti's own prospects of Aintree glory appear just as remote.

Horse and rider began their partnership in January 1975, when Aldaniti won a novices' hurdle at Ascot on his racecourse debut. Now he has become the first Grand National winner since Sundew in 1957 to lead throughout the final circuit.

Mr John Thorne's own example of supreme fitness at the age of 54 may not have ended in victory, but it certainly ended in triumph. Mr Thorne and his beloved Spartan Missile (8-1f) made up many lengths to finish second, four lengths behind the winner.

Royal Mail was a name added to the Grand National's winners' roll in 1937. The New Zealand-bred namesake of that horse made a gallant effort to match his predecessor's achievement, but Royal Mail's (16-1) sustained challenge to Aldaniti started wilting with a blunder two fences from home. He held off Three to One (33-1), however, for third place, two lengths behind Spartan Missile. Last year's winner Rubstic (11-1) finished seventh.

Josh Gifford's wonderful training achievement with Aldaniti is matched on a more personal basis by loyalty to an employee. Champion's long fight against pain and near despair was made that little more bearable by Gifford's repeated promise that Champion's job as stable jockey would be there on his return.

Aldaniti was bred by Mr Thomas Barron at his Harrowgate stud near Darlington, County Durham. Derek H, the winner's sire was a smart Flat-racer and hurdler. Aldaniti's name was provided by Mr Barron's four grandchildren, Alistair, David, Nicola and Timothy. The horse was sent to Ascot sales in May 1974, when Josh Gifford bought him for 3,200 guineas on the advice of his father-in-law, George Roger-

Smith. Aldaniti's first win was in the colours of Josh's wife Althea, but he was then resold to Mr Nicholas Embiricos, a shipbroker who lives in Sussex and has Flat racers trained by Bruce Hobbs.

Mr Embiricos reports that Aldaniti's legs show no signs of the strain to which they were subjected at Aintree. The Grand National winner has returned to Gifford's Findon stable in such great heart that there is even an outside chance of his running again this spring.

Newbury: 16 May

Piggott fined £400 for hitting Reid

By Tony Stafford

The Newbury stewards worked overtime on Saturday, holding enquiries into three of the six races. Twice they overturned the original result, and after the Shaw Maiden Stakes they fined Lester Piggott £400 for striking John Reid's mount Ardar.

Piggott and Reid were each involved in one of the earlier enquiries – the stewards finding in their favour both times – but here Piggott, on Northern Supremo, was adjudged the culprit.

The verdict angered both Piggott and Northern Supremo's trainer Henry Cecil, who said: "My jockey and horse could have been killed." He was referring to an incident a furlong out where Ardar veered veered across Northern Supremo. Piggott's mount ran on to finish first, but the stewards disqualified the horse in favour of Ardar, who crossed the line second.

Lt-Col C.Coaker, stipendiary steward, said that Reid had been hit: "We can't have senior jockeys hitting one another."

Irish Turf Club: 29 May

Turf Club uphold O'Brien appeal: To-Agori-Mou 2nd

By HOTSPUR (Peter Scott)

Vincent O'Brien has won his appeal against the disqualification of King's Lake from first place in the Irish 2,000 Guineas on 16 May. The announcement was made after a six-hour hearing which put To-Agori-Mou back to second place. King's Lake, first home by a neck, was disqualified for bumping To-Agori-Mou, the winner previously of the 2,000 Guineas at Newmarket.

[Nine days later, Major Victor McCalmont, senior officiating steward at the Curragh on the day of the disqualification, resigned from the Irish Turf Club, sure that he and his colleagues correctly interpreted the rules as they stand and feeling his authority had been totally undermined.]

St James's Palace Stakes Ascot: 16 June

Sweet revenge for To-Agori-Mou

By MARLBOROUGH (John Oaksey)

To-Agori-Mou (2-1) beat King's Lake (6-4f) fair and square in the St James's Palace Stakes at Ascot – and, as Vincent O'Brien walked across the winner's enclosure to shake Guy Harwood's hand, an unhappy fragment of Anglo-Irish racing history was laid finally to rest.

The winner received a thunderous, unashamedly chauvinistic welcome and, as they passed the post a neck in front, his rider Greville Starkey raised one arm in an eloquent gesture of triumph. The actual number and angle of his fingers is uncertain, but one enterprising bookie was heard to offer 5-4 Harvey Smith and 3-1 Winston Churchill.

At a subsequent stewards' enquiry after the Prince of Wales Stakes, Starkey was reported to the Jockey Club for a piece of dangerous or careless riding on Bonol – but that had nothing to do with To-Agori-Mou. I understand that the official reaction to the "gesture" was a few quiet words of unofficial advice.

Everyone understands exactly how he felt, but the stewards no doubt feel (quite rightly in my opinion) that racing should take steps to remain a comparatively undemonstrative sport.

Quite apart from the controversy that preceded it, the St James's Palace Stakes, won in a time that broke Brigadier Gerard's record, was quite simply a magnificent race between two very good three-year-old milers. With a lovely clear run round the final turn, Greville Starkey kicked for home fully two furlongs out. These were quite different, much more ambitious tactics than those he used with To-Agori-Mou in either the English or Irish 2,000 Guineas and, without much doubt, they are the right ones. Because now, hard though King's Lake and Pat Eddery struggled to close the gap, they were always firmly held. First and second finished six lengths clear of Bel Bolide and that, taken together with the record time, is a measure of their excellence.

The Aga Khan leads Shergar in through the top-hats

Derby Epsom: 3 June

Peerless Shergar gallops to widest-ever Derby victory

By HOTSPUR (Peter Scott)

Shergar (10-11f) made the 1981 Derby the most one-sided of modern times. His 10-length winning margin was the widest officially recorded for a race founded in 1780, and the result was a foregone conclusion long before he took command early in the straight.

Shergar's time of 2min 44.21sec was the slowest since Airborne won in 1946, but the race was run on softer going than usual.

Riberetto and Silver Season, tracked by Shergar, set a strong early gallop which had the field beginning to string out after half a mile. While his two fellow leaders rounded Tattenham Corner under pressure, Shergar was lobbing along, with young Walter Swinburn standing up in his irons. Riberetto and Silver Season than gave way to Scintillating Air, Shotgun and the Queen's Church Parade, who became the favourite's closest pursuers as he nonchalantly drew clear.

Glint of Gold (13-1) looked a hopeless prospect two furlongs out, but he finished strongly and wore down Scintillating Air (50-1) to take second place by two lengths. Shotgun (7-1) finished fourth, Lester Piggott reporting that the distance was too far for his mount against a colt of Shergar's calibre, while fifth-finishing Church Parade (25-1) also found the distance beyond him.

Shergar's next engagement, the Irish Sweeps Derby on 27 June, should provide a similarly easy conquest for the Aga Khan's superb colt, who will face a much more informative test against the leading older horses in Ascot's King George VI and Queen Elizabeth Diamond Stakes on 25 July. Michael Stoute, who has handled Shergar with such skill, became the first Newmarket trainer to saddle a Derby winner since Sir Noel Murless with Royal Palace in 1967.

Yorkshire Oaks York: 18 August

Fractured skull puts Carson out for the season

By MARLBOROUGH (John Oaksey)

Willie Carson, the champion jockey, fractured the base of his skull, one wrist and a cervical vertebra when Silken Knot fell with him at York. And yet, if such dreadful injuries could be called "luck", he was indeed lucky to escape alive from one of the most horrific falls you ever saw.

The nearest equivalent I can remember was jump jockey Stan Mellor's crash at the first flight of the 1963 Schweppes Gold Trophy – in which he sustained 14 separate fractures of the jaw and face. Everyone will hope that Carson makes as complete a recovery as Mellor – who got married that summer and went on to ride his 1,000th winner.

But however quickly and totally the effervescent champion bounces back, he is officially out of action for at least three months and obviously will not ride again

this season. So Lester Piggott, who took his place and won on the Queen's Height of Fashion in the Acomb Stakes, seems assured, barring further accidents, of his 10th championship. He is now only 10 behind Willie Carson's total and there is no alternative candidate in sight.

Carson, who had started the day with a Royal winner on Church Parade in the High Line Stakes, had Silken Knot in second place on the rails as they turned for home in the Yorkshire Oaks. The unfortunate filly turned out in the end to have broken both her front legs, and presumably it was one of these going that caused her violent headlong fall. Carson was thrown right-handed in front of more than half the field, and they had no chance of avoiding him. For several awful seconds he was being "dribbled" along by flying hooves, and his injuries could

so easily have been far worse.

An ambulance was on the spot in less than two minutes, and the Jockey Club's chief medical adviser, Dr Michael Allen, was the first to examine Carson. He said later that his patient was "conscious, but understandably a bit woozy, in hospital".

Poor Silken Knot was destroyed. Inevitably her fall

caused considerable interference among those behind, and Leap Lively jumped her body on the ground and ran on very well to challenge the leaders. But it was another horse even more interfered with, the Irish filly Condessa (5-1), who made an amazing late rally that brought her storming up the middle to beat Leap Lively (7-1) by a neck.

Arlington Million Arlington Park: 30 August

John Henry home in last stride

By HOTSPUR (Peter Scott)

Willie Shoemaker forced hot favourite John Henry ahead in the last stride in the Arlington Million over one-and-three-quarter miles, in Chicago, to defeat The Bart (407-10), with Madam Gay (123-10), Lester Piggott's mount, in third place, two-and-a-half lengths behind them.

English hopes were high when Madam Gay, second to Shergar in the George VI at Ascot a month ago, turned into the straight, beautifully placed behind Key to Content and The Bart, but she could not really quicken from that stage. "The very soft going was against her. Had the race been run on firm ground, I believe she would have won," said Piggott. According to John Henry's trainer Ron McAnally, the going was not to his liking either, and the six-year-old had an unfavourable draw on the outside of the 12 runners.

The Bart, a five-year-old who had run with credit against Troy in the 1979 Irish Sweeps Derby before his export to the United States, headed Key to Content early in the straight and looked set to win. But Shoemaker's last-ditch challenge on the outside just prevailed. John Henry, coupled in the betting with stablemate Super Moment at 11-10, thus confirmed himself America's champion grass horse in the richest race so far staged anywhere in the world.

Prix de l'Arc de Triomphe Longchamp: 4 October

Gold River (53-1) gives Head 'Arc' win number four

By HOTSPUR (Peter Scott)

Gold River, 53-1 for the Prix de l'Arc de Triomphe, provided the fourth training success for Alec Head in Europe's richest race, but was a personal disaster for his son Freddie, who begged off to ride last year's winner Detroit.

The 10-horse Anglo-Irish challenge was a total failure, Ardross finishing fifth and King's Lake doing next best in 11th place. But earlier Marwell, Sharpo and Rabdan gave England first three places in the Prix de l'Abbaye.

Bikila made a bold attempt to lead throughout. He beat off challenges from Ardross and Perrault in the straight, but Gold River passed him 100 yards out to win by three-quarters of a length. April Run, twice having to switch position, finished strongly to be only a nose behind Bikila, with Perrault fourth another two lengths away.

Detroit, who had beaten Gold River into third place for Longchamp's Prix Foy three weeks ago, was close up entering the straight, but she then faded right out to be twentieth of twenty-four.

Freddie Head, desperate to make the record of Arc wins his own (he shares it on four with the late Jacques Doyasbere), obtained release from Gold River, whom he reckoned would find the distance too short. Gary Moore came from Hong Kong specially for the mount. He rode a winner there yesterday, and his subsequent flight to Paris was stretched to 20 hours by a bomb scare.

Alec and Freddie Head are not the only members of their family to enjoy post-war success in the Arc. Alec's father Willie trained Bon Mot to win and his daughter Criquette was successful with Three Troikas.

Gold River, whose principal success earlier this year was in the two-and-a-half miles Prix du Cadran, became the sixth winner of her sex in the last 10 Arc runnings. She had been destined for Kentucky and a mating with Northern Dancer next spring, but there is now a possibility that she will race as a five-year-old.

OTHER MAJOR RACES

Irish Derby	Shergar	L Piggott	1-3f
Arc de Triomphe	Gold River	GW Moore	53-1
Kentucky Derby	Pleasant Colony	J Velasquez	7-2
Melbourne Cup	Just a Dash	P Cook	15-1
Arlington Million	John Henry	W Shoemaker	11-10
Japan Cup	Mairzy Doates	C Asmussen	11-1

St Leger Doncaster: 12 September

Beaten Shergar is Arc doubt:
St Leger defeat for 4-9 favourite

By HOTSPUR (Peter Scott)

Shergar, the 4-9 favourite, finished a leg-weary fourth to Cut Above (28-1) in a gruelling St Leger, and can no longer be regarded as a certain runner for the Prix de l'Arc de Triomphe. He has been replaced by Ardross as favourite for the Longchamp race on 4 October.

Magikin set an early gallop, and Bustomi took it up six furlongs from home. Shergar entered the straight in third place to Bustomi and Glint of Gold. The favourite was going easily enough at that stage, but distress signals began to fly soon afterwards.

Glint of Gold battled his way past Bustomi two furlongs out, but Cut Above was then really warming to his work. He surged ahead with a furlong left and won by two-and-a-half lengths from Glint of Gold (4-1). Bustomi (13-2) was third four lengths further back, with Shergar another five lengths adrift.

Dick Hern was saddling his fifth St Leger winner, Joe Mercer riding his fourth. Both were associated with the previous St Leger triumph of Cut Above's owner Sir John Astor when Provoke slammed the odds-on Meadow Court in 1965.

Michael Stoute reports that there was nothing palpably amiss with Shergar on the colt's return to Newmarket, but his racing future will not be settled for a few days. "I shall give Shergar a thorough checking out and then discuss matters with the Aga Khan," said the trainer.

While Cut Above's fine performance deserves full credit, Shergar's owner and trainer have some consolation in widespread respect for their refusal to play safe with a high-class horse. Had they kept Shergar at home, he would now be basking in the reflected glory of an Irish Sweeps Derby win over Cut Above, but in preferring sportsmanship to commercialism they honoured the true spirit of racing.

[Two weeks later, it was decided to retire Shergar, so a great racing career ended in anticlimax. But that was by no means the end of the Shergar story.]

Ascot: 24 September

Fault in inquiry rule highlighted by Ascot delay

By HOTSPUR (Peter Scott)

The Queen, visiting Ascot today on the eve of her Australian trip, suffered an agonisingly and unnecessarily long wait during the stewards' inquiry that followed her victory in the Hoover Fillies' Mile with Height of Fashion. This went on long enough to delay presentation of the trophy until after the next race, when the Queen returned to the unsaddling enclosure to receive it.

Leading throughout, Height of Fashion (15-8f) held off a spirited challenge from Stratospheric (7-2) by half a length, but a steward's enquiry was then announced. The film quickly established that neither of the first two placings needed to be altered. Unfortunately, local stewards are instructed not to reveal this until the whole inquiry is over. This is by no means the first time that racegoers and off-course backers of a winner have been kept in unnecessarily long suspense. A request to make their instructions more flexible is to be considered by the Jockey Club Stewards next week.

ENGLISH CLASSICS

2,000 Guineas	To-Agori-Mou	G Starkey	5-2f
1,000 Guineas	Fairy Footsteps	L Piggott	6-4f
Derby	Shergar	W Swinburn	10-11f
Oaks	Blue Wind	L Piggott	3-1jf
St Leger	Cut Above	J Mercer	28-1

1982

15 May At 16, Jack Kaenel, on Aloma's Ruler, becomes the youngest jockey to win the Preakness Stakes, taking the record from Steve Cauthen, who was 18 when he rode Affirmed to victory in 1978.

18 Jun Lester Piggott rides Critique to victory in the Hardwicke Stakes and with six winners is leading rider at Royal Ascot for the 13th time.

26 Jun Willie Carson chalks up his 2,000th winner on Busaco in the Laurie Wills Handicap at Newmarket, and in the evening meeting at Doncaster Steve Cauthen rides 5 of the 7 winners and comes 3rd and 4th in the other two races.

14 Aug Jo Berry rides Relative Ease (20-1) to victory in the Oxo Amateur Riders Handicap (5f) at Wolverhampton, her fourth success in the event in four starts.

2 Oct Century City (20-1) gives Joe Mercer his first William Hill Cambridgeshire victory, carrying 9st 6lb, a record weight for a winning 3-year-old in the race.

19 Nov The meeting at Ayr, in terrible weather, attracts a record low attendance – 362.

8 March

John Thorne killed in point-to-point

By MARLBOROUGH (John Oaksey)

National Hunt racing depends on enthusiasm, and John Thorne, who had as much of it as any man I've ever known, has been killed doing the thing he loved best. He died yesterday [Sunday] in an Oxford hospital, having never regained consciousness after a fall at the Bicester point-to-point on Saturday.

Typically, he was riding Bend a Knee, a young inexperienced horse of his own breeding. It was his second ride of the afternoon, but this was his first day back after breaking a leg in November.

At the age of 54, John got the chance last year to fulfil the ambition of a lifetime with his first ride in a Grand National. His beloved hunter-chaser Spartan Missile started favourite after finishing fourth in the Gold Cup, and was then beaten just four lengths by Aldaniti – the only horse in the field capable of producing an even more romantic and universally popular result.

John Thorne and Aldaniti's jockey, Bob Champion,

celebrated at dinner together that night, and yesterday Bob was as stunned by the news as the rest of John's friends. "It is a terrible loss," he said. "John was one of the nicest people in the game." He was all of that. Indeed, if you tried to produce a prototype of a sporting English countryman at his best, it might closely resemble John Thorne.

A Paratroop officer in the closing years of the War, he came out of the Army to farm in Warwickshire. There he built up the highly successful Chesterton Stud, hunted fearlessly and indefatigably with the Warwickshire hounds, and rode as an amateur for 33 seasons.

That last total would almost certainly have been much smaller but for another family tragedy. In 1963, John's son Nigel was already beginning to show exceptional skill and dash on the family horses when he was killed in a motor accident. Since then, Nigel's sisters Diana and Jane have carried on the family tradition both under rules and in point-to-points.

NATIONAL HUNT

Champion Hurdle	For Auction	Mr C Magnier	40-1
Cheltenham Gold Cup	Silver Buck	R Earnshaw	6-1
Grand National	Grittar	Mr C Saunders	7-1f

Mayfield Novices' 'Chase Uttoxeter: 1 June

Francome 'retires' to give Scu' share in title

John Francome ensured that the 1981-82 National Hunt jockeys' championship would be shared by Peter Scudamore and himself when Buckmaster won the Mayfield Novices' 'Chase at Uttoxeter. Francome, previously three times undisputed champion, pledged when Scudamore was

injured on 26 April at Southwell that if he matched his rival's 120 winners he would retire for the season.

After Buckmaster's victory, which also gave Francome the 800th success of his career, Francome said: "It's a great relief to share the title. That's definitely it for the season."

Geraldine Rees: first woman rider to complete the National

Grand National Aintree: 3 April

Veteran Saunders turns back the clock to win National

By Tony Stafford

History will record the 1982 Grand National as one won by the oldest jockey (48) and in which a woman jockey completed the course for the first time.

But behind the scenes, a poignant moment was provided by Diana Henderson, wife of Lambourn trainer Nicky and daughter of the late John Thorne. Twelve months ago she was part of the group that received her father and Spartan Missile as they returned to unsaddle in second place. Joy and pride, rather than disappointment, was the theme of that party. On Saturday, Diana Henderson was one of the first to greet Dick Saunders and Grittar on their way back to the winner's enclosure. Saunders had been encouraged by John Thorne to continue riding almost 20 years ago, when he was ready to give up for the second time.

The parallels between Spartan Missile and Grittar are remarkable. Both were

ridden by Midland farmers well into middle age, and on the day each was a nine-year-old carrying 11st 5lb. But for the intervention of Saturday's first-fence fallers Aldaniti and Bob Champion in 1981, this would have been a carbon copy, for both Spartan Missile and Grittar are hunter-chasers and winners of the Cheltenham and Liverpool Foxhunters'.

There are many who believe that Grittar would not have beaten Loving Words, who conjured an astonishing rally after unseating his rider, Richard Hoare, at the fourth last. Hoare took quite a time to get back in the saddle and stormed after the others to such good effect that he gained third place – and at least a share of the honours on another epic day at Aintree with Dick Saunders and 26-year-old housewife Mrs Geraldine Rees, who came in eighth and last of the finishers on Cheers.

CHAMPIONS

CHAMPIONS		
Jockey (Flat)	Lester Piggott	188
Jockey (NH)	John Francome	
	Peter Scudamore	120
Racehorse of Year	Ardross	6-y-o
NH Champion of Year	Silver Buck	10-y-o
Leading Trainer	Henry Cecil	£872,614
Leading Owner	Robert Sangster	£397,749
Leading Money Winner	Kalaglow	£242,304

Derby Epsom: 2 June

'Fleece' close to record in sixth O'Brien Derby

By HOTSPUR (Peter Scott)

Golden Fleece, winning the Derby almost as easily as his trial races, returned the Epsom classic's fastest time since electrical recording was introduced in 1964 and the best, excluding wartime races at Newmarket, since Mahmoud's 1936 race record.

Pat Eddery rode the unbeaten Irish colt with complete confidence, having him towards the rear early and swinging wide for room to challenge in the straight. Golden Fleece (3-1f) accelerated with a surge of speed to strike the front 1 1/2 furlongs out. Touching Wood (40-1) was just about to wrest the lead from Norwick when Golden Fleece swept past both and won by three lengths in 2min 34.27sec.

Silver Hawk (14-1) and Persepolis (4-1) finished strongly to snatch third and fourth places.

Vincent O'Brien has now trained six Derby winners. He needs one more to equal the record held jointly by Robert Robson (1793-1823), John Porter (1868-99) and Fred Darling (1922-41). O'Brien's stamp was put even more firmly on the race by the fact that the first three have all O'Brien trained Derby winners as their sires. Golden Fleece is son of Nijinsky, Touching Wood and Silver Hawk are by Roberto. All three colts were reared in the United States.

Irish Sweeps Derby The Curragh: 26 June

Classy win for Assert in Irish Derby

By HOTSPUR (Peter Scott)

Odds-on favourite Assert, trained by Vincent O'Brien's son David, scored a brilliant eight-length victory over Silver Hawk (3-1) in the Irish Sweeps Derby. The crowd was appreciably down on last year, but those who stayed away missed a performance of superb class that fully made up for the race's one-sided nature.

From the time that Christy Roche sent Assert (4-7f) through on the inside of his pacemaker Raconteur to take command entering the straight, the result was a foregone conclusion. Assert has improved tremendously since his two defeats by Golden Fleece, but it would be misleading to measure these champions through Silver Hawk, whom Assert beat twice as far at The Curragh as did Golden Fleece at Epsom.

Lingfield Park: 9 July

Five for Rouse at Lingfield

Brian Rouse won all five races open to him at Lingfield Park yesterday, riding for five different trainers. Rouse, who once left racing to work as an electrician, won on Castle Guard for Ryan Price, to whose Findon stable he is first jockey. His other wins were on Silver Market for Ron Smyth, Nauteous (Peter Walwyn), Welwyn (John Benstead) and Prince of Princes (John Dunlop). The first two started at odds-on, while Prince of Princes (5-1) floored odds laid on To Kamari Mou.

The five-timer would have paid over 170-1, and Rouse received an award of champagne from the Lingfield executive.

Ascot Gold Cup: 17 June

Relaxed Ardross in no hurry to surrender crown

By MARLBOROUGH (John Oaksey)

After welcoming his fourth consecutive Gold Cup winner at Ascot yesterday, Henry Cecil said that Ardross will run in the King George VI and Queen Elizabeth Diamond Stakes only if the going is reasonably soft. So pray for a wet July.

"He has just had too many races on the hard," the winner's devoted trainer said. "Watching him worries me stiff, and waiting to see how he is next morning is even worse." Yesterday – and I am touching wood – Ardross looked happier than in either of his previous races this year.

Despite a moderate gallop set by the Polish-bred, Swedish-trained five-year-old Dzudo, it took Ardross (1-5f) only 100 yards of the straight to take control, and although Tipperary Fixer (10-1) finished fast, Lester Piggott was already pulling up by then, his 11th Gold Cup safely in the bag.

The only sad reflection about the memorable career of the six-year-old Ardross, in which the Arc is his only "failure" since 1980 when Le Moss retired, is that his breeder, Paddy Prendergast, did not live to enjoy it. How he would have loved to see his colours at Ascot on a horse whose great enthusiasm for racing matches his own.

Firm ground, which so signally failed to dampen the enthusiasm of Ardross, had already been demonstrated by record-breaking performances in the first two races. Indian King's decisive victory over Vaigly Star in the Cork and Orrery set a new all-aged mark for six furlongs (1min 13.29sec), and, although the stiff Ascot five furlongs was nearly too far for Brondesbury, his Norfolk Stakes time of 1m 0.75s was the fastest recorded by a two-year-old.

William Hill Stewards' Cup Goodwood: 27 July

Soba puts back worries behind her

By MARLBOROUGH (John Oaksey)

An orthopaedic manual would have been at least as much help as a form book at Goodwood yesterday when Soba and Electric (shock three-year-old Gordon Stakes winner), both recent sufferers from back trouble, won the afternoon's most important races.

Soba, mind you, had been beaten in only one of her seven starts this season – hardly an adequate reason for letting the three-year-old filly start at 18-1 for the William Hill Stewards' Cup.

After that one failure – a dismal fifth three weeks ago at Ayr – she was found to have the equine equivalent of a slipped disc. A Harrogate physiotherapist, Janet Ellis, put it right.

But as Soba bucked and fly-jumped her way to the start, neither she nor David Nicholls looked at all comfortable or happy. On the way back, by contrast, they were always totally dominating the race. The last horse to win a Stewards' Cup from the supposedly hopeless No.1 draw was Jukebox in 1970. But Soba not only made every inch of the running from that position – she took more than a second off the course record in the process, with 1min 9.58sec for the six furlongs.

Bracadale and Celestial Dancer took the minor places on the far side, but Soba had already come home unchallenged. David Chapman, who trains her at Stillington, in Yorkshire, has only ever had one previous runner in the south – eight years ago at Folkestone. His sister, Mrs Muriel Hills, bought Soba's dam (a twin) for 350 gns. Soba is the mare's first foal and, after nine races and only one third last season, she was quite understandably described in Timeform's Annual as "only plating class".

As for David Nicholls, he was leading jockey in Cyprus last winter – and had half a mind to stay there. It was a ride on another handicapper trained by Chapman that lured him back to England, and Soba has made the decision infinitely worth while.

Geoffrey Freer Stakes Newbury: 14 August

Piggott rides 4,000th winner:
Improbable record in reach
By Tony Stafford

Lester Piggott safely negotiated his 4,000th Flat-race winner in England on the Henry Cecil-trained Ardross at Newbury and is within sight of the most improbable record. For, rising 47 and riding for the most successful stable in the country – and seemingly in indestructible health – Piggott is capable of adding the 870 winners he needs to match Sir Gordon Richards' British record.

His striking rate this season is faster than ever – so much so that he could well reach 200 for the first time in 1982. Three more similarly successful years – and in association with Cecil that remains a possibility – would almost see him there. And he would still be younger than the age at which Sir Gordon retired.

That there is no diminution in his powers is self-evident. That jockeys can still be effective well into their fifties is an incontrovertible racing truism.

But just in case the 4,000 mark was the last of the Piggott milestones, Saturday's Newbury crowd rose to join in the celebration as he and Ardross (1-3f) swept clear to beat a hard-ridden Baffin by four lengths. And to show that the sip of champagne in the winner's enclosure in no way impaired his judgment, Piggott then rode an inspired tactical race to lift the ATS Trophy with Balanchine.

It is 34 years, all but four days, since Piggott rode his first winner – The Chase at Haydock in August 1948. But 4,000 is, of course, only Lester's Flat-race total in Britain. Quite apart from 20 winners over hurdles here (from only 54 rides), he must have ridden at least 500 more in the 16 other countries lucky enough to see him in action.

With the years, the public image has softened perceptibly. Piggott has often gone down as the perennial hard-faced professional. Nowadays, the smiles are readily available – and in this summer of 1982, he has happily signed legions of autograph books to confirm just how much he is enjoying his trade.

Budweiser Million Arlington Park: 29 August

British pair gain shock placings behind Perrault in US
By HOTSPUR (Peter Scott)

Be My Native and Motavato, reckoned to be forlorn English challengers for the Budweiser Million at Arlington Park, Chicago, stunned world opinion by finishing second and third to the former French horse, Perrault, in the world's richest race.

Motavato, whose maximum distance on English courses is a mile, stayed this 10 furlongs well enough, and Steve Cauthen made much of the running on him. He was still ahead entering the straight, but then Perrault passed him and went on to win by two lengths.

Plenty of horses in France beat Perrault throughout his European career. But he did improve tremendously towards the end of it and finished fourth in the 1981 Prix de l'Arc de Triomphe. His United States campaign has proved sensational, and yesterday's victory confirmed him as the leading grass horse there.

Be My Native, far from the best three-year-old in England, staged a remarkable late run on the inside to snatch second place from Motavato. Lester Piggott finished seventh on the third British challenger, Noalto.

William Hill Sprint Championship York: 19 August

Late burst gives Sharpo hat-trick in York sprint
By HOTSPUR (Peter Scott)

Evens favourite Sharpo fulfilled the hopes of his many admirers with a decisive victory in the five-furlong William Hill Sprint Championship at York. Winning it for the third year in succession, Miss Monica Sheriffe's champion confirmed himself as the outstanding European sprinter.

Steve Cauthen saved Sharpo for his now familiar burst of finishing speed. This took him ahead a furlong out and then two lengths clear of Chellaston Park, Kind Music and Tina's Pet, who had a furious battle for second place. Cauthen, deputising for the injured Pat Eddery, described Sharpo as the fastest horse he had ridden either in England or in the United States.

It is probable, though not yet certain, that Sharpo will retire to stud at the end of this season. Jeremy Tree, who had trained the five-year-old throughout his career, indicated that Longchamp's Prix de l'Abbaye on 3 October was a definite target.

Haydock Park: 3 September

Levy money is well spent
By MARLBOROUGH (John Oaksey)

Lord Plummer, who retires from the Levy Board at the end of this month, had every reason to feel well pleased at Haydock Park when he opened the last major rebuilding project of his chairmanship. In almost every respect the Board's £2.5 million interest-free loan seems to have been wisely and imaginatively spent.

The stand, named after Tommy Whittle, the track's late and much-missed chairman, provides 1,000 new seats and excellent terraced standing-room for more than 6,000. As in all modern stands, it has been an unfortunate economic necessity to give the best vantage points to 32 private boxes and six hospitality suites, but viewing for the Tattersalls racegoer has been enormously improved, much more, for instance, than at Goodwood.

The bars and restaurants have been developed in partnership with the local Burtonwood Brewery, and the stand contains its own splendid pub, as well as facilities for banquets, wedding receptions and other suchlike jamborees. The pub is open every day, and other rooms provide a vital source of income on non-racing days.

As usual there were a few hiccups on the opening afternoon. The admirable jockeys' changing-room has a luxurious sauna, but no one had put in a drain! Such little local difficulties can soon be solved and, after all, Haydock has continued racing throughout the 18 months of building.

The Grand Opening Celebration Handicap was won cleverly by the Aga Khan's Khairpour (7-2f), who beat some good, experienced older handicappers. Horage has had plenty of compliments this summer and none more graceful than the John Player New Grandstand Stakes victory of The Noble Player (4-1). This, you may remember, was the "nothing" to whom Horage gave 6lb and an easy beating at Newbury before his Gimcrack triumph.

ENGLISH CLASSICS			
2,000 Guineas	Zino	F Head	8-1
1,000 Guineas	On the House	J Reid	33-1
Derby	Golden Fleece	P Eddery	3-1f
Oaks	Time Charter	W Newnes	12-1
St Leger	Touching Wood	P Cook	7-1

OTHER MAJOR RACES			
Irish Derby	Assert	C Roche	4-7f
Arc de Triomphe	Akiyda	Y St-Martin	107-10
Kentucky Derby	Gato del Sol	E Delahoussaye	212-10
Melbourne Cup	Gurner's Lane	L Dittman	8-1
Arlington Million	Perrault	L Pincay	13-10
Japan Cup	Half Iced	D MacBeth	31-1

Prix de l'Arc de Triomphe Longchamp: 3 October

English monopoly foiled only by Akiyda's Arc win

By HOTSPUR (Peter Scott)

English challengers came close to dominating every big race at Longchamp, with Sharpo (4-5f), Goodbye Shelley (35.7-1) and Dione (3.6-1) all winning. But Ardross and Awaasif finished second and third to Akiyda in a desperately fought Prix de l'Arc de Triomphe.

Akiyda, the seventh filly in 11 years to win Europe's richest race, had a good run near the inside throughout, and was always in the first four. She took command halfway up the straight and held off Ardross by a head. Ardross, almost certainly running his final race, answered Lester Piggott's every call with a powerful finish, but the post came just too soon.

Awaasif, who received an early bump from Assert, was prominent all the way. She finished half a length behind Ardross and a head in front of April Run, last year's third. Further rain had made the going heavy, and doubts about whether Assert would take part persisted until trainer David O'Brien and jockey Pat Eddery had made a lengthy inspection of the course before racing. The Irish Derby winner started favourite of the 17 runners and was close up in the straight, but then began to struggle and faded to finish 11th. Eddery blamed the going.

Akiyda (10.7-1) gave Yves Saint-Martin his third Arc

victory and enabled François Mathet to equal Alec Head's post-war record of four training successes in the race.

Runner-up in the Prix de Diane and Prix Vermeille earlier this season, Akiyda returned the second-slowest Arc time in 15 years, 2min 37sec, but this can be blamed on the ground. The filly, who now retires to stud, comes from a family bought by the Aga Khan in a massive purchase of the late M Marcel Boussac's bloodstock.

Sharpo, second in the Prix de l'Abbaye in 1980 and 1981, made no mistake this time. The five-year-old confirmed himself as Europe's top sprinter when beating Fearless Lad, the Kings Stand Stakes winner, by a length. John Dunlop and Willie Carson, who went so close with Awaasif in the Arc, shared in Dione's Prix de l'Opera win. This filly led throughout and held Unknown Lady's challenge by a length.

Goodbye Shelley, unconsidered except by optimists in the large English invasion to Longchamp, gained a momentous victory in the Prix Marcel Boussac, a one-mile Group One race for two-year-old fillies. Trainer Steve Norton had only one previous runner in France and jockey John Lowe had never been to the country, let alone ridden there, before.

---

27 December

Boxing Day dozen for nervous Dickinson

By Tony Stafford

Michael Dickinson produced 12 winners at six Boxing Day meetings to shatter Arthur Stephenson's record of seven achieved in May 1970. Granted continuing good health and provided he retains his seemingly insatiable appetite for success, the 32-year-old trainer is poised to rewrite the jumping record books.

Bank Holidays, with their multiple opportunities, were always a favourite target for his father, Tony

Dickinson, for whom a handful of winners in a day was almost commonplace. Dickinson junior, who, remember, is in only his third season as a trainer, sent out a trimmed-down team of 21, which rewarded him with the 12 winners and, for good measure, five seconds, two thirds, one fourth and, horror of horrors, one unplaced.

Stephenson's tally had been eclipsed by mid-afternoon, by which time Wayward Lad (1st, 7-2) and

Silver Buck (3rd, 1-1f) had, in the King George VI 'Chase at Kempton, all but achieved another of those one-two specials of the Harewood stable. While his big-race owners were taking lunch at Kempton, the young trainer, clearly nervous, kept himself occupied by watching the earlier races and in between happily receiving the regular "good news" bulletins from other

courses. For the record, his other winners were Delius(15-8) and Happy Voyage (8-11f) at Wetherby; W Six Times (1-1f) and Fearless Imp (1-1f) at Market Rasen; Brunton Park (4-6f), Prominent Artist (4-5f) and Slieve Bracken (6-4f) at Wolverhampton; Marnik (8-13f) and Thornacre (2-1f) at Huntingdon; and Londolozi (5-2) and B.Jaski (1-1f) at Sedgefield.

Long John Scotch Whisky Challenge Ascot: 24 September

'Shoe' is match for Piggott

By MARLBOROUGH (John Oaksey)

Bill Shoemaker and Mrs Sally Hindley shared the glory at Ascot yesterday. The great American rode two winners, one of them in his match with Lester Piggott, and, despite a miserable afternoon, Mrs Hindley and her committee raised more than £175,000 for the Multiple Sclerosis Society.

The Long John Whisky Challenge must surely have been the first

"match" ever to involve two jockeys who have a total of more than 12,000 winners to their joint credit.

But hard as Lester and Spanish Pool (trained by Mrs Hindley's husband) struggled to make a fight of it, Prince's Gate (11-8), in front from the start and loving the softer ground, never allowed the 13-8 on favourite to mount a serious challenge.

William Hill Dewhurst Stakes Newmarket: 15 October

Diesis bursts Gorytus bubble: Defeat remains a mystery

By MARLBOROUGH (John Oaksey)

Even three more Lester Piggott winners and Steve Cauthen's first century could not lift the unhealthy fog of mystery, speculation and disappointment which covered Newmarket yesterday [Friday] as Gorytus trailed home last behind Diesis in the William Hill Dewhurst Stakes. At the inevitable stewards' inquiry, neither Dick Hern nor Willie Carson could offer any excuse or explanation.

With some of his horses running below form lately, Hern had Gorytus's blood tested twice this week, on Monday and Wednesday, both tests producing perfectly normal results, and the unbeaten colt ate up well in the racecourse stables after travelling from Berkshire on Thursday.

Gorytus (1-2f) could not possibly have looked better in the paddock – noticeably more powerful and mature in repose than Diesis. But, as was painfully clear from the stands and as a mystified

Willie Carson told the stewards: "When I asked him to go after three furlongs, he just could not produce anything."

Long before Lester Piggott moved behind him on Diesis (2-1), Carson had been scrabbling away without result. Two furlongs out, he looked down anxiously at the favourite's hind legs and, although no symptoms can have been visible, wisely began to pull up. By that time, the race had been majestically decided – with Diesis sweeping through for an effortless five lengths victory.

After being unsaddled, Gorytus walked off to the dope-testing box showing definite signs of distress and exhaustion. Considering the rumours that swept the course on Thursday (William Hill suspended all betting at one time), vague talk of "foul play" and "no smoke without fire" is unfortunately inevitable. Not surprisingly, the colt has been replaced as favourite for next year's 2,000 Guineas.

1983

2 Feb A long-overdue amendment to the Jockey Club rules means that the mount of a jockey found guilty of careless riding may now be placed after the victim(s) of the offence rather than automatically last.

30 Apr The Queen opens the National Horse Racing Museum at Newmarket on 2,000 Guineas day, while the big race goes to the Sangster-O'Brien second string Lomond (9-1), whose stablemate Danzarote was withdrawn 10 days ago when it was the 7-4 ante-post favourite. Tolomeo (18-1) and Muscatite (12-1) are 2nd and 3rd, with favourites Diesis and Gorytus well beaten.

6 Sep Jockey Greville Starkey is suspended for 13 days for reckless riding

(on the disqualified Bluff House last month at Goodwood).

27 Sep The European price for a yearling is broken three times at Tattersalls' Highflyer Sales at Newmarket, finally by Robert Sangster's syndicate, who pay 1.55m guineas for a colt by Hello Gorgeous out of Centre Piece.

12 Nov Arc heroine and "Piggott reject" All Along wins the Washington DC International at Laurel Park, Maryland, to

complete the so-called North American Triple Crown, having taken the Rothmans International in Montreal and the Aqueduct Turf Classic, to earn owner M Daniel Wildenstein a million-dollar bonus, on offer for the first time.

31 Nov Dunette, 7-y-o French classic winner, sets a European record for a broodmare, fetching 840,000 gns at Newmarket from Robert Sangster and partners, her destination the Coolmore Stud, Tipperary.

---

10 February

Shergar demand 'on the way'
Phone call offers talks in Belfast

By A.J.McILROY and ROGER HEYWOOD

A huge hunt was underway on both sides of the Irish border early today for the multi-million pound hero of the racecourse, Shergar, stolen by armed and masked men from the Aga Khan's Ballymany Stud in Co.Kildare on Tuesday night [8 Feb].

At the same time, police were investigating the first apparent lead in the case – a telephone call to the Belfast offices of the Newsletter by a man claiming to speak for those holding the 1981 winner of both the Epsom and Irish Derbys.

The anonymous caller [codenamed "Arkle"], speaking with a "distinct southern Irish accent," said that if one of three well-known English racing journalists turned up at Belfast's Forum Hotel tonight, negotiations for the horse's release could begin. The journalists mentioned were Lord Oaksey of The Daily Telegraph, Peter Campling of the Sun and Derek Thompson of ITV.

Shergar, once wholly and now partly owned by the Aga Khan and whose stud value is put at £10 million at least, was stolen by a gang of up to six men from the stud farm near Newbridge. Two of the men burst into the home of the head groom, Mr John Fitzgerald, held him at gunpoint and locked his wife and seven children in a downstairs room.

They forced him to point out where Shergar was

housed and to help them back the horse out and then load him into a horse box. Mr Fitzgerald, 58, told police that he was forced to lie face down on the floor of the box while it was driven away. He was later transferred to a car and not released until four hours later.

Irish police are working on the theory that Shergar is being hidden in one of the hundreds of small stables and stud farms in the vast plain of the Curragh. It is not believed that any para-military group was involved in the kidnapping.

The timing of the kidnapping could not have been potentially more damaging to the syndicate owning Shergar's stud shares. From next Monday, the start of the stud season, Shergar would have been covering a maximum of 55 mares, earning in nominations from the owners of those mares more than £2.5 million for the syndicate.

Last season, he covered 44 mares, 42 of whom became in foal, and his first son, a bay colt, was born a week yesterday out of Hilo Girl, a half-sister to Ragusa, an Irish Derby winner. The remainder of his foals will be born over the next four months.

11 February

By John Oaksey: At two o'clock yesterday morning I became, willy-nilly, one of the most improbable "contact men" in the history of kidnapping – the nearest I

---

1 February

Bomber tragedy upsets Triumph Hurdle betting

By HOTSPUR

The Grey Bomber, unbeaten in five hurdle races, was a victim of yesterday's severe weather in the north-east. In a freak accident, he was electrocuted when leading Denys Smith's string near the trainer's Bishop Auckland stables.

The Grey Bomber and his rider, Tommy Nevin, Smith's head lad, stopped near power cables which had been blown down by the gales. Melted snow on the ground acted as a conductor and, as The Grey Bomber turned away, three yards from the cable, he dropped dead.

Smith, who was about to bring The Grey Bomber

back to the racecourse following a mid-season break, was naturally upset by the accident: "It's tragic. The Grey Bomber was one of the best horses I've trained," he said. "He was brilliant. Accidents like this always happen to the good horses. The only good thing is that Tommy escaped injury. He's a very lucky man."

The accident, together with general worries about the well-being of David Nicholson's Balanchine, reputedly recovering from a blood disorder, has caused bookmakers to alter drastically their betting on next month's Daily Express Triumph Hurdle.

---

ever expect to be to a Dick Francis story.

Fourteen hours later, 30 miles south of Belfast, the ransom being demanded for the kidnapped Derby winner Shergar had dwindled from £2 million to £40,000 – or £1,000 for each share.

A ransom, of course, is still a ransom, and even if the demand proved to be genuine the Aga Khan and Shergar's 34 other shareholders may well reckon that paying it would set a precedent likely to shake the bloodstock world to

its foundation. But there is still no proof that "Arkle" was not a hoax.

["Arkle" was a hoax and, sadly, after weeks and months of investigation and conjecture, no signs of Shergar were ever seen again. As for his kidnappers – whether they were motivated by some vendetta against the Aga Khan, as syndicate member Lord Derby suggested, or, the more widely held view, were connected with the IRA – they were never brought to book.]

Champion Hurdle Cheltenham: 15 March

Gaye Brief makes light of error

Mercy Rimell first woman to train Champion Hurdle winner

By HOTSPUR (Peter Scott)

Fred Rimell, who rode and trained Champion Hurdle winners before his death two years ago, has now left a further mark on Cheltenham's big race. Gaye Brief, the last horse he ever bought, won it in decisive fashion, trained by his widow, Mercy Rimell, the first woman to triumph in the Champion.

Gaye Brief (7-1) beat the Irish outsider Boreen Prince (50-1) by three lengths. The margin would have been much wider but for a mistake at the last flight which momentarily threatened to

bring him down. For Auction (3-1jf), finishing seven lengths behind Boreen Prince, won a close battle for third place with Broadsword, Ekbalco and Sula Bula. Royal Vulcan, the only horse to have beaten Gaye Brief in his six races this season, was never going well and finished out of the first nine.

Gaye Brief belongs to Sheikh Ali Abu Khamsin, a civil engineer who bought his first racehorse five years ago and was last season's top stakes "earnings" owner under NH Rules.

Bregawn on the way to Gold Cup victory

Cheltenham Gold Cup: 17 March

Dickinson takes first five Gold Cup places

By HOTSPUR (Peter Scott)

Bregawn, Captain John, Wayward Lad, Silver Buck and Ashley House were cheered as a team when they walked back in front of the packed grandstands after giving trainer Michael Dickinson the first five places in yesterday's Tote Cheltenham Gold Cup.

Dickinson continues to break records and

A triumphant Dickinson after the race

exhaust superlatives. His Gold Cup quintet accomplished a tour de force unprecedented in modern big race history, and one which it is difficult to visualise being surpassed. Dickinson had steadfastly avoided predictions about which of his five would prove best, but backers made the correct choice. Bregawn, at 100-30, became the first outright favourite to win the Gold Cup since Arkle in 1966.

Sensing perhaps that a big race is no occasion for foolery, Bregawn showed none of the reluctance to line up that has characterised his recent appearances. Whiggie Geo disputed the lead with him over the first six fences. Bregawn then went ahead and was never passed again.

Captain John (11-1), recovering from a mistake three fences from home, drew nearly level at the last, but Bregawn shook him off and

went five lengths clear. Wayward Lad (6-1) looked the danger rounding the last bend, but could not quite sustain his effort and was beaten another one-and-a-half lengths into third place.

Graham Bradley, who had also ridden Bregawn when he finished second to Silver Buck last year was fully justified in the bold tactics that made full use of his mount's stamina. Silver Buck (5-1) this time began to tire two fences from home and finished a distant fourth, with Ashley House (12-1) a further 25 lengths behind. Eight of the 11 runners finished.

Dickinson, whose first money earnings this season are now an amazing £345,000, began his racing career as a successful amateur rider. A fall at Cartmel damaged his liver and ended his riding career. Three years ago he took over his father, Tony's, stable.

---

18 March

Queen's trainer dies at 95

By HOTSPUR

Captain Cecil Charles Boyd-Rochfort, who has died aged 95, was one of the Queen's racehorse trainers and ranks among the greatest trainers in British racehorse history. He retired in 1968, in which year he was appointed KCVO.

Educated at Eton and a captain in the Scots Guards, he served in the 1914-18 war, was wounded and awarded the Croix de Guerre. He took out his training licence in 1921.

He won every English classic, including five St Legers, excelling in the difficult task of training high-class stayers. For Lady Zia Wernher, he won the fillies Triple Crown in 1955 with Meld. But he had to wait until 1959 for his well-deserved Derby success, Parthia, whose owner was the late Sir

Humphrey de Trafford.

Sir Cecil's association with the Royal family began during the early war years, when he succeeded Willie Jarvis as trainer to King George VI. Their biggest triumph together was the 1946 1,000 Guineas with Hypericum. His series of fine victories with Aureole in 1954 must have done much to strengthen and confirm the Queen's early racing interest.

"The Captain", as Boyd-Rochfort was known throughout the racing world, was not only a great trainer but also a much loved man. He accepted success and defeat with the same gentle good manners. His tall, distinguished figure is etched ineradicably on the memory of countless friends and admirers.

Ascot: 6 April

Walwyn reaches milestone

By MARLBOROUGH (John Oaksey)

Fulke Walwyn and 57 other winners of the Grand National sat down for a special lunch at Ascot with Queen Elizabeth the Queen Mother, the Lambourn trainer's principal owner and the unluckiest Aintree loser of them all. And within a few hours, what was already a day to remember had become a milestone in the career of this remarkable trainer, who took his total to 2,000 winners with a treble.

As one of only two men to have both ridden and trained a Grand National winner – Fred Winter is the other – Walwyn got Ascot's "Focus on Aintree" off to an appropriate start when Gallaher won the opening 'chase. And when hurdlers Desert Hero and Noble Heir followed suit, it became obvious no one could have set up a better set of circumstances as the Aintree Appeal campaign enters its last, most vital, phase.

Grand National Aintree: 9 April

Corbiere stays on lady's day

John Oaksey's insight on the big race

For one awful moment a hundred yards from home in yesterday's Sun Grand National at Liverpool, Jenny Pitman must have relived the nightmare finish in which her then husband, Richard, was caught on Crisp by Red Rum ten years ago. But this time it was different. Ben de Haan and Corbiere hung on to hold Greasepaint's challenge and make Jenny Pitman the first woman trainer to saddle a Grand National winner.

Corbiere (right), the winner

"Crisp's defeat really hurt Jenny almost more than me," Richard Pitman said yesterday. "But this will more than make up for it. She has always been a really good trainer." She has also always been a lady with a strong mind of her own and has been telling us for ages that Corbiere would win.

So those who predicted that this would be the first "petticoat Grand National" were proved right. But from a riding as opposed to a training point of view, their illusions were quickly and painfully shattered. Geraldine Rees, hitherto the only lady ever to complete the course, now became, on Midday Welcome, the first lady to fall at the first fence. And although the American rider Mrs Joy Carrier got quite a bit further, she and King Spruce toppled over at Becher's first time round.

By that time, the 13-year-old

Delmoss, who was last of the 10 finishers and was sold after the race to help the Grand National campaign, had been advertising his talents by blazing merrily away in front.

De Haan had Corbiere (13-1) settled immediately, always near the inside and never out of the first four. They took the lead on the long run to the second last – too soon for Jenny Pitman's peace of mind, as a few lengths behind them Greasepaint (14-1) was still going ominously strong.

But Corbiere is just as resolute as his trainer and, luckily for both of them, the Irish-trained Greasepaint made almost his only mistake at the last fence, landing crooked and losing some momentum. This gave Corbiere an extra two lengths' advantage – just enough, as as the winning post came only just in time for England.

Another Irish horse, Yer Man (80-1) was an honourable if well-beaten (20 lengths) third, and last year's winner and top weight, Grittar, was an entirely undisgraced fifth.

Oaks Epsom: 4 June

Sun Princess scorches Oaks rivals

By John Oaksey

If the Derby was easy, the Oaks was a positive cakewalk. Sir Michael Sobell's Sun Princess had never won until yesterday, but in this £77,178 classic, she and Willie Carson made their opponents look like a pack of overfed corgis chasing a greyhound.

At Newbury three weeks ago, having only her second race, Sun Princess was beaten two lengths by Ski Sailing, who (to some myopic eyes like mine) appeared to have about a ton in hand. Carson had always told me we were wrong, and yesterday, winning his third Oaks for Dick Hern, he proved it with quite unnecessary gusto.

When the front runners suddenly slowed down near the top of the hill, Carson, near the back and towards the outside, said to himself: "I know mine stays – why hang about any longer?" When he released the brakes, Sun Princess (6-1) stormed down the hill, passing at least 10 horses in 200 yards, to lead as they swung out of Tattenham Corner.

None of the others could make even a serious effort at pursuit. Acclimatise (20-1) did best, running on bravely into second place, but even she was beaten 12 lengths, a record distance for any English classic.

Derby Epsom: 1 June

Dominant Teenoso provides Piggott with ninth Derby

By HOTSPUR (Peter Scott)

Teenoso gave a performance of ruthless efficiency to improve Lester Piggott's amazing Derby record. Piggott sent his ninth Derby winner ahead early in the Epsom straight, and from that stage yesterday's big-race favourite was in no serious danger.

Drenching early-morning rain turned the ground heavy, and Teenoso's time of 2min 49.07sec made this the slowest Derby since Common won in 1891, and 15 seconds slower than Golden Fleece's time last year. Piggott had his first Derby ride in 1951 and Teenoso (9-2f) was his 30th. Ireland's Carlingford Castle (14-1) was most capably handled by Michael Kinane, whose first Derby this was, and he finished three lengths behind the winner.

Shearwalk (18-1) was badly hampered five furlongs out when Yawa unseated Philip Waldren, and he made up a tremendous amount of ground to beat second favourite Salmon Leap (11-2) a short head for third place, another three lengths behind Carlingford Castle.

Teenoso's regular rider Steve Cauthen was claimed to ride The Noble Player (11th), and Piggott, left without a ride when winter favourite Dunbeath revealed stamina deficiencies at York, correctly chose Teenoso in preference to Tolomeo, who came ninth.

Hardwicke Stakes Ascot: 17 June

Ascot double and course record is Stanerra's tally

By HOTSPUR (Peter Scott)

Stanerra was the heroine of Royal Ascot this week. The five-year-old Irish mare broke Grundy's course record in the Hardwicke Stakes (at 4-1) yesterday [Friday], adding this to her Prince of Wales Stakes victory (7-1) on Tuesday's opening afternoon.

Old Country and Lafontaine disputed the Hardwicke Stakes lead at a blistering pace. Stanerra took command on entering the straight and went clear. Electric (3-1f), running on bravely, was beaten one-and-a-half lengths, finishing 12 lengths clear of Be My Native (6-1).

Frank Dunne, Stanerra's owner-trainer, has kept her in England since she won at Sandown 19 days ago. She clocked 2min 26.95sec yesterday, beating Grundy's mark, made in his epic King George battle with Bustino in 1975, by three-hundredths of a second.

[These wins projected Stanerra from a tough and useful 4-year-old to one of the leading middle-distance horses, and although she faded to finish 6th in the Arc, she finished in a blaze of glory with her triumph in the valuable Japan Cup in Tokyo.]

ENGLISH CLASSICS

2,000 Guineas	Lomond	P Eddery	9-1
1,000 Guineas	Ma Biche	F Head	5-2f
Derby	Teenoso	L Piggott	9-2f
Oaks	Sun Princess	W Carson	6-1
St Leger	Sun Princess	W Carson	11-8f

OTHER MAJOR RACES

Irish Derby	Shareef Dancer	WR Swinburn	8-1
Arc de Triomphe	All Along	WR Swinburn	17-1
Kentucky Derby	Sunny's Halo	E Delahoussaye	5-2
Melbourne Cup	Kiwi	J Cassidy	9-1
Arlington Million	Tolomeo	P Eddery	382-10
Japan Cup	Stanerra	B Rouse	32-10

Keeneland Select Sales Kentucky: 19 July

Northern Dancer colt shatters yearling record

By Tony Stafford

Two days of unparalleled big spending at the Keeneland Sales reached a barely credible climax on Tuesday night when Sheikh Mohammed's Aston Upthorpe Stud paid $10.2 million (£6,667,000) for a Northern Dancer colt out of My Bupers.

This figure was more than double the previous record set in the same sales ring a year ago when a Robert Sangster syndicate paid $4.25m for a Nijinsky colt. Sangster equalled the previous record on Monday night when he bought another Northern Dancer colt. Both times Sangster was pushed to that hitherto uncharted figure by Sheikh Mohammed, but on

Tuesday night the roles were reversed, with the Sangster party withdrawing when their $10m was exceeded.

Sheikh Mohammed and his brothers, Hamdan Al-Maktoum and Maktoum Al-Maktoum, bought a total of 37 horses for nearly $44m (£28.5m), while Sangster's outlay was nearly $18m (£11.7m).

The Sheikh himself, his country's Defence Minister, is responsible for 21 of them, through his Aston Upthorpe Stud, near Didcot. His chief trainers are John Dunlop and Michael Stoute.

[The record buy, called Snaafi Dancer, retired unraced in December 1985.]

Vernons Sprint Cup Haydock: 3 September

Fast Habibti in line for Racehorse title

By John Oaksey

Habibti put up a spellbinding performance in the Vernons Sprint at Haydock. She is without doubt the fastest horse of any age or sex in Europe and, with the so-called classic three-year-olds either beating each other or sulking unraced in their tents, she must surely be hot favourite for the title "Racehorse of 1983".

Sayf El Arab set a tremendous early gallop, so fast that even Soba had to be content with second place. But Willie Carson was always sitting calmly in full control behind them on Habibti. Soba was allowed a few brief moments in the lead, but that was all. A furlong out, for the third time

this season, Habibti swept past her.

With Carson a willing passenger, Habibti sailed smooth as silk further and further ahead, and her victory by seven imperious lengths in the end represents the finest display of pure speed I can remember.

I never saw Mumtaz Mahal, but her proud title "the Flying Filly" was gloriously usurped at Haydock yesterday.

[A month later, Habibti beat Soba again when they both shattered the Longchamp 5f record in the Prix de l'Abbaye, and Habibti was duly voted top horse by a wide margin, 23 votes to Sun Princess's 2 and Time Charter's 1.]

King George VI & Queen Elizabeth Diamond Stakes Ascot: 23 July

Charter arrives bang on time

By John Oaksey

"Perfect" results are rare in any sport, but the King George came close to that at Ascot yesterday as 48-year-old Joe Mercer rode Time Charter to beat Diamond Shoal (Lester Piggott) and Sun Princess (Willie Carson). Britain's greatest international all-aged prize had, for a change, been gloriously kept at home with only marginal help from the United States.

It was for Joe Mercer, the most stylish Flat-race jockey I have ever seen, his first Group 1 winner for four years. Joe rang the winner's regular jockey, the injured Billy Newnes, yesterday morning to ask the younger man's advice. "Just let her settle and

she will do it when you want her," was the answer – and that was how it looked to us in the stands.

The early gallop was slow and Time Charter lay last at Swinley Bottom. On the turn for home, Piggott took Diamond Shoal (8-1) to the front. Sun Princess (9-4jf) was close and looking dangerous when Mercer pulled Time Charter (5-1) wide for what turned out to be the winning challenge. The distances were three-quarters of a length and a length. The other joint favourite, Irish-trained Caerleon, had both front shoes torn off round the final bend when in a good position to challenge.

Budweiser Million Arlington Park: 28 August

Tolomeo wins in Chicago

By HOTSPUR

An English-trained horse won the world's richest race yesterday, when Pat Eddery landed the three-year old colt Tolomeo a narrow winner of the Budweiser Million.

Starting at the remarkably generous price of 36-1, Tolomeo was in the first three throughout and Eddery kept him close to the inside rail. He passed the pacemaking Nijinsky's Secret to take command just inside the last furlong and then held a challenge from the favourite, the eight-year-old John Henry, by a neck.

[Always finding at least one better at home, Tolomeo nevertheless broke the British earnings record for a season with the £400,000 from this sole victory and £85,162 from his place earnings.]

Vladivar Vodka Trophy Epsom: 30 August

Chief is so close to world record

By MARLBOROUGH
(John Oaksey)

Spark Chief earned £10,000 for the Apprentice School Charitable Trust by winning the Vladivar Vodka Trophy in 53.70 sec at Epsom, and missed a world record, which would have been worth £160,000 to the charity, by a tantalising tenth of a second. Indigenous's 23-year-old five-furlong record was hand-timed from a starting-gate as opposed to stalls, and Spark Chief may now be the rightful world record holder.

But weight should be considered, too, and though 0.19sec faster than Raffingora's electrically timed 53.89sec, he was carrying 30lb less than the famous grey.

Prix de l'Arc de Triomphe Longchamp: 2 October

Piggott reject All Along is Arc heroine

By MARLBOROUGH (John Oaksey)

British fortunes in general and those of Lester Piggott in particular plummeted sadly at Longchamp yesterday when Walter Swinburn rode M Daniel Wildenstein's All Along to dramatic last-gasp victory over Sun Princess in the Trusthouse Forte Prix de l'Arc de Triomphe.

Ten days ago, in circumstances the rights and

wrongs of which are still very much a matter of opinion, Piggott chose to ride Awaasif in preference to All Along. An affronted M Wildenstein promptly took the champion jockey off all his horses. Piggott's reaction to All Along's victory (Awaasif never showed with a chance) was a philosophical "That's life".

But Piggott's fate was not on this occasion the chief concern of the vast British contingent. Three furlongs out, as Diamond Shoal and Sun Princess swung into the straight together, with Time Charter and Stanerra close behind them, any one of several desirable permutations seemed on the cards. But Swinburn brought All

Along (17-1) through first a gap that opened up on the rails and then another between Sun Princess (27-4) and Stanerra to beat the Oaks and St Leger winner by a length, with the French filly Luth Enchantee (17-1) a short neck away third, beating the 13-4 favourite Time Charter into fourth place by a nose.

1984

12 Apr John Francome wins the Railfreight "world championship" at Cheltenham with 17 points, for a 1st and 2nd, beating Belgium's representative Philippe Caus by 3 points with the Italian G.Colleo third a further point behind. Riders from 12 countries, from as far afield as Japan and the Soviet Union, take part, with at least 3 rides each in the 4 sponsored races.

24 Jul The Keeneland Sales end with another record, Sheikh Mohammed's Darley Stud paying more than £41m (£29m) for 29 yearlings. Top price of $8.25m (£6.35m), however, is paid by Robert Sangster for a Northern Dancer-Ballade bay colt. Five of the highest six yearling prices are paid for colts by Northern Dancer. The record price for a stud farm is almost trebled when the Murty Farm, which borders on Keeneland and is owned by the Murty Brothers, goes to a group of Texans for $19.25m (£14.8m).

10 Aug Greville Starkey is suspended for 14 days by the Jockey Club disciplinary committee, who uphold a charge of reckless riding made by the Goodwood stewards after his mount Rousillon had finished 2nd in the Sussex Stakes. Starkey, 44, has been suspended 13 times for a total of 106 days during a career which began with his first winner in 1955. Seven of the bans have been in the last four years.

13 Oct The 9-year-old John Henry wins the last and richest prize of his career, the Ballentine's Scotch Classic Handicap at Meadowlands, to take his total prize money to a record $6,597,947. His US record of 25 Graded-stake wins includes 16 Grade I races.

9 Nov Riding Church Warden to victory in a novice hurdle at Cheltenham, John Francome achieves the fastest 50 winners in a National Hunt season, beating Josh Gifford's 1966 mark by a day.

---

13 January

Epsom future is secured by Derby sponsor

By HOTSPUR (Peter Scott)

BRITISH EVER READY, the battery company whose sponsorship of the Derby and Oaks is for an initial period of three years, will also make a lasting donation to Epsom's future by contributing substantially to the fund for a new grandstand. Built 57 years ago, this stand is rapidly approaching the time when replacement or massive refurbishment becomes essential. Aintree's stands have an even shorter remaining lifespan with only temporary replacements planned.

At least a dozen races in various parts of the world last year were richer than the Derby. Sponsorship will push it up the 1984 ladder despite various new promotions in the United States. Last year's Derby first prize was £165,080, but the winner's share on June 6 should comfortably top £200,000.

Ever Ready's name will be added to the Derby. The Oaks, with its first prize guaranteed to rise above £100,000 for the first time on June 9, will carry the prefix Gold Seal, which is Ever Ready's new longlife battery.

---

24 January

Snaffy Dancer is name for record colt

By HOTSPUR (Peter Scott)

SNAFFY DANCER is the name to be registered for the Northern Dancer colt who set a world record yearling price at Keeneland, Kentucky, last July, and is now being trained at Arundel by John Dunlop for Sheikh Mohammed. I understand that "elegant" is a near translation from the Arabic for the word Snaffy.

This colt's purchase price of $10.2 million dollars was equivalent to £6,258,000 based on the rules of racing exchange rate in force last July. Snaffy Dancer is developing steadily, but Dunlop does not expect him to race until the end of June at the earliest.

Sidbury Handicap 'Chase Worcester: 29 February

Stand-in Francome steps up to 1,000

By MARLBOROUGH (John Oaksey)

Fourteen years and 4,576 races ago, John Francome won on Multigrey at Worcester, the first ride of his career. He went back there yesterday to join Stan Mellor in racing's proudest two-man club as Observe gave him his 1,000th winner in the Sidbury' Handicap 'Chase

Owing to circumstances beyond our control, you may not know the full story of how difficult the final ascent to the summit became. When Country Agent, hot favourite and the champion's only other ride yesterday, was thwarted by Webwood in Div I of the Ferry Novice's Hurdle, the media circus which had been following in Francome's footsteps began to wonder uneasily where it would all end.

Luckily, taking himself too seriously has never been one of Francome's problems. His smile stayed as wide as ever at Plumpton on Tuesday when Dancing Sovereign, widely expected to be the one, not only failed to provide the 1,000th victory, but refused to take any active part in the E.Coomes Handicap Hurdle. Not content with giving the others a 50-yard start, Dancing Sovereign (who had done this sort of thing before) then downed tools completely near the racecourse stables. His evident sympathy with the problems of GCHQ would no doubt have warmed Mr Murray's heart and it also delighted Hugo Bevan, clerk of the course at Worcester, to where the caravan of cameras, microphones and hacks proceeded. Bevan later announced that there will be a race named to mark Francome's achievement at the course next year.

Ben de Haan's weekend injury had left a place vacant on Observe's back, and Mr Tony Gretton's' good horse was in every way an

Francome: prolific winner

appropriate, indeed an ideal, vehicle for the millennium.

Observe is trained by Fred Winter and in the winner's enclosure Francome paid eloquent and grateful tribute to the Lambourn trainer's role in his career. Observe has also been paradoxically involved in two of Francome's brushes with authority this season and, best of all, considering the large advantage given him by the limited handicap weights, he would, as his rider ruefully reminded us, "make a race of it with a clothes horse". Observe duly did just that, but this time all was well.

So, as the corks popped, the cameras clicked and the large crowd cheered their heads off, Francome could look back at 14 memorable years. For most of them, he has been delighting us by doing one of sport's most difficult, hazardous and exhausting jobs at least as well as it has ever been done. And in quite a few people's opinion, better.

20 March

Maximum fine for Francome's riding offence

By HOTSPUR (Peter Scott)

John Francome, whose season has been one of numerous highlights mixed with a fair measure of controversy, was fined £2,500 by the Jockey Club disciplinary stewards in London yesterday for his riding of Easter Lee at Newbury on February 10. Officials considered that Easter Lee would have finished second rather than third in the Stroud Green Hurdle there had Francome ridden him out to the end.

Easter Lee's case is the fifth this season that has seen Francome disciplined for riding offences.

Four of these were for not riding out to secure the best possible minor placing on a beaten horse, and the other for excessive use of the whip on Observe at Chepstow last December.

Francome's fines earlier this season totalled £355. Yesterday's sizeable increase was the maximum that could have been imposed.

NATIONAL HUNT

Champion Hurdle	Dawn Run	JJ O'Neill	4-5f
Cheltenham Gold Cup	Burrough Hill Lad	P Tuck	7-2
Grand National	Hallo Dandy	N Doughty	13-1

Whitbread Gold Cup Sandown: 28 April

Special Cargo delivered

By John Oaksey

AFTER more than 30 years as British jumping's best-loved owner and most faithful supporter, Queen Elizabeth the Queen Mother had her greatest victory at Sandown yesterday when Kevin Mooney and Special Cargo won her the 28th running of the Whitbread Gold Cup.

But as the winning owner would, I am certain, be the first to insist, this magnificent race was much more than just another sporting Royal landmark. With Lettoch and the 13-year-old Diamond Edge 2nd and 3rd, beaten only two short heads, it was also quite literally the most exciting finish I have ever seen, a triumph for the whole sport of steeplechasing and, most of all, for 73-year-old Fulke Walwyn.

Special Cargo was the great Lambourn trainer's seventh Whitbread Gold Cup winner, and the only sad thing about this infinitely happy day was that Diamond Edge should fail so narrowly and gallantly to become the first horse to win the great race three times.

He and Special Cargo both represent masterpieces of the trainer's art. Both have spent most of the last two years on the sidelines recovering from leg trouble. When Special Cargo came out to win the

Grand Military Gold Cup with carbon-fibre implants in his legs, it seemed a miracle. As for Diamond Edge. he has been trained specifically with this one race in mind.

Yesterday, running for only the second time in two years, he rose to the heights of his great days. From start to finish, Diamond Edge behaved as though he owned Sandown — jumping majestically, sometimes with almost hazardous abandon, and always up in the first three.

Behind him, fate struck one damaging blow when Donegal Prince fell at the downhill fence slap in the path of Lettoch. "I just had nowhere to go," Robert Earnshaw said afterwards. "We made up the ground all right, but looking back now it must have cost us the race."

No one could argue with that, but as Lettoch's stable companion Ashley House (7-2jf) led Plundering (7-2jf) and Diamond Edge (11-2) round the final bend, Lettoch (11-2) was only one of half a dozen still in with an outside chance. At the Pond, three from home, Bill Smith with wonderfully cool tactical judgment was sitting motionless, hoarding Diamond Edge's energy for the final hill. At that moment things looked good for

Plundering, who landed just in front, but almost immediately he was challenged and passed by Lettoch.

As these two jumped the second last ahead of Diamond Edge, Mooney could be seen fighting what looked a losing battle on Special Cargo (8-1). Bill Smith had always said that if Diamond Edge could win, this would be his last ride, and now, going to the last two lengths behind Plundering and Lettoch, he threw down the challenge. It

carried him through between the two leaders and his head was definitely just in front a hundred yards from home.

But Lettoch would not give in, and at that moment, with Mooney getting an even more amazing response from Special Cargo, the Royal horse stormed up the far side to thrust his head across the line. Although Diamond Edge was only third, Bill Smith's philosophical reaction was "I will never do anything better than that, so it is time to call it a day."

Grand National Aintree: 31 March

'Dandy' leads home record 23 finishers

By HOTSPUR (Peter Scott)

AINTREE's fortunes, embodying doubts about its future, have fluctuated during the last 20 years in as volatile a fashion as the most incident-packed Grand National. They stand higher now than for a long time. Changed ownership, following protracted negotiations, put the course in secure hands last summer. This has now been followed by a Grand National which provided a record number of 23 finishers and drew a substantially increased crowd. The spirit of good cheer was reflected by a merry choir singing "Hallo Dandy" to the tune of "Hello Dolly" as Saturday's big winner was led in.

The Grand National is also benefiting from a run of well-backed winners since the shocks of Anglo and Foinavon in 1966 and 1967. Only three of the 17 winners since Foinavon have started at longer odds than 15-1, and Saturday's first four finishers were all leading fancies.

Capt. Christopher Mordaunt, the Grand National handicapper, is also entitled to quiet satisfaction with Saturday's result. His 1984 weights were sharply criticised by the stables of Corbiere and Greasepaint for supposedly ruining the chances of last year's first and second, but their splendid efforts against Hallo Dandy showed that both had been fairly treated.

Tudor Line, Wyndburgh and Freddie are now joined by Greasepaint among the Grand National's post-war heroes who have finished second at

least twice without winning it. Greasepaint (9-1f), who so nearly helped Saving Mercy to land trainer Dermot Weld the Spring Double, fought back bravely after Hallo Dandy (13-1) had passed him two fences from home. With Hallo Dandy drifting over to the stand rails on the run-in, Greasepaint drew almost level again, but Hallo Dandy then forged clear once more to win by four lengths.

Corbiere (16-1) and Lucky Vane (12-1) stayed on stoutly to be third and fourth, overtaking Earthstopper (33-1), whose death after passing the post provided the race's only sad note.

Gay Kindersley, who trained Earthstopper, had another Grand National heartbreak 21 years ago when John Oaksey, wearing his colours on Carrickbeg, was overtaken close home by Pat Buckley on Ayala.

The Grand National crowd of 36,500 was 17 per cent up on last year, and the three-day attendance totalled 51,000.

Gordon Richards, of Greystoke, Cumbria, had a meeting that represents the highlight of his training career. Hallo Dandy's victory was preceded by wins for Noddy's Ryde and Little Bay, and he also won Saturday's last race with Jennie Pat.

Hallo Dandy was a 60-1 chance when fourth last year. Much drier ground on Saturday had made Richards as optimistic as any trainer can feel before a Grand National and jockey Neale Doughty played his part to perfection

---

Lavington Challenge Cup Handicap 'Chase Fontwell: 28 May

Perfect Round brings record for Francome

By MARLBOROUGH (John Oaksey)

JOHN FRANCOME climbed to one of sport's highest, most hazardous peaks yesterday when, in the Lavington Challenge Cup Handicap 'Chase at Fontwell Park, Don't Touch became his 1,036th winner, one more than Stan Mellor's career record. The achievement is certain to stand for many years, and it was perhaps appropriate that the landmark should be passed, not on one of his two fancied hurdle-race rides, but on a 'chaser with the ominous letters PPPFU before his name.

The F was a crashing fall suffered by Francome himself. So it was fitting that, with the help of blinkers, his matchless horsemanship should draw from the 10-year-old Don't Touch (6-1) a round of agile perfection.

After accepting a huge bottle of champagne from Piper Heidsieck and some elegant goblets specially engraved by Fontwell, Francome expressed his delight and gratitude, especially to Fred Winter and John Jenkins, with characteristic grace and humour. "At least now you won't have to trek off to Uttoxeter," he told the assembled hacks, and then imparted the best news of the day, that he will ride again next season.

Grande Course de Haies Auteuil: 22 June

Dawn Run in unique double at Auteuil

By MARLBOROUGH (John Oaksey)

EVEN the French did not forbear to cheer at Auteuil yesterday when Dawn Run dominated the Grande Course de Haies from start to finish — becoming the first winner of the British Champion Hurdle to take the French equivalent.

As often happens during the nervous tensions of a Dawn Run big-race day, Auteuil was buzzing beforehand with Dick Francis/Nat Gould rumours of a plot to "murder" the great Irish mare on one of the early bends. On this comprehensively filmed and rigidly stewarded circuit it always sounded a supremely improbable scare. In any case, Tony Mullins and Dawn Run took out the best conceivable insurance policy. As they sailed past the stands on the long run to the first flight, the other nine were at least 10 lengths behind. You would have needed a rifle to stop the leader there, and from that time on the only danger was a fall.

The warmth of the welcome she got from the crowd had little or nothing to do with betting [she was 6-5 favourite]. This is one of those rare horses who can make your heart turn over just by how hard she tries.

The St Leger Doncaster: 15 September

Classical as Piggott rides record 28th

By John Oaksey

Commanche Run (right) by a neck

THe triumphant success story which began in 1954, the day Never Say Die won the Derby, reached an historic landmark at Doncaster yesterday when Lester Piggott drove Commanche Run home to win the Holsten Pils St Leger Stakes. It was his eighth success in the race and his 28th victory in an English Classic, one more than Frank Buckle's 19th-century total and a record most unlikely ever to be equalled.

The circumstances in which Commanche Run's Singapore-based owner Mr Ivan Allan gave Piggott, his long-time friend, the ride in preference to Luca Cumani's American stable-jockey, Darrel McHargue, were, to say the least of it, controversial. But, even if you disapprove of the way the 11-

---

The Derby Epsom: 6 June

Secreto gives David O'Brien Derby record

By HOTSPUR (Peter Scott)

Secreto wore down El Gran Senor in the last few strides of the Ever Ready Derby, enabling David O'Brien to upstage his father Vincent and become the youngest trainer to saddle a winner of the Epsom Classic.

David O'Brien, 27, decided to run Secreto only last Friday, having been disappointed with the colt's Irish 2,000 Guineas defeat. Secreto's short-head success was followed by an unsuccessful objection from El Gran Senor's jockey Pat Eddery for "leaning" on the favourite in the final furlong.

Vincent O'Brien suffered the heartbreak of watching his horse's stamina give out.

El Gran Senor was cantering over his rivals halfway up the straight. He cruised past At Talaq soon after passing the two-furlong marker, with the hard-ridden Secreto in hot pursuit.

El Gran Senor (8-11f) began to tire a furlong out. Eddery went for his whip and the favourite drifted to his right in fatigue. Christy Roche forced Secreto (14-1) in front close home, and would have had his own grounds for lodging an objection had the photo-finish gone against him. Both first and second were sired by the great Northern Dancer. Mighty Flutter (66-1) was third, At Talaq (250-1) fourth.

The Oaks Epsom: 9 June

Plume takes Lester level

By John Oaksey

THE Gold Seal Oaks made happy sporting history at Epsom yesterday when, without even using to the full his famous strength, Lester Piggott rode Sir Robin McAlpine's Circus Plume to victory – his 27th English Classic, equalling Frank Buckle's 19th-century record.

Buckle, who was born in 1766, was still riding winners in his 60s and rode altogether for 48 years. It is only 36 since Lester's first winner in 1948.

The first of his six Oaks winners was the Queen's Carrozza in 1957.

The warm welcome Lester was given by the Epsom crowd was a reminder of the unique place he has so long held in the hearts of the sporting public. Apart from Royalty, in fact, I honestly question whether there is a more famous Englishman alive, and certainly very few if any better known sportsmen in the world.

ENGLISH CLASSICS			
2,000 Guineas	El Gran Senor	P Eddery	15-8f
1,000 Guineas	Pebbles	P Robinson	8-1
Derby	Secreto	C Roche	14-1
Oaks	Circus Plume	L Piggott	4-1
St Leger	Commanche Run	L Piggott	7-4f

times champion got his opportunity, no one can deny the strength and inspiration with which he seized it.

Left in front on the turn for home much earlier than he intended, Piggott was furiously challenged all the way up the straight by the Aga Khan's pair, Baynoun and Shernazar, and by Crazy and Alphabatim. In fact, Commanche Run (7-4f) never lost the lead, but to us in the stands, Baynoun (5-2) and Steve Cauthen looked almost certain to pass him a furlong out, and even Piggott admitted afterwards that he thought he would be beaten.

"But Commanche Run is very game and he knew what was needed," the great jockey said. Certainly they looked a marvellously effective team as the big bay colt kept sticking out his head to hold Baynoun by a neck, with Alphabatim (7-1) passing Crazy (9-1) close home to to take third place.

Cheered to the echo again and again in the unsaddling enclosure, Lester Piggott said quite definitely that he does not intend to retire this season. "I don't intend that to be my last Classic," he says, and to the whole racing world that was the best news of a happy day.

OTHER MAJOR RACES

Irish Derby	El Gran Senor	P Eddery	2-7f
Arc de Triomphe	Sagace	Y Saint-Martin	39-10
Kentucky Derby	Swale	L Pincay	34-10
Melbourne Cup	Black Knight	P Cook	10-1
Arlington Million	John Henry	C McCarron	11-10
Japan Cup	Katsuragi Ace	K Nishiura	396-10

BBC Radio Humberside Stakes York: 10 October

Carson booed after favourite fiasco

Willie Carson received a hostile reception after being left at the stalls on the Queen's Rough Stones, an even-money favourite who trailed in last of four behind Tropical Way in the BBC Radio Humberside Stakes at York yesterday. Boos and cries of "disgraceful, Willie" greeted him as he dismounted and walked to the weighing room, and one irate punter attempted to throw a pint of beer over him.

Rough Stones was left about a furlong, and at the inevitable stewards' inquiry Carson's explanation – that as the stall gates opened the colt stood on his hind legs, screwed himself round, trapping his head briefly over the next-door stall – was accepted.

Carson said "There was just nothing I could do about it," and trainer Dick Hern added: "It can happen to a 33-1 chance or an odds-on favourite."

Nobber 'Chase Navan: 1 November

Echoes of Arkle in Dawn Run victory
By MARLBOROUGH (John Oaksey)

Irish jumping gave its queen a royal welcome home at Navan yesterday when Mrs Charmian Hill's Dawn Run made a majestic start to her new career with a flawless clear round in the Nobber 'Chase. It was at Navan in January 1962 that Arkle won over hurdles for the first time, when he was ridden by Liam McLoughlin and pulled his way past an amazed Pat Taaffe on his stable companion, the evens favourite Kerforo.

Paddy Woods, who later also won on the great horse and rode him in so much of his work, was present yesterday. "I have not heard an Irish crowd buzzing like this for 20 years," he said, and as Tony Mullins rode back on the winner of three Champion Hurdles this year, Arkle's name was on many lips.

Dawn Run led over the first two uphill fences and past the stands. She cleared both with her long ears gaily pricked, then took a good sensible look at the open ditch and measured it like a veteran.

A moment later, we saw perhaps the most significant and hopeful sight of all. Galloping downhill quite closely pressed by the fitter, more experienced Buck House, Dawn Run was not far off full speed when she met the fifth fence wrong. You never saw the proverbial "short one" put in safer or with greater economy.

But then, with three fences left and both Buck House and Dark Ivy hard on her heels, Dawn Run reminded us that brains and agility are only two of her talents. She is also a truly formidable racehorse, and round the turn for home both rivals were simply left standing.

Dinsdale Spa Stakes Redcar: 1 November

Provideo adds to record first season
By HOTSPUR

PROVIDEO turned back the clock 99 years yesterday when winning the Dinsdale Spa Stakes at Redcar, where his 16th success of the season enabled him to claim a second record and emulate another.

Already the winner of most two-year-old races this century, Provideo equalled the all-time juvenile record of 16 set by The Bard in 1885, and

passed this century's all-age best for one season held by Hornet's Beauty since 1911.

Yesterday's price of 8-1 on was also the shortest at which he has started in his 23 races, and his seven-length margin of victory equalled his greatest since he began in the same fashion as the Bard by winning the Brocklesby Stakes, the first race of the season.

Rothmans Invitational Championship Woodbine Park: 21 October

Swinburn out as All Along fails again
By HOTSPUR (Peter Scott)

WALTER SWINBURN, who rode All Along to win last year's Prix de l'Arc de Triomphe and then three big races in Canada and the United States, will no longer be associated with M Daniel Wildenstein's mare. All Along, odds-on to repeat her 1983 success in the Rothmans Invitational Championship at Woodbine Park, Toronto, on Sunday, finished only fourth. Patrick Biancone, his trainer, then claimed that Swinburn had disregarded his instructions.

Biancone says that Swinburn did not make

enough use of All Along. Swinburn's defence is that the five-year-old did not give him "the same feel" as last autumn. Subsequent results suggest that heavy ground at Longchamp took a much more severe toll of this year's runners than did the firm ground on which last year's race was contested.

M Wildenstein fell out with Pat Eddery over his riding of Buckskin in the 1978 Ascot Gold Cup and has refused to employ Lester Piggott since he turned down the mount on All Along in last year's Arc.

Newmarket: 2 November

Cauthen crowned Champion Jockey in sixth season
By HOTSPUR

STEVE CAUTHEN enters the final week of his sixth season since moving to Britain from the United States with the official accolade of champion jockey. He received a trophy to commemorate his achievement at Newmarket yesterday, although there has been little doubt since late summer, when injuries to Willie Carson and Lester Piggott left Cauthen in an unassailable lead.

Cauthen *(right)*, the first American to be champion jockey in England since Danny Maher in 1913, joins an exclusive club of 13 jockeys who have taken the championship since 1914. Steve Donoghue, Gordon Richards and Piggott dominated their generations, with occasional interruptions. In more recent times, Piggott has alternated in winning the title with Pat Eddery, Carson

and, on one occasion, Joe Mercer.

Cauthen, who moves to Henry Cecil's stable next year, has youth on his side and could set up a long sequence of championships, fitness and availability permitting.

Breeders' Cup Hollywood Park: 10 November

All Along beaten in Breeders' Cup Turf
By HOTSPUR (Peter Scott)

The seven-race, multi-million dollar Breeders Cup was inaugurated on Saturday at Hollywood Park, California, where All Along, ridden by Walter Swinburn's replacement, Angel Cordero, was narrowly beaten in the mile-and-a-half Breeders' Cup Turf. She took command two furlongs from home, but was caught in the last few strides and beaten a neck by Yves Saint-Martin's mount

Lashkari (534-10), a Mill Reef colt belonging to the Aga Khan.

Lear Fan and Prego disappointed in the Breeders' Cup Mile, finishing seventh and ninth. The winner, Royal Heroine (17-10), whose time of 1min 32.6sec was a record for any mile race on grass in the United States, was formerly trained at Newmarket by Michael Stoute for Robert Sangster.

The breeding business

By Tony Stafford

The international bloodstock market has undergone an almost cyclic change during the past 15 years. It first soared out of control under the pressure of competition from a number of determined buying groups, but has now settled at a much more modest and realistic level.

It is not difficult to see parallels elsewhere in the modern world. In the mid-nineties heads of the former nationalised industries, now privatised monopolies or oligopolies, are paid massive salaries; footballers are similarly cosseted in financial terms, with clubs, desperate for success at any price, having forced transfer fees into the stratosphere.

These false, literally fabulous, examples from present-day activity echo almost precisely the situation in racehorse breeding in the mid-eighties. Then it was the pressure of the Arab owners vying with Robert Sangster's associates, with interest from a few prosperous American buyers, that caused a spiral which threatened never to end.

Scene of the excesses which promised and indeed brought financial ruin to many previously cautious and prudent breeders was the Keeneland July Yearling Sales, staged in the intoxicating atmosphere of the sale ring in Lexington, Kentucky, at the centre of America's racehorse breeding industry.

Developing equine talent

The Kentucky bluegrass is the ideal nursery land on which to rear young animals. The limestone-based land provides healthy calcium to develop bone in young horses, and the rich grasses produce the requisite nutrition. Kentucky's conditions are similar in many respects to those to be found in the Newmarket area in Suffolk, in the Normandy region of France, and through much of the rolling grasslands of Southern Ireland. It is not an accident that the four countries have become the leading developing grounds for equine talent.

The modern thoroughbred developed into its present form as a result of breeding more than three hundred years ago from Arabian stallions imported into England. All horses officially designated "thoroughbred" still descend from those stallions, and when racing became organised properly in the late 18th century in Britain, the fame of the animals, because of their speed and endurance, quickly spread.

By the early 19th century, Americans were importing some of the top racehorses from Britain to improve their horse breed, a trend which continued almost without interruption until the middle of the present century. Indeed, even after the Second World War, the usual traffic was East to West, with Epsom Derby winners the most typical imports for the New World.

It was not until the late 1950s that there was a significant shift in that trade. Vincent O'Brien was one of the pioneers in acquiring American talent, originally as a trainer of horses already American-owned, and later by travelling across to Keeneland Sales, and the major sales in Canada, to buy unproven young stock.

O'Brien takes the credit for identifying a brilliant young stallion early in its career. He trained the 1970 Triple Crown winner Nijinsky for the Canadian mineral mining millionaire Charles Engelhard, and soon reasoned that that horse's sire,

Sheikh Mohammed of the famous Maktoum racing family

Northern Dancer, was going to be an outstanding success.

Luckily, O'Brien was able to persuade Robert Sangster, heir to the Vernons Pools fortune of the company's founder Vernon Sangster, of the possibilities in buying at the major yearling sales in the United States. For several years, their financial muscle meant that the Sangster-O'Brien group could farm most of the best prospects, with O'Brien's uncanny judgment of what constituted a prospective star and Sangster's cash enough to ensure success.

Headlong inflation

For almost a decade they were able to dominate, but in the late 1970s, a most unexpected development brought an end to their free run and prompted the headlong inflation which caused outsiders to liken the industry to a latter-day South Sea Bubble.

The new buyers who brought about the change were an unlikely bunch at first sight. The tiny state of Dubai, second most important of the United Arab Emirates, is found at the far end of the Persian Gulf, the other side of Saudi Arabia, and a stopping point for jets on the way to the Far East.

Dubai had been a major trading post for many years, but the discovery of offshore oil during the 1960s transformed it into a rich country almost immediately. Its ruling family, the Maktoums, were in reality Bedouin who had lived in the desert, much as their neighbours the Saudis themselves had before their own economic miracle forced its way from under the sands.

The Maktoum family, headed by Sheikh Rashid, but most

significantly his four sons, Maktoum, Hamdan, Mohammed and Ahmed, loved horse racing, and looked to the English version of the sport to indulge their interest.

They quickly acquired a string of talented horses in England and soon turned their attentions to Kentucky, having noted the success which the Sangster importations had enjoyed in the top classic races. Animals such as The Minstrel and Golden Fleece, Caerleon and Sadler's Wells, kept the Sangster bandwagon going.

But once the Maktoums came along, they matched Sangster blow for blow and gradually, when the ante was pushed to its ultimate, blew him out of the water after a series of much-publicised head-to-head bidding battles.

In the early 1980s each July sale at Keeneland featured these bidding sprees. Eventually multi-million dollar prices became commonplace and then crucially, first $10.2 million and then $13.1 million was paid for untried horses a year before they could even race on the track.

Neither the $10.2 million paid by the Maktoums for the original record holder Snaafi Dancer, nor the $13.1 million stumped up by Sangster for Seattle Dancer produced the anticipated super-star – indeed, the former never set foot on a racetrack in public – and from that point, the biggest money days had gone.

Poorer and wiser

The result was that the industry had to self-correct, and the non-horse people who had been attracted by the thought of easy money in the breeding business quickly left it again, usually poorer and wiser.

In the meantime, stallion prices had to adjust accordingly. During the beginning of the 1980s, sons of Northern Dancer with stallion potential were syndicated, usually in 40 shares, for upwards of $40 million. Two of his sons, Storm Bird and Shareef Dancer, the former a Sangster racehorse, the latter owned by the Maktoums, were both sold for massive sums.

El Gran Senor, also by Northern Dancer, won the Irish Derby having narrowly failed in the Epsom Derby. That victory was enough to clinch his $40 million price tag, narrowly beating the figure Henryk de Kwiatkowski secured for his brilliant horse Conquistador Cielo, not by Northern Dancer, but winner of the Metropolitan Mile and the Belmont Stakes within five days in his three-year-old season.

During those days, the level of competition was compromised by the financial considerations. After El Gran Senor won his Irish Derby, he was immediately retired, and a few years later the same happened when Shareef Dancer won the same Classic race.

The 'fall' of Shareef Dancer

Take the case of Shareef Dancer, originally owned by Maktoum Al Maktoum, at the time eldest son of the Ruler, but now Ruler of the Emirate following the death of Sheikh Rashid.

Shareef Dancer retired to stud as a three-year-old having won a race at Royal Ascot and then the Irish Derby, both within a couple of weeks during June. He never raced again, and was syndicated in a deal which valued him at £36 million.

With horses being syndicated in a specific number of shares – in his case 36 – stallion shareholders (or owners) can choose either to send their own mare to the stallion in which they have such an interest, or instead sell their right to breed to him to another breeder who can then send his mare. A single nomination to the stallion was worth £250,000, based on a mathematical formula in which payment could reasonably be recouped within four years.

El Gran Senor: $40m price tag after this Irish Derby win

But when the market dropped, demand for stallions immediately fell, and even the most successful stallions' marketability became reduced. For Shareef Dancer, the fall was particularly steep following a disappointing start. Now, a decade later, despite solid later results, he is available to breeders at a tiny proportion of the original figure.

For a time, Northern Dancer could command a fee of a million dollars for a single nomination, and even at that price mare owners still clamoured for his services. The top stallions in the mid-1990s are available at a fifth of that price.

Double service

But the structure has changed again, fuelled once more by the Sangster-O'Brien team, first by increasing the number of mares covered by the top stallions, and then by their sending some stallions to the Southern Hemisphere to maintain revenue during the breeding close-season in the Northern Hemisphere.

In their Coolmore Stud operation in Ireland, the pre-eminent European-based stallion Sadler's Wells, who is fast becoming the natural successor to his father, Northern Dancer, has received upwards of 100 mares in recent years, maximising the potential income, with upwards of £100,000 being paid for each service.

He has never been asked to do a geographical double shift, but many of the stud's other leading stallions have been sent to either Australia or New Zealand in partnership deals with Antipodean studs, often covering around 80 mares in each Hemisphere.

The result, of course, has been the same as it would be with over-racing horses on the track. Fertility problems have been noted in many stallions, not least Sadler's Wells, whose fertility figures for 1994 were disappointing. Too many examples of a stallion's progeny on the yearling market can also reduce the sire's market attraction, while less talented, less well-bred mares, often with poor conformation, can also be negative factors.

Nowadays, the breeding business is in a less parlous condition than many believed likely just a few short years ago. Stallion fees are now much more in line with what horses can be expected to earn on the track during their racing careers.

The days of the $13 million yearling are long and irretrievably gone. When a yearling goes through the ring at Keeneland and fetches even $2 million, everyone stops, gives a cheer and remembers the good old days. Or were they? Perhaps not.

1985

3 Mar With his victory on Lord at War in the Santa Anita Handicap, Willie Shoemaker becomes the first jockey to amass winnings of $100m (£94.3m).

11 Apr Stefan Wegner wins the Railfreight National Hunt Jockeys' Championship for West Germany, a double on Horn of Plenty and Poyntz Pass taking him 13 points clear of Steve Smith Eccles, John Francome's understudy, while New Zealander Paul Hillis is fined for overuse of what turns out to be an illegal whip.

23 April Princess Anne, riding in her first race, finishes 4th on Against the Grain (11-1) to Elain Mellor on No-U-Turn (11-2jf) in the Farriers Invitation Private

Sweepstakes, a charity event over 1.5 miles. Mrs Mellor, on her 49th winner, becomes the first woman jockey to ride into the Derby winner's enclosure at Epsom.

27 May In winning the Jersey Derby by a neck from Creme Fraiche at Garden State Park, NJ, Spend a Buck, ridden by Lance Pincay, wins a world record $2.6m, which includes a special $2m bonus for winning a series of 4 races, including the Kentucky Derby.

8 Jun Creme Fraiche is the first gelding to win the Belmont Stakes.

14 Jun The American women professional jockeys beat the British amateurs 35-15 in a two-race match at York, Mary Ellen Hickey winning both events.

20 Jul Insufficient on-course betting in the 7.15 at Nottingham means no SP is returned, a lucky break for off-course backers of red-hot favourite Starlite Night,

Robert Sangster

27 Jul Major Dick Hern becomes the first trainer to saddle 4 winners of the King George VI & Queen Elizabeth Diamond Stakes as 3-y-o colt Petoski (12-1) vanquishes unbeaten Oaks winner Oh So Sharp (4-5f) by a neck at Ascot.

3 Aug Handspring (14-1) wins the Bradford Nursery at Thirsk having been left out of the overnight declarations by Wetherbys in error, one of several similar instances in recent seasons but the first to have won.

12 Sep Graham Starkey rides a 7,165-1 five-timer at Salisbury.

31 Nov John Francome saddles his first winner as a trainer, That's Your Lot (25-1) in the Mecca Bookmakers 3-y-o Hurdle Championship at Sandown over 2 miles, ridden by Steve Smith Eccles.

who finishes 5th of 6.

23 Jul The Robert Sangster syndicate pays a world record $13.1m at the Keeneland sales for a Nijinsky colt out of My Charmer.

---

25 January

Bell ban hits Ayr plans

By HOWARD WRIGHT

Harry Bell, 56, the Hawick trainer, yesterday had his licence withdrawn for seven months and was declared a disqualified person as the result of an inquiry by the Jockey Club disciplinary committee. The inquiry followed Bell's conviction at Jedburgh Sheriff Court on Nov.15 last year, when he was fined £500 after being found guilty of failing to provide or obtain proper veterinary attention for a four-year-old filly.

The filly, La Gavina, who was said to have been found in a deplorable state in a field at Bell's Midshields farm last April, was later destroyed. The RSPCA vet who examined her reported that she was emaciated and suffering from malnutrition.

Yesterday the Jockey Club panel heard statements from Bell, who was legally represented, and other witnesses. They found that he had committed a breach of the Rules of Racing and suspended him until Sept.1. Bell is further barred from attending race meetings or being associated with a training establishment.

Bell's suspension is his second as a trainer. In March 1965 the National Hunt Committee withdrew his licence when they inquired into the improved form of Vittorio, who landed a Kelso gamble the month before, only six days after being unplaced at Catterick Bridge. He resumed on Oct.1, 1970, and in January 1975 he was fined the maximum £500 for "using insulting and abusive language in public" to the Ayr stewards.

[Bell announced three days later that he would not be reapplying for his licence.]

Huntingdon: 8 April

Francome 101 after 4 at Huntingdon

By HOTSPUR (Peter Scott)

JOHN FRANCOME, who began the week by announcing he would retire after riding at Cheltenham on Thursday provided he had by then reached 100 winners for the season, passed that total yesterday with a Huntingdon four-timer.

Julesian, backed from 6-1 to 2-1 favourite after Francome's late booking, launched his triumphant afternoon. Gratification (4-6f) provided his second success, and Rhythmic Pastimes (1-1f) brought up

John's century. Fred Winter, trainer of Gratification, also provided the fourth Francome winner in Gambler's Cup (1-1f). Francome, 32, is certain to be champion jockey this season for the eighth time.

While being one of National Hunt racing's great names, Francome will concentrate his training career on the Flat. He, Michael Dickinson and almost certainly Lester Piggott will be joining the Flat trainers' ranks in 1986.

Champion Hurdle Cheltenham: 12 March

See You Then upsets form in Champion

By HOTSPUR (Peter Scott)

FORM was turned upside down in a sensational race for yesterday's Waterford Crystal Champion Hurdle. See You Then won in record time and the odds-on Browne's Gazette lost at least 10 lengths through a swerve at the start. John Francome, due to have ridden See You Then, bruised his right leg when The Reject fell in the previous race. Steve Smith Eccles, his late replacement, sent See You Then ahead after the last flight for a seven-length win.

After interviewing jockey Dermot Browne, the stewards accepted his explanation that Browne's Gazette had tried to anticipate the start and then dived off to the left. Browne attributed this to his mount's keenness. He shouted to the starter to wait but by then the tapes were just going up.

Northern Trial, chased by Desert Orchid, set a scorching pace which made it no easier for Browne's Gazette to

recover the lost ground. Gaye Brief, the 1983 winner, took second place racing down the hill, by which time Desert Orchid (20-1) was beaten. Browne's Gazette (4-6f), under pressure, was in touch entering the straight, but his efforts took their toll. He finished sixth, beaten a total of 14 lengths.

Gaye Brief (4-1) took the last flight in front, with See You Then (16-1) going easily behind him. Northern Trial (200-1), well beaten at that stage, took a heavy fall and was put down. Gaye Brief's lack of a race since December told against him up the final hill. Robin Wonder (66-1) and Stan's Pride (100-1), whose chances on form were remote, came through to finish second and third.

See You Then's time was 3min 51.7sec. His winning margin has been beaten only by Bula and Comedy of Errors in post-war Champion Hurdles.

1,000 Guineas Newmarket: 2 May

Oh So Sharp lands Guineas in last stride

By HOTSPUR (Peter Scott)

OH SO SHARP staged a flying finish to retain her unbeaten record in yesterday's General Accident 1,000 Guineas at Newmarket. She made up about three lengths in the final furlong to catch Al Bahathri and Bella Colora. Separated by only short heads, these heroines provided the closest three-horse finish to any English classic since the war.

It even outdid the 1949 Derby in which Nimbus, Amour Drake and Swallow Tail were divided by heads. A second photo-finish print was required to separate Al Bahathri (11-1) and Bella Colora (7-1), the margin between them being even smaller than Oh So Sharp's winning distance.

Oh So Sharp (2-1f) provided Sheikh Mohammed with his first English classic winner. Mr Hamdan Al-Maktoum, his brother, owns Al Bahathri. The four Maktoum brothers from Dubai represent the greatest ownership power in European racing, with 540 horses.

Yesterday's magnificent race gave further impetus to the wonderful start Steve Cauthen has made as first jockey to Henry Cecil's stable. Cecil, who has now trained three 1,000 Guineas winners, and Cauthen both believe Oh So Sharp will stay at least 10 furlongs. They think she could manage further, and neither the Derby nor the Oaks has been ruled out of Oh So Sharp's programme.

Budweiser Million Arlington Park, Chicago: 25 August

Teleprompter wins 'Million' for Britain

By HOTSPUR

LORD DERBY'S five-year-old gelding Teleprompter landed the Budweiser Million at Arlington Park, Chicago, last night. Making most of the running, he held off the favourite, Greinton, by three-quarters of a length. King of Clubs finished fourth but Free Guest, widely regarded as the main English hope, dropped out quickly after looking dangerous on the last bend.

Teleprompter, who started at approximately 14-1, has now won in four countries. But last night's prize was about five times as much as his combined winnings in England France and Ireland. "This is a tremendous thrill and I hope to bring Teleprompter back to New York for one of the Breeders' Cup races in November," said Lord Derby.

Bill Watts, Teleprompter's Yorkshire trainer, and Tony Ives, whose nerve was totally unaffected by a bad fall at Windsor last Monday, both agreed that the Arlington Park turns suited Teleprompter well. Ten furlongs is reckoned a little beyond Teleprompter's best distance on European courses but, with the ground as yielding as it was at Arlington Park, he still managed it without trouble. Ives said that the bends enabled Teleprompter

Teleprompter wins

to take the occasional breather and thus conserve his stamina.

Teleprompter followed Tolomeo as the second English-trained winner of the Budweiser Million in three years. His time of 2min 3.4sec reflected the ground conditions.

Last night's win is certain to intensify the campaign to allow geldings into the top European races, which are at present barred to them. No such restriction applies in the United States, and John Henry, a gelding who twice won the Budweiser Million, retired early this year with world-record earnings.

The Derby Epsom: 5 June

Slip Anchor in spectacular Derby victory

By HOTSPUR (Peter Scott)

SLIP ANCHOR, leading the Ever Ready Derby field from start to finish, gave a performance that matched those of Troy and Shergar among the three most brilliant which the Epsom classic's last 10 runnings have provided.

Yesterday's victory was even more one-sided than those of his predecessors, because Shergar did not take the lead until reaching the straight and Troy came from behind with a late run that left his rivals standing. Coronach, in 1926, was the last Derby winner to have led beyond dispute from start to finish. Call Boy (1927) and Nimbus (1949) made nearly all the running, but in each case were briefly and narrowly headed in the straight.

Slip Anchor (9-4f), four lengths in front at halfway, rapidly increased his lead going down the hill and rounded Tattenham Corner at least 10 lengths clear. Petoski (33-1) and Phardante (40-1), his nearest pursuers at that stage, then dropped away. Law Society (5-1) moved into

second place, chased by Supreme Leader (10-1). Steve Cauthen, sensibly taking no chances, kept Slip Anchor up to his work. His seven-length winning margin equalled that of Troy, but was less than Shergar's 10 lengths.

Law Society's resolute but unavailing challenge earned him second place. Six lengths behind, the Irish colt Damister (16-1) finished well to snatch third money from Supreme Leader in the last few strides. Shadeed (7-2), who beat only Main Reason (200-1), was virtually pulled up by Walter Swinburn. "The bottom just fell out of him going down the hill," said Swinburn, who had trouble trying to settle him early on.

Lord Howard de Walden, Slip Anchor's owner-breeder, had an offer for him only last week, but "gave it short shrift". Trainer Henry Cecil's confidence in Slip Anchor was completely vindicated, and the colt has followed in the footsteps of his sire Shirley Heights and paternal grandsire Mill Reef as a Derby winner.

ENGLISH CLASSICS

2,000 Guineas	Shadeed	L Piggott	4-5f
1,000 Guineas	Oh So Sharp	S Cauthen	2-1f
Derby	Slip Anchor	S Cauthen	9-4f
Oaks	Oh So Sharp	S Cauthen	6-4f
St Leger	Oh So Sharp	S Cauthen	8-11f

Leopardstown: Sunday 21 July

Leopardstown satisfied with Sunday opening

By HOTSPUR

WHILE racegoers in this country took a day off as usual yesterday, Leopardstown staged the first Sunday Flat-race meeting in Ireland, and a host of British professionals made another of their regular weekend forays to the Continent. The Leopardstown attendance was 12,200, below the figure which had been mentioned in anticipation. British runners picked up valuable prize money in Belgium, France and Germany, with Brian Gubby's sprinter Habitat doing best by

winning at Gelsenkirchen-Horst.

Our Irish correspondent likened the Leopardstown turn-out to "a good Bank Holiday crowd," and a course spokesman said the attendance was "satisfactory if not spectacular". The counter-attractions of three Gaelic football matches and television coverage of the Open Golf Championship were given as reasons for the lack of a record crowd.

Several bookmakers confirmed that betting turnover "was not big".

The St Leger Doncaster: 14 September

Sharp's Leger, Cecil's million

By John Oaksey

Sheikh Mohammed's Oh So Sharp was queen of all she surveyed at Doncaster yesterday, completing the fillies' Triple Crown in the Holsten Pils St Leger and making her devoted trainer Henry Cecil the first Englishman to send out winners of more than a million pounds.

But this was very much a moment for horse lovers, not statisticians. Before, during and after the St Leger, Oh So Sharp was a thing of beauty and a joy to watch. "I don't think I could have kept her in this form much longer," Cecil said. "Another week must have been too late. But as the 1,000 Guineas and Oaks winner strode down to the start, the shine on her chestnut coat and the eager poise of her head were reassuring evidence of how brilliantly he had succeeded.

Riding in his 150th and last English Classic, Lester Piggott on Lanfranco found no one else willing to help him test the favourite's stamina. After only a furlong he went on himself, but the ground was firmer than Lanfranco likes and, although he still led into the straight, that particu-

lar happy ending was never really on the cards.

Steve Cauthen never let Lester get far away, and with more than two furlongs left he asked Oh So Sharp to quicken. It was a bold tactical move because these two furlongs were ones she had never tried before. But, as it turned out, laziness was almost certainly a bigger danger than exhaustion. "She goes to sleep with you," Steve said. "At that stage it suddenly became hard work."

Although Oh So Sharp (8-11f) had to be given a couple of respectful taps and Phardante (18-1) switched inside her to deprive Lanfranco (85-40) of second place, even the dreaded words "Stewards' Inquiry" never put the result seriously in doubt.

So Cecil's great moment came. "I have felt like a batsman in the 90s for a long time," he said. But it is wonderful to have followed my stepfather, Sir Cecil Boyd-Rochfort, who won the Triple Crown with Meld."

Oh So Sharp, the eighth filly to win those three Classics, will not run again this year, but will almost certainly stay in training.

Prix de l'Arc de Triomphe Longchamp: 6 October

Quest awarded Arc as Sagace is demoted

By HOTSPUR (Peter Scott)

RAINBOW QUEST, beaten a neck by Sagace in yesterday's Prix de l'Arc de Triomphe, was awarded France's richest race after the head-on film patrol confirmed that Pat Eddery was justified in claiming that Sagace had bumped his mount twice.

Boos and cat-calls greeted news that the odds-on Sagace had been put back to second place, but the Longchamp stewards defused what might have become an ugly situation by quickly showing film-patrol evidence several times on the closed-circuit television.

Sagace, bandaged on both forelegs as a precaution against the firm ground, took the lead from his pacemaker

Heraldiste early in the straight. Rainbow Quest edged to the right when making his challenge, but Sagace was the culprit. Eric Legrix was till using the whip in his right hand when Sagace veered left and first bumped Sagace two furlongs out, but he had put down the whip before Sagace bumped Rainbow Quest again. Legrix, 20, also lost this year's French 2,000 Guineas in the stewards' room, where Rover Mist was put back from first to fourth place.

Rainbow Quest has run his last race. He will be a stallion in England next year at Mr Abdulla's Juddmonte Farm. Sagace retires to Shadowlawn Farm, Kentucky.

Queen Elizabeth II Stakes Ascot: 28 September

Exhilarating ride for Swinburn on record-breaking Shadeed

By HOTSPUR (Peter Scott)

Walter Swinburn, nursing his injured hand, missed Longchamp yesterday, but had an exhilarating ride on Shadeed, whose Queen Elizabeth II Stakes win at Ascot on Saturday in 1min 38.80sec lowered Chief Singer's course record by one-tenth of a second.

Shadeed (9-4f) passed Teleprompter's pacemaker Show of Hands approaching halfway. Bairn looked the only possible danger entering

the straight, but he was easily beaten off. Teleprompter (7-2) lost ground when squeezed for room after two furlongs. The pace was too strong for him to get on terms, but Lord Derby's gelding finished bravely to be second, two and a half lengths behind Shadeed.

Zaizafon (50-1) also made late headway to deprive Bairn of third place. Shadeed may have been tiring a little at the end, but in view of the scorching pace this was understandable.

OTHER MAJOR RACES

Irish Derby	Law Society	P Eddery	15-8f
Arc de Triomphe	Rainbow Quest	P Eddery	71-10
Kentucky Derby	Spend a Buck	A Cordero	41-10
Melbourne Cup	What a Nuisance	P Hyland	15-1
Arlington Million	Teleprompter	T Ives	142-10
Japan Cup	Symboli Rudolf	Y Okabe	1-1f

Willington Handicap Nottingham: 29 October

5,000-plus crowd sees Piggott's finale

Full Choke makes it 4,349 and out

By MARLBOROUGH (John Oaksey)

They came from far and wide to say goodbye at Nottingham yesterday and Lester Piggott did not disappoint them. A crowd of well in excess of 5,000 was able to cheer Full Choke, his 4,349th and final winner in this country. Predictably, all five Piggott rides started favourite — even Gold Derivative, whose trainer Dan O'Donnell has never saddled a winner in England. But the Bitter End Selling Stakes was not the ideal title for a swansong, and, showing admirable taste, Gold Derivative finished 23rd of 24.

On Full Choke, in the two-and-a-quarter-mile Willington Handicap, by contrast, Lester was able to play one of his favourite games — dictating a slow early gallop from the front and then beating off one challenge after another up the straight. "She takes a bit of riding," he told John Dunlop's assistant Anthony Couch, but even if Full Choke looked slightly half-hearted about it, she had done enough. Hers will be the name in the record books – the last line of the long story which began when The Chase won at Haydock

The end of an era

Park on August 18, 1948.

At a characteristically monosyllabic "press conference" before racing, Lester had said that eating was one of the facets of retirement to which he is most looking forward. "It will be a whole new game," he said. "I may soon have to buy some new trousers." His other replies were typically diplomatic – with Nijinsky, Sir Ivor and Alleged bracketed "in no particular order" as the greatest horses he has ridden.

Pebbles with trainer Clive Brittain

Breeders' Cup Turf Aqueduct, New York: 2 November

Pebbles tops in Breeders' thanks to Eddery's skill

By Tony Stafford

Pebbles and Pat Eddery proved that each is at the pinnacle in world racing when they won the Breeders' Cup Turf race, the highlight for British interests on the seven-race card, offering $10 million in prize money at Aqueduct, New York, on Saturday. The Turf first prize, $900,000 (£629,371), is the biggest ever won by an English-trained horse, although, to secure her place in the field as a late entry, her owner, Sheikh Mohammed Al-Maktoum, had coughed up an extra £240,000.

It needed the opportunism and strength of a master jockey to bring off a memorable neck victory in the face of spirited opposition from Strawberry Road and an insistent Steve Cauthen. It also needed the willing compliance of a champion, for Pebbles (11-5f) was locked on the fence for much of her first attempt at a mile and a half, run at head-long speed, and had to be eased back at what seemed a crucial stage rounding the far turn.

But such is her capacity for acceleration that, when a minute gap appeared inside a faltering Teleprompter on the final turn, the filly was through it and into the lead in half a dozen strides.

In retrospect that was the easy part, for French-trained Strawberry Road (19-5), a veteran of big-race challenges on four continents, harnessed that tough schooling for a desperate final thrust which would have brought victory had Pebbles not responded to Eddery's urgings in the last 50 yards. That she did was testimony to Clive Brittain's sensitive training of this sometimes difficult pupil, who earlier this season became the first filly ever to win the Eclipse. The pair were followed home by Mourjane (55-1), with Lashkari, last year's winner, fourth.

When the winner's time of 2min 27sec was posted on the results board, it brought gasps from the 42,000 crowd, who were not accustomed to seeing a record broken by the 1.2sec which Pebbles lowered this one by.

Shernazar, outpaced for much of the way around the tight seven-furlong circuit and almost certainly disliking the dry, dusty going, finished about six lengths behind the winner in sixth place. He passed a tired but honourable Teleprompter, whose fast gallop produced the extraordinary winning time.

Tote Each Way Handicap Hurdle Lingfield: 21 December

Greyhound 'comes fourth' at Lingfield

By John Oaksey

With Christmas and Boxing Day coming up, it was perhaps appropriate that at Lingfield we had a greyhound finishing fourth in a race won by a pretty girl.

Miss Candy Moore had ridden a highly imaginative race on Windbreaker (12-1), but as she sailed home to win the Tote Each Way Handicap Hurdle, Mrs Vi Cowan's fawn ex-racer slipped his leash and set off in pursuit. His actual target was a challenger, Opening Bars. No contact was made, however, and the dog ran on bravely to take fourth place.

Poor Mrs Cowan collapsed in an effort to retrieve her wayward pet, and had to be given first aid. But both of them went home unscathed.

William Hill November Handicap Doncaster: 9 November

Joe Mercer closes with a big-race winner

By John Oaksey

Joe Mercer's retirement way have been somewhat overshaded in the past few weeks, but in the end his timing was better than his great friend and rival's Lester Piggott. One winner at Nottingham can hardly compare with two on Doncaster's final day of the flat season – especially when one is a 20-1 shot in the William Hill November Handicap.

Storming clear on Bold Rex for his 2,810th and last success in this country, Joe said the perfect goodbye. Only three Englishmen, Sir Gordon Richards, Lester Piggott and Doug Smith, have ridden more winners – and not one of them did it with the same impeccably elegant style.

Joe steered Bold Rex into the winner's enclosure, paused briefly for the clicking cameras, and then said: "That's a nice way to end – on a big-race winner. That's my last ride here, although I've got one more day in Italy tomorrow."

Earlier, Comme l'Etoile (10-11f) had run out an even easier winner of the EBF Armistice Stakes, fulfilling his trainer Jeremy Hindley's declared intention to give Joe an appropriate send-off. "He rode a lot for me when he was with Henry Cecil," Hindley said, "so I told Michael Hills he would have to stand down for this one. After all, Michael has plenty of time."

The late Harry Wragg, whose daughter Susan was married to Joe Mercer's brilliant but ill-fated brother Manny, also chose the November Handicap for his triumphant swan-song, winning it at Manchester in 1946 on Las Vegas.

Unlike the great "Head Waiter", Joe has no intention of taking up training. But whether as a farmer or as agent to the New Zealand-born jockey Brent Thomson, or in any other role, he goes into retirement with the gratitude and good wishes of the whole racing world.

New York: 27 November

Aga Khan's horses disqualified from Breeders' Cup race:

'Doping' of Lashkari revealed

By HOTSPUR

The French-trained Lashkari (fourth) and Shernazar (sixth), trained in England by Michael Stoute, have both been disqualified from their Breeders' Cup Turf placings after traces of the stimulant etorphine were found in Lashkari's urine. There was no similar finding in the sample taken from Shernazar but, as both horses ran in the Aqueduct, New York, race on Nov.2 for the Aga Khan, they are similarly treated under New York Racing Association rules.

Etorphine is colloquially known as "elephant juice" because it is used to sedate large circus animals, but in microscopic doses it is thought to act as a stimulant. The tests were made in the laboratories of Cornell University, and no similar finding was apparent in any of the other six Breeders' Cup races.

John van Lindt, chairman of the New York Racing and Wagering Board, announced the decision at a press conference 24 hours after it had been revealed that the payment of prize money on the $2 million race had been temporarily withheld. Although the news of the delay was accompanied by information that one of the European horses in the Turf race had been doped, connections of Pebbles, the winner, and runner-up Strawberry Road were confident that their horses had not been affected.

The doping of Lashkari, trained by Alain de Royer Dupré, will inevitably refuel suggestions that there is a personal vendetta against the Aga Khan.

1986

2 Feb Mill Reef, 18, whose condition after a heart operation in July last has recently been deteriorating, is put down on veterinary advice. He won 12 of his 14 races over three seasons (1970-72), finishing second in his only two defeats, and was later the National Stud's principal stallion.

10 Mar From today, betting shops are allowed to show live televised races and serve light refreshments. Ladbrokes, with 1,500 shops the biggest of the big four off-course bookmakers, followed by Hills (900), Coral (750) and Mecca (650), are geared to give punters top service, with TV in all their shops. Tomorrow's Waterford Crystal Superior Novices' Hurdle at Cheltenham, broadcast by the BBC, will be the first history-making live TV race.

10 May Amateur jockey Michael Blackmore dies after his mount Silent Shadow fell in a maiden hurdle at Market Rasen.

7 Jun Three days after his Derby success with Shahrastani, Michael Stoute saddles the 2nd, 3rd and 4th in the Oaks, Untold (20-1), Maysoon (12-1) and Colorspin (25-1), respectively, foiled by 15-8f Midway Lady, ridden by Ray Cochrane and trained by Ben Hanbury.

7 Jun Dermot Weld saddles the first 5 winners at Phoenix Park, all favourites and all ridden by Michael Kinane.

5 Aug Princess Anne gains her first success from 13 rides when taking Gulfland to a 5-length victory in the Mommessin Amateur Riders' Stakes (1 1/2 miles) at Redcar.

31 Aug 6-y-o Estrapade, a mare trained by 73-y-o Charlie Whittingham in California, wins the 10-furlong Budweiser-Arlington Million by 4 lengths to pick up the $600,000 (£419,000) 1st prize. Ridden by veteran Puerto Rican Fernando Toro, Estrapade returned 21-10 (coupled with 3 other horses). Pennine Walk, trained by Jeremy Tree and with Pat Eddery up, finishes 3rd. Last year's winner, Teleprompter, misses the break from an unfavourable draw and is never in it.

3 January

Turf authorities lead reform

By HOTSPUR

Geldings, which have been excluded from all European Flat races of Group One Pattern status, will be allowed to contest at least some from this year onwards, and the English turf authorities have led a change of heart in Europe.

All 10 English Group One races that are not confined either to three- or two-year-olds will now be open to geldings. These include the King George VI and Queen Elizabeth Diamond Stakes, Eclipse Stakes, Coronation Cup, Gold Cup, July Cup and William Hill Sprint Championship.

Racecourses staging these Group One events were consulted, and all agreed with the change. This has also received European approval, but when and to what extent France, Ireland, Germany and Italy will follow the Jockey Club's lead is not yet certain.

The Derby and other English classics will remain closed to geldings, but their counterparts in the United States have no such restrictions, and last year's Belmont Stakes was won by the gelding Creme Fraiche. All top races in the United States except those confined to fillies are open to geldings. Lord Derby's Teleprompter who holds the stakes-earnings record for an English Flat-race gelding, went to Chicago last August to make the Budweiser Million the most valuable win of his career.

CHAMPIONS

Jockey (Flat)	Pat Eddery	177
Jockey (NH)	Peter Scudamore	91
Racehorse of Year	Dancing Brave	3-y-o
NH Champion of Year	Dawn Run	8-y-o
Leading Trainer	Michael Stoute	£1,269,933
Leading Owner	Sheikh Mohammed	£830,121
Leading Money Winner	Dancing Brave	£423,601

13 February

Newnes ban to be lifted on July 1

By HOTSPUR (Peter Scott)

Henry Candy, who has given Billy Newnes employment and support since he received a three-year suspension in January 1984, will restore Newnes as his stable jockey when this ban is lifted on July 1. Newnes had appealed to the Jockey Club disciplinary stewards on Wednesday for cancellation of his final year's sentence, but he seemed reasonably satisfied with yesterday's verdict of the proverbial half-loaf.

Newnes' association with the warned-off gambler Harry Bardsley landed him in trouble with the turf authorities. He admitted receiving £1,000 from Bardsley for telling him prior to the Queen's Vase at Royal Ascot in 1983 that his mount Valuable Witness would not like the firm going. Valuable Witness was the beaten favourite for that race and his dislike of firm going has been subsequently underlined. Jeremy Tree, Valuable Witness's trainer, has since spoken in support of Newnes, and I fully expect Tree to provide Newnes with further rides when he returns.

An exultant Jonjo O'Neill taking Dawn Run to victory

Cheltenham Gold Cup 13 March

Echoes of Arkle as Dawn Run lands Cup

By HOTSPUR (Peter Scott)

Scenes reminiscent of the Arkle era greeted Dawn Run's Tote Cheltenham Gold Cup triumph yesterday when this Irish mare achieved the unique distinction of adding a Gold Cup win to success in Cheltenham's other great race, the Champion Hurdle.

Superior stamina at the end of a race run fast enough to lower The Dickler's 1973 Gold Cup time record by almost two seconds enabled Dawn Run to beat Wayward Lad. Dawn Run (15-8f) had a long duel for the lead with Run and Skip. Both looked beaten at the last fence, which Wayward Lad (8-1) jumped slightly in front of Forgive 'n' Forget (7-2, 3rd), and Wayward Lad's string of Cheltenham defeats looked sure to end.

But then he began to tire and edged to his left up the final hill. Dawn Run, summoning fresh reserves and ridden with great determination by Jonjo O'Neill, caught the fading Wayward Lad in the last 100 yards and beat him by a length.

Kerstin and Glencaraig Lady are the only other mares to have won the Gold Cup since the war. Dawn Run did so with the experience of only four steeplechases behind her.

Mrs Charmain Hill, Dawn Run's owner, and O'Neill were lifted shoulder high by the crowd after Queen Elizabeth the Queen Mother had presented their trophies. O'Neill was also mobbed by admirers as he brought Dawn Run back to the winner's enclosure, and some enthusiasts tried to pull hairs from the mare's tail.

Paddy Mullins deserves great credit for training Dawn Run with such skill. The only sad aspect of yesterday's triumph for Mullins was that his son Tony lost the ride to O'Neill.

Mrs Hill, 67, still rides Dawn Run frequently at morning exercise. She has no plans to retire the mare and reckons that Dawn Run will stay in training for at least two more Gold Cup challenges. Yesterday's race, the richest ever staged at Cheltenham, enabled Dawn Run to surpass Wayward Lad as the record first prize money earner under National Hunt rules.

The Grand National Aintree: 5 April

West Tip puts act together for National

By HOTSPUR (Peter Scott)

THEATRELAND'S faith in everything being all right on the night proved well-founded for West Tip in Saturday's Seagram Grand National. His act was put together with maximum efficiency in front of packed Aintree stands and a worldwide television audience. The misjudgment which brought him down when going so well at Becher's second time round last year never looked like being repeated. Richard Dunwoody pursued a well-considered course throughout and delivered West Tip (15-2) on cue to pass Young Driver (66-1) after the last fence.

Dunwoody, 22, was the youngest jockey in Saturday's race. There have been few younger winning Grand National riders since Bruce Hobbs's 1938 victory on Battleship at the age of 17.

Young Driver passed Monanore three fences from home with West Tip in close touch and going well. Young Driver landed a length clear of West Tip over the last fence. He was soon passed, but fought on bravely as West Tip, ears pricked, came home two lengths in front.

Drama, romance or good fortune had been part of almost every Grand National winner's background. West Tip still shows the scars of two injuries, the first when becoming entangled with barbed wire as a three-year-old in Co.Kildare and the second resulting from collision with a lorry in 1982.

NATIONAL HUNT

Champion Hurdle	See You Then	S Smith Eccles	5-6f
Cheltenham Gold Cup	Dawn Run	J O'Neill	15-8f
Grand National	West Tip	R Dunwoody	15-2

ENGLISH CLASSICS

2,000 Guineas	Dancing Brave	G Starkey	15-8f
1,000 Guineas	Midway Lady	R Cochrane	10-1
Derby	Shahrastani	W Swinburn	11-2
Oaks	Midway Lady	R Cochrane	15-8f
St Leger	Moon Madness	P Eddery	9-2

Grande Course de Haies Auteuil: 27 June

Dawn Run killed in Auteuil fall

By HOTSPUR

Dawn Run's distinguished and colourful racing career ended in tragedy yesterday, when this famous Irish mare suffered almost instantaneous death as the result of breaking her neck at Auteuil. She was lying a close third to the eventual winner, Le Rheusois, when she scarcely rose at the fifth hurdle from home and somersaulted on landing.

Dawn Run has a unique place in racing history as the only horse ever to win both the Champion Hurdle and the Cheltenham Gold Cup. The latter victory earlier this year made her the record Anglo-Irish stakes' earner under National Hunt rules, and she later gained her 17th jumping win with a match race victory over Buck House at Punchestown. But more than the records, Dawn Run's charisma made her the most popular Irish jumper since Arkle.

John Oaksey writes (in The Sunday Telegraph): I know I am prejudiced, but none of yesterday's glossy colts, not even Shahrastani, will ever give the human race one-fiftieth as much enjoyment as Dawn Run. Her tragic death at Auteuil on Friday cast a dark blanket of gloom over the sunlit Curragh yesterday — at least for the large part of the Irish crowd which loves a good brave jumper more than anything. With the death not only of Dawn Run, but also earlier of her old rival Buck House, Irish jumping has been deprived of its two outstanding figures. Sympathy is the only worthwhile thing to feel — and it is sympathy with all of us who got so much excitement from their deeds.

The Derby Epsom: 4 June

Favourite Dancing Brave fails Derby punters

By Our Sports Staff

Shahrastani, owned by the Aga Khan and ridden by Walter Swinburn, won the richest ever Derby in dashing style yesterday at 11-2. But runner-up Dancing Brave, the heavily backed 2-1 favourite, will go down in turf history as one of the most unfortunate losers of the race.

The man who came in for all the criticism was its jockey Greville Starkey, 46, who had won the 2,000 Guineas on Dancing Brave. Yesterday, Starkey's performance bewildered punters and left trainer Guy Harwood thunderstruck.

He kept Dancing Brave at the back until the closing stages – then ran through the field to finish just half a length behind the winner.

Marlborough (John Oaksey) writes: As Shahrastani hit the front two furlongs from home, Dancing Brace had only just begun to gallop in earnest. He had at least six lengths to make up in a quarter of a mile, and since he made up five and a half of them, will always have to be remembered as one of the unluckiest Derby losers.

My case for Starkey's mitigation would be that he was fully entitled to expect Dancing Brave to pick up and quicken on demand as he did in the 2,000 Guineas. The jockey may have been betrayed in the first place by his own excessive confidence in Dancing Brave – but he was also let down by the unforeseeable lethargy of the favourite.

Dancing Brave was the best horse in yesterday's race. I confidently expect him to prove it before the season ends, and hope that Greville Starkey will be given the chance to help.

The Irish Derby The Curragh: 28 June

Shahrastani scorches to Derby double

By John Oaksey

No one said "lucky winner" at the Curragh yesterday when Walter Swinburn and the Aga Khan's Shahrastani ran clean away with the Budweiser Irish Derby and a cool £300,000.

"That ought to settle a few doubts," was Swinburn's understandable reaction after he and the Ever Ready Derby winner had pulverised Bonhomie by eight lengths. Apart from Bakharoff's pacemaker, Ostensible, these two had the race to themselves throughout.

Pat Eddery and Bonhomie (7-1) allowed Ostensible six furlongs to justify himself, and then when the pacemaker dropped back exhausted, evens favourite Shahrastani was already a close and menacing second. Looking back for danger, you could find no sign of it — with the whole field including Mashkour, Flash of Steel and Mr John, third, sixth and ninth in Shahrastani's Epsom Derby, all under pressure and getting nowhere.

I honestly cannot recall a race of this value and status where the writing was clear on the wall so far from home. But although the time (2min 32.1sec) was by no means exceptional on perfect going, the early pace certainly looked a lot faster than at Epsom. On balance the result definitely suggests either that a fast early gallop helped Shahrastani to sort out his opponents — or that he has improved abnormally in the last five weeks.

Some had said that without Bering and Dancing Brave yesterday's race, the richest in Europe thanks to Budweiser's sponsorship, was "Hamlet without at least one Prince and maybe two". But now Dancing Brave will have to win next Saturday's Coral Eclipse at Sandown very decisively indeed to satisfy those of his admirers who believe he was "robbed" of the Epsom Derby.

King George VI & Queen Elizabeth Diamond Stakes Ascot: 26 July

Sweet revenge for the Brave

By John Oaksey

No two diamonds are ever the same and only one glittered at Ascot yesterday when Prince Khaled Abdulla's Dancing Brave thoroughly established his brilliance beyond all doubt by winning the King George VI and Queen Elizabeth Diamond Stakes. It was sad that Shahrastani, a distant fourth, should have so obvious an "off day". And even sadder for Greville Starkey that Pat Eddery should be in his place when the Epsom Derby was avenged.

But for Dancing Brave's many admirers and backers, vengeance was sweet. They hope that no one, however "expert", will ever write or say again that he "does not truly stay". One and a half miles is no doubt the outside limit of Dancing Brave's stamina and the three-quarters of a length by which he beat Shardari was shrinking again at the line. But by that time the race was over.

The battle we had all come to see was fought and won early in the straight as Pat Eddery launched Dancing Brave (6-4) a length behind Shahrastani (11-10f), asking for the speed which is his deadliest weapon. In a slow-run Derby it enabled him to cover a furlong in 10.3 seconds — the time of a champion sprinter. Now, after Boldden, Vouchsafe and Dihistan had combined to set a furious headlong gallop, no such speed was needed.

But Dancing Brave's was still more than sufficient. It swept him past Shardari (14-1) and Shahrastani, and with a furlong left he was clear in his glory. The much travelled and hard working French mare Triptych (25-1) came through to be third, but the Derby winner showed no trace of his usual spark and was a bitterly disappointing fourth.

Prix de l'Arc de Triomphe Longchamp: 5 October

Dancing Brave lands 'Arc' in record time

By HOTSPUR (Peter Scott)

DANCING BRAVE'S Trusthouse Forte Prix de l'Arc de Triomphe win at Longchamp yesterday was a performance well worthy of the richest race ever staged in Europe. He lowered the course record in beating the strongest Arc field for years.

'Brave' completes his Arc win in record time, with Pat Eddery up

Prince Khaled Abdulla's champion was backed down to 11-10 favouritism by the massive English contingent. And he produced brilliant finishing speed to win by one and a half lengths.

Dancing Brave and Pat Eddery remained as cool as cucumbers on a hot afternoon and during preliminaries that were even noisier than usual. Dancing Brave and Bering were drawn in the two outside positions. Eddery, who reckoned Bering his chief danger and the horse most likely to avoid interference, correctly chose to track him. They settled down towards the rear as Darara (for a furlong) and Baby Turk made the running, with Nemain and the German hope Acatenango close up.

Shahrastani was the first English horse to make his thrust. Swinburn sent him past Baby Turk to lead one and a half furlongs out. Bering then challenged and for a few strides the English and French Derby winners headed the field. Dancing Brave then swooped on the outside to win going away.

Dancing Brave follows Detroit and Rainbow Quest as Eddery's third Arc winner. His time of 2min 27.7sec lowered Detroit's record of 2min 28 sec which had stood since 1980. Triptych, running her usual brave race, stayed on to finish half a length behind Bering in third place. Shahrastani was a short head away fourth, with his stable-companion Shardari a neck behind in fifth and Darara,

---

13 August

Dope testing methods attacked by Aga Khan

By Hotspur (Peter Scott)

THE AGA KHAN has launched an attack on the accuracy of dope testing in the United States and Europe after more than nine months' investigations which have finally cleared his horse Lashkari of being "doped" before the Breeders' Cup Turf Stakes at Aqueduct, New York, last November.

Dr George Maylin supervised original tests on the Lashkari samples at Cornell University Laboratory, Illinois, but other laboratories in the United States did not support the Cornell findings.

Lashkari, fourth to Pebbles, was originally disqualified after a test that suggested the drug etorphine had been found in his system. Alain de Royer-Dupré, Lashkari's trainer, was given a life ban in mid-January from running any further horses in New York. Royer-Dupré's ban has now been lifted. The New York Turf authorities have completely exonerated him.

Shernazar, trained by Michael Stoute, was also originally disqualified from sixth place in the Breeders' Cup Turf Stakes. Nothing was found amiss with tests on Shernazar, but he also carried the Aga Khan's colours and was coupled in betting with Lashkari.

The Aga Khan said that Dr Maylin deserved some commendation for finally admitting a mistake, but he described security arrangements as "deplorable" at Aqueduct on Breeders' Cup day. He added that the cost of legal, scientific and other expert help in clearing both Lashkari and Royer-Dupré had more than exceeded Aqueduct prize-money earnings now awarded to Lashkari, Shernazar their trainers and jockeys.

The Aga Khan went on to cite the damage this case had done in his all-important first stud season in France, and how those who had taken shares in the horse before the Breeders' Cup were also affected. He added that there had been a "lack of candour" while investigations were proceeding, and said that by no means every owner could have afforded the expenses he had met.

Racing Post Handicap Hurdle Southwell: 3 September

Tuck equals record with Doronicum but 'Brig' fails

By MARLBOROUGH (John Oaksey)

Phil Tuck equalled, but could not break, Johnny Gilbert's 27-year-old record of 10 consecutive jumping winners yesterday. Doronicum, the first of his two rides at Southwell, won easily, but Easter Brig could finish only fifth in the Goverton Handicap Hurdle.

Until Easter Brig, the closest squeak of Tuck's golden spell was at Perth on Saturday, when Atkinsons nearly fell at the fourth last and then had to survive a stewards' inquiry.

But all was well, and Phil's first ride yesterday, Doronicum, gave the expectant crowd remarkably few moments of doubt in the Racing Post Handicap Hurdle. Never out of the first two, they overtook Prince Metternich with four flights left, and from then on the only danger was a fall. Our own Gordon Richards, not to be confused with yesterdays winning trainer, holds the world's longest winning sequence – 12 in succession in 1933.

another of the Aga Khan's runners, in sixth place.

No excuses were offered for any of the beaten horses, and Dancing Brave can be fairly ranked as the greatest English champion since Mill Reef and Brigadier Gerard were contemporaries of such giant stature.

Breeders' Cup Santa Anita: 1 November

Dancing despair

By John Oaksey

FOR THE second time in his life, Dancing Brave was beaten yesterday. But this time there was no valid hard-luck story. Three US-trained horses, led by Manila, just ran faster up the short Santa Anita straight, and the third two-million dollars Breeders' Cup Turf stayed in America.

Drawn on the outside, Pat Eddery settled Dancing Brave with only two behind him as Estrapade made the running. But the favourite moved up easily enough down the back straight, and European hopes were still high as he turned for home, not more than four lengths behind the leader. Dancing Brave has always taken a while to find top gear,

so for a hundred yards of the short straight we could still hope. But then the truth was all too clear – there was no extra gear. And, as Manila passed Estrapade (third) and challenged the ex-Irish Theatrical (second), the best horse in England was for the first and last time made to look ordinary. No doubt the sharp turns did not help, but the real explanation surely is the date. The first day of November is a long, long time from April, and that was when Dancing Brave started his three-year-old racing career. Magnificent though he looked in the sunshine, the fact must be faced that he had gone "over the hill".

OTHER MAJOR RACES

Irish Derby	Shahrastani	W Swinburn	1-1f
Arc de Triomphe	Dancing Brave	P Eddery	11-10f
Kentucky Derby	Ferdinand	W Shoemaker	177-10
Melbourne Cup	At Talaq	M Clarke	10-1
Arlington Million	Estrapade	F Toro	21-10f
Japan Cup	Jupiter Island	P Eddery	139-10

14 November

Ascot mourns death of Jayne Thompson

By MARLBOROUGH (John Oaksey)

THE NEWS of Jayne Thompson's death threw a dark cloud over racing at Ascot yesterday. She had never regained consciousness since falling at the first flight of a selling hurdle at Catterick last Saturday.

Twenty-two years old, a lovely, high-spirited girl who adored her racing, Jayne had been riding for three years and was the leading lady rider two seasons ago. She had 18 winners to her credit

Throughout the racing world the deepest possible sympathy will be felt for her

father, Ron, who trains at Doncaster, for her mother, her brother and her fiancé, Geoff Harker, who, by a bitter irony, rode two winners on the day Jayne had her fall.

This is the first fatal accident to a girl since they started riding under rules 10 years ago, but poor Jayne's head injuries had nothing whatever to do with her sex. It was simply one of those cruel one-in-a-million misfortunes that can happen to anyone who rides racing over fences or hurdles.

Japan Cup Tokyo: 23 November

Jupiter Island leads English Japan-Cup 1-2

By Tony Stafford

PAT EDDERY'S year of almost unbroken success was nicely rounded off with a head defeat of Greville Starkey in yesterday's Japan Cup in Tokyo. Eddery's mount Jupiter Island concluded an honourable career by outbattling Allez Milord in a driving finish.

The principals were involved in two incidents in the closing stages where

each appeared to interfere with the other, but the Tokyo stewards did not consider that the result should be changed.

Clive Brittain's international reputation, guaranteed by the exploits of Pebbles in the Breeders' Cup last year, thus gained another boost. He has brought Jupiter Island back from injury at seven years of age to win his most

important prize. Jupiter Island had been out of action for several months. He cracked a hoof after finishing third in a race in California in April. Brittain's blacksmith had to cut part of the hoof away, and the horse could not run until it grew back again.

The strongly fancied New Zealander Waverley Star was fifth behind the two home-trained runners.

Triptych was 11th and Willie Carson's mount Tommy Way 13th in a field of 14 in the £382,000 race over a mile and a half.

This ending to Jupiter Island's career was an astonishing conclusion as he was bought back by his owners Lord and Lady Tavistock who bred him. Yesterday's victory was achieved in a new track-record time.

Obituary 10 November

Sir Gordon, the best jockey of them all

By John Oaksey

"The most beautiful sight in the world," the late Quiny Gilbey wrote, "is Gordon Richards two lengths in front and his whip still swinging, when you have bet twice as much as you can afford." However large or small your bet, the news of Sir Gordon Richards's death at the age of 82 will bring a lump to many throats from which the cry "Come on, Gordon!" welcomed that "beautiful sight" between 1925 and 1954 – when the most consistently successful British Flat race jockey of all time hung up his boots for good.

Only two days ago, Nov.8 was the 100th anniversary of another great jockey's death, the day Fred Archer shot himself at Newmarket, aged only 28. Archer was champion 13 times and rode over 200 winners in seven different seasons. Only one other man reached 200 before Gordon Richards beat Archer's record total of 246 in 1933, and no one, repeat no one, has done it since Sir Gordon retired.

The year 1933 was the seventh of his 26 championships, but this is no time for futile statistical comparisons. Throughout his long career, and even in the gossip-ridden world of racing and betting – in which any first-class jockey is the object of many and various seductive approaches – Sir Gordon's integrity was unquestioned. He was a rock in an often treacherous sea, and his universally popular knighthood in 1953 was awarded at least as much on account of the example he set as the 4,870 winners he rode.

From the moment I started going racing until the day he retired, the one infallible recipe for making a dull day

Richards rides another winner: at Goodwood, 1951

enjoyable was "Watch Gordon Richards". There were no starting stalls in those days, but you knew Gordon would get off precisely where he wanted. Then, though he preferred to be up near the leaders, any horse that needed relaxing could be "put to sleep" just as effectively as Eddery lulls them nowadays.

And then, best of all, you would see the shoulders start to hunch and the whip begin to wave and, even if someone else was sitting motionless, you would know you still had hope. Because, with a longer rein and much longer stirrups and a much more upright back and an altogether different method from the modern masters, you knew the horse would run home straight and as fast as he was able.

That was "the most beautiful sight in the world," and, like many others, I shall always be grateful to Sir Gordon for creating it and proud that we were there to cheer him home.

1987

28 Feb Princess Anne enjoys her first venture over steeplechase fences, on Cnoc Na Cuille in the 4-runner Portlane Handicap Chase at Kempton Park, coming a respectable last.

17 Mar See You Then (11-10f) completes a hat-trick of Champion Hurdles, trained and ridden as before by Nicky Henderson and Steve Smith Eccles, respectively.

29 Apr Four jockeys are injured at Catterick in an incident in which two horses have to be destroyed, Howards Lad, who was leading the field in the Hurgill Lodge Graduation Stakes when he broke his shoulder and fell, and Rock Pigeon, one of three horses brought down.

19 Jun Henry Cecil beats the post-war training record for winners and first-prize-money earnings at a Royal Ascot meeting as Space Cruiser and Orban take his score to 7 victories worth £2 01,060.

30 Jun Michael Dickinson gets off to a flying start in his new training career in the United States, 2-y-o Bold Magistrate, his

first runner there, winning by 13 lengths at Philadelphia Park.

1 Jul Panamanian Jorge Velasquez's brief spell as first jockey to Mr Mahmoud Fustok in France ends, and he will return to the USA where he has ridden more than 5,700 winners. Their uneasy relationship reached breaking point after Longchamp's Prix de la Porte Maillot last Sunday when Velasquez mistook the winning post on the Fustok-owned Turkish Ruler and was beaten by Balbonella. He was given a 15-day suspension.

14 Aug Martin Pipe sets a record for a jumps trainer, saddling seven consecutive winners, following up his Newton Abbot

four-timer yesterday with the first three winners at Devon & Exeter, all 7 ridden by Peter Scudamore.

23 Oct The Princess Royal rides the Josh Gifford-trained Abbreviation into third place in the British Airways Invitational flat race over 2 miles at Percy Warner Park, Nashville, USA.

26 Dec Nupsala (25-1), an eight-year-old half-bred, routs the home team at Kempton Park to win the King George VI Rank Chase, beating evens favourite Desert Orchid by 15 lengths, to become the first French-trained 'chaser to win in England since L'Empereur at Wincanton in 1963.

Edinburgh: 5 January

Edinburgh has first new course since 1965

By HOTSPUR (Peter Scott)

Edinburgh's jumping track, which Jonjo O'Neill officially opens today, will have entirely portable fences and hurdles. It becomes the first new course in Britain since Ascot began to stage National Hunt racing in April 1965.

No others have been introduced for almost 60 years. Taunton opened in September 1927 and Wincanton moved to its present site a few months earlier. Chepstow began Flat racing in 1926 and jumping in March 1927. Fontwell Park opened in May 1924.

Flat racing at Edinburgh has a long history and moved to Musselburgh in 1816 from Leith, the previous site. Musselburgh's jumping course has been laid out on partly reclaimed land adjacent to the links area and golf course.

The new course's hurdles

are also used at Perth in the spring and autumn. The fences and hurdles will have plastic wings. Grandstand facilities have been upgraded to provide more comfortable internal viewing facilities for the winter racegoer. A new lounge bar overlooks the finishing line and a permanent business entertaining area has been created.

The whole development has cost approximately £90,000. There have been £15,000 contributions from the Levy Board and from Narbol, the bookmaking organisation. Seagram, major sponsors of the Grand National meeting, have provided £10,000 for the new course and Tennent Caledonian Breweries £12,000. Other firms and organisations have sponsored individual hurdles and fences.

20 January

Sunday racing lobby faces strenuous opposition

By HOTSPUR (Peter Scott)

SUNDAY RACING in Britain may still be three to five years away. This is the view held by some members of the Jockey Club Working Party that yesterday published a report on the implications and the difficulties to be overcome.

The first "all weather" racecourse, salvaging days now lost to snow and frost, will surely open well before changed legislation makes Sunday racing practical. Any idea that it could be launched with on-course betting only has become a non-starter. The Home Office will not countenance betting on racecourses while it is banned in off-course shops. Such a distinction would open the

door to a massive upsurge of illegal betting, which would benefit neither the racing industry nor the Treasury.

The Turf Authorities will wait until after the General Election before their Sunday racing campaign is intensified. This concept still incurs hostility not only from church and other religious bodies but also from a section of the general public.

The racing industry has a workforce of about 100,000. By no means all are yet converted or resigned to Sunday racing. They were not adequately represented on the Working Party and their various associations are asked to submit opinions to the Jockey Club by March 31.

22 February

Dickinson to train in US from April 1

By Tony Stafford

Just two days after the final announcement of his break with Robert Sangster and Manton, Michael Dickinson yesterday revealed his plan to begin training in the United States from April 1.

Dickinson is clearly intent on silencing the largely misguided and unfair criticism of his first year's efforts as a Flat-race trainer. He will handle 16 horses, initially for four American owners, at the Fair Hill training centre in Maryland.

Dickinson said: "I very

much regret leaving England and British racing and I am sad to leave my family. But I believe I need to prove to the world and myself that the principles of hard work and dedication, which I applied to 'chasing, will also succeed in Flat racing."

Dickinson has chosen Fair Hill, a facility used by six trainers, which has a one-mile track, a seven-furlong all-weather gallop and an equine pool — he has also private use of a one-mile grass gallop — for carefully thought-out

reasons.

He said, "Most trainers keep their horses in training at a track, but then those trainers have to run at that track. Fair Hill is within easy vanning reach of 10 tracks, and that means a possible 50 races a day to aim at from there."

Dickinson will have 14 two-year-olds and two three-year-olds to start

with, and his owners will include Albert Frassetto, who is in the construction industry in New Jersey.

Dickinson therefore turns his back on any resumption of a jumping career, and that is hardly surprising in view of the fact that, Champion Hurdle and Grand National apart, he had very little to prove in that sphere.

EBF Novice Chase Stratford-on-Avon: 12 March

Stratford chase is declared void
By MARLBOROUGH (John Oaksey)

AFTER an unavoidable tragedy of errors in which two horses were killed and one jockey badly injured, yesterday's EBF Novice Chase at Stratford-on-Avon was declared void. All five finishers had missed the third-last fence and, under Rule 154(1)(b), the stewards were left with no choice.

But nor, it soon transpired, were the jockeys as they approached the final open ditch. Shoemender had fallen there first time round, and his rider, the luckless Carroll Gray, who was later taken to hospital with a suspected fracture of the neck, was still lying motionless on the landing side when the field came round again. An orange disc was (rightly) held in the fence to warn the oncoming field, but jockeys aiming to jump inside it were then waved away.

"That only left a few feet for the whole field," jockey Simon Sherwood told us later. "Not surprisingly, three jumped on top of one another." One of these, Rajen Signal, had to be put down, and his rider Martin Hoad was still being attended to when the field came round again. The racecourse medical officer, Dr Coulton, was on the scene by then and decided that the fence could not safely be jumped. So the six survivors found at least four people waving them round the fence. Nobody in his senses would ignore such signals and, quite rightly, nobody did.

But alas, as the Rules stand at present, even a racecourse doctor does not have the power to say that a fence can be missed out.

Obituary: 9 May

Death of Sir Noel Murless
By HOTSPUR (Peter Scott)

SIR NOEL MURLESS died, aged 77, at his home near Newmarket on Saturday night after a long illness borne with great courage. Sir Noel retired in the autumn of 1976, having established himself as the most successful English trainer of the post-war era.

Petite Etoile, Crepello, Royal Palace, Abernant, Busted, Altesse Royale, Mysterious, St Paddy and Aunt Edith were among many champions he trained. Races to give him special pleasure were a 1957 Oaks victory with the Queen's Carrozza and the 1,000 Guineas of 1968 with Caergwrle, who belonged to his devoted wife, Gwen.

Lester Piggott rode the majority of his big winners, but Murless had an even higher opinion of Sir Gordon Richards, who became his jockey when he took over Fred Darling's Beckhampton stables at the end of 1947. Sir Noel moved to Warren Place, Newmarket, five years later and it was there that 17 of his 19 classic winners were trained.

The son of a Cheshire farmer, Murless rode over jumps and was then assistant trainer to Hubert Hartigan in Ireland before taking out his own licence in 1935. He was knighted in June 1977 and made a Jockey Club member the following month.

Prix de Diane Hermes Chantilly: 14 June

Indian Skimmer routs French in Prix Diane
By HOTSPUR (Peter Scott)

INDIAN SKIMMER sapped the stamina of Miesque in yesterday's Prix de Diane, beating her French rival by four lengths. Miesque, brilliant mile winner of the English and French 1,000 Guineas, clearly found 10 1/2 furlongs too far.

Indian Skimmer's trainer Henry Cecil used Laluche as pacemaker to set a strong gallop. Steve Cauthen sent Indian Skimmer ahead two furlongs out and pushed her into a clear lead.

The Chantilly race, though run over a shorter distance than the Oaks, is France's counterpart classic. Sheikh Mohammed, with Indian Skimmer and Unite, becomes only the third owner to win both in the same post-war season.

The Derby field rounds Tattenham Corner

The Derby Epsom: 3 June

Champion Reference Point close to Mahmoud record
By HOTSPUR (Peter Scott)

REFERENCE POINT (6-4f) dominated yesterday's Ever Ready Derby from start to finish. He beat off a series of challenges to win by one and a half lengths in a time only 0.1sec outside Mahmoud's 1936 record.

Having proved himself the three-year-old champion, Mr Louis Freedman's colt will tackle older horses in his next two races, the Eclipse and Ascot's King George VI & Queen Elizabeth Diamond Stakes. Henry Cecil, who has trained two Derby winners in three years, would gain particular satisfaction from a King George victory, one of the few major races to elude him.

Ascot Knight, Most Welcome, Adjal and Ibn Bey were Reference Point's closest pursuers around Tattenham Corner. Most Welcome's challenge was much the strongest and he drew almost level a furlong out. Reference Point again then showed how hard he is to pass, but, as he began to shake off Most Welcome's challenge, Bellotto came with a strong run on the outside.

Bellotto (11-1) met with interference coming down the hill. Pat Eddery thought this cost him second place, but said the colt was tiring close home. Pat's brother, Paul, kept Most Welcome (33-1) ahead to take the runners-up spot by a short head. The 66-1 shot Sir Harry Lewis was fourth, a further two lengths away.

Queen Alexandra Stakes Ascot: 19 June

Gay Kelleway is Royal Ascot first
By MARLBOROUGH (John Oaksey)

Even Henry Cecil and Vincent O'Brien were pushed, briefly, out of the headlines yesterday when Gay Kelleway won the Queen Alexandra Stakes on Sprowston Boy and became the first woman ever to ride a winner at Royal Ascot.

Kelleway stood in tears at Sandown after the stewards had disqualified Sprowston Boy and given her a three-day suspension for "careless riding" — which starts tomorrow. "Now I really have something to cry about," she laughed as Sprowston Boy (12-1) carried her back in triumph to a warm and well-deserved welcome.

The Queen Alexandra is after all our longest Flat race. After taking over the lead from Kaytu seven furlongs out, Sprowston Boy was never allowed to idle or become unbalanced in the heavy ground.

For Steve Cauthen, who scored an early double on Space Cruiser and Oban, it was a last chance to equal Lester Piggott's post-war record of eight winners at the Royal Ascot meeting. But his mount, the 8-13 favourite Kudz, finished a distant seventh.

On the very day she was disqualified and suspended, Miss Kelleway became the first commercially sponsored woman jockey. At the time it seemed a setback, but her sponsors Weight Watchers, a subsidiary of Heinz, might have spent a million without getting as much publicity as she has given them in the last seven days.

Eclipse Stakes Sandown: 4 July

Mtoto makes his point in Eclipse triumph

By John Oaksey

"LIKE father like son," we thought it might be — and that was how the Coral-Eclipse turned out at Sandown. But it was not the father most of us expected, because Mtoto (6-1) found just too much speed for Mill Reef's Derby-winning son, Reference Point (1-1f), and stormed home three-quarters of a length in front to celebrate the anniversary of his sire Busted's victory 20 years ago.

Mtoto (the M is nearly silent and it means "little one" in Swahili) was the "dark horse" of this field. He has won all his three races this season and there is literally no telling just how good he may be.

So, beaten only three-quarters of a length by a specialist 10-furlong horse racing at his best distance, Reference Point was not in any way disgraced. He finished one and a half lengths in front of Triptych (4-1), and she was 10 lengths clear of Bellotto (6-1), with the others strung out like beaten cavalry.

In fact, Reference Point answered very nearly all the questions. By slamming the Derby third, Bellotto, he proved himself a deserving Epsom winner, and with Milligram (10-1) even further behind, you can certainly call him the best three-year-old of either sex in Europe.

As for the generation gap, Triptych was four lengths behind Dancing Brave in this race last year, and only two behind him in the Arc. That means that Reference Point's Derby was little if at all behind last year's.

But gallantly though the Derby winner acquitted himself, leading for nine of the 10 furlongs, this, above all, was a triumph for Alec Stewart, who, in only his fourth year with a licence, trains Mtoto for Sheikh Ahmed Al Maktoum.

Stewart thought Mtoto was a top-class two-year-old two years ago, but after his first race the colt chipped a bone in a hind leg, an injury that called for the most patient and careful nursing. It is only this year that we have seen the real Mtoto, a four-year-old with an explosive and sustained burst of finishing speed.

The South African jockey Michael Roberts was careful to save up that deadly weapon as long as possible yesterday. Approaching the last furlong, he launched Mtoto alongside Reference Point and, as the two ran home together, the Eclipse produced a spectacle entirely worthy of its long eventful history.

The St Leger Doncaster: 12 September

Reference Point made in Leger

By John Oaksey

REFERENCE POINT made racing history at Doncaster yesterday when he gave his absent trainer, Henry Cecil, a 147th winner of 1987 in the Holsten Pils St Leger and set a new record for prize money by one horse with £774,275. John Day's 120-year-old record was brushed aside, and the Derby, King George VI and St Leger winner now stands poised for another piece of history in the Prix de l'Arc de Triomphe.

No horse, not even Reference Point's late and much lamented sire, Mill Reef, has ever won those four races.

Despite a strong wind blowing dead in his face all the way up the straight, Refer-ence Point (4-11f) achieved a highly respectable time of 3min 5.91sec. But there was one moment to make us catch our breath. Pat Eddery on Mountain Kingdom (9-1) had been able to "slipstream" the favourite up the straight, and just for a second when he pulled out it seemed possible that Mountain Kingdom, not yet shown the whip, might quicken to draw level.

But Steve Cauthen had taken one look behind him and was already waving his whip at Reference Point. It was all the great horse needed, and he lengthened stride to win by a length and a half.

Diamond Day Ascot: 25 July

Royal excitement as Princess romps home

By Tony Stafford

AMONG the massive crowds for Diamond Day at Ascot on Saturday, one urgent voice in the stands exhorted: "Don't be so cool. Do some-thing." This self-confessed plea came not from an ordinary punter, but from the Queen as she shouted home the Princess Royal *(pictured)* on Ten No Trumps (9-1) in the one-mile Dresden Diamond Stakes. Her victory provided the perfect curtain-raiser to Reference Point's spectacular success just over an hour later.

This was not the case of a privileged rider getting on an overwhelming favourite and simply steering the horse home. The Princess Royal showed the fruits of many years' experience at the top of the horse trials world, honed into Flat-racing sharpness by her tutor David Nicholson.

After that, the day had to go well, and nobody present could begrudge either Ten No Trumps' trainer Michael Stoute nor his great rival Henry Cecil, Reference Point's trainer, each complet-ing a treble and making this card their private preserve.

This was Reference Point's finest hour, as he dominated the King George VI and Queen Elizabeth Diamond Stakes. Steve Cauthen set such a gallop that when Reference Point (11-10f) came off the final bend his pursuers were suddenly floundering in vain. He beat Celestial Storm (5-1) and Triptych (5-1) by three lengths and a neck, with last year's St Leger winner Moon Madness (25-1) five-lengths further back and Irish Derby winner Sir Harry Lewis (10-1) and Oaks winner Unite (13-2) trailing in, seventh and eighth, respectively.

Apart from the winner, the hero of the race was the 100-1 Italian challenger Tony Bin, who came fifth despite an exhausting flight which left him battered and bruised and only just passed fit to run.

Phoenix Champion Stakes Phoenix Park: 6 September

Triptych, Miesque maintain brilliance

By HOTSPUR (Peter Scott)

TRIPTYCH and Miesque continued their brilliant seasons with Phoenix Park and Longchamp wins yesterday. And Acatenango, taking advantage of Triptych's absence, beat Moon Madness by half a length in the Grosser Preis von Baden.

Triptych's stable, who made a late decision to tackle the Phoenix Champion Stakes rather than send her to Germany, were delighted by rain in Ireland yesterday morning. The yielding ground proved ideal for Triptych (5-4), whose international first-prize money earnings are now about £750,000.

Tony Cruz, prevented by injury from riding Triptych when she won at York last month, was full of confidence on this wonderful mare yesterday. Keeping her near the inside throughout, he brought her from the rear to pass the blinkered Entitled well over a furlong from home. Entitled, rejected by Cash Asmussen in favour of Vincent O'Brien's other runner, Fair Judgement, fought back well but Triptych won comfortably by a neck.

Miesque, 10-1 on for yesterday's Prix du Moulin, confirmed herself the outstanding European miler when she beat Soviet Star by two and a half lengths.

ENGLISH CLASSICS			
2,000 Guineas	Don't Forget Me	W Carson	9-1
1,000 Guineas	Miesque	F Head	15-8f
Derby	Reference Point	S Cauthen	6-4f
Oaks	Unite	W Swinburn	11-1
St Leger	Reference Point	S Cauthen	4-11f

Prix de l'Arc de Triomphe Longchamp: 4 October

Arc hat-trick for Eddery on Trempolino

By HOTSPUR (Peter Scott)

TREMPOLINO turned spring and summer form upside-down when he smashed Dancing Brave's time record by 1.4sec in yesterday's Prix de l'Arc de Triomphe and the odds-on Reference Point finished 20 lengths behind in eighth place. Pat Eddery, who rode Trempolino, was gaining his third consecutive Arc win and his fourth in eight years.

Reference Point had his lead challenged for a long way by the Aga Khan's pacemaker, Sharaniya, and he faded right out when the other runners closed up early in the straight. Steve Cauthen, conceding that Reference Point was past his best, eased him before the end.

As he was beginning to drop out, Eddery came through on Trempolino (20-1), who quickened to go clear of the field. Tony Bin gave chase but was beaten two lengths. First and second had waited well behind early on while the leaders set a strong pace on the fast ground.

Trempolino carries the colours of M.Paul de Moussac, who sold a half share to the American Mr Bruce McNall a few days ago. Andre Fabre will train Trempolino for the Breeders' Cup Turf Stakes at Hollywood Park California. The colt, who had a spell of back trouble during the summer, will then remain in the United States to be trained by Charlie Whittingham.

Tony Bin, doing best of any Italian-trained Arc challenger since Molvedo won in 1961, beat Triptych by three lengths for second place, with the "ring rusty" Mtoto a head away third.

Doncaster: 7 November

Champion! Cauthen in photo-finish

By John Oaksey

Steve Cauthen did it in style at Doncaster yesterday, but it was not until the sixth race, with the light fading fast, that Pat Eddery finally gave up his crown as champion jockey.

The Irish-trained filly Vilusi was Pat's last chance to stay in the hunt, but when she could finish only fourth in the Remembrance Day EBF Stakes the long, enthralling battle was over.

Cauthen's best British total of 197 put him two up with only one to play, and the Doncaster crowd was able to welcome a supremely popular and deserving champion. Both men would equally have deserved that description, and Eddery, with more than 30 winners abroad this year, can justifiably lay claim to the "European" championship.

Going into the final day with a lead of two, Cauthen had tightened his grip by inspiring Vague Discretion (11-1) to a stylish victory in the EBF Nursery.

As Cauthen and Eddery flew off to ride in Italy today, the racing world was left wondering gratefully how long it will be before we see another battle for the title so long drawn out and so gracefully fought on both sides.

Breeders' Cup Hollywood Park: 21 November

Northern Dancer influence strong

By HOTSPUR (Peter Scott)

NORTHERN DANCER blood, the strongest influence on world breeding in the last 20 years, triumphed again at Hollywood Park on Saturday. Nureyev and Nijinsky, two of his sons, sired the three principal Breeders' Cup winners.

Miesque and Theatrical, who won the Breeders' Cup Mile and Turf Stakes, respectively, are by Nureyev. Ferdinand, successful in Breeders' Cup Classic, is a son of Nijinsky.

Miesque (18-5), better than she has been all season in jockey Freddie Head's opinion, broke the course record when winning by three and a half lengths. Taking full advantage of a good run through on the inside, she again displayed the finishing speed that has made her such an outstanding miler. She became the third French-trained winner of a Breeders' Cup race in the four-year history of this series.

---

23 October

Lester Piggott sent to jail for 3 years: Admits £3 million tax evasion

By Colin Randall, John Shaw and David Graves

Lester Piggott, the greatest name this century in horse-racing and 11 times Britain's champion jockey, started a three-year prison sentence last night after admitting a £3.1 million tax fraud. His solicitor, Mr Jeremy Richardson, immediately announced that there would be no appeal. Although Piggott remained stony-faced, betraying no sign of emotion when he was sentenced at Ipswich Crown Court, his wife, Susan, collapsed in tears in the arms of an usher as he was led to the cells.

The Jockey Club Stewards later granted Mrs Piggott a temporary licence to keep her husband's Newmarket stables open, but made it clear she would have to re-apply for its renewal in January.

Piggott, whose personal fortune has been estimated at £20 million, was said to have used different names to channel his huge earnings in secret bank accounts as far away as Switzerland, the Bahamas, Singapore and the Cayman Islands.

The former jockey, who will be 52 next month, was taken to Norwich prison after being sentenced. He will be eligible for parole after one year or, if early release is refused, could earn remission of one year for good behaviour.

Top racing figures were stunned by the punishment imposed on Piggott, whose genius in the saddle made him a household name throughout the world. But appeals for leniency by Mr John Mathew, Piggott's counsel, had been rejected by the judge, Mr Justice Farquharson, who said he could not "pass over" the scale of Piggott's VAT and income tax evasion without giving an invitation to others tempted to cheat.

Piggott was said to have signed false declarations to the Inland Revenue during three successive inquiries into his tax affairs between 1970 and 1985. The judge remarked that Piggott had even misled his own accountants "until the matter was forced out of you last year".

The large-scale tax evasion which landed him in court arose from his failure to declare the proceeds of a private contract under which wealthy racehorse owners met his demands for huge rewards on top of his officially registered fees and retainers.

The nine times Derby winner was prosecuted in the biggest individual tax-dodging case ever brought in Britain, and the sentence was the highest to be passed for a personal tax fraud. Other leading jockeys and racing figures were also questioned during the inquiry, but the Inland Revenue said it was "too early to say" whether other prosecutions would follow.

OTHER MAJOR RACES

Irish Derby	Sir Harry Lewis	J Reid	6-1
Arc de Triomphe	Trempolino	P Eddery	20-1
Kentucky Derby	Alysheba	C McCarron	84-10
Melbourne Cup	Kensei	L Olsen	12-1
Arlington Million	Manila	A Cordero	1-1f
Japan Cup	Le Glorieux	A Lequeux	76-10

Pebbles (1985) has provided the only English success, and Sonic Lady was the sole English challenger to make much impact on Saturday. Sonic Lady, who will be covered by Blushing Groom in Kentucky next spring, finished third to Miesque. Her stable-companion Milligram, troubled by a sore foot earlier in the week, ran far below form and finished 13th.

Theatrical (9-5f), champion grass horse of the United States since Manila's August retirement, equalled the course record when beating Trempolino (13-5) by half a length in the Breeders' Cup Turf Stakes.

Ferdinand (1-1f) and Alysheba (18-5), the two Kentucky Derby winners in the Breeders' Cup Classic, dominated this 10-furlong dirt race. Ferdinand, ridden with exceptional coolness by veteran Willie Shoemaker, held off Alysheba's late challenge by a nose to take the day's richest prize.

1988

10 Jan Vincent O'Brien ends his association with his first jockey Cash Asmussen because the American's "commitment to ride in three countries was too much". [A week later, John Reid becomes O'Brien's new stable jockey.]

10 Jan Texas owner-breeder Nelson Bunker Hunt's dispersal sale at Keeneland, Kentucky, fetches $46.9 (£26m) for 580 lots, including $1.1m (£611,000) for Dahlia, who remains in Kentucky for a mating with Theatrical.

7 May Wayne Lukas's gamble of running Winning Colors in the Kentucky Derby comes off, as the filly makes all the running to become only the 3rd of her sex to win America's chief classic.

12 Aug The unraced 9-y-o Klute (9-1), touted by its owner as the "fastest horse in the world", is beaten by 25 lengths over 5 furlongs by So Careful (1-14f) in The Philip Cornes Match ("The World Speed Challenge") at Haydock.

19 Aug Lester Piggott's wife Susan, who took over the jailed trainer's string, seriously hurt in accident on the gallops.

Susan Piggott

20 Aug French-trained Mill Native (21-1), trained by Andre Fabre and ridden by Cash Asmussen, wins the Arlington Million (1m 2f on turf) at Woodbine in Canada. Equalize, also trained in France, is second and Sunshine Forever third. Mill Native clocks 2min dead, a new course record. Britain's two runners, Most Welcome and Media Starguest, make no show.

21 Aug Leading French 2-y-o Tersa (49-10) wins Deauville's Prix Morny, the fifth filly in succession to do so.

26 Aug Steve Cauthen escapes serious injury when his horse Preziosa falls at Goodwood, and he is catapulted from the saddle and then kicked aside "like a discarded rag doll". Concussion means a mandatory 3 weeks out, but further complications, including a fractured bone in the neck, cause him to miss the rest of the season.

24 Oct Peter Scudamore's success on Wolfhangar at Fakenham is his 50th of the season, the quickest ever National Hunt half-century, beating John Francome's record by 16 days. The horse was saddled by Charlie Brooks, but 43 of the 50 have been trained by Martin Pipe.

25 Nov Cash Asmussen, with a win on Forest Angel at Maisons-Laffitte, becomes the first jockey to ride 200 winners in a French season.

27 Nov Pay the Butler, a four-year-old by Val de l'Orne, wins the Japan Cup by half a length from Tamamo Cross. Arc winner Tony Bin ends his career by finishing fifth.

---

19 February

Scudamore & Dowling banned for three weeks

By Tony Stafford

Peter Scudamore, almost uncatchable in the jockeys' title race with a 29-winner lead over Phil Tuck, misses the next three weeks of the season in company with Bruce Dowling after an incident at Newbury a week ago. Approaching the fourth-last flight in the February Novice Hurdle, Scudamore, riding Gillie Hills, took exception when Dowling, on King of the Lot, attempted to pass on the inside, and a barging match resulted.

The Newbury stewards felt unable to adjudicate on the incident, referring the matter to the Jockey Club

Disciplinary Stewards, who yesterday found both jockeys guilty of "causing interference through reckless riding".

Scudamore said afterwards that he had a fair hearing. "I was looking towards getting a fine and did not expect the ban to be as long as it was," he said. Dowling was less than pleased. He said: "I'm not particularly happy. It won't help me to pay the mortgage." Scudamore was relieved that the ban, which runs from today, does not interfere with his Cheltenham Festival arrangements.

Doncaster: 24 March

Jockeys refuse to take part in TV interviews

By HOTSPUR (Peter Scott)

JOCKEYS at Doncaster yesterday began the Flat season by refusing to co-operate with television interviews. A statement explaining their attitude is expected from the Jockeys Association on William Hill Lincoln Handicap day, tomorrow.

Some riders are thought to be displeased with the new Jockey Club penalties for "excessive" whipping were announced without their agreement. These took effect from yesterday, with fines replaced by a scale of suspensions.

The television boycott is

thought to stem from fears that different jockeys might express conflicting opinions on the new measures, whereas the Association wishes to speak with one voice. There is a feeling that the new measures will be difficult to interpret fairly, with inconsistencies adding to the sense of grievance.

The Jockey Club has been anxious to get the new measures through in case wider SIS television coverage to new betting-shop audiences should cause misguided agitation for abolishing the whip altogether.

CHAMPIONS

Jockey (Flat)	Pat Eddery	183
Jockey (NH)	Peter Scudamore	132
Racehorse of Year	Mtoto	5-y-o
NH Champion of Year	Desert Orchid	9-y-o
Leading Trainer	Henry Cecil	£1,186,122
Leading Owner	Sheikh Mohammad	£1,143,343
Leading Money Winner	Mtoto	£412,002

Cheltenham Gold Cup: 17 March

Forgive 'n Forget pays the ultimate price

By John Oaksey

AS CHARTER PARTY returned in triumph at Cheltenham yesterday, the screens were going up around another Gold Cup winner. Now, Forgive 'n Forget, who won in 1985, is dead and we are confronted yet again with the price horses pay for our pleasure.

It was going to the fourth from home that Mark Dwyer felt something go desperately wrong. He had no time to avoid the fence but Forgive 'n Forget's off-hind had shattered and there would in any case have been no hope of saving him.

"What might have been" is never much consolation, but Dwyer says sadly that in all their three previous Gold Cups together, including 1985, he had never been so happy with the way Forgive 'n Forget was going. The 11-year-old had made not one mistake and was cruising in third place when disaster struck.

An equally heartbroken Jimmy FitzGerald says that the last time he fancied a horse as much as this was when Forgive 'n Forget himself ran in (and won) the 1983 Coral Golden Hurdle final. "At least he went out on top of his form," the trainer says. "I

suppose if they have to go, this is the place for it to happen."

Forgive 'n Forget stood fourth in the all-time list of jumping prize-money winners, and this was his sixth consecutive visit to the Festival. He is also, alas, the third good horse his owner Tim Kilroy has lost — following Brave Fellow and Fairy King. It was for the latter, destroyed at Kempton Park, that Jimmy FitzGerald bought Forgive 'n Forget as a replacement.

The other, much lesser disaster of the Gold Cup was Cavvies Clown's dreadful blunder at the second-last. It gave Simon Sherwood the opportunity for a wonderfully adhesive piece of horsemanship, but without it the little horse, who had run an heroic race, would have given Charter Party a very much closer fight.

Richard Dunwoody, who rode Charter Party (10-1) with such style and dash, drew clear when Cavvies Clown (6-1) slipped, and won by six lengths. Beau Ranger (33-1) finished 10 lengths away third, and fourth place went to Nupsala (8-1), the French-trained winner of the King George VI Chase.

NATIONAL HUNT

Champion Hurdle	Celtic Shot	P Scudamore	7-1
Cheltenham Gold Cup	Charter Party	R Dunwoody	10-1
Grand National	Rhyme 'n' Reason	B Powell	10-1

The Grand National Aintree: 9 April

No denying Rhyme 'n' Reason
Powell in amazing escape act

By John Oaksey

TRAINER David Elsworth's prediction about Rhyme 'n' Reason came gloriously true in the Seagram Grand National – "If he jumps round he will win" – but not without surviving an horrendous blunder at notorious Becher's Brook and staring defeat in the face two fences from home.

Since Rhyme 'n' Reason had fallen in the Cheltenham Gold Cup, and on his first visit to Aintree, the "if" about his jumping seemed a massive one. As he landed in a sprawling heap over Becher's, quite a few critics were smugly saying to themselves: "I told you so."

But they reckoned without Brendan Powell's adhesive horsemanship and Rhyme 'n' Reason's amazing determination. "He nearly lay down with me, just like he did at Cheltenham," Brendan said. "But then somehow this time he got up."

They were almost at a standstill by then, and when Rhyme 'n' Reason got going again there was only one horse behind him. At that moment odds of 1,000-1 would have looked most unattractive.

But make no mistake, here was far and away the best horse in yesterday's National. From a standing start, after letting all the others go, Rhyme 'n' Reason calmly got back into his stride and, as his grateful rider said, "started jumping from fence to fence." Then, would you believe it, after all that, a second disaster struck.

Lying second five fences from home, Brendan Powell found himself alone in front when leader Little Polveir fell at the 25th. In all his 13 victories, which include an Irish Grand National, Rhyme 'n' Reason had never been in front anything like so far from home.

Powell urges Rhyme 'n' Reason on after they clear the last

Losing his concentration, he began to look about him going to the second last, and Chris Grant launched Durham Edition (20-1) past him with what seemed to be a totally decisive run.

I cannot remember a braver fight back at Aintree than the one Rhyme 'n' Reason (10-1) staged at that point. Switching across behind his rival, Brendan Powell drove the nine-year-old up the Stand side of the run-in and, 100 yards from home, they swept past to pull a lost cause out of the fire.

David Elsworth, who seems certain by virtue of this great victory to land his first trainers' championship, had his most difficult task persuading Rhyme 'n' Reason's owner Juliet Reed to run him in the National at all.

This was only Brendan Powell's second ride in the race – he fell at the third last year on Glenrue and broke his arm.

Only nine of the 40 starters finished. Monanore (33-1) was third, and 1986 winner West Tip (11-1) finished fourth for the second year running.

Festival Stakes Goodwood: 18 May

Mtoto win voided as runners take wrong course

By HOTSPUR (Peter Scott)

Goodwood's first day's racing of 1988 duly provided a vital clue to next month's Ever Ready Derby, but the classic trial was overshadowed by a fiasco which caused the Festival Stakes, the other feature, to be made void.

The six Festival Stakes runners were confronted by incorrectly placed dolls, which misdirected them after half a mile. They should have gone round Goodwood's top bend, but came on the inside loop and thus covered considerably less than 10 furlongs.

A stewards' inquiry was announced after Mtoto had passed the post a length in front of Media Starguest. Voiding the race was a formality, and the matter has been referred to the Jockey Club. Mr Rod Fabricius, as clerk of the course, takes responsibility.

A mile event which preceded the Festival Stakes had been properly run round the inner loop. That stretch should then have been dolled off, but it was not, and dolls also remained to direct the Festival Stakes runners away from their true course.

Mtoto, last season's Eclipse Stakes winner, is a valuable horse who has thus run a wasted race. Goodwood's board will consider the financial implications, and might be well advised to make some reparation by paying full prize-money to the first four.

The Derby Epsom: 1 June

Kahyasi clinches third Derby for Aga Khan

By HOTSPUR (Peter Scott)

KAHYASI displayed courage and stamina in yesterday's Ever Ready Derby to follow Shergar and Shahrastani as the third winner in eight years for the Aga Khan, who is rapidly approaching his grandfather's total of five.

The green and chocolate hooped colours carried by those five winners were worn by Kahyasi yesterday, while third-placed Doyoun carried their owner's usual first colours. The Aga Khan did not wish Kahyasi to carry a distinguishing cap that would have reflected second-string status, since he reckoned Kahyasi (11-1) had as good a chance as the shorter-priced Doyoun (9-1).

Mahmoud, one of the former Aga Khan's winners, still holds the hand-timed Derby record, but Kahyasi set an electric timing record, beating Reference Point's 1987 figure by six-hundredths of a second.

Pat Eddery, riding the 5-2 favourite Red Glow, was criticised for lying too far back. I do not subscribe to that view and doubt Red Glow's heart for a struggle.

If any horse had a hard luck story it was the winner. Sheriff's Star, on Kahyasi's outside racing down the hill, repeatedly hung in towards him. Kahyasi is only a small horse and with Minster Son on his other side he had little room at that stage.

Glacial Storm took command two furlongs out. Doyoun, on the rails, tried a challenge, and Kefaah looked briefly dangerous on the outside before Kahyasi swooped. He passed Glacial Storm (14-1) inside the last furlong to win going away by one and a half lengths. Doyoun was third, in front of Red Glow and Kefaah (25-1).

Kahyasi, named by the Aga Khan after a town in Turkey, is now unbeaten in four races. His most notable previous success in the Lingfield Derby trial had been a rather laboured affair against second-class opponents. This obscured the qualities that became apparent in yesterday's faster-run race.

Former amateur rider Luca Cumani, 39, Kahyasi's trainer, took out a licence in 1976 after assisting his father Sergio in Italy and then Henry Cecil. He made his first mark at Epsom when winning the big bumpers event there in August 1972.

The Gold Cup Ascot: 16 June

Royal Gait disqualified after record Cup win

By HOTSPUR (Peter Scott)

ROYAL GAIT was disqualified after outclassing his Gold Cup rivals at Royal Ascot yesterday. John Fellows, his trainer, is to appeal against this highly controversial decision, as is Cash Asmussen, Royal Gait's jockey, against a seven-day riding suspension. Royal Gait (15-2) broke the course record by more than three seconds as he came home five lengths clear of 7-2 favourite Sadeem.

The stewards' inquiry, announced almost straight afterwards, lasted 25 minutes. Then came news that Royal Gait had been disqualified for interfering with Sadeem's stable-companion El Conquistador.

The original stewards' statement was that Asmussen had been guilty of "careless" riding which caused El Conquistador to fall. This was at least one official error. El Conquistador did not fall but unseated Tony Clark about two furlongs from home. The mistake was pointed out and the stewards were then obliged to reword their notice.

Clark set a very strong gallop on El Conquistador, who was a tired horse when Sergeyevich passed him three furlongs out. El Conquistador, rolling about with fatigue, collided with the rails and he finally unseated Clark shortly after the two furlong marker. Royal Gait was going easily immediately behind El Conquistador when he started to roll. Few of those who saw the official film could agree with the stewards that he had contributed to Clark's mishap. Film evidence, at best, was inconclusive.

Asmussen himself appeared to be squeezed for room by Sadeem on his outside. Greville Starkey, Sadeem's rider, was held blameless and will never be on a luckier big-race winner. The stewards also did not consider that Clark had ridden an injudicious race on El Conquistador by setting a pace too fast for his own good.

[The appeal was unsuccessful. Coincidentally, Sadeem's rider Greville Starkey was thrown when coasting home on 4-1 favourite Ile de Chypre in the last race of the day, the King George V Handicap. Ile de Chypre, who swerved inexplicably, was trained by Guy Harwood, who also saddled El Conquistador and thus had two horses unseating riders on the same day.]

Prix de l'Arc de Triomphe Longchamp: 2 October

Italian delight as Tony Bin holds Mtoto

By HOTSPUR (Peter Scott)

TONY BIN yesterday became the first Italian-trained Prix de l'Arc de Triomphe winner since Molvedo in 1961. His success delighted officials of Ciga Hotels, the Italian-based group who have taken over sponsorship of Longchamp's big race.

Pat Eddery, Tony Bin's jockey for much of this season, was replaced by John Reid after turning down the ride in favour of Indian Rose. Tony Bin and Mtoto waited well down the field while pacemakers for Kahyasi and Unfuwain did their job. Emmson, who went ahead approaching the straight, was passed by Boyatino more than a furlong out. Tony Bin then came flying on the outside. Mtoto finished strongest of all but his luckless run ended in a neck defeat.

Boyatino was third in front of Unfuwain, whose stable had such misgivings about the firm ground that they only made a final decision to run two hours before the race. Kahyasi, having almost certainly his final race, finished sixth. The dual Derby winner was just behind Village Star, but ahead of seventh-placed Fijar Tango, who had beaten him at Longchamp three weeks earlier.

Ray Cochrane said that Kahyasi met with considerable interference, but the unluckiest horse was Mtoto. Diminuendo, also ending her career with a defeat, looked a big danger approaching the straight, but then faded into 10th place. She has clearly passed her peak. Tony Bin, runner-up to Trempolino in last year's Arc, was bought as a foal in Ireland for 3,000gns. Signora Veronica Del Bono Gaucci, wife of a Rome businessman, named this five-year-old after the Italian painter Antonio Bin.

They met when he was at work in the Louvre. Signor Bin, who was then 87, has since died.

Luigi Camici, Tony Bin's trainer, is a cousin of Enrico Camici, who rode Ribot in his two Arc wins. Ribot then sired Molvedo, so there is a link between all Italy's post-war Arc winners.

The St Leger Doncaster: 10 September

Minster Son for Carson
Rider and breeder of Classic winner
By John Oaksey

DICK HERN'S long run of dreadful luck took an overdue turn for the better at Doncaster yesterday when, watching from his hospital bed in London, the great trainer saw Willie Carson and Marcia Lady Beaverbrook's Minster Son make racing history by winning the Holsten Pils St Leger. Carson *(pictured right)* bred Minster Son at his stud near Cirencester, and therefore becomes the first man to breed and ride a Classic winner.

The name in the record books as Minster Son's trainer will be Neil Graham's, but as both he and Lady Beaverbrook were quick to emphasise, all the credit belongs to Major Hern and the infinitely reliable team he has built up at West Ilsley. This was the seventh St Leger winner they have produced there and that total includes Bustino, who won for Lady Beaverbrook in 1974.

Minster Son (15-2) has always been thought to need fast ground, and Carson said on Friday how much he wished they would not water Doncaster. To his even greater disgust it started raining before racing yesterday, but Minster Son turned out not to mind at all. In fact almost certainly the rain told most against his closest rival, the favourite, Diminuendo (4-7). Three furlongs from home, as she cruised up alongside Sheriff's Star (7-2) and Minster Son, Walter Swinburn certainly looked and probably still felt a happy man. Diminuendo was still going easily on a tight rein with all her energy apparently intact.

"But the rain came at just the wrong time," Swinburn says, and, as he began to ride two furlongs out, it was suddenly clear that the favourite had a battle on her hands. Diminuendo was beaten only a length in the end, and since she finished eight lengths in front of Sheriff's Star in the six-runner field it can hardly be right to call her a "non-stayer". But in these circumstances, meeting a good, game colt for the first time, she was simply unable to find the extra speed which against her own sex has made her look such a champion.

"Minster Son has all the guts in the world," his proud breeder says, and this is not just sales talk for the half-brother by Gorytus who goes up to the Newmarket sales this autumn. Head down and battling doggedly on, Minster Son deserved every word of Carson's praise. He certainly stayed every inch of the distance.

ENGLISH CLASSICS

2,000 Guineas	Doyoun	W Swinburn	4-5f
1,000 Guineas	Ravinella	G Moore	4-5f
Derby	Kahyasi	R Cochrane	11-1
Oaks	Diminuendo	S Cauthen	7-4f
St Leger	Minster Son	W Carson	15-2

Breeders' Cup Chase Fairhill, Maryland: 29 October

Jimmy Lorenzo makes mark in United States

By Tony Stafford

IMPORTATIONS from England have long been an influence on American Flat racing and, at Fairhill, Maryland, on Saturday, their significance in jumping terms was emphasised when Jimmy Lorenzo won the Breeders' Cup Chase.

Jimmy Lorenzo, previously trained in Sussex by Peter Hedger, won by three-quarters of a length from Kalankoe to give Graham McCourt a lucky chance ride on a horse passed over by his great friend Graham Bradley.

Jimmy Lorenzo is now trained by Jonathan Sheppard, another English export. Sheppard, who has been the leading jumps trainer in the United States throughout the last 10 years, also saddled the third, Polar Pleasure. Cuckold, whom Bradley rode the previous weekend into second place at Fairhill, made the running, but was pulled up. Rio Clara, partnered by Steve Smith Eccles, finished sixth.

Haydock Park: 15 December

Scudamore reaches 100 in record time

By HOTSPUR (Peter Scott)

Peter Scudamore recorded the fastest century by a jockey in a National Hunt season with his victory on Fu's Lady at Haydock Park yesterday. Her win completed a Scudamore treble for the second day running.

Barring accidents, Scudamore should beat Jonjo O'Neill's 1977-78 record of 149 wins long before the season's end on June 3. O'Neill did not reach his century that season until Feb 8. Even though Scudamore's ratio of wins to mounts this season is better than one in three, a double

century may be too much to expect.

Scudamore, 30, has again ridden many of his winners this season for Martin Pipe's stable, and the Somerset trainer also looks on course for a record. His 1987-88 total of 129 beat Michael Dickinson's 1982-83 figure of 120, and he shared Scudamore's treble yesterday to bring his current score to 89.

[Scudamore lost one of his winners on a disqualification, so his 100th was Sayfar's Lad at Ludlow on 20 Dec, also trained by Martin Pipe.]

---

20 December

French pair out of King George after clerical slip

By HOTSPUR (Peter Scott)

NUPSALA, winner of the King George VI Rank Chase last year, and his stable companion, Nord A.C., cannot run in Kempton Park's big race on Boxing Day. Confirmation of entry details was sent to the wrong Fax number from trainer François Doumen's office.

Non-appearance of these two intended French challengers among the six King George acceptors first raised thoughts that Doumen had misunderstood the new system introduced last month. Original entry procedures were correctly gone through for Nupsala and Nord A.C. by the Dec 7 deadline. The follow-up was also in order except for the all-important Fax

misdirection.

Jockey Club officials established what had gone wrong after they contacted the Societé des Chasses, which governs French steeplechasing. Doumen was yesterday travelling to England by ferry and some confusion remained as to whether he or his secretary made the mistake.

A Jockey Club spokesman commented: "It is very sad, but reinstating Nupsala and Nord A.C. for a big race might lead to problems for every type of race. Such a precedent might cause grievance among English trainers, who may have suffered from entries going astray under the new system or could do so in future."

King George VI Chase Kempton Park: 26 December

'Orchid' makes Christmas vigil worthwhile

By HOTSPUR (Peter Scott)

Desert Orchid *(right)*, the smooth, four-length winner of yesterday's King George VI Rank Chase at Kempton Park, rewarded a vigil by anxious owner Mr Richard Burridge, who had spent the previous night with his dog outside the grey's box at David Elsworth's Whitsbury stable.

Mr Burridge's big-race nerves were not shared by Simon Sherwood, who has still to be beaten on Desert Orchid, and he had a comfortable ride. England's top chaser made a couple of mistakes and Sherwood allowed the hard-pulling Vodkatini two spells in the lead.

Ahead until the ninth, Desert Orchid (1-2f) was finally back in front two fences from home. Vodkatini (7-1) began to weaken there, but Kildimo (8-1) made a spirited challenge and was little more than a length behind at the last. Desert Orchid then quickened away to beat Kildimo for the third time in their four 1988 clashes.

"He paces himself throughout a race nowadays, but seems to get better and better," said Sherwood.

Dry ground helped Desert Orchid set the second-best King George time in more than 20 years. He was clapped from the winner's enclosure after returning 5min 50sec, which is second only to Wayward Lad's 1983 record time of 5min 47.6sec.

The Cheltenham Gold Cup 1-2, Charter Party and Cavvies Clown, finished last of the five runners and fourth, respectively. Desert Orchid is now a 4-1 chance for next year's Gold Cup with Hills-Mecca, who offer the run-guaranteed concession. All other possible challengers are quoted at 12-1 or more.

OTHER MAJOR RACES

Irish Derby	Kahyasi	R Cochrane	4-5f
Arc de Triomphe	Tony Bin	J Reid	14-1
Kentucky Derby	Winning Colors	G Stevens	34-10jf
Melbourne Cup	Empire Rose	T Allan	5-1
Arlington Million	Mill Native	C Asmussen	406-10
Japan Cup	Pay the Butler	C McCarron	139-10

Taunton: 29 December

Mareth Line gives Pipe record for quickest century

By HOTSPUR (Peter Scott)

KABARTAYLAR, long odds-on favourite and runner up in Taunton's first race yesterday, made Martin Pipe briefly look like a batsman in the nervous nineties. His 100th winner this season came with Mareth Line half-an-hour later, and Delkusha afterwards increased the stable score.

Pipe, 43, was born in Taunton and went to school there. The Somerset course provided the first of 578 jumping winners trained by him. This was Hit Parade in Dec 1975. His first full training licence was granted in 1977.

Taunton also played an important part in Pipe's decision to start training and

cease to be an amateur rider. Breaking his thigh there led Pipe to conclude that he was "in the wrong vocation".

Bonanza Boy's Welsh National highlighted five wins for the stable on Tuesday. They had no runners on Wednesday. Pipe's proportion of winners to runners this season is 42 per cent, and beating his 129-winner record of last season seems a formality. Pipe has surpassed the previous record for the fastest seasonal century, set by Michael Dickinson on March 8, 1982-83, with almost 10 weeks to spare. But bookmakers are still offering 8-1 against his double century.

1989

22 Apr Martin Pipe saddles 181st winner of the season, High Bid in a handicap hurdle at Uttoxeter, to beat the record set by Henry Cecil on the flat in 1987.

24 May Triptych, dual winner of both the Coronation Cup and the Champion Stakes, is killed at the Claiborne Farm stud in Kentucky when she runs into a nightwatchman's truck as he does his evening patrol. The 7-year-old was in foal to Mr Prospector.

3 Jun The National Hunt season closes with a record 221 victories for Peter Scudamore, who won with 33% of his rides, and a record 208 winners saddled by Martin Pipe, who succeeded with nearly 40% of his runners.

7 Jun At 500-1, Terimon's 2nd, 5 lengths behind Nashwan in the Derby at Epsom, makes him the highest-priced placed horse in any English Classic.

10 Jun Easy Goer scorches home by 8 lengths from Sunday Silence in the Belmont Stakes, New York, depriving the runner-up of the American Triple Crown and prize money bonuses worth $5m.

25 Aug Stable lass Melody Town is leading Cotton on Quick round the parade ring for Alan Bailey for the first race at Goodwood, a 5f apprentices' handicap, when it is discovered that the jockey of another horse, the Mrs Armytage-trained Damaskeen, is unqualified to ride. So Melody takes the mount and brings the 12-1 shot home by half a length.

15 Sep After the driest, hottest summer on record, autumn rains cause patchy ground, and Able Player is the second horse to fall in 3 days at Doncaster, throwing jockey Billy Newnes. The rest of the programme is abandoned, including tomorrow's St Leger, which is rescheduled for Ayr on the 23rd.

1 Dec The Aga Khan, whose filly Aliysa is threatened with disqualification from her Oaks win in June, resigns his honorary membership of the Jockey Club, dissatisfied with the administrative and scientific methods used by the Club and their forensic laboratory.

---

16 January

Jockey Club issue new guidelines on use of whip

By HOTSPUR (Peter Scott)

PHOTOGRAPHIC evidence of horses' injuries or markings will be required by local stewards from racecourse vets under revised disciplinary guidelines for improper or excessive use of the whip.

These were approved yesterday by the Jockey Club and take effect from Feb 1. Guidelines issued last March stated that veterinary evidence was not essential before action could be taken against a rider. Jockeys' unrest came to a head during late November and resulted in their meeting with the Disciplinary Stewards on Dec 9.

Photographs must be signed for identification by someone in charge of a horse when it is examined in the racecourse sampling unit. Vets will be required to produce such photographs for local stewards, who must then study all relevant parts of the race video before disciplining a rider. Sampling unit photographs will concentrate on whip marks in the wrong area of a horse, and those which have drawn blood, besides the number and severity of weals.

Other changes concern trainers. They are now instructed, rather than advised, that apprentices or other relatively inexperienced jockeys should be taught how to use the whip before riding in public, and to warn all jockeys about horses that mark easily.

CHAMPIONS

Jockey (Flat)	Pat Eddery	171
Jockey (NH)	Peter Scudamore	221
Racehorse of Year	Nashwan	3-y-o
NH Champion of Year	Desert Orchid	10-y-o
Leading Trainer	Michael Stoute	£2,000,330
Leading Owner	Sheikh Mohammed	£1,143,343
Leading Money Winner	Nashwan	£772,045

20 February

Murphy banned for 28 days

By a Special Correspondent

DECLAN MURPHY, stable jockey to Barney Curley, was banned for 28 days by the Jockey Club Disciplinary Committee yesterday for misuse of the whip when Experimenting won at Lingfield Park on Feb 2.

Murphy, who has ridden 18 winners this season, received the ban after the Disciplinary stewards found that he had hit Experimenting with unreasonable force, frequency and severity which caused injury to the horse.

Curley said afterwards: "This is a crazy decision — Declan was only trying to win. There is no justification for such a long ban. Experimenting would not have won but for the whip at Lingfield. Look at what happened to the horse at Folkestone last week, he was hit only three times and was beaten over 30 lengths. We will be consulting with lawyers to see if an injunction can be taken out to stop the ban."

This was Murphy's fifth whip offence of the season — although he was cleared of two of them — and the stewards took this into account in deciding their sentence.

Newton Abbot: 14 February

Scudamore reaches his 1,000 with hat-trick

By HOTSPUR (Peter Scott)

PETER SCUDAMORE *(above)* reached his 1,000th winner in a career that seems destined to surpass all National Hunt riding records when Avionne provided the third leg of his treble at Newton Abbot. Seven days earlier Scudamore had beaten Jonjo O'Neill's 1977-78 record of 149 wins in a season.

Two statistical targets now remain. The first is to ride 200 winners this season, and the second to overtake John Francome's career total of 1,138.

Scudamore's score this season has reached 158. Only some serious accident, which remains a jumping jockey's daily hazard, will prevent his reaching a double century before June 3. Stan Mellor's lifetime score of 1,035 would be overtaken on the way. Mellor became the first NH rider to reach 1,000 victories and his record stood until Francome beat it. "Beating Jonjo's record was fantastic, but to join Francome and Mellor in riding 1,000 winners means still more to me," said Scudamore yesterday.

Wingspan, Let Him By and Avionne, who provided Scudamore's Newton Abbot treble, all come from the Martin Pipe stable. Pipe has supplied 111 of Scudamore's winners this season.

[A previous winner was subsequently disqualified, so Scudamore's 1,000th was Baluchi, ridden the following day at Worcester.]

4 March

Perfection for Pipe as he lands six out of six

By J A McGrath

MARTIN PIPE made it a clean sweep across Britain yesterday, sending out six winners from six runners at three different meetings.

Continuing his domination of jump racing, Pipe took the feature race at Newbury, the Philip Cornes Saddle of Gold Hurdle Final, with Pertemps Network (4-5f), and the important Hochberg Victor Ludorum Hurdle at Haydock Park with Liadett (7-4f), who duly earned a 16-1 quote from Ladbrokes for the Triumph Hurdle.

This added to wins with Kabartaylar (6-5f) at Haydock and Rastannora (15-8f), Silver Ace (1-2f) and Go West (11-10f) at Hereford, and took Pipe's tally to 158 wins this season.

'Dessie' in the lead

Cheltenham Gold Cup: 16 March

Desert Orchid's courage decisive in Gold Cup

By HOTSPUR (Peter Scott)

DESERT ORCHID yesterday summoned every ounce of courage for his finest hour. He wore down the equally gallant Yahoo in a Tote Cheltenham Gold Cup battle that was made gruelling by the heavy ground but enabled the massive crowd to briefly forget the miserable weather.

Mr Richard Burridge, Desert Orchid's principal owner, had considered withdrawing him, but left the final say to trainer David Elsworth, who decided to go ahead.

Neither Elsworth nor jockey Simon Sherwood had feared dead ground, but hours of rain turned it heavy. Snow started falling at breakfast time in neighbouring areas, so Cheltenham were lucky to race. The stewards made a precautionary inspection at noon.

Ten Plus's death marred what was otherwise a great occasion. Leading Desert Orchid three fences from home, he fell and broke a hind fetlock.

Desert Orchid was in front to half-way, but then Sherwood allowed Ten Plus to go ahead. Sherwood was still biding his time when Ten Plus

fell, and reckons the favourite would have won anyway. Ten Plus's departure still did not leave matters easy because the almost unconsidered Yahoo then took command, and had a slight lead over the final two fences.

Desert Orchid (5-2f) refused to give best, and tackling the uphill run-in he inched ahead. The lead steadily increased to one and a half lengths. Desert Orchid edged left towards Yahoo (25-1) in his fatigue, but Sherwood straightened him in time to prevent any interference. "Desert Orchid gave every ounce and I am honoured to be associated with such a horse," said the winning jockey.

Charter Party (14-1), successful in last year's Gold Cup, finished eight lengths behind Yahoo in third place. Bonanza Boy (15-2) was a distant fourth with West Tip (66-1) the only other finisher.

The first grey to win the Gold Cup, "Dessie" was mobbed by his admirers when returning to unsaddle. "He took it all in good part, and knew he had accomplished something special," said Sherwood.

Fairclough Four-Year-Old Hurdle Stratford: 19 May

Anti Matter 200 for Pipe

MARTIN PIPE became the first trainer to send out 200 winners in a season when Anti Matter, ridden by Peter Scudamore, won the Fairclough Four-Year-Old Hurdle at Stratford last night.

Appropriately it was also on this horse, in February, that Scudamore broke Jonjo O'Neill's record number of

winners in a season. Scudamore had his mount on a tight rein for much of last night's race, but made his move as the runners approached the straight for the final time. He dashed Anti Matter past the pacemaking Dwale and went on to gain a five-length victory over Final Flutter.

Scudamore passes 200 mark with Towcester four-timer

Peter Scudamore reached a historic score of 201 winners in a National Hunt season when completing a four-timer on Old Kilpatrick, Canford Palm, Gay Moore and Market Forces at Towcester last night. He had earlier drawn a blank from four rides at Hereford's afternoon meeting.

Scudamore, who in February established a record score for a National Hunt campaign, becomes the first jockey to ride 200 winners in a season since Gordon Richards rode 231 on the Flat in 1952.

Old Kilpatrick (13-8f) and Gay Moore (10-1) both had 12 lengths to spare last night. Canford Palm (4-1) won by 20 lengths and Market Forces (7-2) by seven lengths.

Scudamore's association with Martin Pipe's West Country stable has helped him shatter countless records this season, and many believe his, and Pipe's, may never be broken.

Scudamore, 30, joined Stan Mellor and John Francome as the only National Hunt jockeys to ride 1,000 winners when completing a hat-trick at Newton Abbot on Feb 14. That milestone followed the fastest 50 winners in a season, achieved on Oct 24; a remarkable 100 before Christmas (Dec 15) and the

breaking of Jonjo O'Neill's 11-year record of 149 winners in a season (Feb 7).

Scudamore's unique achievement in one season's jump racing is underlined by the fact that Francome reached four figures in the twilight of his career. His final total of 1,136 should be beaten by Scudamore next season.

Scudamore, who attended Belmont, a Catholic public school, would not be dissuaded from professional race-riding by his jockey-turned-trainer father, Michael. His first winner was Rolyat at Devon and Exeter on Aug 31, 1978. He served his apprenticeship as an amateur rider before becoming stable jockey to David Nicholson and then succeeded Francome as No. 1 for Fred Winter.

By courtesy of Francome's generosity, Scudamore shared the jockeys' title in 1981, but has been outright champion in the last three seasons. Scudamore is first jockey to Fred Winter's successor Charlie Brooks, but most of his wins this season have been for Pipe.

Pipe, who set a record of 129 National Hunt winners last season, has sent out 183 winners so far this season, with six weeks remaining.

NATIONAL HUNT

Champion Hurdle	Beech Road	R Guest	50-1
Cheltenham Gold Cup	Desert Orchid	S Sherwood	5-2f
Grand National	Little Polveir	J Frost	28-1

The Oaks Epsom: 10 June

Gold Seal take-over by Aliysa

By J A McGrath

WALTER Swinburn's dilemma over his Gold Seal Oaks ride ended happily when the Aga Khan's Aliysa won yesterday's fillies' Classic at Epsom with a fine display of staying power and determination.

When it came to the crunch, it was all swinging on whether Swinburn could angle Aliysa through a narrow opening between the leader, Mamaluna, and the well-backed Snow Bride coming into the home straight.

At first the opening did not appear likely to come. But eventually Snow Bride weakened, and Aliysa raced through just over a furlong out and went on to score by three lengths in the exceptional time of 2min

34.22sec, which was 0.68sec faster than Nashwan in the Derby on Wednesday.

Snow Bride (13-2) held on to second, a short head in front of Roseate Tern (25-1), who tracked the winner in the straight and battled on courageously for third place, two and a half lengths ahead of Mamaluna (50-1). Aliysa won well, starting an 11-10 favourite, while stablemate Musical Bliss (4-1), which Swinburn rejected only after much soul-searching, weakened in the straight to finish seventh of the nine runners.

[Aliysa was later controversially disqualified after a drug test, and Snow Bride, ridden by Steve Cauthen, promoted to 1st place.]

Obituary: 12 June

Timeform creator Phil Bull dies at 79

By Peter Scott

PHIL BULL, who founded the Timeform organisation, successfully campaigned for various racing reforms and pioneered race ratings, has died at his Halifax home, aged 79.

Bull started his working life as a schoolmaster. His early writing and tipping went under the name of William K Temple because of professional etiquette prevailing 50 years ago.

Best Horses of 1942, a slim little volume that was forerunner to the now bulky Racehorses annuals, has become a valuable, collector's item. He brought out several more annuals, with assistance from Quintin Gilbey and James Park, but racing's rapid expansion then made it necessary to recruit a full-time staff.

Bull was also a substantial gambler in the 1940s, but his heavy betting never spoiled his accuracy as a race-reader, long before the days when instant TV replays made up for what was missed live. High standards were also demanded from his employees. The Racehorses annuals, as they became in 1950, quickly established an international reputation for accuracy, sound comment and fair ratings. He died with these standards firmly maintained.

Many racing reforms urged by Bull were introduced, but he was too forceful for committee compromises and respectful suggestions. He resigned after only a few months as head of the Jockey Club's Horseracing Advisory Council.

Bull, whose once distinctive red beard steadily turned grey, also owned and bred a number of good horses.

Irish Derby The Curragh: 2 July

Old Vic blazes winning trail in Irish Derby

By HOTSPUR (Peter Scott)

OLD VIC outclassed his Budweiser Irish Derby opponents at The Curragh yesterday. He made most of the running to beat Observation Post by four lengths in very good time. His clear-cut win has increased speculation as to the outcome of his first clash with Nashwan, unbeaten winner of the Epsom Derby and the 2,000 Guineas.

Old Vic, bred at Mr Bob McCreery's Stowell Hill stud, near Templecombe, and bought by Sheikh Mohammed for 230,000gns as a yearling, has won all five races this season.

Pat Eddery, riding Ile de Nisky (5-1), was determined not to give Old Vic (4-11f) the same rope as had his French opponents in last month's Prix du Jockey Club. Ile de Nisky led for a furlong, and then stayed in close touch as Old Vic took command. Zayyani tracked them into the straight, but then dropped away. Observation Post (12-1) made a spirited challenge that took him past Ile de Nisky but without offering serious danger to Old Vic. Ile de Nisky, six and a half lengths behind Old Vic yesterday, had been beaten seven and a half lengths when fourth to Nashwan in the Derby.

Steve Cauthen, who has now achieved the unprecedented accomplishment of wins in the Derby, Irish Derby, Prix du Jockey Club (French Derby) and Kentucky Derby, said he was delighted by the power with which Old Vic finished. Old Vic's 2min 29.90sec was the fastest Irish Derby since Shareef Dancer in 1983.

King George VI & Queen Elizabeth Diamond Stakes Ascot: 22 July

King Nashwan still rules

Unbeaten champion has only neck to spare

By J A McGrath

NASHWAN made turf history when landing yesterday's King George VI and Queen Elizabeth Diamond Stakes at Ascot after a spirited final-furlong duel with Cacoethes. Confidently ridden by Willie Carson, Nashwan won by a neck after persistently finding something extra.

He became the first horse to win the 2,000 Guineas, Derby, Eclipse and King George in one season, doing it with a gritty display that must surely forever silence the doubting Thomases of the racing world.

For British racing, the best news was saved till last. Trainer Dick Hern revealed that when Nashwan retires from racing at the end of the year, he is to stand at Sheikh Hamdan Al Maktoum's Shadwell stud in Norfolk, alongside his half-brother Unfuwain.

For a seven-runner field (including pacemaker) for one of racing's richest prizes, they went a pathetically slow early gallop, which helped make this a tactical battle. Carson, having kept Nashwan on the outside early, then waited for Greville Starkey on Cacoethes to settle in front of him, outpointing his riding rival, and the win was a triumph for the Scot's prowess in the saddle.

The pace had picked up at Swinley Bottom, but they were still going slow enough more than three furlongs out for Top Class to dart around the outside and take it up. "Top Class bumped me when he went past and cost me half a length," recalled Carson. "It could have cost me the race." Nashwan (2-9f) powered to the front inside the two-furlong marker, but then Cacoethes (6-1) loomed large on the outside to throw down a challenge that kept racegoers on their toes for the rest of the race. Nashwan kept pulling something extra out and was able to repel Cacoethes, with the pair drawing seven lengths clear of the third, Top Class (50-1).

Again Nashwan's speed, gigantic stride and class carried him to a memorable victory on lightning-fast ground. He must now rate alongside other greats such as Nijinsky, Brigadier Gerard and Mill Reef. His versatility and tremendous will to win stamp him as an outstanding performer.

Carson wins the King George on Nashwan

Prix Niel Longchamp: 17 September

Nashwan flop leaves stable mystified

By HOTSPUR (Peter Scott)

NASHWAN lost his unbeaten record at Longchamp yesterday, causing his stable dismay and bewilderment when he was only third to Golden Pheasant in the Prix Niel. Nashwan finished two lengths behind the winner after having every chance. His proposed £18 million stud syndication now makes it doubtful whether Nashwan will tackle the Arc (Oct 8) or indeed race again.

Nad Elshiba, Nashwan's pacemaker, led until the straight. French Glory then went ahead, challenged by Nashwan. The blinkered Golden Pheasant then challenged on their outside and went on to beat French Glory by a length and a half.

"Nashwan just did not fire. I cannot explain why, and he felt like a tired horse at the end," said jockey Willie Carson. "I was happy enough until halfway up the straight when it became clear that he would have trouble holding French Glory." Dick Hern, Nashwan's trainer, said the colt had travelled well to France and had been working in good style since the rest that followed his latest Ascot win on July 22.

[Hern had been in favour of aiming Nashwan for the St Leger and Triple Crown, but his owner plumped for the Arc. In the event, after his flop in the Prix Niel, Nashwan was withdrawn from the Arc and never raced again.]

Longchamp: 7 October

Asmussen spells out task facing England's Arc raiders

By J A McGrath

CASH ASMUSSEN gave his rivals something to think about on the eve of the Prix de l'Arc de Triomphe by landing a five-timer at Longchamp as English-trained horses performed dismally. Four of the wins came in Group events as Asmussen, who rides the unbeaten In the Wings for in-form André Fabre in the Arc, completely dominated the first day of the glittering weekend.

He started with a win on Mardonius in the Prix de Lutèce and then took the Prix Dollar on Creator, the Grand Criterium on Jade Robbery, the Prix de Royallieu on Passionaria and rounded off the day by landing the final race, a handicap, on Rough Magic.

Asmussen, cool and confident, rides Longchamp as if he owns the place, and his five successes yesterday took him to 143 wins in France this season.

The English challenge petered out, and the only highlight was the Prix Gladiateur triumph of Hi Lass, owned by Arthur Budgett but now trained by Jonathan Pease in France. Tony Cruz drove the Shirley Heights filly home to score by two lengths from Rachmaninov – ridden by Cash Asmussen.

ENGLISH CLASSICS

2,000 Guineas	Nashwan	W Carson	3-1f
1,000 Guineas	Musical Bliss	W Swinburn	7-2
Derby	Nashwan	W Carson	5-4f
Oaks*	Snow Bride	S Cauthen	13-2
St Leger†	Michelozzo	S Cauthen	6-4f

*Aliysa (11-10f, W Swinburn up) originally won, but was disqualified on 20 Nov 1990.
† At Ayr (Doncaster programme abandoned).

Lingfield: 30 October

Betting-shop regulars give all-weather track the thumbs-up

By Tony Stafford

IF A SAMPLE of half a dozen betting shops in Hertfordshire and North East and East London can be considered representative, then the punters' initial reaction to the delights of Lingfield's all-weather track was a clear "yes".

Starting at 11 a.m., the first shop I visited had the added delights of Derek Thompson as the link-man. The first six heats, mostly with the front-runners staying there, did make for slightly repetitive fare, so it was refreshing when Wizzard Magic came from a long way back in the 1 o'clock race to show that fast finishers could win after all.

Foreigners always cite the variety of English racing as its biggest attraction, but the foibles of the international rich do not fuel the Big Three bookmaking firms' profits; nor do they materially help the Betting Levy, without which racing would inevitably creak.

Midwinter Flat racing will fulfil many functions, not least the useful employment of modest horses which would otherwise stay idle for four months each winter, and cause the temporary lay-off of staff.

The biggest plus was to see the ease with which the horses coped with the bends. Too-sharp tracks were predicted for the two all-weather circuits. Lingfield's seems perfect, especially for the sensibly sized fields. Tomorrow, Southwell and its sand-based (Fibresand) surface has its first public test with a hurdles card, and all concerned anticipate a similar success story.

[Southwell's inaugural all-weather fixture was also a success. The racecourse vet reported that the "kickback" from the surface was less of a problem than with Lingfield's Equitrack, the jockeys were pleased with the surface, and it had no effect on Martin Pipe's vice-like grip on NH racing – he saddled 3 winners out of four runners, all ridden by Jonathan Lower.]

OTHER MAJOR RACES

Irish Derby	Old Vic	S Cauthen	4-11f
Arc de Triomphe	Carroll House	M Kinane	189-10
Kentucky Derby	Sunday Silence	P Valenzuela	31-10
Melbourne Cup	Tawrrific	R Dye	30-1
Arlington Million	Steinlen	JA Santos	53-10
Japan Cup	Horlicks	L O'Sullivan	19-1

Aintree: 23 October

Unveiling of a modified National monument

By John Oaksey

A NEW, fairer and less hazardous Becher's Brook dominated the package of changes announced at Aintree yesterday. Together, they should disarm the famous fence's critics — while improving both the Seagram Grand National and its home.

Although Becher's is still, by any standard, a formidable sight, the gallant Captain would certainly not recognise the Brook to which he gave his name in 1837. "Dammed up to be eight foot wide" in that first Grand National, it has dwindled now to a two-foot trickle, only inches deep. The drop on the landing side, which has always been the great fence's best-known and most spectacular character-istic, remains as big as ever — still varying from 23 inches on the inside to 17 inches on the outer.

But the ditch has been filled in to a depth of only 15 inches and, most important of all, the treacherous "lip", which lay in wait for horses who stood off too far or landed short, has been almost entirely removed.

"Our chief objective has been to reduce the price of failure while allowing the fence to keep its challenge," says Clerk of the Course, John Parrett. Certainly, no fallen horse should ever again be wedged upside-down in the brook as Brown Trix was last year.

Becher's, following the line of the original brook, lies at an angle across the course and many recent disasters have been caused by horses jumping it sharply left-handed. In order to lessen this tendency, the outside running rail has been moved back so that, instead of being confronted by a wall of excited human beings, horses will be able to see clear ahead. Both on the outside and on the inner, special enclosures have been made for photo-graphers, well back from the course itself.

No change has been made to the Grand National safety limit of 40, but no horse rated below 105 by the official handicapper will now be allowed to enter. Almost certainly, that will in itself keep the entries below 40.

As for riders, 15 winners over fences and hurdles is now the minimum qualifi-cation. In exceptional cases, the stewards will consider applications from foreign jockeys or those qualified in some other way.

Kennel Gate Novices' Hurdle Ascot: 18 November

Scu ends record suspense

By J A McGrath

Peter Scudamore rode into racing legend as the most successful jumps jockey ever when Arden won the Kennel Gate Novices' Hurdle at Ascot. This victory, by a neck from the strong-finishing Athens Gate, took Scudamore's career total to 1,139 wins, one more than the flamboyant John Francome, against whom he used to ride regularly.

It also enabled the racing world collectively to let out a sigh of relief after a wait for the inevitable that had seemed an eternity, but was in fact a mere three days and seven rides since he equalled the record last Wednesday.

There was little time for Scudamore to savour his considerable achievement. After a whirlwind round of television and radio inter-views – one conducted in the lift as he descended to the Grandstand basement – he accepted a bottle of cham-pagne from Her Majesty's representative, Sir Piers Bengough, to the warm applause of an appreciative crowd of 10,320.

Then the relentless pursuit of winners started again, with the champion taking a helicopter to Warwick for two more rides – a runner-up and then a heavy fall. Such are the ups and downs of the jumping game.

The 1990s

The organisation of racing in Britain underwent significant changes in the nineties. The formation of the British Horseracing Board (BHB) in 1993 to control both Flat and jump racing signalled the end of Jockey Club rule. And with all-weather tracks already established, both branches of the sport could be seen 12 months of the year when the BHB introduced summer jump racing in 1995 as a two-year experiment. All-weather hurdle racing, however, was discontinued in 1994 because of the number of equine fatalities.

The easing of restrictions on betting shops resulted in longer opening hours and improved facilities and scope. Other changes in the first half of the decade included Sunday racing – the 1995 1,000 Guineas being the first Classic to be held on the Sabbath – and the overnight declaration of jockeys.

Membership of the jockeys' "200 club" more than doubled in the early nineties, with Pat Eddery riding 209 winners in 1990, Michael Roberts 206 in 1992, and, thanks largely to the all-weather element, Frankie Dettori and Jason Weaver becoming the latest double centurions with 233 and 200, respectively, in 1994. The emergence of the latter two coincided with the waning of Willie Carson, but the man to regularly steal the headlines was the granddad of them all, Lester Piggott, who made a comeback in 1990 and rode his 30th Classic winner in 1992.

Sale prices have plummeted in the nineties and stallion fees have dropped more than sixty percent since 1989. Of the outstanding horses so far, Sheikh Hamdan Al-Maktoum's Salsabil became, in 1990, the first filly this century to win the Irish Derby, having already won the 1,000 Guineas and Oaks.

Female trainers have come increasingly into their own, with Jenny Pitman saddling numerous big-race jump winners and Mary Reveley excelling in both National Hunt and Flat. And Lady Herries sent out Celtic Swing to win the French Derby in 1995.

The nineties saw the retirement of two giants of the Turf, trainer Vincent O'Brien and champion jump jockey Peter Scudamore. The latter's title has been keenly contested by Richard Dunwoody and Adrian Maguire, and the National Hunt has provided the most sensational event – the void 1993 Grand National.

A course official forlornly waves his flag, trying to stop the field as the 1993 Grand National dissolves into chaos

1990

3 Feb US jockey Willie Shoemaker retires, having ridden a world record 8,833 winners and amassed prize money of over $123m.

13 Mar Kribensis (95-40) wins the Waterford Crystal Champion Hurdle in record time, beating the mark set in 1985 by See You Then, who finishes last of 19 and is retired, while Past Glories, 3rd at 150-1, is the longest-priced placed horse in the history of the race.

30 Mar Former England football international Mike Channon, granted his training licence on **1 Feb**, saddles his first winners, Golden Scissors (4-1) at Beverley and Wessex Warrior (5-2f) at Wincanton.

13 May Phenomenal NH trainer Martin Pipe takes less than a year to surpass his 208 winners, which was hailed as "a record that may never be beaten," with Huntworth's success at Warwick. He finishes the season, on 2 June, with 224 and a jump record £668,606 in winnings.

13 Oct Dubliners flock to their city track, Phoenix Park, for its last meeting, with a programme offering £1.32m in prize money and featuring the 3rd running of the 2-y-o 7f Cartier Million, won by trainer Dermot Weld for the second successive year, this time with Rinka Das (7-1).

19 Oct Generous (50-1), who had already won over a mile, is the longest ever priced winner of the (Three Chimneys) Dewhurst Stakes, at Newmarket, leaving the three unbeaten fancied colts, Mujtahid (4-5f), Anjiz (4-1) and Sedair (13-2) out of a place. [The future Derby winner, ridden by Richard Quinn and trained by Paul Cole, leaves the bookies unimpressed, however, and is quoted at 50-1 for next year's Guineas.]

23 Oct Pat Eddery, 38, becomes only the 4th Flat jockey to ride 200 winners in an English season when he succeeds on Miranda Jay in a maiden fillies race at Chepstow, but still has to share the limelight with Lester Piggott, who never quite managed this particular achievement, but who gloriously confirms his comeback by landing a 4-timer for Vincent O'Brien at the Curragh as he stands in for sidelined stable-jockey John Reid. At the same meeting, trainer Jim Bolger saddles two winners to equal the Irish record of 134 in a season.

15 Nov Alydar, who finished 2nd to Affirmed in all three US Triple Crown Races in 1978 and became one of the top five stallions in the world, has to be put down after a stable injury at Calumet Farm, Lexington, earlier in the week and a subsequent injury this morning following an apparently successful operation. The insurance pay-out will break records, the total "market exposure" being over $50m, some half of it in the London market.

16 Nov Northern Dancer, 29, widely regarded as the world's most successful post-war stallion, is put down in Maryland. He had already retired from stud duties, and his progeny included Derby winners Nijinsky, The Minstrel and Secreto.

21 Nov Equinoctial, trained by A.Miller and ridden by A.Heywood, wins the Grant's Whisky Novices' Handicap Hurdle at Kelso at a British record SP of 250-1.

Cheltenham Gold Cup 15 March

Shock winner Norton's Coin is one of five record breakers

By HOTSPUR (Peter Scott)

Norton's Coin, whose victory at 100-1 provided the biggest shock in Gold Cup history, was among five Cheltenham winners yesterday to set time records.

Norton's Coin returned 6min 30.9sec to beat Cheltenham's previous 3 1/4 mile record on the New course set by Dawn Run with 6min 35.3sec in the 1986 Gold Cup.

The other record setters were Rare Holiday, Bigsun, Brown Windsor and Moody Man, the last named beating the 2 mile hurdle record set by the first, Rare Holiday, in the Daily Express Triumph Hurdle, the first race of the day.

Desert Orchid and the fine weather were major factors in a crowd of 56,884, which is thought to have been the biggest in Cheltenham history.

Toby Tobias had taken the lead from Ten of Spades before the latter came down two from home. Mark Pitman, riding Toby Tobias, must have felt that he would succeed where his father Richard had failed on Pendil 17 years earlier. Unfortunately for Mark, the closing stages provided a close replica of that race in 1973 in which The Dikler wore down Pendil, as Norton's Coin overtook Toby Tobias (8-1) to win by three-quarters of a length. The 11-year-old Desert Orchid (10-11f) finished third, another four lengths behind.

Norton's Coin (left) overtakes Toby Tobias near the line

CHAMPIONS

Jockey (Flat)	Pat Eddery	209
Jockey (NH)	Peter Scudamore	170
Racehorse of Year	Dayjur	3-y-o colt
NH Champion of Year	Desert Orchid	11-y-o
Leading Trainer	Henry Cecil	£1,519,864
Leading Owner	Hamdan Al-Maktoum	£1,536,815
Leading Money Winner	In the Groove	£459,117

Grand National Aintree: 7 April

Mr Frisk dashes home in National: Red Rum's record broken by 14 seconds

By J A McGrath

MR FRISK, a dashing jumper who seemed destined never to run at Liverpool, produced an outstanding performance to win yesterday's Seagram Grand National for 25-year-old amateur rider Marcus Armytage, after a thrilling battle with old campaigner Durham Edition on the run-in.

Left in front when the American-owned Uncle Merlin went at Becher's Brook second-time round, Mr Frisk (16-1) was 10 lengths clear at one stage, only to have his lead whittled down to two lengths by the fast-closing Durham Edition (9-1) at the final fence.

However, with a powerful surge at the elbow, the Kim Bailey-trained chestnut sprinted for the line and held his advantage by three-quarters of a length. He broke Red Rum's race-time record, set in 1973, by an incredible 14 seconds.

The win was the ultimate triumph for Bailey, who took more than two years to persuade Mr Frisk's owner, 83-year-old Lois Duffey, from Maryland, to let her chaser take his chance at Aintree.

The gods were smiling on 36-year-old Bailey, who spent three years with the four-times Grand National-winning trainer Fred Rimell. The ground was hard and lightning-fast, as Mr Frisk prefers it, and the gelding, once a nervous, flighty type, had settled down beautifully this season to turn in some of his best efforts.

"Mr" Armytage became the first amateur to win since Dick Saunders on Grittar in 1982. He was cheered home by his sister, the professional jockey Gee Armytage, who was nursing broken bones in hospital and had to miss her National ride on Monanore.

Armytage, who works as a journalist on the Racing Post, gave Mr Frisk an excellent ride, as did Chris Grant on Durham Edition, his third runner-up in the National.

Mr Frisk seemed to relish the company after being out in front by himself for so long, found just a little extra and maintained his slender lead all the way to the line.

There was a gap of 20 lengths to the third, Rinus (13-1), with 7-1 favourite Brown Windsor 12 lengths away, fourth of the 20 horses to complete the course.

NATIONAL HUNT

Champion Hurdle	Kribensis	R Dunwoody	95-40
Cheltenham Gold Cup	Norton's Coin	G McCourt	100-1
Grand National	Mr Frisk	Mr M Armytage	16-1

The Derby Epsom: 6 June

Brave's defeat forgotten as Fame swoops to victory

By MARLBOROUGH (John Oaksey)

THE EPSOM fates repaid Prince Khalid Abdulla handsomely for Dancing Brave's 1986 misfortune yesterday with the Derby success of Quest for Fame (7-1), but the other prizes were unkindly shared. Blue Stag (8-1) was Barry Hills' fourth second in the race, and Sheikh Mohammed's Derby record is still one of unrelieved disappointment.

Henry Cecil had always feared that the race might come too soon for Razeen, and Steve Cauthen knew his doom on the 9-2 favourite a long way from home. A May foal, who could not be trained at all last year, Razeen faded rapidly to finish 14th. It seems probable that the wind infirmity for which Razeen underwent an operation last year was found out by the strain of a fast-run Derby.

According to Pat Eddery, Quest for Fame was the easiest of his three Derby winners: "He lengthened his stride and quickened up the hill like only a good horse can." He beat Blue Stag by three lengths, and jockey Cash Asmussen offered no excuses for the runner-up, who follows Rheingold (1972), Hawaiian Sound (1978) and Glacial Storm (1988) in his trainer's catalogue of near misses.

ENGLISH CLASSICS

2,000 Guineas	Tirol	M Kinane	9-1
1,000 Guineas	Salsabil	W Carson	6-4
Derby	Quest for Fame	P Eddery	7-1
Oaks	Salsabil	W Carson	2-1
St Leger	Snurge	T Quinn	7-2

Irish Derby The Curragh: 1 July

Top colts are no match for brilliant Salsabil

By HOTSPUR (Peter Scott)

SALSABIL (11-4) scored a memorable victory over the top colts in yesterday's Budweiser Irish Derby. Sheikh Hamdan Al-Maktoum's brilliant filly passed Deploy (16-1) a furlong out and beat him by three-quarters of a length. Quest for Fame, 5-4 favourite to follow up his Derby win at Epsom, finished only fifth. Pat Eddery said that Quest for Fame was never moving in his best style.

Salsabil had already proved herself Europe's top filly with brilliant successes in the 1,000 Guineas and Oaks. She can now be regarded as the best European three-year-old of either sex.

Deploy, Quest for Fame's stable-companion, made the running. His fine effort bore out the stable's promise that he would compete on his own merits rather than as a pacemaker. Eddery soon had Quest for Fame close up, with Willie Carson tracking him on Salsabil. Quest for Fame came under pressure early in the straight. He could not get past Deploy and, as the favourite drifted to his left, an opening came for Salsabil.

She took full advantage of it and Deploy could not match her finishing speed. Belmez (4-1), who beat Quest for Fame at Chester two months ago but missed the Derby because of tendon trouble, stayed on well to finish four lengths behind Deploy, with Blue Stag, the Derby second and never a real threat here, fourth.

Belmont Stakes New York: 9 June

Go and Go 1st European Belmont winner

By HOTSPUR (Peter Scott)

The shortage of top performers in the United States that are capable of staying a mile and a half was underlined in Saturday's Belmont Stakes, in which Go and Go scored a remarkable eight-and-a-half-length victory for Dermot Weld's Irish stable.

The first European winner this century of America's last three-year-old classic, Go and Go was fourth to Anvari in his previous race, at Leopardstown, and is not top-class by European standards. Unbridled, the 10-furlong Kentucky Derby winner, finished fourth to Go and Go.

Newcastle: 30 June

Carson completes 3,266-1 six-timer

By J A McGrath

The incredible Willie Carson etched his name even deeper into British racing's record books when landing a memorable 3,266-1 six-timer at Newcastle yesterday to become only the third jockey this century to ride six winners on the same card – after Gordon Richards at Chepstow in 1933 and Alec Russell at Bogside in 1957.

Carson's achievements in racing are now bordering on the legend, one of the most extraordinary being his feat in riding a horse he bred himself, Minster Son, to victory in the 1988 St Leger.

Yesterday's feast of success gave him 19 winners in the past six days (11 in two days) and took his seasonal tally to 84. The 47-year-old jockey missed out only in the third race yesterday, when his mount was unplaced. His winners were Arousal (1-1f), Soweto (5-2f), Al Maheb (9-2), Ternimus (8-1), Tadwin (5-1) and Hot Desert (4-7f).

Carson's biggest winner was the Alec Stewart-trained Al Maheb, who took the Newcastle Brown Ale Northumberland Plate by a length and a half from the favourite, Dance Spectrum, to give him his second win in the "Pitman's Derby", the previous success being aboard Lord Derby's Amateur 22 years ago.

Timeform Futurity Pontefract: 4 September

Times equals best – and goes for 17 today

By Tony Stafford

Timeless Times and his trainer Bill O'Gorman yesterday earned their reward for a season's endeavour and astute planning when equalling the record of 16 wins for a two-year-old in the six-furlong Timeform Futurity at Pontefract.

Starting at the remarkable price of 11-2 in a four-horse field, he won easily to equal the record set by The Bard in 1884 and equalled exactly 100 years later by Provideo, who was also handled by O'Gorman. Three defeats, the latest only last week behind the unbeaten Anjiz, have not tarnished the reputation of the supremely tough chestnut colt, who may only have to share his distinction for 24 hours.

Perhaps expecting defeat yesterday, faced as he was by the smart Northern colt Dominion Gold, a 5-2 on chance after massive support, O'Gorman left Timeless Times in today's five-furlong Best Buy Products Stakes at York. Alan Munro, partnering Timeless Times as he has in all the colt's victories, kept him on terms with pace-making Allinson's Mate and sent him ahead rounding the final turn to win by three-quarters of a length, with the one-paced favourite a well-beaten third.

[Timeless Times failed to beat the record.]

Ladbroke Sprint Cup Haydock: 8 September

Dayjur blazes winning trail

By J A McGrath

DAYJUR earned his place in the record books by winning yesterday's Ladbroke Sprint Cup at Haydock, but runner-up Royal Academy looked extremely unlucky. The winning distance of a length and a half would have been drastically reduced had the Irish sprinter managed to obtain a clear run inside the final two furlongs.

Predictably, Dayjur (1-2f) broke fast and headed to the stands rail, where he effortlessly blazed the trail. Willie Carson was careful not to overtax him on the dead ground, holding a little in reserve. Entering the last quarter-mile, Dayjur bounded away, just as Royal Academy (11-2) was blocked for a run on the rails.

When Royal Academy finally got clear, Dayjur was five lengths in front with the prize safely in keeping as he completed a unique treble. He was adding the Ladbroke Sprint Cup to wins in the King's Stand at Royal Ascot and the Nunthorpe Stakes at York.

Winning trainer Dick Hern nominated the Prix de l'Abbaye at Longchamp as the next target for Dayjur. "He's proven today that he handles dead ground and six furlongs as well as he handles top of the ground and five furlongs," said Hern. Carson's tribute to Dayjur was to the point: "He is unbeatable over five furlongs, but defeat is not impossible over six."

Hare Maiden Fillies Stakes Leicester: 15 October

It's just like the old days as Lester gives vintage show

By John Oaksey

"**C**ome on Lester!" the familiar well-loved cry rang out again at Leicester yesterday. And despite three losing rides for the 54-year-old former champion, it sounded far more genuine and persuasive than whingeing weasel words like "they never come back".

Thousands flocked to watch racing's greatest living legend turn back the years in his own inimitable style, and were not disappointed. From the moment Henry Cecil's assistant, Simon Bray, gave Lester Piggott a leg-up on Lupescu in Division I of the Hare Maiden Fillies Stakes, the writing was clear on the wall for all to see. Racing's most famous posterior landed in the saddle light as thistledown, and your immediate impression was of a craftsman thoroughly at ease, happy to be back with his hands on familiar tools.

Except in one respect – about 2 1/2 inches – the race gave the same message equally loud and clear. Out of the gate like a shot, Lupescu was never out of the leading group. The hot favourite and form "good thing" Sumonda (2-5), ridden by Gary Carter,

looked like beating her comfortably a furlong out, but then the old drive slipped back into rhythm and Lupescu (5-1) rallied to lose by only the length of a cigarette.

The finish – even if it did not end quite the way we wished – was a real joy to watch. Although Lester picked up his whip two furlongs out, Lupescu came back without a mark. She had, on the other hand, been given a lovely, tender, forceful ride which proved, to my eyes at least, that Lester has not forgotten.

Needless to say, as we came off the stands, one red-faced, overweight punter beside me sneered, "Five years ago he would have won that easily." Of course, they will say that every time he gets beaten in a close finish, and no doubt on occasion he will make mistakes. But no-one who watched with half-an-eye yesterday can believe that Lester Piggott is past it.

[Piggott's comeback after 5 years somewhat overshadowed Walter Swinburn's performance in bringing home 5 of the 7 Leicester winners, all favourites, for a 39-1 5-timer.]

The St Leger Doncaster: 15 September

Battling Snurge wins St Leger thriller from gallant Hellenic

By J A McGrath

Snurge became the first maiden in 77 years to win the St Leger when he overpowered Hellenic in an exciting finish to the final classic of the season at Doncaster yesterday.

Snurge's victory was a first English classic success and the high point in the respective careers of trainer Paul Cole and jockey Richard Quinn, a combination that has endured despite the odd rocky patch because of "owner pressure".

The colt, a son of Ela-Mana-Mou, is the only horse running on the Flat for owner Martin Arbib, a chartered accountant from Henley-on-Thames, who explained that Snurge was a nickname from school.

The race was the expected test of stamina right to the thrilling last stride, with Snurge (7-2) having the

advantage of the rail after Quinn had gone for a gap on the inside more than 2 1/2 furlongs out as Hellenic (2-1f) took the lead.

An intense battle developed between the two, Snurge taking it up two furlongs out and the filly looking likely to overtake him for a few strides inside the distance.

But Snurge fought back courageously and was clearly in command in the final half furlong, winning by three-quarters of a length, with River God (100-30) four lengths away third of the eight runners.

Quinn, who had taken the inside berth "because the ground was better", said: "Snurge was the class horse of the race, and I always thought I had Hellenic covered. One smack, and he would have gone clear of her."

Breeders' Cup Chase: 20 October

British jumpers land big Belmont double

By J A McGrath

MORLEY STREET, 2-1 favourite, trained by Toby Balding and ridden by Jimmy Frost, completed a glorious double for British-trained runners at Belmont Park over the weekend when blitzing his rivals in an exciting ll-length win in the Breeders' Cup Chase on Saturday.

The victory came only

24 hours after Bokaro (42-10), trained by Charlie Brooks and ridden by Peter Scudamore, won the Queen Mother Supreme Hurdle.

Morley Street, a novice chaser at home, was held up in fifth for most of the way until delivering his challenge before the last. His turn of foot proved decisive as he raced clear of runner-up Summer Colony, with Moonstruck, ridden by Richard Dunwoody, three lengths behind in third. Irish runners, Kiichi (seventh) and Grabel (10th) were both disappointing.

Balding, welcoming his first American winner, said: "Morley Street is as good a horse as I've ever trained. Arguably, he was the best hurdler in Britain last season, but was not quite right when fifth in the Champion Hurdle. He proved what he could do by running away with the Sandeman Aintree Hurdle. Then, in his prep-race for this contest, he beat a St Leger winner on the Flat."

Balding is aiming Morley Street for a big 'chase this year, with the 1992 Cheltenham Gold Cup his long-term target.

Piggott: popular comeback

Breeders' Cup Mile Belmont Park: 27 October

Piggott comeback sensation

By John Oaksey

Even on a day marred by two deaths and the unluckiest big race defeat since Devon Loch, Lester Piggott stole the headlines yesterday at Belmont Park. Swooping from behind on Royal Academy, he won the Breeders' Cup Mile for Vincent O'Brien and underlined his amazing return to the big time of international racing.

Slowly away, Piggott was able to settle the Irish horse nearer last than first, until the turn for home; then, switching to the outside, he began one of those long, relentless challenges which used to be the trademark of so many winning years.

The old cry "Come on Lester" resounded in the Belmont Press Room, much of it with an American accent. Bought for $3.5m as a yearling, Royal Academy is, of course, American-bred through and through: by Vincent O'Brien's great Triple Crown winner, Nijinsky, out of a famously productive mare.

The cruelest defeat was suffered by Dayjur, whose brave American adventure came to a luckless end just 50 yards from the finish, when he jumped his way out of a certain triumph in the Breeders' Cup Sprint. Two shadows thrown across the dirt track by the blazing autumn sun cost him the championship of the world. But there is no longer any shadow of a doubt that the colt is the fastest racehorse in the world.

The winner, the reigning champion Safely Kept, the only filly in the race, was the only one fast enough to match strides with Dayjur in the straight. But until he started jumping, her crown was gone beyond recall.

However, Dayjur's disastrous jump had already been overshadowed when one of the 14-strong field, Mr Nickerson, collapsed and died of a heart attack as they jostled furiously towards the turn and, before that, by the death in the Distaff of the brilliant three-year-filly Go for Wand, who shattered a leg and had to be put down.

Against this background, the comparatively painless bad luck of Dayjur's "phantom jump" seems almost unimportant.

---

4 December

Aga Khan 'to pull horses out of Britain'

By John Oaksey

The Aga Khan stunned the racing world yesterday with an announcement that he is withdrawing all his racehorses from Britain.

The decision is a direct result of the controversial Aliysa affair, in which the Jockey Club's disciplinary committee concluded that his filly had been given a prohibited substance and disqualified her from first place in the 1989 Oaks.

It is the second such incident for the Aga Khan. In 1981, Vayrann was tested positive for anabolic steroids after winning the Champion Stakes, but on that occasion the Aga Khan successfully disputed and reversed the verdict.

Yesterday, six experts assembled by him in London were unanimously critical of the methods used to "convict" Aliysa.

The Aga Khan said: "This is an extremely uncomfortable decision to take. It is not irreversible, but will stand until such effective measures have been instituted to correct the flawed equine drug-testing procedures and administration of the rules sanctioning the use of prohibited substances in racing in this country. Until I am satisfied that basic scientific procedures are applied, I cannot expose myself with all its consequences to a repeat of this. Two cases in eight years is enough."

The Aga Khan, who entered ownership when his father died in a 1960 car crash, has built up the biggest and most successful breeding enterprise in Europe. His decision means that some 90 superbly bred racehorses will leave the Newmarket stables of Michael Stoute and Luca Cumani to be trained next season in France or Ireland.

Jockey Club Inquiry: 20 November

Aliysa loses 1989 Oaks: Aga Khan's filly disqualified

By HOTSPUR (Peter Scott)

Research has failed to establish how hydroxy-camphor came to be present in the post-race urine sample taken from Aliysa after the Aga Khan's filly had won the 1989 Oaks at Epsom, and yesterday's decision to disqualify her could be challenged in the law courts.

As far as the disciplinary stewards are concerned, the rules of racing have been breached because a prohibited substance was revealed.

Snow Bride, beaten three lengths by Aliysa at Epsom on 10 June 1989, has therefore been awarded the Oaks with other horses moved up accordingly.

News of Aliysa's sample was released three weeks after the race. Exhaustive inquiries had already begun at the stables of Michael Stoute, her trainer. These later extended to tests at universities in California and Quebec. Stoute, his stable staff and vets who had looked after Aliysa during the run-up to the Oaks, were all interviewed by Jockey Club security officials. Feed and other products in use at Stoute's yard were analysed, including shampoo and horse oils, but although nine substances were found to contain camphor, only one of them, a leather cleaner, had been in contact with the filly.

A trial was accordingly undertaken to test whether hydroxycamphor could be detected in urine of a horse which had worn tack cleaned with this particular cleaner, but the result was negative.

The Aga Khan and Stoute were fully within their rights to insist on such checks. Stoute said, after the verdict: "Aliysa was favourite for the Oaks... and the Aga Khan sent two of his security men to assist with my own precautions, which ensured that Aliysa was closely and continuously guarded for some days prior to the race." He described the verdict as: "A very big source of future worry for all trainers." The Aga Khan and Stoute may now dispute the verdict in the law courts.

OTHER MAJOR RACES

Irish Derby	Salsabil	W Carson	11-4
Arc de Triomphe	Saumarez	G Mossé	15-1
Kentucky Derby	Unbridled	C Perret	108-10
Melbourne Cup	Kingston Rule	D Beadman	7-1jf
Arlington Million	Golden Pheasant	G Stevens	66-10
Japan Cup	Better Loosen Up	M Clarke	52-10

King George VI Chase Kempton Park: 26 December

Desert Orchid turns on style in record win

By HOTSPUR (Peter Scott)

Desert Orchid (9-4) won his fourth King George VI Rank Chase at Kempton yesterday to beat the previous record which he shared with Wayward Lad, and in doing so demonstrated that all his enthusiasm and agility are still there. His 33 wins in 65 races have been worth £523,536.

Desert Orchid T-shirts were on sale at his fan-club stall below the grandstand. But rain and sleet made it highly undesirable for them to be worn, and many horses of Desert Orchid's age would have preferred a warm stable.

His agility was tested to the full at the 13th fence, six from home, when Sabin du Loir fell in front of him. A sharp sidestep was needed between the faller and the rails, and with Richard Dunwoody's help he reacted quickly to escape being brought down.

Toby Tobias, running for the first time since early April, was now his only realistic challenger, but the testing ground and Desert Orchid's jumping extinguished his hopes and the leader drew away to storm home 12 lengths clear.

1991

8 Apr US trainer and former record-breaking jockey Bill Shoemaker is partially paralysed in a car crash.

15 Apr Martin Pipe becomes the first National Hunt trainer to earn £1m in first prize money in a season when Colour Scheme wins at Southwell.

18 Jun Lester Piggott leads throughout on Saddlers' Hall (7-1) to win the King Edward VII Stakes – 37 years after being stood down for rough riding on Never Say Die in the same race. This is his 114th Royal Ascot win, his 1st for 6 years.

20 Jun Indian Queen (25-1), a 6-y-o mare in foal, wins the Ascot Gold Cup by a neck from Arzanni (13-8f).

30 Jun Generous (1-1f) underlines his Epsom performance by completing a Derby double at The Curragh, beating French Derby winner Suave Dancer (9-4) by 3 lengths, with Star of Gdansk (12-1) 8 lengths back in 3rd.

3 Jul The application by the Aga Khan for a judicial review of the Jockey Club decision to disqualify his 1989 Oaks winner Aliysa is refused.

17 Jul Jack Berry saddles his 100th winner of the season, in record time for the Flat, as Our Fan wins at Hamilton Park.

2 Sep National sponsors Seagram enter into a 7-year agreement with Aintree involving £4m, the race to be known henceforth as the Martell Grand National.

2 Oct The 2-y-o Young Senor (14-1), trained by Geoff Wragg, wins the £23,000 Tiffany Highflyer Stakes at Newmarket, landing a £1/2m sponsorship bonus.

14 Dec It's an eventful day for jockey Dean McKeown on the all-weather at Lingfield, switching from his booked horse Lord Advocate, which wins the first race at 20-1, and breaking a shoulder-bone in a last-race fall, but in between he rides a 7,097-1 treble for trainer James Bethell – Parlemo (20-1), Carpet Slippers (25-1) and Double Echo (12-1).

26 Dec Jump jockey Peter Niven rides a 168-1 5-timer at Sedgefield and becomes the first jockey to achieve three 5-timers in a season, having done it previously at Doncaster and Kelso.

26 Dec Reference Point, 1987 Derby winner, is found to have a broken leg at Dalham Hall Stud and has to be put down.

27 Dec Jump jockey Philip Barnard, 24, dies after sustaining head injuries in a fall at Wincanton yesterday.

Obituary: 19 Feb

Curtain comes down on a golden era as Fulke Walwyn dies
By Bill Curling

FULKE WALWYN CVO, one of the greatest racehorse trainers ever and a former trainer to Queen Elizabeth the Queen Mother, has died aged 80. Walwyn was one of only two men this century to have ridden and trained a Grand National winner. He was champion trainer five times, and won four Cheltenham Gold Cups, a Grand National and two Champion Hurdles.

His wife, Cath, said yesterday: "The Queen Mother was here on Monday and Fulke talked to her. He died very peacefully. He had a wonderful life and wonderful success, but I think of all the horses, Mandarin was his favourite."

Michael Oswald, the Queen Mother's racing manager, said: "He was the greatest trainer of chasers of his time and perhaps of all time. He had infinite patience and his results speak for themselves. I think his training of Special Cargo was brilliant. The horse had appalling leg problems and to have got him back on a course and then win a Whitbread Gold Cup and the Grand Military Gold Cup three times was a most remarkable training performance."

One of the best amateur riders of the last sixty years, Walwyn, a Welshman, won his first steeplechase at the age of 19 at Cardiff in 1930. He rode Reynoldstown to his 1936 Grand National triumph. But in an injury-troubled career, Walwyn fractured his skull severely in 1938 and was forced to give up race-riding. He took out a trainer's licence the following year.

His Gold Cup winners were Mont Tremblant (1952), Mandarin (1962), Mill House (1963) and the Dikler (1973), he won the Grand National with Team Spirit in 1964, and the Champion Hurdle with Anzio in 1962 and Kirriemuir in 1965. He saddled 2,180 winners in his time — some 115 for the Queen Mother.

Trafalgar House Supreme Novices Hurdle Cheltenham: 12 March

Gamble is landed by Furlong
By John Oaksey

THERE was an old-fashioned Irish gamble of gargantuan proportions when Mrs Elizabeth Furlong's Destriero landed the Trafalgar House Supreme Novices Hurdle at Cheltenham. Mrs Furlong's husband, Noel, had reportedly paid half a million pounds to settle a little local difficulty with the Customs and Excise and ease his passage to Britain in general and Cheltenham in particular.

Once there, he backed Destriero to pay his expenses and doubled that horse with The Illiad in the Champion Hurdle. By his own account, half a million pounds was running on to The Illiad, and this brought his price down from 12-1 to 11-2. There was, I'm afraid, no happy ending to this part of the story, because The Illiad finished last.

CHAMPIONS

Jockey (Flat)	Pat Eddery	165
Jockey (NH)	Peter Scudamore	141
Racehorse of Year	Generous	3-y-o colt
NH Champion of Year	Morley Street	7-y-o
Leading Trainer	PFI Cole	£1,256,502
Leading Owner	Sheikh Mohammed	£1,077,215
Leading Money Winner	Generous	£631,480

Cheltenham Gold Cup: 14 March

Garrison foils The Fellow's Cup raid
By Peter Scott

GARRISON Savannah's short-head win over The Fellow yesterday provided the closest Tote Cheltenham Gold Cup finish since The Dikler beat Pendil by the same margin in 1973. Desert Orchid, winner in 1989 and running in his last Gold Cup, finished a gallant third, 15 lengths back.

Richard Pitman, who rode Pendil, watched his son Mark keep Garrison Savannah in front just long enough to withstand The Fellow's powerful finish. Mark, 24, was narrowly beaten last year on Toby Tobias, trained by his mother, Jenny.

A gamble on Celtic Shot (5-2) caused him to displace Desert Orchid (4-1) as favourite, and he went to the front with four fences to jump. But he began to weaken after the next and came home last of seven finishers.

Garrison Savannah (16-1) took over the lead from Celtic Shot. He was three lengths clear at the final fence, but The Fellow's (28-1) strong finish so nearly made this French-trained six-year-old the youngest Gold Cup winner since Mill House in 1963. Garrison Savannah had the advantage of racing by the far rails and he and The Fellow fought out their stirring finish.

[Mark Pitman cracked his pelvis when Run to Form fell in the last race.]

Garrison Savannah is clear at the last

NATIONAL HUNT

Champion Hurdle	Morley Street	J Frost	4-1f
Cheltenham Gold Cup	Garrison Savannah	M Pitman	16-1
Grand National	Seagram	N Hawke	12-1

Lincoln Handicap Doncaster: 23 March

Greaves swoops to land Lincoln

By J.A.McGrath

Alex Greaves, the fresh-faced apprentice who made her name on all-weather tracks, confounded the critics on two fronts at Doncaster when landing the £50,000 William Hill Lincoln Handicap on 22-1 chance Amenable.

Not only did Miss Greaves, 22, excel by riding a smooth, waiting race in the first major handicap on turf this season, but her mount came from stall 23 of the 25-runner field – a draw condemned by most experts.

Miss Greaves, who has steadily improved her riding style, hopes that yesterday's victory, the biggest of her short career, will help her lose the almost inevitable early tag, "Queen of the Fibresand".

"I am a jockey, and I can ride on any surface," Miss Greaves pointed out. "Yes, I have ridden more winners on the all-weather than on turf, but you must realise that I get more opportunities on the all-weather."

Therein lies one of racing's home truths, not often expressed when there is talk of the big stables and million-dollar yearlings. Among other things, the all-weather tracks have provided additional welcome opportunities for many owners, trainers and jockeys through the lean winter months and beyond.

ENGLISH CLASSICS

2,000 Guineas	Mystiko	M Roberts	13-2
1,000 Guineas	Shadayid	W Carson	4-6f
Derby	Generous	A Munro	9-1
Oaks	Jet Ski Lady	C Roche	50-1
St Leger	Toulon	P Eddery	5-2f

The 2,000 Guineas Newmarket: 4 May

Mystiko pays off French pair in Guineas

By J.A.McGrath

CLIVE BRITTAIN, racing's super-optimist, pulled off a long-held ambition when sending out Mystiko to win the General Accident 2,000 Guineas at Newmarket for owner Lady Beaverbrook.

But victory was registered only after an intense battle over the final furlong and a half with the French challenger Lycius, whose final surge took him level with Mystiko 80 yards from the line, only for the Brittain-trained colt to stick his neck out again in the final strides. Only a head separated the pair on the line, with a yawning gap of six lengths back to Ganges, another French raider, in third place, with Generous, having his first outing of the season, a good fourth.

Marju, the 6-4 favourite, was reportedly lame on pulling up, and, as Willie Carson explained: "He left the boxes awkwardly and never gave me a feel. He was not using himself and I think he's gone lame behind."

The stewards ordered that Marju be sent for dope-testing. John Dunlop, the colt's trainer, told the stewards that he was mystified by Marju's disappointing run and also added that he was satisfied that the colt was not showing signs of lameness after returning from the testing.

Stewards secretary Major Peter Steveney said: "In view of the huge liabilities on Marju, the favourite's sample will be tested for everything that might be a stopper." The familiar Carson pumping action was in evidence at the halfway point, but this time Marju was going backwards and eventually finished a distant 11th of 14.

The Grand National Aintree: 6 April

Seagram's Grand National

Garrison fails to withstand Hawke swoop

By J.A.McGrath

SEAGRAM, the New Zealand-bred chaser named after the sponsors, who never took advantage of this clever marketing ploy, won the Seagram Grand National with a powerful late flourish that proved too strong for the Gold Cup winner Garrison Savannah.

Coming to the last of the 30 fences, Garrison Savannah (7-1) was full of running and looking odds-on to become the first horse since Golden Miller in 1934 to complete the Gold Cup-National double in the same season. But heart-break was just seconds away, as the Jenny Pitman-trained jumper's four-length lead at the elbow was transformed to a five-length deficit by Seagram's (12-1) relentless gallop from the outside.

Auntie Dot (50-1), a 10-year-old mare, ran the race of her life to finish eight lengths away in third, with 25 lengths back to Over the Road, who clinched fourth place by a short-head from Bonanza Boy, the 13-2 favourite. A total of 17 horses completed the course after the start had been delayed for several minutes while police arrested nine animal rights activists who staged a demonstration.

Seagram, the horse, well known for his strength and stamina, arrived in Britain as part of the second large shipment of horses imported from New Zealand by Kingsbridge trainer David Barons eight years ago, but after breaking down he was rested for two seasons. The gelding had originally been bought by Peter Brook. Mr Brook reportedly named his new jumper Seagram in the hope of one day marketing the horse, with the huge drinks firm being an obvious target. "But when Mr Brook's company got into trouble, he had to let Seagram go," explained Barons.

The horse was offered twice to Ivan Straker of Seagrams. Each time, Straker reluctantly passed up the offer, and yesterday he watched, obviously with very mixed feelings, from the grandstand as the horse, ridden by Nigel Hawke, gave a galloping display of strength and stamina, staying the four and a half miles to the very last inch.

---

6 May

Pipe calls TV attack on stable 'rubbish'

By J.A.McGrath

MARTIN PIPE, the record-breaking jumps trainer, last night stood accused by The Cook Report (ITV) of operating a stable from which an average of 71 per cent of his horses did not come back into training the following season in the years 1987-91.

The investigative programme claimed this to compare unfavourably with other leading trainers, for whom the average "wastage" rate was 37 per cent. Jenny Pitman, one of a number of racing people interviewed on the programme, was reported to have the lowest average wastage rate in the top bracket of 31 per cent.

Pipe, who has trained more than 200 winners in each of the past three seasons, was said by interviewer Roger Cook to be "loved and loathed" in racing. Cook accused Pipe of increasing his edge by running his horses more often – and especially more often on potentially damaging firm ground – than would others.

Pipe then found himself defending the policy of buying three-year-old horses out of leading Flat stables and trying to convince a puzzled Cook why these types could not go on to win Gold Cups. Pipe argued that there was a place in racing for these types of horses, which could give satisfaction and fun to owners who could not afford to pay the high prices asked for potential Gold Cup and Grand National horses.

Pipe's reaction last night was to declare the programme "total rubbish". "It has been a damaging programme to myself, my family and my staff. The welfare and the care of our horses is always uppermost in our minds," he said.

27 May

Pipe storms past his own record with five-timer

MARTIN PIPE smashed his own record for the number of victories in a season when sending out five winners over jumps and one on the Flat in a Bank Holiday bonanza that took his tally to 229. His previous record of 224, established last season, has been in the champion trainer's sights for several weeks, and with runners on three more days this week before the jumping year ends on Saturday, there is every likelihood that his new mark will be quite exceptional – even by his standards.

Outsider Jet Ski Lady wins the Oaks

The Oaks Epsom: 8 June

Jet Ski Lady in 50-1 Oaks shocker

By J.A.McGrath

IRISH-TRAINED filly Jet Ski Lady, a 50-1 outsider, bolted away with the Gold Seal Oaks at Epsom as the brilliant Shadayid, the even-money favourite, failed to stay and finished a well-beaten third.

Not even a dream run along the inside from last to third place, galloping down to Tattenham Corner, was enough to assist Shadayid. John Dunlop's filly edged closer to the front-running Jet Ski Lady inside the three-furlong marker, but 100 yards further on she was struggling.

Christy Roche, the jockey who upset Pat Eddery and El Gran Senor in the memorable 1984 Derby on Secreto, did it again, and the Irish Champion knew he had this Classic in the bag two furlongs out as Jet Ski Lady powered away, increasing her margin of superiority to 10 lengths by the line. Shamshir (6-1) battled on for second place, three-quarters of a length in front of Shadayid.

Jet Ski Lady was trained by Jim Bolger, who broke the Irish training record last year.

The St Leger Doncaster: 14 September

Toulon takes St Leger for France

By J.A.McGrath

THE HUGE crowd that flocked to Doncaster hoping to see Lester Piggott register a record-equalling ninth win in the Coalite St Leger witnessed instead the French colt Toulon (5-2f) destroy his rivals with a wonderful display of galloping power in a time just outside the course record.

They also very nearly witnessed a tragedy. A little over two furlongs after the start, the 10 runners were forced to veer right, away from the inside running rail, to avoid a man and a young boy sitting in the path of the oncoming horses, who were bowling along at a speed of around 35mph.

As the field thundered past, the man stood up and gave them the V-sign. The man, well known to Doncaster police, was taken into custody, but later released without charge. He had been cautioned the previous day on Town Moor for his behaviour.

Piggott fans were left slightly disappointed as the legendary jockey's mount Micheletti, a half-brother to the 1989 St Leger winner Michelozzo, stayed on to finish third without ever looking dangerous.

The Derby Epsom: 5 June

Breathtaking surge carries Generous to 5-length triumph

By HOTSPUR (J.A.McGrath)

PRINCE FAHD SAL-MAN'S Generous, the colt who thrived on an "old style" preparation, was the hero of Epsom yesterday after pulverising his rivals in the Ever Ready Derby, scoring by a convincing five lengths.

Ridden to perfection by Alan Munro, 24, the cocky young rider who landed the mount and the job as first jockey to Prince Fahd only last month, Generous (9-1) came from third at Tattenham Corner to surge to the front over two furlongs out. From that point, the issue was never in doubt as the Grundy lookalike stormed clear of Marju (14-1), who made up ground well without having the clearest of runs for second, with Irish-trained Star of Gdansk (14-1) seven lengths back in third. The authority displayed by Generous, who was bought for 200,000gns, was completely breathtaking. "At the end of the race, he was not tying up at all," Munro commented.

Generous is a son of French Derby winner Caerleon, but he displayed enough speed and precocity over five furlongs to win first time out as a two-year-old and then run in the Coventry Stakes at Royal Ascot last year. The fact that he finished second, only two lengths behind speedster Mac's Imp, ridden, ironically, by Munro, was an indication of his natural pace.

Despite a seriously interrupted run-up to the 2,000 Guineas, Generous finished fourth to Mystiko, which gave his connections hope of success in the Derby. Mystiko, attempting to become the first grey in 40 years to win the Derby, kept galloping bravely until just past the three-furlong marker, where it became evident that this son of Derby winner Secreto was not going to emulate his sire.

Generous then stormed into the lead, and the Cole stable's followers, who had been bullish about their colt's prospects for weeks, started counting their winnings.

The joint 4-1 favourites Corrupt and Toulon both disappointed, finishing sixth and ninth, respectively.

Prix de l'Arc de Triomphe Longchamp: 6 October

Suave Dancer storms home to head 'Arc' rout

By HOTSPUR (J.A.McGrath)

SUAVE DANCER, the colt who lived in Generous's shadow for the first half of the season, swept to a magnificent victory on home soil when landing yesterday's Ciga Prix de l'Arc de Triomphe at Longchamp, providing the perfect answer to those who felt he would not stay in soft ground.

As Generous sadly faded over two furlongs out to finish eighth, Suave Dancer commenced his winning charge down the extreme outside, a move which, if not as dramatic as that of Dancing Brave in 1986, was every bit as effective and had most of the 35,000 crowd on their feet, screaming encouragement.

Claiming the lead a furlong and a half out, Suave Dancer sprinted away, and although veering slightly right, Cash Asmussen had the trophy as good as in his grasp a full furlong from the line, eventually scoring by two lengths.

The filly Magic Night stayed on for a solid second, a length in front of Pistolet Bleu, with Toulon a further three away fourth. Two horses not to run their race were Jet Ski Lady, the Gold Seal Oaks winner, who beat only one home, and last year's St Leger winner and Arc third, Snurge.

OTHER MAJOR RACES

Irish Derby	Generous	A Munro	1-1f
Arc de Triomphe	Suave Dancer	C Asmussen	37-10
Kentucky Derby	Strike the Gold	C Antley	48-10
Melbourne Cup	Let's Elope	S.King	3-1f
Arlington Million	Tight Spot	L Pincay	18-10
Japan Cup	Golden Pheasant	G Stevens	172-10

Breeders' Cup Chase Fair Hill: 12 October

Morley streets ahead

By J.A.McGrath

MORLEY STREET cruised to a second successive win in the Breeders' Cup Chase at Fair Hill, Maryland, last night, by a distance of nine and three-quarter lengths in a course record time.

After sitting in fourth place in the early stages, the champion hurdler took control at the second last fence and came home an effortless winner for jockey Jimmy Frost. Second home was Declare Your Wish,

ridden by Steve Smith Eccles, with Irish challenger Cheering News a further 15 1/2 lengths away in third.

Morley Street, trained by Toby Balding, ran the two miles five furlongs distance in 5min 10.6sec. "He was almost going too well early in the race," an elated Frost later declared. "The ground was a bit rough and the course a little tight, but he came through it well and we won as we liked."

Melbourne Cup Flemington: 5 November

'Elope' in runaway Cup win

BART CUMMINGS trained his ninth Melbourne Cup winner when 3-1 favourite Let's Elope produced a strong, late challenge to beat stablemate Shiva's Revenge by two and a half lengths in Australia's richest race. The four-year-old, ridden by Steven King, who was celebrating his 22nd birthday, became only the second mare to win the country's top two races, the Melbourne and Caulfield Cups, but had to survive an objection.

The objection, the first in the race's 131-year history, came from Shane Dye on the runner-up. Dye claimed interference by King 400 metres from the finish, but the stewards dismissed the objection

after a 15-minute hearing.

Watched by more than 90,000 people at the Flemington racecourse, the race was televised live to more than 40 countries. To accommodate the race's growing overseas following, the start was put back by 50 minutes so that Hong Kong punters at the Happy Valley racetrack could watch and bet on the race.

Let's Elope was among the tailenders just before the home turn. But Cummings said it was always the plan to settle the mare at the back because he thought there might be a frantic early pace: "I said to Steven before the race that when the rest are stopping, this mare will just be starting."

King George VI Chase Kempton Park: 26 December

The Fellow scorches to record win at Kempton

By HOTSPUR (J.A.McGrath)

FOUR YEARS to the day, French trainer François Doumen wrecked the Desert Orchid party yet again, this time sending out The Fellow for a glorious victory in course-record time in the King George VI Rank Chase at Kempton Park.

With Desert Orchid (4-1) falling three out when struggling in last place, and the fading Sabin du Loir (100-30), another market leader, crashing independently at the same fence, the race proved an anticlimax for many in the 29,178 record crowd who packed the Sunbury course.

But nothing could – nor should – be taken away from the winner who, at the relatively tender age of six, has now taken one of jump racing's

most coveted prizes just over nine months after being runner-up to Garrison Savannah in the Gold Cup at Cheltenham.

Competently ridden from off the pace by Polish-born Adam Kondrat, 24, Doumen's stable jockey, The Fellow (10-1) made his winning move in the home straight, collaring Docklands Express (25-1) to take a clear lead over the last fence and then gallop on to score by one and a half lengths. Remittance Man (3-1f), who looked all over the winner when he jumped his way to the front five out, weakened in the home straight to take third place, two lengths behind the second. The Fellow clipped 1.2sec off Wayward Lad's race and course record.

Arazi storms home

Breeders' Cup Juvenile Churchill Downs: 2 November

Arazi's burst fires dreams of American Triple Crown

By J.A.McGrath

ARAZI, the international horseman's dream, will concentrate on winning next year's American Triple Crown if joint owner Allen Paulson gets his way. Speaking less than 24 hours after Arazi's simply incredible success in the Breeders' Cup Juvenile at Churchill Downs, Kentucky, Mr Paulson made it clear that the Kentucky Derby, the Preakness and the Belmont Stakes – run in the space of five weeks in May and June – will be the target for the colt Americans are now looking to as the new Secretariat.

Sheikh Mohammed, the leading owner in Britain, recently purchased 50 per cent of the Blushing Groom colt for a figure believed to be almost double the $5 million placed on him in reports.

Mr Paulson said: "The prize-money for the Triple Crown is tremendous. Isn't it good to have so many choices? Distance won't bother him, he handles dirt and he's already the European champion two-year-old on grass." He added that he had considered running the colt in both the Kentucky Derby and the Ever Ready Derby. Whatever is decided, François Boutin will continue to train the colt in France.

Arazi's performance on Saturday was remarkable. In the half-mile between the six-furlong marker and the

quarter-pole, Arazi (21-10) weaved his way between horses, making ground from lying 13th of 14 to hit the front on the home turn. The official race-call had the colt making up 13 lengths – a conservative estimate – in just two furlongs.

The chesnut wobbled a little wide as he made the home turn on the wrong leg, but in the final furlong, he effortlessly strode away to score officially by four and three-quarter lengths, a distance that is seriously questioned.

Arazi's success was one of three wins for European-trained horses. Miss Alleged came with a storming finish to win the Breeders' Cup Turf by half a length. And Alex Scott sent out the first British-trained winner of a Breeders' Cup race for six years, and only the second in the history of the series, when Sheikh Albadou (26-1) landed the "Sprint" in convincing style.

Ridden with extreme confidence by Pat Eddery, Sheikh Albadou stormed through to take the lead from the crack American sprinter Housebuster over a furlong out, and sprinted clear to win by three lengths. The winner of his maiden at Pontefract earlier this year, Sheikh Albadou has continued to make staggering progress throughout the season and now joins Pebbles on the Breeders' Cup roll of honour.

1992

8 Jan French-trained colt Arazi is rated the top juvenile since International Classifications for 2-yr-olds were drawn up in 1978, his 130 rating being considered superior to the inflated 131 mark of Tromos in that first year.

3 Mar Peter Scudamore becomes the first jump jockey to ride 1,500 winners.

4 Apr In Election week, Party Politics (14-1), trained by Nick Gaselee, romps home in the Grand National.

7 Apr Arazi cruises in by 5 lengths in the Prix Omnium II at St Cloud on his 3-y-o début to shorten his Kentucky Derby odds to 5-4.

7 May Puerto Rican-born jockey Angelo Cordero Jr, who suffered a serious fall at Aqueduct in January, announces his retirement, having ridden 7,056 winners in the USA.

26 Jun Having notched a treble at Newmarket in the afternoon, Pat Eddery gets to Newcastle in time to win the last 4 races and complete a British record 7 wins in a day.

7 Jul Pat Taaffe, 62, who guided the immortal chaser Arkle to his great triumphs, dies in Dublin. Taaffe won 4 Gold Cups, 2 Nationals and 6 Irish Nationals, and trained 1974 Gold Cup winner Captain Christy.

11 Jul Unbeaten User Friendly (8-11f) completes an Oaks double with a neck victory at The Curragh over Market Booster.

26 Jul Doncaster stages Britain's first Sunday race meeting.

20 Aug The unbeaten Lyric Fantasy is the first 2-y-o filly to win York's Keeneland Nunthorpe Stakes.

13 Sep In a clash of Derby winners, Dr Devious (7-2) prevails by a short head over St Jovite (4-7f) in the Irish Champion Stakes at Leopardstown.

4 Oct User Friendly loses her unbeaten record, beaten a neck by the 4-y-o French colt Subotica in the Arc, with two Derby winners behind them, St Jovite (4th) and Dr Devious (6th).

13 Nov Jump jockey Peter Niven rides the fourth five-timer of his career, when he is successful on all of his mounts at Ayr.

15 Nov Some 15,000 at Cheltenham to see first Sunday jump meeting in Britain.

2 Dec Record-breaking sprinter Lyric Fantasy, whose only defeat has been in the Cheveley Park Stakes, is bought at auction for 340,000gns by a Kuwaiti consortium.

28 Dec Run for Free (11-4jf) wins the Coral Welsh National as Martin Pipe saddles the first 4 home and records his 4th win in the last 5 runnings.

Carl Llewellyn wins the National on Party Politics

Champion Hurdle Cheltenham: 10 March

Justice prevails as Royal Gait survives inquiry

By John Oaksey

The gallant victory of Sheikh Mohammed's Royal Gait in yesterday's Smurfit Champion Hurdle at Cheltenham was dramatically followed by a stewards' inquiry. For several anxious minutes the sad history of the nine-year-old gelding's luckless Ascot Gold Cup disqualification in 1988 looked like repeating itself.

Fidway, with whom Royal Gait appeared to collide soon after the last, dropped out abruptly to finish fourth, but his rider Hywel Davies made no complaint. "If anything, I went over towards Graham [McCourt] and Royal Gait," he said.

Nevertheless, after Royal Gait (6-1) had run on to beat Oh So Risky (20-1) by half a length, with Ruling (20-1) a short-head away third, there were still those who feared that Royal Gait might have hung back left-handed after the Fidway incident and possibly interfered with Ruling.

But, thank heaven, this time the stewards saw it clear. So, at least to this eventful chapter of Royal Gait's extraordinary story there was a happy ending.

Sheikh Mohammed's other representative, Kribensis (12-1), blundered at the third flight, and Richard Dunwoody pulled him up. Morley Street (2-1f), the 1991 Champion, also disappointed, finishing sixth.

Royal Gait, by contrast, jumped a virtually flawless clear round. This, don't forget, was only his fourth hurdle race. The first "novice" (first-season hurdler) to win a Champion Hurdle since Doorknocker in 1956, he is, in fact, the least experienced winner in the race's history.

[Royal Gait (11-10f) collapsed and died after finishing 4th in his next race, in December at Leopardstown.]

Cheltenham Gold Cup (run 12 March)

Pitman horse was a 'spoiler' says Scudamore

By HOTSPUR (J.A.McGrath)

PETER SCUDAMORE has dismissed out-of-hand Jenny Pitman's claims at the weekend that Golden Freeze did not run as a "spoiler" in last Thursday's Tote Gold Cup at Cheltenham. Just as the Jockey Club Stewards prepare to announce today whether they are to inquire into Golden Freeze's role in the race, the champion jockey said that, in his mind, there was one clear intention – to "stalk" his mount Carvill's Hill, the even-money favourite.

"They were perfectly entitled to run a pacemaker, and, as I said before the race, if Carvill's Hill could not cope with that, he didn't deserve to win a Gold Cup," said Scudamore. "But Golden Freeze wasn't a pacemaker, he was a 'spoiler', it's as simple as that. Michael Bowlby, his rider, apologised to me going to the second ditch, saying, 'Look, I didn't want to do this. I hope you win'," claimed the champion jockey. But Scudamore is satisfied the tactics employed did not cost him the Gold Cup. "Carvill's Hill was not good enough on the day," he said.

The Gold Cup issue has divided the racing world like no other in recent years, one side claiming Golden Freeze's role was perfectly legal as the Rules stand and a legitimate aspect of race riding, the other arguing that tolerance of so-called spoilers could pose a threat to the safety of horses and riders.

Scudamore's comments are certain to fuel the fires of controversy which were blazing following Mrs Pitman's television interview on Channel 4 from Uttoxeter on Saturday. She was adamant that Golden Freeze – pulled up before the 16th fence – ran on his merits at Cheltenham.

In the event, Toby Tobias, Mrs Pitman's first string, was a distant fourth after rupturing his near-fore tendon, the race being won by Cool Ground (25-1) by a short head from The Fellow (7-2). Carvill's Hill was fifth.

[Mrs Pitman and her jockey Michael Bowlby were cleared by a Jockey Club hearing at the end of April which found that Golden Freeze had run on his merits. Bowlby, apparently, denied the remarks attributed to him by Scudamore. HOTSPUR, in The Daily Telegraph, felt that, while the rules had not been broken according to the letter of racing law, damage had been done to the image of National Hunt.]

CHAMPIONS

Jockey (Flat)	Michael Roberts	206
Jockey (NH)	Peter Scudamore	175
Racehorse of Year	User Friendly	3-y-o filly
NH Champion of Year	Remittance Man	8-y-o
Leading Trainer	Richard Hannon	£1,154,210
Leading Owner	Sheikh Mohammed	£1,194,380
Leading Money Winner	Rodrigo de Triano	£494,764

Sprouston Claiming Hurdle Kelso: 6 April

Record 5,000-1 odds laid on mare

History was made at Kelso yesterday when Countess Crossett was backed at 5,000-1, the biggest price ever laid on a British racecourse.

The mare, who finished ninth in the Sprouston Claiming Hurdle, was laid at the four-figure price by two Tattersalls bookmakers before being returned at 500-1.

Kelso also holds the record for the highest-priced winner, Equinoctial, at 250-1 in a handicap hurdle in November 1990.

Kentucky Derby Churchill Downs: 2 May

Arazi beaten: European hope 8th in Kentucky Derby

By John Oaksey

HISTORY LOST its way badly in yesterday's Kentucky Derby when Arazi finished a weary eighth to Lil E Tee. The odds-on pride of Europe passed all but two of his 17 rivals in the back straight, only to have seven of them come back past him as his stamina drained away.

"I rode him exactly the same as I did in the Breeders Cup," said jockey Pat Valenzuela, speaking, as far as he went, the literal truth. Arazi's surge from the last to nearly first was indeed a vivid carbon copy of his finest hour. "There he goes," was the cry, but, whereas last year the little chestnut left the others

bobbing feebly in his wake, now all too clearly a mile was as far as he could go. "He simply did not stay," was Valenzuela's explanation, which was hard to contradict.

As all European dreams fell apart, Pat Day, for years Churchill Downs' most successful jockey, took over. Day had finished second in three Derbys but never first. Now, as his old rival Gary Stevens snatched the lead on Casual Lies, he pulled out Lil E Tee and pressed the button. As they stormed away, the best consolation we could find was Dr Devious running his usual honest race to finish sixth.

The Derby Epsom: 3 June

Dr Devious gives Reid first Derby

By HOTSPUR (J.A.McGrath)

JOHN REID, who has endured a number of disappointments in his riding career, put them all behind him to achieve a lifetime's ambition when cruising home a convincing winner of the Ever Ready Derby on 8-1 second-favourite Dr Devious yesterday.

Amazingly, Dr Devious's trainer Peter Chapple-Hyam, 29, has hit the highest possible note in only his second season, but Reid, 36, had hit several dead ends in his chequered career before yesterday. Reid, whose previous best placing in seven Derby appearances was fourth on Sir Harry Lewis in 1987, was enjoying his finest moment as Dr Devious came home two lengths clear of sole Irish contender St Jovite (14-1), with local hope Silver Wisp (11-1) running on strongly in the final quarter-mile for third, a short-head away.

Never out of the first six and always moving comfortably, the tough Dr Devious surged into the lead just inside the two-furlong

marker, passing long-time leader Twist and Turn, and thereafter never gave the opposition a chance.

Dr Devious, who only recently returned to Britain after an abortive raid on the Kentucky Derby, where he suffered from scratches caused by swallowing dirt, showed his durability by recovering from that and from the rigours of a transatlantic journey. On the eve of the Derby, appearing at Epsom with stablemate Rodrigo de Triano, he looked completely relaxed as he and Reid stepped out onto the Downs.

After the race, Reid told how, at the time, he suspected Lester Piggott was taking a shine to his mount. Halfway through the race, Piggott must surely have been wishing that a swap had taken place, for the 13-2 favourite, in his own words, didn't handle the track at all, and eventually finished ninth. Chapple-Hyam, however, warned us not to run down Rodrigo de Triano: "He'll be back."

The 2,000 Guineas Newmarket: 2 May

Piggott takes Guineas
Rodrigo sets up Classic No 30

By J.A.McGrath

Piggott rolls back the years on Rodrigo

LESTER PIGGOTT swept to an amazing 30th Classic victory aboard Rodrigo de Triano in the General Accident 2,000 Guineas at Newmarket.

Coming from some way off the pace, Rodrigo de Triano (6-1) raced into the lead when hitting the rising ground and broke clear to score by one and a half lengths from the strong-finishing Lucky Lindy (50-1). Pursuit of Love (9-2), who travelled in the firing line throughout, held on to be third a further half-length away.

The years rolled back for Piggott as he came into the winner's enclosure after registering this, his first Classic success since Shadeed in the same race in 1985. The smile said it all. Clearly being back with a Classic notch to his belt was the most important achievement so far in what must rank as the most incredible sporting comeback in Britain for years.

"He's the best this century, and probably the last century as well," said elated owner Robert Sangster, for whom Piggott won the 1977 Derby on The Minstrel.

The favourite, Alnasr Alwasheek (5-2), finished a disappointing ninth, while the well-fancied French runner Cardoun (8-1) could manage only 12th of the 16 runners.

NATIONAL HUNT			
Champion Hurdle	Royal Gait	G McCourt	6-1
Cheltenham Gold Cup	Cool Ground	A Maguire	25-1
Grand National	Party Politics	C Llewellyn	14-1

ENGLISH CLASSICS			
2,000 Guineas	Rodrigo de Triano	L Piggott	6-1
1,000 Guineas	Hatoof	W Swinburn	5-1
Derby	Dr Devious	J Reid	8-1
Oaks	User Friendly	G Duffield	5-1
St Leger	User Friendly	G Duffield	7-4f

French 1,000 Guineas Longchamp: 17 May

Rich pickings in France for Cole's Culture Vulture

By HOTSPUR (J.A.McGrath)

CULTURE VULTURE (131-10) made a glorious return to the winning list in yesterday's French 1,000 Guineas, the Dubai Poule d'Essai des Pouliches, at Longchamp, reversing Newmarket form with favourite Hatoof, who could finish only sixth. For Paul Cole, the result was just reward for the faith he has shown in Culture Vulture and

ended the trainer's frustrating run of second placings in big races this season.

Cole said: "If I had thought that the 1,000 Guineas at Newmarket was her true form, I would not have brought her to France." He added: "It was a silly race at Newmarket. This filly needs a good pace, which she had this time."

The Oaks Epsom: 6 June

User Friendly upsets Oaks favourite

By J.A.McGrath

USER FRIENDLY, the result of a dream mating to find an Epsom specialist, produced a superlative staying performance to carry off yesterday's Gold Seal Oaks – giving jockey George Duffield, 45, his first Classic victory.

The filly carried the colours of well-known owner-breeder Bill Gredley, who recalled having dinner with trainer Clive Brittain and Steve Cauthen, just after the jockey had partnered Slip Anchor to win the Derby in 1985. After lengthy discussions, Gredley made the bold decision to mate his mare Rostova, an Epsom winner, with Slip Anchor in a deliberate attempt to breed

the winner of either the Derby or the Oaks.

The race, which beforehand appeared likely to be dominated by All At Sea, the 11-10 favourite, developed into a match in the final quarter-mile as User Friendly (5-1) shot clear, with Pat Eddery working hard to produce a challenge from All At Sea on the outside. But User Friendly fought tenaciously all the way up the straight, running the mile and a half right out to win by three and a half lengths from All At Sea, with an incredibly wide gap of 20 lengths to Pearl Angel (33-1), who clinched third place under Lester Piggott. The field of 7 was the smallest in the Oaks since 1916.

6 July

Roche loses his appeal against 15-day riding ban

By Tony Stafford

THE long-running Christy Roche suspension saga reached at least a temporary conclusion yesterday when the jockey's ban imposed by the Naas stewards on June 13 was confirmed by the stewards of the Irish Turf Club. Roche, who is waiting on legal advice whether to take the matter to the High Court, forfeits his £200 deposit and also faces legal costs which could amount to £5,000.

The jockey was suspended for 15 days by the Naas officials, who ruled that he had been guilty of improper riding

and that he had hit apprentice Robbie Skelly, rider of Freeway Halo. Roche, who partnered Sophisticator, is adamant that he did not aim a blow.

Much controversy has centred on the Roche affair and its implications during the lead-up to the Irish Derby nine nine days ago, which Roche won on the Bolger-trained St Jovite. The Turf Club had planned to convene an appeal inquiry for the Friday before the race, but postponed it to yesterday "in the best interests of the sport of horseracing in Ireland".

Queen Mary Stakes Ascot: 17 June

Pony-sized Lyric scorches home

By John Oaksey

LYRIC FANTASY, who barely measures 15 hands, made her own bit of racing history at Ascot yesterday when she became the first two-year-old ever to break 60 seconds for five furlongs on the Royal Heath. Her 59.72sec in the Queen Mary Stakes justified all the superlatives we had been polishing so busily for

Arazi and Rodrigo de Triano.

Darting clear in the first 100 yards, Lyric Fantasy (11-8f) made all to win by five lengths, unchallenged and unextended. No further description of the race is needed – except perhaps that Mystic Goddess (15-2) and Toocando (10-1) beat 10 others for the honour of acting as ladies-in-waiting.

Redcar: 8 July

Three times a winner as Krone turns on charm and style

By Tony Stafford

A YOUNG American with more than a passing facial resemblance to the Horse Trials rider Ginny Leng, but with a physical stature, mannerisms and riding style more akin to Willie Carson, took an away day from Sweden to captivate the Redcar crowd on a wet evening in the Northeast.

Julie Krone is the name, but it is only coincidence that her surname is the same as the currency of the country from where she arrived yesterday for her first taste of England and its racing. Redcar's executive, headed by Lord Zetland, have proved themselves most inventive in taking the chance to bring Miss Krone over.

Despite the weather, the enterprise paid an immediate dividend when Miss Krone, on Al Karnak, duly landed the opening Julie Krone Maiden Stakes at the far from rewarding odds of 2-11. Whatever you thought of the race as either a betting medium or a contest, you could not disagree with the winning rider's comment, "There's nothing like being on the best horse," after they

Julie Krone: Redcar treble

came home 20 lengths clear.

She completed a stylish treble when pushing home Gant Bleu (9-1) to win the Redcar Motor Mart Handicap and galvanising débutant Cockerham Ranger (3-1) to win the Susanne Berneklint Maiden Stakes.

In a career which began in 1981, Julie Krone has ridden almost 2,500 winners, a tally that would be the envy of all but the leading bunch of domestic riders.

King George VI & Queen Elizabeth Stakes Ascot: 25 July

Sparkling show puts St Jovite in superstar class

By HOTSPUR (J.A.McGrath)

EASILY the best three-year-old in Europe and a conservative 10lb superior to the top-rated four-year-old in Britain; a statement that accurately describes St Jovite (4-5f), the exciting, Irish-trained winner of Saturday's King George VI and Queen Elizabeth Diamond Stakes at Ascot.

A yawning gap of six lengths separated St Jovite and the well-credentialled runner-up Saddlers' Hall, following a performance that emphatically stamped the three-year-old in the world's super league. He seems at least the equal of Generous, last year's brilliant winner, and is certain now to be mentioned without hesitation in the same breath as Dancing Brave, Troy and Shergar, other outstanding horses of the past

to have won the "King George".

Stephen Craine, called in at the 11th hour to deputise for Roche, proved a real star, riding with tremendous judgment and confidence.

Bolger again paid tribute to Roche for his part in the colt's career. "I feel terribly sorry for Christy. What has happened to him is the greatest injustice ever perpetrated in racing," he said. Roche's counsel during the court hearing, Peter Kelly, had pointed out that: "St Jovite might be unplaced if anybody else rode him, but could well win for Mr Roche." It is probably just as well that Mr Kelly pursues a career in law rather than as a racing tipster.

Ayr Gold Cup: 19 September

Balding scoop in Lochsong's treble chance

By J.A.McGrath

FLYING filly Lochsong was absolutely brilliant when making all for a historic victory in the Ladbrokes Ayr Gold Cup, a six-furlong handicap. Ian Balding's sprinter enters the record books as the first to complete the Stewards' Cup/Portland Handicap/Ayr Gold Cup treble – and her growing legion of fans never had an anxious moment.

Blazing the trail throughout, Lochsong was a good four lengths clear of the pack at halfway, with jockey Francis Arrowsmith later admitting: "I didn't want to fight her, so I let her run." The victory shouts went up at the furlong post when it became obvious that Lochsong (10-1) could not be caught, even by the strong-finishing Echo-Logical (33-1), who was two lengths behind at the post. There were 28 runners, and 8-1 favourite Venture Capitalist was unplaced.

Heswall Graduation Stakes Chester: 21 October

Hard-working Roberts joins exclusive 200 Club

By J.A.McGrath

MICHAEL ROBERTS rode into racing's record books yesterday when finally landing his 200th winner of the season at Chester. Jasoorah, a three-year-old filly sent out by his retaining trainer Alec Stewart, was the one to register the long-awaited "double ton" for the South African, who had chalked up only one winner in the previous six days.

Roberts, 38, now becomes the fifth member of the exclusive "200 Club", taking his place alongside Fred Archer (8 times), Tommy Loates (1), Sir Gordon Richards (12) and Pat Eddery (1) as jockeys to have reached this total. Roberts drew a blank with his first four mounts yesterday, but he made sure on Jasoorah, coming home by 12 lengths.

South African champion 11 times, Roberts rode 203 winners in the 1981-82 season, the first jockey to achieve the feat in that country.

OTHER MAJOR RACES

Irish Derby	St Jovite	C Roche	7-2
Arc de Triomphe	Subotica	T Jarnet	88-10
Kentucky Derby	Lil E Tee	P Day	168-10
Melbourne Cup	Subzero	G Hall	4-1
Arlington Million	Dear Doctor	C Asmussen	139-10
Japan Cup	Tokai Teio	Y Okabe	9-1

Dewhurst Stakes Newmarket: 16 October

Impressive Zafonic has bookmakers running for cover

By HOTSPUR (J.A.McGrath)

ZAFONIC (10-11f) lived up to every glowing report issued this autumn with a breathtaking four-length victory in yesterday's Dewhurst Stakes at Newmarket, and the French-trained colt is now as low as even-money favourite for next year's 2,000 Guineas.

Hype or true Classic material? It now seems foolish to have even asked, for Prince Khalid Abdulla's massive brown colt, ridden by Pat Eddery, came charging into the lead, swinging on the bridle, just over two furlongs out and, playing with his rivals, exploded away with impressive acceleration. Inchinor (13-2), who had been under a cloud on the morning of the race, battled bravely to take second, with Firm Pledge (12-1) a short-head away third.

Jockey Club Inquiry: 27 October

10-year ban for Browne

DERMOT Browne, the former trainer and champion amateur rider, was warned off by the Jockey Club for 10 years yesterday after being found guilty of selling information to a bookmaker.

The Jockey Club's Disciplinary Committee found that the Irishman had passed information to Yorkshire bookmaker David Aarons about three horses, Silken Sailed and Argentum, who ran at York in August 1990, and Family at War, a runner at Ripon in September 1990. All three horses were beaten, but none was dope tested.

But a charge that he had been paid for and passed information to Aarons knowing that Norwich and Bravefoot had been doped at Doncaster in September 1990, and that they would not or were unlikely to win, was not proven.

Breeders' Cup Gulfstream Park, Florida: 31 October

Piggott in hospital on grim day for British

By J.A.McGrath

LESTER PIGGOTT was propped up in a hospital bed, nursing a fractured collarbone and broken rib, as Rodrigo de Triano, his intended Breeders' Cup Classic mount, trailed in a dismal last in the finale to the world's richest race-day last night.

Walter Swinburn was given the chance ride after Piggott had taken an horrific fall from Mr Brooks in the opening Breeders' Cup Sprint and was rushed to nearby Hollywood Memorial Hospital.

Piggott was admitted to the intensive care unit, where a spokesman said: "He is doing fine. There is no neurological damage. He is awake and alert." Piggott is expected to be detained for another three or four days as a precautionary measure.

Friends said that the inevitable cries that the Long Fellow's riding career would now be at an end were premature. "The doctors were amazed when they examined him to find that he was only a week away from his 57th birthday," said one. "They could not believe how fit he is for his age."

The extent of Piggott's injuries became known late in the day, shortly before Rodrigo de Triano and the British contingent faced the final humiliation against the best of the Americans in the $3 million Classic. Rodrigo de Triano's defeat completed a whitewash for British runners at the meeting, and Swinburn admitted dejectedly: "You have to wonder whether we should be coming here again. There is a big question mark about this place. I love their beaches here in Florida, but I hate their racecourse."

A total of 21 European horses ran in the seven races, including 12 English, and the best turned out to be the French-trained Jolypha, third in the Classic, and Brief Truce from Ireland, who finished an unlucky third in the Mile. Best of the English were Dr Devious, fourth in the Classic, and Sheikh Albadou, fourth in the Turf.

Piggott's fall took at least 30 yards to happen. He felt Mr Brooks's leg go, immediately looked over his left shoulder to see if horses were following him, and then braced himself for the inevitable fall. Mr Brooks, who was amongst the tail-enders at the time, fell heavily near the inside rail but clear of other runners. Piggott was pitched head-first over the sprinter's neck but sustained his injuries when the horse's hindquarters rolled over and pinned him underneath.

Mr Brooks, who had won both the July Cup and the Prix de l'Abbaye this year, had to be humanely destroyed. The incident cast a long shadow over America's most glittering race day.

1993

14 Jan The remarkable 14-y-o chaser Sabin du Loir, having fretted when he was prematurely turned out to grass in 1992 and then fallen desperately ill, only to make a sudden recovery, runs his 41st and last race – and chalks up his 21st win, in the John Bull Chase at Wincanton.

19 Jan The Home Office announce that betting shops will be able to stay open until 10 pm from April to August to cater for evening racing.

8 Mar Beckhampton trainer Jeremy Tree, who sent out 4 Classic winners and an Arc victor (Rainbow Quest, 1985), dies at 67.

17 Mar Having won the Sunderlands-sponsored Imperial Cup at Sandown on Saturday (13 Mar), Olympian (4-1jf), saddled by Martin Pipe and ridden by Peter Scudamore, wins the Coral Cup to earn owner Jim Neville of M&N Ltd a £50,000 bonus for adding a Cheltenham success.

30 Mar Leading jump jockey Richard Dunwoody apologises publicly for the fracas for which he and fellow jockey Roger Marley were arrested at a London hotel in the early hours of yesterday morning, after he received the accolade of top jump jockey at an awards ceremony – and then, with his damaged right hand strapped up, proceeds to pull off a 14-1 treble from his only 3 rides at Sandown on his return to the saddle.

3 Apr Grand National declared void (see pages 240-43).

17 Apr Frankie Dettori rides a 15,969-1 4-timer at Newbury, including Greenham Sakes winner Inchinor (7-2).

24 May Frankie Dettori's application to ride permanently in Hong Kong is, as expected, turned down, largely because of the adverse publicity surrounding his arrest last month for being in possession of a small amount of cocaine (although he was released without charge).

5 Jun As Prairie Bayou (27-10f) breaks an ankle and has to be destroyed, Julie Krone becomes the first woman jockey to win a leg of the US Triple Crown, partnering Colonial Affair to victory in the Belmont Stakes.

17 Jun Drum Taps (13-2), ridden by Frankie Dettori, beats Assessor (100-30) by three lengths to win his second consecutive Ascot Gold Cup, the third in succession for West Ilsley trainer Lord Huntingdon.

3 Oct French-trained 4-y-o Urban Sea (37-1) beats White Muzzle by a neck to win the Arc, with Opera House 3rd.

Jockey Club Inquiry 25 February

Another doping case confirmed: Latest revelations fuel fear of more 'nobbling'

By HOTSPUR (J.A.McGrath)

THE Jockey Club revealed yesterday that a heavily backed runner, who finished unplaced at Yarmouth last August, was doped. Flash of Straw, trained by Geoff Lewis, tested positive to a prohibited substance, and racing authorities are satisfied the gelding was "got at".

Backed from 25-1 to 4-1 favourite, Flash of Straw was beaten more than two furlongs out and could finish only sixth of 12 to Buzzard's Bellbuoy.

As news of this case became public – just over six months after the race was run – it fuelled the widespread belief that other horses have been doped, and caused punters to ask, how many more cases are there?

Officially, the information had been withheld to protect the image of racing, but unfortunately for all concerned, it has had exactly the reverse effect. Publicity surrounding Her Honour's post-race positive test, and now this latest revelation, has not been good for racing.

The Jockey Club issued a statement yesterday, breaking the news concerning the doping of Flash of Straw. The statement read: "In order to put an end to any further speculation which is harmful to racing, it is confirmed that Flash of Straw, trained by Geoff Lewis, tested positive to a prohibited substance at Yarmouth on August 20, 1992. It has been established that the horse was doped.

"The decision not to reveal this information was part of a deliberate and carefully considered policy to allow the Jockey Club's Security Department and the police to follow up leads and carry out their inquiries without the glare of publicity.

"The overwhelming priority is to catch those responsible, and it was agreed with the Surrey Constabulary that this could be best achieved by quiet investigation. It was to protect this operation that the Press were not given a full briefing when the recent doping allegations were made.

"It is stressed that this is the only confirmed case of doping into which an inquiry is being conducted at the moment by the Jockey Club's Security Department."

This lengthy statement will bring little comfort to the connections of horses involved, not to mention thousands of punters up and down the country who have placed bets on the horses involved.

CHAMPIONS

Jockey (Flat)	Pat Eddery	169
Jockey (NH)	Richard Dunwoody	173
Racehorse of Year	Lochsong	5-y-o
NH Champion of Year	Jodami	8-y-o
Leading Trainer	Henry Cecil	£1,248,318
Leading Owner	Sheikh Mohammed	£1,703,958
Leading Money Winner	Opera House	£502,097

NATIONAL HUNT

Champion Hurdle	Granville Again	P Scudamore	13-2
Cheltenham Gold Cup	Jodami	M Dwyer	8-1
Grand National	Void		

ENGLISH CLASSICS

2,000 Guineas	Zafonic	P Eddery	5-6f
1,000 Guineas	Sayeddati	W Swinburn	4-1
Derby	Commander in Chief	M Kinane	15-2
Oaks	Intrepidity	M Roberts	5-1
St Leger	Bob's Return	P Robinson	3-1

OTHER MAJOR RACES

Irish Derby	Commander in Chief	P Eddery	4-7f
Arc de Triomphe	Urban Sea	E StMartin	37-1
Kentucky Derby	Sea Hero	J Bailey	139-10
Melbourne Cup	Vintage Crop	MJ Kinane	14-1
Arlington Million	Star of Cozzene	J Santos	-
Japan Cup	Legacy World	H.Koyauchi	115-10

Champion Hurdle Cheltenham: 16 March

Granville Again turns on the Champion style

By HOTSPUR (J.A.McGrath)

EVEN by Martin Pipe's incredibly high standards, his victory with Granville Again in yesterday's Smurfit Champion Hurdle was an achievement of which he could be immensely proud. Stepping out after a 78-day absence from the racecourse, Granville Again (13-2) made amends in glorious fashion for the disappointment of last year, when he fell two flights out, by coming home the one-length winner from 50-1 outsider Royal Derbi, with Halkopous (9-1) two and a half lengths away in third.

Many will question the strength and quality of this year's Champion Hurdle field, but there can be no doubting the great triumph gained by Pipe. The champion trainer set out to win jump racing's premier hurdling prize, and achieved it with a certain amount of relish and satisfaction.

Nobody was willing to reveal the exact nature of the problem which had beset Granville Again but, following this success, Pipe paid tribute and extended gratitude to Michael Dickinson, now training in the United States, for the assistance given in this area.

"You can speculate all you like. All I am prepared to say is that Granville Again had a problem and we have been able to sort it out," Pipe said. "I found it a great help in visiting Michael, and he also gave me advice when he came over here," he added.

Rest, it seems, has played a major part, and Granville Again repaid the great skill and time devoted by his connections with a fighting win, holding on well up the run-in to keep Royal Derbi at bay.

Cheltenham Gold Cup: 18 March

Brilliant Jodami has potential to stay at the top

By J.A.McGrath

PETER BEAUMONT'S Jodami, the horse that money can't buy, won yesterday's Tote Gold Cup at Cheltenham in the style of a young chaser capable of defending his crown more than once in the years ahead. Jumping like a stag, from a position never far off the pace, Jodami (8-1) sprinted up the hill for Mark Dwyer to a most popular two-length victory.

Martin Pipe's great ambition to win the race looked like being realised when his Rushing Wild (11-1), ridden by late substitute Richard Dunwoody, kicked clear at the top of the hill, but the former hunter-chaser could finish only an admirable second. Royal Athlete (66-1), sent out by Jenny Pitman, turned in an excellent performance to snatch third place, seven lengths behind Rushing Wild, and so encouraging was the effort that the gelding is now

joint-favourite at 10-1 from 16-1 with Coral's for the Martell Grand National

While Jodami was passing the winning post, the heavily backed French-trained favourite The Fellow (5-4) was battling away in fourth, almost 10 lengths behind. The French contingent were gracious in defeat, but there could be no mistaking their disappointment, particularly as the gelding looked to have the edge on form on his opponents.

Jodami had always shaped as the horse who could win a Gold Cup, but many good judges believed he was too inexperienced to win it this year. What they had not reckoned on was the skilful handling of trainer Beaumont, backed up by his daughter Anthea, her husband Patrick Farrell, and the expert horsemanship of Dwyer, one of the coolest big-race jockeys of the modern era.

The Oaks Epsom: 5 June

Intrepidity swoops to conquer: Record Oaks time

By J.A.McGrath

MICHAEL ROBERTS, the reigning champion jockey, scored one of his most satisfying wins when landing the Energizer Oaks at Epsom on Intrepidity.

Fortunes in racing can change overnight, a fact that Roberts will readily confirm. For, at one stage last week, he looked in danger of being on Sheikh Mohammed's third-string, Iviza, in the fillies' Classic. But following some frantic shuffling behind the scenes, Roberts secured the mount on the Andre Fabre-trained Intrepidity and gave the French filly a memorable ride.

Coming from the rear of the field at the top of the hill, Intrepidity (5-1) looked all-at-sea, as first she tried to negotiate Tattenham Corner and then attempted to remain on an even keel in the home straight. Despite hanging, Intrepidity still proved too strong, swooping close home to pick off both the Irish filly Royal Ballerina (33-1) and Robert Sangster's Oakmead (11-1) – winning by three-

quarters of a length and a head.

Intrepidity's troubles started early in the race, for she was almost on the floor after a furlong. Roberts said: "She stumbled at the road crossing, and I was almost out of the saddle. We were well behind from that point, and I was pushing away, but she picked up brilliantly in the straight.

"This was the first time I've sat on the filly. But going to post she seemed a bit special," he added. Fabre said: "She is a top-class filly with both speed and stamina. I would have liked her to run against the colts in the French Derby, but Sheikh Mohammed decided to go for the Oaks."

Her time – 2min 34.19sec – was a record for the race, being 0.02 sec faster than Time Charter's 1982 mark.

Yawl, sent off the 4-1 favourite, dashed into an early lead, and at one stage held a three-length advantage. But she weakened badly in the straight, prompting a stewards' inquiry into her poor performance.

Alpine Meadow Handicap Hurdle Ascot: 8 April

Scu serves up farewell we all hoped for

By John Oaksey

BEFORE going out to ride his 1,677th and final winner on Sweet Duke at Ascot yesterday, Peter Scudamore accepted an invitation to become a Trustee of the Injured Jockeys' Fund. "I'm delighted," he said. "I would like to pay something back."

Needless to say, as the Ascot crowd and the champion's fellow jockeys all made very clear, any debt of gratitude is ours not his. The whole racing world owes it to a great and lovely man, whose consistent skill and high standards on or off a horse have done nothing but good to the game he loves.

It was entirely appropriate

that Sweet Duke should stay glued to the inside rail throughout the three miles of the Alpine Meadow Handicap Hurdle. Going the shortest way has long been one of the retiring champion's trademarks, and here, with the hurdle course officially "heavy", Scu steered his own course past the stands in search of better ground.

Sweet Duke, who had won here a week before, jumped like a horse conscious of his responsibilities. He went on three flights from home and two more spring-heeled leaps earned a place of honour in racing history.

The Derby Epsom: 2 June

Chief in total command as Tenby bubble finally bursts

By J.A.McGrath

KHALID ABDULLA'S Commander In Chief came home an emphatic winner of yesterday's Ever Ready Derby at Epsom, as the owner's other runner, Tenby, the 4-5 favourite, trailed in 10th and was later subjected to a routine dope test.

Tenby's defeat saved bookmakers a massive pay-out. They reported ante-post liabilities of more than £1 million and, following a remarkable racecourse plunge – £600,000 in recorded major bets alone

– his defeat gave them a "tremendous result".

But the glory belonged to Commander In Chief (15-2), who staged a highly impressive staying performance, coming from ninth approaching Tattenham Corner to win with total authority by three and a half lengths. Two 150-1 outsiders, Blue Judge and Blues Traveller, came in second and third, respectively, with Cairo Prince, at 50-1, finishing late to clinch fourth.

Irish Derby The Curragh: 27 June

'Chief' too powerful for French

By HOTSPUR (J.A.McGrath)

COMMANDER IN CHIEF upheld Epsom form in glorious fashion when proving too powerful for French-trained Hernando in yesterday's Budweiser Irish Derby showdown.

The two stars of this fascinating middle-distance contest lived up to their tall reputations in every respect, the race developing into a match over the final furlong, with the English and French Derby winners drawing clear of their rivals.

But it was the relentless galloping power of Commander In Chief – turned out looking a picture of fitness by trainer Henry Cecil and

backed from 5-4 to 4-7 on the course – that won the day under a vigorous, yet confident, ride from Pat Eddery. Only three-quarters of a length separated Commander In Chief and Hernando (9-4) at the line, and although Eddery had to dig deep into the reserves of the English colt, there seemed no way that he would be overhauled – no matter how his rival tried.

Eddery spoke in glowing terms of Commander In Chief, the star of Dancing Brave's celebrated third crop, pointing out: "If Hernando had come to him, I feel he would have found a lot more. He galloped all the way to the line."

Michael Roberts on Opera House (left) draws away from Commander In Chief in the straight to take the 'King George'

King George VI & Queen Elizabeth Diamond Stakes Ascot: 24 July

Roberts singing Opera House praises at Ascot

By J.A.McGrath

IF a week is a long time in politics, it can seem an eternity in racing. Just ask Michael Roberts, the champion jockey. At Newbury last weekend, Roberts had been found guilty of causing intentional interference and banned for 10 days. A subsequent appeal proved fruitless and Roberts had said that nothing seemed to be going right this season. "Just like a game of snakes and ladders," he quipped. But that statement was delivered before the King George VI and Queen Elizabeth Diamond Stakes at Ascot, in which Roberts came with a beautifully timed run, hitting the front over two furlongs out, to clinch victory on the five-year-old Opera House (8-1).

The Sadlers Wells entire had this glittering Group One prize in his grasp halfway up the straight, proving too strong and mature for the three-year-old generation, who were left toiling in his wake. White Muzzle was beaten a length-and-a-half (9-1) into second, in turn finishing a short-head in front of Commander In Chief (7-4f).

As the field charged towards the entrance to the short home straight, User Friendly, who had made virtually every yard of the running, was still in front, but just seemed to be coming under pressure. In behind her, Opera House and Commander In Chief were travelling best. Turning in, Commander In Chief put in his challenge and briefly went to the front. But the apparent leader of the Classic generation could not withstand Opera House's burst, which carried him to the front two out, and to victory.

Keeneland Nunthorpe Stakes York: 19 August

Trail-blazing Lochsong enjoys her finest hour in Nunthorpe

By HOTSPUR (J.A.McGrath)

BRILLIANT and brave are the most suitable words to describe Lochsong, who enjoyed her finest hour when rising to the occasion to score a popular victory at 10-1 in yesterday's Keeneland Nunthorpe Stakes at York.

For a filly whose first win of last season came off a handicap mark of 73, this Group One success was a staggering achievement. Even her dedicated trainer, Ian Balding, and her enthusiastic owner, Jeff Smith, could hardly believe their eyes, and neither could the opposition.

The Canadian visitor Bold N'Flashy showed enough speed to race upsides Lochsong and Sea Gazer in the first half of the race, with Paris House sitting in behind, and College Chapel hopelessly beaten for early speed on the ground that was significantly faster than on the first day of the Ebor fixture. But at halfway, as Lochsong cruised along at break-neck speed, she had all her rivals toiling.

Approaching the furlong marker, Lochsong's rider Frankie Dettori went for home, and with Paris House unable to pick her up, and College Chapel flying home but with too much ground to make up, the cheers rang out for Lochsong as she recorded the ninth win of her short but spectacular 16-start career.

At the line, she was a length and a half in front of Paris House (4-1), with College Chapel (9-4f) three-quarters of a length away third. "It is just unbelievable," said Balding. "She had no chance on the book, and yet she has done it. She is absolutely amazing."

An emotional Smith admitted he had never experienced anything like the thrill of this marvellous win in his 17 years as a racehorse owner.

Melbourne Cup Flemington: 2 November

Vintage Crop is wizard of 'Oz'

By J.A.McGrath

VINTAGE CROP was responsible for one of the most significant international breakthroughs in racing in the modern era when galloping away with yesterday's Foster's Melbourne Cup at Flemington, Australia.

Shrugging off the gruelling effects of the 10,625-mile journey, Vintage Crop (14-1), assisted by jockey Mick Kinane, exploded a few myths of the Australian Turf when scoring an emphatic victory in the race that "stops a nation".

Australian "experts" said it could not be done – 45 days without a run and going into the country's greatest race ridden by a jockey who had not even seen the course until less than 24 hours before the start. But they were wrong. Trainer Dermot Weld produced the gelding in magnificent condition, considering the 38-hour plane journey and the four-week quarantine period, and Vintage Crop did the rest by charging to the front inside the furlong pole and clearing away to score by three lengths.

Te Akau Nick, a 160-1 outsider, battled on gamely for second, half-a-length in front of Mercator, a 125-1 chance. Our Pompeii was sent off the 5-1 favourite but finished 14th, never posing a threat.

Drum Taps, the other European challenger, trained by Lord Huntingdon, was prominent until the half-mile marker but faded soon after, dropping out to finish a tired ninth. "There was no excuse that I saw," said jockey Frankie Dettori.

As Kinane became only the second jockey to achieve the Epsom Derby/Arc/Melbourne Cup treble – Pat Glennon is the other – this trail-blazing first win by a European-trained horse was hailed as a milestone in the history of the race and is expected to open the floodgates to Northern Hemisphere challengers.

The St Leger Doncaster: 11 September

Tompkins' happy return to his roots

By J.A.McGrath

A DELIGHTFULLY loud and enthusiastic Yorkshire welcome awaited Bob's Return, his trainer Mark Tompkins and jockey Philip Robinson after the colt out-stayed his rivals for a hugely popular victory in the Coalite St Leger at Doncaster.

Tompkins, although born in Leicestershire, grew up in Sheffield and is intensely proud of his Yorkshire roots. For him, it was the ultimate homecoming, and he was quick to recall his first visit to see the Classic, in 1970, when Nijinsky landed the third leg of the Triple Crown.

Bob's Return, bought as a 13th wedding anniversary present for Mrs Jackie Smith by her husband George, is no Nijinsky, but the colt can stay all day and has the heart of a lion. He proved a worthy winner after storming into the lead two furlongs out.

On the line, Bob's Return, confidently ridden by Robinson, had put three and a half lengths between himself and Armiger (4-1), the long-time leader, while Edbaysaan (25-1) plodded on for third, one and a half lengths further back. The betting proved significant, as Bob's Return was backed from 4-1 to 3-1 favouritism before romping to victory.

Mackeson Gold Cup Cheltenham: 13 November

Murphy's stout effort is star performance

By J.A.McGrath

HEROICS aside, big-hearted jumper Bradbury Star and his supremely polished jockey Declan Murphy always deserved to get their name on the Cheltenham Roll of Honour, and it was the 1993 Mackeson Gold Cup that thrust horse and rider into the limelight as they fought for triumph with sheer courage and dogged determination.

Ashen-faced Murphy literally staggered from the unsaddling enclosure in a daze, later explaining: "It was just the adrenalin that kept me going."

What a gallop they went; no wonder they were nearly walking over the line. The testing pace, set most of the way by Egypt Mill Prince, spurred on by the riderless Brandeston, who unshipped his rider at the first, would have broken the best.

On top of that, Murphy had taken a shocking fall from Arcot in the previous heat, rather inappropriately named the Murphy's Handicap Hurdle, and was obviously feeling the effects as he sorted out tactics in a concussed blur from the saddle, "seeing two Jamie Osbornes at one stage," as he later admitted.

So, in many ways, it was almost miraculous that Bradbury Star (13-2) drew alongside Egypt Mill Prince (9-1) approaching the last, and then quickly asserted his authority, striding away to win by seven lengths to the applause of an appreciative crowd. General Pershing, the 11-2 favourite, was four lengths further back, in third.

Breeders' Cup Classic Santa Anita, California: 6 November

Arcangues foils all-American Cup

By HOTSPUR (J.A.McGrath)

WITH a scintillating finishing burst that astounded his rivals, 133-1 outsider Arcangues raced into the record books as the longest-priced winner in the history of America's Breeders' Cup when landing the $3 million Classic, the richest race in the world, for the French here on Saturday.

The telling burst of Andre Fabre's five-year-old, who had come from 10th place at halfway to win, drawing clear, by two lengths, left most of the 55,130 crowd stunned and bewildered. On a day when the seven British runners yet again provided a disappointing challenge – failing even to reach a place – the French proved that they had done their homework and adapted remarkably well to conditions.

Racing in America is very different. The pace and the tightness of the oval tracks are something that most visitors find hard to cope with. When they are facing this task for the first time, at the highest level of competition in the United States, is it really any surprise that they consistently fail?

Barathea finished fifth in the Mile, the closest any British runner managed. His performance in getting so close was remarkable, as he failed to corner at the first turn and almost caused an ugly pile-up. Somehow, they all stayed on their feet.

Wolfhound (10th) and Catrail (12th) both failed miserably, but the race was won by Lure, a true champion who became only the third horse to win back-to-back Breeders' Cup races.

Cartier Awards: 17 November

Lochsong takes the top prize

By Tony Stafford

AUTUMNAL brilliance once again counted more than midsummer excellence when the third Cartier Awards were announced last night. Lochsong, whose most devastating performance was her wide-margin Prix de l'Abbaye win on "Arc" day last month, just edged out Opera House, whose last win came in the King George VI and Queen Elizabeth Diamond Stakes in July.

The awards are the result of three components: the votes of the racing press, those of readers of The Sporting Life, and a points scale based on wins throughout the year in Europe. Sometimes these still cannot establish an outright winner, and in the case of Horse of the Year it took the casting votes of a selected panel to plump for Ian Balding's great sprinting mare. Even more obvious was the last-gasp run of Vintage Crop to foil long-time leader Assessor as Stayer of the Year. The Melbourne Cup, just two weeks ago, was fresh in the voters' minds, and helped overturn Assessor's points advantage.

Grand National 1993
The race that never was

O f all the great races, the Grand National at Aintree invariably produces a story – of triumph or tragedy, heroics or heartbreak, extraordinary good fortune or desperate bad luck. Who would have thought, then, that the most memorable National since the world-famous steeplechase first took place in 1839 would be the void running of 1993, the "race that never was"?

The story ran for days, and recriminations went on for months, and have never really subsided. The on-the-spot reaction was given in The Sunday Telegraph of 4 April by **J.A.McGRATH**, Racing Journalist of the Year, reporting on "the extraordinary big-race farce", under the banner headline:

Grand fiasco stuns Aintree

The 150th Grand National, at Aintree, was declared void in farcical circumstances when, after one false start and a successful recall, almost the entire field failed to realise that a second false start had occurred. Rod Fabricius, the acting clerk of the course, explained: "The starter signalled a false start again, but the recall flag was not shown. It was an error."

The flag man at the centre of the drama was named as Ken Evans, who was officiating, in that capacity, at his third running of the race. Evans, who lives at Haydock, is in his late 50s, and Peter Greenall, the chairman of Aintree racecourse, said: "He has been doing the job for more than 10 years, most of them at Haydock."

At a press conference Greenall said: "Looking at the video, the recall flag wasn't up. The whole starting procedure will be reviewed, but at least we didn't have a tragedy." Questioned on whether the starting gate might have been faulty, he replied: "The starting gate was inspected at midday before racing and found to be in good working order. An inquiry is now taking place. It will decide if it was one or more man's error – or whether it is the equipment that was at fault."

David Pipe, the Director of Public Affairs for the Jockey Club, said: "This will now go to Portman Square for consideration of the Jockey Club stewards."

Captain Keith Brown, the Starter, and Mr Evans declined the opportunity to make statements to the press, claiming that it may be prejudicial to the subsequent inquiry.

The original start had been delayed eight minutes while animal rights demonstrators invaded the course, with police in pursuit. Eventually they were removed, but not until the nerves and temperaments of horses and riders had been severely tested.

In the non-race, seven horses and riders actually completed the four-and-a-half mile trip, and there was heartbreak and tears when John White, who crossed the line first on Jenny Pitman's Esha Ness, realised what had happened. During the "race", Mrs Pitman was reduced to tears. She rushed to the weighing room demanding to see the stewards, and broke down as she called for the race to be stopped.

White said: "I didn't see any flag the second time. When I reached The Chair, I saw some cones and I thought that some of the protesters had got to the fence. I never heard anybody saying that it had been a false start and there were horses around me, so I assumed that it was a race."

There were heated scenes both at the start, when the error was realised, and later in the weighing room. The Starter was the subject of booing and abuse from a hostile crowd, who were outraged when they sensed that racing's showcase event had been reduced to farce.

John Upson, trainer of the heavily backed Zeta's Lad, who completed one circuit of the course before pulling up, approached officials near the starting point to vent his anger. Later, Upson said: "I am absolutely disgusted. This wouldn't happen in a point-to-point field in Ireland *[a statement that was quickly to bring the wrath of the Irish down on him]*. We saw no signs of a flag."

Then, echoing the thoughts, feelings and destroyed ambitions of a host of owners and trainers, he added: "I've spent a year getting Zeta's Lad ready for this race. Now it has all come to nothing."

An estimated £75 million in bets and ante-post wagers will have to be refunded at betting shops throughout the country, and there were chaotic scenes in the betting rings. At the Canal Turn, there was loud booing and hissing and several objects were thrown at the huge video screen.

After the "finishers" had crossed the line, many jockeys remained with their horses in front of the stands, waiting to hear news from officials. Peter Scudamore, who went one circuit on Captain Dibble, said: "People have suggested we turn up next Saturday and do it again – but we can't."

The decision about whether or not to run the 1993 Grand National at a later date is up to the racecourse, not the Jockey Club, according to Mr Pipe, who went on to say that: "The Jockey Club will hold an urgent inquiry – like Monday."

Mr Greenall said: "The Aintree Board is in discussion with the sponsors about running the race again, but there is a very small chance we can do that. Cancelling the race completely is a real possibility because of the difficulty of restaging it."

Observations made after slow-motion re-runs had been studied indicated that Formula One had his head over the tape as the starter hit the lever, thus preventing it from rising on the outside of the long line of horses.

Richard Dunwoody, aboard Wont Be Gone Long, had the tape hooked around his neck as the field thundered off towards the first fence, and he and several others in the vicinity knew it was a false start. Those positioned near the inside, eager for a good position, took off, hell-for-leather, towards the first fence, and there was never any chance that they were going to stop.

The seven horses who completed the course were, in finishing order: Esha Ness, Cahervillahow, Romany King, The Committee, Givus a Buck, On the Other Hand and Laura's Beau.

The following day, in The Daily Telegraph, an army of writers expressed their views and, in the case of jockeys Peter Scudamore and Marcus Armytage, who both rode in the race, described their experiences and their feelings. J.A.McGRATH, expanding on his initial reaction, was scathing in his criticism of the official botch-up:

National humiliation: World looks on as race is turned into a farce

The alleged failure of a casually employed flag man, paid £28 for a day's work, to signal a second false start – and the subsequent failure of seven jockeys to pull up their mounts before a second circuit of the course was completed – reduced the event to farce. The race was declared void, and yesterday at a press conference at Aintree, Peter Greenall, the chairman of the racecourse company, said that this year's race would not be re-run, as trainers overwhelmingly felt it would not be practical from the horse point of view.

The fiasco, which was televised live to millions of viewers worldwide, has cost racing, the betting industry, and the Treasury dearly. Yesterday they were still counting the cost, with bookmakers William Hill threatening to sue Aintree racecourse for losses they claim amount to in excess of £150,000 in their marketing of the race.

The no-race has also cost those involved in the racing fraternity much time and effort, and the heartbreak of the whole episode was hitting home yesterday. The outspoken John Upson, trainer of Zeta's Lad, said the atmosphere in his yard was as if there had been a funeral.

Racegoers who kept their badges from Saturday will be offered free admission at Aintree's November meeting. They will be invited to register with the track by sending back their badges complete with their name and address. Owners and trainers of runners can look forward to being reimbursed their travelling expenses, while owners will also be reimbursed the jockeys' riding fees. All entry fees on the race will be automatically returned.

The prestigious name and reputation of the Grand National have taken an almighty battering this weekend, but Peter Greenall remained convinced that its reputation had not been irreparably damaged.

Many associated with the animal rights

Starter Capt Brown: 'not to blame'

demonstrators will possibly view Saturday's fiasco as a victory, but Greenall pointed out how dangerous and irresponsible their behaviour had been.

Capt Brown at one stage suggested that the race could be re-run, with only the nine horses who had not jumped off with the rest being allowed to compete. This was met with incredulous anger by onlookers, with John Upson shouting: "I'll see you in court."

The stewards eventually declared the race void, and Capt Brown, who was officiating at his last Grand National, and Mr Evans had to be protected by police as they made their way back to the weighing room.

When the inquiries commence, two issues need to be addressed. First, why the riders did not realise the second false start had been called, and, secondly, why the attention of seven jockeys could not be attracted in order to warn them of the false start.

In this age of modern communications, with satellite links and mobile telephones, it is hard to comprehend why there was not something far more sophisticated than a man waving a red flag down the course in front of a 39-runner field charging towards the first fence.

Sharing the front page of Telegraph Sport with McGrath, jockey PETER SCUDAMORE was also critical of the officials:

Blundering officials are only people to blame

It is very difficult to explain the emotions that jockeys experience after a Grand National. There is always an element of danger in a race such as this, and whether you win, finish second or third, or fail to show, you are always pleased for horse and rider to come back safely. You're very happy to be safe and sound.

On Saturday, obviously, things were different, and when I eventually got back to the weighing room, I thought the jockeys were, on the whole, very calm. If anything, we felt disappointed at what had occurred and embarrassment for racing in general.

Personally, I felt that the inadequacies of the hierarchy and racing administration had let the whole sport down. Unfortunately, what occurred is typical of what goes on, and there is growing frustration among those who work in racing concerning the lack of communication between Jockey Club officials and the professionals involved. This Grand National fiasco is just the latest and, unfortunately, most embarrassing of all.

But the one man I do not blame is the starter, Capt Keith Brown. The procedures to start races are perfectly adequate. What is required is a trained man, with decent eyesight, to act as the recall man.

People are certain to come out and say that using tapes at the start is wrong. But 150 Grand Nationals have been run with a start tape, and nothing similar has occurred. I have started with tape wrapped around me at least once in the National. Usually, you find you can just untangle it and slip it off your body.

I am critical of the Jockey Club for not employing someone capable as a recall man. And why on earth were we allowed to do a complete circuit after the second false start? Why were we not warned before that?

Regular Telegraph racing correspondent **MARCUS ARMYTAGE** *provided an eye-witness account of the start:*

A jockey's tale: Impetuosity, delays and noise proved a deadly combination

When I am a grandfather I shall say I was there, and so will the other 38 jockeys who set off once, twice, or not at all for the 1993 Grand National. It will be remembered forever.

I would not want to apportion blame; an official inquiry will do that. However, a combination of factors combined to cause the second false start to be ignored by 30 jockeys. It only registered with nine, who were either tangled up in the starting tape, or near to the outside, where the false-start flag man was standing.

There is always tension at the start of the National, and most jockeys recognise that one of the biggest hazards in the race can be a lack of daylight at the first fence and the consequential chances of being brought down. The answer is to get a good break, to be in that first rank crossing the Melling Road, and besides, nothing irks trainers more than ground lost at the start. For this to happen in the National would be tantamount to incompetence. Yes, we jockeys were impetuous, to say the least.

To add to our impetuosity, we were all ready to start, our girths checked, eight minutes before the official off time. Then there was a further delay while protesters were cleared from the course after we had been called in to line up for the first time. There was some confusion here because those on the very inside of the course were unable to see the protesters and were, to some extent, unaware of why we were waiting. Anticipating a swift clearance of the course, which there was not, many remained waiting, not wishing to lose their "pole" position.

Other factors included a strong wind, a noisy crowd immediately behind the starter's rostrum and an antiquated starting mechanism, the tape of which was not taut across the course.

Keith Brown, the starter, had a megaphone through which he issued instructions. This was fine, but he could not be heard above the roar of the crowd when the tapes went up. Riding Travel Over, I had positioned myself next to Richard Dunwoody on Wont Be Gone Long about seven or eight horses in from the outside of the course and farthest away from the starter. On both occasions, while the horses on the inside got away cleanly, we were caught up in starting tape, either because a horse had put his head over it or because, with such long tape, it was slower coming up in the centre of the course.

Neither time did I see the flag man. I was expecting to see him standing in front of the first fence, but apparently he stood 100 yards down the course on the outside. The second start was identical to the first, with the inner getting off well.

On the outside, Dunwoody was being strangled by tape which had knotted round his neck, while Travel Over had it knotted round his legs, and at one stage, presumably when it became too tight, he jumped five feet in the air as we crossed the Melling Road. I had already lost 20 lengths, and several jockeys around me in a similar predicament steered towards the outside rail to make pulling-up easier.

Dunwoody was screaming "False start" and was being dragged from his horse, imploring us around him to stop. But the majority were gone and the majority, I assumed, were usually right. There was no way they would come back, so I set off in vain pursuit, only to pull up after landing over the first. The tape, it appeared, had injured Travel Over's leg, and the lameness only became apparent with the jar of landing over a fence.

The people you really have to feel sorry for are the owners, trainers and perhaps a few of the jockeys. Those of the last-named group who completed the course on unplaced horses will have been delighted by their rides, as if it was any normal National. Just having a ride in the

Dunwoody: caught up in the tape

National is a thrill like no other, and it was the nine left at the start who were, perhaps, the most disappointed among the riders.

Former jockey **JOHN OAKSEY**, *who is no stranger to Grand National heartbreak, left recrimination to others and tried to see the positive side:*

White puts broken dreams behind him

The only good thing you can say about the humiliating non-event which was meant to be the 1993 Grand National is that no lives were lost and no rider was badly hurt.

But there were no winners in this tragi-comic fiasco and the biggest losers were, alas, the Grand National itself and the worldwide reputation of British racing.

Apart from making sure that no such avoidable disaster is allowed to happen again, there does not seem to be much point in sharing out the blame. Better, surely, to sympathise with those who suffered worst. And of all the many for whom a void Grand National represents such a sour anticlimax after months of planning and hard work, the man I feel sorriest for is Esha Ness's rider John White.

Of course, the abortive result was also a bitter-sweet affair for the winner's redoubtable trainer. But at least Mrs Pitman, who, I understand, described the event with characteristic eloquence, had known the worst all along. When John White passed the post in front, he was fulfilling the dream of a lifetime. It was his 10th Grand National ride (he has never fallen and only once failed to get round) and, as far as he was concerned, it was the win all jockeys long for.

But his blissful ignorance lasted only a few more seconds. "First, I saw all the other jockeys standing about," he said, "and as I stopped, Dean Gallagher shouted that there had been no race. I can still hardly believe it."

He admits to seeing warning cones on one side of The Chair – and to wondering why there were so few horses with the leaders second-time round. "But I thought the cones were something to do with the demo and, as for the numbers, well, horses do fall in a National ..."

White first past the post: "I didn't see any flag."

COMMENTING on the TV coverage, Paul Fox awarded the BBC 1st XI "race" honours, comparing Desmond Lynam's perceptive and wide-ranging interviews with the lamentable lack of information on the course. He put the lie to stories that some 300 million people around the world watched the broadcast, estimating the total world audience at not much more than 25 million, including some 16 million in this country.

The legal situation, according to **EDWARD GRAYSON**, was extremely confused, with claims possibly coming under two overlapping legal areas of contract and negligence.

But the final word on the day must come from Hong Kong, where **ROBERT PHILIP** enjoyed the racing at Happy Valley before witnessing the first live showing of the Grand National there on a giant screen. Bets totalling $25 HK million (£2.2m) had to be refunded. Few of the spectators had seen a steeplechase before, and enjoyed the novelty.

Philip reported that: Maj-Gen Guy Watkins CB OBE, chief executive of the Hong Kong Jockey Club, nearly choked on his gin before fixing his stiff upper lip firmly in place. "People in Hong Kong who are not used to seeing a tapes start might think it all looked a bit of a shambles, what with the lack of hooters and warning lights as we have here. It's a great sadness they never got to see what remains the world's greatest steeplechase. Obviously we're very disappointed."

Similar self-restraint was being shown in the sponsors' [Martell] lounge. But while general feeling was one of good-natured derision at what one expat in the Members' Bar described as a "right old-fashioned English cock-up", political activist Lai Law-kau, a stern critic of Governor Chris Patten, derived smug satisfaction from the embarrassing situation: "It isn't very reassuring that the people who are negotiating the handover of our country to China cannot organise a bloody horse race."

Committee of Enquiry

The Connell Report on the Grand National fiasco was published on 13 June. The 25-page report was compiled by Sir Michael Connell, the High Court judge, Len Cowburn, the former deputy chairman of bookmakers William Hill, and Stan Mellor, the former champion jump jockey and present-day trainer. It listed eight main conclusions, the principal of which were human error and the "Grey Gate" system of starting.

JOHN OAKSEY applauded the breadth of the inquiry and found much more than a desire to "blame it all on the little man", which was the general, tabloid reaction to the report:

After hearing evidence from 34 people and watching all available films and videos, the committee did indeed reach the

conclusion that Aintree recall man Ken Evans failed to wave his flag. But at yesterday's press conference, Sir Michael expressly underlined these words from his report: "To imply that the failure of the advance flag man to act as he should have done was the sole cause of the ensuing problems would be unfair and unrealistic."

It would indeed, because, as the report makes very clear, this whole disaster was to a large extent an accident that was waiting to happen.

Far from blaming it on one man, the committee describe with understandable reluctance the mixture of human error, inadequate equipment and official complacency which, coinciding with an unnecessary delay, a pointless demonstration, a noisy crowd and some unhelpful weather, generated one of the most undignified episodes in the history of the sport.

Averting a repetition

As a result of the 1993 fiasco, a new starting gate and procedures were developed and rigorously tested in race conditions before the 1994 event.

The gate was narrowed from 65 to 40 yards to reduce the problem of tape sagging. Electronically activated, the tape was designed to rise five times faster than before and move at a 45-degree angle away from the horses to prevent riders or mounts becoming entangled. Starter's orders were relayed by loudspeakers.

Instead of pulling a lever, the starter raised the tape by pushing a concealed button, preventing the jockeys from anticipating the off. The start line, on a curve in the course in 1993, was moved forward 50 yards to give the riders a clearer view of the flagmen, three of them now, ex-jockeys in white coats, with fluorescent flags and all maintaining radio contact with the starter.

Security at Aintree was stepped up, with a heavy presence of uniformed and plain-clothes police and an armed response unit in case of terrorists. About £150,000 was spent on security cameras and safety fencing.

The age of the sagging tape and the bowler hat was over.

The start of the 1994 Grand National: a new era

1994

4 Jun Balanchine, owned by Sheikh Maktoum Al Maktoum and Godolphin Racing, and trained by Hilal Ibrahim, is the first horse trained in the Middle East to land a British Classic, winning the Oaks, as the experiment to ship horses to Dubai for the warmer weather in winter pays off.

19 Jul Betting-shop restrictions are to be lifted, allowing them to give more information and broaden the range of their services and facilities.

23 Jul King's Theatre (12-1), ridden in masterly fashion by Mick Kinane, lands an incident-packed "King George" at Ascot, after Ezzoud unseats Walter Swinburn at the start and continues riderless to hinder several major contenders in the home straight, including the Derby winner Erhaab (7-2f) and White Muzzle (9-2), who still manages to finish 2nd.

27 Sep Australian trainer Vic Rail, 49, dies in Brisbane of a heart attack after displaying similar symptoms to 14 horses who had perished in his yard and an adjacent stable in the last week. Racing has been suspended in Queensland until the mystery virus has been isolated.

2 Oct Sheikh Mohammed's lightly raced 3-y-o colt Carnegie, bought as a yearling from Robert Sangster for $1.6m, and trained by André Fabre, becomes the first son of an Arc-winning mare to emulate his dam, while Japanese champion jockey Yutaka Take is heavily criticised for his

handling of White Muzzle (6th) and best of the British runners is Ezzoud (4th).

4 Oct Vodafone, the mobile communications group, is to sponsor the Derby and the whole of Epsom's new-format, three-day Derby meeting for the next three years in a package worth £3.5 million. The Vodafone Derby, which will be worth more than £500,000 to the winner, will be run on Saturday, June 10 next year, along with the Coronation Cup, a day after the meeting has opened with the Vodafone Oaks on Friday. The Sunday programme has still to be finalised.

King's Theatre prevails in the 'King George' at Ascot despite the presence of the riderless Ezzoud

Cheltenham Gold Cup: 17 March

Vive la France as The Fellow finally hits Gold

By HOTSPUR (J.A.McGrath)

One clumsy jump at the final fence ended the dream that Jodami could win Successive Tote Cheltenham Gold Cups; one deadly accurate leap propelled The Fellow and his Polish-born partner Adam Kondrat to victory at the fourth attempt in the race that had so long eluded him.

Kondrat, 27, answered his critics in no uncertain terms, giving a perfect tactical display to land the race he himself calls "the world championship of steeplechasing" and emerging as a man brave and skilful enough to make what was to be the right decision at the crucial moment

With Young Hustler running clearly the gamest race

of his life on the far side of the course, and Jodami bearing down confidently on the near side, Kondrat knew that to get a clean, big jump from The Fellow at the last was the one major requirement if he were to ever lay to rest the Gold Cup ghosts that haunted him. The Fellow (7-1) met the final fence spot on, and while Jodami (6-4f) was struggling to regain his balance and momentum after missing it out, the French combination were sprinting away to the roars of the crowd – registering, in the end, a convincing win by one and a half lengths. Jodami finished four lengths ahead of Young Hustler (20-1), a brave third.

CHAMPIONS

Jockey (Flat)	Frankie Dettori	233
Jockey (NH)	Richard Dunwoody	198
Racehorse of Year	Barathea	4-y-o
NH Champion of Year	The Fellow	9-y-o
Leading Trainer	Michael Stoute	£1,916,932
Leading Owner	Sheikh Mohammed	£2,686,109
Leading Money Winner	Erhaab	£582,828

Queen Mother Champion Chase Cheltenham: 16 March

Viking grabs victory from jaws of defeat

By John Oaksey

IN THE presence of Queen Elizabeth herself, the Queen Mother Champion chase produced the thrill of the meeting at Cheltenham yesterday, when Adrian Maguire and Viking Flagship took defeat by the throat and snatched victory from its jaws. The cliché is honestly no exaggeration here – for if ever a race was won by courage and daring, this was it.

Viking Flagship's last two leaps were bold to the point of foolhardiness. A slight mistake would have meant failure, disaster, or even tragedy. Even when they

both came off, there was still a battle to fight. After Remittance Man's (11-4f) uncharacteristic departure, three fences out, Travado (100-30), Deep Sensation (15-2) and Viking Flagship (4-1) went to the second-last in line abreast. And, bounding over the last, Travado's head was in front. "I looked at Adrian on my inside and thought I had him beaten," Travado's rider Jamie Osborne told me. "That must be a very brave horse indeed." Maguire, not surprisingly, agrees. "The toughest I have ridden," he said.

The Grand National Aintree: 9 April

Miinnehoma and Dunwoody realise Pipe dream in National

By J.A.McGrath

FREDDIE STARR, the well-known comedian, was laughing all the way to the bank when Miinnehoma, the horse he dreamed could land him a Cheltenham Gold Cup, won the Martell Grand National at Aintree instead with a wonderful performance.

The injury-plagued chaser came into the world's greatest steeplechase with only two runs under his belt this season, following an absence because of back problems. But he shook off those worries to land the £115,606 prize, giving Martin Pipe the biggest training triumph of his glamorous career, and something he had always dreamed of.

Running to the final fence, the furious pace and heavy ground had reduced the field from 36 to eight. Two more – Zeta's Lad and Into the Red – departed here, and by The Elbow on the run-in it was

clear that Miinnehoma (16-1), with champion jockey Richard Dunwoody sitting quietly, was moving like a winner as he edged closer to challenge the 5-1 favourite Moorcroft Boy. No sooner had Miinnehoma surged into the lead than Just So (20-1), who carried 31b overweight and had been in the firing line for much of the final circuit, mounted a brave renewed challenge. But the winner produced an unbelievably courageous effort to last home and win by one and a quarter lengths.

There was a gap of 20 lengths to Moorcroft Boy, who tired to take third, with Irish-trained Ebony Jane (25-1) 25 lengths farther away fourth. There were only two other finishers, 100-1 shots Fiddlers Pike, ridden by grandmother Mrs Rosemary Henderson, 51, his owner, and Roc de Prince, a distant last.

Moorhen Handicap Lingfield Park: 6 May

Wood killed in sprint pile-up

By HOTSPUR (J.A.McGrath)

THE British racing world was stunned last night to learn of the death of Steve Wood, a young, lightweight Flat jockey who had grafted hard for a living on the Turf since his teens.

Wood, who was 26, died on the track at Lingfield Park from massive internal injuries sustained in an horrific race fall from the David Chapman-trained Kalar, who stumbled and fell when with the leaders in the five-furlong Moorhen Handicap.

Two other jockeys came down in the pile-up that occurred as the 16-strong field hurtled down one of the fastest sprint courses in the country. Chris Dwyer, who was knocked unconscious for several minutes, and Tony Clark, who was "hung up" in one stirrup iron for some distance, both escaped serious injury.

Paramedics, medical and ambulance assistance, on hand almost immediately, were unable to revive Wood, who suffered suspected rib injuries and lung damage. The diminutive young rider, known as Samson in the weighing room, was based in York and attached to Chapman's yard at Stillington, North Yorkshire.

Racing's rather small, close-knit world has only just heaved a sigh of relief after news that Declan Murphy was making a recovery from the terrible head injuries he sustained in a fall at Haydock on Monday. Now with the death of Steve Wood, a pall of sadness has descended again.

NATIONAL HUNT			
Champion Hurdle	Flakey Dove	M Dwyer	9-1
Cheltenham Gold Cup	The Fellow	A Kondrat	7-1
Grand National	Miinnehoma	R Dunwoody	16-1

ENGLISH CLASSICS			
2,000 Guineas	Mr Baileys	J Weaver	16-1
1,000 Guineas	Las Meninas	J Reid	12-1
Derby	Erhaab	W Carson	7-2f
Oaks	Balanchine	L Dettori	6-1
St Leger	Moonax	Pat Eddery	40-1

Stratford/Market Rasen: 4 June

Dunwoody's title as treble foils Maguire fightback

By Marcus Armytage

RICHARD Dunwoody was crowned champion National Hunt jockey for the second consecutive season last night, but the contest with the dogged Adrian Maguire went to the third-last race before it became mathematically impossible for Maguire to win the title.

Both jockeys enjoyed an eventful and hectic final day, with Dunwoody taking his tally to 197 by virtue of a treble with Errant Knight, Lynch Law and Saraville at Stratford in the afternoon. Maguire, who needed to go through the card at Market Rasen in the evening, sustained the excitement by winning the first two races on Wayward Wind and Its Unbelievable, but when Bobby Socks and then Logical Sun were beaten, it was all over – his score for the season, 194.

The ding-dong will-he?-won't-he? uncertainty of this 10-month title race – Maguire led by as much as 43 in early January and Dunwoody first took the lead in mid-May – has sustained interest in the National Hunt season well beyond its usual sell-by date. It has also camouflaged some of the sheer physical demands made upon both. They have each driven the equivalent of twice round the world, ridden at racing pace over roughly 2,500 miles each on 900 horses. They have jumped roughly 11,000 obstacles – tell that to the jockeys who thought riding in the Derby was dodgy.

The Derby Epsom: 1 June

Carson steers way through 'carnage' to grab Classic

By J.A.McGrath

ERHAAB disappeared off the radar in the first half of yesterday's rough and tumble Ever Ready Derby at Epsom, but the colt lived up to his Arabic name in the second half in every sense, coming with an electrifying finishing burst to land the Classic by a length and a quarter in the style of an outstanding three-year-old.

Sheikh Hamdan Al-Maktoum, the winning owner, later explained: "The name Erhaab has a thousand different meanings in Arabic, but the nearest I could give you to English is 'strong and brave'." An appropriate piece of naming, because Erhaab, the 7-2 favourite, had only two behind him six furlongs out, and was a conservative 12 lengths from the tearaway leader Mister Baileys in the run down to Tattenham Corner

It was an incredible performance. Erhaab cut down his rivals in the final furlong as if they were riveted to the ground. But instead of connections being able to bask in richly deserved glory for this wonderful win, the performance was overshadowed by calls for safety restrictions to be introduced to prevent further incidents such as the one which caused Foyer to unseat Willie Ryan, his rider, six furlongs from home.

Ryan was admitted to hospital with three broken ribs. Willie Carson, 51, who needed all the experience of 25 previous Derby rides to steer Erhaab through the minefield of incident they found, later said: "They'll have to do something about it. There were too many [horses] in there that shouldn't have been in the race. It was murder. I was seeing carnage everywhere coming down the hill."

Two furlongs out, as Mister Baileys galloped on at a furious pace, with Colonel Collins and King's Theatre in pursuit, Erhaab still had almost 10 lengths to make up on the leader. A furlong out, he looked certain to gain a place, but then, 100 yards out, he put his head down, changed legs and produced another surge of power to overhaul King's Theatre (14-1) and record a great victory by a length and a quarter, with Colonel Collins (10-1) third.

Irish Derby The Curragh: 26 June

Oaks heroine Balanchine trounces the colts in Budweiser Irish Derby

By HOTSPUR (J.A.McGrath)

THE Middle East-trained Balanchine became only the third filly this century to win the Budweiser Irish Derby when outstaying her eight rivals at The Curragh yesterday. So easily was she travelling approaching the home bend that she was able to cruise into the lead before Frankie Dettori, her partner, even asked.

"She pulled her way to the front," recalled an ecstatic Dettori. "This filly is very good – and she was much better this time than when she won the Oaks at Epsom." King's Theatre, sent off the even-money favourite, set out after Balanchine (5-1) in the home straight. But the Epsom Derby runner-up could never peg back the filly, and was beaten four and a half lengths into second place. Colonel Collins, carrying the Robert Sangster colours, struggled on to take third, three and a half lengths away.

Balanchine, who had been supplemented to the race early last week at a cost of £60,000, earned a first prize of £348,000. Frankly, she outclassed and outstayed the colts over this mile and a half.

Ralph Hubbard Memorial Nursery Goodwood: 28 July

Piggott hurt in Goodwood fall

By HOTSPUR (J.A.McGrath)

Lester Piggott was taken to hospital with head and neck injuries after a nasty fall which sent the legendary jockey bouncing along the turf in front of a huge holiday crowd at Goodwood yesterday. Piggott, 58, crashed to the ground when his saddle slipped around on the Richard Hannon-trained Coffee 'n Cream, the 3-1 favourite, inside the final furlong of the Ralph Hubbard Memorial Nursery, just as the filly was moving into a challenging position.

Piggott almost had his left leg on the ground as he slid off the horse's back into the path of oncoming rivals, who had to swerve round him, and he bounced several times at high speed before coming to a halt. His riding helmet came

off on impact. An ambulance raced to the scene as Piggott lay prone on the grass. He was given oxygen, and a paramedic checked his chest for injury. But within two minutes, the jockey opened his eyes and said: "Let me get up."

A hush came over the packed grandstand and enclosures as anxious racegoers feared the worst – but word later filtered through that Piggott was conscious and being taken to hospital. Fellow jockey Tony Ives, one of Piggott's close friends, came out of the first-aid room and said: "His neck is in a brace, but he is laughing and joking with the doctor and nurses."

York: 1 September

Dettori on 200 mark after 67-1 York treble

By HOTSPUR (J.A.McGrath)

FRANKIE DETTORI entered the record books as only the sixth jockey to ride 200 winners in a season with a sparkling 67-1 treble at York yesterday. He now has his sights set on Sir Gordon Richards' all-time British record of 269, set in 1947. Italian-born Dettori, 23, has a distinct advantage over the legendary Richards in that he started his season on the all-weather track at Lingfield Park on Jan 1. In

Richards' day, racing did not commence until March, which still marks the start of the Flat season on turf.

Dettori's performance in reaching the double century is nevertheless remarkable – and a credit to his zest for the racing game and his powers of endurance. He is a worthy member of the "200 Club", alongside Richards, Fred Archer, Tommy Loates, and, more recently, Pat Eddery and Michael Roberts.

Jockey Club Hearing: 27 September

Six-month ban for jockey who manhandled rival

By Marcus Armytage

FLAT-RACE jockey Kieran Fallon was suspended for six months yesterday for deliberately pulling a fellow rider from his horse after passing the winning post at Beverley earlier this month. But no action was taken over a weighing room brawl which allegedly followed between Fallon and the other jockey, Stuart Webster.

The Jockey Club's Disciplinary Committee found Fallon guilty of violent and improper conduct. Webster had slowed to a trot after winning the John Mangles Memorial Handicap race on Sailormaite on Sep. 14, when Fallon, who had finished down the field, rode up and dragged Webster from his horse. Both he and

Webster were cleared of other charges under the same rule, as no witnesses came forward with evidence about an alleged brawl from which Webster emerged with a broken nose and Fallon a cut face.

Clare-born Fallon, who is attached to Mrs Lynda Ramsden's Thirsk yard, had been in trouble with the Stewards before for violent conduct. In June he was suspended for seven days after hitting colleague Keith Rutter with his whip during a race. He has been fined three times for striking horses at the start, on one occasion, at Beverley in 1992, for hitting Baladee Pet in a "particularly offensive manner after being unseated," said the stewards.

St Leger Doncaster: 10 September

Moonax springs 40-1 surprise in St Leger

By J.A.McGrath

BARRY HILLS sent the Classic dreams of his sons John and Michael up in smoke when saddling 40-1 chance Moonax for a shock victory over Broadway Flyer in the Teleconnection St Leger at Doncaster, which was run at a furious gallop. The disregarded outsider, the longest-priced winner of the race in more than 70 years, was giving an 11th Classic success to Pat Eddery.

Emotional family scenes in the unsaddling enclosure said it all. Michael Hills, who had set a blistering pace on Broadway Flyer (6-1), trained by his brother John, walked over to his father, hugged

him, and said: "If anyone was going to beat us, I'm glad it was you." Then, as he wandered into the weighing room, Michael Hills added: "It was touch and go whether Dad was even going to run Moonax. I can't believe that he's got up and beat us, but I suppose we've got more years [ahead] than Dad."

Moonax has been only lightly raced this season because of injury. Apart from the long-shot winner, the other major surprises were the poor performances of Red Route, the 15-8 favourite, who trailed in seventh, and Midnight Legend, friendless at 9-2, last of eight.

---

30 September

Trainer is shot dead at home

By David Millward and Rebecca Pike

MR ALEX Scott, one of the country's most respected racehorse trainers, was found shot dead at his home near Newmarket last night.

Police were called to Glebe House Stud in Cheveley, Cambs, following reports of gunshots at about 6.10 pm. They said they were treating the death as "suspicious". It is believed that Mr Scott died after an argument over a former employee.

Mr Scott, 35, who was married with three children, was one of the most successful trainers in Newmarket. His main employers were the Maktoum family, the Arab owners who have dominated the sport over the past decade.

Alex Scott started as an assistant to Mr Tom Jones in the early 80s, and joined Major Dick Hern as an apprentice in 1985. Three years later he branched out on his own, and in 1989 replaced Mr Olivier Douieb as the trainer for Sheikh Maktoum Al Maktoum, who owns about 65 per cent of the horses at the Oak Stables.

Although he continued to train for other owners, the Maktoum horses won him the greatest acclaim in the racing world. In 1991, Sheikh Albadou won the William Hill Trophy and went on to win the Breeders' Cup Sprint, in Kentucky, only the second British-trained horse to succeed.

Prix de l'Abbaye Longchamp: 2 October

Flying mare is back on song

By Tony Stafford

Dettori's delight on Lochsong

ALL the pre-race fears that Lochsong's temperament had effectively curtailed her brilliant career evaporated back on her favourite piece of foreign soil. Jeff Smith's great sprinter repeated her 1993 triumph in the five-furlong Prix de l'Abbaye de Longchamp with a controlled exhibition of power and pace.

Clearly, the meticulous planning of trainer Ian Balding, who last week requested special treatment for Lochsong before the race, was a major factor in her success. Frankie Dettori was on her back fully 20 minutes before the scheduled off time, and the mare was led to the start to ensure that she remained well below the boiling point she exhibited at both Newmarket and York.

Afterwards, Balding and Smith were fulsome in praising Louis Romanet, whose pivotal role in the administration of French racing enabled him to design the pre-race latitude enjoyed by the mare.

As last year, Lochsong (7-10f) was drawn wide, and she soon stretched into a clear lead. By the two-furlong pole, all her opponents were toiling and it was left to Mistertopogigo to chase her home, five lengths behind.

Racing Post Trophy Doncaster: 22 October

Awesome 'Celtic' is only 7-2 for Derby

By Marcus Armytage

THAT never-ending quest to find the horse that doesn't exist, an Arkle among Flat horses, may have come to an end at Doncaster yesterday. Celtic Swing, a black colt with a striking white blaze, not only lived up to his hyped reputation, he actually improved upon it by destroying a field of proven two-year-olds to win the one-mile Racing Post Trophy by a record 12 lengths.

It is a minor point that Annus Mirabilis finished second. He might as well have been at Newbury.

Up until now, the shortest-priced Derby favourite to go into winter quarters in recent years was Reference Point (5-1), who won this race by five lengths in 1986. However, Celtic Swing is as short as 7-2 for the Derby, 2-1 for the 2,000 Guineas and 10-1 for the double.

Cynics might point out that Arazi never won another big race after he did similarly awesome things to America's best in the Breeders' Cup Juvenile. But in Celtic Swing, owner Peter Savill, trainer Lady Herries, jockey Kevin Darley – three new faces at racing's highest level – and racing enthusiasts the country over have a horse to fuel their dreams and shorten the winter.

In the race, Darley, whose first Group One winner this was, sat in second behind Fahal until three and a half furlongs out. In a stride there was no contest, and Celtic Swing (1-1f) continued to extend his lead all the way to the line.

Savill has Darley to thank for the new Derby favourite. His retained jockey spotted Celtic Swing when he rode another horse in a gallop upsides, and he advised Savill to buy it.

Lady Herries was breathless with excitement. "He stepped up in class and did exactly the same as he did at Ascot. Michael Stoute told me his horse Annus Mirabilis was 18lb better than the horse we beat eight lengths there. We beat him 12 lengths here!"

---

5 October

Golden era comes to an end as Vincent O'Brien calls it a day

By HOTSPUR (J.A.McGrath)

VINCENT O'BRIEN, without doubt the greatest trainer of the modern era, is to retire at the end of the current Flat season, bringing down the curtain on a spectacularly successful career that included six Derby wins and three Grand Nationals.

O'Brien, 77, is to transfer most of the horses left at his historic Ballydoyle complex in Co.Tipperary to his son Charles, while the famous training establishment that housed such great horses as Nijinsky, Sir Ivor and Cottage Rake is to be taken over by Coolmore Stud, run by John Magnier, O'Brien's son-in-law. O'Brien and his wife Jacqueline will continue to live at Ballydoyle, while many of their employees will be retained.

Known as the Master of Ballydoyle, from where he notched up an an unrivalled National Hunt record, winning three consecutive Grand Nationals, four Gold Cups and three Champion Hurdles, O'Brien made an even bigger impact on the Flat. He prepared champions such as Sir Ivor and Nijinsky, as well, as his first stars, Ballymoss and Gladness. Other big-race winners included The Minstrel, El Gran Senor and Sadler's Wells.

O'Brien won a total of 44 European Classics, as well as the Prix de l'Arc de Triomphe three times. Peter O'Sullivan, the BBC's senior racing commentator and long-time friend of O'Brien, said: "I cannot think that his achievements will ever be matched by anyone."

Among other tributes flowing in from those involved in the racing world, Lester Piggott, who acknowledged O'Brien's major part in his comeback, said last night: "In my opinion he was the best trainer of all time."

OTHER MAJOR RACES

Irish Derby	Balanchine	L Dettori	5-1
Arc de Triomphe	Carnegie	T Jarnet	3-1
Kentucky Derby	Go for Gin	C McCarron	91-10
Melbourne Cup	Jeune	W Harris	16-1
Arlington Million	Paradise Creek	P Day	18-10
Japan Cup	Marvellous Crown	K Minai	9-1

Breeders' Cup Mile Louisville, Kentucky: 5 November

Barathea makes up for dismal Lochsong

By J.A.McGrath

THE long-awaited British success in the Breeders' Cup came when Barathea raced away with the Mile race under a confident ride from Frankie Dettori. So often unlucky in the big races, the four-year-old colt provided a welcome change of fortune for Dettori – and an army of British supporters – who had earlier suffered a crushing blow when Lochsong trailed in a dismal last of 14 runners in the Sprint.

Taking full advantage of his No.1 draw, Barathea (104-10) began well, took up a prominent position third on the rail, and Dettori then waited until entering the home straight to deliver a devastating challenge which left his rivals with no answers before a record crowd of 71,671.

Barathea scored by three lengths from the strong-finishing Johann Quatz, with Unfinished Symph third, in one of the best performances in a Breeders' Cup race by a European runner. "This is probably the best feeling of my life," gasped an elated Dettori, soon after leaping from the saddle in the style of the legendary Angel Cordero. "This horse has extraordinary acceleration for a furlong and a half," he added.

The fact that only the third British victory in the 11-year history of this series will be delivered by two Italians will matter little in Newmarket, where Barathea is trained by Luca Cumani.

1995

9 Jan Thirsk trainer Lynda Ramsden and jockey Russ Garritty are cleared of all charges in a Jockey Club disciplinary inquiry into the performance of Top Cees at Edinburgh last month.

15 Jan Tweseldown point-to-point is the scene of Britain's first Sunday on-course betting.

18 Jan Champion jockey Richard Dunwoody receives a 30-day ban for "intentional interference" in a race at Uttoxeter on 6 Jan.

19 Jan Celtic Swing is assessed champion juvenile, 6lb ahead of Pennekamp, and earns a 130 international rating.

1 Feb French trainer François Boutin, 58, handler among other great horses of Arazi, Miesque and Sagaro, dies of cancer.

5 Feb Jodami (13-8f) beats Merry Gale (7-4) by 3 lengths at Leopardstown to complete a unique hat-trick of Hennessy Cognac Irish Gold Cups, but jockey Mark Dwyer receives a 7-day suspension for excessive use of the whip.

28 Feb The Home Secretary reappoints Lord Wyatt for a final 2-year term as Chairman of the Tote, and announces that the future of the Tote will be reviewed later in the year.

20 Mar The BHB announce there will be £1/2m added prize money for the 21 new NH fixtures scheduled for June and July. Six courses – Market Rasen, Perth, Southwell, Stratford, Uttoxeter and Worcester – are to hold summer jump racing, Perth opening the season on 8 June with the first of the 13 evening meetings.

30 Apr Champion Hurdler Alderbrook comes 2nd in a Group 1 Flat race, the Prix Ganay, at Longchamp, beaten 3 lengths by Paul Kelleway-trained Pelder, ridden by Frankie Dettori.

7 May Harayir (5-1) wins the first English Classic to be held on a Sunday, the 1,000 Guineas, with on-course betting and betting-shops open, also for the first time on a Sunday. Ridden by Richard Hills and trained by Dick Hern, she beats Aqaarid (3-1f), whose jockey Willie Carson for once makes the wrong choice, both horses being owned by Sheikh Hamdan Al Maktoum.

10 May Another Top Cees row erupts, this time on the Flat, as Kieran Fallon guides the 5-year-old to a 5-length victory in the 21/4-mile Chester Cup at 8-1, seemingly making nonsense of his controversial defeat at Newmarket 22 days ago when he was held up (until too late), reportedly in an attempt to get the trip of half a mile less, The trainer's husband, Jack Ramsden, denies backing the horse or that he had been "laid out" for the race.

23 May An electronic photo-finish camera is used for the first time in Britain (to determine 3rd place in the 4.45 at Goodwood), and produces results in under 30sec.

10 Jun US trainer Wayne Lukas chalks up his fifth consecutive Classic as Kentucky Derby winner Thunder Gulch (6-4f), owned by British-born Michael Tabor, wins the Belmont Stakes after the late withdrawal of the favourite, the other Lukas-trained colt and Preakness winner Timber Country, with a fever.

Master Oats sweetly clears the last to win the Gold Cup

Cheltenham Gold Cup: 16 March

Bailey lands masterly double
Master Oats stamps class on Gold Cup

By J.A.McGrath

KIM BAILEY and Norman Williamson became the first trainer-jockey combination in 45 years to complete the Champion Hurdle-Gold Cup double in the same year when Master Oats outstayed his rivals for a thoroughly convincing victory in an exciting Tote Cheltenham Gold Cup.

But the 100-30 favourite was never travelling well on the first circuit and mistakes at the ninth and 11th fences threatened to put him out of contention. Williamson later admitted that "the horse wasn't jumping well when he was in behind". But after the water Master Oats joined Merry Gale, the Irish jumper with suspect stamina, and galloped with him stride for stride, as they started the descent to the final three fences.

Master Oats' relentless galloping style was soon seen to effect as he drew clear rounding the home bend, with only one left to jump in the straight on the amended course. Alderbrook's sensational Champion Hurdle victory, the first triumph of the week for Bailey and Williamson, seemed an age away as Master Oats approached the final fence at an even pace ready to leap into the history books together with his trainer and jockey.

The jump was straight and accurate, which was all that was required for him to race away from the gallant Dubacilla (20-1), who had run the best race of her career to finish second, beaten 15 lengths. In the stamina-sapping ground, Miinnehoma (9-1) was the only one really staying on behind, making up ground to take third, another 15 lengths away.

CHAMPIONS

Jockey (NH)	Richard Dunwoody	160
NH Champion of Year	Master Oats	9-y-o

The Grand National Aintree: 8 April

Queen of Aintree reigns supreme
Royal Athlete's majestic show gives trainer her second National triumph

By J.A.McGrath

IF she had never formally been crowned the Queen of Aintree, Jenny Pitman took the throne in some style this time by sending out Royal Athlete, one of her six runners, to win the Martell Grand National at odds of 40-1. It was her second triumph in Britain's great steeplechase.

Ridden in inspired fashion by Jason Titley, 24, a fresh-faced Irish youngster from Co.Clare having his first National mount, Royal Athlete took it up at the 17th fence and kept galloping and jumping with tremendous enthusiasm to repel all challengers.

Party Politics (16-1), the 1992 winner, raced into second place nearing The Elbow, but Royal Athlete, showing the heart and courage of a lion, responded admirably to dash away for an impressive seven-lengths win. Over the Deel (100-1) was third, six lengths away. Dubacilla (9-1) was so far back early, she was hardly ever in the "call", but flew home to take fourth in a blanket finish from Romany King (40-1) and Into the Red (20-1), who dead-heated for fifth.

Norman Williamson, the maestro of Cheltenham last month, who looked likely to master Liverpool as well, rode a tactically brilliant race on Master Oats (5-1f), keeping him wide to gain clear sight of his jumps, but the heavily weighted gelding was weakening noticeably before the final fence and came in seventh of the 15 finishers.

An emotional Mrs Pitman, who won with Corbiere in 1983, was in tears as Royal Athlete was cheered into the winner's enclosure at this famous racecourse, a place where she has also known disappointment and despair.

Royal Athlete, now a 12-year-old, has suffered from tendon trouble for the past eight years, and all sorts of other problems, including soft feet and corns. Mrs Pitman has always been a controversial and forthright personality, frequently blasting the media for their opinions, with which she seldom agrees. But even her harshest critics would have to admit this was a training triumph of gigantic proportions both for her and the staff at her Weathercock House yard.

OTHER MAJOR RACES

Kentucky Derby	Thunder Gulch	G Stevens	49-2

NATIONAL HUNT

Champion Hurdle	Alderbrook	N.Williamson	11-2
Cheltenham Gold Cup	Master Oats	N.Williamson	100-30f
Grand National	Royal Athlete	J.Titley	40-1

The 2,000 Guineas Newmarket: 6 May

Local hero falls to French connection

Celtic Swing beaten but not bowed

By J.A.McGrath

FRENCH-TRAINED Penne-kamp came with a brilliant finishing surge to destroy Celtic Swing's unbeaten record – but not his spirit – in a vintage running of the Madagans 2,000 Guineas before a huge crowd at sun-drenched Newmarket.

For three or four tantalis-ing seconds inside the two-furlong marker, hopes and dreams that the much-acclaimed Celtic Swing (4-5f) would maintain clear superi-ority over his generation looked likely to be realised as he swept to the front. Peter Savill's colt drew two lengths clear of the chasing pack, but the maroon and white silks of Sheikh Mohammed, worn by French champion Thierry Jarnet on Pennekamp, loomed up on the far side and, once hitting top gear, he put his ground-devouring stride to great effect.

Initially, Pennekamp's momentum carried him into a lead of three-quarters of a length, but once they they hit the rising ground Celtic Swing started to rally and was pegging back his rival inch-by-inch. Only a head separat-ed the pair after a tremendous duel. Bahri (14-1), who had chased home Celtic Swing in the Greenham Stakes at New-bury, battled on well for third, two lengths away.

Pennekamp, sent off at 9-2 after opening at 7-2, was giving Sheikh Mohammed his first win in the Newmarket Classic. Trainer Andre Fabre, achieving his fourth British Classic triumph, held the view that Pennekamp and Celtic Swing had been engaged in a contest that will go down in the history books as a running of the 2,000 Guineas to rank alongside Brigadier Gerard's defeat of Mill Reef in 1971.

The disappointment in the Celtic Swing corner was plain to see, but there was no sign of despondency. Lady Herries said: "I'm very pleased. If he'd had a race beforehand when he had to battle, it might have been different. At the end, he was coming back at Penne-kamp. Kevin [Darley] said the penny only dropped for the colt to put his head down and start racing about five strides from the line."

Prix du Jockey-Club Chantilly: 4 June

Celtic Swing vindicates Savill's decision with Chantilly victory

By HOTSPUR (J.A.McGrath)

OWNER Peter Savill's decision to by-pass Epsom with Celtic Swing seemed justified in light of the colt's hard-fought victory in yesterday's Les Emirats Arabes Unis Prix du Jockey-Club at Chantilly. The even-money favourite, he scrambled home by half a length in a muddling-run Classic.

After taking the lead more than two furlongs out, Celtic Swing safely held his 10 rivals all the way up the home straight, although the last 100 yards proved heart-stopping moments for the British camp who were present to cheer on only the third British-trained winner of the race in 159 years.

The lack of early pace almost certainly told against Celtic Swing over the final two furlongs, when he was all out to repel the late challenges of horses he should have comfortably beaten on his two-year-old form. Poliglote rallied gamely in the last 100 yards to take second, and Winged Love battled on extremely well to finish third, a short head away.

Savill had been under fire in the 48 hours leading up to yesterday's race for his decision to commit Celtic Swing to Chantilly rather than go for the Vodafone Derby at Epsom. Some said it was a snub for the British Classic; others claimed it was even unpatriotic.

But Savill said yesterday: "I feel justified in going for the French Classic with the result we have seen. There is no question that it was the right decision. We made it in the long-term, best interests of our horse – both mentally and physically."

Walter Swinburn and Lammtarra: emotional victory

The Derby Epsom: 10 June

Lammtarra swoops

By J.A.McGrath

THE astonishing success story of the Dubai-based Godolphin racing team continued when Lammtarra, a 14-1 shot, came with a paralys-ing finishing burst for an emotional win in the Derby at Epsom. From a rails position at Tattenham Corner, he angled his way towards the outside in the home straight and made up at least six lengths in the final furlong and a half to head Tamure (9-1) close home and sweep to victory by one length. Presen-ting (12-1) made up ground for third, three-quarters of a length away. Lammtarra gave jockey Walter Swinburn his third win in the world's most famous Flat race, after Shergar (1981) and Shahrastani (1986).

As Lammtarra passed the post in record time of 2min 32.31sec – smashing the prev-ious best by 1.53sec – powerful binoculars were required to find Pennekamp, the 11-8 favourite, who trailed in a most disappointing 11th after Thierry Jarnet, his young jockey, had him perfectly poised on the outside six furlongs out. Pennekamp came back lame, and Michael Osborne, one of owner Sheikh Mohammed's aides, reported: "He is very sore." Spectrum, the strongly fancied second-favourite, was another to perform poorly on Epsom's equine rollercoaster, finishing 13th.

Astonishing is the only word to describe Lammtarra's success. He had raced only once previously, for a win in the Washington Singer Stakes over seven furlongs at Newbury last August. And when he faced the starter in the Derby, he was having his first outing for 302 days, pointing to an incredible training feat by the Godolphin team. Lammtarra is owned by Saeed Maktoum Al Maktoum, 19-year-old student son of the ruler of Dubai.

The winner is trained now by Saeed bin Suroor, a former policeman who became the licence-holder for Sheikh Mohammed's Godolphin stab-le only three months ago. In his first year with a British licence, he has completed the coveted Derby-Oaks double, as Moonshell had taken the fillies' Classic 24 hours earlier.

The most poignant mo-ments came when interviews were being conducted and Sheikh Mohammed and Swinburn both remembered Lammtarra's former trainer Alex Scott, who died in a shooting incident near Newmarket last year. Scott had believed strongly in Lammtarra, even backing him ante-post for the 1995 Classics before he had raced.

While Pennekamp and Spectrum both came back physically amiss, Daffaq, who had been in the race as a pacemaker for Munwar, fractured his nearside knee and was later put down. The irony was that Daffaq could never get the lead in a very fast-run race.

ENGLISH CLASSICS

2,000 Guineas	Pennekamp	T Jarnet	9-2
1,000 Guineas	Harayir	R Hills	5-1
Derby	Lammtarra	W Swinburn	14-1
Oaks	Moonshell	L Dettori	3-1

Index

**Index compiled by
Norman Barrett**